Reversing the Gaze

Reversing the Gaze

Amar Singh's Diary,
A Colonial Subject's Narrative of
Imperial India

Editing and Commentary by

Susanne Hoeber Rudolph
Lloyd I. Rudolph

with

Mohan Singh Kanota

Copyright © 2002 by Westview Press, A Member of the Perseus Books Group

Copyright © for diary extracts by Susanne Hoeber Rudolph, Lloyd I. Rudolph, Mohan Singh Kanota.

Westview Press books are available at special discounts for bulk purchases in the United States by corporations, institutions, and other organizations. For more information, please contact the Special Markets Department at The Perseus Books Group, 11 Cambridge Center, Cambridge MA 02142, or call (617) 252-5298.

Published in 2002 in the United States of America by Westview Press, 5500 Central Avenue, Boulder, Colorado 80301–2877, and in the United Kingdom by Westview Press, 12 Hid's Copse Road, Cumnor Hill, Oxford OX2 9JJ

Find us on the World Wide Web at www.westviewpress.com

A CIP catalog record for this book is available from the Library of Congress.
ISBN 0-8133-3626-0

The paper used in this publication meets the requirements of the American National Standard for Permanence of Paper for Printed Library Materials Z39.48–1984.

10 9 8 7 6 5 4 3 2 1

CONTENTS

List of Illustrations

PART VI

Acknowledgments

Selecting, editing and interpreting Amar Singh's diary has involved many encounters during the twenty-eight years that we have intermittently worked at
completing the project. Here we want to acknowledge the persons and institutions who helped us see the project through to completion.

We start with the gang at "Redcombe," a large charming house in Kasauli, a
hill station in Himachal Pradesh. In 1971, we retreated there from the heat of the
plains below with the diary volumes for 1898 to 1905. Three came to help: Jim
Womack, a University of Chicago College student sufficiently enamored of India
to earn the travel money by driving a CTA (Chicago Transit Authority) bus;
Linda Streeter, an India Fulbrighter bitten by the diary bug who stayed on to help
out; and M. L.. Sharma, an accomplished secretary of the old school, adept at
shorthand, Hindi, Urdu, and English, whose flying fingers then and for some
years transcribed diary selections from Amar Singh's longhand into typed words.
Back at the University of Chicago, Kathy Anderson, Susan Lenth, and Ed Carr did
the second cut typescript, the twenty-nine chapters that constituted our
mid–1970s version of the diary. We remember with respect and fondness the late
Philip Lilienthal, editor of the University of California Press, a diary enthusiast
who, on the advice of a skeptical board, regretfully turned down our then 1600-
page typescript. Too costly. Hildred Geertz, a declared reader of the mid–1970s
MS, made comments and suggestions that are reflected in the current version. So
are the insightful suggestions of anonymous readers for Oxford University Press
and Westview Press. Finally we acknowledge University of Chicago graduate students from a variety of disciplines who became co-conspirators in the Amar
Singh diary project: Joan Erdman, now an established scholar of Indian performing arts and culture, helped us experiment with interpretive introductions for
thematic parts; Laura Jackson, while writing a dissertation on marks of
sovereignty, took on the arduous task of "cleaning" a scanned version of the erstwhile typescript, when scanners were not what they are today; Daisy Rockwell,
while writing a dissertation on Hindi novelists, researched Amar Singh's reading
and its context; Andrea Towle, and aspiring historian, and Kara Murphy, a student of international relations, began an extended process of copyediting.

In the many years of quadrennial visits to Jaipur to work on the diary and on-
Rajasthan politics and culture we were helped by friends; the late Raghubir
Singh, Thakur of Bissau, whose haveli was our first home in Rajasthan and who
helped us find the diary by introducing us to Amar Singh's younger brother,
Colonel Kesri Singh; the late Colonel Kesri Singh, whose wit and flare were said
to charm even the Queen of England; Mohan Mukherji and his wife Reena, he
erstwhile finance secretary and then chief secretary, Government of Rajasthan, an
intellectual among the bureaucrats, who extricated us from various bureaucratic
and political entanglements, she an elegant and handsome woman whose hospi-
tality lent warmth to our Jaipur stays; Raghu Sinha, a gallant, generous, ever-sup-
portive friend; the late A. K. Roy, whose life in the Indian Administrative Service
was relieved by devoted scholarship; Francine Krishna, a Kipling scholar whose

literary curiosity went along on outings to ancient monuments; the philosopher, Daya Krishna, whose "seminars" in the university or in his or others' living rooms were the heart of Jaipur's intellectual life; Mukund and Neerja Lath, whose appreciation of art, philosophy, design and good talk invigorates a wide circle of friends; Rajendra Joshi, whose passion for Rajasthan studies has produced three international conferences, three volumes of conference papers and the Institute for Rajasthan Studies; Indu Shekhar, whose intrepid historical curiosity produced a remarkable collection of archival material and rare books [now in Regenstein Library], his wife Radha, his ever-hospitable mother and his daughter Nina, author of a pioneering study of Shyamaldas.

Our anchor since 1971 in the usually calm but sometimes turbulent Jaipur waters has been our steadfast friend and collaborator, Mohan Singh, Thakur of Kanota. He arranged for the cataloguing of family papers which made it possible for us to fill in important details of the diarist's career and that of his family. Mohan Singh's immediate family, his wife Narendra, known to us as Bhabi; his sons, Man Singh and Prithvi Singh; the daughters, Krishna, Vijay, Uma, Marudar and Madhu; their wives and husbands; his uncles and cousins, particularly the late Thakur of Naila and the Thakur of Santha, helped us imagine what extended family life in Amar Singh's haveli 100 years ago might have been like. His friend and fellow amateur historian, the late Thakur Devi Singh of Mandawa, like Mohan Singh, helped solve many textual, archival and genealogical puzzles.

Johannes and Elfriede and Francis Hoeber read early drafts of the selections. Their responses and comments helped us imagine the intelligent lay reader who is one of our intended audiences. The feisty students of Social Sciences 232, South Asian Civilization, at the University of Chicago served as testing ground for the diary as a pedagogic device. We received early encouragement from a doyen of the Indian publishing world, Ravi Dayal.

The photographs in this volume have come mostly from Amar Singh's photo albums. Some were taken by Amar Singh himself. He was an early practitioner of what at the time was a new technology. His ancient camera and glass negatives are part of the Kanota family archive. Subhash Bhargava skillfully transformed Amar Singh's photographs into images for this volume. Jack Davis and Robin von Breton have permitted us to use a few photographs they took in 1971. Christopher Muller-Wille adapted or drew maps for use in the volume.

Our work on the Amar Singh diary has been made possible by a variety of granting agencies. We are grateful for their help. They include the American Philosophical Society, the American Institute of Indian Studies, the Fulbright Foundation, the Smithsonian Institution, the National Endowment for the Humanities and the National Science Foundation. The University of Chicago sometimes supplemented these grants. Three presidents of the American Institute of Indian Studies have been exceptionally supportive, Edward Dimock when the diary was in a fledgling state, Ainslee Embree when it was a substantial project, and Frederick Asher when it came time to publish. Francine Berkowitz of the Smithsonian Institution, a long time supporter, helped to fund both research and publication. Susan Wadley, chair of the AIIS publication committee, facilitated use of the Smithsonian funds. The energy and diligence of Laura Parsons and Rob

Williams at Westview Press, and Bela Malik and her team at the Oxford University Press added greatly to the quality of the text and the appearance of the book. We want especially to acknowledge Pradeep Mehendiratta, Director General of the AIIS, who, since we encountered the diary twenty-eight years ago, has been an invaluable friend, advisor and constructive critic.

Selections from Amar Singh's Readings

Duty—Samuel Smiles

Creative and Sexual Science—G.S. Fowler

The Mysteries of London—George W. M. Reynolds

Plutarch's Lives—Thomas North

The Mahabharata—Edited by Manmatha Nath Dutt

Problems of the Far East—George N. Curzon

The Strand Magazine (Vol. XIX)

Elements of Social Science—Rev. George Drysdale

Memoirs of Baron De Marbot—Translated by Arthur John Butler

Napoleon and His Marshals—J. T. Headley

Washington and His Generals—J. T. Headley

The Hoghunters' Annual (Vol. IX)

A Short History of the English People—John Richard Green

Text Book of Military Topography (Part I)

Complete Etiquette for Ladies and Gentlemen

Cosmopolitan Hinduani—Depicting Muhammedan and Hindu Life and Thought in Story Form—Susila Tahl Ram

Reversing the Gaze

INTRODUCTION

"A Rajput who reads will never ride a horse," says the well-known proverb. But ride he did, and read he did, and wrote voluminously for forty-four years. From September 3, 1898, in the waning days of the Victorian era, until his death on November 1, 1942, three years into World War II, Amar Singh kept his diary every day except one, the day his horse threw him and he lay unconscious. Writing daily became an integral part of his being, a way to know and construct himself, an activity even more compelling than the demands of his several military careers or of his extended family.

Eighty-nine bound volumes, each about 800 pages, can be found at the Kanota fort, 12 miles east of Jaipur on the Agra road, in the rooms Amar Singh called his library. Even by the generous standards of seventeenth- and eighteenth-century Europe, his is one of the longest continuous diaries ever written.[1] The selections in this volume represent the first seven years, from 1898 when he was twenty until 1905, his twenty-seventh year: the days of his youth, when life was still full of surprises.

We read Amar Singh as an ethnographer as well as a first-person narrator of daily life. He speaks as author and observer, about himself as subject, object and native informant. He tells stories about himself, about his kind and others, about

PHOTO 1   The diarist reading. Amar Singh's photo albums.

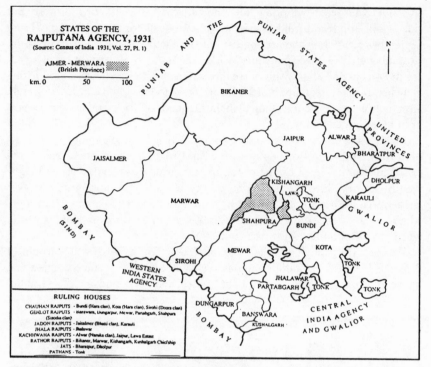

PHOTO 2   Map, princely states of the Rajputana Agency, 1931; Census of India 1931, vol. 27, Pl. 1.

the quotidian and the anomalous. His stories deal with the contestations and strategic interactions that shape his own motives and those of others. Written at the dawn of an unknown future, his daily entries escape the retrospective rationalizations of autobiography. They tell us a special kind of partial truth, the truths of daily living in the present. As a self-conscious agent located in a particular time, place, and circumstance, Amar Singh reflects upon and contests culture even as he enacts it; his daily entries show culture in the making as well as in the doing.

Amar Singh was born and bred a Rajput, then the dominant social order in the princely states of Rajputana.[2] How is it that a Rajput whose virtues were said to be martial, not literary, living in an India that lacked conventions of diary writing, should have begun a diary and continued writing for forty-four years? He wrote for himself, not for a reading public or its critics and markets. The diary became an alter ego and his best friend. An autodidact and self-created intellectual who loved books, good conversation, and ideas but was surrounded by the ennui and philistinism of Rajput and British acquaintances, he wrote "to keep myself amused."

More important, he wrote in response to his liminal positioning between two societies, Rajput and English, the first "black," princely, and subordinate, the second "white," colonial and dominant. We hear an interior dialogue as he explains to himself, and to invisible Rajput and English auditors, the intricacies and virtues of the sometimes contradictory modes of life he experiences. Although symbiotic, the two worlds in which Amar Singh lived were in tension with each other. His efforts to grasp and master the differences between them defined the cultural borderland that finds expression in his diary.

Amar Singh "reverses the gaze." It's him looking at them, not them looking at him. This is not an account about a native subject composed by agents of the colonial master. It is a reflexive "native's" narrative about the self, the master, and the relationship between them.

1

Provenance:
Making a Self at the Jodhpur Court*

Noble families in feudal England often sent a male child for "fostering" to the household of a superior lord. It is in this spirit that Narain Singh of Kanota in 1888 sent his son, Amar Singh, as a ten-year-old from his home in Jaipur to the Jodhpur court. For the next ten years Sir Pratap Singh, the prince regent and the raj's emblem of princely India,[1] saw to his training and education.[2]

When Amar Singh begins his diary in 1898 he is living in Sir Pratap's ample bungalow on the Ratanada palace grounds. The horizon is dominated by the formidable Jodhpur fort Situated atop an 800-foot butte that thrusts up from the desert floor, the fort towers above the walled city below. The arid expanse of the Ratanada palace grounds accommodates two royal residences and the bungalows of numerous legitimate and natural sons of the late Maharaja Takhat Singh.[3]

The Jodhpur fort was built in 1459 by Rao Jodha, founder of the city and state that bear his name.[4] A Rathore clan leader, Rao Jodha reaped successes in battle that enabled him to refound Marwar, the kingdom's ancient name. His realm lay astride the great Thar desert between the Indus river (now in Pakistan) and the Aravalli range that bisects Rajasthan from the northeast to southwest (see map of Rajputana). Jodhpur's desert setting was said to account for its people's character and physique and for much of its wealth. For centuries the desert trade routes that crossed Rajasthan from Cambay on the Gujarat coast and from Baluchistan via Sind linked northern India to the entrepots of the Persian Gulf and the Mediterranean world.[5] "Protecting" and financing trade provided much of the revenue for Jodhpur's rulers and helped make the fortunes of its merchant families-today's "Marwaris."[6]

Sir Pratap's is a strictly male society; those living in the bungalows on the Ratanada grounds are offspring of the Jodhpur royal family, Sir Pratap's brothers, nephews, and cousins, the progeny of his father, the late Maharaja Takhat Singh. The Jodhpur women, secluded in the *zenana* (women's quarters), are barely mentioned in the first years of the diary. Squadron drill, polo, and hunting make up the daily round. Amar Singh's calendar is busier than the others; his extra responsibilities include serving as the regent's private secretary, taking tutorials with Ram Nathji, and, of course, writing his diary.

Ram Nathji, who had been principal of the Nobles School in Jaipur before his arrival in Jodhpur, has been employed by Sir Pratap to educate his nephew, Sardar Singh, the young maharaja. He finds Amar Singh the more promising student.[7]

---

* Indian names and terms are explained in the glossaries.

PHOTO 3   View across Jodhpur city to Jodhpur fort, *circa* 1930; Amar Singh lives at Jodhpur with his guardian, Sir Pratap Singh, from 1888 to 1901; his Champawat lineage is a branch of the Rathore royal lineage of Jodhpur. Amar Singh's photo albums.

PHOTO 4   Camel encampment, Jodhpur. Amar Singh's photo albums.

Sir Pratap's admiring biographer, R.B. van Wart, has sketched a portrait of the prince-regent and his world:

> Who that has seen it will forget the race course?—that dusty, animated track thronged with Thakurs, Europeans, syces [grooms] exercising their horses, and Sir Pratap in charge, ordering, dictating, instructing, missing nothing— not one person but received his or her orders, and woe betide him who failed to carry them out to his mentor's satisfaction. Before the lash of his tongue strong men quailed and crept away like terrified children. . . .
> In the afternoon [Sir P] either rode or else there was polo. . . . When spectator he was wont to sit in the red stone and marble stand at the end of the ground near his house watching every movement of the game, saluting the players chukker by chukker, and, above all, silent. . . . Opposite him on the stone benches sat a row of glum and silent Thakurs—the Trappist monastery, as one well known political officer happily described them. . . . Dinner was an early meal, taken in the garden, for the weather was hot, with horses cropping the grass all around us, greyhounds thrusting up appealing heads for some choice morsel. . . . After dinner Sir Pratap betook himself early to his bed, a long, wide wooden plank like a table top . . . at the foot was a small platform . . . where the dogs slept. . . ."[8]

Jodhpur is an imperial outpost of the British empire in India, its princes and nobles, as constructed in colonial narratives, are loyal vassals of Queen Empress Victoria. Jodhpur's role in India's subcontinental empires did not begin with the British empire; its princes commanded armies of the Mughal empire, governed Mughal provinces, and were central figures at court. Jodhpur princesses married Mughal rulers and became mothers of Mughal emperors.[9]

When Amar Singh begins his diary in 1898 his guardian, Sir Pratap, the picturesque "Sarkar"—the personification of "government"—has been for many years the best known and most honored of the Indo-Victorians, by appointment, as it were, the "beau idéal"[10] of the Indian prince. The most talented member in generations of the Jodhpur royal family and Jodhpur's de facto ruler for two generations, "Sir P" was much in demand at the imperial durbars [royal courts] and jubilees that celebrated and legitimized British rule in India.[11]

Sir Pratap played a leading role at the Queen Empress's golden jubilee of 1887 and at her diamond jubilee in 1897. The colorful, exotic Jodhpur regent was perceived as both an imperial "other" and as a (native) Edwardian gentleman. He attracted the admiring gaze of court and county society and celebrity attention from the press. What they saw and talked and read about was a dashingly handsome man whose imperfections added to his appeal: his limp reminded them of hunting accidents, his trademark Norfolk jacket and jodhpurs were well-worn and rumpled, his speech in English was home-made and pungent. Celebrated as a founder of modem polo in western India and as a world-renowned player, he was known as the designer of the "Jodhpur breeches" that had quickly become the sport's approved habit. "Sir P" was known too as a daring and skillful *shikari* (hunter, huntsman) and extraordinary horseman; a reformer who was declared

PHOTO 5   Sir Pratap Singh, Amar Singh's mentor and patron. Serving intermittently for fifty years (1873- 1922) as first minister or regent of Jodhpur state, he became the Victorian and Edwardian era's most admired Indian prince. Sir Walter Lawrence described him as "a typical Rajput, a great horseman, a gallant soldier, a very astute administrator . . . what lent special charm to his Rathore turban . . . was the sacred miniature of Queen Victoria set in pearls." His notorious casualness is displayed in the "uniform" beneath the martial accouterments. Amar Singh's photo albums.

to have rescued Jodhpur from "anarchy and decay" by transforming its administration and checking ruinous social practices, a "dedicated and gallant" soldier who, in 1888, raised and afterwards commanded the Jodhpur Lancers. This imperial service regiment, to which Amar Singh belonged, fought on behalf of the empire on the North-West Frontier, in China during the Boxer Rebellion and on the western front and in the Middle East during World War I.

Featured in the pages of *Punch* (one cartoon showed him with polo mallets crowning his head), in sporting magazines, and in *Vanity Fair*, Sir Pratap's name became a household word in England. At the high noon of imperial consciousness, he seemed simultaneously to personify gentlemanly public school virtues, attractive forms of eccentricity, and the exoticism and romance of the imperial "other." Victoria often wore the *sirpesh* (jewel-studded decoration) he presented to her in 1887 on the occasion of her golden jubilee. He wore on his turban the miniature self-portrait she had given him.[12] Here is his account of how this improbable romance began:

> The august Queen Empress was pleased to send for me; and in obedience I presented myself. Reaching near her, I made my salute, Indian fashion, placing my sword on the ground: then, coming closer, I kissed her gracious hand, extended in English style; and immediately I raised it to my eyes. All English officers present were astounded at the eccentricity of this salutation: and after the reception was over they asked me about it. I explained that, according to Indian ideas, it was thought ill to salute one's master bearing arms. So I laid down my sword. Further, after kissing Her Majesty's hand, I raised it to my eyes, because there is nothing dearer to a man than his eyes. This explanation seemed to satisfy everyone.[13]

From 1888 when, at the age of ten, Amar Singh first came to live at Jodhpur, he recognized Sir Pratap as his "master." Narain Singh, Amar Singh's father, had sent the two eldest of his seven sons, Amar and Sheo Nath, to join Sir Pratap's household. The two men were old friends. In 1873, the twenty-eight-year-old Pratap, who was not then on good terms with his brother, the Maharaja of Jodhpur, came to live at Jaipur. His sisters, *rajkumar's* of Jodhpur, were married to Maharaja Ram Singh of Jaipur,[14] counted by *raj* officials and his fellow princes as one of India's most successful rulers.[15] Pratap came to learn from his brother-in-law and to find a congenial exile.[16]

Under Maharaja Ram Singh's tutorship the young Pratap "learned the art of administration." On the advice of Ram Singh and the British-controlled Political Department, responsible for the viceroy's overseeing of the princely states, Maharaja Jaswant Singh of Jodhpur, in 1878, appointed the thirty-three-year-old Pratap prime minister of Jodhpur. This was the beginning of Pratap Singh's extended (off and on for forty-four years) tenure as the *de facto* ruler of Jodhpur state.[17]

In the mid-1870s, while the young Pratap was living in "exile" at the Jaipur court, he met Amar Singh's grandfather and two granduncles, then ministers of Jaipur state and leading members of the Jaipur court. Amar Singh's father, twenty-five-year-old Narain Singh served as the maharaja's head of household and commander of his bodyguard. Responsible for the maharaja's comfort and security, he performed such intimate and confidential tasks as preparing the maharaja's *hookah* (waterpipe, hubble bubble) and cooking his meat, not inconsequential tasks in an age that feared poisoning and physical threats to the maharaja's person. Narain Singh and Pratap Singh, both young men in the circle around the maharaja, became fast friends.

After Pratap left Jaipur in 1878 to become prime minister of Jodhpur, he and Narain Singh kept up the friendship through occasional visits and a frequent if somewhat one-sided correspondence. Pratap wrote penitently:

> Though you have written me about twenty to twenty-five letters, I could not write you even one. Please pardon me. If we had both been alike, the affection between us would not have lasted. Even though I do not abandon my bad habits, please don't abandon your good habits. Put my faults under your seat.[18]

PHOTO 6   Amar Singh's father, Narain Singh, and friends in their youth. The apparel, from Rajasthani angarkhi (dress shirt) to French uniform, suggests a wide repertoire of possibilities and no insistence on uniformity. From left: (uncle) Bhim Singh; (father) Narain Singh; (father's good friend) Pratap Singh, not yet Sir; (uncle) Mukend Singh of Gondher; unknown. Circa 1872–1878, when (Sir) Pratap lived at Jaipur and he and Narain Singh were companions of Maharaja Ram Singh. The photo-portrait hangs in Narain Niwas Palace Hotel.

About the time this letter was written, probably in 1888, Pratap Singh, now Sir Pratap and a leading figure in princely and imperial India, visited Narain Singh in Jaipur. Narain Singh's eldest son, the ten-year-old Amar, was said to be "naughty," a usage that usually conveys that a boy is spirited and adventurous. The oral history of the Kanota family has it that Sir Pratap, who had only natural sons, was taken with the boy and asked whether he might be sent to live with him in Jodhpur. Narain Singh sent Amar Singh to Sir Pratap in Jodhpur in the manner of a page, to learn martial arts and rulers' ways, and to endow him with a wise and powerful patron.

Amar Singh gives a somewhat different gloss in his diary to why he was sent to live in Jodhpur with the great but strict Sir Pratap. He speaks about it from the perspective of his querulous uncle Roop Singh of Naila who did not always pull on with Amar Singh's Kanota family. Roop Singh "complained," Amar Singh writes, "that I was very naughty and mischievous and that was the cause of my being taken to Jodhpur." It is plausible that without the disciplining hand of the father who was often posted on service away from Jaipur, the independent-minded boy was a handful for his mother and aunts.

When Maharaja Ram Singh died in 1880, the Kanota family lost its court connection. The new maharaja, Madho Singh, proved unfriendly, later hostile, a stance encouraged by his prime minister, Babu Kanti Chander Mukerjee. The prime minister, having succeeded the Kanota family at court, was suspicious of their designs. Narain Singh was posted as *nazim* (police chief) at remote Jhunjhunu, a headquarter town of Shekhawati, the unruly northern marches of Jaipur state. Populated by over-mighty subjects, Shekhawati's great *thakurs* (nobles) often asserted their independence from the Jaipur durbar and its *dacoits* (robbers) were particularly troublesome and bold. It was a difficult and delicate assignment. As the Jaipur court's officer, Narain Singh fit uncomfortably between the Jaipur court's claim to overlordship and the thakurs' claims to greater autonomy. The formidable Babu Kanti Chander continued his vendetta against the Kanota family and its collaterals by stoking his master's apprehensions about Narain Singh's loyalty. Despite a convention that bureaucratic lineages should be accommodated somewhere in state service,[19] Madho Singh remained adamant about ridding himself of Narain Singh.

In 1899 Narain Singh was dismissed from service at Jaipur on charges that he had conspired with the thakurs. The Political Department immediately appointed him guardian to the then minor Maharaja Jai Singh of Alwar, signaling its support for the Kanota family in the struggle with the Maharaja of Jaipur.[20] Later, after Jai Singh was given his powers, Narain Singh served as a leading minister in the Alwar government. For almost fourteen years, from 1888 to 1901, when Amar Singh leaves Jodhpur to marry and to enter the Imperial Cadet Corps (ICC), he rarely encounters his father, grandfather, or other family members at Jaipur.

Amar Singh knows himself as a Champawat Rathore. The Rathores, like other Rajput exogamous "clans"—Shishodias in Udaipur, Kachhawas in Jaipur—had centuries ago established their suzerainty over previous inhabitants of the area that would become Jodhpur state.[21] Rao Jodha founded Jodhpur city in 1459[22] with the help of many brothers, including Champa, founder of the Champawats. The brothers became the eponyms of Jodhpur's five royal lineages.

Under the spell of nineteenth-century British medievalist enthusiasms, bardic accounts of Rathore lineage heroes became colored with neo-medieval symbolism. Escutcheons were invented; that of Jodhpur state, a product of British heraldic art, invoked feudal monarchies and chivalric societies. It bore a coat of arms and the motto, "Ran Banka Rathore" (Battle Valiantly Rathore).

Amar Singh's Champawat ancestors left the family estate of Peelva in the mid-nineteenth century. Jodhpur's desert ecology yielded a precarious living. Under the prevailing system of primogeniture, younger sons, particularly those from small, impecunious estates such as Peelva, often sought their fortune elsewhere. Amar Singh's grandfather, Zorawar Singh, and two great uncles, Shambu Singh and Fateh Singh, the first in 1861, the latter two in 1854, all younger sons, migrated to Jaipur. Entering state service under Maharaja Ram Singh, they quickly rose to prominence and prosperity as ministers and members of court. Each was granted an estate and title; Shambu Singh became Thakur of Gondher, Zorawar Singh Thakur of Kanota, and Fateh Singh Thakur of Naila.[23] All three wore the gold anklet of the honored *tazimi sardar* (high-status court honor). All retained ties to Peelva, their Jodhpur home *thikana* (estate). In Jaipur they were considered a "foreign" clan and were referred to collectively as "the Champawats."

Under Sir Pratap's tutelage, Amar Singh has learned to think of himself not only as a Rathore and Champawat, but as a Rajput. In the unselfconscious categories of official British ethnography, the term Rajput came to possess both Indian and English connotations: *kshatriya*, the warrior-ruler *varna* (caste) of India's ancient texts,[24] and aristocrat, the landed noble and gentry status familiar to English discourse. British understandings of caste conflated culture and biology; genetic codes were seen to determine character and status. Rajputs were perceived to be "by nature" rulers and warriors. In nineteenth-century readings, to be a Rajput was a condition outside history, essential and timeless.

From at least Mughal times Rajput identity has been shaped by the oral and written panegyrics of court bards. Ironically, by Amar Singh's time, Rajasthan's paramount bardic authority was not a native *charan* (bard) but a voice reexported from England, that of Colonel James Tod. His two-volume work, *Annals and Antiquities of Rajasthan*, illustrated with arresting contemporary engravings,[25] was published in 1829 and 1832.

The research and some of the writing for his imposing work of scholarship and romantic imagination had been done between 1818 and 1822 while Tod served in Mewar (Udaipur) as the East India Company's first political agent to the western Rajputana states. It became not only the authoritative version through which older bardic accounts of Rajputana were filtered for nineteenth-century Indian and English consumption, but also the dominant historiography of princely India. Those who wished to know what a Rajput was consulted Tod. The ethnographic eye replaced the indigenous account. When, in 1901, Amar Singh leaves for the ICC, he is reading Tod to understand the tradition to which he belongs.

Tod's *Rajasthan* dominated in quite different ways both raj and Indian nationalist perceptions. The post-Mutiny raj, which had taken over the direct rule of India from the East India Company, was in need of an ideology to legitimate itself. Tod's account of Rajputana's ancient dynasties, feudal kingdoms, and chivalric honor provided the actors and the backdrop furnishings for a *mise en scène* in which devoted and genealogically qualified Rajput vassals justified the imperial project with their support and loyalty. In time, in the words of Lord Curzon, viceroy when Amar Singh began writing his diary, India's princes and nobles came to be construed as the country's "natural leaders."

Tod's account of the chivalric Rajput also opened the way for the imperial theory of martial races.[26] Prior to the rebellion of 1858, much of the army in India had been built across caste lines. After the rebellion, it was reconstructed on the basis of caste. Rajputs, who had proved mainly loyal in the rebellion were favored, and were declared to be martial, by contrast with the Brahmans of the Bengal Army who, having been disloyal, were declared non-martial. Tod proved serviceable in naturalizing and historicizing a warrior-ruler ideal by celebrating 1,000 years of Rajput bravery and valor.

When, in the years after the rebellion, it proved congenial to English notions of gender as well as politically expedient to construct an ideology of martial (masculine) and non-martial (effeminate) races, Rajputs served as the prototype. From Lord Roberts' reconstruction of a post-Mutiny Indian Army on "racial" lines"[27] to Lt. General Sir George MacMunn's *The Martial Races of India* (1932),[28] Tod's Rajputs served to valorize a racial theory of fighting men. The legitimacy of British rule in India and subcontinental security in the era of the "great game"[29] in Asia came to rely on coopting, rewarding, and celebrating "martial races."

Indian nationalists brought a different interest to their reading of Tod and their understanding of Rajputs. They were in need of a genealogy of resistance. Tod's account of the legendary Mewar (Udaipur) ruler, Rana Pratap (1572–1597), featured his resistance to the blandishments and power of the Mughal empire. At Haldighati (1576) Rana Pratap had challenged the emperor Akbar's mighty army.[30] For twenty-five arduous years Pratap's guerrilla warfare held Mughal power at bay. Tod's bardic-inspired accounts of Pratap's fight to preserve Mewar's autonomy and honor nourished nationalist historiography and metaphors. The subject of plays, poems, and histories, Rajput history provided plausible narratives about India's first "freedom fighter" against imperial rule.

These cultural enthusiasms and panegyrics furnish Amar Singh with an appropriate self-image in the late nineteenth-century imperial *mise en scène* within which he acts. That they have been overtaken by recent critiques of Rajput historiography and identity is more of interest to the scholar of the 1990s than the diarist of 1900.[31] Dirk Kolff's historical unpacking of the term "Rajput" in the sixteenth and seventeenth centuries concludes with the opinion that the aristocratic Rajput of ancient lineage is a creature of the seventeenth and eighteenth centuries when, under the influence of the Mughal court culture, "something like a new Rajput Great Tradition" takes shape.[32] Raj officials after 1858 willingly endorsed the Rajput Great Tradition story, a story that justified placing Rajput princes at the center of the imperial ensemble as loyal but independent feudatories. It was an arrangement that suited the often socially ambitious British middle-class members of the Indian Civil Service (ICS) eager for deference from the exotic princes and aristocrats with whom they hobnobbed and from whom they expected compliance.[33]

Tod's framing of Mewar's struggle to preserve its freedom had an enduring impact.[34] By 1928, when Sir Walter Lawrence, Viceroy Lord Curzon's private secretary and Sir Pratap's loyal friend published his memoirs, *The India We Served*, the myth of the noble Rajputs had reached its apogee. For Lawrence,

> The highest type [of Indian] with which I am acquainted . . . is the Rajput of Rajputana. . . . I like to think that the . . . Indians of ancient times . . . resembled closely the fine thoroughbred men now living in Rajputana—whether they be called Kshattriyas . . . or Aryans . . . still always great and chivalrous gentlemen, with whom it is a privilege and an education to associate.[35]

After 1857, the raj relied increasingly on princely India as a source of legitimacy and political support. The princes in turn came to rely on British recognition and power to legitimize and secure their rule. They were accorded pride of place in a new imperial cosmology that recognized them as India's "natural rulers." Prevalent stories and metaphors about Rajputs help us to understand Amar Singh's Rajput identity and provide the backdrop for how he was perceived by British military officers and civilians.

2

Liminality: Making a Self Between Two Cultures

From age ten to twenty, Amar Singh lives at the Jodhpur court in the male society surrounding the regent, the formidable Sir Pratap Singh. He is there for intensive cultural training—how to conduct himself as a Rathore and Rajput, the first Jodhpur's ruling lineage, the second the social order that dominated Rajputana's princely states. The Rajput order at Jodhpur is not hermetically sealed. It mixes its cultural conventions with the cultural and administrative practices disseminated from British India. Unlike British India, where transgressions of the colonial divide were severely sanctioned and a source of conflict, in princely India they were more tolerated, even encouraged.

Pursuit of a military career in colonial India brings Amar Singh into British cultural and political space for a different regime of intensive cultural training—how to become an officer and a gentleman. In 1900, as a *rissaldar* (junior commissioned officer) in the Jodhpur Lancers, he is sent to China with other Imperial Service Forces. The Lancers join an Allied Expeditionary Force sent to quell the Boxer Rebellion and to lift the Boxers' siege of foreign legations in Peking. His companions on the long voyage from Calcutta to China and during the severe winter of 1900–1901 at Shan Hai Kuan include several British officers of the Indian Army deputed to the Jodhpur Lancers. Amar Singh becomes their friend; he drinks their tea; he reads their magazines; he observes their military practices and is drawn by their discipline and professionalism. He both confronts and evades choices—of private conduct, of professional practice—forced upon him by the tensions and jealousies between the Indian and the British officers.

The military career becomes the site of his liminality, to adapt, to refashion or to resist—the choice is up to him. During three years (1902–1905) as one of the first batch of young men to enter the Imperial Cadet Corps, designed by Lord Curzon, the viceroy, to make achieving aristocrats out of "idle" princes and nobles, he is continually exposed to British manners and professional standards. The same is true during his nine years (1905–1914) as a staff officer at Mhow, a divisional and command headquarters in central India, where he lives as the lone Indian officer in the cantonment.[1] Photographs show him at weddings and garden parties, wearing the only turban in a sea of broad-brimmed women's hats and men's boaters, the single Indian face in an array of white stiff upper lips.

Frequent leaves from the ICC make him an adept at switching cultural codes. When he visits his wife and daughter in the midst of the extended family in the Jaipur *haveli* (mansion), he enters the relatively autonomous Rajput and princely world embedded in imperial India. Amar Singh masters the complex family politics of the haveli of which he will one day be the master. He acquires the skills of propelling an ambitious family to greater social and political heights, through carefully arranged marriages, through strategic responses to a hostile maharaja, and through sturdy alliances with British agents to the princely states.

With the outbreak of World War I in August 1914, Amar Singh leaves Karachi for France as a captain in the Indian Land Forces (ILF). He serves in Flanders and Mesopotamia and receives the medal of gallantry. When he returns to Bombay in 1916 as aide-de-camp (ADC) to General Knight[2] he is still a staff officer outside the chain of command. It is the same Indian Army that, as Lord Curzon found when he tried to give king's commissions (exclusively held by English officers) to the graduating cadets of the ICC, would not countenance "a black commanding a white."[3] The rigid racial boundary betrays Amar Singh's hopes of playing on both sides of the line between princely and British India.

In 1917, in response to nationalist demands for Indianization of the Army, and in recognition of the crucial role played by the Indian troops who fought the war in Europe and the Middle East, some concessions are made: Amar Singh and eight other former cadets of the ICC are given regular king's commissions. Austen Chamberlain, secretary of state for India, supports the innovation: "Early action seems to me desirable," he writes in 1915, "in order to mark the part played by Indian troops in the war and refute the colour bar theory."[4] It is a deviant sunny moment, soon obscured.

With the war's end military budgets, appreciation for "the part played by Indian troops in the war," and fear of nationalist agitation decline precipitously.

PHOTO 7 "The Ormerod-Westcott Marriage, Mhow, 1910." Amar Singh is serving as a staff officer to Sir O'Moore Creagh, general officer commanding, 5th Division, Western Army Corps, Indian Army. For nine years, 1905–1914, he is the lone Indian among the officers of the cantonment's British society. His white Jodhpuri *sapha* (turban) is just visible above the clergyman at the right. Amar Singh's photo albums.

PHOTO 8   Amar Singh's bungalow in the Mhow cantonment. "My house, Northwest view." Amar Singh strides toward the waiting servant. In World War I he sees combat in Flanders when Indian Army divisions helped halt the German drive to the Marne. Austen Chamberlain, secretary of state for India, proposes king's commissions for Amar Singh and eight other Indians "in order to mark the part played by Indian troops in the war and refute the colour bar theory." Amar Singh's photo albums.

Amar Singh continues on active service in the Indian Army. He serves as a major and senior squadron commander in the 16th Cavalry Regiment during the Third Afghan War (1919–1921). In the absence of the British colonel, he commands the regiment. With the return to post-war colonial "normalcy," the racism of "military opinion" resurfaces in judgments about the fitness of an Indian to be in a command position in the Indian Army. His career ends abruptly and ambiguously as he resigns over an (unexplained) unfavorable confidential report: ". . . when Col. Mears came to Tank and showed me my confidential report, we had hot words over it. . . . I was so annoyed with him that I told him plainly that the best he could do was to get me a year's leave [pending retirement] .. . . He agreed to this. . . ."5

Amar Singh's interpretation of liminality, that the permeable boundary between forms of life allows him to play both British and Indian culture and roles, is betrayed by the ending of his first career. His borderline position is redeemed,

PHOTO 9   Amar Singh's Edwardian drawing room at Mhow. Amar Singh's photo albums.

on the other hand, by his second career in the princely state of Jaipur. In September 1922, Maharaja Madho Singh dies. Actively hostile to the Kanota family, he had blocked an appointment for Amar Singh in Jaipur state. The nine-year British-controlled minority administration that takes charge of Jaipur state's affairs[6] radically alters his prospects. The administration sees an experienced Indian Army major from a prominent Jaipur family as an ideal candidate to raise and command a cavalry regiment, the Jaipur Lancers. On his father's death in 1924 Amar Singh becomes Thakur of Kanota and assumes a prominent position in Jaipur's court society. His borderline position between British and princely India forms the basis of a new career.

He develops an intimate fatherly relationship with the minor Maharaja Man Singh. In 1931, when Man Singh is given full powers, Amar Singh remains his friend and adviser. He turns over the day-to-day management of his Kanota estate to a younger brother, Sardar Singh, but retains an active interest in progressive farming, buying books, subscribing to journals, experimenting with improved seeds and methods, and investing in irrigation. Head of Kanota's 100-person joint-family household and entangled in relations with his Naila and Gondher uncles' households, Amar Singh finds himself deeply engaged and often

PHOTO 10   General Lloyd Payne, *circa* 1912, inspecting retired viceroy's commissioned officers (VCOs, like US noncommissioned officers), ordinarily the highest rank available to Indians in what was an apartheid army until the mid–1930s. The positioning of the actors highlights the contrast between Amar Singh's status as a king's commissioned officer (KCO), standing with the white British officers, and that of the VCOs.

troubled by extended family diplomacy. When he retires in 1936 as commander of the Jaipur state forces, Maharaja Man Singh makes him a major general. Until his death in November 1942, he remains active as a respected elder statesman. On the evening before his death he welcomes Jaipur's new prime minister, Sir Mirza Ismail, at a carefully planned dinner party at Kanota fort.

We have spoken of Amar Singh's positioning between two overlapping but distinct worlds, princely and British India. Rather than experiencing liminality as rite of passage,[7] as a temporary disruption between one condition and the next, he experienced it chronically. That Amar Singh continually encountered the contradictory faces of the colonial state, helps to explain why he persisted in writing his diary and how he came to shape its "self as other" ethnography. In the diary's early years we see him trying to learn and master the manners and outlook of two societies, the Rajput society of his birth and the British society to which he is introduced at a relatively young age. It is a game of double mirrors; he sees not only the Rajput ways of his elders and the English ways of British Indian Army officers but also the Rajput image constructed by the British and the British image imagined by his master and mentor, the Jodhpur regent, Sir Pratap Singh.

An Indian and a Rajput, Amar Singh sometimes observes, sometimes resists British practices and worldviews. Compliance and resistance do not exhaust his responses; more often than not he contextualizes: "Well cooked British food is just as much to my taste as the Indian. I might say that if there is Indian food and one has to eat with knives and forks, then there is no fun. In the same way if there is English food and one has to eat it without knives and forks then it loses enjoyment."[8] He finds that each tastes best when eaten in its appropriate fashion. In the privacy of the diary he can congratulate, scold or debate with himself about the choices he has made and the actions he has taken. His diary helps him to clarify the meaning and consequences of living on the border.

3

How We Encountered the Diary

It was largely fortuitous that two political scientists should have become enamored of a humanistic project like editing and interpreting Amar Singh's diary. Our involvement is proof of the seductiveness of "the field" in general, Rajasthan's in particular and *our* liminal positioning between the social sciences and the humanities.

We first encountered the diary in 1971 while living in Jaipur during our fourth visit to the princely state city that in 1949 became Rajasthan's capital. In 1956, as freshly minted Ph.D.s trying to write our first book about India we had chosen Rajasthan, a princely state in the north, and Madras, a province of British India in the south, as the sites of fieldwork for a book that became *The Modernity of Tradition*.[1] We had driven overland from London to India in a Land Rover. From Belgrade to the Khyber we bounced along unpaved roads and unmarked tracks. We slept in the Land Rover and ate off the countryside. The journey took six weeks.

Crossing over the Khyber pass from Afghanistan into Pakistan we were startled by the subcontinent's relative orderliness; the roads were paved and well-marked, government offices and dak bungalows punctuated the countryside, bazaars were well stocked. The arid, mountainous landscape and desert stretches were similar to what we had seen in Turkey, Iran, and Afghanistan but the physical and cultural continuities were contradicted by pervasive signs of governmental authority and commercial vitality.

Colonel Kesri Singh was a frequent visitor at Bissau House, our Jaipur home in 1956. A younger brother of Amar Singh known for his wit and storytelling, he would introduce us to Amar Singh's diary and help us imagine the diarist as a person. We were living in Bissau House at the invitation of the late Thakur Raghubir Singh of Bissau. In search of accommodation in pre-tourism Jaipur, he had made available a ground-floor suite of rooms in his sprawling bungalow. This chance encounter put us in the heart of the old regime whose resistance and accommodation to democratic rule we meant to study.

Our verandah opened on a well-kept garden whose watered green lawns, flower beds, shrubs, gazebo, and sparkling fountain invited romantic contemplation of the charms and comforts of aristocratic living. Beyond the garden walls on a distant horizon we could see Nahargarh (Tiger Fort) perched on the ridge of hills that ring the walled city of Jaipur. The compound's walls sheltered the Bissau family from the shops and ateliers of a lively bazaar adjoining the nearby city wall.

Jaipur takes its name from the astronomer and patron of learning and religion, Jai Singh, the maharaja who planned and built the city. As the Delhi-centered Mughal empire's power and patronage began to fade after the death of Aurangzeb in 1707, local sovereigns, markets, and patrons filled the spaces left vacant by Mughal decline.[2] Jai Singh, nominally a *jagirdar* (landed magnate) of

the Mughal emperor, saw opportunities for independence and territorial aggrandizement. By 1727 he had decided to move his capital from Amber in the Aravalli
hills to the plains below. Before his death in 1743 Jai Singh had presided over laying out and building one of the world's most striking planned cities.[3] In the context of Mughal decline Jaipur quickly became a haven for artists and religious
sects seeking patronage and merchants in search of commercial opportunities.

As the British left India in 1947, India's princes were cajoled and coerced by
the "iron *sardar*," Deputy Prime Minister and States Minister Vallabhbhai Patel,
to surrender their sovereignty to the Government of India. All were rewarded
with privy purses and token marks of sovereignty. A few were asked to occupy
prestigious but largely ceremonial offices. Jaipur's maharaja, Man Singh, became
Rajpramukh (ceremonial head of state) of the newly formed state of Rajasthan,
and Jaipur city was selected as its capital.

Rajasthan's Rajput jagirdars and lesser gentry were next on the agenda of a
state and national government committed to land reform and to dismantling
India's old regime. When we moved into Bissau house in 1956 its master, Thakur
Raghubir Singh, was a major figure in Rajasthan society and political fife and his
city home an important gathering place for the old regime's lords whose large
estates were being "resumed" with compensation by the recently elected Rajasthan government. A steady stream of anxious *rajas* and *raos* and *thakur
sahibs*[4] along with a sprinkling of princes were frequent guests. Over drinks and
dinner that lasted past midnight they teased and ragged each other by reciting
dohas (couplets) that impugned an ancestor's courage or honor, and discussed
strategy and tactics. As houseguests of the thakur sahib we sat in on their discussions of how to adapt to land reform and democracy.[5]

Kesri Singh was more bemused than anxious. Unlike Amar Singh, who as the
eldest son eventually inherited the Kanota title and estate, Kesri Singh was a *chota
bhai* (younger brother) who had to live by his wits. Like many younger sons of
Rajput noble houses, he had spent many years in princely state service—in
Gwalior, Jaipur and Kashmir—where ability and charm helped make a man's fortune. In the late 1930s as guardian of the Jaipur royal children, he had lived for a
time near Badminton, the duke of Beaufort's estate, and the Badminton school
where "Mickey" and "Bubbles,"[6] the two eldest children of the Jaipur maharaja,
Man Singh, were being educated.

We found the stylishly eccentric Kesri Singh affable and charming. He affected
a Loden cape and flourished an ivory cigarette holder. As a student in Mayo College he had designed a Kanota coat of arms and referred to himself as Kesri Singh
de Kanota. "Kesargarh" (Tiger Mansion), which he built for himself near the
walled city, was a confection of a castle; his chauffeur-driven car had a springing
tiger painted on each side. Known as a great shikari, author,[7] raconteur, and conversationalist, he could be counted on to keep royalty amused, as when Queen
Elizabeth and Prince Philip visited Jaipur in 1961. Being a younger son gave him
a certain perspective on his noble peers.

We thought we were pursuing a Tocquevillian-style inquiry about the fate of
India's old regime under democratic rule. In the 1950s and 1960s, when western

scholars and policy intellectuals swarmed into "new nations" such as India with the salvational message of modernization and development, our interest in India's old regime appeared at best as exotic, at worst irrelevant. Earlier, before independence and democracy, both Indian nationalist and British imperial scholars for quite different reasons had ignored or denigrated the society and politics of the princely states. Progressive nationalist intellectuals were inclined to dispatch princes and "feudal classes" to the dustbin of history. British writers tended to patronize the princes and nobles as loyal feudatories even while deprecating them as idle and decadent or sensationalizing them as globe-trotting high society celebrities.

We wanted to look behind such stereotypes. Perhaps the relative independence afforded by "paramountcy's" "subordinate cooperation"[8] allowed more freedom to be Indian than did the more direct domination of the colonial relationship in British India. Perhaps those born and bred in princely India might be less subject to what Ashis Nandy calls the "intimate enemy," less assimilated, less afflicted by a residual colonial mentality.[9]

Having served in three states, including a spell as inspector general of Jaipur state's police, Kesri Singh knew a lot about the government and politics of princely states. He was an intelligent "informant." In 1971, as on previous visits, we pursued him with questions about the details of his experiences. This time, fifteen years from the time we first met in 1956, he pointed us to a fuller source. Why he waited so long we do not know. Perhaps he expected us to grow weary of our subject, perhaps our persistence made him more confident that we could be trusted. In any case he told us about his brother's diary and introduced us to his nephew, Mohan Singh, heir to Amar Singh's title, estate, and diary.

General Amar Singh,[10] it seems, had kept a diary between 1898 and 1942, the year he died. Mohan Singh showed us two glass-fronted shoulder-high bookcases filled with eighty-nine folio-size leather-bound volumes. For us, this proved to be the beginning of a thirty-one year relationship with Mohan Singh as a friend and as a collaborator. Mohan Singh had already begun working on the diary. He showed us typed excerpts of his selections. They featured public life, great persons and events, such as a viceroy's visit or a maharaja's installation; sport such as a polo match at Mhow, the Kadir Cup competition, a tiger hunt at Alwar, pig-sticking in the Jod of Bali. For the most part they mirrored raj representations of life in princely India. We asked to see more. With Mohan Singh's help and guidance, we began reading bound volumes of the diary manuscript and found there was more, much more.

An "amateur" historian—he has no degree in history—Mohan Singh is the author of a comprehensive three-volume genealogical history in Hindi of his and Amar Singh's lineage, the Champawats.[11] The work has made him a much demanded speaker at well-attended meetings of a recently constituted Champawat association. His eldest sister, like Mohan Singh an autodidact, had introduced her much younger brother to Rajput and Mughal history. Once launched, he kept going; he and the late Thakur Devi Singh Mandawa,[12] author of several works on Rajasthan history and editor of an historical journal, became a self-constituted

PHOTO 11   Susanne Rudolph, Mohan Singh and Lloyd Rudolph at Amar Singh's *chattri* (cenotaph) in 1971. Photo by Lloyd Rudolph.

historical society, meeting regularly to explore and debate Rajput and Mughal history and culture. Mohan Singh has history at the ready; he supplies on-line responses to our queries about historical events and personalities, and supplies detailed information about lineages, families, ritual practices, and manners, which he calls "etiquette."

As we read more bound volumes of the diary text, we found extensive candid accounts of family life and personal relationships. Initially Mohan Singh did not share our growing enthusiasm for selecting passages dealing with private life in the big house, the kind of writing that can be found in Part V. It was not so much a question of confidentiality as it was what was interesting and worth knowing. Family accounts were too obvious, too self-evident. As Mohan Singh was wont to say in those days, "but everybody has a family."

For us, Amar Singh's candid accounts of life in the joint family exposed and articulated what for Mohan Singh was tacit knowledge. We saw gripping narratives, tragedies, dramas, quotidian triumphs—persons in motion and motives in context. Sometimes they illuminated, sometimes they challenged conventional abstractions about the nature of patriarchal society, female agency, colonial subjection. Watching Amar Singh's scripting and staging of cousin Bhoj Raj Singh's marriage; the conventionally problematic relationship between "my mother" and "my wife"; the Naila thakur, his uncle Roop Singh's efforts to dominate the extended family was as enlightening as it was engaging.

Writing about family disputes, discord, even chicanery can be read as compromising family honor and as revealing disharmony in the lineage to the outside world. Would such accounts and others that portrayed the expressive life, intimate scenes of love and affection, jealousy and anger, expose to public gaze what should not be recognized or acknowledged? When diary excerpts were serialized in Hindi translation in *Rajasthan Patrika*, an outraged reader wrote to protest Amar Singh's candid account of the characterological weaknesses of his guardian, Sir Pratap Singh, regent of Jodhpur. He insisted that having such thoughts, even in the privacy of a diary, much less publishing them ninety years after the fact, was an act of *lèse majesté* that threatened Rajputs' moral standing and public reputation.[13]

Such reactions gave us pause. As outsiders and scholars we were keen to pan for gold in the diary's reflexive ethnography of private life in the big house. At the same time, we began to see the diary project increasingly through Mohan Singh's Rajput eyes.

Over the years, as we considered together the value of Amar Singh's diary accounts and talked about their relation to the wider world of scholarship and literature, as those among his extended family and in Rajput society who might take offense died, and as we became more drawn into the ethos of the Kanota lineage, Mohan Singh's views and ours have increasingly coincided. We recognized the need for prudence, he became more sanguine about being candid in print.

4

Reconstructing the Text

This volume is a kind of second coming. Between 1971 and 1976 we had pruned the first seven years to about 2 percent, prepared glossaries of persons, events, and unfamiliar terms and written a 100-page introduction. We approached the diary in the spirit of Ranke's "wie es eigentlich gewesen ist," of positive truth and unmediated authenticity. We would use Amar Singh's diary to improve on archival history and anthropological ethnography. It would provide more and better "factual" evidence about what happened and how people behaved. Where necessary, we would "correct" Amar Singh's facts and ethnographic readings.

For a variety of reasons we did not publish the 1976 version of the Amar Singh manuscript. Instead we worked on other books and published seven articles based on the diary, four of them in *Essays on Rajputana*.[1]

We have a different view in the 1990s of the 1970s selections. Influenced by versions of the postmodern turn in literary and historical scholarship we no longer believe that positive history and public life encompass all of what the diary has to say about meaning and truth. To be sure, we live in the shadow of positive truth, the facticity that is sometimes taken as all there is to "reality." We now recognize that the subjective truths and imagined worlds found in personal documents share something with those found in novels and poetry and with the constructed "realities" deployed by historians and social scientists.[2]

While preserving the factual apparatus of the 1976 Ms we adopt a different epistemological stance: we accept that Amar Singh is constructing an era, places, persons, and himself. We now view his diary as a particular kind of text, a personal document that captures multiple and partial truths, a representation of Rajputs, of princely and imperial India, and of the colonial condition. In 1976 we dimly recognized what now guides our editing effort, that Amar Singh is telling us *what he knew*, not objective truths or the whole truth, that the diary is more like a painting than a photograph, more mediated than transparent, more figurative than literal.

Liberated from the epistemological claims of positive truth, we have felt more free to intervene in Amar Singh's text The most obvious way is cutting out what is not to be presented. Our 1976 Ms represented about 2 percent of the first seven years (1898–1905), this one about 1 percent. As we condensed and concentrated, we shaped a particular Amar Singh, one who seems less concerned with hunting and riding, bathing and exercising, and paying routine visits to relatives than with constructing ethnographies of family and court life.

We intervene too in our introductions and commentaries. In Part 1, when Amar Singh is learning to tell a good story and his writing legs are a bit wobbly, we appear as co-narrators. Our narrative voice fades out (around 1900) but our editorial voice, in bracketed material and in endnotes, appears throughout.

In the 1970s Ms we were careful to preserve the ordering and rhetoric of the daily entries not only because of our positivist epistemology but also because we valued the daily entry's "open-endedness." It is the daily entry's open-endedness that saves diaries from the retrospective rationalizations that beset autobiography and biography. Daily entries are written in present time, innocent of future knowledge and the path not taken. Where will an event or conversation lead? Will it gather force, fade, disappear? Diarists writing in the present do not know the outcome of the stories they tell day by day, autobiographers and biographers writing retrospectively do. They can tell their stories teleologically, as if the outcomes were immanent in the beginnings. Particular events can be fitted into known trajectories, depicted as pieces needed to complete a puzzle or shown as links that enabled everything else to happen.

Our 1990s perspective freed us to disrupt the diary's chronological linearity, its day-to-dayness, without losing the daily entry's open-endedness. We now imagine ourselves as film editors ruthlessly cutting and arranging rushes for plot, character development, and dramatic tension. The result is six thematic parts. In formulating part and chapter titles we have chosen a language, sometimes our own, sometimes Amar Singh's, that typifies narrative themes. Readers can pick and choose among them according to their tastes and priorities.

Why depart from the diary's chronological structure? Our reasons have to do with rhetoric and theory. Viewed from a distance, daily diaries tend to speak in a staccato rather than a connected fashion. Accounts of events, persons, and conversations, often as not, are dispersed over separate entries. References to a favorite cousin or a detested officer can be separated by days, months, even years. How is the reader to remember who is who and what is what? Unlike novels, plays, operas or film scripts, diaries are weak on flow and continuity, the downside of open-endedness. Written without knowledge of outcomes or consequences, diaries lack explicit plots or causal connections. The diarist cannot string his entries on the thread of a story with beginning, middle and end. As editors making and arranging selections, we can.

Bringing together entries about persons, events, and conversations so that they tell stories also helps to advance social science explanations. Stories can suggest why and how things happened—the likelihoods that arise from sequence, conjunction, and association and from the consequences of intention and agency.

Our thematic rearrangement should make it easier for a variety of readers, western "others" and Indians separated by generation, place, and cultural difference from turn-of-the-century Rajput and imperial societies, to "be there," to imagine what these distant, alien contexts are about, to spot and remember *dramatis personae*, to follow motives, and experience relationships. We expect them to have less need to consult the persons glossary or the family tree when they encounter cousin Bhoj Raj Singh and Amar Singh's "bhabee," hero and heroine of one of the diary's longer connubial dramas.

Sometimes our rearrangements and bracketed interventions may resemble docudrama[3]—a burgeoning practice on television, in film, and in print that blends imaginative and positive truth to fill narrative and informational gaps, develop plot, heighten tension and deepen character. In so far as we have engaged in docudrama, we have tried to do so constructively by maintaining the integrity and centrality of Amar Singh's voice and by not putting words in his mouth and/or thoughts in his head.

The epistemological doubt generated by the postmodern turn has led us to privilege Amar Singh's knowledge over ours. While we think we know more about Rajasthan and imperial India than most of our readers and sometimes question Amar Singh's version of things, we have abandoned our 1970s practice of playing expert by second guessing and correcting what he has to say about practice and belief. In an era that has dethroned the author and recognized reader sovereignty we count on the readers to bring their knowledge, experience, and imaginations to bear on Amar Singh's claims and ambiguities. These days dealing with ambiguous knowledge, even mystery, is often better left to readers than experts. Other than situating him and supplying absent facts, why should we try to challenge or go beyond Amar Singh, a reflexive native informant, when he says of a practice, "it is Rajput etiquette"?

Of course not all readers are the same; they bring different backgrounds and expectations to what they read. "Indians" at home in India are different from diasporic "Indians" at home abroad, Americans are different from Europeans, scholars are different from lay persons. We put the term "Indians" in quotes because we think of transnational persons like Salman Rushdie or Bharati Mukerjee, or our Indo-American students at the University of Chicago, as being at "home" simultaneously in several places and contexts. Then there are those "Indians" who hold that knowing and telling the truth about India and its way of life requires the "authenticity" of being Indian, an authenticity that, by their lights, the likes of us are said to lack.[4] Who are we, American scholars of India, to instruct those who learned what it meant to be Indian at their grandmother's knee—in Bangalore, Pune, Jaipur or even in Skokie or Downers Grove? By contrast, non-Indian readers—Americans, Europeans and others—may fault us for not telling them how it "really" is with "Rajputs," for not talking like "scientists" who have "been there."

Our response to such dilemmas has been to provide facts and interpretations in bracketed material, endnotes, and glossaries, in language that will hopefully allow readers to join us in constructing or imagining what Amar Singh's diary means.[5]

5

An Indian Diary in English[1]

To study the rhetoric of the British raj . . . is . . . to attempt to break down the incipient schizophrenia of a critical discourse that seeks to represent domination and subordination as though the two were mutually exclusive terms. Rather than examine a binary rigidity between these two terms—which is an inherently Eurocentric strategy—this critical field would be better served if it sought to break down the fixity of the dividing lines between domination and subordination, and if it further questioned the psychic disempowerment signified by the colonial encounter.

Sara Suleri[2]

The borderline work of culture demands an encounter with "newness" that is not part of the continuum of past and present. It creates a sense of the new as an insurgent act of cultural translation . . . refiguring . . . [the new] as a contingent 'in-between' space.

Homi K. Bhabha[3]

When we were young one could still find in a variety store such as Woolworths little pastel-colored diaries locked with a golden hasp and key. Adolescents, mostly girls, bought them to commune in private with their secret selves. Such rituals of privacy and secrecy mark the diary as a particular form of first-person document. Diaries differ from public, retrospective first-person writing such as journals, autobiographies, and memoirs because they are written in the present and in confidence.

The boundary between public and private that separates autobiographers from diarists is hard to discern and often transgressed. Selves are social as well as individual constructions. Secrecy does not prevent society and the times from seeping in; they penetrate consciousness and mediate reflexivity. Diarists cannot invent themselves out of whole cloth. They may be more at liberty than autobiographers to dodge constraining social voices but such voices cannot be wholly silenced. Significant others perch on Amar Singh's shoulder, judging, even scolding. He explains himself, justifying what he has said and done, to interiorized presences—Ram Nathji, his father, Captain Cameron, Major Turner, even Sir Pratap. Sometimes Amar Singh's pen "refuses to write"; sometimes he withholds from his diary "subjects which are too tender and . . . sacred."[4]

Amar Singh's pen is also affected by the shadow of the future-imagined readers, more grandly, posterity. There is an implied expiration date on confidentiality, an implication that when he is no more, his confidences may become public. While reading Samuel Pepys' diary, he speculates "whether in the future someone would print my diary and whether anyone would care to read it."[5]

Secrecy allows him enough space to confess his indiscretions, lapses, and failures and to grumble about, even to curse and criticize, those he encounters daily. But secrecy does not remove his concern to represent himself and others in ways that will pass muster with posterity—the future readers.

Rajput society in Jodhpur and Jaipur was not hospitable to privacy. Pursuing privacy signaled that those involved might be trying to evade social control by hegemonic collectivities such as family, caste, court, and by the raj establishment. Young men and women in patriarchal family settings were under special surveillance. Efforts to establish private space and engage in private acts were suspect as potential arenas of resistance or subversion. To write a diary in private about the self and for the self, as Amar Singh did, was a culturally deviant act that smacked of a rebellious consciousness.

Why Did He Write?

Why did he write? For whom did he write? Why did he continue without interruption for forty-four years? Were there salient cultural warrants or literary models in Rajput or pan-Indian practices which led him to the diary form? Does his liminal positioning between two worldviews and their languages help explain why Amar Singh made diary writing a lifelong commitment?

At one level, there may be a rather straightforward narrative answer to the question of why he wrote a diary. We imagine a remark by his teacher, Barath Ram Nathji. "Amar Singh, you should keep a diary in English." From Ram Nathji's perspective a diary would help to perfect Amar Singh's English; it would give him experience in writing; it would give him a vehicle for critiquing his assigned reading and reflecting on his experiences, and it would be a form of discipline and self-control.

As headmaster of the Jaipur Nobles School,[6] Barath Ram Nathji had become familiar with the Victorian public school practice of using diaries for pedagogic purposes and as means to instill discipline and self-control. The spread of public school practices to India also helps to explain why, when Amar Singh in 1902 joined the first class at the ICC, he and his classmates were required by their instructors to keep diaries.

Ram Nathji's hypothetical injunction to Amar Singh may help to explain why he wrote in English rather than in Hindi, his mother tongue which would seem more compatible with a diary's interiority and self-communication. His choice of English for his diary—he did write in Hindi for *Saraswati*, a leading journal of the north India Hindi revival—may have had something to do with a liminal consciousness responsive to imagined English-speaking interlocutors and audiences.

Ram Nathji's assignment may indeed have been the proximate cause of the diary. But it does not address whether Amar Singh's cultural context or personal motives helped or hindered his vocation as a diarist. Many schoolboys had to write diaries but most seem to have abandoned them on the morning after graduation.

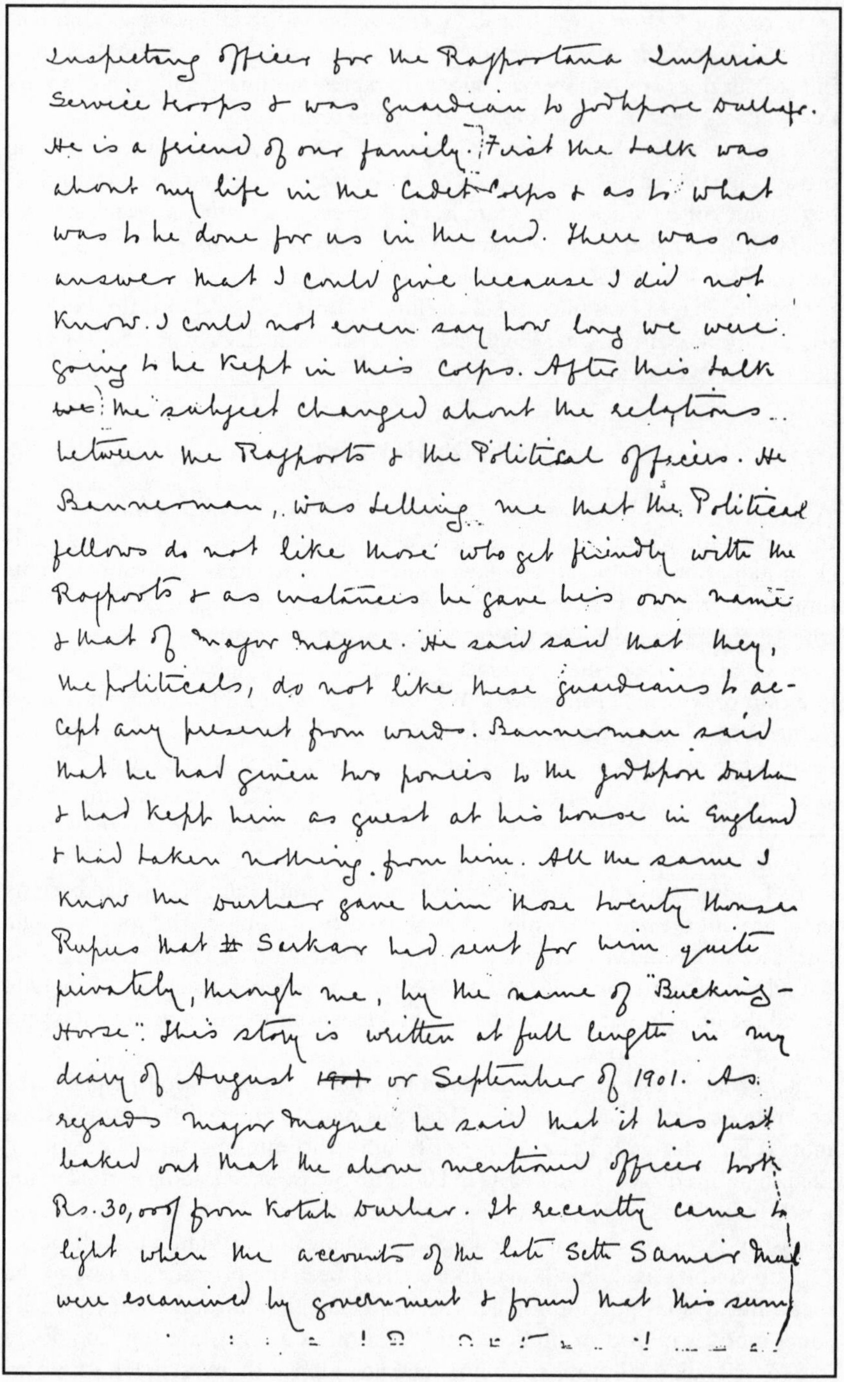

Inspecting Officer for the Rajpootana Imperial Service troops & was guardian to Jodhpore Durbar. He is a friend of our family. First the talk was about my life in the Cadet Corps & as to what was to be done for us in the end. There was no answer that I could give because I did not know. I could not even say how long we were going to be kept in this corps. After this talk we the subject changed about the relations between the Rajpoots & the Political Officers. He Bannerman, was telling me that the Political fellows do not like those who get friendly with the Rajpoots & as instances he gave his own name & that of Major Magne. He said said that they, the politicals, do not like these guardians to accept any present from wards. Bannerman said that he had given two ponies to the Jodhpore Durbar & had kept him as guest at his house in England & had taken nothing from him. All the same I know the Durbar gave him those twenty thousand Rupees that # Serkar had sent for him quite privately, through me, by the name of "Bucking-Horse". This story is written at full length in my diary of August 1901 or September of 1901. As regards Major Magne he said that it has just leaked out that the above mentioned Officer took Rs. 30,000 from Kotah Durbar. It recently came to light when the accounts of the late Seth Samir Mul were examined by government & found that this sum

PHOTO 12   Page of the diary. *Alwar, Sunday, 13th December, 1903.* "XIX. Talk with Bannerman." (Former British Resident in Jaipur.)

Cultural Warrants for Diary Writing

We have already noted that conventional readings of Rajput culture do not find literary pursuits, much less diary writing, among its features. More broadly, Indian civilization has been read as indifferent to the individuality that subjective writing entails. Amar Singh frequently affirms a Rajput identity,[7] more often than not by criticism of Rajput failures, but never speaks of Rajputs as practicing first-person autobiographical writing. British official ethnography and historiography celebrated Rajputs as a "martial race," brave and bold men on horseback—on the battlefield, at the hunt and, in Amar Singh's day, on the polo-field. Stereotypes? Probably. But in the seven diary years that follow, Amar Singh often complains that he cannot have a conversation with fellow Rajputs about books or ideas; "they do not read; they do not know how to converse."

Rajput culture was not of a piece, was not homogenous and monolithic. Alternatives were available, some more conducive to the writer's calling than others. Among the most important alternatives was charan culture, the culture of Barath Ram Nathji, Amar Singh's guide to Rajput as well as English culture. Charan loosely translates as bard. *Charans* or *baraths* were literary persons. Through oral performances and written texts they were expected to preserve, transmit and cultivate Rajput civilization. As guardians of Rajput codes of conduct, they told *charit* (biography), and reported on *charitra* (character and conduct). At courts, both large and small, they instructed by entertaining. They performed key roles in major rituals such as coronations and death ceremonies. A few, like Ram Nathji's maternal uncle in Jodhpur, served as *diwans* (first ministers) to maharajas. Charans accompanied trade caravans as guides and protectors; killing a charan, like killing a Brahman, was believed to bring divine punishment on the perpetrator.

Charans composed and recited dohas, narrative poetry in couplets, that through celebration, irony, and satire praised and criticized Rajput conduct and character. Amar Singh was introduced to dohas by Ram Nathji; between March 24, 1898, when Amar Singh begins his notebook, until September 3, when it becomes "The Diary," Amar Singh fills its pages with dohas written or assigned by his tutor. It was an induction into the literary vocation. He collects dohas for years thereafter; he and an intellectual Rajput friend at the ICC value each other in part because they share a common passion for dohas, recording them in copy books and reciting them to each other.

The standing of charan poetry in Rajput consciousness and culture may have legitimized Amar Singh's literary bent but, as a *genre*, it did not provide a warrant for first-person autobiographical writing such as a diary. Charan ballads about Rajput heroes addressed their conduct; they dealt with honor and courage in public space, not thoughts, attitudes, and feelings in private space.

Amar Singh's liminal positioning offers another explanation for why Amar Singh became a diarist. Today, at the end of the twentieth century, a century after Amar Singh began his diary, hybridity has more or less been accepted as normal. Global processes have made the forging of multiple, transcultural selves a common, though no less complex, experience. Coming to grips in his diary with his liminal positioning in imperial India, Amar Singh provides an account of hybridity formation before decolonization and hyper-globalization. Because he writes in English, the diary seemed to privilege British ways but it immediately becomes apparent that his English medium was not his message, at least not his whole message. In the early years particularly, Amar Singh is preoccupied with negotiating the dual cultural terrain of princely and British India. Evaluating options and recording adaptations, straddling and crossing cultural and moral boundaries, he considers what manners, food, music, words, forms of address, and responses to authority are morally right or instrumentally useful. His diary records his effort to find out what is contextually appropriate for the kind of person he wants to be.

Liminal positioning can favor but not ensure diary writing. Many in late nineteenth-century India were similarly positioned but few kept diaries and even fewer kept diaries that grappled with hybridity. Diaries began to be written in Europe in the seventeenth and early eighteenth centuries as secret documents. They were written in private by individuals who wanted to hide their thoughts from powerful, disapproving others, unorthodox communicants with God, women living under severe forms of patriarchy. Like the early use of the mirror, the diary made it possible for individuals to view and imagine themselves directly instead of through the mediating eyes and voices of collective others. Only in the later eighteenth and nineteenth centuries did the diary emerge as a form of literature, a *genre*, "a new type of narrative"[8] that featured individuality and subjectivity in the context of conventions of self-understanding, self-discipline, and the development of private realms open to public scrutiny.[9]

In Amar Singh's time, agents of patriarchal joint and extended families and of caste and religious corporate groups enforced rules and scrutinized behavior in ways that inhibited individuality and blocked privacy. Diary writing was difficult and dangerous in Amar Singh's 100-person joint-family household.

The formulaic conventions of Rajput art and manners were not conducive to diary writing either. Stock images and language shaped perceptions and attitudes in ways that were at odds with the diary's quotidian particularity and specificity. Quentin Crewe, while researching for his biography of the Jaipur maharaja, Man Singh, *The Last Maharaja*, almost ran aground on the iconographic conventions of Rajput society. Those who knew Man Singh persisted in telling him formulaic tales about the maharaja rather than what they knew about him; they "remembered the royalty, not the man."[10] Vishaka Desai in her essay "Images as Icons" comparing Mughal and Rajput miniatures shows us how deep-rooted such conventions were: paintings of Mughal emperors and eminent courtiers capture and reveal distinctive persons while the rajas and courtiers in Rajput court painting are so highly stylized that it is difficult to distinguish one raja from another. For Rajput court painters too it was more important to convey royalty than the man.[11] Breaking loose from such conventions Amar Singh writes about men and women as he knew and experienced them, distinctive persons located in space and time with their own ideas and attributes.

Literary Warrants

Were there literary models for autobiographical writing, exemplary works to which educated persons might turn for inspiration and guidance? The answer is, very few, and Amar Singh is unlikely to have known about them. Mughal imperial memoirs and court histories were in Persian,[12] a language that he, like most educated Indians of his time, did not command. The sixteenth-century *Baburnama*, the greatest Mughal autobiography and a work of consummate individuality and reflexive subjectivity, was written in Chaghtay Turkish, the Timurids' spoken language, and was not conveniently and authentically available in English until 1912–1921, well after Amar Singh began his diary.[13] Nor did other eighteenth-century Indian autobiographical works, of which there were several, serve as models or influence him.[14] Apart from *Plutarch's Lives*, of which more later, Western exemplars entered his life after he had become a committed diarist.

One might argue that the widely used and well-known *roznamcha* (daily record) was—and is—a form of diary. Kept by rulers, merchants, *zamindars* (masters of landed estates), and heads of households, they record the arrivals and departures of persons, weddings, deaths, births, important events, and finances—money paid and value received. They are particular, not formulaic, but they tell us about the surface of human behavior, leaving motive and meaning untouched. Similarly, it might be argued that *charitra* (accounts of the character and conduct of deities, kings and exemplary persons), provide models for autobiographical writing. But like the charans' poetic accounts of Rajput heroes, charitra engages in a form of biography that attributes formulaic motives to persons and stereotypical consequences to their deeds. Persons are constructed as social objects from models found in honored and familiar texts and play prescribed roles.

According to Mukund Lath, a keen student of Indian literary and philosophical texts, "True [auto]biography in which a person reveals himself through his actions, aspirations and strivings, is completely missing" from charitra.15 But Lath has edited, translated and interpreted a "true autobiography," Ardhakathanaka (Half a Tale), the remarkable seventeenth-century diary written by Banarsi, a north Indian merchant, poet, and influential Jain theologian. Lath's 100-page introduction masterfully locates the Banarsi text in a critical examination of well-known and lesser literary texts from the seventh to the seventeenth-century and beyond. He finds that "long centuries [were] almost totally devoid of meaningful autobiographial writing."16 This absence, Lath argues, is often attributed to the ". . . widely-held view that Indians were deliberate anonymity-seekers" who, until modern times, placed "little value . . . on the individual or his achievement."17 He challenges this reading of motives and values: it neglects, he argues, considerable evidence that literary authorship existed and mattered and, more important, that creative artists—sculptors, painters, architects, musicians—were deeply concerned about individual recognition and made efforts to achieve it.18

Western attention to the formulaic and to anonymity in Indian cultural productions tends to exaggerate and mis-specify differences between western and

Indian civilization, to render the contrast between them in black and white rather than shades of gray. Western eyes often see India through the lens of Renaissance humanism, an image that features self-generating individual creativity by great artists like Michaelangelo or great writers like Machiavelli, and find India wanting in individuality and originality. But it does not follow that Renaissance humanism can account for the secret diaries written in seventeenth-century Europe or public ones in the nineteenth century. Similarly, formulaic representations and anonymously created culture do not necessarily account for the paucity of premodern autobiographical writing in India.

The growth of communications and the spread of literacy in the later years of the nineteenth century generated growing numbers of self-reports in journals, diaries, autobiographies, and *atma kathas* (stories of the self). Those who wrote them, particularly if they were women, had to defy conventional social pressure.[19] These accounts, often written in regional languages other than Hindi such as Bengali and Marathi, had to be translated if they were to achieve all-India circulation. Amar Singh, who follows his teacher and mentor Ram Nathji in ordering books from shops in British India and who recorded those he read in annual registers, does not seem to have encountered Indian autobiographical writing in the early years of his diary.

It seems that Amar Singh became and remained a diarist without the benefit of Indian or English models of autobiographical writing. But his early and enduring attachment to English literature may have helped him to write subjectively and reflexively. The novel, new to India as a genre, became a visible part of the literary landscape in the later nineteenth century. "The autobiographer," according to Philippe Lejeune, "came into his own only . . . by imitating novels."[20] Amar Singh was a voracious reader not only of novels but also of works of nonfiction.[21] In the years after 1900, he records sixty books or more per year in his annual registers, many of them novels.

More important than the influence of novels in making him a diarist may have been his response to *Lives* by Plutarch, the one author whose work seems to have been an enduring *vade mecum*—a model to emulate even if never realized. We suspect he began reading Plutarch just about the time he switched from his notebook to "The Diary" on September 3, 1898. We know that he acquired the Langhorne edition on September 22, 1898, three weeks after he began his diary.[22] He continued reading Plutarch throughout 1899, 1900, 1901, and into 1902. He marked passages, copied many into his diary interspersed with his favorite dohas, and occasionally made comments on particular passages. Mixing dohas with passages from Plutarch may not have been entirely fortuitous. Plutarch's command of character, context, and narrative seems to have impressed him in part because it resembled the charan literature he knew so well, tales of famous men, rulers, commanders, and warriors whose conduct brought honor or disgrace to those in whose name they acted. When early on he portrays the young Maharaja of Jodhpur, Sardar Singh, we hear echoes of Plutarch, echoes that reverberate in subsequent characterizations of persons in context. The intensity and duration of his interest in *Plutarch's Lives* during the initial years of the diary suggest that this reading was more important than other literary influences for consolidating his commitment as a diarist.

For Amusement

Finally, the answer to the question, "why did he write?" may lie less in cultural influences than in self-realization. Why do people climb mountains, go trekking, travel to distant lands, play the flute or the guitar? Because adventure or health is fashionable, travel is affordable, some social circles and some generational cadres declare flutes and drums seductive or "cool?" Or because some practice has taken hold of the self in ways that sustain life, give meaning, provide joy, enhance well-being?

Alain Corbin writing about "The Secrets of the Individual" tells us that "For those who savored interior monologue, keeping a diary was also a source of sophisticated pleasure" and the French diarist, Maine de Birand, that

> I have plenty to do in following the movement of my ideas and impressions, in exploring myself, in examining my dispositions and my various ways of being, in drawing the best out of myself, in registering the ideas that come to me by chance or that are suggested to me by my reading.[23]

For Amar Singh "writing to my heart's content"[24] was amusement and pleasure. Being kept from writing—and reading—brought lassitude, degeneration, boredom. In December 1900, Amar Singh is in China with the British Expeditionary Force, serving as ADC to Sir Pratap Singh, regent of Jodhpur and commander of its Imperial Service Troops. He meets his master and commander on the parade ground. "He asked me where I was during the whole of the day yesterday . . . . I explained that I was in mine own room reading books." Amar Singh explains the purport of Sir Pratap's question:

> . . . instead of sitting comfortably in our rooms we ought to loaf about after him doing nothing but staring at his face. Now this is too hard for me. I honestly say that this is the thing I hate most of all. He does no work that would occupy him. He cannot read, and cannot sleep the whole day through, and so naturally must pass his time somehow or other. It is quite different with me, who love reading as much anything in the world.[25]

Amar Singh dreaded the boredom of being trapped into mindless talk by empty-headed military peers or philistine courtiers as much as he chafed at being obliged to attend Sir Pratap by standing silently in his presence. In July 1905, at Mount Abu, a hill station in western Rajasthan, he finds himself in the midst of a swarm of royals and their entourages escaping the intense heat of the plains. Asked to share space with his father he finds that "the room where my father was put up is much too small" and over-run. He retreats to a nearby bathroom where he devotes "hours and hours writing my notes . . ." and trying to "concentrate his mind on reading and writing." "How can a man enjoy his life," he asks, "when he has to go shut himself up in a bathroom to escape the constant noise. . . ."[26]

The [bath]room was quite a small one and the table was an awful thing. It was a small round rickety thing with room hardly enough to put my diary and an inkpot on. I had to put it against the wall to prevent it from moving up and down. . . . The others never would get me a table though I begged of them repeatedly to do so. They merely laughed. Even this table I brought against their will. They were an idle lot indeed. They never realised how much I wanted this piece of furniture.[27]

Eventually the Maharaja of Alwar, master of Amar Singh's father, intervenes to give father and son more space:

He said we were cramped up and that I can come up in the house and occupy the room [recently vacated by Captain Smith].. . . I was very happy indeed. There was a fine table and I enjoyed writing to my heart's content.[28]

Perhaps the overriding factor in Amar Singh's keeping of a diary is this: the diary is his best friend, his constant companion, a portable alternate self that keeps him alive and amused.

What fate does Amar Singh expect for the diary? His name, Amar, *a mar*, means without death. Does Amar Singh expect the diary to live after him, to speak to future generations? Apart from going to great lengths to keep the diary confidential and out of the hands of those seeking access to it, he makes no mention for eighteen years of what future if any he has in mind for the diary. But in 1916, in the Mediterranean on a troop ship taking him from Flanders to Basra, he confronts the question of the diary's future. He is reading Samuel Pepys' multi-volumed diary and is aware of its fame and that it was written almost 300 years ago. His interest sometimes flags but he keeps going according to his rule that a book once started must be finished. When he has finished he wonders ". . . whether in the future someone would ever print my diary and whether anyone would care to read it."

6

Reversing the Gaze: The Diarist as Reflexive "Native" Ethnographer

Every life mirrors to some extent the culture and the changes it undergoes. The life of every individual can be regarded as a "case study," and who is better qualified than the individual himself to study?

M. N. Srinivas[1]

As we read and re-read the diary, it gradually dawned on us that the diary was as much an ethnography as it was private writing about a self in formation. We have named what Amar Singh wrote during the first seven years of his diary, his twentieth to his twenty-seventh year, self-as-other ethnography. As he writes daily diary accounts about the manners and mores of turn-of-the-century princely and British India he comes to know and construct himself.

As a participant, an observer, an informant, a narrator, and an author, he constitutes an ethnographic other in constituting an ethnographic self. Who had he been? Who did he mean to be? Who might he become? Querying and analyzing his own and others' motives, expectations, and conduct in many settings—weddings and funerals, court and raj society—he explores how and why rules and roles are enacted, contested or constituted among the generations and between the genders and the races. What he says, thinks, and does is shaped by what others say and do.

Amar Singh's ethnographic propensities arise in part from his youth. Between twenty and twenty-seven (1898–1905) we find him shaping an identity by making cultural judgments and choices and learning from the meaning and consequences of speech and action. What kind of person does he want to be—as son and husband, soldier and sportsman, courtier and Rajput, princely subject and raj feudatory? Should he adapt to English models and if so why, when, and what models? The diary shows him making minute and major judgments as he positions himself among quotidian practices and moral differences. As he writes his diary day by day we see culture in the making as well as in the doing—how agency and structure interact, how culture shapes self, and how self shapes culture.[2]

How Amar Singh represents himself and his world resembles the way anthropologists as ethnographers seek to know, represent, and write about the "other."[3] But there are differences. The conflation of self and other spares him some of the obfuscating mediations that plague anthropology: the subjectivity and projection that affect observation and knowing; the fortuitous or calculated resistance and/or compliance of the native subject; the objectivist fictions of scientific narration and authorial rhetoric.

How did anthropological ethnography get that way—and how have the "natives" responded? The "us" in the early days of ethnography were "Europeans" from imperial metropoles, the "them," natives living usually under colonial domination in what were deemed cultural isolates, denizens of remote islands, villagers living behind mud walls, tribals hidden away in the bush. Natives were objects to be studied, subjects of alien rulers, peoples whom colonial administrators had to control and, in time, improve morally and materially—the white man's burden in Kipling's unintendedly ironic phrase.

After World War II and decolonization, "them," the other, the "people with culture" whose powerlessness gave them "cultural visibility," had not yet become extinct.[4] They could still be found in what came to be called "third world" countries as well as among a new category, "minorities" at home, marginalized, dispossessed underclasses, and downwardly mobile or displaced élites, for example, WASPS in America, gentry and aristocracy in Britain.[5]

The claim that Amar Singh qualifies as an "ethnographer" runs counter not only to expectations about professional training but also to expectations about the cultural positioning of ethnography. In the anthropological canon of the classical era, natives, the other, were not supposed to be ethnographers—informants perhaps but not ethnographers. They could be observed enacting their culture, fulfilling cultural "obligations," behaving in culturally appropriate ways, but they were not expected to be self-conscious or reflective, capable of subjectivity, choice or contestation. The cultural scripts that constructed them were written by "us"; these told them who they were and how they should behave.[6]

In the not-so-distant past, before the recent challenge of "authenticity" to the claim that only outsiders could know and represent the other, anthropologists fancied that they had a professional license, a guild monopoly, a scientific calling, to study, know, and write about the other. Today, as we traverse the 1990s, the anthropologist's monopoly claim has been reversed; the natives abroad and minorities at home now insist that only they can give an authentic reading of who they are and what they are about,[7] that only the reflexive (and not so reflexive) "other" can speak for natives and minorities. But authenticity's counter claim to a representational monopoly is recent.

When Amar Singh wrote his diary, natives were not thought capable of representing themselves—much less of being reflexive. This is no longer so. In his 1975 essay "On Living Intimately with Strangers" T.N. Madan[8] explained to himself and his anthropologist colleagues that an ethnographic anthropologist can go home again *if* he can render the familiar unfamiliar. Madan recognized that "detachment" distinguished his way of knowing from the "empathy" called for by participant observation among an "other." What he did was closer to "objective subjectivity" than it was to the "subjective objectivity" or the earlier "observation" of an anthropology that claimed to be human science. Studying not only his own society but more importantly his own community of Kashmiri pandits led him in time to the more general view that anthropologists should "not divide humankind into 'ourselves' and 'others.'"[9]

Madan's critique opens the way to configuring Amar Singh's diary as ethnography. The other is not, it seems, debarred from the capacity of self-understanding; the epistemological barrier between self and other is lowered. "Critical self-awareness," Madan says, may be vouchsafed to some anthropologists—those who have acquired the "distance," the "sense of surprise," the "anthropological doubt" required for "critical self-awareness."[10]

Amar Singh was not a professionally trained anthropologist. Unlike T.N. Madan or M.N. Srinivas, he could not place himself in the intellectual history of ethnography. Like Molière's Monsieur Jourdain who did not know he was speaking prose, Amar Singh, when he began writing in 1898, did not know he was writing ethnography. (Nor does he use the kind of academic, intellectualized language that some readers may associate with reflexivity.) In any case, "doing" ethnography in the Edwardian era before Malinowski invented ethnographic fieldwork in 1914–1915[11] makes him something of an anachronism and, as a "native," certainly an anomaly.

In the 1980s, anthropologists' immaculate conception of knowledge and the scientific narrative style lost credibility; the natives became restless, gained power and voice and claimed to be part of "us," denizens of the modern world. Scholar anthropologists were revealed as authors and rhetoricians whose work was more literary and philosophic than scientific. Their subjectivity, critics argued, colored what they saw, heard and "represented," and their language relied on the arts of persuasion.[12]

Clifford Geertz highlights the role of rhetoric and persuasion:

> The ability of anthropologists to get us to take what they have to say seriously has less to do with either a factual look or an air of conceptual elegance than it has to do with their capacity to convince us that what they have to say is a result of having actually penetrated (or, if you prefer, been penetrated by) another form of life, of having, one way or another, truly 'been there.' . . . Persuading us that this offstage miracle has occurred . . . is where the writing comes in.[13]

Amar Singh does not have to convince us that he truly has been there. He is there, liminally positioned between princely and British India, speaking in an "authentic voice" (his own) about forms of life of which he is a part. His writing is not burdened by the need to produce an "offstage miracle" that convinces us that he commands another form of life.

If there is a miracle it occurs on-stage in sharing through his diary accounts the experience of the self as other. We have been spared the mediations that separate an anthropologist *from* a form of life. But we have not been spared the mediations involved in constructing a diarist-ethnographer *within* a form of life. The "self as other" disposes of one conundrum only to reveal another, how does the self as diarist-ethnographer construct his own form of life? Where does the necessary self-reflexivity come from?

One source of his reflexivity is his liminal condition. He lives between princely and British India, routinely crosses the boundary that separates them and is "penetrated" by both forms of life. This liminal positioning allows him to denaturalize and problematize the "etiquette" of both forms. An instance is when his recently married sister experiences seizures after she is married, uprooted from the household of her birth and sent to live in the unknown territory of her husband's family in Alwar. The seizures are interpreted by her in-laws as ghost possessions. Her father, Narain Singh, a minister at Alwar, cannot speak to his daughter about being alone and isolated among strangers, nor tell her that, in his view, there are no ghosts, because Rajput "etiquette" bars intimate conversations between father and daughters. Amar Singh speaking as insider tells us such etiquette is natural: "this [being alone and miserable after marriage] is a customary thing; women of India always do this . . . [it] is looked upon as etiquette. Girls have to do it." But then he recognizes it is natural only in some places: "All this trouble arises through this Rajpoot etiquette. Englishmen talk straight off to their daughters and sisters." Having "seen" that his father was barred by Rajput etiquette from comforting his daughter he reluctantly "chooses" the Rajput way: "However good the latter may be I am not in its favor. I like my own country's customs." The condition of the "native" and its alternatives are both reported and represented as choices for a self-reflexive actor.

The secrecy of private space also seems to generate reflexivity. To be a diarist and write as a diarist entails writing in secret for the self.[14] Away from public gaze and censure, from the pressure of producing culturally sanctioned responses, a diarist, can see, hear, and say things not allowed or not recognized by conventional society. Secrecy for the diarist, like "science" for the anthropologist studying the other, is a way of realizing objective subjectivity.

On this reading, the diary becomes the ethnography of secrets of and about the self. Like the women and dissenters who wrote diaries in seventeenth- and eighteenth-century Europe and the Bengalis who wrote journals in nineteenth-century India, the young Amar Singh feared discovery by powerful persons in his environment.[15] Amar Singh too had "secrets" to tell about himself and about his contemporaries' lives, secrets that they were unable to recognize or unwilling to acknowledge publicly. Secrecy allowed him to circumvent the fictions required by public civility. Amar Singh may not have had the "distance" that a trained ethnographer engaging in participant observation might claim but his position between two cultures and as a diarist writing reflexively in secret enabled him to render the familiar unfamiliar. He saw and wrote at a distance from within.

In recent decades the dichotomies between participant and observer, between subjectivity and objectivity, have eroded. The cleavage between the self and the other, the ethnographer and the natives, was expressed in the "rhetoric of experienced objectivity."[16] It has given way to first-person fieldwork accounts that replace third-person accounts of the theater of the other.

In "polyphonic" "dialogic" textual production both ethnographer and subject are on stage in a reconstituted theater of the other. They engage each other, sharing the conversation built into a script But they do not share the production of the script's text. Despite the appearance on stage of reciprocity and mutual determination, the writing of the play, however literary and "partial" it may be, remains the task of the ethnographer. Politically he or she retains authority over the text about an other. But Amar Singh, a reflexive diarist writing about his culture from within, realizes a more symmetrical relationship by conflating self and other. He can be participant, observer, informant, narrator, and author rolled into one. He writes the play and speaks its lines; it is his text, his script, his performance.

PART I: GETTING STARTED

Part I, "Getting Started," introduces the opening phase of the diary's text and many of the persons, places and practices that are to follow. We have intervened more in Part I than we do later, topically rearranging Amar Singh's groping first attempts to write daily narratives. Our headings aggregate related diary entries strung out over many months in a format that anticipates the extended essays that Amar Singh himself soon comes to favor.

Amar Singh begins his diary writing somewhat in the manner of a *roznamcha*, the day books kept by scribes at rajas' courts and merchants' *havelis* (mansions or big houses). They provide a record of who comes and goes and of noteworthy events. It is a bare bones account rather than the kind of reflexive, ethnographic writing that Amar Singh adopts as he develops his diary voice, a voice that narrates and attends to personality and character, motive and manners. The diary becomes a friendly listener to his feelings and opinions, his criticisms and explanations of his own and others' intentions and actions.

From September 1898 through December 1900, we see the reader and Amar Singh through this apprenticeship phase. We share more in the narration here than in the parts that follow, providing context and background, invoking persons, clarifying events. Our voice will fade as Amar Singh finds his.

Dramatis Personae

Sir Pratap Singh, known as *Sarkar*, "Government." Regent of the princely state of Jodhpur. Brother of the late Maharaja Jaswant Singh, guardian of the minor Maharaja Sardar Singh and mentor and patron of Amar Singh. "He is at present in every respect the Nestor of Rajputana."

Barath Ram Nathji, Amar Singh's teacher and confidant. Thirty-eight-year-old poet, bard, and former principal of the Rajput Nobles School at Jaipur, now in Sir Pratap's service as tutor to the Maharaja of Jodhpur.

Hurjee, Thakur Hari Singh of Deoli, renowned polo player. Favorite of Sir Pratap and Amar Singh's rival for Sir Pratap's attention.

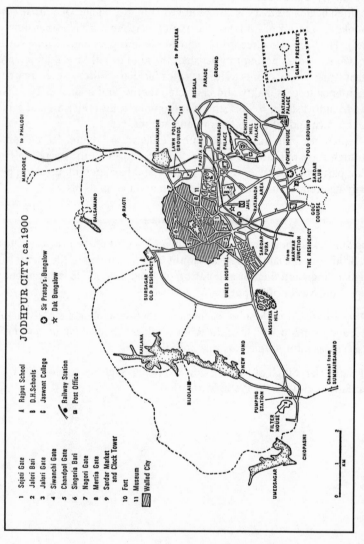

PHOTO I-1. Map of Jodhpur city, *circa* 1900 showing locations that figure in the diary, such as the walled city and Sir Pratap's bungalow near Ratanada and Chitar Hill Palace. Map by Christopher Muller-Wille adapted from *Jodhpur*, Jodhpur Government Press, Jodhpur, 1938.

1

About the Diary

The diary's eighty-nine volumes reside in glass-fronted cabinets of Amar Singh's library at the fort in Kanota village, 10 miles east of Jaipur on the road towards Agra. They begin as a "Memorandum Book" on March 28, 1898. Like contemporary users of digital organizers, Amar Singh records useful information, stray thoughts and literary quotations on the lined pages of an ordinary school copy book. When Amar Singh begins "The Diary" six months later, on September 3, he uses the same medium but soon switches to folio-size, high-quality, lined foolscap. Quires of lined paper are with him wherever he goes. At the end of the year he asks his brother, Sheo Nath Singh, to have the loose leaves bound in Jaipur. He counts on Sheo Nath to respect the diary's confidentiality.

Memorandum Book

[The first entry in the "Memorandum Book" is written at Jodhpur and dated March 28, 1898.]

1. Remedies for the boil in the arm-pit.[1] Opium, white pebble, and sugar to be compounded together, and made a little warm over the fire and then applied.
2. White Arab pony Raja gelded on the 22nd of March 1898.
3. [Partly illegible *doha* (couplet), heard from Jamadar Khichi Mal Singh]
4. Army Signalling

A oo -	K - o -	X - oo -
B - ooo	L o - oo	Y - o - -
C - o - o	M - -	Z - - o o
D - o o	N - o	
E o	O - - -	1. o - - - -
F o o - o	P o - - o	2. o o - - -
G - - o	Q - - o -	3. o o o - -
H o o o	R o - o	4. o o o o -
I o o	S o o o	5. o o o o o
J o - - -	T -	6. - o o o o
	U o o -	7. - - o o o
	V o o o -	8. - - - o o
	W o - -	9. - - - - o
		10. - - - - -

[Between March 1898, when he begins the "Memorandum Book", and its close at the end of August Amar Singh devotes twenty-three daily entries to inscribing from one to as many as sixteen dohas (in Hindi or Rajasthani) interspersed with quotations in English from books he is reading. At the end of December 1898— and for forty-three years thereafter—he creates an annotated bibliography of the books he has read during the year.]

Jodhpore, 29th March, 1898

> "The inexpert doctor is dangerous for your life
> The inexpert mullah (divine) is dangerous for your religion."[2]
>
> Dr Sirajuddeen

8th April, 1898

> "The tiger has no homeland;
> Wherever the tiger lives, that becomes his homeland."[3]
>
> Barath Ram Nathjee[4]

> "As the tiger mates but once,
> As a gentleman gives his word but once,
> As the banana tree bears fruit but once,
> And the virgin is anointed with nuptial oil but once,
> So Hamir's resolution once taken is irrevocable.[5]
>
> Barath Ram Nathjee

Grey Arab pony Raja who had been gelded on the 22nd ultimo got all right and ridden on walk only today.

12th April, 1898

> Medicine for horse's mange: Soak fig leaves in buttermilk, mash with a little salt and place in sun four to five hours. Then apply to horse's body.
>
> From Jaswant Singhjee of Agunta[6]

[On September 3, 1898, abruptly and without explanation, a new page in the erstwhile Memorandum Book is titled "The Diary." Ram Nathji, his much admired and respected teacher, was probably the source of the project. Ram Nathji had kept a diary himself in 1894 while traveling in Europe.[7] As a teacher and, later, principal of the recently founded Nobles School in Jaipur, Ram Nathji had followed the English public school practice of assigning diaries as a means of discipline, self-knowledge, and moral development. We imagine him saying to his promising and receptive pupil, "Now Amar, your English needs practice. Why don't you keep a diary?" As he reads Ram Nathji's tutorial assignments, particularly *Plutarch's Lives*, which he takes up about the time he begins the diary, he gains the confidence to try a diary format.[8]]

The Diary, 1898

Ratanada, Saturday, 3rd September, 1898

I am now living in the bungalow which is between those of Rao Raja Bharoon Singhjee and Rao Raja Sowai Singhjee. Sarkar [Sir Pratap] . . . departed for Mount Abu to see the A.G.G. [Agent to the Governor General] . . . on the night of the 2nd.[9] We [the Jodhpur Lancers] had squadron drill in the morning and after that I went to my haveli of Peelva[10] and brought my rifle and some other things. The whole day I loaded cartridges.

In the evening we went out for shooting. I shot one chinkara [gazelle]. The bullet struck him on the belly and he dropped. . . . When we went near him he got up and began running and so I rode my pony (Chestnut Arab, Earl) and galloped after him. . . . He sat down in a bush where Hurdeojee caught and I finished him with the lance. Maharaj Sher Singhjee also had three shots after one female. . . .

[This is Amar Singh in his minimalist mode. As he goes beyond his initial bare bones format, he finds he needs and likes his diary's company. It becomes both an alter ego and a best friend. Amusement or pleasure is "writing to my heart's content." Boredom is being kept from writing or reading. It means being trapped into mindless talk by empty-headed or philistine peers or being obliged to attend to one of his patrons when he could be reading or writing. "I like Lichman Singh coming to me," he writes in July 1905, "because he is not a bore. If I am busy I go on with my work and he does not mind."[11] At the hill station of Mount Abu in summer (see Introduction) he complains about his noisy companions,[12] and they laugh at his need for a writing desk.[13] But when the Maharaja of Alwar offers him space with a fine writing-table he can spend "hours and hours writing my notes."[14]

Writing becomes a habit, a daily affair. When he misses a day, he catches up later. "In the noontime, I wrote with the pen all the account of the 9th, 10th, and 11th which was first only by pencil."[15] "During the whole of the noontime I wrote my diary of the four days past."[16] "These two habits of mine I am trying my best to carry on. They are the writing of my diary and never to read a book by half but always to go through it from one end to the other."[17] Over the diary's forty-four years, he misses just one day, when he falls from his horse in a hunting accident and lies unconscious.

Daily entries usually open in a standard manner, reiterating the routines of the day, for example: "In the morning I got [up] early and after the ablutions had the dumb-bell and the Indian club exercise."[18] We learn that he drills with the squadron, talks with Ram Nathji about books and ideas, performs his duties as Sir Pratap's private secretary, reads avidly, hunts or plays polo, writes his diary.

In 1900, on an inspection tour with Sir Pratap, he tries a new format: a five-page essay about the unconventionally informal relationships among the male members of a family that hosts the royal party.[19] The entry is the prototype for long essays written over several days or weeks. His longest, a 129-page essay in 1904, gives an account of his sister-in-law's wedding at Satheen.

Premeditated and carefully crafted, the essays are organized beforehand under Roman headings and Arabic subheads:

Last night after writing my diary I arranged the headings for my "Notes about My Last Visit to Satheen." I had about an hour and a half at my disposal and even then I could not finish the work. The thing is so complicated that it took a lot of time and still greater bother.[20]

And a day later:

> Last night before and after dinner I arranged all the headings about my "notes" for the last visit to Satheen. To begin with I was rather puzzled how to arrange them but when I took to it in earnest I did it pretty well.[21]

Amar Singh keeps the essay format going for twenty-two years. In 1922, after retiring from the Indian Army, he returns "home" to Jaipur where, on the death of his father, he becomes the Thakur of Kanota, a prominent member of court society and begins a second military career with the Jaipur State Forces. It is the kind of career that his grandfather, Zorawar Singh, had foretold and that he hoped to begin when, in 1905, he graduated from the Imperial Cadet Corps (ICC). He drops the essay format and begins the practice of writing more fully each day, perhaps twenty or more pages. As a forty-four-year-old householder he may have been more concerned to record his interpretation of daily life than, as a twenty- and thirty-year-old, he had been to master it.

Amar Singh's turn to an essay format may be related to his tutorials with Barath Ram Nathji. Early tutorial assignments included books by Samuel Smiles (*Duty; Character; Thrift*) as well as *Plutarch's Lives.* Amar Singh treats Plutarch as he does dohas, entering epigrams at the head of daily entries. From Shakespeare onward, Plutarch had shaped England's literary imagination. In Amar Singh's time, Plutarch was much admired as an interpreter of the "classic" age by public-school-educated, empire-building Victorians.[22] Plutarch had shaped the literary and martial imaginations of two of the most famous proponents of empire, Sir William Napier, the eminent author, and his brother, Charles Napier, conqueror of Sind.[23] The Napiers helped to make Plutarch an icon of the Victorian and Edwardian reading public by infusing their words and deeds with references to Plutarch. Samuel Smiles, perhaps the most widely read writer of his time, was another Plutarch admirer. His account of Plutarch in *Character* seemed to speak directly to Amar Singh: "He had an eye to see and a pen to describe the more prominent events and circumstances in [the lives of all classes and ages] . . . and possessed the power of portraying the individual character of his heroes."[24]

Amar Singh attempts his own version of a "Life" two weeks after the diary begins.]

Sunday, 18th September, 1898

. . . As I have now made up my mind to depict if possible the features and manners of any man I come across who interests me I think I can do no better than first begin with his highness himself. His Highness Rao Raja Swor Maharaja Sardar Singh Bahadoor is of middle. . . .

[Here the account ceases abruptly. Two pages are cut out of the diary. Three days later he reveals the reason.]

Wednesday, 21st September, 1898

. . . I also received a letter from my father, and though it was not so private yet he had directed me to destroy it after reading. So I thought that if anybody were

D U T Y

WITH ILLUSTRATIONS OF

COURAGE, PATIENCE, & ENDURANCE

By SAMUEL SMILES, LL.D

AUTHOR OF 'LIVES OF THE ENGINEERS' 'SELF-HELP,' 'CHARACTER' 'THRIFT,' ETC.

Not once nor twice in our rough island story,
The path of Duty was the way to glory. TENNYSON.

The stern behests of Duty,
The doom-books open thrown,
The heaven we seek, the hell we fear,
Are with yourselves alone.
J. G. WHITTIER.

A NEW EDITION

LONDON
JOHN MURRAY, ALBEMARLE STREET
1883

To do our duty in this world towards God and towards man, consistently and steadily, requires the cultivation of all the faculties which God hath given us. And He has given us everything. It is the higher Will that instructs and guides our will. It is the knowledge of good and evil, the knowledge of what is right and what is wrong, that makes us responsible to man here, and to God hereafter.

The sphere of Duty is infinite. It exists in every station of life. We have it not in our choice to be rich or poor, to be happy or unhappy; but it becomes us to do the duty that everywhere surrounds us. Obedience to duty, at all costs and risks, is the very essence of the highest civilised life. Great deeds must be worked for, hoped for, died for, now as in the past.

We often connect the idea of Duty with the soldier's trust. We remember the pagan sentinel at Pompeii, who died at his post, during the burial of the city by the ashes of Vesuvius, some eighteen hundred years ago. This was the true soldier. While others fled, he stood to his post. It was his Duty. He had been set to guard the place, and he never flinched. He was suffocated by the sulphureous vapour of the falling ashes. His body was resolved to dust, but his memory survives. His helmet, lance, and breast-plate are still to be seen at the Museo Borbonico at Naples.

This soldier was obedient and disciplined. He did what he was appointed to do. Obedience, to the parent, to the master, to the officer, is what every one who would do right should be taught to learn. Childhood should begin with obedience. Yet age does not absolve us. We must be obedient even to the end. Duty, in its purest form, is so constraining that one never thinks, in performing it, of one's self at all. It is there. It has to be done without any thought of self-sacrifice.

to see this memorandum and tell his highness, or any of the persons whose character I had written and intended to write, they might be displeased, so I cut off some papers and scratched some words and don't intend to write any more. . . .

[Almost two years later, away from the dangers of the Jodhpur court, he resumes the abandoned character sketch of Maharaja Sardar Singh.[25] But questions of privacy, secrecy and confidentiality persist over the years. A diary can provide private space for secrets of the self that makes its written pages a stage for a theater of inner thoughts and states of mind. Yet the very act of putting pen to paper, of writing words, is a form of publication. It allows for the possibility that someday the words might and can be read by others. In 1916, while on a troop ship carrying him from the Western front to Basra to fight the Ottoman Turks, Amar Singh reads Pepys' diary. "I wonder," he muses to his diary, "if someday others will read my diary as I am reading Pepys's?"

Twelve years earlier such a possibility had occurred but the potential reader was neither distant, hypothetical nor disinterested.

> I got a letter [in October 1904] from the private secretary of the Maharaja Sahib of Idar [Sarkar] asking me to send my China diary to help the people who are writing the biography of Maharaja Sir Pratap Singhjee. This was a surprise and a blow to me. I cannot possibly send the diary to any man, and Sarkar would be the very last man to whom I would send the thing, because there are pages and pages written that would reveal the inner life of the man. I am sure he would never speak to me if he once heard[26] my diary.[27]

Amar Singh does have a listener whom he is willing to admit to the private space of "the inner life," whom he trusts and knows to be sympathetically responsive, his respected and admired tutor. "No one has yet seen what I write except Ram Nathjee and he never tells anyone."[28]

Diarists may not be prepared to put certain thoughts on view even to themselves. The written word concretizes thoughts in ways that make them less secret and more public. An account of "talks with Ram Nathjee" on different subjects shortly before his marriage signals that certain things are being withheld.

> Last night before going to bed I had many talks with Ram Nathjee on different subjects and chief among those was about my marriage. These points are not to be discussed here but will on some further day when everything will have been over.[29] . . . I also had long talks with Ram Nathjee on my family subjects which are too tender and yet far more sacred to be put in here and so I shall never do so. . . .[30]

Some years later in a similar vein Amar Singh censors the contents of a long discussion with Kaloo, his long-serving, faithful servant, about behaviors and motives that his grandfather and parents would have regarded "out of etiquette": "There were lots of other private things which I told him but refrain from writing here. I don't want them known to anyone."[31]

Sometimes, when Amar Singh is ambivalent about what he is telling the diary, he transfers responsibility: "My pen refuses to write." Alternatively, that same ingenious pen sometimes tells stories its master did not quite intend, as when he reports on a conversation with a royal person who tells him that he "had" forty-nine men and fifty-six women in a particular year. "I cannot stop my pen which wants to write all that I come across." Often Amar Singh ducks a delicate issue or one that pains him with a lame remark: "I will write this at some other time."[32]

After completing his diary for 1899, Amar Singh seems to have asked Ram Nathji to review the text. "Good," "Shame," "Extremely good of you, Amar," appear in the margins of several early volumes. Ram Nathji pencils in an overall judgment on the 1899 text. Amar Singh retraces it in ink:

> Sorry to say that though this diary has been written at its end during the months of the greatest famine of the century yet nothing has been written about it or the suffering humanity. Very sorry to say that you have left to the world only a record of so many animals killed in such and such a manner. A writer must always bear in mind that it is his duty to give something very profitable to his readers for the time they spend in reading his works. With very few exceptions here and there the diary contains nothing worth reading in it except a record of butchery in some form or other. My dear Amar, here was an opportunity for you to devote some part of your time in thinking over the famine and pointing some remedies for the same, thus making the diary not only very amusing but very useful to mankind. Now don't you be cross when you read these remarks of him who loves you sincerely.
>
> R.N. Ratnu

To which Amar Singh replies:

> My dear Master Sahib,
>   I am indeed very grateful for the trouble you have taken to read the whole of my diary and [to] have written remarks on it. I feel very much honoured by it. You know this perfectly, that you are the only man who has yet been at liberty to do what you like with these pages which, though quite rot and a record of butchery as you say, can yet put me to great inconvenience if known to bad characters. I ought surely to have written about the famine but you must bear in mind that no opportunities were given me to study or watch it and consequently I could not write anything and I [did] not write, fearing that I may put in something quite out of the place. What I have written is of which I am an eye witness or have heard from very reliable sources. You must have observed that nothing has been written about the administration of Jaipore or Jodhpore, not even about the case and confiscation of our villages.

Like his teacher, Ram Nathji, Amar Singh becomes a proselytizer on behalf of diaries. He succeeds in recruiting two of his brothers. Sheo Nath Singh keeps a diary for twenty-five years, from 1901 to 1926, and Sardar Singh for fifty-two years, from 1901 to 1952.[33] Sheo Nath's is bound in eight volumes, Sardar Singh's in twenty-five. Both record in English daily accounts of events. Both brothers follow Amar Singh in putting charts of hunting bags by type of game and month at the end of each year but neither follows his practice of inserting charts of books read nor do they engage in self-examination or reflexive ethnography.

At the end of each year, after the December 31 entry, Amar Singh prepares two charts, one listing by month and type the game taken, the other books read by title, author and remark. The rational and calibrated form of the charts makes explicit the roles diaries can play in the regularization of life and the disciplining of self.

> As I have plenty of time at my disposal today I intend writing a retrospect on my diary. I had commenced writing it from the 3rd September, 1898 which is now more than a year. . . . From the 9th October to the 31st December, 1898 I shot or speared or hunted 70 heads of game. And before that time and the commencement of my diary, that is the 3rd September, 1898, I had killed four heads of game only.[34]

Here are Amar Singh's first two charts.

TABLE 1.2   Register of the Shikar I had in the Last Four Months of 1898[*]

Names of the animals	September	October	November	December	Total
Hares	0	0	1	8	9
Foxes	0	0	1	2	3
Jackals	0	1	1	0	2
Chinkaras	1	0	0	1	2
Black-bucks	1	0	0	0	1
Pigs	0	5	4	5	12
Partridges	0	0	7	5	12
Lavas	0	0	2	2	4
Wild cocks	0	0	4	4	8
Grouse	0	0	3	10	13
Snipe	0	0	0	1	1
Monthly total	2	6	23	40	72

[*We follow Amar Singh's arithmetic.]

TABLE 1.3   List of the Books Read

Names of books	Authors	Remarks
1. Elizabeth or Exiles of Siberia	Ram Nathjee	Translated to Hindi.
2. Character	Samuel Smiles	Very good.
3. Heroines of India	Samuel Smiles	Good.
4. Duty	-do-	Very good.
5. The Mysteries of London, Vol. I	G.W.M. Reynolds	Very good.

(continued)

TABLE 1.3   *(continued)*

Names of books	Authors	Remarks
6. The Mysteries of London, Vol. II	-do-	Very good.
7. The Mysteries of London, Vol. III		Very good.
8. Sport in Many Lands	The Old Shikarry	Good.
9. The Mysteries of London, Vol. IV	G.W.M. Reynolds	Very good.
10. Fights for the Flag	W.H. Filchett	Good.
11. Deeds that won the Empire	-do-	Good.
12. With Kitchener to Khartum	G.W. Stevens	Good.
13. Achievements of Cavalry	General Sir Evylen Wood	Good.
14. Round London	Montagu Williams	Good.

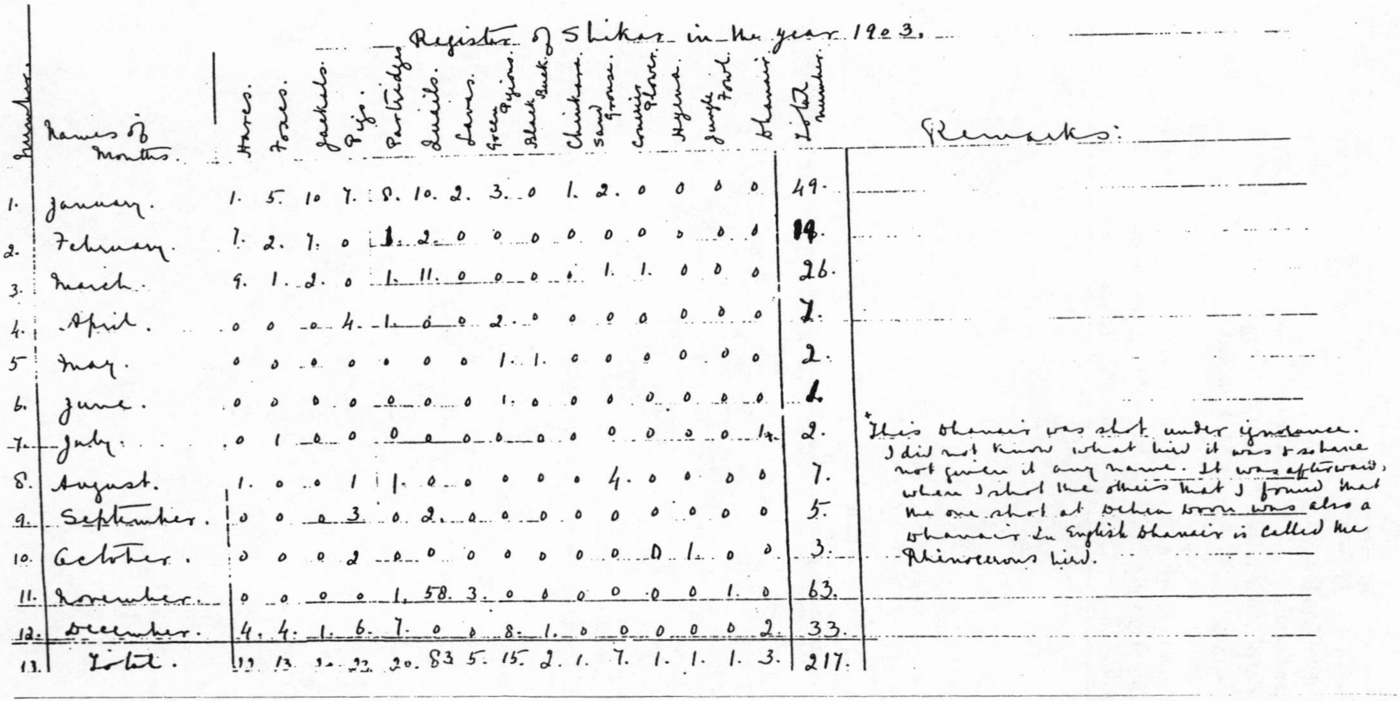

Register of Shikar in the year 1903.

Number	Names of Months.	Hares.	Foxes.	Jackals.	Pigs.	Partridges.	Quails.	Lavas.	Green Pigeons.	Black Buck.	Chinkara.	Sand Grouse.	Coursier Plover.	Hyena.	Jungle Fowl.	Dhanesir.	Total number.	Remarks:
1.	January.	1.	5.	10	7.	8.	10.	2.	3.	0	1.	2.	0	0	0	0	49.	
2.	February.	7.	2.	7.	0	1.	2.	0	0	0	0	0	0	0	0	1	14.	
3.	March.	9.	1.	2.	0	1.	11.	0	0	0	0	1.	1.	0	0	0	26.	
4.	April.	0	0	0	4.	1.	0	0	2.	0	0	0	0	0	0	0	7.	
5	May.	0	0	0	0	0	0	0	1.	1.	0	0	0	0	0	0	2.	
6.	June.	0	0	0	0	0	0	0	1.	0	0	0	0	0	0	0	1.	
7.	July.	0	1	0	0	0	0	0	0	0	0	0	0	0	0	1*	2.	*This Dhanesir was shot under ignorance. I did not know what bird it was & so have not given it any name. It was afterwards, when I shot the others that I found that the one shot at Dehra Doon was also a Dhanesir. In English Dhanesir is called the Rhinoceros bird.
8.	August.	1.	0	0	1	1.	0	0	0	0	0	4.	0	0	0	0	7.	
9.	September.	0	0	0	3.	0.	2.	0	0	0	0	0	0	0	0	0	5.	
10.	October.	0	0	0	2	0	0	0	0	0	0	0	0	1.	0	0	3.	
11.	November.	0	0	0	0	1.	58.	3.	0	0	0	0	0	0	1.	0	63.	
12.	December.	4.	4.	1.	6.	7.	0	0	8.	1.	0	0	0	0	0	2.	33.	
13.	Total.	22	13.	[illegible]	22.	20.	83	5.	15.	2.	1.	7.	1.	1.	1.	3.	217.	

PHOTO I-2 “Register of Shikar in the Year 1903.”

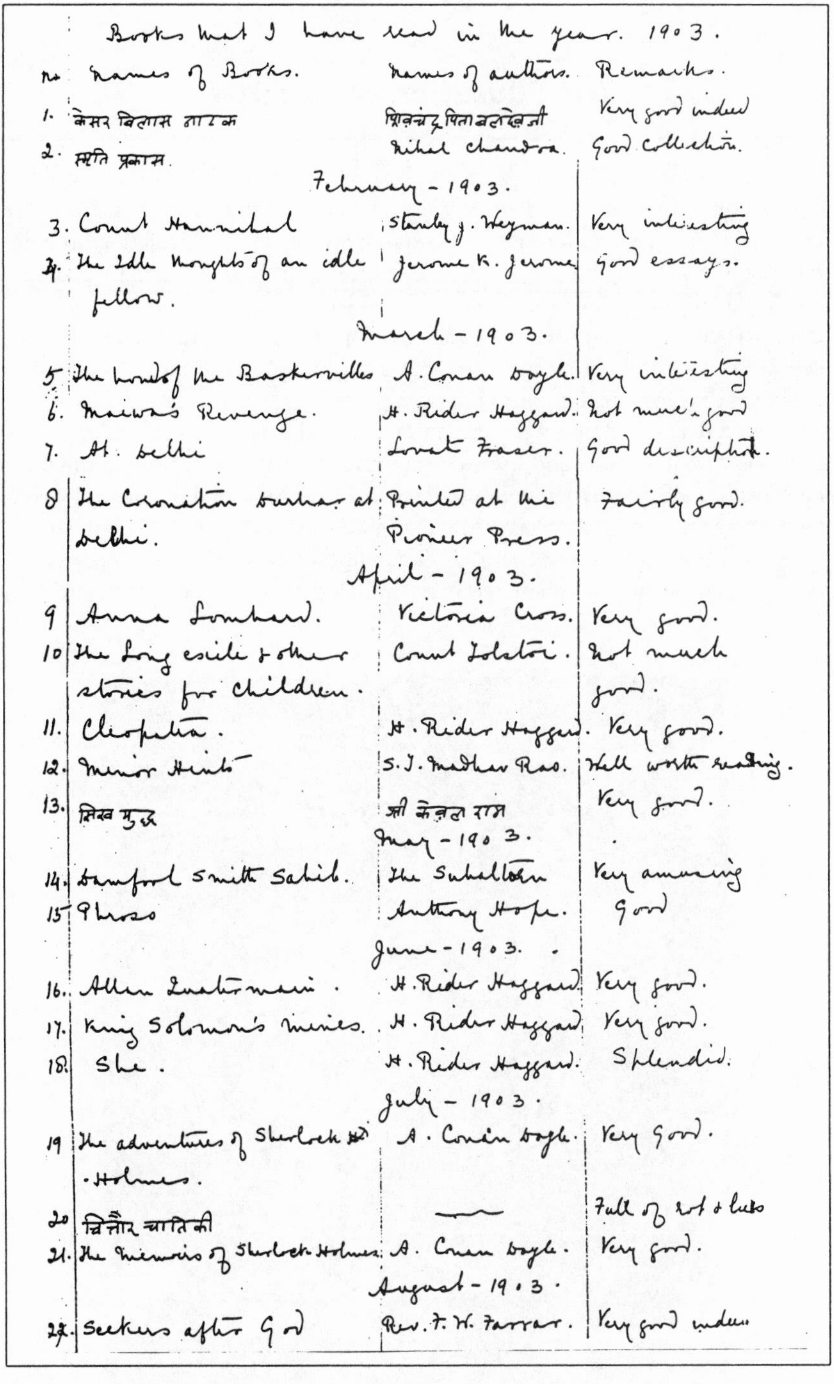

Books that I have read in the year. 1903.

no.	Names of Books.	Names of authors.	Remarks.
1.	केसर विलास नाटक	शिवचंद्र पिता बलदेवलाल	Very good indeed
2.	स्मृति प्रकाश	Nihal chandra.	Good collection.

February – 1903.

| 3. | Count Hannibal | Stanley J. Weyman. | Very interesting |
| 4. | The Idle thoughts of an idle fellow. | Jerome K. Jerome | good essays. |

March – 1903.

5	The hound of the Baskervilles	A. Conan Doyle.	Very interesting
6.	Maiwa's Revenge.	H. Rider Haggard.	Not much good
7.	At delhi	Lovat Fraser.	Good description.
8	The Coronation Durbar at delhi.	Printed at the Pioneer Press.	Fairly good.

April – 1903.

9	Anna Lombard.	Victoria Cross.	Very good.
10	The Long exile & other stories for children.	Count Tolstoi.	Not much good.
11.	Cleopatra.	H. Rider Haggard.	Very good.
12.	Minor Hints	S. J. Mathew Rao.	Well worth reading.
13.	शिव गुरु	श्री केरल राम	Very good.

May – 1903.

| 14. | Sandford Smith Sahib. | The Subaltern | Very amusing |
| 15 | Phroso | Anthony Hope. | good |

June – 1903.

16.	Allan Quatermain.	H. Rider Haggard	Very good.
17.	King Solomon's mines.	H. Rider Haggard	Very good.
18	She.	H. Rider Haggard.	Splendid.

July – 1903.

19	The adventures of Sherlock Holmes.	A. Conan Doyle.	Very good.
20	चितोर चातिकी	——	Full of rot & luts
21.	The Memoirs of Sherlock Holmes.	A. Conan Doyle.	Very good.

August – 1903.

| 22. | Seekers after God | Rev. F. W. Farrar. | Very good indeed |

PHOTO I-3 "Books that I have Read in the Year 1903."

2

The Education of a Diarist

[The diary both records and contributes to Amar Singh's education. He writes down what he learns about manners and mores even while articulating his judgments and evaluating his responses. We see him learn by observing. A wedding is a cultural education for him who cares to observe and reflect. So is a conversation, particularly a controversial one. Early on he begins a practice at which he gets better and better, reporting, without privileging his voice, conversations as dialogues that capture diverse and opposing views.

A good deal of Amar Singh's education is autodidactic; he reads all the time, thinks and writes about and uses what he reads. Soon after beginning the diary he is reading fifty or sixty books a year. He reads Marie Corelli, scorned by contemporary critics but appreciated by the newly educated Board School generation, Gladstone and Queen Victoria. Victorian literature supplies his adjectives. Persons can be "noble," their tempers "mild," their characters "upright" and

PHOTO I-4   Amar Singh reading, 1907. Amar Singh's photo albums.

"pure-minded," their features "expressive of gentleness and goodness." His early reading molds his moral stance. Samuel Smiles' discourses on "Character" and "Duty" mesh well with the moral climate created by Sir Pratap's asceticism and Ram Nathji's cosmopolitanism. Ram Nathji puts in his way G.S. Fowler's *Science of Life* and Dr George Drysdale's *The Elements of Social Science*, widely read but "underground" books on sexual life that help to liberate him from some of the inhibitions of a repressive Rajput-cum-Victorian moral universe.[1]

Amar Singh's formal education consisted of eight years, from the age of ten to the age of eighteen,[2] at the Powlett Nobles School, Jodhpur. Founded by Sir Pratap in 1886, it catered to boys unable or unwilling to attend the "Eton of India," Mayo College in Ajmer.[3] Powlett costs were borne equally by the maharaja and the nobles whose sons attended.

Amar Singh seems to have performed respectably. When in 1890 the Resident, Colonel Powlett, inspected the school, he noted "very satisfactory" beside the names of five of eleven boys, including Sheo Nath Singh, Amar Singh's brother. Amar Singh is among the "Others [who] are doing fairly well."[4] The school was a small affair with no more than eleven sons of landed noblemen or maharajas' relatives in attendance. Five years later, its modest enrollment of twenty-four was taught in six classes by six English and two Hindi instructors, and examined twice yearly by the superintendent of Jodhpur schools. A principal aim was to make the boys literate in English, which was becoming the language of administration and national discourse in the princely states, as it had in British India. The superintendent wrote:

> The improvement in the English pronunciation is reported to be remarkable though there is still some room for further progress. The classes were however weak in English composition and grammar, which defect, it is hoped, the teachers would endeavour to rectify.[5]

The average age of the boys was twelve; they boarded, and were subject to a spartan living and hazing not unlike that experienced in British public schools. The school reflected too the spirit of Sir Pratap who "was a great believer in making youth fit and hard."[6] Some were subject to harassment:

> We used to be forced to eat our food whether hungry or not. I remember several boys who hated Kheer [sweetened rice pudding] and when forced to eat they used to vomit. . . . They were compelled to eat back what they had vomited. . . . This was done in case of a very few who were believed to be pretending to vomit. . . . The object of our guardian was to make us fat.[7]

There was some sadism: Amar Singh recollects what happened to a former "tentmate" in a tent shared "with four more." The guardian, Zalim Singh

> used to joke with one of the boys, Bhatee Durjon Singhjee of Lavara. . . . One evening at dinner the boy said something about it. Zalim Singh then and there began beating the poor fellow and so badly did he beat that the poor

fellow cried piteously and begged of everyone, even the servants, to relieve him of his oppressor. . . . We had hardly gone to sleep . . . (in a tent for six) when we were waked by the noise occasioned by the beating of the poor fellow. He was not allowed to cry while being beaten and if he cried he was hit on the mouth. I never remember anyone being beaten so very badly.[8]

After leaving Powlett Nobles School in 1898 Amar Singh begins training with the Jodhpur Lancers and continues his literacy education through a tutorial-like relation with Ram Nathji. Ram Nathji has been engaged by Sir Pratap Singh, the regent, to educate Jodhpur's minor prince, Sardar Singh, a teenager who will soon acquire his powers, and knows it. Ram Nathji's royal pupil's recalcitrance stands in marked contrast to Amar Singh's aptitude and willingness to learn.]

Jodhpore, Monday, 5th September, 1898

Early in the morning I went to Jodha Squadron [of the Jodhpur Lancers] . . . On my return I stopped in the way for two hours with Barath Ram Nathjee who gave me a nice translation [into Hindi] of *Elizabeth or Exiles of Siberia*. It was only one half [of] which he had made a fair copy; I read it in the noon and at about . . . seven . . . we went for shooting. I had one shot after a chinkara but missed. . . .

PHOTO I-5   Students of Powlett Nobles School Jodhpur, *circa* 1888. Amar Singh is fourth from the left, standing. The seated boy in the middle is Maharaj Kumar Sardar Singh of Jodhpur, heir to the throne. Amar Singh's photo albums.

[This entry fixes his early routines.

On September 8, Amar Singh intersperses five pages of dohas with quotations from Defoe, forty-four dohas in all, most taken from "Ram Nathjee's copybook." like stories and images found in the 1960s music of Bob Dylan, Bruce Springsteen or Joan Baez, the metaphors and parables found in dohas and *sawaias* (couplets and quatrains) framed the attitudes and behavior of young Rajputs of Amar Singh's generation. Dohas were learnt—and "known"—by heart. They were used by Rajputs of all ages as part of their oral, aural, and visual vocabulary. They figure in competitive recitations, identify experiences, praise or damn adversaries, and impress and challenge peers. When Amar Singh finds that Jorji "thinks too much of himself and knows himself to be the strongest and the best of all mankind [and has] very mean ideas too," he concludes that "the [following] proverb suits him very well: 'A petty man can no more digest straight talk than a pint pitcher can contain a quart.'"[9]

There is a brisk trade in dohas. Jivraj and Jodhji have collections. Amar Singh and Jivraj spend happy hours during the heat of the day, or in the evening, after some energetic pig-sticking, copying out each other's dohas. "After polo Jive Rajjee came to me and I learned the two dohas written above and one sawaia." In December 1898, Amar Singh spends several days copying "Rajya" dohas written by a well-reputed eighteenth-century poet of uncertain provenance but attributed to a servant, Rajya.[10]

> In the Malagiri [forest], every tree that grows becomes a sandalwood tree;
> Thus, says Rajya, [virtuous] company transforms even the trees.

Or, as Amar Singh remarks on meeting Maharaja Jai Singh of Alwar who is said to be "improving in character":

> No matter how much it is watered with sugar syrup,
> the Neem tree will never grow sweet;
> Bad habits once formed perish only at death.[11]

The doha gains a new lease on life toward the end of the nineteenth century when, initially in Bengal,[12] nationalists turn to legendary tales about those Rajputs who resisted Mughal rule for models in their own struggle against British rule. Amar Singh's entry on March 16, 1903, presents a famous doha celebrating the refusal by Mewar's sixteenth-century hero, Rana Pratap, of the Mughal emperor Akbar's blandishments and his resistance to Akbar's armies.[13] The doha, which has accumulated a polemical history in Indian nationalist and communal discourses, is ascribed to Prithvi Raj, a poet and favorite of the emperor and younger brother of Akbar's general, Raja Rai Singh of Bikaner.[14] The context of Prithvi Raj's poem is Rana Pratap's twenty-one-year guerrilla resistance to Akbar's imperial armies. Legend asks us to imagine Rana Pratap in the hills of Mewar's Aravalli wilderness, living as best he can off the land. He sees his little daughter crying because a cat had taken away her last coarse grain *chapatti* (unleavened flat bread). It is more than he can bear. He writes a letter of surrender to Akbar. The emperor shows the letter to Prithvi Raj to confirm the handwriting.

[Inquires Prithvi Raj]
Will Pratap stoop to call Akbar "emperor"?
Will the sun, son of Lord Kashyap
Rise in the West?

Tell me, Pratap,
Should my hand stroke my mustache [in pride]
or let my sword slay my body [in despair]

[Responds Pratap]
So long as Pratap breathes
By Ekling I swear that Pratap will call Akbar "Turk"
And the sun will continue to rise in the East

O Rathore Peethal
Let your hand twirl your mustache
While Pratap is there to slay the readers of Kalam [Muslims][15]

On September 8, among five pages of dohas he includes sayings attributed to Defoe.

35 For fame of families is all a cheat,
     'Tis personal virtue only makes us great
36 When kings the sword of justice first lay down,
     They are no kings, though they possess the crown.
     Titles are shadows, crowns are empty things,
     The good of subjects is the end of kings.
     To guide in war and in peace to protect,
     Where tyrants once commence, the kings do cease,
     For arbitrary power's so strange a thing
     It makes the tyrant and unmakes the king.
                    From Defoe, from Ram Nathjee's copy books

Along with classics of the English and Indian canon, Amar Singh reads best-selling authors of the English book trade.]

Saturday, 10th September, 1898

In the noon time I read some pages of Smiles' *Character*.[16] In the evening we had polo.

Wednesday, 14th September, 1898

. . . I saw mallis [grooming of horses] and then went to Sarkar's house [where] I passed about an hour with him and about one with Ram Nathjee who gave me such nice advices and lectures on a point which I shall never forget. [He] also gave me a book, *Science of Life*, by Prof. G.S. Fowler, and pointed out a certain subject and chapter by which even now though I have seen only about a dozen pages it seems to me as if my knowledge and experience has vastly improved. . . . If I continue reading it I hope it will make me a man as a man ought to be. . . .

[*Science of Life* is an alternative title for G.S. Fowler's *Creative and Sexual Science or Manhood, Womanhood, Their Mutual Interrelations . . . as Taught by Phrenology and Physiology.*[17] His recommendations concerning healthy sexual practice appear to be the focus of Amar Singh's discussion with Ram Nathji.

Ram Nathji, as one of the few persons to keep abreast of intellectual and literary currents in Britain, is an avid bibliophile.[18] While thoroughly embedded in Rajputana cultural traditions, he is not burdened by them. He seems to regard an ethical and rationalist critical stance as part of his vocation as charan. His discussion with Amar Singh of sexual practice bypass the stringent Rajput etiquette governing frank exchanges between older and younger persons.]

Thursday, 15th September, 1898

. . . I passed about one and a half hours with Ram Nathjee talking on different subjects but chiefly on Homer and Mahabharata. . . .

[Ram Nathji's charan community often served as genealogists and poets at Rajput princely courts and noble houses. As genealogists, charans kept lineage and clan records; as poets they shaped "history" and reputation through their poems (dohas) and performances about Rajput deeds. Traditional intellectuals, like their rivals, court and temple brahmans, charans[19] were the conscience of their masters. More often than not their poetry and performances were designed to please more than to criticize their masters. What charans said and how they said it defined what particular Rajput lineages, clans, and individuals believed about themselves and other Rajputs.

Ram Nathji was what might be called a "new" charan, that is one of the few who, in the last quarter of the nineteenth century, transformed their traditional calling. New charans such as Shymaldas, court poet, prime minister, and historian at Udaipur[20] and the cosmopolitan intellectual, teacher, and state servant, Ram Nathji, found new ways to serve and critique power.

Ram Nathji's experiences fitted him to be a cultural translator in Rajputana. He had studied for eight years in Ajmer, the British enclave in the center of Rajputana, and attended the English-medium Government College there. It is likely that he was among the first subjects of a Rajputana princely state to receive an English-medium education and to travel in Europe. In 1881 he had withdrawn before completing the F.A. (Fellow of Arts) degree to go to Jaipur where he taught the resident, a Mr Talbot, Hindi, and, through Talbot, was appointed headmaster of the newly founded Nobles school. His stewardship made it clear that he was familiar with the curriculum and methods of English public schools.

After thirteen years as headmaster, Ram Nathji, in 1894 at the age of thirty-three, took the unconventional, pioneering step of viewing the raj at "home" on an European tour. The tour took him to Paris and Scotland as well as to London and its environs. Ram Nathji hiked the highlands around Oban, attended the

CREATIVE

AND

SEXUAL SCIENCE

OR

MANHOOD, WOMANHOOD, AND THEIR
MUTUAL INTERRELATIONS

LOVE, ITS LAWS, POWER, Etc.

SELECTION, OR MUTUAL ADAPTATION; COURTSHIP,
MARRIED LIFE, AND PERFECT CHILDREN

THEIR

GENERATION, ENDOWMENT, PATERNITY, MATERNITY, BEARING.
NURSING AND REARING; TOGETHER WITH PUBERTY, BOY-
HOOD, GIRLHOOD, ETC., SEXUAL IMPAIRMENTS
RESTORED, MALE VIGOR AND FEMALE
HEALTH AND BEAUTY PERPETUATED
AND AUGMENTED, ETC.

AS TAUGHT BY

PHRENOLOGY AND PHYSIOLOGY

By Prof. O. S. FOWLER

PRACTICAL PHRENOLOGIST AND LECTURER; FOUNDER OF FOWLER AND WELLS; AUTHOR
OF "HUMAN SCIENCE," "SEXUAL SCIENCE," "SELF-CULTURE," "LOVE AND
PARENTAGE," "MATRIMONY," "OFFSPRING, AND THEIR HEREDITARY
ENDOWMENT," "MATERNITY," "AMATIVENESS," ETC., ETC.

Prof: O. S. Fowler

330   MARRIAGE: ITS DUTY, ADVANTAGES, ETC.

riage.⁶⁰ Every male requires his female, and every female her male. "It is not good for either to live alone." Each was made for the other, as much as eyes for light, and are about as useless isolated. Paul meant you, and every one of you, when he said, "it is better to marry than burn."

FATHERS OF FAMILIES, ever since "society" existed, have been the aristocrats, dignitaries, and privileged classes, enjoying special honors and immunities in civic life; while the unmarried have always been looked down on, ridiculed, put off with "second-class" fare, accounted nobodies, edged around, left out in the cold, except when bated, or wanted as makeshifts. Do they ever "lead off" in society? Can they give select parties, or "entertain"? Only a married woman can ever administer style. Preposterous all attempts. Society originates in the family, which embodies humanity into one homogeneous sheaf, every kernel clinging to its head, and all bound together into one golden bundle by the magic girdle of marriage; excepting those scattered celibates "lying all around loose," as if not worth gathering.

670.—THE CAUSES AND EXCUSES OF CELIBACY CANVASSED.

ITS CAUSES make it all the worse; of which self-abuse is the greatest.⁶⁰ By sickening, nauseating, disgusting, and weakening the Love element, it makes its victims so feasty, dainty, extra particular, offish and repellent towards the opposite sex, seeing their faults before appreciating their virtues,⁶⁰ that, neglecting these and discarding those opportunities, they drift along down the current of time into the gulf of cross-grained celibacy; besides repelling the other sex. Yet some are born natural old bachelors and old maids, through maternal sexual indifference or disgust. This last and one other great cause, told to old maids,⁶⁰ deserves more pity than censure.

IT HAS NO VALID EXCUSE. Many say, "Its evils are great, but those of marriage, much greater." Others say:

"I WOULD DISCIPLINE my mind; accomplish these and those desirable ends; go to college, &c., which marriage would prevent."

DOES WEAKENING FEET strengthen hands, or starving stomach develop muscle? Improving and stunting either of the mental powers similarly affects them all. Starving the social to strengthen the intellectual is like stifling the lungs to improve the brain. Affectional culture promotes intellectual.⁶⁰ ⁶⁰

CELIBACY: ITS CAUSES, EVILS, EXCUSES, ETC.   331

"LOSING EITHER of the senses surely quickens all the others, as blindness touch. Then why not love-inertia increase intellectual vigor?"

BLINDNESS redoubles sensation by compelling its increased action; yet what prevents exercising touch even more with sight than without?

ACTIVE Love disciplines all the Faculties.⁶⁰ ⁶⁰ Engaged collegians can study best, and married preachers preach, lecturers lecture, writers write, naturalists study, better than unmarried; and all others prosper better in all other pursuits. What! God enjoin marriage on all,⁶⁰ ⁶⁰ yet punish obedience with inferiority! The fact is, helpmeets help, not hinder.

"MANY OF THE BEST and most gifted in all ages and pursuits have remained unmarried, or else married after having attained their celebrity. Pope, Cowper, Watts, Addison, Whittier, Halleck, &c., among the poets: Swift, the Johnsons, Irving, the most gifted and finished among authors: Newton, and both the Combes, among the philosophers; 'Queen Bess,' one of the most distinguished among sovereigns; Peabody, among the self-made millionaires; and hosts of others, go to prove that celibacy rather promotes than impair human excellence. At least, celibates but pattern after our Great Teacher and Exemplar; and the Catholic clergy piously and properly forego marriage, that they may serve 'The Virgin,' and her celibate Son, the more completely than they could if trammelled with family cares."

ARE YOU SURE Catholic "Fathers" were born without manhood, or crucify it, or exercise no passion in any way? At least you have no such pietarian excuse, nor any other. Irving loved early and too devotedly to love another after his idol died;⁶⁰ yet late in life showed how much he craved and needed female sympathy; as did Peabody.

671.—RESPONSIBILITIES AND EXPENSES OF MODERN FAMILIES.

"TAKING A WIFE NECESSITATES HER SUPPORT, with that of children; and a clinging, dependent family is a serious responsibility."

WHAT A POLTROON, to let this prevent your marriage! Suppose a young lion, shaking his head moodily, should say, "I can hardly hunt for myself, and can't afford to obligate myself to hunt for a lioness and parcel of blind, howling whelps besides, lest they or I might come to want," would n't the other lions reply—

PHOTO I-6   Barath Ram Nath Ratnu (Ram Nathji), Amar Singh's teacher, traditional bard (*charan*), principal of the Rajput Nobles School at Jaipur, European traveler, tutor to the Jodhpur maharaja. "I passed about one and a half hour with Ram Nathjee talking on different subjects but chiefly on Homer and *Mahabharata*. . . . " Amar Singh's photo albums.

PHOTO I-7   Amar Singh's study and library at Kanota fort, with *punkah* (hand-operated fan), as seen in 1971. The study is on top of an underground vault that accommodates much of the 2,400-volume library Amar Singh accumulates over forty-four years of reading. Photograph courtesy of Robin von Breton.

theater in London, met Lords Ripon and Rosebury, and for some weeks shared in the lively conversation of an international boarding house in Kent.[21]

It was after he returned from his European tour that Sir Pratap Singh called him to Jodhpur to act as guardian and tutor to his nephew and heir to the Jodhpur throne, Sardar Singh. Ram Nathji served subsequently at Idar as Sir Pratap's diwan (first minister) and at Kishengarh as head of the judiciary and member of council. While suffering from what his grandson, Kesri Singh, believes to be eczema, he died at forty-nine in 1910.

Amar Singh benefited from Ram Nathji's literary repertoire, which included western and Indian classic texts, Homer and Plutarch as well as the *Ramayana* and *Mahabharata*, and from his scholarly cast of mind. In 1892 Ram Nathji published *Rajasthan ka Ithihas* (History of Rajasthan), one of the first publicly available "modern" (that is, non-bardic, "professional") histories of Rajasthan.[22] Ram Nathji's unconventionality and broadmindedness introduced Amar Singh to a peerly relationship that was rare if not unique in Rajputana's hierarchical *hukum* (your order) culture.]

Monday, 17th April, 1899

. . . I again resumed my reading the *Mysteries* until five in the afternoon when I finished it. I have gone through the whole of the volumes of both the series, viz. the eight volumes of the *Mysteries of the Court of London* [and *The Mysteries of London*].[23] These are indeed the most interesting and at the same time moralizing books I have seen up to this time. M. George and W.M. Reynolds well deserve the esteem of all its readers. . . .

[*The Mysteries of London* offer stories in a Dickensian vein, taking gentlemen protagonists down narrow alleys into the London underworld, where they learn about its denizens' humanity and their artful—or deceitful—ways of evading the social control and economic exploitation of their betters and experience the joys and dangers of seduction. *The Mysteries of the Court of London* offer, among other tidbits, the delicately prurient adventures of a rake named Florimel.]

Wednesday, 19th April, 1899

. . . Barath Juktidanjee came and brought a book composed by himself called *Sardar-Sujass* [a work honoring Maharaja Sardar Singh of Jodhpur]. It is nothing but a composition of flattering lies. I told him that instead of losing his time in such idle and useless things he must devote himself to some substantial work. As an example I showed him the work of Barath Ram Nathjee's *Itihas Rajasthan*[24] [*History of Rajasthan*] and directed his attention to the prologue in which he has showed or rather fully exposed the folly of Rajpoots. I told him that his work would rather help to spoil than correct anybody's character. . . . He asked me to see his book but I told him that it would be throwing time uselessly. He went away rather dissatisfied.

I think that the twelve volumes of the *Mysteries of London* and the *Mysteries of the Court of London* has done wonders with me. It has given me quite new ideas from what I had before.

THE

MYSTERIES OF LONDON.

BY

GEORGE W. M. REYNOLDS,

AUTHOR OF "PICKWICK ABROAD," THE MODERN LITERATURE OF FRANCE,"
"ROBERT MACAIRE," ETC.

WITH NUMEROUS ILLUSTRATIONS
BY G. STIFF.

VOL. II.

LONDON.

GEORGE VICKERS, 3, CATHERINE STREET, STRAND.

MDCCCXLVI.

THE MYSTERIES OF LONDON.

CHAPTER CXXXVII.

RATS' CASTLE.

RICHARD MARKHAM, though perfectly unpretending in manner and somewhat reserved or even sedate in disposition, possessed the most undaunted courage. Thus was it that, almost immediately recovering himself from the sudden check which he had experienced at the hands of the Resurrection Man, he hurried in pursuit of the miscreant, followed by the policeman and the people whom the alarm which he had given had called to his aid.

The people were, however, soon tired of running gratuitously for an object which they could scarcely comprehend; but the police-officer kept close to Markham; and they were speedily reinforced by two other constables, who, seeing that something was the matter, and with characteristic officiousness, immediately joined them.

From an inquiry put to the waterman of the adjacent cab-stand, who had seen a person running furiously along a moment or two before, Markham felt convinced that the object of his pursuit had plunged into the maze of Saint Giles's; and, though well aware of the desperate character of that individual, and conscious that should he encounter him alone in some dark alley or gloomy court, a fearful struggle must ensue between them, he did not hesitate, unarmed as he was, to dash into that thicket of dangerous habitations.

Soon outstripping the officers, who vainly begged

The prologue of Ram Nathjee's *Itihas Rajasthan* is also a wonderful thing, comprising in a very few pages all the bad ideas together with examples, which [are] characteristic to the Rajpoot with a very, very few exceptions, which also he has shown there. . . .

Jaipore, Sunday, 23rd April, 1899

. . . I was trying to read *Plutarch's Lives* when my eyes closed in slumber. . . .

Deoli, Sunday, 14th June, 1899

"As debauchery often causes weakness and sterility in the body so the intemperance of the tongue makes conversation empty and insipid."

Plutarch's Lives, Lycurgus

Saturday, 26th June

2. When a Roman divorced his wife, his friends remonstrated, and asked him, Was she not chaste? Was she not fair? Was she not fruitful? He held out his shoe, and said, is it not handsome? Is it not new? Yet none knows where it wrings him, but he that wears it . . .

Plutarch's Lives, Paulus Aemilious

Monday, 8th January, 1900

3. The man who would be truly happy should not study to enlarge his estate but to contract his desires.

Maxim of Plato, *Plutarch's Lives*, Demetrius

[Marginal note by Barath Ram Nathji, "Very good."]

Monday, 15th January, 1900

. . . In the noon time I saw a little of *The Strand Magazine*[25] which Capt. Patterson has kindly arranged for six months from England. It is very amusing indeed. . . . After polo Mr Latouche [consulting engineer, railways] gave me the journal of the Bombay Natural History Society.

Saturday, 3rd March, 1900

. . . In the noon time I saw a little of *The Pioneer*[26] and then slept for a long time. Now that I have no book to read with me at present I feel very dull and that is why I go to bed. . . .

Sunday, 21st April, 1900

. . . I read a few pages of *The Life of George Washington* by J.T. Headley. . . .[27]

Sunday, 29th April, 1900

A portion of a letter of Washington to Lafayette:

At length I am become a private citizen on the banks of the Potomac and under the shadow of my own vine and fig tree, free from the bustle of a camp

PLUTARCH'S LIVES ENGLISHED BY SIR THOMAS NORTH IN TEN VOLUMES VOL ONE

MCMX · PUBLISHED · BY · J · M · DENT & SONS · L? · ALDINE · HOUSE · LONDON · W-C

The words of the Sabine women they)

and requests that could be any way imagined, passing wise persuasions and reasons to induce them to a peace. For what offence (said they) or what displeasure have we done unto both you, that we should deserve such an heap of evils, as we have already suffered, and yet you make us bear? We were as you know violently (and against all law) ravished by those, whose now we remain. But our fathers, our brethren, our mothers and friends have left us with them so long, that process of time, and the straightest bonds of the world, have tied us now so fast to them, whom mortally before we hated, that we are constrained now to be slighted thus, to see them fight, yea and to lament and die with them, who before unjustly took us from you. For then you came not to our rescue when we were virgins untouched, nor to re.over us from them when they wickedly assaulted us, poor souls: but now you come to take the wives from their husbands, and the mothers from their little children. So as the help you think to give us now doth grieve us more, than the forsaking of us was sorrowful to us then. Now, such is the love they have borne unto us, and such is the kindness we bear again to them. But if ye did fight for any other cause than for us, yet were it reason ye should let fall your arms for our sakes (by whom you are made grandfathers and fathers-in-law, cousins and brothers-in-law) even from those against whom you now bend your force. But if all this war began for us, we heartily beseech you then that you will receive us with your sons-in-law, and

restore Romulus and Tatius imparle together

your sons by them, and that you will restore unto us our fathers, our brethren, our kinsfolk and friends, without spoiling us of our husbands, of our children, and of our joys, and thereby make us woeful captives and prisoners in our minds. These requests and persuasions by Hersilia, and other the Sabine women being heard, both the armies stayed, and held every body his hand, and straight the two generals imparled together. During which parle they brought their husbands and their children, to their fathers and their brethren. They brought meat and drink for them that would eat. They dressed up the wounds of them that were hurt. They carried them home with them to their houses. They shewed them how they were mistresses there with their husbands. They made them see how greatly they were accompted of and esteemed; yea how with a wedlock love and reputation they were honoured. So in the end peace was concluded between them, wherein it was articled, that the Sabine women which would remain with their husbands should tarry still, and be exempted from all work or service (as above recited) save only spinning of wool. And that the Sabines and Romans should dwell together in the city, which should be called Roma, after Romulus' name: and the inhabitants should be called Quirites, after the name of the city of Tatius King of the Sabines, and that they should reign and govern together by a common consent. The place where this peace was concluded, is called yet to this day Comitium: because that *coire*, in the Latin

and the busy schemes of public life, and am solacing myself with those tranquil enjoyments of which the soldier who is ever in pursuit of fame, the
statesman whose watchful days and sleepless nights are spent in devising
schemes to promote the welfare of his own, perhaps the ruin of other countries, as if this globe was insufficient for us all, and the courtier who is always
watching the countenance of his prince, in hopes of catching a gracious
smile, can have very little conception. . . . Envious of none, I am determined
to be pleased with all; and this, my dear friend, being the order of my march,
I will move gently down the stream of life until I sleep with my fathers.

Life of George Washington

. . . This is a nice little book though the language is not so sweet and endear-
ing. The subject of the book is very noble, for beyond any doubt Washington's
character through the whole course of this life is free from even the slightest spot
or blemish of infamy. He is an incomparable character indeed. . . .

3
Sarkar

[Two persons occupy the most emotional space during the opening years of his diary: Amar Singh's "master," Sir Pratap Singh or "Sarkar", regent of Jodhpur and Queen Victoria's model prince,[1] and Hari Singh of Deoli or "Hurjee," handsome, talented, dissolute, Sir Pratap's favorite.

For Sir Walter Lawrence, private secretary to the Viceroy, Lord Curzon (1899–1905) and voice of high raj piety, Sir Pratap was the most admirable Rajput, the greatest kshatriya-Aryan gentleman of them all. He "was a typical Rajput, a great horseman, a gallant soldier, a very astute administrator. He had a wonderful way with the Indians and was universally loved by the English." No one ever took "a liberty with Sir Pertab. . . . When he and other rajas visited

PHOTO I-8   Sir Pratap Singh, regent of Jodhpur, favorite of Queen Victoria, and patron of Amar Singh. He is with his close friend, the famous polo player Thakur Hari Singh ("Hurjee"). The portrait hangs in Narain Niwas Palace Hotel, formerly Amar Singh's country house.

British India its leading citizens . . . so free and easy in British and official circles . . . [became] humble and deferential in the presence of a real Raja. Their manner and attitude changed at once—instinctively they recognized their natural leaders and were glad and proud to see them."[2] Or, as General Sir Horace Smith-Dorrien, another leading voice of raj enthusiasm, put it, he was "a man whose name spells chivalry and all that is highest and noblest in the human race."[3]]

Jodhpore, Tuesday, 27th September, 1898

. . . At two I went to the office. I, Baboo Raghubans Narainjee, Maharaj Akhai Singhjee[4] and Munshi Moizuddeen of Ahmedabad had a good talk on Sarkar's character. They all agree that he is very severe to those under him, and overdoes anything he wants to do. By his strictness he spoiled and displeased each and everyone. H.H. the maharaja sahib [Sardar Singh, who only recently has been granted his powers] was himself kept in such strictness that he could not ever get a hearty meal, nor a ride or drive, and neither a free talk with anybody. The result came out that when he managed to get a little from under his control . . . he [did not] care a fig for [Sarkar] though before he used to tremble at his very name. . . .

Though he is a very wise man with some very high principles in his character . . . he lacks in education. If a good education had been given to him, as all agree, he would have nearly doubled his fame and good name.

From morning till evening and . . . even in dreams at night he has nothing in his head except Hurjee and polo. *Punch* drew a very good picture of him in his paper, with polo sticks pricking out from every quarter of his head like hairs. If [*Punch*] had known his real personal character he would most surely have made Hurjee's pictures between the sticks. . . .

Deoli, Sunday, 16th October, 1898

[Sir Pratap's militantly rationalist views were much noted in the literature of Anglo-India. In the 1880s he had abandoned Hindu orthodoxy to become a spokesman for Swami Dayanand's Arya Samaj movement. In the name of a return to the "original" theism of the *Vedas*, purported to be the earliest "Hindu" texts, the Arya Samaj opposed polytheism, "idol worship," and the mediation of Brahmanical authority.[5]]

. . . Before breakfast Sarkar gave a lecture about the Hindu gods and Brahmans. He then asked me on my honour if I believed in them. I said that I used to believe until very lately when Barath Ram Nathjee dispelled the thought from my mind. He did not like the mode in which I said and told that . . . All his lectures were given in vain for so many years, to which I said that I could not argue with him while I did [argue] with Ram Nathjee. Then there was a talk about the books *Ramayan* and *Mahabharat* [two great Indian epics] in which I said that the former had very good characters while the latter has none.[6]

He did not like both of them. After this he asked Jodha Chhimunjee who is havaldar [estate clerk] there whether he believed in gods or demons. He declined both, but by this time his son of the age of about twelve years came and Sarkar asked him if his father worshipped anything. The boy readily said that he kept

A PROSE ENGLISH TRANSLATION

OF

THE MAHABHARATA

(TRANSLATED LITERALLY FROM THE ORIGINAL SANSKRIT TEXT.)

ADI PARVA.

EDITED AND PUBLISHED BY

MANMATHA NATH DUTT, M.A., M.R.A.S.,

RECTOR, KESHUB ACADEMY;

Author of the English Translations of the Ramayana, Vishnupuranam,
Srimadbhagabatam, Bhagabat Gita and other works.

CALCUTTA.

PRINTED BY H. C. DASS, ELYSIUM PRESS,
65/2, BEADON STREET.

1895.

from all directions ;—even those who were eating and drinking came leaving their food and drink.

13—14. Like blazing fires taking faggots to increase their splendour, those best of men, the great car-warriors of the Vrishni and the Andhaka races, possessing the lustre of the blazing fire, took their seats on thousands of golden thrones, covered with excellent carpets and adorned with gems and corals.

15. When they were all seated like an assembly of celestials, the Savapala with his followers narrated all about the conduct of Jishnu (Aryuna).

16. Having heard it, the proud heroes of the Vrishni, with their eyes red with wine, rose up from their seats, being unable to brook the conduct of Partha.

17—18. Some cried, "Yoke our cars", some "Bring our weapons," some "Bring our costly bows and strong armours," some loudly called upon their charioteers to yoke their horses adorned with gold to their cars.

19. While their cars, their armours, and their standards were being brought, the uproars of those heroes became exceedingly great.

20. Then proud and intoxicated with wine, Valadeva, who was like the Kailasha mountain, adorned with the garlands of wild flowers and attired in blue robes, thus spoke to all.

21. "O senseless men, what are you doing when Janardana (Krishna) is sitting silent ? Without knowing what is in his heart, you are vainly roaring in wrath.

22. Let the high-minded (Krishna) speak out what he proposes to do. Accomplish with all alacrity what he desires to do."

23. Having heard these words of Hala-yudha (Valadeva) which deserved, to be accepted, they all exclaimed, "Excellent," "Excellent." They then became silent.

24. Silence have been restored by the words of the intelligent Valadeva, they again all took their seats in that court.

25. Then the chastiser of foes Rama (Valadeva) thus spoke to Vasudeva (Krishna), "O Janardana, why do you not speak, why are you silently gazing ?

26. O Achyuta, it was for your sake that Partha had been welcomed and received with all honour by us. It appears that wretch, that fool, does not deserve our welcome and honour.

27. Is there a man born of a respectable family who will break the very plate after having dined off it ?

28. Even if one desires to have such an alliance, who is there who desiring happiness will act so rashly remembering the services he has received ?

29. By insulting us and disregarding Keshava (Krishna) he has carried away Subhadra by force wishing to compass his own death.

30. He has placed his foot on my head. O Govinda, how shall I bear it, (shall not resent it) like a snake trodden b...

31. I shall alone to-day m... the earth free of all Kauravas. Never shall I put up with this insult offered to us by Aryuna.

32. Thereupon all the Bhojas, Vrishnis, and the Andhakas, assembled there approved of every thing that Valadeva said, and they roared like the sounds of kettle-drum or the clouds.

Thus ends the two hundred and twenty second chapter, the wrath of Valadeva, in the Subhadraharana of the Adi Parva.

CHAPTER CCXXIII.

(HARANA HARANA PARVA.)

Vaishampayana said :—

1. When the powerful Vrishnis all began to speak in this strain, then Vasudeva (Krishna) spoke these words of deep import and true morality.

Krishna said :—

2. Gudakesha (Aryuna) has not insulted our family by what he has done. There is no doubt he has enhanced our glory.

3. Partha knows that we are never mercenary. The Pandava (Aryuna) also regards a *Saimvara* as doubtful in its results.

4. Who also would approve of accepting a bride in gift as if she were an animal? What man again is there on earth who would sell his offsprings?

5. I think the son of Kunti (Aryuna) saw these faults in all other methods, therefore the Pandava took the maiden away by force according to ordinance.

6. This alliance is very proper. Subhadra is an illustrious girl and so is Partha. Thinking all this, he has taken her away by force.

7. Who is there that would not desire to have Aryuna as a friend ? He is born in the race of Bharata and the illustrious Santanu, and he is also the son of the daughter of Kuntibhoja.

two images of Pabujee with him tied to his turban. Sarkar then saw his turban and found both tied to it . . . [Jodha Chhimunjee] felt very foolish and ashamed when it was found out.[7] . . .

Jodhpore, Friday, 3rd February, 1899

. . . It was time to dress for polo. The 11th and the 20th Hussars teams, our teams and other Europeans had a nice fast game. I played only one round.

I was a little late on the ground and so could not join in the first round though Sarkar had called [me]. In the remainder rounds he did not call [me] thinking I was not come. I sent the other ponies [away] and kept Deo Roop to ride home.

When there was time for only one more round I went and stood before Sarkar. I was in a very bad temper. . . . When he asked me whether my horses were come or not, I simply told him that I had brought them with me. He told me to play.

I did play but only to show him that I was not pleased to play. . . . Sarkar gave me his own shirt which he was wearing at that time. I purposely played very badly, and took [off] the shirt . . . in the middle of the ground when the time was over. Sarkar saw all this but did not say anything. He simply told someone who was standing there to take it.

The manner in which he told the man to take the shirt from me and the little glance he threw at me, still touches my heart. Nor shall it be forgotten by me for some time to come. It was indeed a very foolish and boyish act on my part. I ought to have acted prudently. I purposely played badly, but it was nothing in comparison to the rudeness in which I returned back his shirt. I ought to have gone [to] my horses and there put it off and given to Girdhari Singh or Hazibux. But the mischief was done. . . . I repented the very [moment] I met Sarkar's eyes and heard him tell the man to receive the shirt. I acted very rudely and shall repent for it for a long time to come. What must he have thought of me. What opinion he must have formed of me. . . .

Sunday, 17th June, 1900

It is rather difficult to judge about Sarkar, for I have never seen him play in a match or tournament, but still I hear that he plays ten times better on those occasions than ever seen here. He is at present in every respect "The Nestor of Rajpootana."[8] He is called "The Father of Polo" by nearly every good English player. He is a beautiful, hard and straight hitter and plays very steadily. Next to never he tries to hit on the near side either back or straight. . . . He is the best judge to watch a game and can nearly recount all strokes done by each player, which is rather a difficult thing. He is unquestionably the best teacher of this game if he had not a few notions of his own.

4

Hurjee

[Hurjee, Amar Singh's rival for Sir Pratap's attention, is Sir Pratap's constant companion and confidant. Tall and handsome, an outstanding polo player, Hurjee starred on the team Sir Pratap led to victory in the national championship at Poona in 1893.

As regent and royal prince, Sir Pratap showers Hurjee with his favors, making him *Thakur* (Lord) of Deoli; arranging a marriage with a proper if impecunious Rajput girl; having him appointed aide-de-camp (ADC) first to General Ellis, then to Sir William Lockhart, commanders of British forces which, in 1897 and 1898, in a resumption of the "great game" with the Tsarist empire in Central Asia, are trying to "pacify" "tribal" resistance on the North-West Frontier;[1] arranging for a fine bungalow; making him colonel of the Jodhpur Lancers' first regiment. In 1890, Sir Pratap, stretching raj protocol, arranges for a unique honor: the viceroy, Lord Lansdowne, is quartered in Hurjee's bungalow.[2]

Amar Singh is troubled by Hurjee's pretensions to Rajput status and by his character. Having begun life as a *daroga*, a community of household servants, Hurjee, with Sir Pratap's backing, is trying to be accepted in Rajput society.[3] Amar Singh regards Hurjee's claims as at best anomalous, at worst as fraudulent. And he finds it difficult to abide Hurjee's indolence and alcoholism.

Hurjee relies on Sir Pratap's patronage and friendship for establishing his social position and excusing his dissolute ways. Sir Pratap's efforts to have Hurjee treated like his son in Jodhpur court society and in British raj protocol become a matter of some notoriety but usually succeed. Amar Singh thinks that Sir Pratap is compromising Rajput honor and betraying his reformist principles.

When Hurjee dies of drink at thirty-four, Sir Pratap makes Hurjee's son, Dalpat Singh, his ward. Dalpat Singh dies heroically at Haifa in World War I while leading a Jodhpur Lancer charge on the Ottoman Turks' impregnable defenses.[4] Sir Pratap arranges to have his own *chattri* (cenotaph) erected next to Hurjee's memorial stone near the parade ground at Jodhpur. Hurjee's descendants continue to live in the penumbra of Jodhpur royalty and to carry on Sir Pratap's legacy of outstanding polo.[5]]

Jodhpore, Monday, 26th September, 1898

. . . In the evening we had polo. It was a better game than usual, sometimes fast and sometimes slow. I and Hurjee had again very hard riding off [in which one player crowds another's pony off the ball.] I myself know and all my friends say as well [that I should not], but I am quite helpless. I can't resist the temptation when I see a chance to get at the ball. I know very well that Sarkar takes it ill when I ride [off] with Hurjee. He always takes care to come in the ground after our party has come. Whenever he sees me coming he takes his best horse and often gets down to change another if he has taken a bad one. He never allows Hurjee to ride a new horse when he sees me coming. I don't know any other cause of his displeasure except that I don't care for Hurjee in the game. . . .

Deoli, Saturday, 15th October, 1898

[Sarkar with a contingent of Jodhpur Lancer officers go on a three-month inspection and training tour. Throughout they take every opportunity to hunt.]

We reached Javalia at half past seven. Here arrangements had been made for horses, as we had wired to the thanadar [official in charge of a *thana* or police post]. We reached our destination, Deoli, which is Hurjee's village, at half past eight. [Hurjee is Thakur of Deoli. Much of his income is drawn from this revenue-bearing village.]

Just as Sarkar got down and went in Hurjee came and they met in the gate. Sarkar said, "Well my boy, how are you." The brute made no reply; he was drunk to excess. Sarkar embraced him, and we sat on the choatari [a raised platform, commonly set in a courtyard, where the men meet to smoke and converse].

Monday, 17th October, 1898

. . . One very shameful event on Sarkar's part also occurred this day. It was that as I was sick, he told Thakoor Sahib [of Bera, his son-in-law] to eat with Hurjee. Thakoor Sahib declined and Sarkar . . . forced him to submit, though unwillingly, to his will. . . . [Barath Ram Nathji writes in the margin, "Yes, it was a shameful deed." Ram Nathji is upholding a Rajput convention of commensality that allows fellow Rajputs to eat from the same thal (large metal platter) but bars them from doing so with a non-Rajput. Here Sir Pratap insists that his son-in-law acknowledge Hurjee as a Rajput.]

Deoli is a very big but at the same time a very dirty village too. The koat [fort] itself where we were stopping is one of the dirtiest and filthiest places I have ever lived up to this time. It has a small pol [gate] covered with wood work and the roof is white-washed with cow dung. [Prepared cow dung provides a smooth hard surface to mud construction.] The building or rather a wretched hut is covered with tiles placed on bamboos. It is all black, for the [men] who live in [it] also cook by their bedside and thus render it more horrible. The cow dung made damp by the water used in washing kettles and dishes and in bathing imparts a nauseating [stench] capable of making the healthiest man sick. In one corner of it there are the ashes used in cleaning plates etc. This is all about the upper story.

Now I begin with the lower [story] on the ground. Where you enter the gate on your left there is a brick dais on which a dirty carpet with a rotten gaddi [cushion, used for sitting or reclining] is spread for the kamdar [estate agent] to sit It is also dotted with ink spots like a clump of stars. . . . The inside of the . . . koat is full of mares, goats, sheep, luggage, gram [a grain], grass, kitchen store and lastly a tarut [latrine] of the dirtiest kind. I [cannot] think how Sarkar likes this place. He is only obliged for the sake of the wretched gola [slave] to stop here and bear all these hardships. . . .

5

The Apprentice

[Amar Singh who is being trained as a *rissaldar* or junior commissioned officer of the Jodha squadron, a unit of the Jodhpur Lancers,[1] and as ADC to Sir Pratap who commands the Jodhpur Lancers' two regiments, also acts as Sir Pratap's private secretary, conducting correspondence, making arrangements, and reading newspapers to him.]

Jodhpore, Saturday, 8th October, 1898

. . . At ten I went to Sarkar's house where he told me to give my charge [as an officer] to Rissaldar Dhokal Singhjee and accompany him [Sarkar] in his camp to Sevari.

[For three months during the "cold weather," Sarkar and his aides, like Mughal officials earlier and ICS (Indian Civil Service) officers in British India, go on tour to inspect the training of the Jodhpur state's forces. Their headquarters are at Sevari, *pargana* (revenue district) Bali, the hilly, forested eastern portion of an otherwise arid state, where they can hunt. The rains have failed again. Jodhpur has begun to experience the disastrous famine of 1898–1899. Its population declines by 500,000, a 20 percent drop, and half its cattle die.[2]

The Jodhpur Lancers have been an imperial service unit since 1889 when, with help from Major Beatson of the Indian Army, Sir Pratap inaugurated the scheme. Major Henry Turner, who, in 1900, accompanies the Jodhpur Lancers to China and is currently the Indian Army officer on deputation for training and inspection, goes on tour with the Lancer units. The Lancers are meant to be trained and equipped for imperial service on India's frontiers and beyond. Critical to the expedition, and to the movement of troops, food, and fodder, is the railway that Sarkar, with encouragement from the raj, has had built.]

Mori, Sunday, 9th October, 1898

In the morning we awoke [on the train] at Marwar Junction and had tea and biscuits. We got down at Mori at about ten, where Bera Thakoor Sahib [Sir Pratap's son-in-law] and his younger brother came to receive us. The tents were pitched near the station where we stopped. . . .

Sevari, Wednesday, 12th October, 1898

[The party establishes permanent camp at Sevari.] In the morning we went to [build] the musketry range and worked till ten. There were about four hundred men in all [*sowars* (horsemen), *syces* (grooms), and villagers]. We did a good lot of work, and nearly made half of it. We came back at half past ten. In the noontime . . . read the dak [post] letters [to] Sarkar.

[Sarkar's English reading and writing skills are indifferent. His spoken English, replete with Marwari syntax and artful malapropisms, is one of his trademarks, and amuses and charms his British counterplayers.[3] Citing "Sir P" became a minor industry in raj publications. For the next few years we find Amar Singh reading letters and newspapers to Sir Pratap and writing his letters.]

In the evening . . . I also wrote one telegram for Sarkar to Baboo Saroop Narainjee to send Rs 7,308 out of the regimental horse fund for the assami [wages] of the . . . sowars.

Deoli, Saturday, 15th October, 1898

. . . At half past four we started by the goods train in the brake-van for Javalia station. As it was evening we opened the doors of the brake-van and sat on a blanket which the guard had supplied us. We had nothing with us except three saddles, and as we were only three, namely Sarkar, Thakoor Sahib Bera, and myself we passed the time very agreeably. Even Sarkar's temper was very good and he pointed out and told the names of all the villages that could be seen from the way. I never before enjoyed a railway journey so much as on this time. The forts of Kumbhalgarh and Bali and the Aravalli range was the best view.

[Rajasthan's countryside is festooned with forts; hardly a mountain or promintory is without one. Kumbhalgarh was built by Rana Kumbha of Mewar in the fifteenth century. Perched on the highest of the Aravalli's thirteen peaks (2,800 feet), its 40-kilometer circumference features battlements and crenellated walls. Rana Pratap, the legendary Mewar ruler, withdrew to the impregnable Kumbhalgarh after the Battle of Haldighati (1576) against the armies of Akbar, the Mughal emperor. For thirty years, until his death in 1597, Rana Pratap resisted Mughal rule by fighting a "scorched earth" guerilla war.[4]]

Desuri, Friday, 28th October, 1898

. . . Major Turner inspected the horses and afterwards the recruits. For the latter he got very angry or rather disgusted. . . . He asked . . . [one] . . . how long it is since he was enlisted and was answered that the sowar was enlisted about eight months. Then he asked whether he knew anything. The answer was that he knew nothing except a little lance exercise and the riding school drill on foot. He said it was only the work of one week. Then he ordered the instructor to dismiss them. This also was done in a very bad way and showed very clearly that the recruits knew nothing up to the present time. . . .

Mekranis, Thursday, 3rd November, 1898

. . . We . . . stopped at the thana of Mekranis. All the bunyas [merchants] of the city came and a school and a municipal committee were organized. People came in flocks simply to have a look of Sarkar. . . . As a great injustice is done to the poor inhabitants about their bedsteads, they had come and pleaded about it in the noon time. Their appeal was granted. . . . Sarkar issued an order that no one, even the durbar [maharaja] should take their bedsteads. And, if they did, they must be fined. We all and Sarkar himself slept on the ground.

Jodhpore, Saturday, 15th April, 1899

[Five months later, in the spring of 1899, Amar Singh has completed a year of probationary training in the Jodhpur Lancers under Turner's supervision. Some trainees succeed; some do not. Amar Singh anxiously awaits judgment on his own performance.]

... Sarkar came back from the course to change [his] horse. He asked me whether I had seen the letter of Major Turner. ... All the officers who were here [were] called to attend and ... it was read. This had occurred on the 13th and although I had gone to attend I was sent to bring Khanjee and so could not hear. Its purport was that Major Turner [told] Sarkar that some officers were ready and could be sent in the rissala [the Jodhpur Lancers].... He moreover hinted that some officers viz. Rissaldar Bishan Singhjee ... Achaljee, Bahadurjee, and Jamadar Rirmaljee, were not fit for service.

Sarkar had twice told me to read [the letter] but as I could find no opportunity I could not see it. Now that I saw him telling [me] the third time I thought that he wanted to tell me indirectly that Major Turner was also not well pleased with me when he was here. I hinted this and then a painful scene took place.

PHOTO I-9   Jodhpur landscape. "If I had spent my childhood in Jodhpur, I would be taller and stronger." Amar Singh's photo albums.

I was so overcome that I could restrain my feelings no more and . . . gave vent to tears. The scene was a most touching one indeed and lasted for some time. I could only answer him in broken words and sobs. He himself was touched greatly. It ended in my satisfaction, that Major Turner had never told anything about me while he was here. I was too overcome to follow him [Sarkar] to his house but came back. One thought was uppermost in my mind and that was when he said on some subject that "I ought not to entertain such thoughts [about] him." . . .

I must leave it now, for it grieves me to the very heart to dwell on it. After I came back I washed my face and head to cool myself for my head was burning. Then to relieve myself from my thoughts I read the *Mysteries of London.* . . .

Thursday, 14th September, 1899

. . . Capt. Patterson [assistant inspecting officer, Jodhpur Lancers] . . . showed me the report he had sent for last year. I asked him to give me a copy of what he wrote about me. He very kindly did so and it runs as follows: "This young officer has first rate abilities, a good knowledge of English and is a fine horseman. He however does not know his work and takes no trouble to learn it. It is a pity he is not made to."

I think it was all right and much more than I expected. . . .

Friday, 2nd March, 1900

. . . We had the lance exercise of the regiment on foot and then mallis. Sarkar came to see the latter and got very angry with Pemjee for he had kept some Rajpoots as syces contrary to Sarkar's order. The first thing that Sarkar did in turning out the syces [who have been serving ever since the regiment was organized] was quite unjust. The poor fellows who had resigned all other professions and were entirely dependent on this service were turned out in this trying famine to starve and die. This was too bad. Suppose the regiment was ordered to go on active service in the Transvaal,[5] how could they have managed without syces. If new ones are ordered to be enlisted it would take some time before they can be obtained and would be quite useless for want of experience. [Ram Nathji comments in margin, "True, quite true."]

Secondly, . . . it was ordered that [when Rajputs were enlisted] instead of one syce between two horses there should be one for each horse. This put everything in confusion. Many who had enlisted before now deserted. The cause of their desertion was that when they served two horses they got six rupees. Now in serving one horse they got only three. The men who were serving had some relatives with them who were also in want of something to eat. Three rupees can hardly satisfy a man for one month. Still some old men and children who could not earn anywhere else came and enlisted. The work was dragging [on] fairly well. . . .

Col. Wyllie [the resident at Jodhpur], is giving a tea party in honour of the surrender of General [Paul] Kruger with eight thousand men and the relief of Ladysmith in the Transvaal.[6]

6

Manners and Mores

[The cold weather inspection trip places Amar Singh in the country fort of the Raoti family, members of the royal lineage. Their unconventional informality in intergenerational relationships surprises and disturbs him as does the Jodhpur maharani's relaxed practice of *purdah* (literally "veil", "female seclusion"). While playing in a polo tournament at Mhow he dines with several princes whose arrangements suggest the different ways that Indian notables were adapting to British social practices.]

Jodhpore, Monday, 19th February, 1900

Comments Upon My Trip To Heeradeosar And Birai. I think it would not be out of place to write a few comments on my trip to Heeradeosar and Birai both of which belong to Maharaj Fateh Singhjee [a grandson of Maharaja Takhat Singh of Jodhpur[1]]. We had gone to the former village for pigsticking and black buck shooting in both of which we were disappointed. To the latter we had gone for pigs and imperial grouse. . . .

The Raoti family is rather too fond of telling very big stories and imitating the raj [court] customs but their habits or rather their conduct between themselves or their servants is too mean for such big persons.

Maharaj Fateh Singhjee and his two sons are on a familiarity which is very near to companionship; and far different to what would be in other well-to-do Rajpoot families. They joke together and sometimes or rather often use such slang words (though not in anger) between themselves as I would blush to utter even before my companions or even subordinates. There is no doubt that they live in great harmony between themselves yet to a certain extent I do not like their mode of living. According to our customs sons should have a great respect and restraint towards their parents.

The members of this family are also known to be misers. A man should be an economist but by no means a miser. They would rather have presents from others than give to any one. For instance when we passed through Aratio there were two fat goats lying before the thakoor's house and the eyes of . . . all at once rested on them. The place was only five miles from Salwa and there was no necessity of halting there but they simply stopped in hopes that the thakoor would present one of the goats, which he did not. Had he let fall any hint they would assuredly have taken away the goat. Even Sher Singhjee (who is the best polished of the whole lot) wished to shoot the goat on a plea that it was quite accidental. . . .

The time there in their company was most agreeably passed. They were also very attentive [to] me indeed. Their one great peculiarity is that they are very happy and jovial among themselves. . . .

Mhow, Saturday, 25th November, 1899

. . . Last night I did not go to bed until a late hour for we had gone to dine with the Maharaja of Rewa. . . . [Today] at half past seven we went to dine with the Alwar durbar. . . . At the Rewa dinner it was half Rajpoot and half European fashion. There we sat in the drawing room but the wine goblets began circulating very soon though I and Sher Singhjee kept aloof from them.

Healths were drunk in the Rajpoot fashion though in European style. Dinner was served on the table but instead of the plates, knives, forks and spoons, only one plate was put to hold bread while all around in rows [small bowls] . . . were arranged . . . containing different dishes as they would be in a Rajpoot plate or salver.

At the Alwar house we were received in the drawing room in a purely English style. [The maharaja] also came to receive us on the door of his house. [The maharaja is playing "host," who advances to receive guests, rather than "durbar," who would be approached by inferiors.] The talk in the drawing room and the style of eating and even the eatables were purely European. At Rewa about a dozen men sat [at] the table whilst at Alwar three of us and the maharaja completed the party.

7

A Mania for Polo

POLO IN JODHPORE. *... I have not as yet during the lapse of nearly twenty-two months since I began to write my diary ... devoted one single page separately to write anything about the game of polo which is "all in all" at Jodhpore, and one of my chief pursuits of life jealously contested at present.[1] Here in Jodhpore and specially with Sarkar, or when we all companions and polo players chance to meet, we have next to [nothing] to talk but only polo! Polo!

PHOTO I-10   "We play Polo, we talk Polo, and we even dream Polo." In 1893, the Jodhpur team won the Indian Polo Championship at the Challenge Cup tournament at Poona; in 1897, it challenged English teams on their home ground at Hurlingham. From left to right: Zalim Singh; Dhokal Singh of Gorau; Major Stuart Beatson; Sir Pratap; Hari Singh (Hurjee). Courtesy Jaipur Polo Club.

It is nearly twenty years when polo was introduced first in Rajpootana at Jaipore by Sarkar. I still perfectly well remember when I saw the Jodhpore polo for the first time when Sarkar brought me from Jaipore to keep with him in 1888. At that time polo used to be played once a week, that is, every Monday, which is a holiday. What excitement it was, and how happy they all used to feel at the mere thought of polo. Instead of that we have now polo every day and have no excitement for it, but when we have no polo, we feel dull, and don't know what to do. . . .

At that time it was not so well and systematically played as it is now. Even the riders had not their full accoutrements.[1] *Polo began to be played properly when Major Beatson came here [in 1890] and also reached its zenith [of] proficiency while he was here. When he went away it began to decline gradually and is still going down, though bravely resisted by Sarkar.

[In the 1890s as polo became a world sport Major (later major general Sir) Stuart Beatson and Sir Pratap made Jodhpur the "home of polo" in India. Some version of polo has been played in Asia for centuries.[2] Perhaps the earliest mention of the game is in the eleventh century by the Persian writer Firdusi in the *Shanamah*, a Persian "Mirror of Princes" text. A fifteenth-century Persian miniature in the British Museum depicts what can pass for a polo match. A mounted game using mallets appears to have come to India with the incursions and conquests of the Afghan and Turkic chiefs. Sultan Qutb-ud-din Aybak's death in 1210 is attributed to a fall from a polo pony. Abul Fazl tells us in the sixteenth-century chronicle of the life of Emperor Akbar, the *Ain-i-Akbari*, that *chaugan*, as it was called, "tests the value of a man, and strengthens bonds of friendship. Strong men learn in playing this game the art of riding; and the animals learn to perform feats of agility and to obey the reins."[3]

Polo seems to have declined on the subcontinent with the decay of the Mughal empire but survived in Tibet and among the peoples of Manipur, sometimes conjectured to include some Tartar groups. The Jaipur polo club in 1996 still had on its walls a photograph of a "jungly" looking Manipur team, in local dress, their heads wrapped in knotted scarves. Its caption describes the Manipur team as playing at Calcutta in 1864, a date that approximates the beginning of the sport's revival in India. The Calcutta Polo Club celebrated its hundredth anniversary in 1967.

In 1890, when Major Beatson arrived in Jodhpur to work with Sir Pratap in raising, organizing, and training two cavalry regiments of Imperial Service Troops,[4] they found a common bond in the enthusiastic promotion of polo. Together, they played a leading role in establishing modern polo in northern India. By 1893, a legendary Jodhpur team of Sir Pratap, Hari Singh (Hurjee), Dhokal Singh and Major Beatson won the Indian Polo championship at Poona, defeating the British regimental teams.[5] Dhokal Singh is said to have carried the sport to Jaipur where he taught the young maharaja, Man Singh, how to play.[6] By the mid-1930s, Man Singh, then captain of India's team, frequently led it to victory in world competitions.

In 1897, a second Victoria Jubilee year that put the empire on display in London, the championship Jodhpur team challenged English teams on their own ground. Now, one year later, Amar Singh finds Sarkar's circle obsessed with polo, for better or worse.]

Ratanada, Monday, 26th September, 1898

All the players of our team dislike the game and so do I. Not because we dislike it, but because we don't like the way in which the game is played and we are treated. Every one of us knows that we are simply to give a little exercise to Sarkar. They always beat us, sometimes with ten and sometimes with fifteen loves, but we don't care as we are accustomed to it. He and Hurjee often turn round and give a free hit and we poor and pitiable things have to turn and run away even before they hit the ball. He always keeps the best players on his own side and the weakest against him because he doesn't like to be beaten. Whenever any of us and specially I get a goal by fluke, or even a good run, Hurjee doesn't like [it] and puts the whole blame on Sarkar, who doesn't give him any rebuke but submits to his anger by a word or two of flattery. . . .

Jodhpore, Wednesday, 25th October, 1899

["The Jodhpur Army Team" enters several tournaments in the fall of 1899, giving Amar Singh his first tournament experience. If he bridles at playing courtier while playing polo in Jodhpur, away from home he finds his level on an all-India stage, playing against the best teams.]

. . . As arrangements are being made for a team to go to the Mhow [national championship] tournament we following are selected: 1. Jiverajjee; 2. Sher Singh-jee; 3. Myself; 4. Bharjee. This team is to be entered by the name of the "young-sters team." . . .

Monday, 13th November, 1899

[Mhow, headquarters of the Fifth Division, Western Army Corps, Indian Army, is located in central India, now Madhya Pradesh.]

. . . [B]y the noon train we [started] for Mhow. . . . Sarkar and we all were in very good spirits. In the train at Luni Junction, Mr Latouche [consulting engineer, Jodhpur Railways], gave us tea in his carriage. Capt. Patterson, who is going to Mathura was also in the train and joined the tea party. It was very amusing and both the sahibs were very kind to us all.[7] After tea I stopped in their carriage to talk, which was mostly on England and London. . . .

Mhow, Saturday, 18th November, 1899

. . . After polo we went to the club where there was drawing for the first ties. They came out as follows:

Monday 20th	2 p.m., Alwar vs. Malwa.
	4 p.m., Royal Fusiliers vs. 20th Hussars' 2nd team.
Wedns. 22nd	2 p.m., Royal vs. Hussars' 1st team.
	4 p.m., 3rd Bombay Cavalry vs. Jodhpore Army team.

Mhow, Wednesday, 22nd November, 1899

. . . At four was the game between the 3rd Bombay Cavalry and ourselves. We beat them by four goals and two subsidiaries to two goals. In the first chukker I scored two for my side and in the third Sher Singhjee added one to the score. The game was all along very hard and in full speed too. Old colonels and majors said that they had never seen such a fast game played before.

Friday, 24th November, 1899

. . . At two p.m. commenced the first match between ourselves and the 7th Royal Fusiliers. We beat them by three goals and three subsidiaries to one goal and two subsidiaries. Though the game was not so fast as we had with the 3rd Bombay Cavalry yet we won with a great difficulty for our arms were quite stiff and we could neither hit hard nor straight. . . . In the next match Alwar beat the 20th Hussars by four goals and five subsidiaries to two goals and two subsidiaries.

[The Jodhpur team, having won all its matches, enters the finals against Alwar.]

Monday, 27th November, 1899

. . . The game was played in the worst form. Everyone was leaving his place. Our arms were still stiff though we had them well rubbed. At first Alwar scored a subsidiary and a goal. In the third chukker we scored two goals. In the remaining chukkers they scored two more and so beat us by one subsidiary and three goals to two goals. The game was neither in good form nor so fast as it was with the 3rd Bombay Cavalry. They were hitting very hard and straight. . . .

Thursday, 28th November, 1899

. . . We then went to the Alwar house to see my father [Indian guardian to the Maharaja of Alwar, Jai Singh[8]] who is going off to Nasirabad[9] with the Alwar durbar [where there will be another tournament]. The [Alwar] durbar himself came to see us but was rather too proud of his victory and joked in indirect ways. If my father had not been present I would have given him some good cutting answer which would have stopped his mouth. . . .

Ratlam, Wednesday, 29th November, 1899

. . . At the Ratlam station we received a telegraph from Sarkar in which we were ordered to stop at Nasirabad and play the tournament. The joy was indeed boundless. We all caught each other in embraces and congratulated each other on the happy occasion. I shall never forget the joy experienced on that occasion. . . .

Nasirabad, Wednesday, 13th December, 1899

. . . In the second match at 4 p.m. we played the Alwar team. They beat us by three goals and five subsidiaries to two goals. In reality we had three but the damned umpire would not accept [it] and gave a foul against us. He is the same Capt. Swiney of the Fusiliers who used filthy language when they played against us at Mhow. All the lookers-on and specially two colonels and one major said that the umpire was quite against us. . . .

Thursday, 14th December, 1899

. . . I stopped at the Alwar house . . . until my father came. The maharaja also came and talked for some time with me. He said that though we three played very quietly yet Bukhtawar Singhjee made a great noise and said too much in the game yesterday afternoon. He often repeated these words that "Bukhtawar Singh had too much to say." At last I told him that he used the most filthy language. At first he denied . . . but at last had to acknowledge though reluctantly. . . .

Mhow, Saturday, 16th December, 1899

. . . We went to see the final of the tournament at half past three. . . . The 20th Hussars were beaten most shamefully. They very narrowly escaped being beaten by love. The score was Alwar six goals and three subsidiaries to the Hussars one goal only. The Maharaja of Alwar is no doubt a brilliant player. He hits very hard and straight. . . .

PHOTO I-11   The Mhow polo tournament of 1899. Amar Singh's notes indicate that the six teams that played in the tournament are in the photograph but only five are identifiable by jerseys: three Indian teams, Jodhpur Army Team [black *saphas* (turbans)]; Alwar (grey jerseys with crossed tiger daggers); Malwa (black jerseys with escutcheon); and three English teams, of which two are apparent in white and black jerseys. Amar Singh at left end, second row from the back. H.H. Alwar, seated, second from left, second row from the front. Amar Singh's photo albums.

Jodhpore, Sunday, 24th December, 1899

Comments Upon My Stay At Nasirabad.   . . . Except the Mhow friends who had come here we had no one to talk to us. The [English] officers that enlist in the infantry regiments are never of high birth. That was the reason they never took care of us. They regarded us as menials or something lower than themselves, but the cavalry and the artillery officers were always attentive to us even here. Though for courtesy's sake they made us honorary members of their club yet we simply went there twice and considered that enough. . . .

The tournament here produced only one good game and that in the semifinal between ourselves and Alwar. We would certainly have won but there were a few things wanted and they were these. The umpire was quite against us. He blew his whistle when we scored the third goal and said that our No. 1 had hooked the opponent's stick from under his pony's neck but it was all false. . . .

Look at the perfidy of Capt. Roberts of the 7th Fusiliers who was the honorary secretary. I think he must be called the dishonorary secretary. We knew beforehand and so asked him whether we could have Major Turner [military adviser to the Jodhpur Lancers], who was soon expected, as our umpire. . . . He agreed to all this but at the last moment put Swiney and refused the others. This is open bribery indeed. . . .

Sher Singhjee and Bukhtawar Singhjee showed the greatest signs of discontent at being beaten and I and Sheonath Singhjee the least, which put us in a better esteem of Major Turner and some other officers. . . .

Sunday, 17th June, 1900

Polo in Jodhpore.   [If canonical British social theory holds that "games" shape culture and character, Amar Singh suggests the possibility that culture may transform the game.]

One of the chief causes of the decline [of polo at Jodhpur] is, as Sarkar always says, and I with my humble experience quite agree with him, "Everyone here thinks himself the best judge and player." . . . "Funny strokes, instead of straight and hard hits, have also contributed to its downfall." . . . [Another of his opinions is] that "Jodhpore plays too selfishly and everyone tries to score a goal even at the risk of upsetting the combination of his party." The fourth remark is [in Hindi]: "They play rash, foul, and without rules." . . .

Capt. Patterson's remark once was that "they play too roughly." Capt. Patterson was no doubt quite right . . . for here in Jodhpur "riding off" is considered as a first duty and "hitting the ball" as a secondary one, which is quite contrary to Sarkar's opinion too. "Riding off" is only to be used to ride a man off the ball, but not off the ground as is usually seen here. The ball may be at one end of the ground, but at the other the opposing No. 4 [principal defensive position] and No. 1 [leading offensive position] are seen hustling one another, each trying to put his adversary out of the ground which is considered as a great feat of horsemanship. . . . Capt. De Lisle of the Durham Light Infantry says that "it is not the duty of No. 1 to ride a back off the ball, but [is to] . . . never . . . let him come up or on the side of the ball. . . .

PHOTO I-12   Mhow polo tournament, December 1912. Amar Singh at left. Amar Singh's photo albums.

I myself used to like riding off very much but after seeing Capt. De Lisle's remarks in *The Polo Magazine* I consider it useless and waste of horse spirit. However good or spirited a horse may be, he is sure to get sick of it in some time.

Flattery spoils the game in Jodhpore. . . . Nobody goes near Durbar and if anyone rides off Ogumjee or Mobjee [his favorites] he is soon out of temper and tries to ride him off even though he be No. 3 or No. 4. . . .

8

Blood and Other Sports

[Polo is not the only game in town. Jodhpur society, like British society, is much taken with a variety of sport: game hunting, tiger shooting, pig-sticking, tent pegging, and goat cutting. Amar Singh reads polo magazines and subscribes to the *Hog Hunter*. If "Games" are said to prepare English school-boys to govern, blood sports are said to prepare Rajputs to fight and rule. And sporting events make society happen.

Sport cultures vary by locale. Blood sports and polo are de rigueur at Jodhpur, where the spirit of Sir Pratap prevails. It is otherwise at Jaipur, where a sedentary maharaja, Madho Singh, avoids blood and other sports in part because of their association with British lifestyle, in part because of his languid character and sybaritic tastes. While at home in Jaipur [Part V] Amar Singh learns to cycle and plays tennis and croquet at garden parties given by Sir Swinton Jacob, the public works department executive engineer responsible for some of Jaipur's most important buildings.

In the cold season of 1898, Sir Pratap and his aides are on tour, camping mostly at Sevari.]

Deoli, Wednesday, 26th October, 1898

. . . In the morning we had tent pegging. [Mounted competitors armed with lances attempt at a gallop to spear and lift "tent pegs" fixed into the ground. An artful rider will twirl his lance with panache as he gallops toward the peg, spear it and bear it off triumphantly on the tip of his raised lance.] I tried with the left hand, and though I touched the peg many times . . . could not get it up, nor could Jiverajjee though he was doing with the right. It was because the peg was dry and the spear was [for] pigsticking and too blunt. . . .

Sevari, Monday, 7th November, 1898

In the morning we had goat cutting. [A goat is suspended by the hind legs from a pole; the object is to sever the head with a single sword stroke. To be able to deliver such a blow from horseback while holding the sword with one or two fingers is regarded as particularly demanding.] . . . Jiverajjee cut one goat by one finger. . . . Kishorejee cut a few hairs and I about two inches and all the rest missed. After this I cut one sheep with one finger. My hand trembles so much today that I can scarcely write. . . .

Thursday, 17th November, 1898

. . . Twenty goats and sheep were brought for the Jodha Squadron by the hakim sahib [head of the pargana]. . . . Duffadars Buchan Singh and Buddan Singh cut a goat each with one finger. I tied two goats together and then struck with one finger. I cut the near one clean but the off [one] remained half . . . Jiverajjee went next and cut half. After him Buchan Singh went, but missed and his hand went so low that he gave a slight cut on Butta's [his horse's] tail. After this Kishorejee went and gave a slight cut. After him Akhai Singhjee went on the same goat but missed. He went for the second time and cut clean through from the very place where the former had given a cut After this another goat was hung and I went. Only about two inches of skin remained in it. . . .

Roopawas, Wednesday, 4th January, 1899

Early in the morning we started for Roopawas. . . . In the way about two miles from Chanod we stopped for a short time in a field where we lighted a fire to warm ourselves. When the morning began to dawn we started on. . . . We drove the hill of Bala with fifteen sowars. The [wild] pigs all gathered in one place and did not come down so one sowar fired a rifle and they all came down. Boars, sows, and young ones were nearly a hundred in one herd. I was alone after them. I selected a big one and killed him about a couple of hundred yards below the hill. I was looking about when I saw another one at the foot of the hill and went after it. This proved to be a sow but still I killed her about a hundred yards further from the first one. I was coming back when I saw the whole lot going on towards the big hills. I immediately chased and killed one big boar in a very short time. He dropped in one spear only. I again saw another but as it proved to be a sow I let it go unhurt . . .

Sher Singhjee and Buchanjee . . . told me that the shikarkhana men [the maharaja's gamekeepers] were coming. [Most forest was royal hunting preserve; unauthorized hunting was not allowed.] We all gathered and were arranging to carry the pigs when [the *shikarkhana* (hunting department)] men arrived. We told them that we had killed only one pig. We took them with us and began to go on our way towards Roopawas. From the way I [made an excuse] and came back and showed the pigs to Buchanjee and Bhagootjee who brought them on mules to our camp. . . . We gave four rupees to the shikarkhana men who were quite pleased and took me for black-buck shooting. . . .

[The winter tour has ended. Sir Pratap and his party return to Jodhpur city.]

Jodhpore, Saturday 14th January, 1899

Oh, the nice runs in the Jod of Bali, at Dadai, and at Madri will not be forgotten for a long long time to come. . . . Within a month and a half I have learnt more of pigsticking than in eleven months I have learnt of polo .

. . . Within three months while out in camp I have speared nearly twenty-three pigs which has nearly doubled my interest in it. In the whole of the way I was hunting for some sport. I like to ride after a thing more than shoot it. Even the partridges and quails I like to ride and catch rather than shoot. I would rather like to spear a jackal or fox than see it caught by dogs. . . .

In the book entitled *Sport in Many Lands* by the "Old Shekarray" I saw that General Outram and Colonel Skinner both speared a tiger separately on different occasions. Please heaven if ever I get an opportunity I would also try and imitate those daring sportsmen.

Wednesday, 25th January, 1899

. . . After polo I asked Sarkar what horse I was to ride in the parade for Driffield was lame. He gave me one big Australian horse of a bay colour. He said it was a thoroughbred and much more than I could think. He has a large head and seems to be a well . . . bred animal. I have given him the name of Ghatotguch which I think suits him very well. [Ghatotguch, son of Bhim, one of the ambiguously heroic Pandava brothers in the Mahabharata. Ghatotguch soon becomes Amar Singh's favorite horse. Over the next five years, in India and in China, they win many riding and hunting competitions.]

Monday, 27th March, 1899

. . . Nizar Mahomed . . . [and I] went to Bakhat Sagaur [and killed a boar]. . . . I managed to spear him nearly six times when he fell down and died. We were meditating how to carry the boar when we saw a shikarkhana man coming towards us. . . . If I had been alone I would have run away with my horse. Now if I could manage to get out, the two who were on foot were sure to be caught. Again there was fear of the dogs being caught and recognised. Considering all things I stood to meet him. When he saw [my] . . . hat [possibly signifying either that he was a gentleman or that he was in the maharaja's service] he became very submissive and I, taking the opportunity, ordered him to clear the pig of his entrails. This being done I went and brought a boy with a donkey on which we tied the boar and returned. It is about two years old. The shikarkhana man, never suspecting that I feared exposure, and taking me for one of durbar's favourites, asked [me] to help him in one of his mokudmas [legal suits]. I promised and gave him my address. At the time of separation I told him to keep it a secret from everybody which he promised. . . . [Ram Nathji's marginal comment. "Very bad of you, Amar."]

Thursday, 31st May, 1900

A Few Comments About My Personal Experience of Tiger Shooting. . . . (1) The first experience that I ever had [while still a school boy at the Powlett Nobles school] was at Desuri, when I went there with Maharaj Zalim Singhjee. The late durbar, Maharaja Jaswant Singhjee [of Jodhpur] and Sarkar had gone on before. . . . On the very day of our arrival there was to be the shikar at Ghora Dara. It is a beautiful and well arranged [place] for shooting. A large mountain glen is enclosed with a very high fence [that] runs parallel for some distance and then begins closing. The end where the fences close is about a hundred and fifty yards open and there at the mouth of the outlet, but inside it, is constructed an "Odi" [shooting box] . . . where the shooters sit silently in wait. The place where a buffalo is tied to entice the tiger is on the hill from where the two fences have their commencement. All around the hill and the likely places are constructed small roads with fine sand to find out by the foot prints whether the tiger is there or not.

Sarkar, who had the management of the beaters this time, posted men at intervals on trees alongside the fences with orders that if the tiger seemed inclined to go over the fence they were to whistle slightly to distract him. It was in this line of men that a few other of the Powlett Nobles School boys and myself were posted. It was a tiresome task for a boy like me but there was no getting down.

At last the beating began and the sentinel from a hill informed us with his flag that the tiger had started and was coming down. . . . I distinctly saw the tiger coming . . . at a fast pace down the hill. After reaching down it stopped, turned to the right, and got into a cave in the hill. Every method that could be devised was tried to force it out, but proved unsuccessful, and so in the end, the evening coming close, the mouth of the cave was stopped with thorny bushes and stones and a sentinel and guard placed to watch it.

Next day was built a cage of bricks and a goat tied in it with some water in a basin to entice the tiger into it. On the night of the tenth day (counting from the day it had got in) hunger and thirst forced him to quit his retreat and enter the cage. But no sooner it was in then the gate closed and barred his way [back] into the cave. For a long time it roared and struggled but with no avail.

Next morning . . . the durbar . . . posted himself on a rock about a hundred yards off with some of his followers and Sarkar. The cave had two mouths and a man entered from one side and coming to the other barred by the cage drove it out, though with great difficulty. Thrice it thrust its head out and went back again, but the fourth time it jumped out with a terrific roar followed by the cracking of about a dozen or score of rifle shots. One of them hit it on the head and dropped it dead about fifteen yards from the cage. I was an eye witness of it from a short distance on the right of the riflemen. It was no doubt a very pretty sight. . . .

Jaipore, Thursday, 5th April, 1900

[For twelve years, since 1888, Amar Singh has lived at Jodhpur as ward to Sir Pratap Singh. When he makes one of his periodic visits to his natal household at Jaipur, he encounters quite different sports, those of the smart set of British officers and Jaipur nobles who gather around the British residency.]

. . . In the evening I went for lawn tennis at Col. Jacob's house.[1] I played one game of it but was quite out of practice and could hardly hit in the right place. I had also two games of badminton in which I played a little better than I expected.

Saturday, 7th April, 1900

. . . At three p.m. I took a little lesson about cycling with Ram Nathjee. I hope to learn cycling in about a week and master it in about a fortnight. In the evening we went to the residency for lawn tennis. I played two games. I think it was easier today than the day before yesterday.

Monday, 9th April, 1900

. . . I talked with Roop Singhjee [of Naila, Amar Singh's uncle] until past twelve p.m. and then learned cycling from Ram Nathjee. Today I have mastered it after trying hard for nearly two hours. In the afternoon at about half past three p.m. I went to Kiam Khanjee and took my lessons in Urdu. . . .

Thursday, 12th April, 1900

In the morning after the ablutions Bhoj Raj Singhjee [the Gondher cousin] and myself went out cycling on the Tonk Road as far as seven miles. We went very easily but the journey back was very tiresome for the whole way we were ascending. I went straight back to the haveli where I stopped for some time with my mother and took my breakfast with my grandfather.

9
My Family

[Amar Singh does not fully "go home again" until after his marriage in 1901, when his wife, in line with conventional expectations, moves into her husband's family's household. During his Jodhpur years, 1888 to 1901, Amar Singh pays periodic visits to his natal joint family—Kanota—and the extended family—the Naila and Gondher branches. Below a surface of formulaic relationships, we encounter his stern and distant but caring grandfather, Zorawar Singh; his proud and jealous uncle, Roop Singh of Naila, the British residency favorite; cousin Bhoj Raj Singh of Gondher, who becomes his close friend; mother, a role more than a person, whose cause in haveli politics he champions but whose proper name, according to etiquette, he does not mention even in the confidential pages of the diary.[1] His father, Narain Singh, dismissed in 1898 from his post as inspector general of police at Jaipur, is appointed in 1899 at the behest of the British of-

PHOTO I-13   The men of Kanota. In the middle, grandfather Zorawar Singh, flanked by two of his three sons, Gambhir Singh and Bhim Singh. At the left end, grandsons Amar Singh and Hem Singh, at the right cousin Bhoj Raj Singh. Amar Singh's photo albums.

ficers of the Political Department to the sensitive post of assistant guardian to the difficult but promising Maharaja of Alwar, Jai Singh.

"This is a great example of the self-interestedness of the Hindus," writes Amar Singh of his father's dismissal from Jaipur service. "For his own purpose Kanti Chander [Mukerjee, prime minister of Jaipur State] had dismissed my father from his service without the slightest thought how much valuable his services were to Jaipore. Look at the result. My father was dismissed on the plea of a misconduct (though there was none, as everyone will say) and the government of India has appointed him guardian to look after the conduct of the Maharaja of Alwar. Is not this a [comment on] the Maharaja of Jaipore and his prime minister Babu Kanti Chander Mookedee? I should say it is!"[2]

The three branches of Amar Singh's family are descendants of three younger brothers who left the small estate of Peelva in Jodhpur in the 1860s to seek their fortunes at Jaipur. They became ministers in Maharaja Ram Singh's government, *jagirdars*—titled estate holders—and *tazimi sardars*, leading personages at court. The three families are known by the names of estates granted to them by Maharaja Ram Singh: Gondher, held by Shambhu Singh, the eldest of the three brothers; Kanota, held by Zorawar Singh, Amar Singh's grandfather; and Naila, held by Fateh Singh, Maharaja Ram Singh's diwan until the maharaja's death in 1880.

Real estate expresses the success of the lineage. Each family occupies a large haveli in Mani Ram ki Kothi ka Rasta, a lane off Johri bazaar in the walled city of Jaipur. Ranked by seniority, not size, Gondher house is known as *badi haveli* (large house); Kanota as *bichli haveli* (middle house); and Naila as *choti haveli* (small house). The families have built forts near their principal revenue villages and, as the diary opens, are building "garden houses" on forest tracts near the Rambagh, the Jaipur royal family's "Sans Souci," palace and hunting preserve, and since the 1960s one of Jaipur's leading hotels.]

Jaipore, Sunday, 1st April, 1900

[Amar Singh has been ordered to Jaipur by Sir Pratap, and proceeds on calls to renew family connections.]

We reached Jaipore at about seven p.m. where my uncle Roop Singhjee and my [cousin] brother Bhoj Raj Singhjee came to see me. From the station we went [outside the walled city] to the garden of my uncle Roop Singhjee where we shall all stop as long as we shall remain in Jaipore. . . . [My brother] Sheonath Singh and I went to haveli [in the city] to see our mother and grandfather. The latter was at Kanota but I saw the other members of my family. The gun of nine p.m. having fired the city gates were closed and so we left the carriage outside and walked home.

Monday, 2nd April, 1900

. . . In the morning after the ablutions I went to the three other havelis to see the other members of my family. At all the places I was very well treated. . . . After

PHOTO I-14   The Champawat connection at Jaipur. Three younger brothers from Peelva, a small estate in Jodhpur state, sought their fortunes in Jaipur. Entering the service of Maharaja Ram Singh (died 1880), they became ministers and were granted estates, Gondher, Kanota and Naila. The lifesize colored photo-portrait (*circa* 1875) reproduced here shows Shambhu Singh (Gondher); Fateh Singh (Naila); Zorawar Singh (Kanota), Amar Singh's grandfather. The portrait hangs in Narain Niwas Palace Hotel.

seeing all my relations I went to my garden to see the house that is being built there. [Kanota bagh's (garden) 25 or so acres[3] are forested and home to game and abut the royal Rambagh.] It is very nicely laid out and when it will be all finished it shall be a splendid place to live in. . . .[4]

Thursday, 5th April, 1900

. . . I went to the haveli where I talked with my grandfather [Zorawar Singh] for a long time. All the time I was with him and he was giving me advice on different subjects. He also asked me to learn Urdu and I have promised him to fulfill his orders as soon as possible. After stopping a short time with my mother I came back to the garden.

[Since 1864, Urdu has been Jaipur state's court and official language, English the language of communication with the Government of India, particularly the raj's

PHOTO I-15   Zorawar Singh, Thakur of Kanota, he founded the Kanota lineage at Jaipur and headed Jaipur state's *Jagir Bakshi Khana* (estate office) from 1876 to 1898. "My grandfather also told me that he had a dream and saw me administering the Jaipore council work and was sure of its fulfillment." Zorawar Singh wears French epaulettes, Rajasthani *angarkhi* (dress shirt), Mughal style pearls and silk sword scarf, and the gold anklets of a *tazimi sardar* (high status court honor). He leans on the literary paraphernalia of a Victorian gentleman, with the Parthenon, a classical icon, to the rear. Colored photoportrait in Narain Niwas Palace Hotel, Jaipur.

Political Department. Maharaja Madho Singh is resistant to British influence in cultural as well as political and administrative affairs.[5] He may well have preserved Urdu as a vehicle to resist English. Even though Amar Singh's family is no longer in favor at court, Zorawar Singh, who nurses hopes of a ministerial career for his eldest grandson and heir, seems to regard Urdu as "a passport to State Service."[6]]

Tuesday, 17th April, 1900

. . . [I]n the morning I went with Roop Singhjee to choti haveli [Naila] where I went in to see my grand [aunt]. . . . After stopping a short time . . . we went to the bari haveli [Gondher] and then after a short while I went to mine or "bichli" [Kanota] haveli. . . .

Tuesday, 8th May, 1900

. . . [Grandfather] told me that if I regarded his advice worth anything, I should never leave Urdu until I had thoroughly mastered it. He also said that Sarkar does not like it but still I must anyhow learn it by stealth."[7] . . . He [Zorawar Singh] also told me that he had a dream and saw me administering the Jaipore council work and was sure of its fulfilment. I beg heaven that this prophecy would be fulfilled. . . .

PART II:
THE JODHPUR LANCERS IN CHINA: IMPERIAL SOLDIERS OR COOLIES OF THE RAJ?

On August 11, 1900, Amar Singh learns that he will be sent to China. The war in which he is to fight is part of the great competition for empire which mesmerizes the Atlantic powers toward the end of the nineteenth century. Britain which accomplished its imperial expansion with the navy, and then with troops recruited in the colonized lands from among subject peoples is, in 1900, already at war in South Africa against the Boer Republic of the Transvaal.[1] The empire now calls on its Indian Army, including Imperial Service Forces such as the Jodhpur Lancers, to cope with the Boxer Rebellion and the struggle for influence in a vanquished China.[2]

For the diarist, the China experience provides the backdrop for another encounter, a micro-conflict over imperial hegemony played out on the stage of individual choice. A complex and subtle drama pits two contenders against each other: Sir Pratap, Amar Singh's patron and "master," royal regent of Jodhpur, and general officer commanding the Jodhpur Lancers,[3] versus Major Turner, British officer in the Indian Army seconded as "adviser" to the Lancers. Theirs is a political struggle to define the nature of imperial subordination and a cultural and personal struggle for Amar Singh's devotion. The contrasting models teach Amar Singh that his "master" is fallible, a lesson he allows himself to confide to the diary. He is torn by divided loyalties as he finds himself attracted to the military professionalism, English social style, and moral imperatives represented by Turner.

By June 1900, the anti-Christian and anti-foreign "Boxers"[4] enter Beijing, help to besiege the legations, kill the German minister, Baron von Ketteler, and turn back a British relief column. The Qing (Manchu) dynasty, dominated by the inept dowager empress, Tz'u-hsi, is in disarray and China threatened with imperial occupation. Under the nominal command of Field Marshall Count von Waldersee, an eight-nation (Britain, Germany, Japan, Russia, France, the United States, Italy and Austria) expeditionary force is formed which relieves the Beijing legations on August 14, and begins peace negotiations in October. By 1901, ministers of the dowager empress have signed the Peking Protocol that imposes a severe annual monetary indemnity[5] to be paid to the "Great Powers" as recompense for the Boxer "crimes" and permits the powers to station troops in China. Rivalry among the imperial powers leads them to restore the dowager empress and support the US "open door" policy rather than carve up China along the lines of their respective spheres of influence.

The Boxer movement provoked domestic political struggle and international war. Over the few years that the movement occupied the historical stage, the motives and strategies of the Chinese government varied considerably as it responded to the demands and actions of domestic forces and foreign powers. Retrospectively, it can be interpreted as sectarian, messianic, xenophobic, and reactionary—in the sense of seeking to avert a Western future and to restore the Chinese past. It can also be interpreted as revitalizing, nationalist, and progressive. Thus Mao Tse Tung's early admiration for a literary work about "good" bandits, *Water Margin*, suggests why he declared the Boxers a progressive force, honest peasants struggling against rich, parasitic, effete feudalists.[6] Like other late nineteenth- and early twentieth-century responses to European colonialism and imperialism in Asia and Africa, the Boxers repudiated and attacked those European ideologies and technologies (such as Christianity, railroads, and paper money) that they perceived as immediate threats to vital aspects of Chinese culture, domestic authority, and economic interests. The Boxers practiced self-strengthening by boxing and adhered to miraculous formulae and intricate rituals in the belief that these would render them invulnerable and invincible. Negotiations conducted between September 1900, when the Jodhpur Lancers first arrive in China, and September 12, 1901, result in the Chinese government's acceptance of the debilitating and degrading Twelve Protocols. On January 7, 1902, the empress in pageant re-enters Peking to the applause of the foreign community stationed on the walls above the main gate. The Boxers, in court and out, are repudiated and the old regime, although fatally encumbered, struggles on for another decade to come to grips with adversity and change.

Part II begins three days before the relief of the foreign legations at Beijing, when a telegram reaches Sir Pratap in the middle of the night with the "joyful news" that Jodhpur is to make available to the paramount power one regiment (approximately 500 men) of its Imperial Service Forces for active service in China. Imperial Service Forces are part of a larger project on the part of the British government to externalize the cost of empire by casting the major burden of acquiring, expanding, or defending British overseas territories onto the fighting personnel and budgets of the colonies. Until Indian independence in 1947, the Indian Army secured tranquility within India and imperial objectives around the world with a volunteer force of Indians that numbered two million by 1945. In World Wars I and II, nearly 100,000 Indians were killed.[7] Most of these troops were *sepoys* (soldiers, ordinary ranks) in the Indian Army, raised and trained by the Government of India. But some were soldiers and officers of forces like the Jodhpur Lancers, raised and paid for by the princely states, semi-autonomous entities constituting something like two-fifths of the territory of British India. The training occurred under the supervision of British officers seconded as advisers, subject to inspection by the inspector general of Imperial Service Troops.[8]

A memo from the inspector general of Imperial Service Forces sets the stage for the micro-struggle that follows the arrival of the Jodhpur Lancers in China. The regiment is to be under the "general command" of Sir Pratap Singh, and under the "direction and control" of Major Turner, inspector, Imperial Service Troops, Jodhpur, a division of labor that is less than transparent. Sir Pratap happily turns over his duties as prime minister of Jodhpur to a special committee of ministers.

The regiment, known in Jodhpur as the Sardar Rissala and abroad as the Jodhpur Lancers, becomes part of the British component of the Allied Expeditionary Force. By the time the Jodhpur Lancers arrive in China in September, most of the serious fighting associated with the relief of Beijing in August 1900, is over. The sporadic engagements Amar Singh reports are the remnants of guerrilla warfare that even at its height lacked effective centralized direction. The Jodhpur Lancers are stationed in Zhili province at the outskirts of Shan Hai Kwan, an ancient fortified city adjacent to the point where the Great Wall meets the sea. Beijing is about 100 miles due west, Tianjin 40 miles to the south and the border of Shandong province, the epicenter of the Boxer movement, another 40 miles further south (see map).

The political struggle between Sir Pratap and Major Turner is played out in the ambiguous liminal space between British-ruled India and princely-ruled India. Whenever colonial subjects in British India encounter British masters in 1900, the rules structuring the relationship are relatively clear. Questions of status and power in the Indian Army are a settled matter; Indian officers, from *subedar major* (highest non-commissioned rank held by an Indian in the Indian Army) downward, while trusted and respected, are firmly subordinate to the least British subaltern. But when British masters encounter princely state subjects, the rules are less clear. The Indian officers of the Jodhpur Lancers are an anomaly; they do not fit into the Indian Army's categories of subordination and inferiority. They are officers of an allied power ostensibly committed at home to "subordinate co-

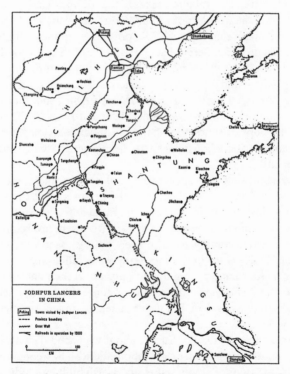

PHOTO II-1   Map of places visited by the Jodhpur Lancers in China. The Lancers spent most of their time camped near Shan Hai Kuan, a walled city on the Yellow Sea where a spur of the Great Wall meets the ocean. Map by Christopher Muller-Wille, adapted from Victor Purcell, *The Boxer Uprising*, Cambridge, Cambridge University Press, 1963, p. xiv.

operation." Where do they fit in when they are beyond the frontiers of India on imperial service?

The raj recognized princely autonomy; the princes recognized British suzerainty and viceregal discretion. In the raj's informal constitution, the princes appear as blue blooded ancient rulers. Often revered by their subjects and loyal to the British crown, they legitimized British rule in India. To treat them in the same manner as subjects in British India would be to endanger this legitimation.

The problem as posed in China, where both Sir Pratap and Major Turner had jurisdiction over the Lancers, had two aspects: (1) who was in charge militarily and (2) who was socially superior. The second was a question of greatest interest where two "caste"-conscious societies, the British and the Indian, abutted. The question of who was in charge surfaces surreptitiously and often: is it Sir Pratap as general officer commanding, a prince of Jodhpur and preeminent figure in raj and British society, or Major Turner, the military adviser seconded by the Indian Army to Jodhpur in 1898 whose job it is to see to it that the Lancers as Imperial Service Troops are combat-ready?

Major Turner could claim that an 1899 agreement between Jodhpur state and the Government of India provided that an Indian Army officer—British by definition—would "direct, control and manage" the Jodhpur Lancers whenever the unit served beyond the frontiers of India.[9] Crosscutting the 1899 agreement and supporting Sir Pratap's claim was a "Note on the Discipline of Imperial Service Troops Employed on Active Service" sent on the eve of the Lancers' departure for China by Colonel Stuart Beatson, then inspector general of Imperial Service Forces, to the "Commandant, Jodhpore Lancers." The note states that "Imperial Service Troops are not a portion of Her Majesty's Army, and, therefore, are not subject to any Code of Military Law applicable to that Army. . . . Their position is simply that of troops of states, maintained in *subordinate cooperation with the British Government* [our italics], which have been placed at the disposal of the Indian Government. . . ."[10]

So far as issues of status are concerned—and they are intertwined with issues of power—Major Turner views them with the perspective of the Indian Army. The Army's rules institutionalize national and racial differences by sharply distinguishing king's commissioned officers (KCOs), who were invariably British and "white," from viceroy's commissioned officers (VCOs), who were invariably Indian and "black." KCOs in the Indian Army were called major, captain, lieutenant; VCOs *subedar major, subedar,* and *jamadar* in the infantry and *rissaldar major, rissaldar,* and *jamadar* in the cavalry. A convenient fiction held that KCO and VCO ranks were equivalent, but it was generally understood that the Indian ranks were inferior.

Sir Pratap's contest with Major Turner about who should sit at which dining table and who should sleep in first class cabins and who in second raised, in concrete form, the questions of power, status, and worth built into Indian Army rules and conventions. Did the Indian Army's rules about separateness and inequality apply to Sir Pratap and his Lancers? Were they black Indians or blue-blooded Rajput nobility?[11]

Turner, the middle-class professional, did not hold all the cards in the contest with the Indian soldier aristocrat Sir Pratap over status rules at the dining table. Turner could not have been unaware of Sir Pratap's standing as an Indian prince. Singularly representative of the princely state mystique, he is a principal object of Queen Victoria's improbable romance with India. Turner has to cope too with the mentality and expectations of educated, English-speaking Indians who, like Amar Singh, thought of themselves as gentlemen, superior, for example, to a non-commissioned English officer who "is not a gentleman and we can not expect him to behave like one. . . ."[12]

Turner is a model officer, efficient, brave, and morally persuasive.[13] Sarkar is a model Rajput, but hampered in China by the lack of activity and a supportive court. Both men think well of the skillful, engaging, intelligent diarist, and would prefer him exclusively in their own social and moral circle. The code governing the social scene seemed to be: be English and be with Turner; be Indian and be with Sir Pratap.

When Amar Singh returns to India in July 1901, his assessment of the Indian Army worldview is surprisingly bitter, given the sanguine daily reports about his relations with English officers:

> The Indian are looked upon as inferiors in the scale of humanity. . . . However young or junior a British officer may be he always looks down upon the other as an ignorant fellow. . . . I do not know what would have happened to the regiment if [Sir Pratap] had not been with it. . . . I would not like to be treated like a coolie. . . .[14]

Dramatis Personae

"Sarkar," Sir Pratap Singh, honorary commandant of the Jodhpur Lancers in China. Amar Singh's guardian, regent of Jodhpur state. "I am to be with him in the field to earn his esteem, which I value much more than anybody else's."

Major Turner, officer deputed to inspect the Jodhpur Lancers at Jodhpur in 1898, and to "direct" them in the field. He "is well known among the highest circles in India" and "has mentioned my name particularly to his friends."

Hurjee, colonel in the Jodhpur Lancers. Renowned polo player. Intimate and favorite of Sir Pratap.

Jasji, subedar major and "native" commandant of the Jodhpur Lancers.

Maharaj Akhai Singh, son of Sir Pratap's brother. Officer in the Jodhpur Lancers.

Bukhtawar Singh, brother of Sir Pratap's son-in-law, the Thakur of Bera. Officer in the Jodhpur Lancers.

1

Getting There: With the
Allied Expeditionary Force to China

Jodhpore, Saturday, 11th August, 1900

In the morning Sarkar called for me. I hastily put on my clothes and went. He showed me the telegram which he had received about two in the morning. It contained the joyful news of the sanction for Sarkar to go to China and in full command of his own regiment [the Jodhpur Lancers]. Major Turner will act under him. Sarkar told me to get ready. . . .

Sunday, 12th August, 1900

. . . I had my horses saddled in full marching order and saw that everything was complete. I also bought a watch for forty rupees. During the greater part of the daytime before and after breakfast I had my things put aright and mended all that wanted repairs. . . . By the night train eighty horses started for Calcutta among whom Ghatotguch [Amar Singh's favorite horse] also went.

Thursday, 16th August, 1900

Last night after our coming back from dinner the rain set in heavily and fell the whole night through. It was accompanied with great thunder and lightning was seen all along the skies such as has not been witnessed since some years. . . . Altogether the rain fell four inches and a half. [The torrential rains of the 1900 monsoon end the terrible drought of the previous two years.]

[Sir Pratap orders Amar Singh to go to Mathura, in Uttar Pradesh, where the Jodhpur Lancers are temporarily quartered because the famine has made horse fodder scarce at Jodhpur.] After dinner I bid goodbye to all and went to the station where we started for Mathura.

Monday, 20th August, 1900

Comments Upon My Journey from Jodhpore to Mathura. [Amar Singh proceeds by train to Mathura to "arrange about the kit of [Sir Pratap's] staff."] In the night we were in a great fix for on both sides the train was unable to pass on. We were going via Marwar Junction but the Guia Bala [River] stopped us [torrential rains having converted the drought-stricken Marwar desert into a flood plain]. . . .* *Luckily Mr Latouche [consulting engineer to the Indian Railways] was also in the train . . . [he] promised to send us over in trollies [small, open inspection cars used by railway staff] and so we accompanied him. . . . When he went to inspect the road I went out for shooting. It was a fine cool day and the grass on all sides being green and the ground wet and full of nullas [streams] with mountains on two sides made the scenery quite charming. . . .

At about six we started in four trollies for Kuchaman Road. In the middle where the bridge had been swept away we stopped, for Mr Latouche had to inspect the construction. . . . In a clear moonlight night or on cool mornings and evenings and cloudy and cool days I would like very much to travel in these [trollies rather] than in trains. For two or three friends it is a capital drive and keeps one in high spirits. . . .

Wednesday 22nd and Thursday, 23rd August, 1900

. . . [At Mathura we had] the horses put in the [wagons] and all the goods loaded. We started at quarter to three by a special [train for Calcutta]. . . . In the morning I awoke at Sarsnel station where the horses were watered. At Fatehpore we took a little tea and at Allahabad I had a bath and wrote my diary of yesterday. [The Indian railways were a self-contained, predictable form of life, with elaborate locales and services. Railway retiring rooms provided reassuringly anglicized and standardized amenities throughout the subcontinent for bathing, resting, writing, and dining. Amar Singh used them for undisturbed diary writing.]

. . . While we were on the table taking our breakfast Col. Beatson[1] of a sudden came in and was followed by Sarkar and his suite. It was quite unexpected and caused a good feeling.

Calcutta and S.S. Mohawk, Saturday, 25th August, 1900

[At Calcutta] we took our horses out of the [wagons] and after having them watered loaded them . . . on board the *Mohawk*. Col. Beatson also came to see the work done. I was myself very busily engaged in giving rupees and receiving the receipts. I had also some rupees exchanged for sovereigns. The rate was fifteen rupees for one sovereign. After this I went to the shop of Whiteaway, Laidlaw and Co. . . . and bought some warm clothing. At R.B. Rodda's I bought a Mauser pistol and at Thackor and Co. I bought a book called *Problems of the Far East: Japan, China and Korea*, by Lord Curzon [the incumbent viceroy].[2]

. . . All the officers were also photographed in a group. After this we went on board the ship *Mohawk* and as soon as it sailed we gave three hurrahs in the Queen's and the government's name and then in the general's and last though not least in Col. Beatson's name.

It was intensely hot. In the evening after sunset we had a heavy rain.

[On October 11, almost two months later, Amar Singh finds an article about the departure, and reproduces it in the diary: "I saw the *Pioneer* of the September 8, 1900, and found something concerning us. I read this over to Sarkar and have cut it out and will fix it here for I have taken a fancy to it. . . . The presentation of the 'China Cup' is all a bosh."

[From our own correspondent] 5th September 1900

The 4th Brigade of the China Expeditionary Force, chiefly composed of Imperial Service Troops had nearly all started on its way. General Cummins and Staff left in the "S.S. Wardha" on Saturday, September 1st. General Pipon is still at Fort William. The Headquarters Squadron of the Jodhpore Imperial

Service Lancers left for China in the "*Mohawk*" on the 29th, having arrived from Mathura early this morning. Calcutta had apparently not realised that they would be leaving at once, and it was only after their departure that the public awoke to the fact, otherwise such a gallant corps would have had a more enthusiastic sendoff. There were few spectators beyond the military authorities, and even Major Turner's personal friends, of whom there are many in Calcutta, missed the opportunity of seeing him off. The band of the 7th Rajputs played the troops on board. We have heard so much about the Jodhpore Lancers and their gallant leader, Sir Pertab Singh, that it must have been great disappointment to many not to have had a glimpse of them.

The sporting Maharaja said he had hunted most things from a rat to a tiger and stuck many a pig; but he had never killed a man, and he intended giving a "China" cup to the first of his followers who had the luck to stick a Chinaman. . . .]

S.S. Mohawk, Sunday, 26th August, 1900

In the morning when I woke it was still raining. . . . I went up on the deck where Sarkar was standing. He was having the horses groomed and the stables cleaned. I myself went all round the ship to see it. It is a nice ship indeed, and is one of the transport lines of the Atlantic. . . . After breakfast I again wrote three letters for Sarkar and Hurjee. [Amar Singh, who is assigned as Sir Pratap's staff officer, acts as his secretary as well as regimental adjutant throughout the China campaign.]

Monday, 27th August, 1900

. . . In the noon time I . . . sat and helped Major Turner to write the regimental orders. Towards evening the orders were given to me and I translated them in Hindi in another book. This took a long time and I had to sit up even after dinner. . . . At about ten p.m. when all others had slept Major Turner took me with him when he went round to see the horses.

Tuesday, 28th August, 1900

Last night when Major Turner went down to see the horses everything was in disorder. The windsails[3] which had been provided for giving some air to the horses were robbed from the dumb beasts and appropriated by the sowars [soldiers]. He had, however, put this to rights and then went to see the 2nd troop where there were no sentries, and even the one that was, was found reclining on an easy chair. The windsails were not properly fitted and he had to do all this with his own hands. I am ashamed to say that even I who was there could not help him, for I had my writing case and books which I could not place anywhere, for all the floor was drenched by the rain. Some horses had no head stalls, while some had their buckets and grass strings knocked down and were standing without anything to eat. He did a lot of it with his own hand but still no sentry appeared, though often called for. Major Turner is no doubt a hard working and painstaking man. I fear very much [in] what condition the horses of the other three squadrons will reach China.

Wednesday 29th August, 1900

In the morning when I awoke I felt very bad and frightfully giddy. It was with great difficulty that I reached the water closet. On coming back from there I had to lie a short time before I could wash my hands. Another rest and I washed my face, and so I continued resting and working during the dressing process until I reached the top and retired on one of the sofas in the library. There I passed the whole day reading *Pearson's Magazine*. When I went for the breakfast I was unable to sit and there being none except Major Turner and two other officers I laid myself down on the sofa and ate a small bit of bread and a cup of tea. I took no luncheon and no dinner, except a couple of . . . small plantains. . . . I kept myself up for a long time in the night reading *Problems of the Far East*.

Friday, 31st August, 1900

Comments Upon My Stay At Mathura and the Journey from Thence to Calcutta Until We Go on Board the Mohawk. . . . I had been sent [to Mathura] to look after the staff work but I found there was nothing to look after except to arrange for the mess. This was a most bothersome task and puzzled Major Turner very much, though I did not find what he was puzzling for, except that he wanted that none of the other officers should dine in it, except we few who have eaten with him, and even in this he wanted to have two separate parts in which one was to consist of himself, Capt. Hughes, Sarkar and Hurjee or Dhokaljee [a Jodhpur Lancers officer who ultimately does not come to China] while the other was to hold the rest of us such as Bukhtawar Singhjee, Akhai Singhjee, myself, and one or two others, while the rest of the officers were to have their separate mess. I knew very well that Sarkar would not at all appreciate this and had the greatest difficulty in persuading him to have it big enough to hold ten men. Capt. Hughes is a very good man and at once assented to anything reasonable while Major Turner wanted some circumlocution to have the thing assented.

[The background for these maneuverings is the practice in the Indian Army of strict segregation, expressed in messing, between KCOs who, until 1917, are exclusively English, and VCOs who are Indian. Turner is attempting to substitute one principle of interdining, based on rank and type of commission, for another which prevailed in Sir Pratap's jurisdiction at Jodhpur, where all Rajput officers dined together. The division Turner proposes would create two tables, one for the two British officers and the senior Indian officers of the Jodhpur Lancers, and one for Sir Pratap's less senior staff officers including Amar Singh—"we few who have eaten with him." The rest of the "native" officers would eat in a separate mess.]

Next he asked me about the passage of the officers on board ship. His opinion was that only the staff will be in the first class while the other officers, including Jasjee, and all squadron commanders, were to be in the 2nd class. This also I had a great difficulty in settling and at first had Jasjee and Bhabootjee [a squadron commander] put in the first class, though he would not consent that they would dine on the first class table but with the other officers.

All this arrangement of his was dismissed, I don't know by what authority, for all the officers are put up in the first class and dine just as the others do on first class tables. I think this was all arranged by Sarkar and Colonel Beatson [who has had long experience with the arrangements of the Jodhpur Lancers], and which I think must have irritated the major a good deal. . . .

Calcutta is a grand and magnificent city and far superior to Bombay or any other city I have up to this time seen. Here in the end I am affixing two papers. One is a note on the discipline of Imperial Service Troops employed on active service and the other is "Hints for Horses and Baggage Animals on Board Ship in Tropics" [not included here].

> To the Commandant, Jodhpore Lancers.
>
> Note on the Discipline of Imperial Service Troops Employed on Active Service.
>
> 1. Imperial Service Troops are not a portion of Her Majesty's Army, and, therefore, are not subject to any Code of Military Law applicable to that Army.
> 2. Their position is simply that of troops of States, maintained in subordinate co-operation with the British Government, which have been placed at the disposal of the Indian Government, and they remain subject to the Military Law of their own states and to that only.
> 3. The command of each corps remains for disciplinary purposes in the hands of the State appointed Commandant, who holds all trials and awards punishment, in accordance with the rules adopted by the state as its Military Code.
> 4. Should the State appointed Commandant be for any reason unable to form a court for the trial of an accused person, then recourse maybe had to the summary powers of the General Officer in Chief Command.
> 5. These summary powers the General Officer in Chief Command exercises, by virtue of the delegation of power made by the chief of the State and assented to by the Government of India.
> 6. When in camp, Imperial Service Troops are not under the jurisdiction of the Provost Marshal, his authority for punishment—the Indian Articles of War—being inapplicable to them.
>
> Stuart Beatson,
Inspector General,
Imperial Service Troops

[Beatson's document is evidently intended to define the autonomous space occupied by princely state forces, and to protect them against being subsumed to the imperial practices usually applied to the Indian Army. The "State appointed Commandant" is Jasji; the "General Officer in Chief Command" is Sir Pratap. This memo does not even mention the role of Major Turner, the military adviser, in "directing and controlling" the forces.[4]]

Monday, 3rd September, 1900

Before breakfast I took a telescope and was quite busy in looking at the various ships and steam boats, the picturesque scene presented by the many islands and hills through all of which we were passing. These are the Straits Settlements of the Malay peninsula and presented us an enchanting view. This was the most southern portion or point of land in Asia. . . .

Tuesday, 4th September, 1900

. . . Before breakfast I read and finished the *Problems of the Far East.* . . . This book, though I went through it, I did not find so interesting for it was all about politics and hence quite dry reading. Moreover, it is also a difficult book, containing some words quite difficult for an Englishman to understand. . . . Major Turner for instance said it was a too bad way of writing a book. His opinion is that the simpler the language the better the book. I also agree with him.

Hong Kong, Sunday, 9th September, 1900

. . . In the morning when I awoke I saw the city and the harbour which was full of ships, and [it] presented a most beautiful and picturesque view. . . . [The *Mohawk* proceeds to Wai Hai Wei and Wusung, the ocean port of Shanghai, at the mouth of the Yangtze. Amar Singh reads and finishes *Montezuma's Daughter* by H. Rider Haggard which made him "sick while reading for it describes many cruelties." He also "passed the time until breakfast by looking at the man-of-war ships of Germany, America and Russia," and landed at Shanghai on September 24.]

Shanghai, Monday, 24th September, 1900

. . . We reached the Hong-Kew Wharf . . . General O'Moore Creagh [commander, British Expeditionary Force] came to see us on board. He is a friend of Sarkar. . . .

Sunday, 30th September, 1900

[There is a fourteen-day lull, as the regiment waits for an assignment.] . . . I took my chair outside and began to read *A Man's Foes* but was interrupted by visitors who always crowd in such masses in the evenings as if they were going to some public fair. A cavalry regiment is quite a novelty here in Shanghai. . . .

Wednesday, 3rd October, 1900

. . . After breakfast I wrote one letter for Sarkar and then went out to the town. I am getting quite sick of this job for I have to go to the same place and do the same sort of business every day. Moreover the rickshaw coolies are a great botheration and often I have to go to the policemen to settle the hire. Seeing us strangers they ask three and sometimes four times the hire that is their due. . . .

Thursday, 4th October, 1900

Tragedy. . . . There was a Chinese theatre . . . which our esteemed Shekawat Thakur Hari Singh of Deoli [Hurjee, Sir Pratap's staff officer and favorite], the so called Lieutenant Colonel, went to honour with his presence. Captain Cooper was also with him. I knew he had gone there and nothing more until after breakfast when I was talking with Major Turner. He let fall a hint about this matter. I

PROBLEMS
OF
THE FAR EAST

BY THE RIGHT HON.
GEORGE N. CURZON, M.P.

LATE FELLOW OF ALL SOULS COLLEGE, OXFORD, AUTHOR OF 'RUSSIA IN CENTRAL ASIA' AND 'PERSIA,' AND GOLD MEDALLIST OF THE ROYAL GEOGRAPHICAL SOCIETY

JAPAN—KOREA—CHINA

NEW AND REVISED EDITION

'And first we must begin with Asia, to which the first place is due, as being the place of the first Men, first Religion, first Cities, Empires, Arts; where the most things mentioned in Scripture were done; the place where Paradise was seated, the Arke rested, the Law was given, and whence the Gospell proceeded: the place which did beare Him in His flesh, that by His Word beareth up all things.'
PURCHAS, *His Pilgrimes*

Westminster
ARCHIBALD CONSTABLE AND CO.
14 PARLIAMENT STREET
MDCCCXCVI

---

do for Russia in Central Asia, and for Persia, or the countries on this side of India, i.e. the Near East—what I hope to be able to do hereafter for two other little-known Asiatic regions, directly bordering upon India, i.e. the Central East —I attempt to do in this volume, and in that which will follow it, for the countries lying beyond India, i.e. the Far East. As I proceed with this undertaking, the true fulcrum of Asiatic dominion seems to me increasingly to lie in the Empire of Hindustan. The secret of the mastery of the world, is, if only they knew it, in the possession of the British people.

No Englishman need grudge the splendid achievements and possessions of the mighty Power whose hand is outstretched over the entire north of Asia, from the Ural Mountains to the Pacific. He need not be jealous of the new-born Asiatic zeal of our next-door neighbour in Europe. He may respect alike the hoary pride of China and the impetuous exuberance of renascent Japan. But he will find that the best hope of salvation for the old and moribund in Asia, the wisest lessons for the emancipated and new, are still to be derived from the ascendency of British character, and under the shelter, where so required, of British dominion. If in the slightest degree I succeed in bringing home this conviction to the minds of my countrymen at home, I shall never regret the years of travel and of writing which I have devoted and hope still to devote to this congenial task.

My sincere thanks are due, for revision or advice in different parts of this work, to Mr. Cecil Spring-Rice, of H.B.M's Diplomatic Service, the delightful companion of my later journeys; to Mr. W. C. Hillier, H.M. Consul-General in Korea; and to Mr. J. N. Jordan, of the British Legation at Peking.

July 1894.

did not ask him much more but what I gathered from him was that last night, after the theatre was over and they were coming out the colonel asked the captain to wait for ten minutes until he came back. The captain . . . waited for about an hour and a half and then finding the colonel not returning . . . came home.

. . . Bukhtawar Singhjee . . . told me more fully about this matter. Hurjee had not come back last night, as I had thought, but only came at half past eight this morning. God knows where he was and what he had been doing, but one can be sure that he had been drinking and had passed the night at some brothel house or in the company of some prostitute. Even now at the dinner table he was full drunk and talking as if he was the wisest and the most sober of the company.

. . . The European officers were winking and smiling at Bukhtawar Singhjee for they all know that it was he who had the honour to conduct the colonel back to his tent. This damnable brute is tarnishing Sarkar's reputation as Major Turner says and I quite agree with him.

Friday, 5th October, 1900

Comments Upon Girdhari Singh.   [Girdhari Singh is a *daffadar*, non-commissioned officer in the Jodhpur Lancers who is one of the group of young men whom Sarkar keeps in service about himself. After Hurjee's death, Girdhari Singh becomes Sarkar's favorite, and his chief of household when he becomes Maharaja of Idar (see Part VI).]

Having a few minutes to myself I pondered for some [time] how to occupy them best until this thought of writing something about Girdhari Singh occurred to me. I must first begin by describing him as fully as I can. He is a tall, thinly built fellow. . . . His cheek bones . . . protrude . . . and make his face quite unbecoming. He is good at nothing except as a marksman. At the annual musketry course he always has good points.

His bearing while with Sarkar is quite of a sort as you would call sickly and innocent, never smiling or speaking but always as serious as any could imagine a man to be. If Sarkar asks a question it is three times after it has been repeated that he will answer and even that not quite sufficient to be audible and as short as possible. . . . He is not active and has next to no . . . energy. Sarkar has been trying his best to make a man of him but has not yet succeeded and my opinion is that he will never do so. . . .

Before he selected Girdhari Singh [Sarkar] had another boy named Mool Singh, who is now a duffadar in the Jodha Squadron and at present in the Transvaal [Boer] War. The talk turned on both these boys and Sarkar said that Girdhari Singh will beat Mool Singh and I contradicted him. He got rather annoyed and told me that he would send Girdhari to England if necessary and beat [Mool Singh]. I had already gone too far, for we are not supposed to contradict anything, and so thought it best to hold my tongue. . . .

Girdhari Singh, though he seems quite innocent, is not so in reality but is cleverer though not wise enough. Although quite calm before Sarkar he is the most talkative in his absence and far surpasses Jiverajjee in his chattering, though he cannot support his argument to that extent.

Of late Sarkar has been trying to raise him higher and Hurjee is full of jealousy with him. I wonder he has not yet prevailed on Sarkar, though I know he has been trying to get rid of this poor fellow. . . . He is a Jodha Rathore Rajput of Loadsar . . . third son of the father who owns the property. . . .

Monday, 8th October, 1900

In the morning we all awoke very early at about half past two and then got ready. The whole of the squadron was in field service order and so was I. We went out for reconnaissance all around Shanghai, for this is the day appointed by the dowager empress of China [Tz'u-Hsi] for the extermination of all foreigners from Chinese territory. [The perception that she issued such a proclamation runs counter to the events of the time. The dowager empress and her court had fled Beijing in August and did not resume rule until January 1902. On September 12, 1901, the court accepted the Twelve Protocols imposed by the allied powers.[5]]

Aboard S.S. Mohawk, Wednesday, 10th October, 1900

A Few Remarks About the Reconnaissance. . . . I must begin first by writing out the orders which are as follows:

> . . . In accordance with brigade orders of yesterday's date the squadron will parade tomorrow at 4 a.m. in field service order in order to take part in a combined movement of the Shanghai field force. . . .

[There follow directions to four patrols.]

> . . . No. 4 Patrol will consist of a field troop and one section under the command of Jamadar Bhaboot Singh and will proceed along the road and railroad towards Wusung distant 10 miles. Rissaldar Amar Singh will accompany this patrol.

. . . We reached the railway station at about half to six and at six started for our business. Jamadar Bhaboot Singh was with me together with twenty sowars and non-commissioned officers. Mr Burkill was also sent with us to show the road as far as the Wusung village. . . .

From here we took the road which led us straight up to the village and we passed through it. It is small . . . but densely crowded. People were rather amazed to see us and some even ran away at first sight. Ghatotguch being the biggest horse excited their curiosity very much. I told Mr Burkill that he had made a mistake in bringing us to this town for our instructions were to avoid as much as possible the inhabited places. However there was nothing more to be done and we had to go on through the narrow street which was their main hazard. It was very dirty and was paved with stones and was so narrow that two horses could not walk side by side. . . . The smell was very bad. After passing through the village we came to the railway line and passing the gate stopped on the other side. . . . From here Mr Burkill went back and I sent the following report with him:

> Way is all clear. No signs of hostility appear at all. . . . Country all flat but full of canals and ditches. . . . Horses take to the stone bridges quite willingly. In some places the path lies alongside the line of houses. Will go further on and let you know later on. . . .
>
> Amar Singh

. . . Now from this place to the Wusung railway station we encountered very bad paths. They are quite narrow and at every fifty yards are cut by ditches which are passed by a piece of flat stone or a piece of wood for the conveyance of wheel barrows. To add to this they are all overgrown with grass and cannot be properly seen and so there is every danger of the horse putting his legs in them and breaking [a leg]. Long rows of houses were passed and children ran away and hid themselves at first sight of us.

At length we reached the railway station. The warships were also lying quite close to the shore in the river. Now when we reached the station the rain began to fall heavily and so the men were ordered to put on their great coats to protect them from getting wet or cold. . . .

Now we began our journey back but it was no easy matter. . . . I wrote the following report:

> Had been out reconnoitering up to Wusung Station. There seems not to be the slightest signs of hostilities. The ground is absolutely useless for riding. Every fifty yards you encounter a ditch of some sort or the other. All around in the fields are houses with enclosures in which the enemy can hide and put us at disadvantage. We had to go quite close to them for there was no other way. It is drizzling and for some time it also rained. The sowars ought to carry water-proof sheets. They have got wet. The ground too is slippery owing to the showers. We cannot trot and can hardly ride safely even at a walk. . . .
>
> Rissaldar Amar Singh

Now I think I have no more to write than that we all arrived safely and had a jolly good sleep. Those that were with me . . . rode more than 50 miles [in a day].[6] . . . I will write too a copy of the letter from Capt. J.M. Stewart, D.A.A.G., to Major Turner.

Headquarters. 2nd Brigade, British Contingent, China,
8th October, 1900, 10 p.m.

My Dear Major,
    Your letter with Rissaldar Amar Singh's report have just been received. The General wishes me to write and thank you for both. He would be glad if you would express to Sir Pratap his appreciation of the way the Jodhpore

Lancers worked today. He is afraid they must have had a very long and trying day for both men and horses. The country he knew was a very bad one for cavalry but he had every confidence, which has not been misplaced, that the Jodhpore cavalry would get over it, if anyone could. . . .

Yours sincerely,

J.M. Stewart

[As Amar Singh is the only one of the Jodhpur Lancers officers who can write a respectable English letter, his squadron has the advantage that its actions can be brought to the attention of the English commanders. He goes on to provide the Lancers with a distinguished fighting genealogy embedded in vintage imperial ideology about the martial races.]

I think it will not be out of place to write the report of Lord Roberts [then commander in chief, Indian Army] . . . when he inspected our regiment [in 1889] even while it was in her infancy. I am copying it from "The Navy and Army Illustrated" of December 10, 1897. It runs as follows:

> The cavalry were specially fine. The gallant Rajpoot horsemen of Jodhpore had always been famous for their chivalrous bravery, unswerving fidelity, and fearless self-devotion in their wars with the Marathas and the armies of the Moghul emperors, and I felt, as superbly mounted squadrons passed before me, that they had lost none of their characteristics, and that blood and breeding must tell, and would, if put to the test, achieve the same results now as of old.[7] . . .

By some chance I have been able to write together the opinion of two generals among whom one is unquestionably the best and the most renowned of the modern times. Let those who read it judge for themselves.

[On October 9, the *Mohawk* proceeds to Shan Hai Kwan, where the Lancers will make permanent quarters for the winter.]

S.S. Mohawk Friday, 12th October, 1900

. . . We reached [Wei Hai Wei] and anchored in the harbour at about eight a.m. Shortly after our arrival the ship bearing the Bikanere camel corps which is come as an infantry also arrived from Hong Kong. An hour later the Maharaja Major Ganga Singh also came to see Sarkar. [Ganga Singh of Bikaner was regarded by British opinion of his day as one of the most effective of the maharajas. He was a "loyal" ruler and occupied a position similar to that of Sir Pratap, an "ideal prince" in the British iconography of princely India.[8]] He liked our ship very much and said that their ship was only a sort of hovel in comparison to the *Mohawk*. Sarkar made him a present of two Mauser pistols. . . .

2
Tensions in the China Garrison

[The exhilarating months of a sea journey to China, and the introduction to routine military activity in the Shanghai area, give way to a long, cold, uneventful winter. The Lancers move into quarters at Shan Hai Kwan, in Zhili province, where Boxer activity has been pronounced. The city, northeast of Peking, lies in an area which, according to historical tradition, was guarded by seven forts, at the northernmost corner of the Great Wall. It played a historic role in the defense of China against invasions from Manchuria. Most of the remaining fortifications were destroyed by the limitless plundering of the (European) barbarians, but some of the area has recently (1990s) been restored through financial donations from the overseas Chinese community.

For months nothing happens, except that the weather gets colder. Amar Singh observes the sleazy side of war, as he sees plundering and brutality by ex-

PHOTO II-2 Officers of the Jodhpur Lancers at the stables at Shan Hai Kuan. Cavalry was ill suited to the rice fields further South, but did well on the open plains near Shan Hai Kuan. The officers wear black arm bands in mourning for Queen Victoria's death which occurred on January 22, 1901. From left, Amar Singh, Hurjee, Sir Pratap, Bukhtawar Singh, Akhai Singh. Amar Singh's photo albums.

peditionary force troopers. His comrades, the men from the desert, forced by the cold into their tight quarters and with nothing to do but "loaf about," get on each others' nerves. The personal becomes political. Amar Singh's associating with British officers, especially with Major Turner, arouses Sarkar's resentment, expressed as a subliminal disapproval of cross-cultural fraternization. Meanwhile, the "Hurjee problem" chips away at Sarkar's reputation with Amar Singh and the British officers.]

S.S. *Mohawk* and Shan Hai Kwan, Sunday, 14th October, 1900

It was raining and . . . fearfully cold. We were shivering. At about seven a.m. we anchored in the harbour of Shan Hai Kwan. The other three squadrons were also here. At about one p. m. we began to disembark first in a lighter which took us to the beach and from thence we landed. . . . The Kaim Khani Squadron was already in camp and helped us a great deal.[1] . . .

Shan Hai Kwan, Monday, 15th October, 1900

In the morning I had to . . . have the tents moved about according to Sarkar's whimsical notions. Hardly had this been finished when . . . Sarkar came and ordered that the first squadron was to get ready in full marching order. I was also ordered to accompany Sarkar . . . to the city of Shan Hai Kwan. . . . There was some fighting in the city and some men of the Chinese were killed. We saw their corpses lying in one of the city gates. We went all round and through the city to awe the enemy and establish confidence. . . .

*I. Shan Hai Kwan City

[Toward the end of his stay, on July 4, 1901, Amar Singh summarizes his experience at Shan Hai Kwan. We have moved the passage here (between asterisks).] I had landed at Shan Hai Kwan on the 14th October, 1900, for the first time and . . . finally left on the 2nd July, 1901. It consists of a period of exactly eight months and nineteen days. . . .

The city of Shan Hai Kwan is situated between the hills and the sea, as is denoted by the name in the Chinese language. It is quite square and has very high walls and strong gates. The latter at present are guarded by the allied troops who each hold one of them, and no one except officers bearing arms can go in. . . . The four gates are at each cardinal point of the compass and a broad street runs from each one of them [joining] in the very centre where there is a square tower with four gates for men and carts to pass. This is a strong brick tower and has a big bell on the top.

The city is a dirty and filthy one. It is also very smelly. There were very few things to be bought and the few . . . were very dear. . . . There are lots of cheap things for show in stalls but foreigners [are] swindled unless they take away a thing by force in which case they give anything they like. There are very many obscene pictures for sale as well. The Chinese magistrate lives here and it is the seat of the district [government].

PHOTO II-3   "A group of Chinese officials with Japanese and Chinese officers," 1901.
Amar Singh's photo albums.

II. The Great Wall

The Great Wall of China which is considered among the seven . . . wonders of the
world was our daily view.[2] I had walked for weeks continually on it and was won-
dering what sort of man he must have been who started this enormous work. It is
the end here, where the wall runs into the sea. . . .

III. The Forts

There are numerous forts found here. It seemed to me as if it was a cantonment.
What a pity the inside of all the unoccupied ones is pulled down by the foreigners simply for the sake of bricks and wood. These are mud forts and beautifully
built. . . . No. 1 fort which is near the great wall on the seashore is the biggest
and is well defended with the latest pattern siege guns. . . . These guns have been
divided between the powers who will each ship his share to [his] respective
home.

IV. The Country Round

The country round is all hilly . . . but is all cultivated and there are many small
hamlets. . . . The roads are very nicely built [with] trees on both sides. Unluckily
nearly all these trees have been cut down. The [black] soil is very productive, and
the people mostly cultivate Kaoliyang [Indian *jawar*, an edible grain]. It was quite
barren when we arrived . . . but as soon as the rains commenced the fields were
ploughed and there stand nice green crops. . . .

VII. The Climate

The climate was very healthy. There were next to no sick [people] in our lines. I
for myself am greatly improved in health and so is everybody else. The winter was

PHOTO II-4   The men from Jodhpur's desert suffer from the severe cold of Shan Hai Kuan's winter, wrap their heads in scarves, and muffle themselves in wool and fur. Amar Singh admires the snow and learns "sliding." Back row, from left, Bukhtawar Singh, Hurjee, Sir Pratap, Major Turner, a Japanese officer (?), Akhai Singh. Front row: Amar Singh, Captain Pinchard, Captain Hughes, Captain Alexander, the captain's dog. Amar Singh's photo albums.

no doubt a very severe one. It was simply too awful. The record is forty-two degrees below freezing point. . . . The fruits, bread, and everything used to freeze. The ink also froze twice inside our rooms. The men's moustaches used to freeze with their breathing [no small thing, given the prevalence of mustaches among Rajputs]. . . . Even sometimes the perspiration used to freeze on the bodies of the horses while they were still hot and working around the course. . . . There was no limit to the clothes we wore. Bathing had become quite scarce. . . .

VIII. Our Quarters

Our quarters [which were in a fort] were quite nice and good. The stables too were nice and warm so far as winter was concerned [but] they were absolutely useless for the rains. They had been dug underground and thatched and plastered with mud. . . . Stoves and kongs [clay platforms heated by a small fire under-neath] had been provided to make fire and keep warm. . . .

X. Games

. . . During the whole of the winter time I had whiled away the time by sliding. I found it rather too difficult at first but soon got used to it and began enjoying it very much. However cold it might be I soon warmed myself by this process. . . . It was done by stealth because I know Sarkar does not approve of it. . . . [It is not clear whether Amar Singh has iceskates or is simply sliding on his boots.] During the whole of the winter I had one horse to ride [Ghatotguch] and one horse is not quite sufficient for me. . . . [End of Shan Kai Kwan Summary]*

Tuesday, 16th October, 1900

. . . An order came for us to start at once with (200) two hundred lances to the railway station from whence we are to proceed on to a place where the Boxers have risen and cut off a Russian patrol. We have to reach the station at 9 p.m. . . .

Wong Kun Ying, Thursday, 18th October, 1900

. . . We had an early breakfast and then went out for a reconnaissance. . . . Two troops were with Major Turner and I was with him. I led an advanced scout in the centre for some distance until all the troops halted and formed into three columns. The right was composed of the Russians, the centre of Germans, and the left of the French Zouaves with whom was Major Turner and myself . . . We first searched a village but found no arms there. In the second village a few rotten firearms of the oldest fashion were found and for this reason only the French set fire to a few houses. There were no men to be seen except a few old ones, all the rest having run away to the hills. No women were seen at all. The inhabitants seem quite gentle and friendly and offer fruits, walnuts, chestnuts, tea, and liquor to all the troops, but the Russian brutes still maltreated and abused them. The Cossacks plunder like devils.

Friday, 19th October, 1900

. . . We went out for the same business as yesterday, that is, of searching villages for arms and to burn them if any were to be found. . . . The most pitiful sight of all was that of scores of women hiding or rather trying to hide in the fields with their infant babes clinging to their breasts. When we were ordered to search their carts which were full of their clothes for arms they ran hither and thither and be-hind the bushes. It is quite a shame to bring so many troops to fight or rather to frighten such poor and harmless women.

Hung Chow, Saturday, 20th October, 1900

This morning the orders were to retire back to Hung Chow station. . . . All through our way back the Russians plundered every village they passed of all its cattle, sheep, or mules. Sometimes they even took away their clothes. They were too brutal.

Shan Hai Kwan, Wednesday, 25th October, 1900[3]

Experiences from the Wong Kun Ying Expedition. There is I think not much to write about . . . except . . . the cruelty and mismanagement of the Russians. To my opinion [they] are quite heartless brutes. . . . They had sent news that a Russian section had been cut off and that many Boxers were in great force. . . . All this trouble was for nothing. It was found that no Russian section was killed at all and that all this was invented by them simply as a pretext to plunder the poor inhabitants. The Russians have very bad management and they cannot live if they do not plunder.

I am almost sorry or rather ashamed to say that I too brought a mare and a mule foal as a plunder though it was done with orders. Still I was the man to blame for I set them to this task. Afterwards we had to leave that mare and the foal, for the general would not let us have it. The Germans had brought in [a] good many sheep which the general had also sent back. . . .

The poet had truly said: Even heaven would be ruined if it had no master, if its masters were too many, or its master were weak, a minor, or a woman. What, then, of the world?[4] This same thing is happening in China. If under able hands, China can put in the field an army that would compete with any power in the world. . . .

The Russians thrashed them whenever they could not make them understand. They said that some Boxers had assaulted their outposts and that a man had been wounded. We saw him too. It was a cut on the head he had received and who can say whether it was a Boxer or a poor inhabitant whose wife or daughter had been raped before his very eyes and who had struck the blow. . . . On the first day after our disembarkation . . . we had been sent to ride through and about the city to terrify the people because the Boxers were said to have made an assault [the previous] night on the Russian gate. . . . Among the eight people who were called Boxers, six were women. Probably they had been robbed, raped, and then slain to cover the whole thing.

. . . The people of China are, as all know, very industrious and clean, but I think great cowards. Their villages are most beautifully built and have separate rooms. . . . Their houses are also clean and well built but contain one storey only. I have not seen a single city belonging to the Chinese people that has two storeys. . . . The most extraordinary thing is that they don't milk their cows. They don't know what milk is. All their things are cooked by fat. . . . [The lactose-free diet of the Chinese astonishes the Indians, avid consumers of milk products.]

Tuesday, 23rd October, 1900

. . . After breakfast and up to five p. m. I lay idly on my bed reading *A Man's Foes*. I am in a good fix indeed. If I don't go out and stand idly I fear to incur the displeasure of Sarkar who might say that I was lying idly and at the same time if I do go out I waste my time idly which I don't want to do. . . .

Friday, 26th October, 1900

. . . It is the first time that I have seen [our winter] quarters and . . . they are quite comfortable. They can hold two squadrons. It is one of the Chinese forts and now they are making reparations to suit us. . . .

Sunday, 28th October, 1900

. . . After breakfast I . . . went out for felling trees and chopping them. About this Capt. Hughes had told me and I had gone simply to have some exercise. . . .

Monday, 29th October, 1900

. . . When [Sarkar went out to call on the Russian general] he had warned me to look after Hurjee that he may not drink whisky. This was rather a troublesome task for me. However keen I was he slipped twice while I was trying to learn a game called The Indian Golf. I saw him drinking but I was not supposed to stop him but only be at his side that he may not drink. What would he care for me when he never cares even for Sarkar. By the time he returned back Hurjee was full drunk. . . .

Wednesday, 31st October, 1900

I am attaching a copy of the standing orders. [The printed copy is bound into the diary.]

STANDING ORDERS

By Lieutenant-General Sir Alfred Gaselee. K.C.B., A.D.C., Commanding the China Expeditionary Force (1900)

1. Discipline: The strictest discipline will be maintained in the Force, and men are warned that any looting or ill-treatment of the inhabitants will be severely punished. The great danger of straying outside the lines or cantonments and of straggling on the line of march when in China must be impressed on all ranks as kidnapping is a favourite practice of the Chinese. Men should be warned that stragglers thus kidnapped will probably be tortured by the enemy and never seen again. Ill-treatment of transport coolies will be severely punished. . . .

2. Tactics: . . . the General Officer Commanding wishes to point out that the conditions of warfare with the Chinese are very dissimilar to those ruling in the Transvaal or on the North West Frontier of India. The Chinese, however well armed they may be, are very indifferently trained and are little accustomed to their weapons, consequently we have no cause to fear the enemy's musketry fire and can, as a rule adopt formations that would be quite inexcusable when operating against Boers or Afghans. Again, the Chinese will probably operate in masses offering suitable targets and consequently volley firing will, as a rule, prove more efficacious than independent fire, especially as regards its moral effect, and this is a point which should constantly be borne in mind by Brigadiers and Commanding Officers.

    As regards the general attitude of the troops in action, it is hardly necessary to remind officers of the Indian Army that with Orientals, especially Mongolians, a prompt offensive is usually the most efficacious method of dealing with the enemy and that there is nothing to which the Oriental is more susceptible than a threatened flank or rear. . . .

By Order, E. G. Barrow, Major General,
Chief of the Staff, China Expeditionary Force,
Hong Kong, 24th July, 1900

Saturday, 10th November, 1900

. . . The Chinese Governor here at Shan Hai Kwan had asked General Reed [major general commanding the Third Brigade, British contingent, China Field Force] to send an escort with his men who were to bring the revenue money from shimungtsai. The purport of the escort was a guard against the probability of its being looted by the [Russians or the Japanese].* It was about six hundred dollars and some five Chinese men carried it on their ponies.[5]* Even the enemy has [more] confidence in the British Government than any other power and I am glad to say that . . . they fully deserve it.

Sunday, 11th November, 1900

. . . Sarkar seemed . . . very cross with me because of my going with that escort the other day. Although he is such a big man yet some of his ideas are quite bad. He is not so pleased with me as he was at Jodhpore and all because Major Turner likes me so much. However, let this alone. . . .

During the whole of the noon time I sat outside in the sun and read *The Review of Reviews*. In the evening I went out for a walk with Major Turner and Capt. Pinchard. We first went to the railway station and then to Mr Rickett's house where we sat for some time. There was a goodly company of Cols.—MacSweiny, Cooke, Collis and some others. The house too was quite warm and comfortable. . . .

Friday, 23rd November, 1900

During the noon time we received the mail from India. I had no letter for myself but there was one for Sarkar from my father which ran as follows:

> Jaipore, 4th October, 1900
> Dear Sir,
>
> Thanks for your kind letter of the 8th Sept. which I received but a day before yesterday. It made me happy and I would have replied it immediately had I not been prevented by the serious illness of my brother Gumbhir Singh. He was feeling much agony at the moment. His case was an intricate one which at last proved itself deadly, and very sorry to say that yesterday he expired leaving all of us wailing. Much care had been taken for his treatment. Formerly he was under the treatment of Dr Pank, but when he declared the case quite hopeless, and left the treatment, we engaged a Hakim [who works in the Unnani tradition of medicine associated with Muslims] and when he pronounced the case quite hopeless a Baid was employed [associated with Ayurveda, a medical tradition associated with Hindu texts], but all these cares were useless and futile. . . . Alas! during his illness he often used to say, "All these pains are a revenge as I have not accompanied my cousin [nephew] Amar Singh." No one can avert Fate! Resignation to the will of God is on such circumstances becoming from our nature.
>
> What should Amar Singh do on receiving the news I leave to your discretion. The worldly custom wants that he should come out of his dera [tent] and have himself shaved at a distance of nearly ten or twelve yards from the lodging place; and he should bathe. I say, if he can perform the above as-

serted duties with convenience he should do them provided you think proper. I do by no means mean to bother him about it if there is some inconvenience. Hoping success in your voyage and the object of your voyage.

Yours faithfully,
Narain Singh

One can imagine what a thunderbolt it was because it came quite unexpected. . . .

Saturday, 24th November, 1900

. . . At about nine a.m. I shaved myself and had a bath. After this, . . . I went and sat in the open where mats and blankets had been spread out. All the officers of the regiment, Sarkar, Hurjee, Major Turner, Captains Hughes, and Pinchard and some others came and sat there for a few minutes while Bukhtawar Singhjee circulated the plate containing opium of which all partook. When this ceremony was over we all disassembled but Capt. Hughes did come in my room and stopped for a short time. . . .

Tuesday, 27th November, 1900

In the morning I . . . went out to Sarkar who was talking with Major Turner. He gave me two telegrams of which one was mine containing the shocking news that the Jaipore Durbar had confiscated the three jagirs [estates of Amar Singh's extended family], leaving barely anything at all. Sarkar had seen it before me and said that I should not care much about it. Of course there were my grandfather, father, and other elders to look about it yet this was too terrible a news. I am sorry that Sarkar is not in India at present to help us in this difficulty. What cannot be avoided is to be suffered.

[The news that Amar Singh has received means that the prosperous and respected position that the Kanota family and the two related houses have built for themselves in Jaipur since the 1860s is in the gravest danger. The Jaipur government charges that the better portion of the estates of Amar Singh's grandfather and his two brothers, who served as Maharaja Ram Singh's ministers, was fraudulently acquired. The government's object is to extract compensation for the alleged fraud and to seize the impugned portions of the three estates. The case drags on for four years, from a Jaipur law court to the viceroy's office at Simla. The news comes to Amar Singh at the midpoint of the adjudication.

The adverse decision of the Jaipur law court holds that the brothers have used the position of the eldest brother, Shambhu Singh of Gondher, who controlled the jagir-granting office, and of the second brother, Amar Singh's grandfather Zorawar Singh, head of the same office at a later time, to falsify the papers and mislead Maharaja Ram Singh into making grants which he did not mean to make. The brothers argue that the maharaja was acting with full knowledge, and intended to raise their incomes to a level commensurate with their dignified position at court as *tazimi sardars* (high-status court honor). They assert that the maharaja's visit to the Gondher estate demonstrates that he knew all about the *jagirs* (landed estates).][6]

Wednesday, 28th November, 1900

[The combination of a death in the family and news of the confiscation seems to hit Amar Singh harder than he lets on.] . . . Sarkar asked if I would come out for tent-pegging, but I was too unwell to stir out. As soon as I laid myself down on the bed I began to feel sleepy and closed mine eyes. I continued to sleep undisturbed until dinner time when they wanted to wake me but I was not at all feeling inclined to eat and so did not leave my bed. I had no fever at all but felt . . . dull.

Saturday, 1st December, 1900

. . . Sarkar gave me a letter written by Major Turner to Mr Lawrence [the secretary to the viceroy, and a good friend of Sir Pratap] as a sort of recommendation concerning the case [of the family's property]. I stamped [it] and sent it away. Next I wrote another letter to Colonel Beatson from Sarkar's side for the same purpose. . . .

. . . [Bukhtawar Singhji] told me . . . what mean ideas Hurjee has. He once told Bukhtawar Singhjee in a confidential manner not to have any intimacy with me, . . . meaning that I was a crafty or cunning brute or I don't know what. Of late I think I have done nothing to irritate him. Of course there was one thing which might have offended him . . . while we were at Shanghai Sarkar ordered me to wire for 5,000 (five thousand) rupees for his expenses. When Hurjee knew this he told me to wire for two thousand more for him. The money was to come from Sarkar's treasury and so how could I take such a responsibility without his sanction, though Hurjee said there was no need to ask Sarkar about it. I however did inform him to which he turned a negative answer and said that five thousand would do quite amply. As far as I can see there was no fault of mine. When the five thousand arrived he asked for the other two thousand which he had ordered but they had not come.

Thursday, 6th December, 1900

In the evening I again went to the pond where I tried sliding. It is rather a difficult job but [I] hope I shall soon learn it unless I . . . get hurt by falling. . . . I again fell twice in the evening but was not hurt at all. The whole of the day was very fine and especially after the sun had come out. This is the first time I have seen the snow falling and I enjoyed it very much.

Thursday, 13th December, 1900

I dressed and went out for a walk. . . . I met Major Turner and Capt. Hughes coming back from the commissariat. I returned back with them. I had an intention of breaking off their company for fear Sarkar might see me with them. There was not the slightest chance of it and so I did go with them but as the proverb says "When the eye is destined to burst, a mote will be sure to pierce it." I saw Sarkar coming down from the fort. This was the most unusual time for him. . . .

Saturday, 15th December, 1900

. . . Major Jasjee came and sat down chattering which annoyed me greatly. I don't like anybody to disturb me when I read but these fellows have not the slightest regard for another's feelings. . . .

Monday. 17th December, 1900

. . . When Sarkar went out, I followed after him. . . . After a while he had his horses saddled and also told me to work mine. . . . He was very rude in giving me the order. What harm had there been if he had ordered me in a mild or rather a fair and common-day language. He seems rather displeased with me though I do not see the slightest ground for it. . . . His temper is getting [more] irrita[ble] every day. . . .

Tuesday, 18th December, 1900

. . . I . . . went out after Sarkar who had preceded me to the parade ground. . . . He asked me where I was during the whole of the day time yesterday. I had of course gone nowhere and so replied that I went out for a walk in the evening and as for the noon time I was in mine own room reading books.

The whole purport was that instead of sitting comfortably in our rooms we ought to loaf about after him doing nothing but staring in his face. Now this is too hard for me. I honestly say that this is the thing I hate most of all. He does no work that would occupy him. He cannot read, and cannot sleep the whole day through, and so naturally enough must pass his time somehow or other. It is quite different with me who love reading as much as anything else in the world. . . .

Wednesday, 19th December, 1900

. . . I went out for a walk with Capt. Pinchard up to the railway station. On my way back I separated from him. . . . The main object of my separating from him was the dread of encountering Sarkar in his company.

Sunday, 23rd December, 1900

. . . I came and stood with Sarkar who ordered me to bring the list of those gentlemen [to] whom letters were to be written. He added some more to the list which now numbers fifty-one. . . . I was ordered to begin writing them. . . .

Tuesday, 25th December, 1900

[On Christmas day, the Allied Expeditionary Forces arrange a sports competition] . . . [I] dressed myself smartly for the gymkhana. . . . All the nationalities were invited . . . The whole day was a very fine one. The sun was bright and it was quite warm. . . . The dinner too was a grand and a nice one too though only one guest was invited. . . .

Today's Gymkhana Fully Described.   In trying to describe the gymkhana I must give a list of all the games we had and then describe them at length:

1. Tent pegging by sections.
2. China pony race.
3. Japanese Cavalry race.
4. Cossack race.
5. Spearing a Musack.
6. Tug of war on foot.
7. Tug of war on horse back.
8. Tent pegging by sections
9. Lloyd-Lindsay.
10. Cossack Tricks.
11. Goat cutting.
12. Tug of war.
13. Mule Race.

[Descriptions of only some of the events are included here.]

3. The Japanese cavalry race was not so good. The Japanese are not good horsemen. God has not given the Chinese and Japanese the gift of horse-riding. . . .

8. In the tent pegging by sections of officers there was a great interest. [This is a sport in which a rider at full gallop is expected to lift a peg fixed in the ground with the tip of his lance. Skilled riders accomplish the charge with much flourish and bravado.] It was not only our regimental officers that competed but all the other English officers had their sections. In this the staff section of Sarkar won. It was composed of Hurjee, Akhai Singhjee, Bukhtawar Singhjee, and myself. We went three times and there was only one miss by Bukhtawar Singhjee. The dressing was also very good. . . .

9. In the Lloyd-Lindsay race there were all officers. It was open to all nations. . . . The conditions were that we were to start with empty pistols, dismount, give our horses to the sowars that were in wait for us, load our pistols, and fire and try to hit the bottle at a range of twenty-five yards. After hitting the bottle, empty the pistol, mount, and ride back to the winning post. . . . At the start we went in good speed. I for myself had taken a handful of cartridges out of my pocket and springing from my horse hastily loaded and fired. By good luck I broke mine bottle at the very first shot. I hastily [mounted] my horse [and] came home in an easy canter. I was quite an easy winner. . . .

10. The Cossacks' tricks were quite amusing. . . . The tricks were such as picking up a dead man, carrying another behind him, standing high up on a pony while going at the gallop, dismounting and mounting at the gallop. . . . They were all good tricks and very well performed too. I rather like them. . . .

11. Goat-cutting . . . [The goat is suspended head down from a high pole, and the galloping rider seeks to behead it with the sword—a form of practice for hand-to-hand sword combat]. Hurjee cut his goat clean and so did Mr Alexander [that is, they beheaded it in one stroke]. Sarkar was to go but he gave his chance to Mr Alexander who cut clean. . . .

. . . There were all nationalities assembled, British, Germans, French, Russians, Italians, Austrians, and Japanese. . . . One very seldom gets such a chance of seeing such a gathering. . . .

Wednesday, 26th December, 1900

. . . Major Turner presented me with a silver bottle and two tumblers that were fitting into it, as the trophy of my yesterday's winning the Lloyd-Lindsay. . . .

Thursday, 27th December, 1900

A Queer Thing.   . . . Every day we hear some new queer or strange thing but this surpasses all. About a week ago Sarkar had told Akhai Singhjee to tell Capt. Pinchard not to call him Akhaijee but Maharaj Akhai Singh. Sarkar, or rather Hurjee, and Major Turner not being on good terms are the cause of all this humbug. In my opinion Sarkar was quite wrong in giving this order. . . . Poor Akhai Singhjee was in a fix. For a couple of days he kept quiet, but Sarkar again hearing him named Akhaijee asked if he had told them or not. On declining he was ordered the second time to do so but still he kept quiet. The other day when Gaussen addressed him as Akhaijee Sarkar was there and told Mr Gaussen not to address him in that way but as Maharaj Akhai Singh or Maharaj. When he went away Akhai Singhjee was reprimanded the third time and so the poor fellow was obliged to tell Capt. Pinchard in the best manner he was able to do.

The result of this was that on the 25th when we were on the race course Major Turner came and asked me in what manner I wished to be addressed, for he said that there had been an objection about it. I of course told him that the way in which he usually talked to me was quite right and that I saw no cause why he should change it . . . What harm was there in calling us Akhaijee, Bukhtawarjee and Amarjee . . . I was fumbling about in quite an embarrassed manner . . . and was telling him that I had personally no objection to it when Hurjee came up to my great relief . . . What could Hurjee say? He too could make no answer and was fumbling and blubbering about when Sarkar came and Major Turner began talking with him on this point. I hastily drew away, but whatever I could see was Sarkar making gesticulations and finding some excuses and giving some groundless reasons. . . . I do not know what they (I mean the four Englishmen) must have thought of it. . . .

[Marginal comment by Barath Ram Nathji:] "Hurjee, Dhokaljee and Amarjee are persons having no titles but Maharaj Akhai Singhjee is a titled person, consequently to call the Maharaj simply Akhaijee is a direct insult. Call Major Turner by the name of Mister Turner and you will find the difference. It would be quite right to call him Major Turner or Major simply; likewise Akhai Singhjee should be called Maharaj Akhai Singhjee or Maharaj simply. I think Sarkar was quite right in making this suggestion."

Sunday, 30th December, 1900

. . . I was sent for by Sarkar. I went and had all the letters signed. It took nearly the whole of the daytime for additions were . . . in several of them. After this it took me the remainder of the time to write "yours sincerely" on them all. . . . After dinner . . . I . . . addressed all the envelopes. It took me a long time. . . .

Monday, 31st December, 1900

Comments Upon My Visit to the Arethusa.   . . . The captain and the officers of the *H.M.S. Arethusa* had given a [New Year's] luncheon party and invited four officers from all the British regiments out here in Shan Hai Kwan. From the Jodhpore Lancers were Captains Hughes, Pinchard, Akhai Singhjee and myself. We

PHOTO II-5   "A group of some soldiers of all nations collected in China." Amar Singh at right rear, left of tree. Amar Singh's photo albums.

started from here at about a quarter past eleven. . . . My winning the Lloyd-Lindsay has made me quite a conspicuous figure among the officers both naval and military. They were congratulating me very cordially. The general and his staff had also come. . . . There were tables in three rooms and all were . . . full. The luncheon was quite satisfactory. . . . After all was over there were cheers for the general and the captain of the *Arethusa* and last though not least for the queen. Everything was on a grand scale and splendidly carried out. . . .

Wednesday, 9th January, 1901

. . . Sarkar does not dine with us on the mess table because he is in a fix. He does of course like to come and dine with us but there is the ever-apparent difficulty of Hurjee. If that gentleman comes in the mess he drinks too much as usual and makes a fool of himself. If on the other hand he is left alone in the room without Sarkar he drinks so much that there is no limit to it. . . .

Then there are two more difficulties. First he must make some excuse for his not coming, which he finds by saying that he is always desirous of going to bed early. Next he wants to make Hurjee sleep early, as that Johnny drinks as long as he does not retire for rest. Thus compelled by circumstances he takes his dinner as early as half past five or six. Nowadays the nights are very long and so one gets quite tired of lying down. . . . Thus he rises up very early, as early as three or four a.m. . . . and wakes the poor syces and Rajpoot boys who groom his horses, and then commences stables which last as long as he thinks it . . . time to work the horses. . . . just fancy these poor boys, not sufficiently clad (for they are made to put off their coats during the stables) shivering in this bitter cold. . . .

He does not like our going to the mess and yet would not tell [us] to desist. He does not like our talking or going out with Major Turner or any other European and yet would not say so. He does not like our sitting in our rooms and yet would not say so. We cannot go out to call on any one for he would not like it though [he] will never mention it . . . While Sarkar is present, no matter where, either in or out, we are not supposed to speak, not even among us. He would not say anything about it but will never like it. All these things the officers see and ask us and though we defend him as best we can yet the thing leaks out, for after all the truth is truth and lie is lie.

Nowadays Sarkar has practically left the company of the English officers. . . . Nearly the whole of the morning he spends with his horses and only comes to the breakfast table for form's sake. After breakfast we do not see him because during the noon time he sits in his room to keep company to Hurjee, who next to never comes out and even then for a short time. . . . He is the laughing stock of Major Turner and the other Englishmen [which] makes Sarkar's reputation bad. English people have a great society and out here everyone knows these things and laughs and cracks jokes at our expense. Isn't it miserable?

A List of All the Books That I Have Read During the Year 1900. [Amar Singh's readings, both his fiction and magazines, are a fair sampling of the tastes of an Edwardian gentleman, modified by India. Most of these books can be found in his library at Kanota. We provide a selection here.]

TABLE 2.1   A List of All The Books That I Have Read During the Year 1900

S.N. Names of Books	Names of Authors	Comments
(February 1900)		
1. Plutarch's Lives		Very good
. . .		
(March 1900)		
4. Rasselas	Samuel Johnson	Very good
5. The Page of the Duke of Savoy	Alexandre Dumas	Very good
. . .		
8. Life of George Washington	J.T. Headley	Very good
. . .		
(May 1900)		
10. Rajasthan Ka Itihas	Raja Shiv Prasad Hind	Good
. . .		
12. Life of Maharana Pratap Singh of Odeypore	Munshi Devi Prasadjee	In Hindi and Urdu Not well-written

(continued)

TABLE 2.1 *(continued)*

S.N. Names of Books	Names of Authors	Comments
(June 1900)		
13. Itihas-timir-Nask	Raja Shiv Prasad Hind	Good
14. Schiller's William Tell	Translated by Major Patrick Maxwell	Very good Excellent
...		
17. Brief History of Jaipur	Thakoor Fateh Singhjee Champawat of Naila	Not much good
...		
(August 1900)		
20. Problems of the Far East	Rt. Hon. Lord Curzon	Very good
21. Montezuma's Daughter	H. Rider Haggard	Very interesting
...		
24. A Maker of Nations	Guy Boothby	Very interesting
25. The Talking Horse	F. Anstey	Very amusing
...		
(November 1900)		
28. The Strand Magazine of July [and August]–1900		
29. The Wide World Magazine of [August and] September–1900		
(December 1900)		
32. The Review of Reviews of July–1900		
33. The Man Who Didn't or the Triumph of the Snipe Pie	Mrs Lovett Cameron	Small but amusing
35. Helbeck of Bannisdale	Mrs. Humphrey Ward	Rotten
36. A Social Highwayman	E. P. Train	Good
39. The Strand Magazine of October–1900		
40. The Chevalier D'Auriac	L. Lovett Yeats	Very interesting
...		

TABLE 2.2   Register of the Shikar I Got in the Year 1900[*]

Animals	Jan	Feb	Mar	Apr	May	June	July	Aug	Sep	Oct	Total
Foxes	14	2	4	0	0	1	0	0	0	0	21
Hares	1	1	0	1	1	0	0	0	0	0	4
Jackals	3	0	4	1	0	0	0	0	0	0	8
Chinkaras	8	3	0	0	1	1	0	1	0	0	14
Black Bucks	0	1	0	0	0	0	1	0	0	0	2
Imperial Grouse	1	39	0	0	0	0	0	0	0	0	40
Pigs	1	0	0	0	0	0	0	0	0	0	1
Partridge	4	0	1	4	1	0	0	0	0	0	10
Sandgrouse	0	7	3	2	0	0	0	0	0	0	12
Ducks	0	3	0	0	0	0	0	0	0	3	6
Bustards	0	1	0	0	0	0	0	0	0	0	1
Green Pigeons	0	0	0	10	0	0	0	0	0	0	10
Hyenas	0	0	0	0	1	0	0	0	0	0	1
Nil-Gai	0	0	0	0	0	0	1	0	0	0	1
Monthly Total	32	57	12	18	4	2	3	1	0	3	132

[*We go with Amar Singh's arithmetic]

THE STRAND MAGAZINE.

Vol. xix.   JANUARY, 1900.   No. 109.

The Brass Bottle.

By F. ANSTEY.

Author of "Vice-Versâ," etc., etc.

CHAPTER I.

HORACE VENTIMORE RECEIVES A COMMISSION.

 HIS day six weeks—just six weeks ago!" Horace Ventimore said, half aloud, to himself, and pulled out his watch. "Half-past twelve— what was I doing at half-past twelve?"

As he sat at the window of his office in Great Cloister Street, Westminster, he made his thoughts travel back to a certain glorious morning in August which now seemed so remote and irrecoverable. At this precise time he was waiting on the balcony of the Hotel de la Plage—the sole hostelry of St. Luc-en-Port, the tiny Normandy watering-place upon which, by some happy inspiration, he had lighted during a solitary cycling tour — waiting until She should appear.

He could see the whole scene: the tiny cove, with the violet shadow of the cliff sleeping on the green water; the swell of the waves lazily lapping against the diving-board from which he had plunged half an hour before; he remembered the long swim out to the buoy; the exhilarated anticipation with which he had dressed and climbed the steep path to the hotel terrace.

For was he not to pass the whole remainder of that blissful day in

Sylvia Futvoye's society? Were they not to cycle together (there were, of course, others of the party — but they did not count), to cycle over to Veulettes, to picnic there under the cliff, and ride back— always together—in the sweet-scented dusk, over the slopes, between the poplars or through the cornfields glowing golden against a sky of warm purple?

Now he saw himself going round to the gravelled courtyard in front of the hotel with a sudden dread of missing her. There was nothing there but the little low cart, with its canvas tilt, which was to convey Professor Futvoye and his wife to the place of *rendezvous*.

"THE PICNIC UNDER THE CLIFF."

Vol. xix.—1.   Copyright, 1900, in the United States of America, by D. Appleton & Co.

3

Under Fire at Lijapoo

[The months of routine are broken in January of 1901 by one of the few engagements the Lancers experience in China. Amar Singh fights his first battle—an event he records with the eye of a historian and the enthusiasm of a Champawat Rathore Rajput. He grasps that the history of any battle is observer-dependent, providing accounts of separate observers: "the guard that was with the carts . . . gave this account." In the slack periods, the tug of war between Sir Pratap and Major Turner continues. Sir Pratap, self-excluded from the society of the officers mess because of the "Hurjee problem," attempts similarly to dissociate Amar Singh from it.]

Shan Hai Kwan, Monday, 21st January, 1901

The Incidents of the 12th January Fully Described.   To begin with I must first describe what I was doing before the news arrived. I was in my closet and had ordered Maharaj Akhai Singhjee's black Irish horse to be got ready. . . . When I came out and was washing my hands Girdharijee [the servant of Akhai Singhjee] told me that some shots have been just fired on Capt. Hughes while he was coming from the city and that all were going after the offenders. I too hastily buckled on my sword and revolver and taking my spear rushed out. Just in the doorway I found the black horse waiting for me. There was no time to change the saddle and so I jumped on its back and galloped off in the direction pointed by our men. As the troop had already started before me and they were within my sight, I rode very fast and soon overtook them.

The Origin

The men who had gone with the mules and carts to collect wood for our regiment and the commissariat were informed by the inhabitants that the enemy was in the neighbourhood and will attack them, and advised them to clear off as soon as they could. Naturally our men paid no attention to their advice and, having loaded their carts, were just starting when some shots were fired at them. Some mules were hit and so the men dispersed. The syces hid themselves in the nullahs [streams or drains] and made for the camp at their best pace. The sowar with the commissariat mules was on horse-back and galloped hard amid a hot shower of bullets for the camp to inform us about the attack. . . . His name was Sheoram Singh and he was a Mertia [Rajput lineage]. The camp being informed, a troop had been sent as described before. The rumour about the shots being fired on Hughes was quite wrong. . . .

The guard that was with the carts bringing in wood for the regiment [gave] . . . this account. When the shots were fired they hastened to take shelter in the village. Only three succeeded and fared the worst. The other three that could not reach mounted a hillock and kept a constant fire and thereby kept the enemy at a respectable distance. These three were under Duffadar Dul Singh who has the credit of all this. But it was not so with the other three in the village. Having reached it they went into a house and locked the door from inside. This put them in a trap, for they were unable to see the enemy. While they were loading their magazines some of the enemy got up on the roof of an adjoining house. From thence they had a view of our men through a window, whose paper was unluckily torn.

Three Men in a Trap

While their attention was occupied in loading their magazines the enemy fired two shots simultaneously from the top of a house through the broken window. Both bullets hit Jodha Mengaiz Singh and he fell down mortally wounded. While falling down his balance was towards the window and consequently his carbine fell out through the aperture and was captured and taken away by the enemy. Our two remaining sowars divided the wounded one's ammunition and, taking cover, began firing aimlessly in the direction from whence the enemy were firing.

The enemy now came to the back of the house and began to dig a hole in the wall to shoot in. Just as the man from the outside drew out his crowbar after the final stroke, our men fired a shot through the hole and most certainly wounded the operator, as is proved by the fact that they desisted from this and took to another method. They mounted the roof and began scraping off the covering. Our men fired at the sounds overhead and wounded one, for his groans and sprawlings were distinctly heard by those down below. Though wounded, they set fire to the roof, which was all wood and stalks.

Now was a critical moment. There was no more disturbing by the bullets but the smoke was choking them and the burning flames were scorching their clothes. To add to this they were very thirsty. Driven to desperation, they opened the door and rushed out to sell their lives as dearly as they could in the open. Imagine what their relief must have been when instead of meeting the enemy they encountered Capt. Pinchard and our men under Pratap Singhjee amounting to half a troop. The sick man was taken out and inspected by Pinchard who said it was quite hopeless and that the man will expire before morning. All his bowels had been blown out. He however expired on his way back to the camp. The village where all these incidents had happened is known by the name of Lamasu.

The Man in the Nullah

. . . We were riding on and just as we reached the top of a high hill we saw a man on horseback beckoning us towards him. . . . He had been sent by Hurjee saying that they had a man with a rifle in a nullah. . . . Here I must leave off my account and describe the fight of the man in the nullah.

When Hurjee saw the man he had sent word that he had a man with a rifle. The major misunderstood and thought that the man was already his prisoner and so told the sowar to tell Hurjee to keep him. Hearing this they tried to catch him alive. All this while he was firing but no one was hurt. Bukhtawar Singhjee knocked him twice with his spear. Once the fellow fired pointblank but missed, and so Bukhtawarjee was saved. All this while Hurjee was a spectator and Bukhtawar Singhjee and the Chinaman the performers. [Having] knocked [him] down the second time our men, that is to say Hurjee, Bukhtawarjee, and the sowar, jumped off their horses and wanted to catch the man alive. Bukhtawar Singhjee was on him and motioning him to throw away his rifle but he would not. Hurjee shouted to the sowar to run on and help Bukhtawarjee. At that instant the prostrate man fired a shot and hit our sowar who was wounded but still advanced on. Seeing this, Bukhtawarjee struck the Chinaman with his sword on the head and thereby finished him. To make sure, Hurjee fired his Mauser pistol on the inanimate body. The sowar was Mertia Sheoram Singh, the same who had brought the news home. He was mortally wounded and expired within five minutes.

This scene had taken place in a nullah about half a mile from Lamasu. The body of Sheoram Singhjee was carried to Lamasu in blankets. Hurjee and Bukhtawarjee walked back to Lamasu, for all the three horses had bolted as soon as they had got off their backs. Thus ended the story of the man in the nullah. Had Bukhtawar Singhjee not delayed but given the final blow a few moments before, the life of Sheoram Singh might probably have been saved, but death cannot be averted. We must not be sorry, for such a death is worth dying and especially to a Rajpoot.

The Engagement of Lijapoo

To resume the thread of my personal account. I must say that I was leading at a brisk trot, because Major Turner's pony was not going well. . . . We were going along the bank of a nullah . . . when we came up of a sudden on a village where there were two red flags with some white in [them] . . . floating. How I wished to possess one of them, but it was too dangerous.

We rode up a hill overlooking it and saw the same men [as had been near the red flag village] with rifles slung on their shoulders and riding Chinese ponies, making for the village further on. [Our] men were dismounted and ordered to unsling their carbines. I hastily jumped off and taking a carbine, loaded and fired at twelve hundred yards. The cartridge misfired. Seeing them too far off, the men were ordered to mount again and we rode on with an intention of charging them. The major and myself got away very soon for we were free but it took some time before the sowars could come up, for they had to buckle and sling up their carbines. The major was on the point of dismissing the idea of charging but I urged him and he agreed. The major was riding on ahead and I about a hundred yards behind trying to form the sowars in a line for the charge. Seeing this [was] quite hopeless, as they were all scattered one behind the other, the major called and . . . asked me to come on that we may charge on and let them come on as best they could.

I galloped on and soon passed the major. I was about fifty or seventy yards ahead when I reached the rear of the enemy and looked back. The major shouted "go on into him" and the next instant I closed up. The last man was riding a mule and had no weapon and so I let him go. The second had jumped off his horse and was running alongside the third one who seemed to me their leader. I speared him in the back and down he rolled. I left him and took myself to the other one who was thrown off in the same manner when, looking to my right, I saw a man falling off his horse by the revolver shot of Major Turner. I went further on and dropped another with my spear. This time my spear fell from my hand and so I drew out my revolver and fired at two men and they both rolled down from their ponies but got up again.

Of the whole lot these two acted like heroes. One was some fifty and the other eighty yards off. The nearer one was quite in the open while the other was in a cover afforded by the bank of a nullah. Like a fool, I too stopped and began to fire my revolver. I fired the remaining four chambers and looked around. While all this was happening, the two were busy firing on me with their Mauser rifles. Each must have fired some five shots separately. but I got off scot-free. Looking around, I saw the major and the others standing under cover of a low nullah bank some two or three hundred yards off. I galloped off and joined them with the farewell bullets of my friends whizzling around me. This is my personal account. . . .

Now something about what the others had done. . . . Unluckily [the other sowars] all stopped to finish those whom I had dropped and so many escaped scot-free. Had they moved on without finishing the wounded ones and secured fresh victims we would have got many more. . . .

On my rejoining, the others mounted and we prepared for the retreat, for the place was too hot for us. The enemy were firing heavily from the village, and seeing so few of us were advancing . . . in great strength. . . . Bullets were falling on every side and were whizzling over our heads, but luckily none was hurt. They only stopped firing when we were out of sight. . . .

The party that we attacked were from seventeen to twenty. The people firing from the village Lijapoo are estimated from eighty to a hundred. Anyhow, it was a good day's work and the retreat was quite light and full of talk. All were very excited and each said that he had killed some two, some three, and some one. But they had only finished the wounded ones. . . .

My Feelings and Experience

. . . As soon as we got down the hill and intended to form [a] line [to charge] I had no other thought than of calling the men on. When I was on the point of closing up with the enemy I had no excitement at all. I had no hatred, no anger, nothing that I can describe in my mind. Looking behind was quite involuntary and the voice of the major, "go on, into him" and my leaving the first unarmed man is all I felt. The faces of the three men whom I speared, and when they looked at me while falling down, is a sight never to be forgotten. They had an expression of great pain and horror or fear whatever it may be called. It was also the same with the other two that were knocked with the revolver. I can safely say without exaggeration or boasting or self-praise that my temper and nerve seemed to me to be quite calm. Of course I was a little excited.

As regards fearing from bullets I say that I never found out until I went to Major Turner and the others standing in the cover that any one was firing from the village. . . . I had not the slightest notion of the bullets passing near me, though one had passed through my coat, as was found out on the third day. Of course when I turned to join the major and the others in the nullah, I galloped hard and quickly, for then I had time to think of the danger of being shot by the two men who were firing as fast as ever they could. . . .

I was going on to the parade ground . . . when near the quarter guard Pratap Singhjee asked me how it was that I had got my coat torn. On examination it was found that a bullet had passed through it on . . . the 12th instant. Up to the present no one had noticed it, not even I. . . . On the breakfast table Major Turner showed the bullet holes to Sarkar.[1] . . .

As far as I can see I do not find anything to blame myself except that I, instead of drawing my revolver, ought to have drawn my sword. I am sure that I would have killed some more and so would the sowars when they had no one to finish, for the blow from the sword would have meant instant death. It was as sharp as a razor, and the goat-cutting practice would have done everything. One more thing I find is . . . never to ride a pony [as Major Turner did]. . . . I feel confident in myself that had I been using my sword from the back of Ghatotguch I would have done nearly double the execution. But what is done is done.

Miscellaneous

Under the heading of miscellaneous I shall first describe the general opinion. Every one praises me but few the major. I honestly say that the major did all he could and had [a] very cool temper and was never behind at the fighting, though he could not keep up with me as he was riding a small polo pony and I on a big Irish horse. People have even misrepresented to Sarkar about the conduct of the major. Sarkar questioned me about it and I said plainly that he was not in the least to be blamed as far as I could see. The argument [is] that when the enemy was found in force why a retreat was ordered. I think it was a most safe and a sensible thing under the circumstances, and I would not blush to do so under the same conditions a next time if I had the full command. Foolhardiness is . . . of little value. Even in Marwari we have a proverb, meaning that "that fellow's bravery reaches blindness." [Sarkar was evidently disappointed to have missed the expedition during which the sole command lay in Turner's hands. A second and larger party, including Sarkar, went out the next day to the same village, but "there was none to be seen except a few old people."]

I do not know what opinion Sarkar had [of] me but as far as I can make out he has not a bad one. He has never spoken a word to me about it though he praised Bukhtawar Singhjee and complimented him. There was no word for me because I was not with Hurjee. Hurjee praised Bukhtawarjee and so Sarkar praised him. The English officers praised me and so there was no word for me. Just imagine what my feelings must be. But I don't expect praises when I know the circumstances. I did what I consider I ought to have done and I am satisfied.

When we came back each described his tale and Hurjee I hear exaggerated himself though he did practically nothing. . . . Sarkar had very little sleep, for he was sorry he had not accompanied us. I wish he had been with us in the charge at Lijapoo. . . .

[With the passage of time, the story of Sir Pratap's role in this engagement came to coincide more closely with what Sir Pratap's admirers would like it to have been. His biographer writes: "The officers and men were absolutely devoted to him. In their first action, when charging a band of 'Red Beards,' as certain of the Boxers were named, the cry was heard all over the field, 'Has Sirkar killed?' and not until he had did any of the regiment use the right end of their lances."[2] This imagined dialogue draws on pig-sticking etiquette, according to which the honored guest or senior person is often allowed the first spear.]

Monday, 21st January, 1901[3]

· · · Sarkar called me and ordered [me] to write a letter to Mr Lawrence. The purport of this letter was that Sarkar wanted that [a] district [be given] as a grant for himself in compensation of the work done by our men on the 12th instant, though he did not mention [the battle] at all. . . . It took me the whole of the evening to write and rewrite this letter as I had to think a great deal over such an important letter. . . . [Sir Pratap's request should be read in light of pre-British traditions in Rajputana, when special service to the ruler, especially in war, was often rewarded with the grant of revenue-bearing lands.]

Here is a copy of the letter written.

My dear Mr Lawrence,

I hope my letters that I have been writing now and then have been reaching you in due course of time. Since a few days the cold increased very much, but the health and condition of my regiment is quite as good and perfect as can be wished. As I consider you to be a great friend of the Rajpoots and specially my own, I am always troubling you now and then for something or the other. Can I ask you a favour? I think I can without any hesitation.

If you will kindly look into the book called *Aitchinson's Treaties Of India or Rajpootana*, I am sorry I don't know the name perfectly well, but you can see in any book containing an account of the treaty between the British government and my grandfather Maharaja Man Singh, and you will find an account about [the district of] Umarkote and the conditions concerning it. [This district fell to the possession of Jodhpur in 1780 during Maharaja Bijai Singh's time, but was wrested from that state by the Talpur Amirs of Sind. When the British government annexed Sindh in 1843 Jodhpur put in a claim for Umarkote. But as the fort of Umarkot was a valuable frontier post, the British kept it, and Jodhpur was given a monetary compensation.[4] It is this Jodhpur claim to Umarkot that Sir Pratap is exploring implicitly as a reward for the service of his regiment.] I wish that it be granted to me during the term of the viceroyalty of his excellency Lord Curzon for you know perfectly well that one gets very few opportunities, I mean lucky ones, in one's life, and I am sure that I can never expect a better viceroy than H.E. Lord Curzon as regards a just [man] and a well-wisher of the Rajpoots, with a friend like you to lay before him [the] petition in its best lights.

You also know perfectly well that a Rajpoot sets much more value on landed property than on anything else in the world. [There] is a common saying among us [expressed in Hindi] . . . which [means] that the "Jat," family, or the clan of a Rajpoot is his strip of land. Those who have no land are of no consequence. You know her majesty is no longer a queen but an empress and can grant this. Even during the Indian mutiny the government had granted districts to Patiala, Jaipore and Khetri, but Jodhpore got nothing, though it had rendered as much service as any of them. Now this is an opportunity for us to be favoured. . . . I hope [H.E. the Viceroy] will have this granted to me . . . and thereby render his name ever dear in the memory of many future generations of the Rajpoots to come.

. . . Please present my respects to their excellencies Lord and Lady Curzon and also remember me to Lady Lawrence.

This letter had been written by me for Sarkar and I have striven to my utmost to write it as nicely and fairly as ever I could. I had never paid any letter so much attention. Just imagine this request granted and the joy it would give me. My name would ever be mentioned with it and I would be proud of it. . . .

[Sir Pratap had a special friendship with Sir Walter Lawrence, the viceroy's private secretary, who liked and respected him greatly.[5] The request must be read in light of the fact that Sir Pratap's role as prime minister at Jodhpur has come to an end, and that he is casting about for a new and respectable responsibility worthy of his status. If Sir Pratap's request had been granted, he would in fact have been the independent chief of a new small state. Amar Singh infers that the request is only for Sir Pratap's own lifetime, with the implication that he would will it to Jodhpur at the end of that time. As it was common for Rajput and Mughal rulers to reward their fighting men with grants of land after a successful engagement, Sir Pratap appears to think that Lijapoo provides such an occasion. The request is not granted but Sir Pratap soon succeeds as maharaja of the small princely state of Idar (See Part VI).]

Which Is The Best Place For Me. . . . An argument . . . took place between myself and Bukhtawar Singh. While we were reciting our adventures I happened to drop a hint to the effect that I had been in a better and a [more] fitting place than he had been [by being with Major Turner, whereas Bukhtawar Singh had been with Hurjee]. He disagreed. He said that Hurjee would feel more for us than Major Turner and that we bear love to him much more than Turner, and that if we are in danger he would try much more than Turner. All this may be true but I doubt very much.

Bukhtawar Singhjee was right in his own way and I in mine as will be shown by the results. Hurjee praised him to Sarkar but took most of the credit for himself though he had done nothing. After all Hurjee did praise him and so Sarkar became quite pleased and praised him to his face a good deal though not so much as we expected. Except Sarkar and Hurjee nobody knows what Bukhtawar Singhjee did and whether it was creditable or not. He cannot himself say and Hurjee, when he does say, wants a share himself too. This is the result of his work.

Now to take [my case] I can safely say that nearly every English officer in Shan Hai Kwan knows that I did something and [they] always congratulate me when they meet. Major Turner has written all about it to India and has mentioned my name particularly to his friends. . . . I am sure he shall continue doing so on every dinner table and give me credit as is proved already here. . . . Practically speaking, I have no interest in this fight. Sarkar has brought me with him and I am to be with him in the field to earn his esteem, which I value much more than anybody else's. Next business is this, to gain some good name for myself and my family which can be obtained after Sarkar from the English officers and especially those who are well known. Major Turner is well known among the highest circles in India and has a good position among them. . . .

Friday, 25th January, 1901

. . . We . . . heard the sorrowful news of the death of Queen Victoria of England and Empress of India. It was quite too sudden. . . .

Monday, 28th January, 1901

. . . After breakfast I borrowed Capt. Hughes' eye-glasses and taking an orderly with me went to No. 1 fort on the seashore. There mounting on the highest parapet I had a good view of the sea. Within about half a mile of the shore the ice had melted but beyond it was all frozen hard and the snow having fallen over it, it was glistening in the sun and presented a most lovely sight. Except one, all the other ships were frozen in the ice and quite unable to move. One ship was also firing the minute guns of the queen's death. . . .

Tuesday, 29th January, 1901

. . . Sarkar ordered me to write a letter to Col. Beatson for him. The purpose of the letter was that the regiment be sent to England on the occasion of any procession in honour of the coronation. The news also reached us about the coronation and proclamation of the Prince of Wales [Edward VII] as King of England.

Thursday, 31st January, 1901

. . . Last night was the coldest that we have had since coming here. The thermometer fell to seven degrees below zero and the frost was thirty-nine degrees. . . . To add to this the wind blew the whole night at such a high rate as we very seldom see. The urine in the piss-pots was all frozen. The ink was frozen hard in the inkstands and the soap that we usually use froze so hard to the plank on which it was lying that try what we might but we could none of us remove it until we poured some hot water on it. The sentries had the worst time. One of them got quite benumbed. He was hardly able to speak. Luckily he was soon found and put into the room and rubbed and some blankets thrown over him. Thank God no harm was done to him. . . .

Sunday, 10th February, 1901

. . . I read over to [Sarkar] my father's letter [concerning the confiscation of the family's Jaipur properties (see November 27, 1900)]. He was really grieved to hear of it and has done and is doing all he can to help us in this difficulty. . . .

Before and after dinner I wrote a very long letter to Ram Nathjee all about our case which is unluckily not at all encouraging as I found from what Mr Lawrence writes to Major Turner ... [this was in answer to Turner's letter sent on Amar Singh's behalf. In the event, Sir Walter was not fully informed; the case is about to take a turn for the better. On February 12 Sir Griffith Evans, member of the viceroy's executive council, reviews Jaipur state's decision and declares it untenable, opening the way for a compromise.[6]].

Tuesday, 19th February, 1901

... Before dinner I read over the ... letters to Sarkar which had arrived today. Mr W. Lawrence writes that Babu Kanti Chander Mookerjee [the prime minister of Jaipur] is dead. It is also in the *Pioneer*.... [As the babu was the driving force behind the case against Amar Singh's family, his death may create a more favorable climate for the family.]

Wednesday, 27th February, 1901

... The general [Major General G. Richardson, commander, Cavalry Brigade] went round the lines and the horse stables and the men's quarters. He was pleased very much and said that what more could he want. It could not be better. The lines are surely very clean. I can safely say that our fort and quarters are the cleanest and tidiest in the whole of Shan Hai Kwan.

Tuesday, 5th March, 1901

Here I want to describe ... as summarily as possible the talk that was between Sarkar and Jasjee this morning. [Jasji, the native commanding officer of the Jodhpur Lancers, is supposed to answer to Major Turner and Sarkar.] Sarkar had issued an order to Jasjee the other day that the ponies are not to be worked in the course with the horses because they get cramped and the horses, having a faster action than the ponies, jumble everything. This was quite right indeed. Now this morning Sarkar again found some horses being worked with the ponies. Sarkar was very angry with this and told Jasjee many things. Of course Sarkar was quite in the right. ...

Poor Jasjee is in a fix: he has to listen to what Major Turner says who is a very artful fellow. Though in fact Sarkar [as general officer commanding] is in command of this regiment [Turner] always has the things done in Jasjee's name [as commandant]. Of course he can command what he likes with Jasjee but not so with Sarkar. He has quite excluded Sarkar and the staff from the regiment which is a policy of his own. For all this doing on the part of Major Turner Jasjee is not to be blamed at all, though Sarkar expressed indirectly that he was initiating, which I am quite sure is not right. Jasjee was so sorry and shocked that tears began to trickle from his eyes, which is the first time I have heard or seen him do. Sarkar does not like all the promotions that have been given by Major Turner, and especially that of the adjutantship of Pudumjee, which I have heard him express more than once. When Major Turner goes away some fellows will have a bad time.

Sarkar does not like when Major Turner always shoves Jasjee forward as the commandant of the regiment. From one point [of view] I think [Turner] is quite right. Except in formal parades [such] as march pasts, Jasjee ought to command, for he is the only man at present who can do it satisfactorily. Sarkar cannot drill the regiment and he must look on unless he wants to make a mess of it. I will finish my account with the proverb [a Hindi proverb follows] that means, where elephants fight ants are trampled . . . which is at present happening here. . . .

Wednesday, 13th March, 1901

By continuing today's account I mean to describe the talk that I had with Major Turner. . . . One most curious thing was that Major Turner told me that Sarkar was very jealous of all of us. For . . . instance, he said that [Sarkar] had [asked him] why did [he, the major] give the register of the men present on parade to Jasjee instead of to [him, Sarkar] when General Richardson was inspecting the regiment. The major told me that if he had not so much respect for Sarkar he would have laughed [at] him in his very face.

The major remonstrated that it was the business of either the adjutant or the commandant, whereas he [Sarkar] was the general officer commanding. To this Sarkar said that if Jasjee was treated in this manner he would soon be assuming airs and grow quite reckless and disobedient. The result of this was, as the major told me, that he had come to the conclusion that Sarkar fears to trust anyone for fear that one day he might turn against him. Do what I might I could not shake that belief from his head. . . .

[Turner and Sarkar appear to have a different understanding of the division of labor between a general officer commanding and his subordinate officers. Sarkar, accustomed to the more intimate patrimonial environment of Jodhpur, does not believe in vesting significant authority in his officers, an attitude which Turner interprets as mistrust. Amar Singh, who is usually inclined to picture Sir Pratap as jealous and mistrustful, does not seem to agree on this occasion, but credits Sarkar's ideas about authority as the source of the disagreement.]

Monday, 18th March, 1901

. . . While I was on the breakfast table Major Turner asked me if I would tell Sarkar to see that when horses are lent to officers like Generals Gaselee [commander of the British contingent of the China Expeditionary Field Force in 1900] or Richardson care must be taken that they are well cleaned and the saddlery is spotlessly clean. Now this morning when a horse was sent for General Gaselee its bit was as dirty as can be imagined for nobody cleans Sarkar's saddles and bridles and no one else can interfere in it for he would not like it. [Turner] asked me to take charge of it voluntarily and be brave enough to ask for it, but unluckily I had to deny for I know that instead of being pleased [Sarkar] would be offended and even then would never [let] me . . . do it . . . When hard questioned I had to leave the room for I could not describe our position satisfactorily, but the major understood it because he is thoroughly acquainted with Sarkar's manners, among which, I am sorry to say, some are quite unworthy of him. . . .

Tuesday, 26th March, 1901

. . . We saw in one of the newspapers about the death of the Maharaja of Idar. Directly after breakfast was over I was sent by Sarkar to the station to send a telegram to Mr Lawrence, the private secretary to the viceroy. It ran as follows:

Hear Maharaja Idar is dead. Am nearest relation. Hope viceroy will support my rights.

[Sir Pratap stakes a claim to Idar-Ahmednagar, a small Indian state to the south of Jodhpur, ruled by princes of the Rathore lineage which also rules Jodhpur.[7] Maharaja Takhat Singh of Jodhpur, Sir Pratap's father, had been adopted in 1843 to the Jodhpur throne from Ahmednagar. For Sir Pratap, Idar would make a nice alternative to Umarkot, which he had requested earlier.]

Wednesday, 27th March, 1901

. . . After this I waited on [Sarkar] for some time and then went to the station to send a telegram to the governor of Bombay about the death of the Maharaja of Idar and Sarkar's claims to it. . . . After coming back I had breakfast after which I made a rough copy of a letter for Sarkar to Mr Lawrence asking his help in the Idar adoption case. I doubt very much of his succeeding. [Sir Walter Lawrence reports: "When Sir Pertab was out in China, during the Boxer rising, he wrote to me saying he was the next heir to the State of Idar. I made over his letter to the Foreign Office at Simla, and was somewhat surprised to hear next day that Sir Pertab had strong claims, and when the Maharaja of Idar died Sir Pertab succeeded."[8]]

Sunday, 31st March, 1901

. . . We waited on Sarkar for some time while he was standing in the open court between our rooms. The three British officers, Capts. Hughes and Alexander and Lieutenant Gaussen, were also present there and the latter coming near, began to talk and ask questions because he had just come for the night from Ching-Wang-Taii. I was in a fix for Sarkar was watching with a frowning eye. He does not like to see any of us talking with any person at all. I am as sick of this inhuman and slavish life as a man can be.

[The long inactive winter in the Shan Hai Kwan garrison, broken only by the engagement of Lijapoo, finally draws to an end. Military action having subsided, Sarkar tours the Far East with his staff. In April 1902, they visit Peking where horse races and an assault at arms have been arranged for the armies of the International Expeditionary Force. Amar Singh wins the international steeple chase on Ghatotguch, to the great glee of the British officers, who feared "The Germans would win it." Sarkar wins the Railway Purse [prize money]. In May, Sarkar and his staff set out once again, this time to visit Japan as honored princely tourists. The high point of the trip is the visit to the court, where the emperor graciously receives the visitors. Amar Singh concludes that the grand tour "to me personally . . . was of great importance and has done immense good. . . . I have seen a bit of the world and have acquired some experience. . . . Now [at] any sort of meeting I can talk on a subject that most men would be eager to [hear]. . . . "]

4

Thinking It Over:
"Tried Warrior" or "Coolie of the Raj"?

[The grand tour of the Far East is over, the China experience is drawing to a close. Amar Singh assesses what it has meant to him: he believes he has become more accomplished, sophisticated, cosmopolitan. He has been exposed to a varied society in China and Japan, and found himself in heady and distinguished company.

His sponsors in these experiences are Sarkar and Major Turner and his estimate of their contributions is contradictory. Despite the cordial relations he has developed with the British officers, his judgment of the raj is highly critical. On the one hand he is grateful to Major Turner "for praising and introducing me everywhere" and for teaching him "manners and customs." On the other hand, he credits Sarkar with protecting the Jodhpur officers against the demeaning treatment often meted out to Indian officers in the British Indian Army, and securing for them the respectful reception to which the semi-autonomous nature of the princely states entitles them. Because of Sir Pratap's efforts, he says, the Jodhpur officers were not viewed "in the same light as native regiments are regarded."

The Lancers build up a distinguished record as does Amar Singh personally: at Lijapoo; at the steeple chase; at the Lloyd-Lindsay Cup. But there is a sting at the tail-end of the experience. Amar Singh becomes more conscious of the race-based differential which will color much of the remainder of his career. He makes a resolution to avoid the (British) Indian Army, which has a dual line of status in which Indian officers are inferior. "I would not like to be treated like a coolie."]

Shan Hai Kwan, Sunday, 23rd June, 1901

. . . We reached Shan Hai Kwan at seven in the evening where Major Turner and several other officers had come to see us. We were all very glad to get back to our dear old Shan Hai Kwan after an absence of more than a month. We found it greatly changed. It is all green on every side. Ghatotguch is also in splendid condition.

Wednesday, 26th June, 1901

. . . I went with Sheonath Singhjee to his quarters and weighed myself. My weight is 130 pounds.

Sunday, 30th June, 1901

I . . . bid goodbye to Capt. Alexander and Major Turner. . . . * After coming back I had breakfast and then saw a little of *A Complete Manual of Manners for Ladies and Gentlemen.*[1]* . . .

Aboard the Transport Ship *Kai Fong*, Wednesday, 3rd July, 1901

The Dispatches. . . . Major Turner told me something about the dispatches . . . the names of none of the commanders of the Imperial Service Troops [the princely states forces] had been mentioned in the dispatches. . . . Major Turner was very keen about Jasjee. . . . [He] had spoken to Sarkar about this. The latter said that Hurjee ought to get something and as regards Jasjee, what has he done to deserve it? Major Turner was sneering and jeering at it, and told me how could a man be mentioned who has done nothing except lying in bed and occasionally riding in the course. Anyone can see that he deserved nothing. This sort of thing is very disappointing. . . .

Aboard *S.S. Itria*, Thursday, 4th July, 1901

. . . We traversed twelve miles in the river and ten in the open sea [in the Kai Fong] before we reached [the] *Itria* which is the ship that is to take us back home. . . . After reaching the *Itria* we had some trouble in putting up the gangway but once it was put up we took the horses on board in no time. . . .

MY STAY AT SHAN HAI KWAN FULLY DESCRIBED[2].

XI. The Regiment

During this period . . . the regiment has done good work. It has given every satisfaction expected from it. It underwent the winter most admirably. . . . The men bore all hardships very well. Jasjee gave good account of his abilities and so did the other squadron commanders except Bhabootjee who was always slack.

Major Turner took great pains and was the sole cause of making them smart. Unluckily Sarkar is not on good terms with him though there is not any ground for this [ill] feeling . . . The sole cause of this ill feeling is Hurjee The regiment has earned the praises of Generals Gaselee, Barrow [chief military officer of the China Expeditionary Force, and secretary to the Government of India in the Military Department, 1901.] Richardson, Reid and all the foreigners. . . . Of course all this praise has been due to the presence of Sarkar who is very keen for pleasing everyone.

XII. Society

. . . I had the best European society. It has done me an immense good. I know their ways and habits and am acquainted with . . . their ideas. We used to live with them as pals. It has improved my knowledge of English. It has given me a taste for reading. I now know a little how I should behave when among them. All the other British officers used to treat me as their equal and not in the same light as native officers in native regiments are regarded. This was all due to the kindness and influence of Sarkar. At dinner table whenever there was a talk on any business I was often considered as an authority on Indian customs but I am sorry to say I know very little of these. However, I used to give a good account of the little I did know. Now if I ever go to England I would, I think, not be an idle or ignorant company in conversation whether it is English or Indian.

This society has given me a good character in all my acquaintances and next to Sarkar I am grateful to Major Turner for praising and introducing me everywhere. It is from him that I learned . . . manners and customs. Unluckily I could not associate much with him for fear of displeasing Sarkar. . . .

XIV. How I Passed My Days

As soon as the winter set in with some rigour, then commenced the real trouble. Sarkar and Turner were at variance and as the latter had a liking to me and often talked [to me] . . . Sarkar . . . soon got angry though never said a word. . . . This sort of thing continued for a long time and [ended] only . . . when, after our return from Peking, Major Turner went off on that expedition of surveying. Then all at once [Sarkar] became quite pleased and I got as many horses to ride as I could. He was always smiling and talking on different subjects. . . .

I had regular and nice meals, and the consequence is that I am entirely changed for the better both in health and vigour. I am looking quite fat though in Jodhpore I was always thin.

XV. My Experiences

Though it was not real fighting yet I have now a little idea what active service means. . . . Now I feel confident that I can at least command a squadron with some credit independently if entrusted to my care. . . .

Sunday, 14th July, 1901

The Allied Armies in China.   Having myself partaken in the international show where nearly every great nation of the world was represented, I intend to write a couple of lines about every one of them. . . .

I. The Russians

Of all the foreigners I like the Russians most. Of course I have heard that the Russian government has carefully selected the best troops, and so have the other nations, except Great Britain who could not possibly do it owing to their being seriously engaged in [the] South African [Boer] campaign.

The Russian cavalry or rather the Cossack, whom I had a great opportunity of observing, is a true soldier in the truest form. There is no smartness in [him]. There is nothing glittering, and every small particle that [he] carries is useful. . . . [The] uniform is quite light. There is no pride in him. He is an innocent looking soldier and very obedient, though . . . reported to be very poorly paid. They loot the Chinese a good deal but I do not blame them because it is the policy of their government who do not supply them sufficiently and so, whenever they run short of provisions, an expedition is organized and they bring in what supplies they want.

The Cossacks are good riders though very poorly mounted. Their horses are all Mongolian or Siberian ponies who are very powerfully built, . . . useful for long marches and stand the climate very well. The soldiers do not groom them much and often they are seen in quite a dirty condition. Their saddles are quite light . . . like our Indian kathi. . . . The accoutrement is well oiled but never cleaned. . . .

. . . They do not have swagger and useless parades. . . . When first they come on the ground the officer stands in the centre and the men ride in a big circle at a trot by single file which is very good, because the officer can then find out if there are any lame horses and whether every one is in good order or not. Their next parade is riding in double and single ranks and doing charges which are not quite so effectual.

. . . They have also their practice of vaulting while the horse is running at a gallop. . . . It may seem quite easy, but just imagine a man riding at full speed and then jumping down and jumping again in the saddle on the off as well as the near side with the sword dangling on his side and the rifle on his back and at the same time wearing a heavy long coat. . . . It must also be considered that the saddle stands a good foot high on the back.

After parade when they go to their lines they are always singing in one chorus. In march past, when they come on the saluting line, they salute speaking in three words at intervals and quite unanimous which sounds very nice. . . . The Russian officers are very fond of riding and are all a good lot. They are though great drunkards, which is no vice among them. They are all very polite. Some people have not a very high opinion of them but I have.

II. The Germans

The German Army is very nice. I am sorry to say I have not seen their cavalry or artillery but their infantry only. The men are squarely and heavily built. Their drill is . . . approaching to machinery. Their march-past step, usually called the goose-step, looks quite fine but is a waste of energy. . . . It certainly is good to make them strong, otherwise for long marches I do not approve of it. While marching past their legs and arms are quite in harmony with each other. . . . Their uniform is very gaudy though of late they are copying the British by wearing khaki. On their helmets they wear their national crest which is of brass and is kept very clean. This is a useless thing in war, for it exposes the man though even under cover. . . . They still wear some gaudy breast plates and other nonsense.

III. The French

. . . What I saw was their infantry. The Zouaves, as the regiment is called, is a very fine regiment indeed. The men are very strong and march very well. They are very quarrelsome. In Tientsin there were always rows and twice there were at Shan Hai Kwan. Their uniform resembles Mohammedan clothes whom they have copied. The dress is not attractive but I think very comfortable. . . . The officers as well as the men are very proud. They . . . seldom came to our lines. They too are not much of horsemen. Of course Britain stands at the top in horsemanship. . . .

IV. The British

[The "British Army" and the "Indian Army" served the British government and the Government of India respectively. Both were officered by Englishmen, but the

Indian Army recruited Indian as well as British soldiers while the British Army recruited only British. They represented separate career lines, marked by caste distinctions that favored the British Army. "Members of regiments from Britain, which were not part of the Indian Army," Raleigh Trevelyan tells us, "considered themselves a caste apart." It was not done for an officer of a British regiment "to marry someone connected with the Indian Army."[3] In China, Amar Singh only encounters members of the Indian Army.]

The British, though here represented by the Indian Army, are very nice. The men are all strong and of one height. They are well trained. The officers are nearly all of them very good horsemen though I do not much approve of the riding. . . . They are made to sit straight and stiff which gives them a look of rather statues then men. The uniform is nice and serviceable. . . . Smartness is much looked after and consequently the real thing required in fighting suffers in some degree. . . . I do not approve . . . too much stiffness of mien.

V. The Indians

Now I will try and describe a little the Indian Army that I have had a good opportunity of observing here. [In the previous paragraph Amar Singh was referring to the British officers and soldiers of the Indian Army; now he is referring to the Indian officers and soldiers in that army and to the Imperial Service Troops, to which the Jodhpur Lancers belong, and which constitute a different category from both the British and the Indian Army.] Both in the cavalry and infantry the recruits are carefully picked, the chief point being good physique. Unluckily very little or rather no attention is given to collect men of good birth.

The Indian Army here made a good show and as far as I can see was never behind any other foreigners though there was no English regiment. Everywhere the men behaved very well. [They] were stouter and taller than many of the Europeans. . . . For my own regiment I can say that it is better than any cavalry I have seen here. . . . The men are better horsemen and the horses too are of better quality and better trained. . . . Rajpoots did and can stand much more hardships than others. The British can excel so far as dressing and wheeling is concerned but in the actual heat of the fight they would not. . . .

VI. Some Other Members of the Allied Army

. . . The Americans are quite an independent sort of people. The soldiers do not much respect their officers. Officers and men consider themselves on equal footing and hence discipline suffers. . . .

VII. Difference Between the British and Indian Army

. . . The Indians are looked upon as inferiors in the scale of humanity. The British are better treated, supplied, fed, clothed, and paid than the Indians. Even they are better armed though they have now found the mistake and are arming them on the same principle. No Indian can rise above the rank of a rissaldar or subadar major, and however young or junior a British officer may be he always looks down upon the other as an ignorant fellow, even though he may be much [more] experienced and possessed of [a] better head.

[Amar Singh first reported his encounter with the invidious distinction between the KCOs (English) and the VCOs (Indian) in the entry of August 31, 1900. The status of the VCOs is comparable to non-commissioned officers in the British Army, both with respect to their class origins and the leadership role assigned to them. In August 1900, Sir Pratap and Colonel Beatson, who had served at Jodhpur, prevented Major Turner from applying the distinction to the Jodhpur Lancers in the dining and sleeping arrangements on the *S.S. Mohawk.* Now, as then, Sir Pratap intervenes on behalf of the status of the Indian officers, skillfully using the anomalous position of the Imperial Service Forces as products of the semi-autonomous princely states.]

As an example I will write on my own regiment, with which I am well acquainted and which is on a better footing than any other composed of Indians. The lieutenants, Alexander and Gaussen, always commanded over our captains. Captain Hughes always considered himself much more senior to Jasjee and even went so far as to take away his sword without any trial. Hughes is merely a captain while Jasjee is a major. The difference lies that the one is British while the other is an Indian. [The princely states and the British officers in the Indian Army give different interpretations to the same ranks. Jamadar, rissaldar, rissaldar major and subedar major, the titles carried by the Jodhpur officers, are read in the princely state forces as equivalent to lieutenant, captain and major; the British officers of Indian Army consider them titles of non-commissioned officers, such as sergeants.]

The taking away of Jasjee's sword is a great blow to our pride. There was clearly written in the orders that the special service officers [Hughes, Turner] had no other business than to see that the orders of the general officer commanding [Sir Pratap] are understood and to give counsel and not to interfere in any way at all. The charge against Jasjee being that he was drinking on the line of march. He had no doubt drunk a little, which every other British officer does. He was quite sane, and yet Capt. Hughes took away his sword. Just fancy a junior punishing a senior. Nowhere, either in the British or foreign armies, a junior can punish a senior. Then what business Hughes had? If Jasjee is not to be considered a major why does the government allow or empower the states to confer these ranks in the Imperial Service Forces? Either there ought to be no captains and majors in the imperial service or, if they ought, then they must be treated on the same footing which is rather difficult. [Amar Singh's objection is grounded in "A Note on the Discipline of Imperial Service Troops Employed on Active Service," which he enters in his diary on August 31, 1900 (see Part II, 1). Apart from the issues of power and command, drinking, whether by Hurjee, for whom excess is habitual, or Jasji, for whom it seems to be occasional, appears to be a specially sensitive point for the British officers.]

Had it not been for Sarkar this thing would have gone too high. Major Turner never objected to it. On the other hand he sent a bad report of Jasjee to Jodhpore. I do not know what would have happened to the regiment if Sarkar had not been with it. Hurjee would never be considered on the same footing as a British colonel nor I as a lieutenant. Whatever may happen, I for myself will never serve in the army except in imperial service [meaning the princely state forces, which are commanded by Indian officers]. Even if any one offered me a direct rissaldar majorship in the British Indian Army I would straight away reject. I would not like to be treated like a coolie.

. . . Here is another proof of the slight treatment that the Indian officers receive. Jasjee and Bhabootjee, who are both a major and a captain respectively, are kept down in a wretched hole in the second class with six others. The four other British sergeants are there in a separate cabin . . . but on better footing. Major Turner and Capt. Hudson had a greater anxiety for these four sergeants than they had for the others whom they merely put down as native officers, which means nothing worth bothering.

We four, that is to say Hurjee, Bukhtawar Singhjee, Akhai Singhjee and myself, are put in the first class cabins because we are on Sarkar's staff and consequently big swells, though in reality not an ounce bigger than Jasjee and Bhabootjee, with the exception of Hurjee, who is a colonel.

Again there is another example. British sergeants and soldiers never salute Indian officers, no, not even . . . Sarkar. They look as if they expect the others to salute them. . . . It is a mark of great favour on the part of the sergeant or soldier if he even condescends to say good morning. Now if an Indian officer did not salute a British officer there would be a hell of a row and the Indian would be punished for his impunity.

I do not blame the French soldiers for calling the Indians coolies, considering the way the British treat them. They of course know what they see or hear. If a foreign soldier sees a British soldier not saluting an Indian officer, they naturally come to the conclusion that the latter is a coolie and so they call him. The British make a great row when they hear the foreigners calling Indian soldiers and officers coolies, though they do not mind treating them as such themselves. Major Turner would not send our names for the military order of the dragon (which is an American thing) on the ground that Indians are not supposed to subscribe for it. . . .

Saturday, 20th July, 1901

Some Regimental Reports.   Informal Report on the Jodhpur Lancers, inspected at Shan Hai Kwan on March 1 and 2, 1901 by Major General G. Richardson, C.B., C.I.B. Commanding Cavalry Brigade, China Expeditionary Force.

> *Drill and Manœuvre*: Three squadrons paraded for my inspection. The regiment was drilled by the commanding officer and the squadron commanders. The pace was smooth and steady, the direction and distance carefully maintained. Dismounted practice was well and intelligently performed. . . .
>
> *Equitation*: The riding was good. The men sit still and are evidently well instructed. . . .

Equipment: Is mostly English manufacture, carefully cleaned and looked after.

Discipline: Is well maintained, conduct good. . . . The Jodhpur Lancers are a very fine regiment of imperial service troops, fit for service in every respect.

S[igne]d/- G. Richardson, Major Gnl, Commanding Cavalry Brigade, China Expeditionary Force, Peking, 1st March, 1901.

Confidential: 5 C "Inspections" Jodhpur Lancers, Dtd. Shan Hai Kwan the 26th February, 1901

From: General Officer Comdg, 3rd Brigade,
British Contingent, China.

To: The Chief of the Staff, British Contingent,
China Field Force.

Sir,

I have the honour to report as follows on the Jodhpur Lancers. . . . A very fine regiment, animated by a very fine spirit and Sir Pratap Singh is the beau ideal of a native prince. The Lancers were largely represented in the expeditions to the Laushan Hills and Chimunsai and a field troop behaved very well when engaged with marauders outside the great wall last January.

(1) Conduct and discipline in the field. Very good.
(2) Dress and turn out. Smart and neat.
(3) Sanitary condition. Excellent.

The Regiment is thoroughly efficient and fit for service. I have etc. etc.

S[igne]d/- A.I.F. Reid, Major General, Commanding 3rd Brigade, British Contingent, China Field Force, Dated 7th March, 1901.

[We have omitted the report from General Alfred Gaselee.]

Tuesday, 23rd July, 1901

. . . In the evening I read and finished *From Sea to Sea*, vol. II by Rudyard Kipling. Some stories in it are quite nice. . . .

Thursday, 25th July, 1901

[I] waited on Sarkar and was ordered to go and measure the cabin in which the other regimental officers are put up. There are eight of them in it including a major, a captain, and an adjutant [while another such cabin is shared by only four non-commissioned British officers]. What a shame for those who treat native officers like this. Then I enquired where they ate their food and had their baths etc. All these things were required by Sarkar who I think will speak about it to the viceroy. I wish some good would come out of this. . . .

Calcutta, Friday, 26th July, 1901

The ship was now in the Hoogly river and we were approaching Calcutta. The men were all in uniform and there was great bustle over it. . . . At about one in the afternoon we reached Kidderpore Docks and there were gathered most of the big men of Jodhpore, chief among them being Maharaj Zalim Singhjee [Sir

Pratap's brother], Maharaj Arjon Singhjee [Sir Pratap's nephew] and Thakoor Sheonath Singhjee of Bera [Sir Pratap's son-in-law], the Thakoor of Lamia, Rao Raja Raghu Nath Singhjee [natural grandson of Sir Pratap's father, and thus his nephew], Pandit Sukhdeo Prasadjee [the prime minister and, Sir Pratap's political rival], Barath Ram Nathjee, Singhi Buch Rajjee, Ratan Lalljee, Rodda Muljee and many more. I never expected to see so many of them. We all met very jovially and were congratulated by them all. . . . I followed [Sarkar] to the Great Eastern Hotel. . . . All this while I was in the carriage of a big and respectable Marwari merchant whom I introduced to Sarkar. . . . Sarkar starts off tonight for Simla and I am stopping for the night in the ship and will take his horses and baggage in the special tomorrow.

[The reception at Calcutta is the first of numerous such events for the returning Lancers and their peerless leader. The merchants who come are mostly "Marwaris," that is, men from Marwar or Jodhpur, who have settled in Calcutta and made their fortunes there, but retain ties of family and sentiment to Jodhpur.

Sir Walter Lawrence provides a glimpse of Sir Pratap's unconventional appearance at Simla: "When he returned from the war in China he came straight to my house in Simla. He left his followers at the foot of the mountain and arrived in Simla dusty and travel-stained, without any baggage. . . . Tired as he should have been, and clad only in his Khaki dress, in the Jodhpur breeches of his own invention, he was the figure and the centre of the party."[4]]

. . . I hastened back to the station and had the horses loaded in the trucks and at about five in the afternoon started by the first special train. . . .

Jaipore, Tuesday, 30th July, 1901

. . . During the whole of the journey I talked with Jasjee on different subjects and the talks were mostly about Sarkar and nearly all confidential [reminding us that Amar Singh does keep some secrets from the diary]. . . .

Jodhpore, Friday, 2nd August, 1901

[Amar Singh meets Sir Pratap at Jaipur and proceeds with him by train to Jodhpur] . . . [A]t three in the night we reached Kuchaman Road [the first rail stop in Jodhpur state] where the maharaj kanwar sahib[5] and most of the state officials were present to receive Sarkar. Among the leading nobles were the Thakurs of Pokran, Asope, Daifa, and Kuchaman. . . .

I . . . helped Sarkar to dress and then he went in the saloon with the maharaja kanwar. At Merta Road [the next station] the Maharaja Sahib of Bikanere came to see Sarkar.*[He] added another knot of the wreath of glory by coming on this occasion. It was very nice of him indeed to come. Bikanere is the next great state of the Rathores and at the present time he was [in the absence of the Jodhpur maharaja][6] . . . the leading Rathore chief.[7]* . . . We reached Jodhpore where there was a great crowd at the station. . . . The platform was chokeful and we were so much buffeted about that when once any one of us looked around he could not reach the other fellow. We were perspiring with this business and with the greatest difficulty reached the carriage. The resident and other Europeans had just as bad a time as anyone else. . . .

Saturday, 3rd August, 1901

All the people looked very happy at having Sarkar back again after such a long time. During his absence they had a good experience of what it was without him. I had never expected that he would have a grand reception.

There was a great crowd that and the next day of people. . . . *An address [was] given by the citizens of Jodhpore and was read by Kavi Raj Murardanjee [chief bard of Jodhpur, and a minister] and then several other poets recited their poems which they had composed in the praise of Sarkar and I am proud to say that my name was also mentioned in nearly all of them.[8]* . . . The country is all green and the year seems to be a promising one.

. . . Would to God Sarkar would go to many more campaigns and take me with him. This going to China has made a man of me. I am now known by Englishmen and have plenty of subjects to talk with them whereas with my people I am quite a tried warrior.

Excursus on Hurjee. [Amar Singh memorializes Hurjee in the diary at his death in 1903. We have moved the obituary to this part in which Hurjee has played such a visible role.]

Meerut, Friday, 6th March, 1903

Notes About Hurjee[9]. This morning when I went to Jodhpore Durbar I heard that Hurjee has died. This was a sad news indeed but we must console [ourselves] with the only means in our power, "God's will be done." As I have been with him and have learned horsemanship under his tuition I think I know him enough to write a few notes in his memory in my diary [see also Part I, 4]. . . .

I. The Origin and Gradual Increase

Hurjee was a daroga by caste, and had been given in dowry when Sarkar (as I shall write the Maharaja Sahib of Idar for the sake of shortness) was married at Nawalgarh, a thikana in Shekawati. [*Daroga*[10] is the name widely used in Rajasthan for a category of servants of princes and noblemen. Amar Singh, when he is angry with Hurjee refers to him as a *gola*, a slave.] Hurjee was a mere child at that time but was plucky, active and at the same time very mischievous. A few month's training showed that he would turn out a good rider and this he did. At that time any lad who was a good rider earned the favour of Sarkar, and Hurjee was not backward in this instance. By degrees he became the greatest favourite, until he was treated with respect and awe by the others. He got a jagir from the state. His social rank was very high and among Europeans he was considered a first class fellow and mingled in the best society. Sarkar carried him to the topmost steps of the ladder.[11] The only point on which he failed was he could not become a Rajpoot in spite of all the exertions that Sarkar put forth. This was an utter impossibility. . . .

II. Hurjee as a Horseman

There is no doubt that Hurjee was one of the best horsemen that ever sat on the saddle. He was quite a master. Of course he failed in some points. He was a very good race rider both on the flat and the steeple chase. . . . He trained horses by mere force and strong will. . . . He was a brave and fearless rider and never lacked courage to mount a vicious animal. Not only in India, but in England as well he won some races and got the nickname of Fred Archer who has been one of the best race riders. . . .

III. Hurjee as a Sportsman

. . . He was a first class pigsticker, polo player, and a good shot either with the rifle or the gun. He had done a lot of pigsticking and it was very hard to beat him. Unfortunately he never competed in any cup except once for the Jodhpore Cup, which he would most probably have won, but for a disagreement on one point, for which he got angry and went home. . . . It was this point. He and Capt. Cameron speared the pig almost at the same time. Sarkar was the umpire and decided in favour of Capt. Cameron. Now, this was an injustice which he would not stand.

As a polo player, he was the best back that I have ever seen yet. He won, I think, four tournaments. So long as he won a game he was alright, but whenever he lost he was no good. He got out of temper and spoiled the whole show. He was very good at foot-games and was a very fast runner. As Sarkar was against tennis, cricket, etc., the poor fellow had no chance of showing his merit in this respect. [Sir Pratap's prejudices—perhaps the prejudices of a cavalry man against foot-sports?—are persistent and contagious. Amar Singh later refuses to participate in these sports at the Imperial Cadet Corps.]

IV. Hurjee as a Gentleman

This is rather a difficult point to solve. He was a very good gentleman in some ways whereas in some others he was quite mean. In order to distinguish him more easily his life may be divided in two halves. During the first half, which includes his boyhood, he was very riotous, but as he grew up he had some points. One good point he had and this was that he never used foul language. . . . His bearing towards Europeans was mild and friendly but with natives not so good. He was rather boyish even late in life. There were few gentlemanly manners about him. . . . He was not a real gentleman. . . .

VIII. Hurjee as a Soldier

Without doubt Hurjee was a first class soldier. . . . He was proficient in all the arms. . . . not heavy but . . . strong enough for any work and as hardy as a soldier ought to be. Three times he went out on active service, viz. Black Mountains, Tirah, and China. He earned a good name during the first campaign but during the latter two he was a source of constant trouble. . . . He neither did any work himself nor allowed Sarkar to do any. Besides this, Hurjee was present at all the disturbances that took place in Marwar and was the constant companion of Sarkar who used to go to quench them. . . . Hurjee was a perfect soldier, but he was no good as an officer. He was brave to fight but not wise to command. . . .

XV. His Influence with Sarkar

Hurjee had the greatest influence over Sarkar, who never dared to do a single thing without Hurjee. . . . Whenever this fellow used to get cross there was an end of all work whether sporting or stately. . . . This went very hard with Sarkar. . . . At last Hurjee took to living at his village which relieved Sarkar. . . . Sarkar is still looking after his children, the eldest of whom is being educated in England. I do not know on what was this influence based. . . . I think it was much more on affection than anything else.[12] . . .

XVII. Wonderful Physical Strength

Though thinly built and not very tall Hurjee was very strong and could wrestle very well. . . . Even when he used to drink such a lot and eat opium, he could just come and have some chukkers at polo just as well or rather much better than most others. If he kept sober for a week he was alright again and was able to do his work well. . . .

XVIII. His Villages

Hurjee had been given three villages, Deoli and two villages called Tavali. . . . [From these villages he would receive land revenue, as overlord of the cultivators of the villages. Sir Pratap, as regent, was in a position to make such grants]

XXI. Concluding Remarks

On the whole Hurjee was much better as a favourite than any other that I have come across. Even at this position there were not much traces of pomp, pride or show. He was a thorough soldier and lived like it. He was always the bulwark of Sarkar as far as sports were concerned. He has been called ambitious and [grasping]. I say he was, but not to that extent as the others. Whatever Hurjee took was by permission of Sarkar and not what may be designated stealing. He enjoyed life thoroughly in every sense of the word so far as his limited knowledge would let him think. He was the very idol of Sarkar's life during his youth but towards the end was neglected. For this Sarkar cannot be blamed. He endured more than a man can do. . . .

PART III:
TRANSGRESSION AND RECONCILIATION: BECOMING A HOUSEHOLDER

For thirteen years Sir Pratap, regent of the princely state of Jodhpur, has been Amar Singh's master and mentor, taking responsibility for his training and appointments. Now, in 1901, as the two return from the China expedition, Sir Pratap once again shapes his life: he arranges Amar Singh's marriage, and nominates him for the Imperial Cadet Corps (ICC). The two events propel Amar Singh into a new stage in life, one in which he is no longer Sir Pratap's protegé and part of the Jodhpur royal ménage. His life bifurcates into a public arena controlled by Englishmen and their cultural and professional demands, and a more private, Indian arena controlled by the cultural demands of a Rajput family on the eldest son and heir.

Amar Singh becomes a husband and householder. His universe shifts to the princely state of Jaipur, to the *haveli*, the big house occupied by his joint family as it reaches out to incorporate the young bride Amar Singh brings home. It shifts at the same time to the tents, camps, and classrooms at Dehra Dun and Meerut, home base of the ICC.

Part III includes Amar Singh's detailed account of his wedding with Rasal Kanwar, second daughter of the Thakur of Satheen, an important but indebted *thikana* (estate) in the distant deserts of the princely state of Jodhpur.[1] Sir Pratap takes the opportunity to choreograph a strikingly unconventional wedding ceremony in line with his own "whims and ideas," ideas derived from his commitment to the reformist Hinduism of the Arya Samaj.

Marriages in Rajput society define the participants. This wedding is designed to contest familiar definitions. Amar Singh's mother, father, and other close relations do not attend. The family agrees that arranging the marriage is an appropriate culmination of the many years that Sir Pratap has mentored Amar Singh, bringing him up as though he were his son. When Sir Pratap takes over, he uses the marriage to express a Hindu identity that breaks with the conventional orthopraxy of Amar Singh's Kanota family.

The Arya Samaj responded to the onslaught by European rationalist critiques, Christian challenges, and Muslim alternatives by sponsoring a "return" to the vedas, reimagined as a pure and rational monism. It incorporated into its Hinduism a critique of polytheism, rituals, caste, priests, and their "superstitious excrescences." Sir Pratap's Arya Samaj marriage ceremony reflects his support, as head of state, to the Walter Krit Hitkarni Sabha, a Rajput association that tries to reduce the ruinous costs of rituals, not only of weddings but also dowries and death ceremonies. Named after Colonel C.K.M. Walter, political agent in Jodhpur from 1875 to 1877 and supporter of the association's objectives, the sabha targets Hindu orthopraxy through an associational form that claims no religious presuppositions.[2]

In the conduct of Amar Singh's marriage, the conventional content of a Rajput wedding, such as the composition of the *baraat* (groom's party), the ceremonial dinners, the dress, the time spent, all are subjected to Sir Pratap's austere and minimalist construction. Amar Singh's prose is replete with the adjective "plain" as he strives to convey Sir Pratap's intent—plain khaki rather than ornamented silk and satin; uniforms with buttons and belts rather than *achkans* (a long coat) with pearl necklaces. An appropriate Rajput marriage requires a large attendance, especially in the baraat. This requirement triumphs over even Sir Pratap's austerity standards. The challenge to Sir Pratap's choreography is how to shape an event worthy of his own status and of one who stands in a filial relationship to himself, while adhering to his faith in simplicity. In default of the many relatives from the joint and extended family who would supply a plentiful baraat were the marriage held under their auspices, Sir Pratap substitutes the resources of the dynastic state that he commands. He drafts Amar Singh's fellow officers in the Jodhpur Lancers as companions, men who can be commanded to dress simply without damaging their dignity. Jodhpur state's *farash khana*[3] supplies equipment for the five-day mounted expedition to and from the bride's desert estate. The result is the outline of a conventional Hindu wedding filled in with purged or modified representations and reformed rituals.

When Amar Singh returns to Jaipur to install his wife in the joint-family haveli, his family attempts to reverse Sir Pratap's transgressions of conventional Hindu marriage practices by trying to put him through the missed rituals. Amar Singh protests, then flees, leaving Ram Nathji, his friend and teacher, to pacify the disappointed family.

Amar Singh's is an arranged marriage, the product of negotiations on behalf of two families more concerned with suitability, with status and wealth, than with compatibility. Readers who expect love to precede marriage may find it hard to imagine the quality of love that the selections in this part reveal.

Dramatis Personae

"*Sarkar*," Sir Pratap Singh, younger son of Maharaja Takhat Singh of Jodhpur, former prime minister of Jodhpur, guardian and "master" of Amar Singh.

Thakur Kishore Singh of Satheen, brother of the bride, young lord of a distinguished but debt-ridden estate.

Rasal Kanwar, eldest daughter of the late Thakur of Satheen, Amar Singh's bride.

Ram Nathji, bard, tutor, and staunch older friend of Amar Singh. Now coach to the newlywed.

The wedding party, forty young noblemen from the Jodhpur royal lineage, plus a squadron of Jodhpur Lancers.

1

An Uncommon Wedding

Notes About My Marriage¹.

I. A Faint Idea

To begin with, I had no idea that my marriage would take place so soon after my return from China. I had not the least thought of it, though at my arrival in Jaipore [his family's home state] people used to say that I would soon be married, but I took them all as mere guesses. At last when Sarkar came from Simla he talked about it in the atish [office of the royal stables, where he was staying] before all [the] people. Sarkar had no wish to marry me [off] so soon, but when he learned from my father that it was one great wish of my grandfather, he consented and said he would do everything. He allowed me only one day in Jaipore [after their return from China] and then took me with him to Jodhpore. There his views began to develop gradually and the marriage day was fixed as well. During all this time I was under the impression that I would be sent to Jaipore for the observance of certain rites, but at the last few days I found out that I was mistaken.

During all this time I was not at all treated as a bridegroom but as a mere common man as usual. There was the . . . usual working of horses in the race course and the playing of polo . . . without the least thought of . . . an accident. . . . These were great strokes of a firm resolution and a firm belief in God who would spare in the greatest calamities and injure even when the utmost care is taken.

All these things were to my liking and did me an awful lot of good. Had I been in Jaipore I would have been shut up for a long period with nothing to do but sit idly in my room and either stare about in the faces of people or talk, a talk which has no interest for me because most of our men are unluckily ignorant of the ways of talking on particular occasions.

II. The Arrangements Made

Sarkar's arrangements were no doubt grand. His first point was that none of my family members should come and consequently none came at all, not even my father. . . . Sarkar's ambition was to make this marriage on his own account and expense with all his whims and ideas. . . . There was no one to oppose or contradict him. My family left everything [to] him and he did a first rate father's duty. He used to say that Amar Singh's father and mother were both alive and so there was no need of his [Amar Singh's] going to Jaipore. His meaning for a father being he himself and a mother his own wives. He fully fulfilled it. Another idea of his was to take men of simple tastes like himself. He collected most of the young maharajas [brothers of the late maharaja of Jodhpur], rao rajas [natural sons of the late maharaja], thakoors [lords], and kanwars [heirs] of high rank and birth. All the officers of both the regiments were taken and only koat duffadars; [lower officers] were left behind. Then there was one full squadron from the regiments taken as well.

The eating arrangements were simple but good and profuse. The cooks were Goanese, Mohammedans, and [of the caste of] barbers as well. The dinner table and chairs for the officers and nobles was a mud platform with a ditch all round. The platform served as a table and the ditch for putting in the feet and using it as a chair. Knives, forks and spoons were used. There was a plate and a tumbler for each one separately. [Sarkar chose to serve in English style rather than provide thals, round salvers off which people might dine Rajput fashion.] There was no wine or liquor to be seen at all of any kind whatever. The . . . expenses were all incurred by Sarkar. . . .

Tents had been sent for accommodation and everything was done to secure comfort and ease. Nothing was uselessly spent on unnecessary show of profuse elegance. Everything was to be extreme plain and good taste.

III. The Marriage Dinners

Of these there were four big ones given, two breakfasts and two dinners. At every table there were present some fifty men of high rank and standing including the Imperial Service regimental officers. . . . *Beside them there were nearly all the maharajas, rao rajas, and some of the thakoors that were at present in Jodhpur.²* At one end of the table sat Sarkar with the chief, big and elderly nobles and at the other myself with nobles of my age. . . . The regimental officers and most others wore their undress uniforms or plain khaki coats. . . . The food consisted of meat and polao [a rice dish], bread and sweets. It was quite a plain and common food served in plates and eaten with knives and forks.

The dining saloon in Sarkar's house was never before seen so much crowded except in the Jodhpore polo tournament and pigsticking weeks when there used to come nearly [one] hundred Englishmen besides natives of high rank. The waiting on the table was performed by the khansamas [cooks] and some of the Rajpoot sowars [soldiers] of the regiment.

IV. The Bana Ceremony

. . . In the evening . . . I was presented with a photo of Sarkar by himself. In giving it to me he said that it was my first spear cup for sticking the first Chinaman among the Jodhpore Lancers. [Amar Singh speared several Chinese during service in the Boxer Rebellion. See Part II.] It is a picture of Sarkar on China clay and mounted with gold and encircled with a row of pearls. [Amar Singh wears this cameo on his turban, as Sir Pratap wears one of Queen Victoria on his.³] It was a very nice present indeed and given at a very timely occasion. . . . He spoke very kindly while giving it and ordered me to wear my full dress uniform for the dinner. . . .

At last . . . I was conducted to Sarkar's own room where the gods had been drawn on the wall. I was made to sit on a chair because it was considered more convenient with long-boots on. [It is usual to sit cross-legged and shoeless on the floor at ceremonies. The long-boots problem continues to surface frequently during the wedding ceremonies. Leather is an impure substance. Moreover, all the ceremonies assume that one can tie things to the ankles, or sit cross-legged next to other participants. But Sarkar's distinctly un-Brahmanic conception of this wedding requires military dress, and how can a cavalry officer be without long-boots?]

The Brahman uttered some Sanskrit words and with a red paste made a small mark with his finger between my brows and afterwards stuck some rice on it. Then I was made to sprinkle some water and throw some rice at the gods. . . . I never understood what he was uttering or doing but blindly followed his doing. Sarkar with all others was standing at my back observing these rites. He is quite against them and said that these were only observed in consideration of Thakoor Zorawar Singhjee, meaning my grandfather.

. . . [Certain] ceremonies are performed by a mother and this place was taken by Sarkar's wives. They came in and after stroking my chin with their hands like a mother made me sit on a chair. They performed the oil ceremony which is called tel chhadana, meaning oil is being put on. Then there was the Pithi ceremony observed [in which turmeric paste is applied to the body to soften and brighten the skin. Normally the female members of the groom's family perform these cleansing and anointing tasks on a bare-bodied bridegroom dressed only in dhoti]. . . . As I was wearing the full dress they just touched my boots and applied some on my cheeks. Then they tied the Kakan doras [red and yellow auspicious threads braided together and tied on the right leg and wrist of the groom, and the left leg and wrist of the bride]. One piece was tied on my right hand and then they searched my legs but there were the long-boots, and so it was given to me to tie it on when I [took] those boots off. Lastly the elder wife of Sarkar gave one coconut with one gold mohur [coin] and two rupees, the second wife another coconut with one gold mohur and seven rupees. The "purdait" who is the mistress gave five rupees.[4] . . . It was indeed very kind of Sarkar to make his wives do these ceremonies of a mother for me. It was a great and rare honour. . . .

VI. The March From Jodhpore to Bisalpore and Thence to Satheen, Together with the Reception There

. . . *In the morning I awoke very early at two a.m. and after washing myself dressed in my full dress uniform. . . . The orders for all were to collect at 3 a.m. . . . One by one the people began to come till all were collected by half past five when Sarkar came and photographs were taken. One was of all of us in a group. I was sitting on a chair and the others were standing. . . . [5]* When we started from Sarkar's house . . . a small escort of sowars [was] leading the way. After them at some distance was my party of five [consisting of several young members of the royal family, Amar Singh's friends and age mates].[6] . . . Behind us was Sarkar and Sheonath Singhjee Bera [Sir Pratap's son-in-law] and then all the nobles and regimental officers followed by the squadron. . . . *In the way, the pace was always regulated by Sarkar with the sounding of a bugle. . . . The pace was mostly walk and trot . . . a long file of two and two riding side by side . . . with proper distances between the different parties.[7]* We were [spread out] to the distance of about a mile and the show was quite imposing.

[The 50 or so kilometer distance to Satheen is traversed expeditiously on horseback in one day.] We went in so early that they (I mean the Satheen people) were caught quite unawares. It was only the dust flying that gave notice of our approach. . . . The reception was . . . [by] the three brothers [of the bride] who are thakurs of three different thikanas[8] . . . and after them were all their clansmen and followers and servants, some mounted on horses and some on camels.

The village people had also come out in dense crowds but none of them could make out the bridegroom [who would normally be wearing showy clothes and riding on a caparisoned horse]. I was wearing just the same clothes and . . . hat [as the others]. I had of course Sarkar's picture on my [turban] but the people were too ignorant and were looking [for] clothes of pink or yellow colour, of which there was no sign at all. Most of them thought that the bridegroom had

PHOTO III-1   The wedding party, *baraat*, that accompanied Amar Singh on the five-day journey to the desert estate of Satheen where, in 1901, he marries the young lord's sister. Participants observed the ascetic rules of Amar Singh's guardian, the Jodhpur regent, Sir Pratap. Instead of Rajput finery they wore uniforms. The wedding budget conformed to new state rules prohibiting the lavish expenditures that had often proved ruinous. The wedding party is assembled in front of Sir Pratap's bungalow, Amar Singh seated in the middle. Amar Singh's photo albums.

not yet arrived but was to come afterwards. . . . Best of all was that there was no beating of tomtoms or unnecessary noise caused by the singing of dholis [traditional singers] which is a thing I hate from the very bottom of my heart. . . .

VII. The Marriage Ceremonies

[The baraat is accommodated in a tent camp near the fort of Satheen.] Having had dinner early the bugle sounded at ten p.m. to get ready. By eleven we were all ready, and about half past eleven the [groom's] procession started on its way to the koat [fort]. I was mounted on the black horse Dunwell and all the rest, including Sarkar himself, were walking. Sarkar and the regimental officers were in their full dress uniforms and so was I . . . with the flags of the lances furling in the slight breeze. . . . On one side of my horse walked Sarkar wearing all his medals and decorations and on the other was Thakur Sheonath Singhjee of Bera. . . . My horse who had never seen these things and sights before was a little fidgety. There were no gold or silver ornaments on [my horse] but simply a new saddle of parade recently sent by Messrs Arpwood for Sarkar from England. . . .

At last we reached the gate where there was a check of a couple of minutes. The toran [a symbolic decoration suspended over the gateway to the bride's quarters] was at last slung down from its top with a rope and then Sarkar gave me a long and thin green branch which someone had brought out from inside the koat. Seeing the slinging down of the toran, Dunwell got . . . fidgety and I feared very much that he might . . . turn back and bolt. When Sarkar handed the green bough the horse became a little more restive. Sarkar told me to touch the toran with that bough thrice. I did that with some difficulty because I had to manage the horse while passing under it.

Arrived inside the koat, we stopped near the steps of a platform. At that time Sarkar instructed Maharaj Daulat Singhjee[9] to go on my off side and mount the horse immediately on my getting off. I was instructed not to leave the saddle until he (Daulat Singhjee) had his foot in the offside stirrup. When this was all done I got off. . . . These precautions are taken against the mounting of the manda people immediately after a bridegroom (which means people of the bride's family or service or their guests). If by some chance this occurs then there are great jokes cracked at the jan (which means the bridegroom's party).

Having dismounted I was led on the platform which was covered with . . . a green carpet richly embroidered with gold and on this I was made to sit. All others, including Sarkar, sat either in the front or on both sides. As soon as we sat down cigarettes were circulated but very few partook of them owing to Sarkar's presence.[10] After about five minutes I was led inside. No one was allowed, not even my brother Sheonath Singh. As soon as I reached the zenana [women's quarters] door I was [faced] with a screen of pink colour. Some big lady of the house, probably the wife of Thakoor Kishore Singhjee of Satheen [brother of the bride], did some ceremonies. A big mark with a red paste was drawn on my nose reaching from the point of my nose to the middle of eyebrows. On it were stuck some rice and then a small mouthful of lapsi [dish specially prepared from ground wheat and cooked with sugar for the bride and groom to feed each other] and then of dahi [curd, yogurt] were shoved in my face which I swallowed blindly. . . . Now the curtain was drawn aside and arti ceremony was done [in which a small flame is rotated around the groom by the mother-in-law].

. . . A few minutes afterwards my wife was brought in and made to sit on my right. We waited for some time until a gold mohur came and with it the gath jora was tied [a long piece of cloth attached at either end to groom and bride]. After its having been tied there was a worship and at that time someone whom I afterwards found to be a big lady of the house came and having surveyed my face passed a remark to the effect that the bridegroom was beautiful. I tried my utmost but could not help smiling, seeing which they began to laugh a little because I was not expected to laugh but keep as sullen as possible. It was the tone of the words in which she passed her remark which made me smile and not the compliment paid to my beauty because I know I am not beautiful but at the same time I own that my features are exactly like my father's . . . which are just what ought to be in a good Rajpoot. . . .

From here we went to another place where the marriage was duly performed. . . . The bride was [seated] on my right. In front of us was a small fire kept alive with a few thin pieces of fuel but mostly ghee [clarified butter]. Some Sanskrit words were uttered and we both were also made to do . . . sundry ceremonies and at last the pheras (walking round that fire) came. My wife was leading in the first three and I in the last and fourth one. . . . [Then] I was made to sit on the right of the bride, because after this ceremony she was acknowledged as my wife by the law. Both the Thakurs of Satheen and Khejarla [bride's brothers, substituting for the deceased father] came in and performed the kunnia dan which means the giving away of a daughter in the form of . . . charity.

The whole of this time it was very hot and women were chokeful in the small place. The singing was a thing that annoyed me most. It was a great shout in my ears and I did not understand a single word of what they sang. . . . The ceremonies having got completed we, I mean my wife and myself, were taken out and made to sit in the rath [a decorated cart, drawn by bullocks, fitted with two-and-a-half domed, curtained canopies]. According to the common usage I ought to have returned [to my camp] in the rath with her but Sarkar insisted that I should ride back. Who could have dared to contradict him? I was made to sit in [the rath] for a couple of minutes and even in that short time I managed to see my wife's face in spite of her resistance. I am glad to write here that her features are as mild, beautiful, and as much to my taste and liking as I could have wished. In the whole circle of my family, including [my cousin] Hem Singhjee's wife whom I have seen afterwards, there is none to surpass her in nobleness and mildness of features though there may be of a fairer colour, about which I do not much care nor is that much to my taste. Anyhow, I was quite satisfied with her looks at that time and her manners and temper by now. She is exactly what I thought she would be by the look of her features. . . .

These ceremonies had been very briefly observed and the greatest haste was done. People said that never was a ceremony concluded so soon and specially in such big places. On the whole it took me about an hour inside the zenana instead of four or five. Even the . . . ladies were telling me that to take a bride was not an easy matter but that they feared Sarkar [and hence did not insist on the full panoply of rituals].

VIII. The Adoption Ceremony

This . . . ceremony [recognizes] . . . that as the bride has left her father's house she should have some one to help and advice even in her husband's house. . . . However, Sarkar had sent Ram Nathjee to me to ask whom I liked most to have for a father to my wife. . . . I said that I would have Sarkar for this purpose and if he could not on my account accept it then my next choice would be Thakoor Sheonath Singhjee of Bera. Rain Nathjee was very much pleased with my answer and said that this was exactly what he himself would have advised. When this was reported to Sarkar, that I wanted him to become a father to my wife, he was very much pleased and began to laugh. He also said this remark [in Marwari] . . . which means "I want to get free but [that rascal] wants to entangle me." Then Ram Nathjee told my second wish, with which he was also very much pleased, and said that "I . . . am an old man but he (meaning Sheonath Singhjee) will pull through." . . .

Thakur Sheonath Singhjee and my brother both went in and the ceremony was performed by the former. . . . Now . . . [my wife] has a big and noble person for a father and protector and one whom I respect. . . .

IX. Breakfasts and Dinners

. . . Next morning . . . the women came singing and rejoicing to call me to their house [for breakfast]. . . . Once inside the zenana I was conducted in a small but a nice room of the deshi [native] fashion. . . . I walked straight up and sat with a reclining posture on the *same green velvet carpet embroidered with gold on which I was made to sit that night. The back was supported by massive round cushions.[11*] . . . In a couple of minutes the room was chokeful of women. They crowded one over the other simply for the purpose of looking at my face. I soon got tired of it and wanted very much to clear them out, but simply bore up with them with the thought of not wounding and hurting their feelings. Ten minutes later my wife was conducted in supported by a couple of women on each side, and as many behind. Near the foot of the carpet they stopped and I was . . . asked to get up and conduct [her] myself on the carpet. After a short deliberation I had to do it. Next the women wanted us to sit quite too closely, but try what they may, we did not do that. Ten minutes more and they all cleared out and my wife and myself were left alone for about an hour, after which I opened the door and ordered breakfast. Their purpose to give this time in the day was because they were very much doubtful as to Sarkar's sanctioning my stopping for the night with my wife. Breakfast over I soon hastened out though they wanted me to stop for some more time and have an hour's sleep. . . .

[That night when I went to the fort] . . . a curtain was drawn across the room, and the ladies of the house came in and sitting behind it began to ask questions which had no plain meanings to them but were all riddles . . . [and] silly questions.

There were many to which I turned a deaf ear. In the very beginning, when these questions were commenced, I told them that I had passed my years all through with Sarkar and had never been in the company of women and consequently knew not a single riddle of theirs. They would not hear this objection of mine but continued to ply question after question and I was obliged to turn a deaf ear by which they seemed a little annoyed. . . .

They had also stood against the door and asked me to open the door which was closed. In fact the door was ajar but the woman standing in it wanted me to repeat some silly verse which is meant as the key to it. I did not know it but said simply that the doors of this house were now quite open for me since they had married me their daughter. They began to laugh and got out of the way. Then they asked many other questions but I knew none and so there was no answer from me. To show their silliness, I will write a few here. How can a man understand them? I have myself now learned their meaning from my cousin Lichman Singh the other day when we all sat joking together.

Kharvar Khopo [old person, meaning father-in-law];

Kaag Godawani [she who makes crows fly; meaning mother-in-law. When a crow comes and crows on the house, it is an omen for a guest to come; a son-in-law is the most important possible guest. Hence, when a crow comes, the mother-in-law makes him fly as a good omen, that her son-in-law is coming.];

Sirakh-Mai-Li Sarkahi [thin and gentle, meaning wife];

Tam-Tami Ra Beej [seeds which open and close, meaning eyes].[12]

Now just think of the silliness of these questions. How can a man unexperienced like me understand them and give a proper answer? Many persons had told me that I ought to learn these things but I did not, though they had even volunteered to teach me. [In a subsequent wedding reported in the diary, the groom arrives with a manuscript containing all the questions.]

After the wine cups had been circulated the dinner came, and when it was over, they all went out and so we went to bed undisturbed. I use the word undisturbed, because there is a custom prevalent in Rajpootana that when the husband and wife sleep for the first few days, women peep through the holes in the doors to watch what takes place. Now this is a really bad custom. Luckily I was free from it, because the doors were all closed and bolted from inside by me and to prevent from seeing through the holes there were thickly padded curtains hung on the inside.

. . . At about two in the night I was awakened by the rattling of the door from the outside and, on opening, the women brought in food. I was not at all hungry but had to partake of it as a custom. This food is called the adrithia, which means the midnight food. This is I think . . . to keep the bride and the bridegroom from starving in case they might not have eaten to their heart's content with all the women watching all round. . . .

X. The Teeki Incident

After I had passed my first night in company with my wife and awoke in the morning it was rather too late. . . . The horse too had come much later than had been ordered. Anyhow, I hastened out. . . . Having reached the camp I hastily threw off my achkan and turban and went and sat with Sheonath Singhjee Bera. We were talking when his eyes fell upon a teeki [colored grain, used in ceremony] which had [come] off from my wife's forehead and got stuck on my shirt. He snatched it away before I was aware of it and then laughed and gave it to Sardar Singhjee of Bhadrajoon who showed it to many others, and then commenced the jokes all round at my expense. This was quite an accident but it warned me for hastily changing my shirt which was coloured pink from my wife's clothes by our mutual perspirations. Had they observed this they would have found another thing to laugh at me. . . .

XII. The Worship of the Gods

This is a usual custom, that when a couple is married they go to nearly all the village gods and worship them to secure their protection. . . . My wife had been brought out in the rath and we moved out of the koat. I will refrain here from giving the names of the gods because I am sorry to say I don't remember. . . .

At one of the worships there was a Bhopa [wandering singers and storytellers; many tell stories of the hero Pabuji]. Now these Bhopas are priests but of the lowest class. The one that was present at this ceremony was an old and disgusting man. My very soul revolted against sitting near him. He pretended as if the deity had come into his body and spoke as if he were the God himself. He even went so far as to say that such and such sacrifices and presents should be made to the God and then all would be well. If I had anything to do with this business I would never let my wife see such a false and revolting scene. . . .

XV. My Talk with Thakoor Kishore Singhjee

The last day that we stopped in Satheen the thakoor sahib, my brother-in-law, sent word to me through Barath Jookti Danjee that he would like to have a talk with me for a quarter of an hour if I had no objection and felt no inconvenience. I sent back the answer to the effect that I was ever ready at his service. The talk at first was through Jookti Danjee [following etiquette] who was quite a bore for me. I hated his very presence there and at last asked him to sit out for a short while.

Kishore Singhjee was very polite and his talk was very obliging. I told him plainly that I was ever ready at his service and to have made me a brother . . . was a great deed of kindness on his part and honour for me. I further told him that I was thoroughly satisfied with each and everything and as regarded the few discontents about a couple of points, I had nothing to do. Everything was done either by Thakoor Sheonath Singhjee or Ram Nathjee under the supervision of Sarkar. I was merely as a machine working at their orders or will. More, I was not at all acquainted with any of the customs and so if any ceremonies were not observed and if any mistake . . . was done by me through ignorance [it should be] forgiven. He very kindly said that there was none though I think there were several.

As regarded the dowry, I said that I did not care a blow. If they gave me a couple of thousands more it would not increase my wealth much or if on the other hand they gave me less it would not diminish. It would just be the same for me.

By God's will I have everything available in my house and there was only one thing lacking which he had supplied, and that was my wife. I was satisfied with this thing of his in every way and wanted nothing else. . . .

XXI. The Dress

In Jodhpore just a few days before the marriage my dress was plain khaki undress uniform. . . . During the whole of the way I wore the khaki clothes which were as follows: Black Russian boots of the Cossack pattern and khaki breeches. The coat was the regimental khaki undress uniform. On the head I wore my hat[13] which had on it the picture of Sarkar and which was the only distinction I had from others. . . . For the marriage ceremony I had the full dress uniform complete with long boots and spurs. . . . I carried Sarkar's wish to the last point and even now wear nothing else but khaki. People quite wonder at it when they hear all this. . . .

XXIII. The Dowry

[The definitions in parentheses are Amar Singh's, those in square brackets ours.]

TABLE 3.1   The Dowry
[The definitions in parentheses are Amar Singh's, those in square brackets ours.]

Value		
Rupees	*Annas*	*Names of the things*
344	12	Ornaments for myself
6020	1$^{1/2}$	Ornaments for my wife
605	00	Silver things and vessels
354	8	Ornaments for the slave girls [Amar Singh is referring to the women attached to the bride's family who are sent with her as part of the dowry.]
598	8	Siropaos [sets of clothes for a man] numbering 76
1398	8	Bais (which means clothes for my wife)
129	2	Miscellaneous clothes for my wife
87	8	Bais numbering 40 (to be distributed in the family)
44	8	Bais for the Dholan (who is the wife of the family bard)
308	11	Carpets, etc., etc., together with beds and beddings
25	12	Bais Bina sia (which means unsewn clothes)
186	10	Miscellaneous
156	5	Mugad (a sort of sweetmeat to be distributed in the family)
112	8	Rath (a sort of female carriage)
200	00	One pair of bullocks for the above
1311	00	Seven horses
115	7	Brass vessels and things of iron

(continued)

TABLE 3.1   *(continued)*

Value		
Rupees	*Annas*	*Names of the things*
242	00	Clothes for the four slave girls and other things for them
355	00	Gold mohurs in the Samela [the reception at which the bride's relations receive the bridegroom's family] and Jawari ceremony [at which money is given to the groom by the bride's family] and rupees
20	00	Lace: Gold lace for putting on clothes.

The above is a complete list of nearly everything given in a dowry and the whole total amounts to [Rs] 12,615 [annas] 12.1/2, which is I think quite enough. . . . [The value of this dowry exceeds the annual valuation, Rs 11,000, of Kanota thikana, Amar Singh's family's estate.[14]]

XXIV. Conclusion

. . . [The estate of] Satheen has an income of some forty thousand rupees annually and has a Rekh of eighteen thousand.[15] Khejarla [an estate belonging to a branch of the same family] has an income of some fifty thousand rupees annually with a Rekh of twenty-two thousand. The latter is the only thikana among the eight first-class nobles of Marwar of foreign, I mean ganayat, family. [The leading nobles in most of the Rajput states belong to the same lineage as the maharaja of that state. *Ganayats* are "foreign" in the sense that they belong to a lineage other than that which founded the state. Jodhpur, the home of Sir Pratap and site of the wedding is ruled by the Rathore lineage. Bhatis, Amar Singh's wife's lineage, belong to the ruling lineage of neighboring Jaisalmer state.]

Their family is very good and high. They have a sort of rule never to marry their daughters to a maharaja. They are Urjanot Bhattis. I hate or rather despise the Rawalot Bhattis who do not marry their daughters to any one except a raja or maharaja.

The late Thakoor of Satheen had three sons. The eldest was adopted in Khejarla and is the present Thakoor Madho Singhjee. The second is the present Thakoor Kishore Singhjee of Satheen. The third is quite a boy yet and is adopted in the thikana of Kharia. His name is Sawai Singhjee. [When there is a failure of issue in the family, Rajputs usually arrange succession by adopting a boy from a collateral branch of the family.] Madho Singhjee and Kishore Singhjee had been educated at Ajmere in the Mayo College [which provided English-medium education at the pre-college level for princes and nobles]. They are both, I hear, of very good character but are gradually getting in the common Rajpoot destructive habit of wine and opium intoxication. What a pity.

The thikanas are, I hear, also in debt to some sixty thousand. But this I think is owing to the last famine. . . .

Now to conclude the whole thing I will say that Sarkar has done me a great honour by his personally coming and bringing so many of the maharajas and big nobles with him. His having the bana ceremony . . . performed by his wives was a much greater thing and his not allowing any of my family members to join and doing the whole thing on his own account was an honour that has never been given to anyone so far as I know in the Jodhpore history. . . .

He had two ornaments made for my wife, an aad [necklace] and a nuth [nose ring] which are both very nice and expensive. His making one wear the ordinary clothes was also a great convenience and comfort for me. The *tyag* money [payment to a bard] was also given, fully twelve hundred, which is the exact sum allowed by the committee. [The groom's family was expected to give tyag money, to the *charans* (bards), of the bride's side. The amounts tended to escalate due to status competition fueled by the bards, creators of reputation, who might vary their ballads depending on the generosity of donors. The "committee" refers to the Walter Krit Hitkarni Sabha.[16]]

My family has not been put to a single pice's expense. Even the railway hire has been paid by him. I conclude my narrative with heartfelt thanks and gratitude to Sarkar for his kindness.

2

Becoming a Householder

[A bride becomes a daughter to her husband's family as much as she becomes wife to her husband. Amar Singh brings his bride home to Jaipur to be incorporated into the joint family he left behind thirteen years ago when Sir Pratap took him away to Jodhpur to raise him like a son. Amar Singh confronts the fact that henceforth his primary affiliation will be to his natal family where his wife will bear children rather than to the men's society which dominated Jodhpur. He finds that his social self is defined in part by the corporate front his extended family presents to the world of the princely state of Jaipur. The reputations and possibilities of his own Kanota household overlap with the two related families, Gondher and Naila, all branches of the Champawat lineage.

Amar Singh enters society at Jaipur as the future Thakur of Kanota, a status which dictates the geography of his daily life. The center of activity is *bichli* haveli, middle haveli, the family's three-story mansion in the walled city built by Maharaja Jai Singh in the early eighteenth century. The city still closes its gates at 9 o'clock at night, obliging Amar Singh to make special arrangements for admission if he reaches the train station outside the city at a late hour. *Bichli* haveli is one of three belonging to the three brothers of the Champawat clan from Jodhpur who became ministers to Maharaja Ram Singh of Jaipur in the 1860s. *Bari* haveli (big mansion) belongs to the senior Gondher branch and *choti* haveli (little mansion) to the junior Naila branch.[1] The ranking is appropriate to seniority among the three families, but not to their relative wealth. Naila, founded by Fateh Singh, chief minister to Maharaja Ram Singh, is the wealthiest. Kanota, the middle lineage, owes its prosperity to the thrifty loan business carried on by Amar Singh's grandfather, Zorawar Singh. Gondher has been hard hit by Maharaja Madho Singh's efforts to expropriate the lineage's villages on a charge they were fraudulently acquired.

Most of Amar Singh's social exchanges occur in the three mansions. If members of small nuclear families satisfy their gregariousness by moving out into the world, denizens of large joint families find plenty of company at home. The haveli is a small village, populated by some 100 family members and servants. Several collateral families live together. The inner courtyards, divided into *mardana* (men's portion) and *zenana* (women's portion), are occupied by uncles and aunts and cousins in profusion, as well as the retinues appropriate to each.

Amar Singh and his cousins form a generational set of young bucks who have a good deal in common and continually tease each other. Teasing is a highly developed Rajput sport, sometimes just short of a blood sport. There is much to-ing and fro-ing among the adjoining havelis. One is expected to call upon grandfather, mother, uncles, and aunts both within one's own and in other houses. These exchanges recognize and constitute the corporate solidarity of the Champawat lineage. Social activity is carried on in gendered groupings. The uncles and

182

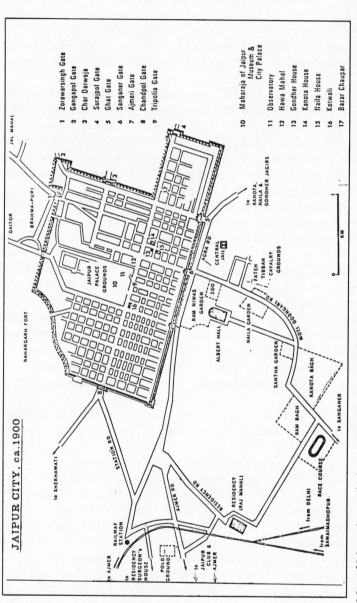

JAIPUR CITY, ca.1900

1 Zorawarsingh Gate
2 Gangapol Gate
3 Char Darwaja
4 Surajpol Gate
5 Ghat Gate
6 Sanganer Gate
7 Ajmeri Gate
8 Chandpol Gate
9 Tripolia Gate

10 Maharaja of Jaipur Museum & City Palace
11 Observatory
12 Hawa Mahal
13 Gondher House
14 Kanota House
15 Naila House
16 Kotwali
17 Bazar Chaupar

PHOTO III-2   Map of Jaipur city to which Amar Singh returns after his marriage. The three related Champawat lineages live in neighboring mansions (13, 14, 15 on the map) inside the old walled city, not far from the Jaipur maharaja's palace. They create "gardens," then country houses, in the countryside beyond the walls. And they take the Agra road to reach their *jagirs* (landed estates) at Kanota, Naila, and Gondher, some 10 to 13 miles beyond the city. Map by Christopher Muller-Wille, adapted from the tourist map, *Jaipur*, distributed by the Rajasthan State Tourist Department in 1973. (No date, no place.)

PHOTO III-3   Jaipur *circa* 1907; view of Tripolia Bazaar with Victory Tower. Amar Singh's photo albums.

nephews of the three houses participate in social activities at the gardens of the three families south of the walled city.

Having a garden outside the walled city began in the time of Maharaja Ram Singh. After he built himself a garden palace, the Rambagh, his nobles followed suit. The three Champawat families have gardens in various stages of development, as do more senior nobles of the state. Eventually, in the 1930s, Amar Singh will spend much time and money building his garden house, the palatial Narain Niwas which survives in 2000 as an active hotel.[2]

The uncles and cousins from the related houses move with the fashionable set of "smart" noblemen who come to be seen playing tennis and racquets on late afternoons at the British residency. At Jodhpur, there had been two centers of Rajput society, the rough-and-ready polo-playing set around Sir Pratap and a "fast" set which patronized racing, dance, and music, around the young Maharaja Sardar Singh, considered decadent by Amar Singh and Sir Pratap. At Jaipur, things are different. The smart set can be found at the residency, not at the palace. Unlike his cosmopolitan predecessor Maharaja Ram Singh, and successor, Maharaja Man Singh,[3] Maharaja Madho Singh is ostentatiously unenthusiastic about English society.[4] In contrast to Sir Pratap, who scoffs at many Brahmanic practices, Madho Singh is an orthodox Hindu. He tries to keep his English guests at a distance. He prefers not to dine with them or have them in his palace. He discourages his nobles from consorting with them. The intimate friendships that Sir Pratap developed with British residents or other English civil and military officers are not seen at Jaipur in the time of Madho Singh.[5]

Maharaja Madho Singh and his prime minister, Babu Kanti Chander, carry on a struggle with the three Champawat families. Although eventually exonerated, they are accused of fraudulently acquiring their estates. The maharaja may have been prevented by the British from seizing their estate, but his unrelenting opposition, especially to Amar Singh's father, Narain Singh,[6] excludes the Kanota family from court service or favor. Narain Singh takes service "in exile" in the adjoining princely state of Alwar as native guardian to the minor maharaja, Jai Singh. He rarely appears at his home in Jaipur.

Ram Nathji, Amar Singh's teacher, introduces a topic appropriate to his new life stage, the conduct of a healthy sex life. Amar Singh reads George Drysdale's euphemistically entitled, *The Elements of Social Science,* at mid-century "the most notorious book of its age." Despite the fact it is "out of etiquette" in Rajput society for younger persons to discuss sexual topics with older persons, Ram Nathji makes it possible for Amar Singh.

Jodhpore, Thursday, 12th September, 1901

[The wedding party returns to Jaipur via Jodhpur.] . . . At about nine we went to the station. . . . Sheonath Singhjee of Bera saw us [off] in the railway carriage. Ram Nathjee accompanied me to Jaipore as my guardian and that of the bridal party.

Jaipore, Friday, 13th September, 1901

Last night I had gone to bed very late because it was awfully hot in the carriage. I was up as late as four in the morning and then went to bed. I was in the compart-

PHOTO III-4 Narain Niwas. The Kanota family, like Naila and Gondher, established a "garden"—a 40-acre walled recreation and hunting area—in the countryside beyond Jaipur's city wall and near the Rambagh, the royal family's much larger garden (now the site of a prestigious hotel). In the 1930s Amar Singh built Narain Niwas, named after his father, inside the garden compound. Today it is Narain Niwas Palace Hotel. Amar Singh's photo albums.

ment with my wife. I awoke at half past seven and came in the other compartment with Ram Nathjee and Sheonath Singh and washed myself. We had a slight
breakfast on biscuits and a cup of tea at Merta Road. After that I sat talking with
Ram Nathjee on different subjects and also showed him some of the photographs
that I had brought out from China. After twelve I went in the other compartment
with my wife and we talked for a long time until I fell asleep with my head resting
in her lap. I had a very long and a very sound sleep. After waking I came in the
other compartment and talked with Ram Nathjee who gave me long lectures of
different subjects among which reading was most prominent. We reached Jaipore
station at about seven in the evening.

My cousin Bhoj Raj Singhjee was the first to see me and after him came my
uncles Roop Singhjee, Chhiman Singhjee, and Mehtab Singhjee. There were
some other of my younger cousins who all went to look after my wife. We came
to the dharamshala or the inn made and supported by my grandfather Thakoor
Fateh Singhjee. I will have to stop here for the night and until twelve tomorrow
when is the [astrologically auspicious] time fixed for our entry in our house.

*XX

[Amar Singh's arrival at the family home is complicated by the fact that the
household has not fully accepted Sir Pratap's spare and rationalist approach to
the marriage, and is bent on making up for the omitted ceremonies. His grandfather feels that certain additional events are essential. Amar Singh, on the other
hand, is convinced that Sir Pratap has met all ceremonial requirements. At Jaipur
he discovers that he is an important ceremonial object. He is expected to act with
reserve and restraint, and submit to the appropriate rituals.]

. . . On my arrival at the door of my haveli when I got out of the carriage I
walked straight in. The purohit who is our family priest wanted to stop me and
do some ceremonies but I did not [listen] to [him]. . . . [When] I hesitated for a
moment in consideration of displeasing my grandfather, the purohit made a
round mark with his forefinger between my eyebrows with the red paste. I hastily
wiped it off and walked into my grandfather's room whom I met midway and
saluted. Then I found that I had made a mistake in coming straight on after my
marriage. I felt ashamed but what was once done was done and would not be undone. Ram Nathjee soon came to my relief and he began to talk with my grandfather. A short while afterwards the latter relieved me by saying that I might go.

Though relieved here I was soon wanted inside. I declined but when they said
that it was my grandfather's desire I had to go, though I soon . . . found that it
was all an invented thing to beguile me in. As soon as I got into the zenana gate or
rather porch I found it cramful of women. Most of them were ladies of our
household. My wife was standing with her full suite of the slave girls that had
come from Satheen and my mother was doing some rites. She also did some rites
to me but the situation was becoming too critical and so I insisted on going out
on the plea that none of the ceremonies had been left undone. I meant that all
had been observed at Jodhpore and consequently there was no need of any of
them. Once outside the curtain I rushed up to my room and never went in again

PHOTO III-5   Entrance to *Bichli Haveli* (middle mansion) on *Haldion ka Rasta* (Haldion's street) in the heart of the walled city of Jaipur, first of the three mansions of the Kanota family, photographed in 1971. In 1901, Amar Singh brought his new bride here, to the 100-person joint-family household, densely populated with three generations of family members, their servants, accountants, and hangers on. The *haveli* is now occupied by small business. For the three-level floor plan of this expansive establishment, see Part V. Photo by courtesy of Robin von Breton.

though repeatedly sent for. Ram Nathjee kindly made my grandfather understand that all had been done and so I was bothered no more.[7*] . . .

Tuesday, 17th September, 1901

[Weddings tend to concentrate in certain periods of the year designated as astrologically auspicious. Hence it is not surprising that cousin Hem Singh, son of Amar Singh's father's brother living in bichli haveli, has also just been married.]

... Bhoj Raj Singhjee [the cousin from the Gondher house] had come and we chatted and gossiped and joked at the expense of Hem Singhjee, who when he came out in the morning, had all his shirt coloured. This was caused by his perspiring while sleeping with his wife and the colour of her clothes sticking to his clothes. This was nothing very odd but it gave us a good pretence to laugh and crack jokes at him. . . .

Bhoj Raj Singhjee and myself rode to the garden of Roop Singhjee where we all brothers and cousins collected together and the cracking of jokes commenced at each others' expense. I was not at all troubled because there was nothing to laugh at me, owing to none of them being with me at the time of my marriage. Of course Sheonath Singh [his younger brother] was, but he never went in, and moreover he has great respect for me and never utters a single word of joke in my presence. At last Hem Singhjee came and then we each and all turned on him and had a merry laugh. He makes most blunders and somehow we come to know of them. Our meeting dissolved at ten. . . .

Saturday, 28th September, 1901

Having washed and dressed I was about to go when I was wanted in by my mother for something to eat. I do not at all like eating at this time, but had to do to please her. I never so much as hurt her feelings in the least because she is my mother and moreover loves me best of all the seven brothers. I then went to the bari haveli . . . from whence I sat in the carriage of [my uncle] Mookend Singhjee [Thakur of Gondher] and drove down to the residency where there was tennis. The courts were full when we arrived and so Mr Cobb suggested that we should go and try racquets. We wanted nothing better. I had two games at it and two at lawn tennis. I like the former for at the latter I am utterly bad and awkward. I feel ashamed while playing it.

[The residency constitutes a political as well as a cultural arena. Politically, it gives recognition to British power and influence in the state; culturally, it represents a space in which English speech, manners, and games are practiced. It is a society of insiders, of those who stand in favor with the raj, or hope to do so. By contrast with cantonment society in British India, which had enough British officers and families to be able to function as a British ghetto, the British official and unofficial contingent of a middle-sized princely state is too small for self-sufficiency. There were about thirty English persons living in Jaipur in 1936, many of them—the maharaja's English driver, an English nurse—ineligible for sociability.[8] As a result, princely Jaipur was a more integrated society than those found in British India.

H.V. Cobb is currently the resident. Residents and political agents resemble diplomatic representatives, in that the princely states claimed a limited and ambiguous sovereignty within the ambit of British "paramountcy." As representatives of the paramount power, they could become decisive in the politics of a state. Imprudently independent maharajas, or fiscally irresponsible and ineffectual ones, might attract the attention and intervention of the Government of India. Subjects of princely states had an interest in the resident's favorable opinion.]

Wednesday, 2nd October, 1901

The man
Of virtuous soul commands not, nor obeys.
Power, like a desolating pestilence,
Pollutes whatever it touches, and obedience,
Bane of all genius, virtue, freedom, truth,
Makes slaves of men, and of the human frame
A mechanized automaton.

Shelley's *Queen Mob*

Let no one for more loves pretend,
Than he has hearts in store;
Love once begun should never end
Love once and love no more. . . .

The above . . . are copied from
Ram Nathjee's note book. . . .

In the evening I went for polo. There were four chukkers played and I joined in them all. The game was also faster and better played than usual. After it we sat talking with Mr Cobb for a long time. I was interpreting for Roop Singhjee [Amar Singh's uncle, Thakur of Naila; a regular at the residency and an officer in Jaipur's judicial service].

Friday, 4th October, 1901

. . . . In the morning I . . . went out with Bhoj Raj Singhjee to the residency where [we] had some [four] games at racquets. . . . There was rather too much crowd this morning because, besides us, there was the Thakoor Sahib Devi Singhjee of

PHOTO III-6   "Tennis at my garden," 1907. Until the building of Narain Niwas, the garden was used mainly for sport and hunting. At the time, the wild country outside Jaipur's city wall supported a variety of game, including tigers. Amar Singh's photo albums.

Chomu and his brother and Mr Garret and some others. I do not like [it] when there is a great crowd. After the game was over we drove straight for home and as soon as I reached haveli I changed my clothes and began reading *The Elements of Social Science*, which I continued until breakfast and even afterwards until at about half past one in the noon time. . . .

[Behind this innocuous title, *The Elements of Social Science* by "A Doctor of Medicine," lies one of the more liberating sex instruction texts of the nineteenth century. The author, Dr George Drysdale, published his numerous editions anonymously. *The Elements of Social Science: or Physical, Sexual and Natural Religion. An Exposition of the True Cause and Only Cure of the Three Primary Evils-Poverty, Prostitution and Celibacy* is a polemic against abstinence. Originally published in 1854, it is one of the first of its *genre* in English nineteenth-century writing. A descriptive account of sexual activity and problems, it treats them as natural and subject to scientific investigation and knowledge. By the time of Drysdale's death in 1904, it had sold 100,000 copies. This is the more astounding as "it was never reviewed in the respectable press, never stocked by a bookshop, and was publicised and sold entirely by secularist agencies—and even some of these repudiated it as obscene."[9] Ram Nathji, who has long talks about this time with Amar Singh about sexual conduct and morality, presumably put the book in his student's hands.

Drysdale preached in the mid-nineteenth century what in the mid-twentieth would be regarded as a sane council of moderate sexual expressiveness. His scientific language and moral tone satisfies Amar Singh, raised in Victorian-cum-Sir Pratap asceticism. Drysdale believes Christianity has led men away from understanding the body and urges "physical religion"; chastises Malthus for preaching abstinence when birth control would achieve the same result at lower psychic cost; notes that abstinence is bad for the health, especially that of women, who become hysterical if they are allowed sexual lives in fantasy only; decries "rosewater morality," which, by blocking healthy sexual appetites, creates unhealthiness—masturbation, "sodomy," and prostitution. He urges "preventive intercourse."[10]]

Thursday, 17th October, 1901

. . . We [rode] to the Jeensi ground where . . . the Jaipore cavalry was practising at the march past drill, which was the most grotesque thing that can be imagined. Some [were] in khaki, some in white. Some had coats and some shirts while some wore angarkhis [traditional hip-length coat with fitted sleeves, deeply cut out in front, and tied with strings]. Some wore breeches and some dhotis [long piece of cloth tied as nether garment, usually white] . . . some of them carried swords, some spears, and some sticks only. The turbans were of all descriptions and colours.

[Maharaja Madho Singh's forces do not live up to the standard Amar Singh has grown accustomed to at Jodhpur. When Amar Singh is asked to raise the Jaipur Lancers in 1923, he creates a professional military force, including the headquarters facilities for the Indian Army's 61st Cavalry.]

Friday, 18th October, 1901

. . . We all drove down to the residency for racquets. The racquet-court was all too wet and quite unfit for playing. Bhoj Raj Singhjee and myself were . . . of this opinion, that we should [not] be going on such a wet day but the others would not listen to it. This sort of thing gives a low opinion of us in the eyes of Europeans and shows us as mere flatterers coming to please them and not to enjoy playing. . . .

I went in during the whole of the noon time and talked with my wife. I want to have some time to talk to her so as to let her know my ideas. . . .

Saturday, 19th October, 1901

. . . We went back to Roop Singhjee's garden where I had a long conversation with Ram Nathjee on physical and sexual subjects. He is indeed very kind [to] me and gives hints and explanations on all the utmost important subjects and which are such that very few people understand and even if they did, would not and could not make others understand. I consider myself the luckiest fellow for having earned the confidence of such a man as can very rarely be found. He has been, on some subjects, more than a father to me. It is through him only that all my family members have begun to regard me as a promising youth.

. . . During the whole of the noon time I was in with my wife and informed her on many subjects which I wanted her to avoid and which I had learned from Rain Nathjee this morning. The most important being masturbation by women and the laws of impregnation. . . .

Sunday, 20th October, 1901

. . . Before breakfast I saw a few pages of *The Elements of Social Science* and then went in and passed the whole of the noon time in company with my wife. I read her over some two hundred dohas from my copy book and also talked for some time and then slept . . .

Monday, 21st October, 1901

. . . Returned back to Ram Nathjee and talked with him. I confessed of my own free will that I take a little liquor and he gave examples and forbade me from this practice. I have promised and hope to carry the point to the last end.

Tuesday, 22nd October, 1901

. . . I saw a chapter of *The Elements of Social Science*, and then went into my wife. I also took my brothers Bari Sal and Kaisar Singh with me. We joked for about an hour and then sent them out. [Rajput etiquette permits a bride to have friendly relations with her husband's younger brothers, while social relations with his older brother, where there is one, or his father, are forbidden.] I then read over some selected dohas from my copy book to my wife. I try to make her mind and feelings equal to those of mine but that requires some time and a good [deal] of constant company which is rather too hard to get unless we live by ourselves. . . .

CONTENTS

PART I.
PHYSICAL RELIGION.

PART II.
SEXUAL RELIGION

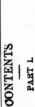

EVILS OF ABSTINENCE.

It is most unwise to suppose that our chief duty with regard to our appetites and passions is to exercise self-denial. This quality is far from being at all times a virtue; it is quite often a vice; and it should by no means be unconditionally praised. Every natural passion, like every organ of the body, was intended to have normal exercise and gratification; and this it is to which every individual and society at large should aspire. It is always a sign of imperfection in an individual, or in society, that the normal requirements of all their members be not duly provided for. Abstinence is much more frequently a natural vice than a virtue; and instead of deserving praise, merits condemnation, as we may learn from the mode which all-just nature punishes it. Wherever we see disease following the violation of conduct, we may be certain it has been erroneous and sinful, for nature is unerring. Sexual abstinence is frequently attended by consequences not one whit less serious than sexual excess, and far more in our moralist can paint in all its horrors the evils of excess, how few vigor are there that the reverse of the picture is just as deplorable to the instructed eye!

On our and dangerous, as they are not so generally recognised. While the young man enters on the period of puberty with an imagination excited with the ideas of love and romance he has read of, or conceived in his mind, the visions of happiness, and all these receive ten-fold intensity from the realms of the new bodily development. If this have no natural way, the consequences may be most fearful and deplorable. Thrown as he himself by the sensualism of our morality, the baneful effects of which will describe under the head of the abuse of the sexual organs. If he do not; if, persuaded by the theoretically received, but by no means generally practised, view on moral subjects which surround him, he abstain from all sexual gratification, he is exposed to the following evils, of which, if we look around us, we may see too many examples. Haunted by amatory ideas, and tormented by frequent erections of the sexual organ, the spirited youth wars manfully for the citadel of his chastity; or takes refuge in study, in severe bodily exercise, in platonics, the un-

---

FIGURE 3.1 Dr. George Drysdale, *The Elements of Social Science: Or Physical, Sexual and Natural Religion. An Exposition of the True Cause and Only Cure of the Three Primary Evils—Poverty, Prostitution and Celibacy*

Thursday, 24th October, 1901

. . . I found a telegram waiting for me. It was from Sarkar and ran as follows: "You have been admitted in Imperial Cadet Corps. Come sharp to Jodhpore." This was rather too sudden. I wanted to stop at least another fortnight.

Friday, 25th October, 1901

. . . I awoke early and after washing myself went with Bhoj Raj Singhjee in his tandem to the residency where we had racquets . . . Mr Cobb having come we played with him. He took me for his partner. . . . To [Captain Commeline] and Mr Cobb I showed Sarkar's telegram and they were both very much pleased and congratulated me on having entered the Imperial Cadet Corps. On our way back we stopped at Roop Singhjee's garden and he and Ram Nathjee were both of them very much pleased at this news. . . .

Saturday, 26th October, 1901

. . . Having reached [the] haveli I went straight in to my wife and spent the whole of the time from one to four p.m. with her. She was too sorry to part with me. I however took my leave of her which I said would be the last before I left unless I could find an opportunity. In spite of all my instructions and advices that I had been giving her and gave her at that time, tears came in her eyes. However, my advices had a great effect on her, otherwise she would have been very bad indeed. I again encouraged her to keep heart as her tears would not make me postpone my departure and even if I did that, I must and would go some day or the other. My firm bearing gave her some heart and she having composed herself we parted. . . . I had some rings sent for from the city and made her a present of a couple of them which she liked and that fitted her. . . . I started by the nine o'clock passenger train for Jodhpore. . . .

Jodhpore, Monday, 28th October, 1901

. . . Last night I was up until midnight talking with my servant Kaloo. . . . Having sorted the clothes [I must take to Meerut with me] I applied myself to the books which took a much longer time. I had some of the best ones packed up in small boxes that can be easily carried while going and coming. . . . There are too many books with me and will take some time before they all reach safely to Jaipore. . . .

Saturday, 9th November, 1901

. . . I read and finished *The Elements of Social Science*. . . . This . . . has opened mine eyes as to what real life is. I had been rather in a hurry while going through the book. I . . . am fully resolved to re-read it some time afterwards. . . . I know how much harm has been done to myself and now that I have come to know it, I feel the more and want to spend some time in company with my wife, but this is rather too difficult for me.

Sarkar does not approve of such things [as spending time with one's wife], and I do not want to do anything contrary to his wish. I was very eager on going [back to Jaipur] and had asked Bera Thakoor Sahib to ask for my leave, but it is through the kind advice of Ram Nathjee that I have dismissed that idea. Though I would have been doing nothing out of the way yet I would have fallen in Sarkar's eyes and that is a thing I would not do for anything. . . .

My Recent Stay of a Month and a Half in Jaipore. . . . I stopped there for about a month and a half and during this time I enjoyed myself thoroughly. . . . Besides [riding, cycling, driving or racquets] I used to spend about an hour or two in the company of Ram Nathjee who always used to give me some good advice or the other and especially used to warn me against falling into any bad habit as it was just the time when I had turned a new page in my life.

I must say that I had begun to take a little wine [a word used for all alcoholic drinks] every night in company with my wife and when I confessed it, it was he [Ram Nathji] who explained the matter fully to me, described and pointed out its mischiefs, with the result that I was fully convinced of my error and promised to give it up and never touch it unless in an assembly of friends or relatives and even then very little. I am glad to say that I never again touched it and hope will not.

My wife too, when I fully explained the matter to her just as Ram Nathjee had done to me, agreed that it was of no use. In fact she always used to prevent me from drinking at all. . . . The wine I used to drink was always liquor of the best obtainable kind in Jaipore and consequently very expensive too. [The context for these reflections is that alcoholism and opium smoking were the scourge of Rajputs. Amar Singh's wife's brother, the young Thakur of Satheen, dies of the two addictions at twenty six.]

Cycling was a thing that I enjoyed every morning. . . . It used to give me good exercise, of which I was always in great need and used to save my horse. . . . Bhoj Raj Singhjee had lent me this machine. . . .

. . . Yes, I hate sleeping in the day time, but could not help there because I was always up talking with my wife until twelve and sometimes one in the night. It was necessary for me to talk to her and try and make her mind on the same level and footing as mine own. This thing can only be done gradually and to do it one must first grow quite familiar and win another's confidence and love.

I am glad to say we do not disagree on anything at all. Of course she has some superstitions still in her head, but they will gradually all die out if I have occasion to stop and talk to her for a long and continuous time. Then I used to wake her gradually on the many sexual evils which Ram Nathjee used to describe to me and I used to read in *The Elements of Social Science*. These things have somewhat convinced her that I am well educated and know of more things than most others. I am indebted for this to Ram Nathjee according to whose guidance I am working.

. . . She is a very mild woman and not at all disposed to mix up and make rows with others. She is very obedient to my will and orders. I only wish she would continue to behave herself as she has done up to the present all throughout her life. . . .

Twice a day I used to go in and see my mother. I very seldom used to go to the other female members of my family because the result is often not good. [Amar Singh, raised in a very male society for the last ten years, follows the reserve observed between men and women in this *purdah* (female seclusion) society, even in relationship to aunts and female cousins.]

... I enjoyed myself thoroughly. Still, if I had been sent away to Kanota fort for this short time [with my wife], I would have been much more free. Our etiquette is too strict and puts a strain on us to move freely about. So long as my uncle was in the haveli, I was unable to go in. A little more freedom would be ... preferable.

[Rajput family etiquette restrains the young married adults not only from publicly showing their feelings towards each other or their children, but also from having any conversations with each other in public. A husband should not be seen, especially by an older male, going to his wife's room. Amar Singh takes elaborate precautions not to be seen, and becomes adept at using the back passages and stairs of the large mansions to escape detection.]

Thursday, 14th November, 1901

... I sat ... [and] wrote two letters, one to my father and the other to my wife. This is the first time I have written to her in reply to her first one which I had received the other day. I showed mine letter to Ram Nathjee and he quite approved of it. Though I have just as much respect for him as for mine own father yet he treats me in such a familiar way that I keep no secrets from him. ...

PART IV:
SOLDIER FOR THE RAJ?
ACCOMMODATION AND
RESISTANCE AT THE IMPERIAL CADET CORPS

Amar Singh begins his military career by becoming a soldier for the raj. He is among the first to cross the seemingly insuperable barrier of a "black man commanding a white man" which, Lord Curzon tells us, "no one will look at."[1] Philip Mason in his panegyric of the Indian Army, *A Matter of Honour*, reminds us that the British Empire and the nation were dominated by an "imperial class, servants of the Queen and of the Empire, rulers of the subject peoples and of about nine-tenths of their fellow countrymen." At the center of this imperial class are the British officers of the Indian Army, that "military brotherhood," that "monastic order," which embraces the myths of hardiness and self-denial elaborated in the family and in public schools. These virtues are believed to be uniquely British. Indians, soft rather than hardy, indulged rather than disciplined, and without the characterological benefits of a public school education, are made of different stuff.[2]

The Imperial Cadets Corps (ICC) was set up to remedy these failings and to temper the exclusion of Indians from the officer corps of the Indian Army. A small and only moderately successful institution, it was the "dear child" of that remarkable viceroy, Lord Curzon, and aspired to train aristocratic Indians for officer status. Sir Pratap, Amar Singh's patron, lays the foundations for the latter's career by arranging for his protege to receive formal training at the ICC. This Part consists of the diary accounts of the seven terms that made Amar Singh an officer and gentleman.

Why did Lord Curzon create the ICC? Were his intentions realized? How did Amar Singh fare as a soldier and officer? We trace his military career in an Indian Army whose British officers, mostly from public schools, are convinced that Indians, even Indian princes and noblemen, cannot be officers and gentlemen. Amar Singh's career is an anomaly; Indians were virtually excluded from the officer corps until the late twenties. On August 25, 1917, he is one of the first nine to become a king's commissioned officer (KCO) in the Indian Army.[3] He is probably the first Indian to command a regiment when, on three occasions during the "Third Afghan War,"[4] he takes temporary charge of the 16th Cavalry.[5] While other Indians are commissioned over the next twenty years, none is given command authority until 1929 and then over Indians only. Not until World War II are they given command over other British ranks. But four years after Amar Singh's commissioning, his career as a KCO in the Indian Army comes to a dead end.

Sent in October 1919 to the front in Waziristan during the Third Afghan War, Major Amar Singh encounters insubordination by a junior British officer, a Merrick-like,[6] socially mobile lieutenant who chafes at having to obey an Indian officer. It is an encounter that draws its heat from both race and class. Yet he carries on, sometimes in command positions. Exactly why his career ends in April 1921 remains mysterious. He and Colonel Mears, his regimental commander, exchange "hot words" over his annual confidential report. He resigns without revealing the details to the diary.[7] The career for which the ICC has prepared Amar Singh is cut short. It is his second career, from 1922 to 1936, as commandant of the state forces of princely Jaipur, an Indian among Indians, that engages his full potential.

When Amar Singh begins his first term at the ICC in 1902, it has just been established by George Nathaniel Curzon, Marquis of Kedleston.[8] As a young man at Balliol, the future Lord Curzon inspired several contemporaries to pen this much-cited lampoon:

> My name is George Nathaniel Curzon
> I am a most superior person.
> My cheek is pink, my hair is sleek
> I dine at Blenheim once a week.[9]

Why did Lord Curzon, spectacular, energetic, politically unastute, establish a Cadet Corps? The doggerel provides an entry to the man and his times, particularly his relationship to the ICC. In 1901, aristocracies in Britain and India are already an endangered species, on the verge of becoming anachronisms in their respective historical contexts. Is Curzon's perception of being a "superior person" viable in late Victorian, much less post-Victorian times? Can a person born to a title who chooses to sit in the House of Lords become prime minister when middle-class values and politics are in the ascendant? Can he, as viceroy of India, salvage India's "natural aristocracy," its princes and nobles, by training them as modern professionals? Is it possible to be an achieving aristocrat? Does being one provide a way to survive as a "governing class" in a Britain or India in which middle-class morality has come to the fore?"[10] Or are Lord Curzon's self-image and the ICC both improbable?

The Curzons had "ruled" at Kedleston in Derbyshire for 800 years, its elder sons providing its squires and younger sons its vicars.[11] As a youth Curzon decided that the only goals worthy of pursuit were to be viceroy of India and prime minister of England, at the helm of what was then the world's greatest empire. In 1898 at the age of thirty-nine he became viceroy of India and continued to be so for seven years. He "responded readily to the magnificence of Empire . . . and thought it, 'under Providence, the greatest instrument for good that the world has seen. . . . [T]here has never been anything so great in the world's history.'"[12] The prime ministership ultimately escaped him.

Tory imperialists like Curzon and Lytton who preceded him as viceroy by twenty years, counted on the "natural aristocracy" to cement British rule. As they saw it, India's princes and nobles, among whom Sir Pratap Singh, prince regent of Jodhpur and Amar Singh's patron, was a paragon, were the "real Indians," respected, honored and obeyed not only in princely but also in British India. The Cadet Corps under its honorary commandant Sir Pratap Singh would help India's natural aristocracy become achieving aristocrats, military professionals whose knowledge, skill, and discipline would enable them to rule at home and serve the empire abroad. In the face of mounting middle-class criticism in Britain and nationalist criticism in India that the upper classes were "indolent, corrupt and immoral,"[13] aristocracy could remain natural, *noblesse oblige* viable, hierarchy and paternalism credible, if their claims were justified by accomplishments and service.

Here is Sir Pratap voicing his version of this credo—perhaps tutored and edited but nonetheless his—about the time he was appointed honorary commandant of the Cadet Corps:

> Indian princes should . . . attend to every business with forethought and industry. . . . One great lesson taken out of the experiences of my life which I wish to place before my brother princes is this: Give up love of ease and luxury, make yourselves in every respect fit to rule, and take personal interest in the work of your state."[14]

The ICC became one of the elements in the symbolic and ritual world Curzon constructed. Like that other high Tory imperialist and superior person, Lord Lytton, Curzon believed that political theater, the pomp and pageantry of power and incorporation, particularly those modeled on Britain's Mughal predecessors, would buttress British rule in India.

Lytton had proclaimed Victoria Queen Empress of India, Kaiser-i-Hind, on January 1, 1877, at a grandiose durbar in Delhi[15] attended by an estimated 84,000 persons. It was a tableau at centerstage of which were sixty-three princes, advertised as rulers of 40 million people whose domains were larger than France, England, and Italy.[16]

Lytton's durbar became a standard by which public ceremony from then on was known and measured. Two more imperial durbars followed at the same location, the first in 1903 when the viceroy at the time, Lord Curzon, proclaimed the recently crowned Edward VII emperor of India, the second in 1911 when George V traveled to India to crown himself emperor. Curzon scrupulously followed the forms laid down by Lytton and felt obliged to explain and justify changes and additions.[17]

At the "Curzonation" of 1903, Amar Singh and his ICC classmates, mounted on black chargers and resplendent in their "strikingly beautiful uniform of white with sky-blue and gold facings, . . . formed a constant contingent in the Viceroy's escort."[18] The Cadet Corps' presence helped paint in some of the figures in the imperial social portrait, which included the "real Indians." At centerstage was the queen empress, the viceroy, and the native princes; in the background, the Indian peasants, sturdy and loyal. In the middle ground, mediating between the grand figures at the center and those behind, were the "native gentlemen." Educated but respectful of authority, the talents and services of native gentlemen made raj rule a going concern. In Curzon's eyes, some cadets, the royals, would reinforce the moral quality at centerstage while Amar Singh and other fellow cadets would reenforce the native gentlemen in the middle ground.

Altogether out of the picture were the professional, literary, clerical, and teaching Indians, summarized as *babus*. Curzon, like other Tories, feared the nationalist products of the universities. They were considered superficially clever urban youths, their heads turned by anglicization and bookish learning so that they thought they knew more and better than their imperial masters. The respectful title, babu, designating a scribe, a literate gentleman, became a term of contempt. It was the loyal princes and native gentlemen who would command respect and obedience.

Given this kind of social portrait, what were the prospects for an Imperial Cadet Corps? There was a model. Lord Lytton as viceroy had tried in 1879 to create a "native" Indian élite of civilian officeholders, the Statutory Civil Service, its incumbents selected for their social distinction rather than by merit, which he considered a vulgar certification. It was meant to parallel the highly visible and prestigious Indian Civil Service (ICS), the "steel frame" of raj rule, whose ranks in principle had been open to Indians since the Queen's proclamation in 1858.[19] The ICS was selected by competition, through examinations that for Lytton emphasized the deplorable quality of clerk-like cleverness. Lytton's Statutory Civil Service would stress other virtues. Its incumbents were drawn from backgrounds similar to those Curzon now hoped to tap for military service, and recruited in a similar manner—through recommendation by knowledgable officials, such as the British residents at princely courts, or other British notables, which would guarantee appropriate social background, character, and loyalty. But the Statutory Civil Service failed to live up to Lytton's—or Tory imperialist—hopes and expectations. By 1900, it had long been reduced to a provincial service, overshadowed by an ICS that now included a handful of Indians, English-educated and anglicized.

The ICC had an even thornier path before it. British military opinion was opposed to Indians becoming KCOs in the Indian Army by competing for admission to Sandhurst, the Royal Military Academy. Allowing this would inevitably lead to a demand that Indian graduates, like those who entered the ICS via merit, be given positions equivalent to those held by Englishmen. Most distasteful to the British was the possibility that Indian officers would command English troops and eventually, English officers. The cabinet affirmed this view in 1897, when the Maharaja of Cooch Behar who had pressed for his son being allowed to try for Sandhurst was denied permission; the son later joined the ICC.

Despite this resistance, Curzon thought some means could be found simultaneously to strengthen British rule and imperial security by associating "Indian gentlemen of the highest birth and position . . . who are bound to us by every tie of self-interest, if not of loyalty," with the military leadership and command of native troops.[20] He proposed to create a corps of twenty or thirty young men drawn from the four chiefs' colleges, an approximation of English public schools, who would be trained at a Sandhurst-like Cadet Corps and, upon graduation, be given king's commissions. They could hope to become officers in the Indian Army or serve as officers of the Imperial Service Forces, that is, the forces of the princely states,[21] or in the Indian Army as staff, or in imperial regiments if such were created. The scheme was twice rejected by the cabinet.

In 1901 Curzon tried again, more successfully. Invoking the record of Imperial Service Forces in China during the Boxer Rebellion, he argued that an Indian aristocrat, prince, or nobleman must have an occupation "suitable to his rank, congenial to his tastes, and free from danger to our own military and political system." Commissioned service, not immediately in the Indian Army—"for that would or might involve a black man commanding a white man, which no one will look at"[22]—but with Imperial Service Forces or on the staffs of general officers, would give recognition to the substantial contributions and loyal support that the Indian princely states had extended to imperial interests.

Curzon managed to gain approval for a scheme that would allow those who passed examinations at the end of a three-and-a-half-year course modeled on Sandhurst to hold a special kind of commission, presumably to be signed by the king, Edward VII. This would allow princes and nobles to be distinguished from the viceroy's commissioned officers (VCOs), who were the solid backbone of the Indian Army, but clearly subordinate and inferior to KCOs. Nothing more precise could be agreed upon.

From the beginning, uncertainty about the nature of the commissions and the career that would follow cast a pall over the ICC, hindering recruitment and accounting for dropouts. "We have not much to expect from the Corps," Amar Singh tells the diary in the fourth term. "All the big swells were gone," he reports in the sixth term, surveying the shrinking student body, and the departure of the young princes. Lord Kitchener, who became commander in chief in India in 1902 and Curzon's nemesis in 1905, rigidly opposed king's commissions for Indians.[23]

The initial class of twenty-one recruits who enter with Amar Singh in January 1902 contains six royals: four maharajas and two heirs apparent. The rest are, like Amar Singh, noblemen or noblemen's sons, or from respectable families.[24] None of the rulers or heirs stays the course or receives a commission. When the first class graduates in 1905, only four cadets are commissioned.

Amar Singh is one of the four. At the graduation ceremony Lord Curzon presents Amar Singh and three of his classmates, Aga Kasim Shah, Vali Udeen Khan, and Zorawar Singh, commissions signed by King Edward. They and subsequent graduates of the ICC are to serve in a newly-created Native Indian Land Forces, the NILF or ILF. In this anomalous service, created to accommodate Curzon's compromise solution, officers hold king's commissions but their command authority is limited to "native officers, soldiers and other persons belonging to the said Native Indian forces." In compliance with war office and entrenched "military opinion," NILF officers would not command British troops or officers.[25] Cadets commissioned in the NILF were to make careers in the princely states as officers of Imperial Service Forces. But Maharaja Madho Singh of Jaipur resists considerable pressure to appoint Amar Singh to a command in Jaipur; consequently he has to be assigned as a staff officer, that is, without command authority, in the Indian Army.

General Sir Garret O'Moore Creagh, commander in chief of the Indian Army writes in 1910:

> The Imperial Cadet Corps was originally started with this object in view ["to provide for the military aspirations of Indians of noble fighting families or clans"], but for various reasons it has not fulfilled what was expected of it. In the first place the commissions given to young men were not of a nature to satisfy their ambitions, or to make them feel, as they think they have the right

to, that they have the same opportunities as their British confreres. Then it was common talk, whether true or not I am unable to say, that the Cadet Corps was used by the Political Department as a penal settlement; and again, it was under the Foreign Department and in no way connected with the Army, which latter fact gave grounds for the belief that it was never seriously intended for a military institution. Whether these statements made to its detriment were untrue or not, they were certainly believed by the great majority of Chiefs who have spoken to me on the subject.[26]

Amar Singh spends nine quiet years at Mhow,[27] mostly under General O'-Moore Creagh, then commander of the 5th division, Western Army. He is the sole Indian in a British officers' mess. When World War I erupts in August 1914 the Government of India responds quickly by dispatching an Army Corps (the Lahore and Meerut Divisions) to the western front. Captain Amar Singh is attached as aide-de-camp (ADC) to the commanding officer, Sirhind Brigade, Lahore Division.[28]

The story of the war on the Western front has often been told but usually without mentioning the Indian Army. Its role was crucial. At a critical moment in the early months of the war, when the British II Corps in Flanders was exhausted, demoralized, and without reserves, apparently unable to prevent an imminent German breakthrough, Indian reinforcements arrived. From the middle of October 1914, through the second battle for Ypres at the end of April 1915, units of the Indian Corps made the difference between stalemate and defeat. "It is hard to see," Philip Mason writes, "how the Germans could have failed to pierce the line" if the Indians had not been there and held.[29] According to John Buchan's contemporary fortnightly account, ". . . it was the performance of India which took the world by surprise and thrilled every British heart."[30] And a German soldier writes to the *Frankfurter Zeitung*: "Today for the first time we had to fight against the Indians. . . . At first we spoke with contempt of the Indians. Today we learned to look on them in a different light."[31] Amar Singh was there, at Betheune, St Omer, Hazebrouck, Neuve Chapelle. In June 1915, he is mentioned in dispatches.[32]

These events affect the commissioning process. In November 18, 1915, the secretary of state for India, Austen Chamberlain, telegraphs the viceroy, Charles Hardinge, about how to acknowledge India's contribution to staving off the German thrust through Flanders and beyond Lille. The mood is one of strategic urgency tinged with repentance. Now was the time to make amends for Kipling's racial and civilizational slur in the *Recessional* on the lesser breeds without the law.[33]

Here is the text of Chamberlain's telegram:

No. 2012.
Secretary of State to Viceroy. Telegram P., 18th November 1915,
7 p.m. [Recd 19th, 10 a.m.]

Private. Question of Commissions for Indians. Your private letter of October 14th appears to reserve question till after the war. But on Imperial grounds early action seems to me desirable in order to mark the part played by Indian troops in the war and refute the colour bar theory. I would propose selection of a few officers now in the Indian land forces, preferably from amongst those who are serving in the war, for commissions in Indian regiments. The selection would be based on merits and would have the advantage of giving concession as act of grace and not in response to agitation.

The following have, I understand, all proved their fitness for commissions in Indian regiments both as officers and comrades [note "comrade" rather than the more conventional peace-time usage, "gentleman"]: Captain Amar Singh, lieutenants Bala Sahib [Daphle] and Rana Jodha Jang. . . . lieutenant Malik Mumtaz Mohammed Khan and Captain Aga Cassim Shah also commend themselves by their past record, and there are doubtless others whom you could recommend. . . . Offer of commissions should be confined to those who will seriously take up soldiering as a profession.

. . . [A]s far as possible [selection] should be representative of principal fighting races.

I hope you will be able to concur, and if so be able to nominate a few suitable officers. I hold the view that, while some action is politically urgent, it will not, if confined as proposed to individual cases, prejudice the details of any considered scheme hereafter.

I should like to make the announcement on January 1st, and as I have not yet consulted Army Council or made submission to His Majesty, should be glad of an early reply.[34]

It did not happen—at least not on January 1, 1916, when Austen Chamberlain thought it could more easily be made to appear as an "act of grace and not in response to agitation."

By 1917, however, the impulses of 1915 had gained steam due to increasing nationalist agitation. They had also gained two important Liberal supporters. A new viceroy, Lord Chelmsford, and a new secretary of state for India, Edwin Montagu, were responding to the "powerful and increasing demand for a greater share by Indians in the administration of the country." King's commissions were offered to Captain Amar Singh and eight other former cadets on August 25, 1917, five days after the "momentous declaration" of August 20, 1917, committing Britain to "responsible government" in India.[35]

These nine were the first Indians to hold regular KCOs. Of the nine, four served longer than Amar Singh, Bala Sahib Daphle the longest, till 1929.[36] Their date of rank, August 25, 1917, preceeds by four years General Carriappa's,[37] the senior-most officer at independence who, in consequence, became India's first commander in chief.[38]

The backlash within the Indian Army against the politicians' notion that Indian officers could, by a stroke of the pen, be made equal to British officers becomes immediately apparent.[39] If liberal policy could not be blocked politically it could be sabotaged bureaucratically. The Indian Army's first countermove was to offer the initial seven newly-minted Indian KCOs disadvantageous terms of appointment, terms that would discourage them from accepting. Without consultation with the commander of their service, the inspector general of Imperial Service Troops, the seven former cadets, since 1905 officers in the NILF were informed in the telegrams announcing the commissions that they would all lose seniority, that is, be demoted, and as result receive less pay and smaller pensions.

Amar Singh, for example, was commissioned in the NILF on July 4, 1905, promoted to captain on July 4, 1914, and, in the ordinary course of events, would be promoted to major on July 4, 1920. Without warning, he was gazetted captain with promotion to major not due for ten years, that is, August 25, 1927, when he would be forty-nine. In other words, his date of rank as Captain after twelve years of service was made equal to that of British officers with four.

On August 5, 1918, Amar Singh writes to Zorawar Singh, his closest friend at the Corps and its top student, about their common problem. Zorawar Singh replies on August 18:

> My dear Amar Singh,
> I was delighted to receive your letter of the fifth.
> I had myself written to the I.G. Imperial Service Troops in January 1918 to find out whether our commissions in the Indian Army will be antedated so as to tally with the dates of our Captaincy in the NILF. I received a reply identical to the one you . . . received. . . .
> This hits us hard [over Rs 20,000 in pay in addition to the loss of seniority].
> I am thinking of sending a memorial to the secretary of state in the matter. Joint protests are against King's Regns. [Regulations] but it does not prevent us from sending identical individual protests, and I think that is the best course for us to follow. Failing a favourable reply to my memorial . . . I propose to resign my commission as a protest. I do not know how many may be prepared to follow my example in the matter for the sake of principle. However that will not alter my decision.
> Your way of protesting appears to me a bit mercenary if you will excuse my using that word. It is not a case of not having an ambition to Command B.O.S.; it is one in which principle is involved.
> They have partly recognized the justice of our case by granting us commissions in the Indian Army as Captains and not as 2nd Lieutenants. Why should they not go the whole hog?
> Hoping you will see the justice of my contention and do as I am doing. I feel sure Prithi [Singh], Bala Saheb [Daphle] and Mumtaz [Mohammed Khan] will do the same.
>
> Yours very sincerely,
Zorawar Singh
>
> P.S. If necessary I am prepared to go to England to work on our case.

Zorawar Singh's efforts fail. He resigns but the others remain. Amar Singh's "mercenary" way of protesting may have borne some fruit; pensions were to count from July 4, 1905, the date of the former cadets' commissions in the NILF.[40]

From August 25, 1917, Amar Singh is on active duty as a KCO in the Indian Army, first as a staff officer to General Knight in Bombay but soon as a squadron commander in the 16th Cavalry Regiment. He ends his Indian Army career fighting in Waziristan during the Third Afghan War. An acting major, he is probably the first Indian to command a regiment: in his diary he reports that on three occasions between September 28, 1920, and March 15, 1921, he assumed officiating command of the regiment.[41]

He tells us about an incident of insubordination by a junior British officer. It seems to have been an isolated incident, in part because of the way Amar Singh, his colonel and his fellow officers, all of course British, handled the situation. Class seems to have been as important as race in positioning the protagonists, Squadron Commander Major Amar Singh, his subordinate, Lieutenant Wilks, and Colonel Mears, the regimental commander.

It is late October 1919. The 16th Cavalry Regiment has been transferred from Delhi to Dehra Ismail Khan, on the west bank of the upper Indus, now a district headquarters in Pakistan's North-West Frontier Province. Lieutenant Wilks is a junior officer in Amar Singh's squadron.

> This fellow has been in the ranks and then for years as a clerk up at Simla. He got his commission lately. . . . I have never liked him . . . or the way he talks. . . . He gets on my nerves.[42]

Amar Singh may have had in mind an incident which occurred eight months earlier. In March 1919, while the regiment was posted in Delhi during Gandhi's first civil disobedience campaign, Wilks invited himself to dinner at a restaurant, left before the bill was paid, got "roaring drunk," arrived at the hotel "half unconscious and then, this morning, started drinking again as it was St Patrick's day. This is a fine way of celebrating the memory of a saint."[43]

> [Wilks] was posted to my squadron. He did not take much notice of me and showed his independence a great deal as he considered himself a favourite of the colonel. . . . Since coming here [Dehra Ismail Khan] he has hardly ever attended parade when the colonel was not on it. . . . The other officers were watching . . . and told me that Wilks was getting too bumptious and I must show him his proper place. . . . [Scott] said that it was absolutely necessary I should do it and that I could be sure of everyone backing me if I caught him at the right time.
>
> This made me take the step. . . . I was [putting on] my belt [when] I told him to . . . see that the squadron was alright and I would be down in a few minutes. On this he told me that he was going [on patrol] on a totally different road [from that ordered by Amar Singh the night before]. He then told me that the troops that were going with him had fallen in at a different place. I said that I had not ordered them to do so. He said he had done it. I then said that he might have asked me before doing it.
>
> This was too much for Wilks. He turned quite red and said, "Good God, man. I am on a totally different job and had received direct orders from the colonel." I said I did not care. I was commanding the squadron and he ought to have asked me. On this he said that we will have to go to the colonel over this. He had lost his temper, but I quite quietly said, "As you please."
>
> [After the reconnaissance] . . . he said that he was awfully sorry for making an ass of himself this morning and that it will never happen again. . . . I

thought he had considered that he was wrong and had no chance if he went to the colonel. In this I was wrong. . . .

When I came back . . . the colonel . . . took me to his room and began saying that this morning while he was dressing Wilks came to see him and told him that he was not going to take orders from me. The colonel told me he told Wilks off, ordered him to go back on parade and not to be a bloody fool. I was his squadron commander and he had to take orders from me. . . . He said that if ever he does it again I must jump on him. . . . If I found that any of them did not pay [me] the same attention as they do to Hill and La Touche [the other squadron commanders] I was to bring them before him. . . .

I shall be pleased when Storey comes and I get rid of Wilks who is really a dirty, low breed swine for whom I do not care in the least though I keep up appearances.[44]

Amar Singh's prominent role in the Indianizing of the Indian Army raised questions about nationalism as well as race and class. In March 1919, seven months before his encounter with Wilks, his regiment was sent to Delhi "in support of the civil" to deal with disturbances that might accompany the call by Mohandas K. Gandhi, a new voice in the nationalist movement, to join a satyagraha, a non-violent civil disobedience movement, to challenge and resist the authority of the recently passed Rowlatt Act. The Act was the extension of a draconian wartime measure permitting summary police action to combat "subversion."[45]

How should Amar Singh act as an Indian officer whose squadron's mission, to keep law and order, might involve firing on fellow Indians?

. . . [A]ll the leaders of Indian unrest and the majority of the thinking Indians were against [extending the Rowlatt act]. . . . The leader of them all is supposed to be Mr Gandhi. . . . a great fellow for passive resistance . . . [and] the most popular man in India at the moment . . . His suggestions are taken up much more promptly than even the commands of the viceroy. . . .

All the shops were closed and the poorer people known as "the mob" had free range. . . . If any of the shop keepers did not shut up they looted their place. They even went to the length of trying to stop running of the trains.[46]

The police was inadequate to cope with them and so the military were called out. . . . The mob collected in large force and would not disperse when they were ordered to and so the British soldiers fired on them—officially they killed about a dozen and wounded another two dozen or so. The Delhi people say that there were about sixty killed and over a hundred wounded.

This shooting quieted the rising . . . a great deal but it raised a great indignation in the mind of the public. All those there killed, were made martyrs, and the new thing was that Hindus were carried by the Mohammedans and the Mohammedans by the Hindus to their cremating and burying places respectively, with bands playing and flags waving. . . . Such sympathy had never before been heard of . . .

Now I will write some personal experiences. The first day when the riots broke out and the mob had been fired on we were discussing the matter in the mess. I just casually said that I was not quite sure whether they were right in firing and cited as an example a case that I had heard had happened in some former Dublin riots. The military had been called out and one of the junior officers had given the order to fire, on which he was badly told off and very nearly run in for manslaughter.

This story at once put the whole of the mess against me and they made up their minds that I was in sympathy with the rioters. They even reported this to Colonel Mears who subsequently told me about it.

The 16th Cavalry men were at Delhi for some time but I was never sent [from the cantonment, a residential area in which military live in times of peace]. I did not volunteer either because I did not want to undergo all the inconvenience. Besides this, though I had no sympathy with the rioters, I certainly am against the passing of the Rowlatt Bill for which all these troubles had taken place.

I was left to command the depot at the cantonments. [When I spoke to the commandant about the reason] . . . he told me that he had not sent me to Delhi during the riots and had selected me to stop with the depot because some people mentioned to him that I had said that I was well pleased to be out of the Delhi riots. He also said that the riots were mainly against Europeans and had nothing to do with Indians. Then different people had different opinions. . . . It was from these considerations that he had not sent me to Delhi.

The Colonel told me that he had no doubt whatever that I would have acted up to the moment but at the same time he did not want to put me in a position which was not to my liking. I thanked him very much for these kind thoughts.[47]

From his sketchy account, the end of Amar Singh's career as a soldier for the raj was unpleasant, ambiguous, even mysterious. It reveals, among other things, that Amar Singh's commission was the fruit of a moment of madness, of a temporary British elation about the Indian contribution to the war, and anxiety to reward and sustain it. As the euphoria of the Great War evaporated, its idealism lost in pointless destruction of life and military spending, the impulse to include Indians in the officers' brotherhood also faded. The moment of initiative by the Liberals in the English government had passed, their views reduced to a minority.

1921 is a year of financial stringency and severe retrenchment for the military establishment in India.[48] The Indian contribution during World War I disappears from public view, so much so that the story of KCOs for Indians in August 1917 is not mentioned in standard accounts of the Indian Army. Normalcy, which returns with a vengeance, means an Indian Army without Indian officers. The Esher Committee, which reported in 1920, indefinitely delayed if it did not entirely reverse the policy inaugurated in August 1917, by recommending that "the grant of king's commissions [to Indians] would be pre-mature at this stage."[49]

At the beginning of April 1921, Colonel Mears, still in command of the 16th Cavalry Regiment, visits Tank,[50] about 30 miles north of Debra Ismail Khan, where two of the regiment's squadrons, one under Amar Singh, are posted. During the course of this visit he shows Amar Singh his annual confidential report. "He had not given me a good report this year. We had some hot words over it. . . .

I was so annoyed with him that I told him plainly that the least he could do was to get me a year's [ordinary] leave and then I would take another [pending retirement] and go away altogether. He agreed to this."[51] We hear no more about the content of the report, which he seems to find so unacceptable that he cannot tell the diary. He resigns.

The nine cadets, commissioned in 1917, are eventually retired as officers in the Indian Land Forces, not in the Indian Army. The action seems to indicate that their commissioning as KCOs in the Indian Army is ultimately undone and, in that sense, "temporary."

It was not until 1929, that Indian officers with KCOs were given command authority but a "black man" still could not command a "white man" until World War II. Indian officers were assigned to segregated, that is all-Indian, units under the so-called eight-unit scheme.[52] It was Field Marshall Sir Claude Auchinleck, commander in chief of the Indian Army during the war, who ended discrimination. From his time, all Indian units, except Gurkha batallions, accepted both British and Indian officers.[53]

This is the story of the Indianization of the Indian Army which starts in January 1902, when twenty-four cadets, princes and nobles representing, in Lord Curzon's view, India's natural aristocracy, begin their first term at the ICC. Amar Singh "tell us what he knows" day by day, for seven terms and three years, about this first experiment in creating soldiers for the raj.

Dramatis Personae

Sir Pratap Singh. "Sarkar," regent of the princely state of Jodhpur, honorary commandant of the ICC, and patron of Amar Singh.

Major W.A. Watson. 1st Lancers, Central Indian Horse. Commandant of the ICC. "He is very mild and of a feeling heart."

Captain D.H. Cameron. 1st Lancers, Central Indian Horse. Adjutant of the ICC. "A thorough gentleman . . . [who] listens to the griefs of the cadets. . . . [and] a great horseman."

Wordi Major Deep Singh. "Native" adjutant of the ICC.

His Highness Maharaja Madan Singh of Kishengarh. The "baby maharaj." Cadet and constant companion of Amar Singh. A "thorough gentleman though a mere boy"; a fine horseman.

Kanwar Zorawar Sigh of Bhojpura. Highest ranked cadet and "The only man with whom I would have enjoyed conversation, but he is not a good rider."

Maharaj Akhai Singh. Amar Singh's old friend from Jodhpur, nephew of Sir Pratap. "We used to talk for hours . . . "

Nawab Iftikhar Ali Khan of Jaora. Imperial Cadet "He is the boss of the whole corps [and] . . . is good at nearly all [the sports]." Jaora and Amar Singh are rivals for the informal leadership of the teenage society of cadets.

His Highness Sardar Singh of Jodhpur. Reluctant cadet. "He lay the whole day on his bed talking to . . . his flattering servants."

1

"An Example for Others": First Term in the Imperial Cadet Corps

[The account opens with the news that a Cadet Corps is about to be formed and Sir Pratap, as regent of Jodhpur and reliable friend of the raj, will do his best to recruit suitable boys. This small group of some twenty cadets and three officers will create an institution that is something between an English public school and a military academy. Amar Singh's first term at the ICC has a honeymoon flavor: he is praised and admired, his comrades seem benign, his friendships rewarding. But his position with respect to both his peers and his teachers is peculiar. He has had only six years of formal schooling, and is in competition with others who have behind them the equivalent of a full higher secondary education. Yet he is more widely read than any other, and has the best or next to best command of English. Some of his peculiarities presage future difficulties. He is a twenty-three-year-old married war veteran inserted into the company of inexperienced adolescents five to six years his junior; he is an experienced soldier whom his teachers feel they have to retrain. Some of the younger fellow students, the maharajas, are his social superiors and expect recognition of their status.]

Jodhpore, Friday, 16th August, 1901

. . . At about four in the afternoon the [British] resident at Jodhpore, Capt. Erskine, came to see Sarkar about sending some boys for the Imperial Cadet Corps.[1] The following were shown today as fit for going: Maharajas Rattan Singhjee, Kishan Singhjee and Akhai Singhjee, Thakoors Gopal Singhjee of Gundoj, Kishor Singhjee of Bicamkore, my brother [Sheo Nath Singh] and myself. . . .

Tuesday, 27th August, 1901

. . . My brother could not go for the Imperial Cadet Corps owing to his not having studied in the Mayo College.[2] [It was Lord Curzon's intention that those admitted to the Imperial Cadet Corps should previously have studied at one of the four chiefs' and nobles' schools, of which Mayo College at Ajmer was one; the others were the Chiefs' College in Lahore, College for Chiefs in Indore and the college founded by Chester McNaghten in Kathiawar. Amar Singh too had not studied in one of these schools, but was presumably exempted in recognition of his war experience, strong command of English, and special favor of Sir Pratap. Amar Singh and his friend, fellow Jodhpur Lancer and comrade of the China days, Maharaj Akhai Singh, proceed to the Cadet Corps at Meerut, in Uttar Pradesh.]

Meerut, Friday, 3rd January, 1902

. . . I was up and after washing myself dressed and went out. There was a sergeant from some regiment, specially told off to drill us. . . . There are at present including myself only seven cadets. . . . He took us for a long double [time] . . . which finally ended in a run. The sergeant was leading and we all followed. After this he drilled us. He was simply teaching the timings and a few elementary things.

While we were at this drill Major Watson [W.A. Watson, commandant] came and so did Captain Cameron [D.H. Cameron, adjutant]. The latter introduced me to the former. Here I also obtained permission to get Ghatotguch and keep him as an extra horse. Of course the rules only allow . . . three private ponies but there is always a let out and so I am to keep it in the name of Deep Singhjee [native adjutant] who has only one pony.

. . . Captain Cameron called me and took Maharaj Akhai Singhjee and myself to ride with him. He also lent us his own ponies. After it was over I went to take my lessons. I am given to write a history of my family and an essay on my favourite game, polo.

Saturday, 4th January, 1902

. . . For dinner we had all of us collected in one tent and dined together. We are trying to start a mess and the beginning is quite hopeful.

Monday, 6th January, 1902

. . . In the morning I awoke early and sat down to read *The Memoirs of Baron De Marbot*, which I continued until half past eight when we were taken for that long run and then drilled at marching and turning. . . .

Today Captain Cameron . . . made each one of us read his own [essay]. I was the first to commence. Akhai Singhjee, Sardar Singhjee and myself had written about polo, Zorawar Singhjee on cricket, Basant Singh on football [soccer] and Pratap Singhjee about tennis. Zorawar Singhjee's and mine he chose and thought fit to show to Major Watson. I am quite satisfied to see myself not only compete but be rather a little ahead of Zorawar Singhjee who has passed the university degree of F.A.[3] examination whereas I do not know anything. I only read up to the sixth book [of English] without any mathematics, grammar, history, geography or any other thing. Captain Cameron was not only pleased but rather surprised at it.

After coming back I was just changing my clothes when Captain Cameron came to me and began to talk. That essay of mine about polo has given him a very good opinion of my abilities. He said that he looked upon me as the leading file among the cadets and asked me to set an example of mine conduct for the others to follow . . . He expressed himself thoroughly well satisfied with my conduct and . . . promised to look upon me as a father. What more could I want?

After giving me many more advices he went away but after a short while Pratap Singhjee of Kama [a relative of the Maharaja of Jaipur] came and I had to talk to him. He asked me my opinion about his not joining the mess because he fears that Maharaja of Jaipore [who observes stringent rules against intercaste dining[4]] would not like it and had sent word, though indirectly, to this effect. I advised him not to leave it as there was no excuse and even then if he did he would be chaffed . . . by the others. . . .

THE MEMOIRS

OF

BARON DE MARBOT

LATE

LIEUTENANT-GENERAL IN THE FRENCH ARMY

TRANSLATED FROM THE FRENCH

BY

ARTHUR JOHN BUTLER

Late Fellow of Trinity College, Cambridge

IN TWO VOLUMES

VOL. II.

WITH PORTRAIT AND MAPS

LONDON

LONGMANS, GREEN, AND CO

AND NEW YORK: 15 EAST 16th STREET

1892

---

about his disappearance, but I could give them no more than I have told here. He was an excellent officer and a good comrade.

But this digression has made me forget Tchichagoff, who, having been beaten by Ney, did not venture to attack us again all that day.

Having thus explained briefly the position of the armies on the two banks of the Beresina, I must say a few words as to what was taking place upon the river while the fighting was going on. The masses of unattached men—who had had two nights and days to cross the bridges, and who, in their apathy, had not taken advantage of them because no one compelled them to do so—wanted to cross all at once as soon as Wittgenstein's cannon-balls began to drop among them. The vast multitude of men, horses, and wagons got completely clubbed at the entrance of the bridges, blocking them without being able to reach them. Many were pushed by the crowd into the Beresina, and of these nearly all were drowned. As a crowning disaster, one of the bridges broke under the weight of the guns and ammunition wagons. All then made for the other bridge, where the confusion was already so great that the strongest could not withstand the crush, and a great number were suffocated. Seeing the impossibility of crossing the encumbered bridges, many of the wagon drivers urged their horses into the stream. But this method of crossing, which would have been very useful if it had been carried out in an orderly way two days before, was fatal to almost all who attempted it, because, pushing wildly forward, they hustled and overturned each other. Still, some reached the opposite bank, but as nothing had been done to prepare a landing by sloping away the banks—as the staff ought to have done—few vehicles succeeded in getting up, and many people perished there also.

During the night of the 28th, these horrors were increased by the Russian guns playing upon the wretches who were struggling to cross the river. At nine in the evening the cup of misery was overflowing, when Marshal Victor began his retreat, and his divisions came up to the bridge in good order,

Friday, 10th January, 1902

Today Major Watson taught me algebra. This is the first day that I have done it or rather seen the way in which it is done. It does not seem much difficult in the beginning. After a short while I began to understand it a little.[5] Then at about two we were called and measurements were given for our full-dress uniform.[6] It is going to be white.

Saturday, 11th January, 1902

I came back to my tent and having read the remaining few pages of *The Memoirs of Baron de Marbot*, finished it . . . Marbot was a lieutenant general in the French Army and was with Napoleon in nearly all his wars. He gives a very good description of every battle and the causes by which it was gained or lost as the case may be. . . . It suited my taste very well.

At half past eleven we went to take our lessons. Major Watson taught us English. First he examined our diaries which he has ordered every one of us to write daily and having corrected them gave a small dictation from the *Pioneer*.[7] After this he gave us a small composition and then we were allowed to go. By this new management of a diary which is to be shown to him, I have to write two. I cannot of course show this one in which I insert many private things and so have to write another one for that purpose.

Sunday, 12th January, 1902

Last night after dinner we played one game of cards and then began the recitation of Sanskrit. We all of us listened and Zorawar Singhjee recited it. This led on to singing. Kunwar Ram Singhjee sings very well. His t[u]ne being Gujarati sounds very sweet to the ears. They all recited a song or other except Akhai Singhjee, Gopal Singhjee and myself . . . I liked the singing of Jahawar Singhjee of Jaisalmere. Though I did not understand him much yet his t[u]ne being of mine own country and somewhat familiar I was greatly taken in. . . . [Amar Singh's response is unexpected. He has acquired a distaste for music from Sir Pratap, whose Spartan asceticism and rough-riding masculinity are repelled by the association of singing with the women's world, with the *nautch*, whose dancers are seductive and available, and with decadent drinking and carousing].

Monday, 13th January, 1902

In the morning I awoke early and after washing myself dressed and sat down at my table and began to do some examples of algebra. Sometimes I got the right answer but mostly wrong ones. Somewhere or other I miss the real point. . . .

Major Watson had to go and receive the Maharaja Sahib of Kishengarh. . . . He came at about one and I saw him for the first time. He is a handsome boy and a promising one too. Sham Sundar Laljee who is the prime minister of his state . . . asked me to take care and help his master in everyway. I . . . am myself delighted to be of some use to a Rathore prince.[8] . . . The maharaja sahib took me to his tent and showed his baggage. I said it was rather too much and he has promised to reduce it. Some superfluous furniture that he had ordered was also returned by my advice.

Tuesday, 14th January, 1902

Last night after dinner the Sanskrit tutor of the Maharaja of Kishengarh read us a lecture about religion. . . . There was not much in this lecture worth writing down. Sham Sundar Laljee dropped a few hints to me, though indirectly, to the effect that no one ought to criticise these things. I understood the hint alright . . . his view was the cadets who have not the proper knowledge and experience would naturally begin to slight their own religion and follow others . . . and so to keep them a bit stuck fast to the old ideas would be better. This was, I think, his view, specially for his own master, and I approve very much of it.

I drove with the Kishengarh maharaja in his trap. His age is seventeen years. . . . Of course he has always [been] living in his own house and requires lots of teachings. I take a special interest in him because Sarkar, my father, Ram Nathjee and Sham Sundar Laljee have asked me to take care of him. The last named gentleman has directed his master to take every help and advice from me.[9]

Wednesday, 15th January, 1902

. . . Sardar Singhjee and myself . . . went to call on the Maharaja of Rutlam. . . . I find that he does not in the least like . . . coming here but had to come when invited by the viceroy.

Tuesday, 21st January, 1902

. . . I was . . . called by H.H. the Nawab Sahib of Jaora[10] to listen to his phonograph which is a really nice one. I . . . intend getting one for myself.

We were . . . shown the full dress uniform. Capt. Cameron asked me if there was anything that I did not approve of. I said it was all right but on the kumerbund [cummerbund] there ought to be a belt, otherwise we would look like so many chaprasis [uniformed servants].[11] He is thinking the matter over and might . . . have it changed.

Wednesday, 22nd January, 1902

. . . After dinner there was a lecture[12] in the [Hindu] mess but I not caring to hear it went over to the other [Muslim] mess[13] and talked with the Jaora Nawab Sahib and his cousin.

Saturday, 25th January, 1902

. . . Last night after dinner we had good singing. . . . I was myself never fond of singing but now I am getting fonder. The more I listen the more I understand, and the more I understand, the more I am liking it. After all it is an innocent amusement.[14]

Saturday, 1st February, 1902

. . . I went to give a telegram to Sukhdeo Prasadjee [first minister of Jodhpur state, who has brought Maharaja Sardar Singh, to the Corps] I thought it would be rude to leave . . . the tent, especially when I had come there, without seeing the [Maharaja of Jodhpur]. After a quarter of an hour's waiting he did come and

PHOTO IV-1   Amar Singh in his "strikingly beautiful uniform of white with sky-blue and gold facings," the full-dress uniform of the Imperial Cadet Corps, *circa* 1902. Amar Singh's photo albums.

though I saluted again, there was neither a response nor even a nod or smile. However, like a fool, I waited for five more minutes.

The durbar asked Deep Singhjee to take a chair while he seated himself on his bed. Deep Singhjee hesitated, seeing that Gopal Singhjee of Gundoj and myself were standing. He was about to sit on the ground saying that the other two were to sit as well. There was no answer from the durbar but I hastened to say that he should take the chair and not mind about us. He took the hint and sat down. The durbar began to converse with him but as regarded us two, there was neither a word nor a look. Now, this was [more] than I could stand and so I returned to my tent without asking leave or saying good night.[15]

I repented myself for having waited on him, and vowed myself never again to go to his tent unless specially sent for or when ordered by my officers. If he does not care for me, what do I care for him?

Monday, 3rd February, 1902

Last night after dinner I went to the tent of Jodhpore durbar. He received me very kindly and talked until ten when he went to bed. He even said that I may come and talk to him whenever I had nothing else to do because he was always sitting idle. All his pride of being a maharaja has and will gradually disappear when he finds himself lonely. . . .

Sunday, 9th February, 1902

. . . I had a game of lawn tennis on the court presented by the Maharaja of Kishengarh to the cadet corps. I was however called by Capt. Cameron and talked to him until dinner time. Whenever he feels lonely or wants to have gossip, he sends for me. We talked on different subjects and he also made me read out of a small book written by an ancient Roman emperor [Marcus Aurelius]. It was [a] very nice and moralizing one indeed.

Monday, 10th February, 1902

. . . After dinner I . . . was sent for by the Maharaja Sahib of Kishengarh. I talked to him about his warming method. It was of course a little cold but not much. He was lying covered with blankets and a couple of servants were making him warm by applying cotton that was being warmed over fire. He listened to what I said and the process was stopped for the time. . . .

Tuesday, 11th February, 1902

Kishengarh Maharaja and myself went out for a drive. First we went into the city [Meerut] but found it very unpleasant, and so afterwards went over the outer roads. I had a talk with him whether he was betrothed or not. On his answering in the negative I advised him to care where he got engaged, and not look for money, as a good wife was the sole cause of a happy life. I also advised him not to marry more than one wife. . . .

[Maharaja Madho Singh of Jaipur has come to visit the Imperial Cadet Corps at the invitation of Sir Walter Lawrence, secretary to Viceroy Lord Curzon. Lawrence, who is soliciting support from the princes for the Cadet Corps, had considerable respect and affection for the maharaja, especially for those aspects that made him most emphatically an orthodox Hindu other. In his memoirs, *The India We Served* he recounts the much told story of the maharaja's sea voyage to England, accompanied by three enormous silver urns of Ganges water. Upon his arrival in England, elaborate steps were taken to guard the maharaja against seeing beef cattle in the countryside lest he enquire about their use.[16]

Madho Singh, a singularly unmilitary Rajput who does not like to ride, has allowed himself to be persuaded to make the visit. It provides an eagerly sought opportunity for Amar Singh. He hopes that, after qualifying in the Cadet Corps, he might receive an appointment in Jaipur state to build up and lead its old-fashioned and unprofessional military forces. Eager to ingratiate himself with Madho Singh, he starts with a considerable handicap.

A year earlier, while Amar Singh was in China, the maharaja's officers confiscated Kanota, Naila, and Gondher, the revenue-paying estates belonging to Amar Singh's grandfather and uncles, on the grounds that they had been fraudulently acquired when the brothers were ministers of Jaipur state. When the three

Champawat families bring a case contesting the confiscation, they lose in the Jaipur court. But on appeal, in a decision humiliating to Jaipur, the Government of India sets aside the judgment and orders the estates restored. Narain Singh, Amar Singh's father, having been the most persistent family member in pursuing the case, was very much in the maharaja's bad books, a hostility inherited by his son.]

Wednesday, 19th February, 1902

At half past two I went to the railway station to pay my respects to the Maharaja of Jaipore who came at twenty minutes past two. His private secretary, Baboo Sansar Chanderjee having come yesterday was there ready to receive the maharaja sahib.[17] . . . I explained my object to him and he promised to do what I wanted. [Presumably Amar Singh spoke of his desire to serve Jaipur state after finishing at the Cadet Corps.]

The special [train] was a very big one. The durbar is going to Hardwar [a sacred city and pilgrimage center on the upper Ganges]. Though there were some who knew me [in the maharaja's party]. . . . they none of them dared to come near or talk [to me].* . . . In the Rajpoot states . . . if the ruling chief is angry with a man no one goes near him and if one does it is in private when no one is watching. Here I shall give an example of an upright and truly noble mind. Baboo Kanti Chander, the prime minister of Jaipore, once told Mr Stothard, the assistant engineer, not to talk or mix up with the Champawats, meaning my family, as the maharaja sahib was not pleased with us. Stothard replied that if I don't do my work properly the durbar can make me do; but he has no business to choose . . . [my] friends . . . That must be left to . . . [my] own choice. Just think of these noble words. . . . People might say that Stothard is an Englishman and does not care for the maharaja as the latter can do no harm to him. . . . [But] it is moral courage and nothing else.[18]*

I was kindly allowed to escort the maharaja to Major Watson's house. When the maharaja sahib came out of his railway carriage I saluted him and presented two rupees [the conventional *nazar*, a symbolic offering that shows respect]. He did not say a single word to me. . . .

Tuesday, 20th February, 1902

Visit of the Maharaja of Jaipore.   . . . H.H. the Maharaja Sahib Madho Singhjee of Jaipore . . . had been induced to come and visit the cadet corps by Mr Lawrence.

When I went to see [the Maharaja of Jaipur] . . . I was called into his presence and ordered to sit down beside him. I refused thrice but at last obeyed his commands. He asked me how many cadets there were and why was Pratap Singhjee of Kama [a relative of the maharaja] not at the riding school. To the latter question I answered that he is not as yet a good rider. He directed me to help him and keep up the name of Jaipore. To this I answered that by his kindness everything would go on satisfactorily. When taking leave I asked if there was any service for me. To this he said that at present the only service he required of me was to study and drill hard. I promised to do all in my power and then took my leave.

I knew beforehand he would talk to me because Captain Cameron had told me the night before that Mr Lawrence had forced him to show me kindness and talk a little as the government had an eye on the case. I had no hopes that he would even look at me but contrary to that he even seated me beside him and asked a few questions as to how I was getting on.

The special [rail] carriage of the maharaja sahib was quite a big one and there were over two hundred men with him including a couple of his mistresses.

Sunday, 23rd February, 1902

I came to my tent and read a little of *Napoleon and His Marshalls*.

Saturday, 1st March, 1902

Our diaries having been corrected beforehand we were given a lecture on the uses of the words "will," "shall," "may," "might," and "to do." After that we were made to read a little of *Treasure Island*. . . .

Tuesday, 4th March, 1902

I . . . commenced reading *Washington and His Generals*. I was reading the account of Washington himself and was so interested that I went right through it. He is the noblest and highest character that I have yet read about. I was greatly taken by it. . . .

Thursday, 6th March, 1902

Last night after dinner I stopped in the mess for some time until all others dispersed. I was feeling rather melancholy because I had heard from Capt. Cameron that some of the boys are grumbling that I am too hard on them. I could not understand this because I am as kind, gentle, and friendly with nearly all of them as best I can. Through Zorawar Singhjee and Johar Singhjee I found that it is Sardar Singhjee [of Shahpura] who is grumbling. *He went so far as to tell some of the other cadets not to speak to me.[19]*

Saturday, 15th March, 1902

[A horse show and riding exhibitions are organized at Meerut. Sir Pratap sends Amar Singh a big chestnut waler gelding, Cockchafer, for his use in addition to Ghatotguch.[20] "He is as kind to me as a man can be."]

. . . I won a first prize on Cockchafer for the hunters and hacks [saddle horses] competition. . . . I again won the first and second prizes for pigstickers and the horse jumping on Cockchafer. The pigsticking competition was won by Ghatotguch and the second was Cockchafer.

The horse show was a very nice one and there was a collection of some of the finest specimens of horseflesh. Many officers were congratulating me on all sides. My officers, Major Watson and Capt. Cameron, and my father [who had accompanied the Maharaja of Alwar to observe the competition] were very pleased with me. All the people were admiring the generosity of Sarkar in giving such nice horses for presents as Ghatotguch and Cockchafer. After the show was over the lieutenant governor distributed the prizes. . . .

men would have stopped an army. Soldiers of the 39th and 85th, you are no longer French soldiers. Chief of the Staff, let it be written on their standards, '*They are no longer of the army of Italy.*'"

Nothing could exceed the stunning effect with which these words fell on those brave men. They forgot their discipline, and the order of their ranks, and bursting into grief, filled the air with their cries,—and rushing from their ranks, crowded, with most beseeching looks and voices around their General, and begged to be saved from such a disgrace, saying, "Lead us once more into battle, and see if we are not of the army of Italy." Bonaparte wishing only to implant feelings of honour in his troops, appeared to relent, and addressing them some kind words, promised to wait to see how they should behave. In a few days he did see the brave fellows go into battle, and rush on death as if going to a banquet, and prove themselves, even in his estimation, worthy to be in the army of Italy. It was by such reproaches for ungallant behaviour, and by rewards for bravery, that he instilled a love of glory that made them irresistible in combat. Thus we see the Old Guard, dwindled to a mere handful in the fearful retreat from Russia, close round him as they marched past a battery, and amid the storm of lead that played on their exhausted ranks, sing the favourite air, "Where can a father be so well, as in the bosom of his family." So, also, just before the battle of Austerlitz, in his address to the soldiers, he promised them he would keep out of danger if they behaved bravely, and burst through the enemy's ranks; but if they did not, he should himself rush into the thickest of the fight. There could not be a stronger evidence of love and confi-

---

NAPOLEON

AND

HIS MARSHALS.

BY J. T. HEADLEY.

IN TWO VOLUMES.

VOL. I.

SIXTEENTH EDITION.

NEW-YORK:

BAKER AND SCRIBNER,

36 Park Row and 145 Nassau Street.

1848.

WASHINGTON

AND HIS GENERALS

BY

J. T. HEADLEY

VOLUME I

NEW YORK

CHARLES SCRIBNER'S SONS

1899

---

ife, and without the power to order a single company, stood and saw his brave Virginians fall. At length Braddock was struck down, and his two aids borne wounded from the fight, leaving Washington alone to distribute orders. Here his military qualities shone forth in their greatest splendor. Galloping through the disordered host, his tall and commanding form towered amid the smoke of battle, and presented a constant mark to the sharp-shooters. Men were falling like grass on every side of him, yet reckless of danger, he spurred his steed over the dead and dying alike, straining every nerve to stay the reversed tide of battle. At length his horse sunk under him, and he fell amid his wounded and dead companions. Springing on the back of another, he pressed amid the throng, pointing in this and that direction with his sword, and sending his calm and resolute voice amid the frightened ranks, but without avail. A second horse fell beneath him, and he leaped to the saddle of a third, while the bullets rained like hail-stones about him. Four passed through his coat, and he knew that he was a sure mark for the Indian rifles as he thus rode from point to point. But he seemed to possess a charmed life; for while nearly half the entire army that had three hours before crossed the Monongahela in such beautiful order and proud array, had sunk on the bloody field, and three-fourths of the whole eighty-seven officers were dead or wounded, he still remained unhurt. Cool as a rock, his inward excitement was mastered by his judgment, and he galloped hither and thither as calmly as if on a parade. Absorbed in the fate of the army, and intent only on saving it, he seemed to forget he had a life to lose

Thursday, 20th March, 1902

At about half-past eight the Maharaja Sahib of Kishengarh and myself drove to T.A. Rust, art photographer, where we had some photos taken. First of all we both had a photo taken on horseback. The durbar rode Cockchafer and I Ghatotguch. After that we had another group taken in our plain coats and breeches. (See photo VI.4.) The third group was with our deshi achkans on ["native" coat, long and with a raised collar]. I had forgotten to take mine but the Durbar sahib was kind enough to lend me one.

Gurmukhtsar, Friday, 28th March, 1902

Notes About the Kadir Cup.   [During this first term in the Cadet Corps, Amar Singh is encouraged to enter the competition for the Kadir Cup. It is "one of the principal sporting trophies of India. . . . This tremendously exciting sport, in which a single man on horseback with a spear is pitted against boars . . . had been popular among the British since the early days of the East India Company. . . . On the great day of the Kadir Cup sometimes a hundred spears competed, and the men and their horses settled in gay tented camps . . . practising their runs with stampeding hoofs and dust-clouds in sunshine, like knights before jousting."[21]

Pig-sticking generated a cult almost as devout as that of polo, but rougher and more "jungly." The competition takes place in riverine or marshy country, where the pig hides in tangled thickets, and the chase is over difficult and uneven terrain. In 1902 the competition took place at the Meerut Tent Club. It was staged in the grassy marshes on the banks of the Ganges, at Gurmukhtsar, the port for the city of Meerut. The *jheels*, or lagoons, Amar Singh tells us, were full of water and long grass "which cooled it very much and made a real home for the wild boar." The ground is quite unpredictable: "This morning I had the experience of riding over a bed of melons. I was very near down with my horse."

Pig-sticking, like polo, creates a society of persons who share a passion for the sport, and a program of familiar activity: transporting the horses, laying out the terrain, sending out the beaters and elephants to drive the pig, drinking the health of the sport and its participants. It is a society that brings together gentlemen who hold with the English public-school understanding that manly sports, like cold baths and Latin, develop character. In raj memorabilia, pig-sticking at the end of a long, hard day is featured as one of the worthy routines of the peripatetic "collector" who settles disputes and administers justice for grateful rustics at camp tables set before tents in sylvan groves.[22]

Like polo, it creates a pantheon of heroes, an anthology of hair-raising tales and heroic performances, and a gallery of etchings and witty cartoons. Amar Singh's introduction to formal competition in 1902 leads to a long attachment to the sport and its mystique. His library at Kanota fort houses multi-year runs of *The Kadir Cup Journal* and *The Hog Hunters Journal*, as well as many books on pig-sticking.[23]]

II. The Camp

The camp had been beautifully laid under a grove of mango trees just at the foot of the sand hills. Most of the people competing had their own tents and arrangements. Those who had informed the honorary secretary before were provided with big tents. . . . I do not yet know what the hire will come up to. In these tents there was a bed, two tables, a wash-hand-basin, lamp and a tub. . . .

III. The Mess

The mess tent was a very big one with a long table in it. The food was just as good as could be expected under the circumstances. I was rather sorry to have joined it, because the natives do not like my doing this . . . [that is, dining with Englishmen. It is not clear whom Amar Singh has in mind when he speaks about "the natives." Sir Pratap would not object; Maharaja Madho Singh would.]

VII. The Heats

. . . Suffice it to say that . . . the winners were Col. Shiva Singh and Mr Barrett of the 15th Hussars who ran for the final, which was won by the native gentleman who is a nobleman of Patiala and commands the body-guard of that state's ruling chief.

VIII. Arrangements for Beat

The tract of the jungle that was beaten was in some part very long. It stretched for miles and miles. The beating was arranged as follows. There was a long line of twenty-six elephants which actually did the beating. Besides them there were about a couple of hundred coolies who marched in a line in front of the elephants. They did very little of the business, except making a great noise to no purpose. . . . As soon as a pig breaks out, the heat at the nearest . . . begins, and the beating ceases.

XVI. The Drinks Out Hunting

We got free [drinks]. Three or four coolies walked behind the elephants carrying bottles of soda water on a bamboo sling called the kawar. There was ice with them as well. Every now and then these coolies were called and people slipped off their elephants and stood round enjoying their drinks. It was quite a nice scene. . . .

XX. My Chances

My first chance was on Ghatotguch in which I got the spear in a very short time. The horse went very well. The pig . . . was quite a small one. He wanted to run across my horse and was speared. The other competitors were not very good ones . . . The second chance was on Cockchafer. He started very fast and I was the first man on the pig but the horse got so much afraid that, try what I may with spear and whip, he would not go within twenty yards. *I think it was the long grass waving to and fro as the pig moved through it that frightened my horse.[24]*

[At] the third chance . . . we found the pig nearly as soon as we were on the line. He ran straight for some time and I was leading at the time by at least three lengths. The others could not keep up the pace. I was just about to spear when the pig jinked to the right and ran right into Col. Shiva Singh, who was following at

"THE JINK"

The

HOGHUNTERS' ANNUAL

Editors:

Captain H. NUGENT HEAD, M.C.,

Major J. SCOTT COCKBURN, M.C.,
4th Q. O. HUSSARS.

VOLUME IX.

Copies obtainable from:

THE EDITOR, "THE HOGHUNTERS' ANNUAL"
24, Park Street, Calcutta.

THE AGENT, "THE HOGHUNTERS' ANNUAL"
Withington House, Andoversford,
Glos., England.

BOMBAY:
THE TIMES OF INDIA PRESS,
1936.

the proper pace, and got the spear. I am sorry to have been knocked out of it but am perfectly pleased that it was an Indian who beat me. I pray[ed] to God that he may give the cup to him in the end. Next to myself I wanted him to win. . . .

I made a mistake by going so fast. . . . I was over hasty. I had only one thought, of going faster and faster, and not of the chance of a jink. By this I lost my last chance of the Kadir this year.

XXI. The Hog Hunter's Cups

These are a sort of race run not on a regular course but across country. . . . I am almost sure that Ghatotguch would have won had he not fallen. Someone in front of me came down and my horse tumbled over him. I tried my best but could not stop as the pace was too fast. . . . The ground over which I fell was quite soft and nice. It was a river bed of fine sand. . . .

XXII. The Last Dinner

I am writing this short account to show how jovial the whole party was. As soon as the eating business was over, the bottles began to go round. First of all Capt. Balmain, the honorary secretary, got up and having made a short speech about the show, thanked the committee and suggested their health which was drunk unanimously. Major White then rose and thanked the honorary secretary. Then commenced the suggesting of healths all round. Every man round the table was mentioned and had to get up and make a short speech to thank in his turn the health drinkers and the man who proposed it.

Capt. Cameron made a short speech and suggested the health of those who had fallen down and mentioned my name and the manner in which I pluckily got up and rode the race. I hesitated for some time to answer but when asked from every side I had to get up. I thanked them all for the kind manner in which they had drunk my health and ended by saying that I could not have chosen a better place to fall on. At this they all laughed very much.

Capt. Balmain speaking about all the visitors mentioned Col. Shiva Singh and myself as the two representative from the natives of India and said that none could have represented the natives better.

There were two songs such [as] "The Boar" and "The Valley." When we were about to leave the table all of us stood and, crossing our arms, caught hold of one another and sang a beautiful song. This was all very nice fun. Every one was jolly and cheerful. I enjoyed myself thoroughly.

Dehra Doon, Monday, 21st April, 1902

Notes About My First Term in the Imperial Cadet Corps.

I. Rules

As regards rules I am attaching a printed copy to save the bother of writing them over again. I am sorry to write that these were not quite so strictly observed as I had thought they would be. However we went on all right.

Draft Rules for the Imperial Cadet Corps

I.   The Imperial Cadet Corps has been organized by His Excellency the Viceroy with the main object of providing a military training for selected members of the aristocracy of India, and of giving them such a general education that, whilst in course of time they may be able to take their places in the Imperial Army as British Officers, they may never lose their character and bearing as Indian Gentlemen. With this object in view the Cadets will be expected to acquire during their training a good knowledge of the English language, and at the same time to maintain an enthusiasm for their own history and traditions.

II.   The Cadets will be treated in every way as soldiers, and will be required to behave as such. Discipline will be strict. The moral side of their character will be closely watched; and tendency to immoral or [un]manly practices will be sternly suppressed; and, as the education is to be essentially military, every endeavour will be made to keep the Cadets in good physical condition.

III.   The Corps will remain under the direct surveillance of His Excellency the Viceroy, who takes a deep personal interest in its welfare, and will himself inspect it periodically.

IV.   The Cadets will be in attendance on His Excellency on occasions of State. [The model Viceroy Lord Curzon has in mind here seems to be the King's Bodyguard or Horse Guards, also an aristocratic military service prominent on ceremonial occasions. The ICC made its debut as the Viceroy's Bodyguard at the 1903 durbar held on the occasion of Edward VII's assuming in *absentia* the title Emperor of India.[25]]

V.   The Staff of the Imperial Cadet Corps will consist of:

(a) A Commandant. Major W.A. Watson, Central India Horse, has been selected for this appointment.

(b) A British Adjutant. Captain D. Cameron, Central India Horse, has been selected for this appointment.

(c) A Native Adjutant. Thakur Dip Singh, Commandant, Bikaner Camel Corps, has been selected for this appointment. A small establishment of servants, bhishtis [water carriers], and sweepers will be entertained.

VI.   Colonel Maharaj-Dhiraj Sir Pertab Singh, G.C.S.I., K.C.B., has accepted the position of Honorary Commandant of the Corps.

VII.   (a) Selected youths between the ages of 17 and 20 will be admitted to the Corps as Imperial Cadets. Education at one of the Chief's Colleges of Rajkot, Ajmere, Indore and Lahore, will, with rare exceptions, be made the basis of selection. At the start the age limit may be somewhat relaxed, but it will be strictly adhered to in future. [Amar Singh has not attended a chief's college and is overage. Although he was born in July

1878, the army and ICC records show his year of birth as 1881.]

    (b) Ruling Chiefs will not be excluded. . . .

VIII.   The selection will be made personally by His Excellency the Viceroy, in consultation with the Principals of the Colleges, with the local Governments, and with the authorities of the States to which the Cadets may belong. . . .

IX. . . .   (f) No Cadet will be allowed to bring with him any member of his family.

X.   The Corps will be located in camp at Meerut during the ensuing cold weather, and in the hot weather in quarters at Debra Doon. . . .

XI.   It is proposed that the course of instruction in the Cadet Corps shall last for between two and three years. . . .

XIV.   At the end of each term an examination will be held by the Commandant . . .

XVI. . . . (c) Any serious case of misconduct will be reported direct to His Excellency the Viceroy with a view to the offender being forthwith removed from the Corps.

    (d) The strictest attention will be paid to caste rules, and any infringement thereof by a Cadet will be treated as a serious offence.

    (e) No women will be allowed in or near the camp or quarters. . . .

II. Our Studies

These were not much. In the beginning we were taught . . . arithmetic and algebra for a few days but these were done away [with] and only English was kept. We were divided into three classes. . . . The first class was taught Green's *Short History of The English People* and *Treasure Island* by R. Louis Stevenson. [Green's *Short History*, the *Cambridge History of English Literature* reports, met with "a success unprecedented since the days of Macaulay . . . [and] assisted greatly in spreading and sustaining a living interest in our national past."[26]] Besides this we used to have dictation, writing summaries of what we had read, some Greek and Latin roots and English idioms.

Major Watson used to teach us. The lessons usually lasted for about two hours. The major sahib was always kind and I never saw him get out of temper with us. . . . We had no lessons to prepare at home except to write the usual diary which was corrected, or summaries . . . sometimes. The pronunciation was . . . corrected and explanations given on general topics or important subjects.

The second class was taught by Captain Cameron. Their studies was *Treasure Island*. They used to have dictation, a few Greek and Latin roots, and diaries.

The third class was taught by Professor Paonaskar, the private tutor of H.H. Kishengarh. . . . They were . . . beginners . . . during this first term.

A

SHORT HISTORY

OF THE

ENGLISH PEOPLE

BY

JOHN RICHARD GREEN

HONORARY FELLOW OF JESUS COLLEGE, OXFORD

WITH MAPS AND TABLES

London
MACMILLAN AND CO., LIMITED
NEW YORK: THE MACMILLAN COMPANY
1898

---

liberty and justice with the townsmen. The franchise of the town was extended to the rural possessions of the Abbey without it; the farmers "came to the toll-house," were written in the alderman's roll, and paid the town-penny."

The moral revolution which events like this indicate was backed by a religious revival which forms a marked feature in the reign of Henry the First. Pious, learned, and energetic as the bishops of William's appointment had been, they were not Englishmen. Till the reign of Henry the First no Englishman occupied an English see. In language, in manner, in sympathy, the higher clergy were completely severed from the lower priesthood and the people, and the severance went far to paralyze the constitutional influence of the Church. Anselm stood alone against Rufus, and when Anselm was gone no voice of ecclesiastical freedom broke the silence of the reign of Henry the First. But at the close of Henry's reign and throughout that of Stephen, England was stirred by the first of those great religious movements which it was afterwards to experience in the preaching of the Friars, the Lollardism of Wyclif, the Reformation, the Puritan enthusiasm, and the mission work of the Wesleys. Everywhere in town and country men banded themselves together for prayer; hermits flocked to the woods; noble and churl welcomed the austere Cistercians, a reformed outshoot of the Benedictine order, as they spread over the moors and forests of the North. A new spirit of devotion woke the slumber of the religious houses, and penetrated alike to the home of the noble Walter de l'Espec at Rievaulx, or of the trader Gilbert Beket in Cheapside. London took its full share in the revival. The city was proud of its religion, its thirteen conventual and more than a hundred parochial churches. The new impulse changed its very aspect. In the midst of the city Bishop Richard busied himself with the vast cathedral church of S. Paul which Bishop Maurice had begun; barges came up the river with stone from Caen for the great arches that moved the popular wonder, while street and lane were being levelled to make space for its famous churchyard. Rahere, the King's minstrel, raised the Priory of S. Bartholomew beside Smithfield. Alfune built S. Giles's at Cripplegate. The old English Cnichtenagild surrendered their soke of Aldgate as a site for the new priory of Holy Trinity. The tale of this house paints admirably the temper of the citizens at the time. Its founder, Prior Norman, had built church and cloister and bought books and vestments in so liberal a fashion that at last no money remained to buy bread. The canons were at their last gasp when many of the city folk, looking into the refectory as they paced round the cloister in their usual Sunday procession, saw the tables laid but not a single loaf on them. "Here is a fine set-out," cried the citizens, "but where is the bread to come from?" The women present vowed to bring a loaf every Sunday, and there was

III. Our Games

... Besides polo we used to have football [soccer] and lawn-tennis ... [and] the Hindusthani game Khari-Kunda which was started very late but played with great ardour. On dark nights they used to collect lamps and place them all round.

VIII. The Mess

The mess arrangements were not good. In the beginning Sardar Singhjee of Shahpoora started it but soon got disgusted because Deep Singhjee was always a hindrance. He wanted to employ his own private servants to save their food expenses. Besides this he was always dealing underhand with the modi [merchant who sold produce to the kitchen]. . . .

The food was quite simple. We used to sit round tables in groups of twos and threes as suited one another best. We used to have two sorts of meat, vegetables, chapaties [unleavened wheat pancakes] and sometimes kheer [a dish of sweetened milk and rice]. Some of the cadets who had been accustomed to good food always complained. For me it was just the same.

The Mohammedans had another mess of their own. They had English food and it was supervised by Capt. Cameron who also was a member of it. Arrangements were made to have a big mess for the Rajpoots after the English style and have food of the same style. They are even now proposing and we hope to have it soon.

IX. The Camp

This was very handsomely laid out. The tents were pitched on the three sides of the house in two rows. All round ran a road in the middle of the tent lines. The tents were quite nice and we lived most comfortably. The furniture was quite enough. The whole compound including the stables was always kept nice and clean. The house contained the office, the store and the Mohammedan mess.

X. Daily Life and How I Passed My Days

The daily life was full of work and I passed my days most agreeably. . . . I formed many new acquaintances and had a good name in the society. Most of the cadets liked me and the others respected me thinking me as one of the leaders. Capt. Cameron always considered me as such. . . . I never absented myself from drill or school. There used to be religious lectures on Saturday and Wednesday nights but I never attended. . . .

XI. The Society

Our society was high and good. All the Englishmen with whom we mingled at polo or other sports were good men and of high position. The cadet corps had a high society. . . . Big chiefs and nobles from all the parts of India had collected. . . .

PHOTO IV-2   The cadets' "Lines" at the Imperial Cadet Corps. These were "very hand-somely laid out. The tents were pitched on the three sides of the house in two rows. The tents were quite nice and we lived most comfortably. The whole compound was kept nice and clean . . ." Amar Singh's photo albums.

XII. The Officers

There were three officers and I shall take them separately.

1. First comes Major Watson not only because he was the commandant but also in all other respects. He is a short, well made man, neither too thin nor too fat. He has fine features, good temper and agreeable manner so he treated all the cadets alike, never showing favour to any one specially. All that I have heard and seen of him is good. . . . He is a religious man and wants everyone to stick to his own.

. . . He used to live in a house of his own where he used to entertain us all who cared to go on Sunday evenings to tea and badminton and croquet. His wife is a very agreeable woman and [whenever I went there] I used to play croquet with her. Unfortunately she is short sighted.

2. Next comes Capt. Cameron who is our adjutant. Like Major Watson, he too belongs to the 1st Lancers, Central India Horse. He is a tall, strong and fine look-ing man. He is hot tempered and gets out of it on the slightest mistake without considering . . . whether he himself is in the right or wrong. His anger does not

last long because he is good at heart. . . . He does not like to hear of other people's opinions when he is bent on doing something [but] if properly explained, then he does listen. . . .

He is very fond of horses and keeps a good many of them . . . but lacks in training. . . . He wanted his ponies to be as nicely trained as mine own and yet not trouble them. Thus . . . he used to ask Akhai Singhjee to work them instead [of me and] used to say that I was too hard on them. . . . He was more kind to me than most other cadets and often used to ask me to dinner. . . .

3. The third is Wordi Major Thakoor Deep Singhjee.[27] I am sorry to say he is not at all fitted for this post. He used to command the Camel Corps of Bikanere and his services have been borrowed. He was not on good terms with the maharaja sahib of that state. Deep Singhjee has a good name among Englishmen though not with us. Englishmen only see the outer things and not the real ones. He is good at flattering and talking. Though he has won the favour of his officers, yet his subordinates were never pleased with him. . . .

He has the bad habit of grabbing money whether by right or wrong means, so much so that in our mess he wanted to play the game. We knew of it and opposed his schemes hotly. He wanted to put in his private servants in the mess and we had some difficulty in putting a stop to it. He being an officer, we cannot say what we want pointblank but have to go round and round and tell things having two meanings. His education is not much and his pronunciation of English is simply too horrible. He is not at all a good rider, though he plays polo a little. He keeps following the others at a slow canter. . . .

XIII. The Cadets

[Amar Singh here provides a full list of the cadets.]

The following are the names of the imperial cadets and they are given in the same order as they joined the Corps:

1. Sardar Basant Singhjee of Atari, Amritsar District, Punjab.[28]
2. Kanwar Pratap Singh of Kama, Jaipore, Rajpootana.[29]
3. Raj Kanwar Sardar Singhjee of Shahpoora, Rajpootana.[30]
4. Kanwar Zorawar Singhee of Bhojpoora, Bhavnagar, Kathiawar.
5. Maharaj Akhai Singh [of Raoti,] Jodhpore, Rajpootana.[31]
6. Thakoor Gopal Singhjee of Gundoj, Jodhpore, Rajpootana.[32]
7. Banwar Amar Singh of Kanota, Jaipore, Rajpootana.[33]
8. Kanwar Jawar Singhjee of Jaisalmer, Rajpootana.[34]
9. Kanwar Ram Singhjee of Virpoor, Kathiawar.
10. Kanwar Khuman Singhjee of Dabri, Kotah, Rajpootana.
11. Kanwar Deo Singhjee of Palkia, Kotah, Rajpootana.
12. H.H. Maharaja Madan Singhjee of Kishengarh, Rajpootana.
13. Raja Samandar Singhjee of Weir, Bharatpore, Rajpootana.
14. H.H. Raja Sujjan Singhjee of Rutlam, Malwa.
15. Kanwar Bharat Singhjee of Amleta, Rutlam, Malwa.
16. Sahibzada Amanat Ullah from Tonk, Rajpootana.[35]

17. Kanwar Rai Singhjee from Chhota Udaipur, Gujarat.
18. H.H. Nawab Iftikharali Khan of Jaora, Malwa.
19. Nawab Vali Uddeen Khan from Hyderabad, Madras.[36]
20. H.H. Maharaja Sardar Singh of Jodhpore, Rajpootana.
21. Mohammed Akbar Khan of Hoti, Hoti Mardan, on the frontier [the North-West Frontier Province].[37]

. . . Some of these cadets are big swells. We all used to live harmoniously. There was no quarrelling though towards the end of the term there were ill feelings. Naturally we divided into separate groups and parties. . . . I will here give a detailed account of the parties.

Deo Singhjee and Khuman Singhjee are both from Kotah and not in good circumstances. They had no ponies and used to live a retired life among themselves. They seldom joined in any game but passed their days in each other's company. . . .

Then come the four cadets, Pratap Singhjee, Salamander Singhjee, Rai Singhjee and Gopal Singhjee. . . . These four have been coupled together because their temperaments are somewhat similar. . . . They are all four very quiet, timid and retiring boys. . . .

Now I will deal with the Maharaja Sahib of Jodhpore. As regards his character I need write nothing here because I have done so often and often. Suffice it to say that he only twice came to the school room and about four or five times to drill during the whole of the term. He was nearly always sick or pretended to be such. . . .

. . . About the two Kathiawar boys, Zorawar Singhjee and Ram Singhjee: The former is a very well educated boy and handsome looking. He is well and strongly built. He is not much of a rider but is good at tennis, football and other foot games. He is one of the leading cadets and mixes with us in society very much. His character is good and there is no fault to be found in him, He is on very friendly terms with me. . . .

Vali Uddeen is the second son of Nawab Vicral Umrao of Hyderabad. Vali Uddeen had been sent to England and had just returned when he was entered in here. He has studied at Eton College and so his education must be good. Here in the cadet corps he had a bad time of it. Some of the boys used to joke at him and gave him the name of "Rosy." Poor fellow. He does not know Indian things and is practically an Englishman. We none of us liked him. . . . He was quite unable to put on his own turban.

H.H. Rutlam, H.H. Jaora, Sardar Singhjee [of Shahpura] and Amanat Ullah come now in a group. I have given these four names together because these four are intimate friends of one another. H.H. Rutlam is a good horseman, a first class polo player and good at nearly all the games. . . . The Nawab of Jaora is a thinly built little fellow. He talks a good deal. He is a good rider and polo player. His education is fairly good. He is fond of singing and playing on the phonograph. . . .

Lastly I come to my real and dear friends Maharaj Akhai Singhjee and H.H. the Maharaja Sahib of Kishengarh. The former, that is to say Akhai Singhjee, has been my school fellow, brother officer and companion for the last fourteen years.

He is short and handsome looking. He has always been on very good terms with me. Though we have sometimes quarrelled on petty subjects we came out all right in the end. His temper is mild, good, and gentle and the more I observe of him the more I like. I am sorry to write that whenever I have quarrelled with him the fault has been mostly on my side. . . . He had a better education than I had but since he left the school he has not read a single book, with the consequence that he now lags far behind me. . . . I esteem his moral character very much. In fact he is one of the few whom I consider to be far superior to me in this respect. . . . I consider myself a brute when I compare myself with him. I can say nothing but complimentary [things] of him and will desist from writing any more for fear of overdoing and spoiling the whole thing.

Now I shall give the account of Kishengarh Maharaja, for whom I feel a sort of paternal love. He had been practically put under my charge by his prime minister, Baboo Syam Sundar Lalljee. I have always done and will ever do my best to help him. He is short in stature and thinly built. He is a nice looking little boy with good manners. He is very anxious of learning something and is quick at it. He has a sort of manner by which he seems as if not caring what the other man is explaining and this puts me out of temper often. . . . Many trifling habits which were rather vulgar he has left off by my advices. He is altogether too good and places a great confidence in me. I hope he will one day turn out to be one of the best ruling chiefs. . . .

[Amar Singh concludes his account of cadets by grouping them by what he calls "caste." Only one of his categories, Jats, refers to a caste as that term is conventionally understood, the rest being Rajput lineages and religious communities. It may be that because Rajputs comprise fourteen of the twenty-one cadets, Rajput lineage seems to him the most salient principle of organization. However, unlike persons from different castes, Rajputs from different lineages eat together and intermarry, that is, they treat each other as belonging to the same endogamous caste. For the officers organizing the corps the division which seems most salient is that between Hindus and Muslims.[38] Amar Singh early on mentions the possibility of a common mess. The diary does not tell what led to Mohammedan cadets eventually eating in one mess and all the other cadets, including the Sikhs and Jats,[39] in what Amar Singh refers to as the "Hindu"[40] mess, with some individual cadets making solitary arrangements. However, there is frequent participation by boys of the Rajput mess in the Muslim mess, brokered by the neutralizing force of "English" styles of eating.]

Here I will write the cadets' names with their castes.

TABLE 4.1   Cadets' Names with Their Castes

Rathores*	Bhatees*	Sisodia*
H.H. Jodhpore	Johar Singhjee	Sardar Singhjee
H.H. Kishengarh	Ram Singhjee	Sikhs**
H.H. Rutlam	Chauhans*	Basant Singhjee
Akhai Singhjee	Rai Singhjee	Jats***

(continued)

TABLE 4.   *(continued)*

*Rathores**	*Bhatees**	*Sisodia**
Gopal Singhjee	Khuman Singhjee	Samandar Singh
Bharat Singhjee	*Kachhawa**	*Mohammedans***
Deo Singhjee	Pratap Singhjee	H.H. Jaora
Amar Singh	*Gohil**	Vali Uddeen Khan
	Zorawar Singhjee	Mohamed Akbar Khan
		Amanat Ullah Khan

[*Rajput lineages
**Religious communities
***Caste]

2

"The Results of Sodomy": Second Term in the Imperial Cadet Corps

[The second term at the Cadet Corps opens at Dehra Dun, then a handsome retreat at the northern edge of the Siwaliks just below the Himalayan hill station of Mussoorie. Unlike Meerut in the plains below, Dehra Dun at 3,000 feet makes an active life possible despite the onset of the summer. The mellow beginnings of the first term for Amar Singh give way to more testy relations with fellow cadets and officers. Some of the adolescent cadets come to resent the imperious and pedagogic style which is the fruit of Amar Singh's greater age and experience. The Corps prepares for a visit from Lord Curzon. A scandal reveals British sternness over social mores and sexual practices in the era of Oscar Wilde; it also demonstrates the minuteness of British control over the quasi-autonomous princes.]

Dehra Doon, Saturday, 19th April, 1902

We were taken round for a ride on the roads in the form of an escort [in which Amar Singh feels honored to be included]. At a bridge, from whence we are to escort the viceroy, we were made to stand in a line and practised several times at the formation. The horses, being quite new, do not start quick enough and so we get jumbled up. . . .

[Sir Pratap, honorary commandant of the ICC, also arrives for the viceregal visit.]

Monday, 28th April, 1902

At half past nine we had stables at which H.H. Idar [Sir Pratap] inspected. . . . In the evening I put on my full-dress uniform and then went over and helped H.H. Kishengarh. Neither he nor his servants having done this before [they] find it an awful job to do. I soon did the thing right for him. At about five we were called in by Capt. Cameron and placed in exactly the same order as we shall have to stand when the viceroy comes. The escort was mounted and the rest of the cadets were on foot. Sarkar's horse . . . standing since a long time, began to jump and the durbar had to jump down and while doing it fell. Luckily he was not at all hurt and pluckily mounted again. . . .

Wednesday, 30th April, 1902

At about a quarter to seven the escort and the officers went to the bridge and had to wait for about an hour when the viceroy arrived. [His] bodyguard went aside and we took their places and escorted H.E. [His Excellency] to our quarters. In the short space in front of our mess the rest of the cadets were formed up. The viceroy on getting out of his carriage first came and looked round the escort. Everyone's name was called as he went along. He made a few remarks at each and went on.

After this the escort was galloped and trotted about in files and finally moved in line at a walk. . . . Afterwards we . . . were each one of us presented. When it was over the viceroy made a short but very nice speech and dismissed us. . . .

Thursday, 1st May, 1902

Notes About the Viceroy's Inspection.

V. What Was Said About Me

When I was presented [to the viceroy] Major Watson said that I belong to Jaipore and had been a soldier. His excellency asked whether I required reteaching, to which Major Watson answered that I had been in an irregular regiment and don't much care about fineness and show and that when one can ride well and is brave enough they don't think there is any necessity of learning anything else. Lord Curzon asked whether I would be all right by the time the Delhi durbar came. Major Watson answered that I was sure to [be] as I was a beautiful rider. Then His Excellency inquired if I knew English. Major Watson said that I knew it well and was very well grounded in it. He said that I was the best in it. The viceroy was pleased to see the China medal ribbon and Major Watson explained that I had been in the expedition with Maharaj Col. Sir Pratap Singhjee . . . I have not written a single extra word for self praise. I have, as far as possible, used their own

PHOTO IV-3   Viceroy Lord Curzon inspecting the Imperial Cadets, 1905. He considered the empire "under Providence, the greatest instrument for good that the world has seen." Founder of the Imperial Cadet Corps, he defended his "dear child" in the face of "military opinion" in Great Britain and India. Amar Singh's photo albums.

words and these only as a memorandum and not for show as some would think. Of course this diary is quite a private thing and not to be shown to other people.

Wednesday, 7th May, 1902

Major Watson sent Akhai Singhjee to the second ride as a punishment for not looking at the right and being unattentive. This was a very sad incident. . . . I had some difficulty in consoling Akhai Singhjee, who was sobbing and weeping like a child at the degradation.

Thursday, 8th May, 1902

Last night after dinner Swami Prakash Nandjee gave us a lecture about the existence of God and some other facts of our daily life. His chief aim being that we Indian people are very apt to copy the Englishmen in their dress and other superficial things but not the real good habits and manners. Major Watson attended the lecture. . . .

Monday, 12th May, 1902

I was about to go to bed when Akhai Singhjee came in and we began talking. The talks were on common subjects in the beginning but towards the end they turned on the most private ones. We began to compare our experiences. It was a damn fine pleasant time too for us. We laughed at each other. This talk made us late for polo. . . .

 A Few Notes About Captain Cameron.   For some time past I have been intending to write some notes about Capt. Cameron. A man's thoughts and ideas are continually changing and so I am hastily sketching a little of his character as [it] is at present impressed upon my mind. I used to like Cameron while we were at Meerut in spite of being warned that he was not a man to be relied on. I now find my mistake. Ever since my coming to Dehra Doon I have found him not quite pleased with me. Nor does he like Akhai Singh now. He is very fond of the Jaora Nawab [whose tutor he was before coming to the Cadet Corps] and H.H. Rutlam. He takes an interest in the Mohammedan boys but not the Rajpoots. At riding school the Nawab of Jaora is put on the right as the leading file though he does not know anything and he has absolutely ruined his horse. If anyone else had done so, I do not know what [Cameron] would have done. The nawab always gives a curt reply and Cameron keeps silent whereas we poor fellows have to keep quiet. Akhai Singhjee who has passed the riding school examination as an instructor with the 16th Lancers is not considered fit for a leading file.

Akhai Singhjee and myself are continually worried at riding school. This is merely to show that we don't know anything and that swab of a fellow is teaching us. I can quite safely say that for some time to come I can teach riding and horsemanship to Cameron and Major Watson. What do they know? They cannot train their own polo ponies. They do not know how to teach young horses to jump. They know only to crack whips or shout. If we suggest anything it is disregarded.

I have become quite sullen here. I [have] not much to complain against Major Watson but enough against Cameron. I am beginning to hate him though for decency and flattery I have to keep up appearances. . . . This beggar does not like my playing of polo whereas all the good Jodhpore players do. He thinks I cannot play as a No. 1.[1] The fool. If I once played with all vigour and was kept well supported from behind by my No. 2, he will soon find out his mistake. I am considered not good enough for a tournament and neither is Akhai Singhjee. Good God! With all this self esteem and boast of his, he does not feel that the other day H.H. Kishengarh, Akhai Singhjee and myself gave an equal game to Jaora, Rutlam and Cameron. Think, they are going for the Simla Tournament. What fine fellows.

Once I plainly told Cameron that I would not play as a No. 1. This greatly displeased him. Nowadays I always take care and bump about Jaora and Cameron just to show them what I am worth, whereas if I play on their side I simply canter about, hit wide and don't leave the ball when called from behind. Cameron knows this all. At Meerut he used to talk to me a good deal; now he does not even look at me. . . .

Thursday, 15th May, 1902

Notes About the Tea Party.   . . . We had been invited four or five times to tea by Zorawar Singhjee and Ram Singh. Now we thought it proper to call them some day and we did so. There were Zorawar Singhjee, Ram Singhjee, Gopal Singhjee, Sardar Singhjee, Jawar Singhjee and two of us, that is Akhai Singhjee and myself. All of us partook of the butter and bread, sweets and tea except Zorawar Singhjee, who absolutely refused on the ground that he just had his tea and would have nothing more. Well, this was a downright insult and I knew its cause as well. It would have been better if he had not come at all.

The cause was this, that last time when we went to tea with them Zorawar Singhjee and Sardar Mohammed Khan began eating out of the same plate, just as if they were Rajpoots of the same sort. I was quite surprised at it. What do you think were my ideas when Zorawar Singhjee got up and began to give mouthfuls to every one? This giving of "mouthfuls" is an Indian custom and denotes great love and friendship. I had to refuse and did refuse on the ground that I had enough. Akhai Singhjee and Gopal Singhjee did the same when they saw me do it. I just hinted Gopal Singh about it. Zorawar Singhjee had to sit down but was quite ill at ease.

Now I will never eat with Zorawar Singhjee, not because he did not take tea with us but because he eats with Mohammedans and out of the same plate too. There is no objection to my dining with him in the English way but there is in that of the Indian. However great a friend may be he has no right to ask his friends to eat with one of the other caste. I don't know what put this into his head. He must be crazy to think we would accept his mouthfuls from out the plate in which a Mohammedan is eating. How foolish and ridiculous.

Sunday, 18th May, 1902

. . . I was invited to tea by Zorawar Singhjee, I had also a short nap for about an hour. In the evening we went to Major Watson's house and had tennis and badminton. . . .

Monday, 19th May, 7902

I was alone and amused myself with my thoughts. Sometimes I was at Satheen and sometimes Jaipore. . . .

Wednesday, 21st May, 1902

Last night after dinner Akhai Singhjee and myself talked for a short while and then wrote a couple of Hindi songs into my copy book. These are the ones that Akhai Singhjee's wife had sent. I corrected them all which was not at all an easy task as they were full of mistakes and some of the verses had been omitted altogether. . . .

Monday, 26th May, 1902

. . . 2. Wasting other people's time is wrong, yet common. Time is life, and as no one has any right to take another's life, so he has none to occupy his time, except by consent and to advantage.
3. To waste time in bed not required for sleep is especially pernicious, because it often begets impure thoughts and feelings, which lead to sinful conduct.
4. An idle head is Satan's workshop.

From *Science of Life*
by G.S. Fowler

Sunday, 1st June, 1902

Among my letters that I found on the table was one from my sister announcing the sorrowful news of my mother's illness. I am very sorry. My sister wrote that my mother wanted me to come. . . . When I thought over all the love she has for me and for the little brothers and my sister I began to weep. Tears ran copiously and the sobs came involuntarily. I had a bath which cooled me a bit . . .

Tuesday, 3rd June, 1902

At about five Major Watson came and having called all of us together told the news about the peace in the Transvaal. So the Boer war is at an end at last.

Major Watson gave a nice little speech and in the end before dispersing we gave three cheers. . . .

Saturday, 7th June, 1902

. . . Tonight we had a big dinner given by H.H. Kishengarh in honour of the declaration of peace in South Africa. The Mohammedans had it in their own mess though the arrangements had been made by him. Then there was a big dinner in the Rajpoot mess where all the cadets assembled. . . .

After dinner we had a good speech by Swami Prakash Nandjee. He simply explained at large all the comforts and benefits conferred by the British government on India. . . .

. . . It was a very nice dinner and the arrangements too were very good. We dined in plates on the table. These were deshi plates and nearly all of us sat down two and two together.

Just at the end of the dinner H.H. Jodhpore and myself were about to come to high words. He wants to impose on me as he does on others but I am not the man to listen to such nonsense.

Tuesday, 10th June, 1902

1. All thoughts, all passions, all desires,
   Whatever stirs this mortal frame,
   Are ministers of Love,
   And feed his sacred flame.
2. Impatience, irritability, and fretfulness are sure signs that lads or lasses are secretly abusing themselves. Till then they hear everything; afterwards, nothing. Any boy who has contracted this direful habit is sure to manifest its consequences either in his looks or his acts or both. He is entirely unable to conceal its results. . . .

> From *Creative and Sexual Science*,
> by Professor G.S. Fowler.

When I went to lessons and just before Major Watson came I learned that some of the cadets had nicknamed me "Rough Rider Sergeant Major." I told them all that I neither joke with anyone and nor like anyone doing the same to me. None has as yet called me by this name. [The epithet may carry a double load: that Amar Singh is too bossy, and that he is more like a non-commissioned officer than a "gentleman."]

Wednesday, 11th June, 1902

I woke at four and while I was shaving H.H. Jodhpore came in. Seeing him alone I asked him why he was displeased with [me]. He said that he was so before but not now. The cause of his being so before was that I never used to go to him. . . .

Sunday, 29th June, 1902

Last night I had dinner in the Mohammedan mess as Aga Kasim Shah had invited me . . . he is the nephew of H.H. Aga Khan, and . . . will one day fill that place, which is the head of the Khojas"[2]* [an important Muslim religious community]. Besides myself the Maharaja of Jodhpore, Akhai Singhjee and Sardar Singhjee had been asked as well. . . .

Tuesday, 8th July, 1902

We were given a lesson in topography. We were shown how to draw a map and what were the different signs of the different places. This subject is rather a difficult one though interesting. *I, having not learned arithmetic am very dull at it. Capt. Cameron was trying all he was able to do to teach me but I could catch nothing of it at all.[3]* . . . I drew a map of Ratanada, Jodhpore, as we had been given as a home lesson. . . . I chose the place where I had passed nearly all my life up to the present.

four hours' run up-stream an error of 2 miles in the total distance was made, or an average of half-a-mile an hour, whilst in the three hours' run down-stream an error of 2 miles was made, or an average of $\frac{2}{3}$ of a mile every hour. Hence the rate of the stream is clearly somewhere between $\frac{1}{2}$ and $\frac{2}{3}$ mile *less* than it was estimated to be, and taking it roughly at $\frac{1}{2}$ mile, the true distances run will be as follows:—

$$4 \times (10 - 1\tfrac{1}{4}) = 4 \times 8\tfrac{3}{4} = 34\tfrac{3}{4} \text{ miles.}$$
$$3 \times (10 + 1\tfrac{1}{4}) = 3 \times 11\tfrac{1}{4} = 34\tfrac{1}{4} \text{ ,,}$$

The mean of these giving 34·25 miles. (The correct distance by calculation is 34·28 miles.) Since this distance is shown on the reconnaissance sketch by 32 inches the true scale of the latter is about $\frac{32}{34\cdot25}$, or ·93 inch to a mile.

To continue this reconnaissance at a scale of 1 inch to a mile, with the average rate thus ascertained to be 8½ miles up-stream, each 1-inch space on the sketch should be reckoned as seven minutes, and to continue it down-stream, each 1-inch space should be reckoned as about five minutes.

The main point in such a method of measuring distances by "time" as the preceding is to adopt a *definite* space (shown by parallel lines $\frac{1}{2}$ inch or 1 inch apart) and give it its correct value by experiment. The converse method of making each space represent a fixed number of minutes is not suitable for this class of work, as it entails measuring decimals of an inch and using parallel rulers or marquois scales to divide the paper into the required spaces.

Sketches based on time measurements have also been made with great success from free *balloons*—working on much the same system as when sketching from a steamer.

The paper is divided into 1-inch spaces, and the rate of the balloon having been taken over a measured distance, or otherwise ascertained, each 1-inch space is given a certain value in minutes. For example: With a balloon running at 20 miles an hour, to sketch at 1 inch to a mile, each 1-inch space on the paper would be marked as three minutes.

In sketching from a balloon the work is done *with reference to the course already run*, and not by attempting to look ahead.

The paper, which is rolled on a cavalry sketching board, is ruled into 1-inch squares, the line down the centre being taken to represent the course of the balloon. The magnetic bearing of the course run is taken from time to time by observing with a compass the direction of any farm, tree, &c., over which the balloon has passed some minutes previously.

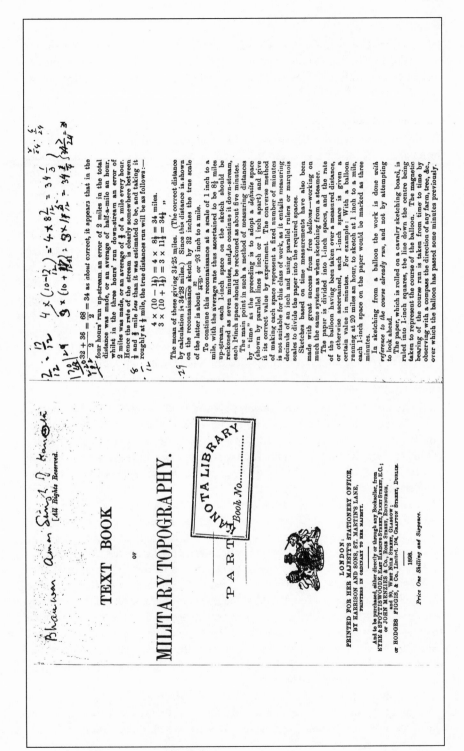

TEXT BOOK

OF

MILITARY TOPOGRAPHY.

PART

LONDON:
PRINTED FOR HER MAJESTY'S STATIONERY OFFICE,
BY HARRISON AND SONS, ST. MARTIN'S LANE,
PRINTERS IN ORDINARY TO HER MAJESTY.

And to be purchased, either directly or through any Bookseller, from
EYRE & SPOTTISWOODE, EAST HARDING STREET, FLEET STREET, E.C.;
or JOHN MENZIES & Co., Rose Street, Edinburgh,
and 90, West Nile Street, Glasgow;
or HODGES FIGGIS, & Co., Limited, 104, Grafton Street, Dublin.

1898.

Price One Shilling and Sixpence.

Monday, 14th July, 1902

After stables I went to Capt. Cameron. . . . while there the conversation turned about the dismissal of [Karan (a pseudonym)] Singhjee.[4] Capt. Cameron told me all about the dismissal. It was owing to the nasty habits of sodomy and masturbation that he was turned out. . . .

Tuesday, 15th July, 1902

While on our way from the mess Zorawar Singhjee and myself compared our notes about the dismissal of [Karan] Singhjee. Major Watson had told all about [it] to Zorawar Singhjee with instructions to acquaint all the cadets with it without mentioning his [Watson's] name. . . .

Thursday, 17th July, 1902

Last night after dinner I went to Kishengarh maharaja and talked to him. While I was there Jodhpore durbar came and we had a few cross words. He is proud that he is acting wordi major[5] but what does that matter to me? Not one damn. . . . Akhai Singhjee came in. . . . He said that I did not do . . . well to argue with the durbar. He says so because the durbar is kind to him. . . . Why should I not keep up my manly bearing, instead of flattering like a courtier. . . .

I woke at three and after washing and shaving myself went to the smaller polo ground where we had cricket. I hate this beastly game very much. I would never play it if it was not compulsory. It spoiled the whole of my afternoon. . . .

Thursday, 17th July, 1902

Notes About The Dismissal Of [Karan] Singhjee.   [The prevalence of homosexuality—a recurring subliminal theme in the diary—Amar Singh's homophobia, and British and Indian attitudes toward homosexuality are not the only themes of this account. It also features the minute monitoring of the private behavior of princes by members of the Political Department, the raj's representatives in the princely states.]

. . . My father had dropped me a hint about the bad habits of this unlucky cadet at the very beginning. I was not only warned to keep from this boy only but from the Raja Sahib of [Rohari] as well. Besides this I had known this boy to be bad from beforehand and was informed by Jawar Singhjee as well.

Having all these warnings I began to watch this fellow. Knowing my father well, he kept on good terms which bordered on friendship. Then I began to see that he was making friends with Akhai Singhjee but there he found that that boy was not of his habits and so he had to leave off all hopes. By this time they formed their own party with some others of that sort. Luckily at Meerut there was not much bad work done. However these fellows in this party began to hate me because I would not mix up with them. They even went so far as to report to the officers that I was harsh and strict to them.

The brutes, what business had I with them? I began to see there that matters were going on too much ahead. Masturbation and sodomy had commenced in the corps. I did not actually see anyone but there was no doubt about the suspicions that I had. It was not I alone who suspected, but most others did the same. I watched them very closely. . . . I had told my father how someone had reported against me to my officers and how I afterwards found it out that this was [Karan] Singhjee. Of course my father was sorry to hear of this, and a father's love prompted him to acquaint Capt. Cameron and Major Watson about the real conduct of [Karan] Singhjee, which ruined the poor fellow's character. My father did this only for my love. He thought, and rightly too, that by letting the officers know that [Karan] Singh was a bad character he (my father) would secure me against petty complaints. This was at least what he told me. [We find out, from the entry of August 9, that Amar Singh's reconstruction here overestimates his father's role. It was a letter intercepted by the Political Department monitoring one of [Karan] Singh's correspondents, a prince, that put the ICC officers on [Karan] Singh's trail.] However, this had its full effects which were not at all meant. Capt. Cameron told me the other day, while acquainting me about [Karan] Singh's dismissal, that my father knew very well about all this.

. . . When we arrived here [Dehra Dun, second term] I found that these fellows were forming a closer friendship and that their number was increasing. One night Deep Singhjee had come to me to tell [me] that I had better attend the mess regularly as the others were also not coming by following my example. While we were talking about it the conversation turned on the characters of the cadets and Deep Singhjee told me plainly that with the exception of a select few nearly all were bad. . . . This fact shows that at least one of the officers was well acquainted with this business. . . .

The very morning that Major Watson returned from Simla, and even before coming to school, [Karan] Singhjee was sent for from the class and we never saw him again. During the five minutes' interval we heard that he had suddenly left for [his home]. After school we all began to enquire and knew for certain that he had been dismissed. . . .

We were all very keen to ask the reason but none dared to ask the officers. . . . I was the first who dared to put this question to Capt. Cameron. I had gone to show him my cousin Bhoj Raj Singhjee's letter. Cameron asked me whether my father would send Sheonath Singh [the second of Amar Singh's five younger brothers] here or funk owing to [Karan] Singhjee's dismissal. This was the opportunity.

I said that I did not know why he had been turned out. On hearing this, sahib took me out in the open and began to explain. This was a delicate subject and he did not know how to begin. . . . He said that he knew [Karan] Singh had this bad habit from long before but it was thought that he had probably forgotten it. It is now found out that he has not done so but during the holidays some letters or some sort of proofs have been got which lay the charge fully at the culprits feet. By those letters it is proved that he had been trying to induce some of the others to this business.

The captain said that nothing bad had actually been done. I informed the sahib that I knew all about [it] but still he insisted that I did not. The cause of his insisting this point was probably to convince me that nothing actually happened.

Sahib would not tell me any names but there was no need of that. Probably I knew more things than the sahib did.

In the end I was told to inform if I knew of any other bad fellow and never hide it as the honour and good name of the corps was not only in the keeping of the officers but the cadets as well. . . . His point is that it [should] be known that this is an institution where such things are most rigorously stopped, that nothing bad has actually happened, and that on the slightest proof of a bad character, even while on leave [such behavior] has been punished by dismissal within an hour's notice.

He asked me what I thought as to the feeling of the Rajpoot chiefs and whether they would hesitate to send their children. I said that when this fact is known they would most willingly send their boys and that it was this cause which has lowered Mayo College in the eyes of all Rajpootana. . . .

Friday, 18th July, 1902

During this time I read and finished the *Meditations* of Marcus Aurelius,[6] translated from the Greek by Jeremy Collier, revised with introduction and notes by Alice Zimmerman. It is a very nice little book. I liked it very much indeed. It contains spiritual and saintly ideas. What sound principles and judgment Aurelius had. He was a truly great man.

Monday, 4th August, 1902

This morning we were all of us ordered to be present at nine o'clock as there was the examination. . . . In arithmetic . . . I could only do four [questions] and even they were not rightly done. Time was three hours. I fear I shall fail in this subject. . . .

Tuesday, 5th August, 1902

At nine we went to school as it was examination. Major Watson was punctual and the papers were distributed. There was only English composition with 300 marks. For subject we were given to write a letter to any friend about the life in this cadet corps. The time was three hours. . . .

I find that out of the 300 marks of arithmetic I have got 145. This was quite unexpected. I never thought I would get anything over thirty. . . .

Wednesday, 6th August, 1902

. . . The first class [was examined] in Green's *Short History of the English People*. . . . I did all the questions though I fear not so well as some of the others. I have never learned or read history before and that is what makes matters worse. . . .

Friday, 8th August, 1902

I went to Kishengarh durbar and gave him a paper in which I had written down the most important things that were likely to be asked in the drill examination . . . [and] went to bed at eleven. In the morning I . . . went over and taught a few more things to Kishengarh maharaja. Sergeant Chapman came there and pointed out some more things. . . . At ten we collected in the school for the last day's examination. First there was a military paper in which there were two hundred marks and the time was two hours. . . .

Friday, 8th August, 1902

I Become A Father.   Yesterday I received a letter from Jaipore, written by Umaidjee [the family priest] in which he informs me that my wife has given birth to a girl on . . . the July 30 last. All my family were expecting a son and so was I. It is rather a disappointment to them all. As regards myself I do not much care whether the child is a male or is female. What I most care is for my grandfather. What a disappointment it must have been to him. . . .

I have kept this thing very secret in this corps and had told to Akhai Singhjee who in his turn has informed the Maharaja of Kishengarh. Why I have been so keen to keep the matter quiet is that I do not want to be talked about and congratulated from everyone. Then besides this, people crack jokes at you. These are the things. Ram Nathjee is the only other man who shall hear from me about it. [See also Part V, 1.]

Saturday, 9th August, 1902

Something Old And New.   . . . Akhai Singjee told me that H.H. the Maharaja of Jodhpore had once dropped the following hint, in private, that [Karan] Singhjee had not been dismissed for any misconduct in this corps but because he had written a letter to the Maharaja of [Anantpur] in which there were several silly things which proved, without a doubt, that these two fellows had and were still having this beastly connection of sodomy. Now, this letter was, by some chance, intercepted by . . . the guardian to the Maharaja of [Anantpur] and was forwarded to the foreign [and political][7] office through the proper authorities. Major Watson did not know anything about this matter until the time he went to Simla where he received his orders to dismiss [Karan] Singhjee and which order was at once carried into effect on his coming back.

Now, this information through Akhai Singhjee has put the things in its clearest light. . . . I was thinking that it was my father who had told the captain sahib and the major sahib. . . .

Sunday, 10th August, 1902

The Result Of The Summer Examination.   Here is the sketch of the summer examination of the first class [the most advanced class]. I am glad to write that I stand second. I had no hopes of it at all. I was greatly handicapped in arithmetic and it was owing to this that I lost my marks in drill. Then history was quite a new subject for me. I had never learned or even read it before. . . . However, thank God, I have done the thing creditably. There is only one subject in which I stand first and that is the first paper of composition for which we had to write a letter to a friend, giving an account of our life in the cadet corps, and describing the specially marked events of which, I am sorry to say, there were not many.

TABLE 4.2   Result of the Summer Examination

Names	Arithmetic	Composition	Do. 2	History	Drill	Total
Full Marks	300	300	400	300	400	1700
Zorawar Singhjee	292	220	330	300	387	1529
Amar Singh	145	250	323	258	293	1269
Amanat Ullah Khan	187	210	183	236	319	1235
Basant Singhjee	242	160	242	219	341	1204
Mahomed Akbar Khan	231	175	244	219	278	1147
Vali Uddeen Khan	162	230	256	177	291	1116
Nawab of Jaora	130	200	305	177	304	1116
Sirdar Mahomed Khan	156	200	168	172	242	938
Kasim Shah	93	205	263	118	292	971
+ Bharat Singh	90	195	65	0	287	557
+ Rutlam Raja	0	160	111	0	185	456
+ Dholphore Rana	0	170	80	0	0	25

[+These three cadets were not at school for a long time.]

Thursday, 14th August, 1902

I sat down and talked with Major Watson. Seeing his wife buying some things to take to England I asked the sahib if he would like something from Jaipore. He thanked me very much but denied on the plea that it would not look well as I was his subordinate. After some time he asked me to get him six small buttons of the Jodhpore gold mohar [coins] but insisted that I must let him pay for them. I came to my room, took the buttons, and made him a present with two Jaipore cloisonne shirt links. . . .

Friday, 15th August, 1902

At three o'clock Akhai Singhjee and myself . . . bid [Captain Cameron] and the others good-bye and galloped off to the station.

Wednesday, 29th October, 1902

Notes About My Second Term In The Cadet Corps[8].

II. School

. . . We were not worked hard. The chief thing taught us was the correct way of speaking and writing . . . The major sahib never got angry but always treated us with the greatest possible love. He was always in good humour and tried his best to make us understand. Some of the cadets used to quarrel about the seats. I was of course very eager for a seat under the punkha [fan], but fortunately had never any occasion to quarrel. Some used to send their books first and reserve a seat. . . . Among the studies may be counted the diary, which we had to write regularly, and dictation and composition. Sometimes we were given to write summaries on some chapters of Green's *Short History of the English People*. Taken all together it was quite a satisfactory work.

III. Riding School

. . . So long as there was riding school I used to have a very bad time of it. Both Major Watson and Capt. Cameron used to get angry and shout at me for not keeping my legs still and riding with a hollow back, that is to say, a non-military seat. Besides these, we were ordered to turn our toes inwards and upwards and the heels were to be sunk below. It was all right for those who were beginners but an old rider has a bad time of it, and specially if he has been taught to ride in quite the contrary style. New ones have only to learn whereas the old ones have to forget some and learn other ones.

I was often [reprimanded] with words like an "old soldier," "a medal wearer" and several others. I had become quite dull by constant reproaches. . . . I was of course considered as a very good rider but one that had his own opinion and was indifferent to . . . orders. Whenever the sergeant used to drill us I was quite comfortable but Cameron was simply furious, most probably because he was displeased with me in those days. Like a fool I became quite sullen to him.

IV. Foot Drill

Of this we had plenty. I was never any good at it though I was not considered the worst. The slow marching always used to put me out and sometimes I used to get out of step. . . . I am in a very bad habit of thinking about something else while doing some work. I know it is very bad but cannot help it. . . . Anyway, I was never made to work with the second squad, though I was always in fear of that. . . . It is considered as a degradation and I would have felt it very keenly as I have been a soldier, seen active service, and am considered very clever. Besides this there were too many whom I had displeased and who would have chuckled at me.

V. Mess

We could not have English food because we could not get a Hindoo cook [who could cook English food]. The native food was simply disgusting. . . . [Presumably it was possible to get a Muslim or Christian cook for the English food, but the more orthodox boys might have objected.]

X. Games

. . . Every Sunday there was tennis at [the] major's house and nearly all the cadets used to go. . . . I was no good at all but used to play all the same. . . . During the later part of the term two new games, hockey and cricket, were introduced. . . . As regards the latter I was hopelessly bad. I could not field and was a very bad bat. I never made a single run. I never took any interest in this game and this was one of the causes that my officers became displeased with me. . . .

Of all the games polo was greatly played and encouraged too. . . . The imperial cadet corps team was getting fit for the Delhi tournament and there used to be great talks and arrangements. Though they all wanted me to join I absolutely refused to play as a No. 1. This offended my officers a good deal and they in their turn were determined not to ask me any more. . . .

XI. The Officers

I. Major Watson was quite pleased with me during the first term but 'not this time. . . . The commandant was a very impartial man though his views once formed were not easy to be changed. He had got this into his head, that I was a proud and headstrong boy, and nothing would shake his belief . . .

He is very mild and of a feeling heart. He never wants to hurt other peoples' feelings. As an instance, when he had sent Akhai Singhjee to the second ride and he [Akhai Singhji] began crying, the major sahib came to his room to console him and while doing so looked very much touched. . . . Now, just think of this.

To me personally he never showed any consideration. He did not even talk to me much. It was most probably because he had got such a bad opinion of me and for which I do not blame him in the least and neither myself because I never did anything to my knowledge. It was what we call circumstantial evidence.

He was very keen on our keeping strict to our old rules and for that purpose used to call Nathu Lalljee and Prakash Nandjee to give religious lectures. . . .

II. Now comes Capt. Cameron. He is very fond of horses, is a better rider, knows much about buying and selling and [is] better [in] every way so far as horses go. He was rather too fond of Jaora Nawab which is, of course, quite natural. [He had been Jaora's guardian.]

I fear he was not quite impartial. Those that were the friends of Jaora were well considered and not the others. I was a special case because my father is a great friend of Capt. Sahib and I have known him for a long time as well. Though not quite pleased with me he had a regard and estimation which the Major Sahib had not. . . .

III. The third and last is Deep Singhjee . . . He is very mean, proud, grasping and wily fellow. . . .

XII. The Under Officers

Of these there were four appointed from amongst us. They were H.H. Jodhpore, H.H. Kishengarh, H.H. Rutlam and H.H. Jaora. While appointing them, sahib said that they have not been promoted because they are ruling chiefs but because they have been the best cadets. This may very well be said of the other three but Jodhpore is quite out of the question. He very seldom went to drill or school and was most of the time either on leave or the sick list. . . .

I. Jodhpore durbar got a good name in the corps. The good reports of Major Watson will do him good and help a great deal in his getting his powers as a ruling chief sooner. . . . He became a great friend with Jaora Nawab, Amanat Ullah and Sardar Singh [Shahpura]. . . . Durbar was on the sick list for nearly the whole time.

Just fancy he was given the charge of wordi major. This shows clearly that consideration for the chiefs was shown. . . . I did not go there much though all my friends wanted me to do so. I cannot get along with the durbar and we soon get dissatisfied. . . . He often kept [to] his room and lay the whole day on his bed talking to a silly racing fellow called the captain sahib or to his flattering servants such as the wrestlers Chirag or Gubboo. . . . Durbar did not spend much money and kept within limits considering his former extravagances. There were two letters written regularly, one to Ogumjee [his favorite at Jodhpur] and the other to his wife whom the durbar used to call Baijee Lall, meaning his daughter. . . .

II. H.H. the Maharaja Sahib of Kishengarh is a thorough gentleman though a mere boy. He is gentle, smart, good humoured and not at all proud. All the corps likes him and so do the officers. He is industrious and very good at learning things. . . . He learned to play polo much quicker than one can expect. He is a first class rider and I can trust him with my best horse. . . . Most of the boys used to call him by the nickname of the baby maharaj or durbar. . . .

He is just the sort of companion for me, light, quick, strong to endure fatigue. . . . He . . . looked upon me as his guardian and well-wisher. In everything that he did he used to take my advice. . . . During the few months that we had been together we became so fast friends that one could not imagine we had never seen one another six months ago. . . .

He eats his own food and does not dine with Englishmen or Mohammedans though he never objects to tea.

IV. . . . The last though not the least is the Nawab of Jaora. He is the boss of the whole corps. He always leads everywhere. At polo, at tennis, at cricket, at riding school and at football he gets the lead. No doubt he is good at nearly all of them, but all the same, too much partiality is shown. . . . His will is the will of most of the corps and whatever he wants to be done is often done. . . .

The Nawab Sahib is not popular in the corps except with a few. . . . I for one hated him and he had the same opinion of me. We used to get out of our tempers at polo. That was one of the causes that made me determined not to play as a No. 1. . . . He is a better student than any of the [other] under officers. . . .

In the end I shall write that the Nawab Sahib is not a bad or mischievous boy even though we never agreed. He has polite manners. . . . He does not mix or talk with low people . . . but keeps his dignity and thinks of his position.

XIII. The Cadets

First of all I shall give a list of all the cadets and then write about them separately. I shall take them first by Hindoos and then by Mohammedans according to their rank. [There follows a list of twenty-two. Amar Singh ranks the Maharaja of Jodhpur and the other rulers first among the eleven Rajputs, and himself last.]

I. Akhai Singhjee is the first whom I shall treat . . . In the corps he was regarded as a very quiet boy though disliked by some owing to his friendship with me. The Jodhpore Durbar used to like him very much and fed him in his own room. Poor Akhai Singhjee was sick of this kindness and used to get very little time to himself. He used to come to me at the first opportunity to have a chat but before ten minutes were over he was called and had to go. . . . In my room we used to talk for hours whenever the durbar was away and used to write dohas in copy books. We got very familiar and friendly. . . .

Akhai Singhjee stood first in the examination of the second class. He cannot speak English well and his Urdu speaking is just as bad. . . . Marwari is the only language he can use fluently. . . .

V. Kanwar Zorawar Singhjee, who comes from Bhavnagar, is about the best cadet here. He has passed the F.A. degree of the Bombay University and is a clever boy. He does his work very well and nearly all the people like him. The officers and specially Major Watson is very fond of him and of course he deserves it all. He is of a cool and mild temper, never bothers with other people and has always a cheery disposition. He is my great friend and indeed [of] most of the others. . . . His caste is Gohel [a Rajput lineage in western Gujarat].

XIII. Now I will take the Mohammedans, commencing with Vali Uddeen. This fellow has been educated in England and is much more an Englishman than an Indian. . . . I think it is a great mistake to send children to be brought up in England. They remain half way, neither fully English nor fully natives. They look very funny in both societies. The officers were quite pleased with Vali Uddeen. He belongs to the Piagha family in Hyderabad and has a large income. . . .

XIV. Aga Kasim Shah had only just joined the corps at the beginning of the term. The first day that he came, several of us took him for a merchant and I was one of them. He was dressed like them and looked an exact picture. Kasim Shah is not a good rider but at the same time he can not be ranked among the worst ones. . . . His English pronunciation is the best in this corps. . . . Kasim Shah . . . never offended anyone. Of the whole lot of Mohammedans he is the best gentleman. . . . He is the nephew of H.H. Aga Khan, and as the latter has no son, this fellow is the nearest relation and will one day fill that place, which is the head of the Khojas. . . .

XIV. Divided into Parties

During the last term we had formed ourselves into small parties which were distinctly separate from one another. One of these was composed of Zorawar Singhjee, Ram Singhjee and Sardar Mohammed Khan. . . . Their habits and moral conduct [were] very good. . . . What they did most was . . . to collect together in one room, have tea and gossip the live long day. All three of these were old school fellows at Rajkot and are neighbours in their native homes.

Another party was composed of Basant Singhjee and Deep Singhjee. The former used to follow the latter and so we gave them the names of "chakwa chakwei," which is a pair of birds that never separate from one another. This was rather a subordinate flattering a superior than a party. . . .

The third party consisted of Kishengarh durbar, Akhai Singhjee and myself. We were looked on by some as great badmashes [trouble-makers]. Kishengarh and Akhai Singhjee were not hated but I was the culprit that was taken to be most proud and haughty. Many used to think that I was always making the other two of my companions do what I liked. Anyway, we used to be very happy together and very seldom went out without one another. This was of course a party of whom all the rest stood in awe. We used to hunt, shoot, and ride a good deal on our own. . . .

The last though not the least of these parties was formed of Jaora, Rutlam, Sardar Singh, Amanat Ullah and Bharat Singhjee. . . . I hated their very sight and they of me. . . . The head of this party was the Nawab of Jaora, whom they all feared and flattered. The officers, and specially Capt. Cameron [were] very much pleased with these fellows as their head was the nawab. . . .

I cannot say as to which was the most powerful. The nawab's was the most numerous and popular. . . . My party was awe inspiring to the others. None dared to contradict us as I was thought to be a man who had better be left alone. . . .

XV. Dinners and Singing

There was [any] number of times we had singing. The Nawab of Jaora had sent for a professional man who used to sing several times. Once or twice the Major Sahib came to listen as well. The Raja Sahib of Rutlam sent for a man who was good at playing on the harmonium. Besides this, there were four phonographs in the corps and these machines had hardly any rest. . . . In the Nawab of Jaora's room this machine was started as early as six o'clock. . . .

Some of the boys were good singers and used to sing either in the mess or their own rooms. . . . [I] never tried it myself before others, though sometimes when either alone or with Akhai Singhjee and Kishengarh durbar, I used to amuse myself . . .

XIX. My Own Experience

[My] experience . . . clearly showed me the difference between the well-educated British officers and the native rank holders. While out in China and even after our return I was under the impression that if natives were only allowed the higher ranks they would be just as well filled. It is now that I have come to know that there is a vast difference between them. I myself know nothing at all when compared to them. Their education, their military knowledge, is far superior, and I fear it would take me twenty or at least five years to learn all.

Besides this, I am now coming to know what a bad English writer and speaker I am. My pronunciation is simply awful and I make several mistakes in writing which I ought not to. Then I have come to know what good there is in drill and doing things neatly and cleanly. How hard it is to learn and do things properly. . . .

Then I have now begun to understand a bit of English ideas, as to how they like one another and behave. Why they do so is because they have been taught to do so. What is real sport is dawning on me, as well as the way in which it ought to be enjoyed. Then the social ways, in which I have acquired very little knowledge. The respect which juniors pay to their seniors is simply wonderful. These people respect but at the same time retain their independence. There is nothing like the Indian customs that when there is a big person we must all flatter him. Englishmen don't do so. Where respect is due they pay it and where self-respect or inde-

250

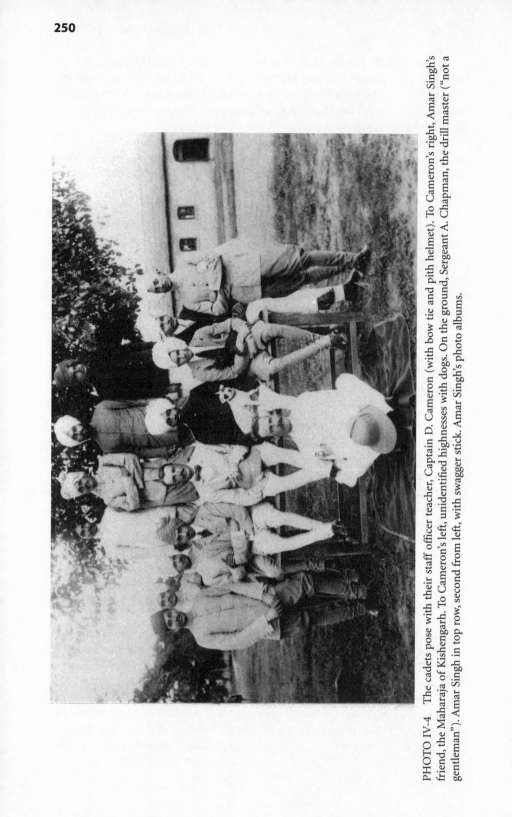

PHOTO IV-4   The cadets pose with their staff officer teacher, Captain D. Cameron (with bow tie and pith helmet). To Cameron's right, Amar Singh's friend, the Maharaja of Kishengarh. To Cameron's left, unidentified highnesses with dogs. On the ground, Sergeant A. Chapman, the drill master ("not a gentleman"). Amar Singh in top row, second from left, with swagger stick. Amar Singh's photo albums.

pendence is necessary they maintain it. These are . . . a few of the numerous things that I have been learning.

XX. Conclusion

May God bless Lord Curzon for starting such a fine thing and giving an opening to the aristocratic families of India for a good service in the British Army. May his successors follow the same policy.

Daurala, Sunday, 16th November, 1902

Notes About The Dismissal Of [Karan] Singhjee. [The Political Service officers dealing with the "sodomy" scandal are torn. They are worried that the scandal will affect the reputation of the Cadet Corps; they want to evict a culprit to show the uprightness of their standards and their institutions. On the other hand if the officers succeed in proving what they regard as the misbehavior of their wards, their own trusteeship of these young men comes into question. Hence compromises are devised. But no one seems to have any compunction about violating the privacy of the minor princes and nobles.]

Twice during my [second] term I had written notes about this subject but there was always something wanting as I came to know the particulars by degrees and not at once. Now, I think I know nearly every detail of it which begins thus. The Maharaja of [Anantpur] is almost the worst character of the present ruling chiefs and of this all the people know. His English guardians are so strict that every letter that the Durbar writes or receives is first read either before being handed to the maharaja or before being posted respectively. Now there came a letter from [Karan] Singhjee in which there were some obscene jokes about certain people. . . . These jokes were written in such a manner that nothing could be made out of them. It was the opinion of [the English guardian] to destroy the note but [the Indian guardian] said that if he wanted to get to the bottom of the mystery he had better let the durbar read the thing and wait as to what its answer would be as that may throw some light.

Most probably the durbar got wind that something was suspected and in the answer he wrote back that such things ought not to be written in letters. Great care had to be taken that the answer was not sent without being seen by the guardians and to make assurance doubly sure, it was arranged with the post-office people that [no] letter bearing this address was to be dispatched before being sent to [the English guardian]. The sahib when he read the answer could not understand a bit and brought it to [the Indian guardian] who too could not make out anything. There was nothing left but to wait for another letter and see what came in it.

Not a long time elapsed before one did come full of filthy jokes, messages, facts and many other indecent things. This letter proved as to who the bad characters were. . . . So bad and indecent indeed was the whole thing that both the [guardians] got furious. The letter was sent to Capt. Cameron at Dehra Doon with instructions to inquire of [Karan] Singhjee as to why and for what he wrote such letters. Capt. Cameron was very sorry when he saw the note. . . .

COMPLETE ETIQUETTE

FOR

Ladies and Gentlemen.

A GUIDE TO THE

RULES AND OBSERVANCES OF GOOD SOCIETY.

Illustrated.

LONDON:

WARD, LOCK & CO., LIMITED,

WARWICK HOUSE, SALISBURY SQUARE, E.C.

NEW YORK AND MELBOURNE.

1900.

---

14   ETIQUETTE FOR GENTLEMEN.

it is damp or suffering in any way through the weather. The right hand should be ungloved.

When you are shown into the drawing-room, if the mistress of the house is present, at once advance towards her. Should she offer her hand, be prompt to receive it, and for this purpose take your hat, stick, and right-hand glove in your left hand as you enter. On no account place your hat on the chairs or table. There is a graceful way of holding the hat which every well-bred man understands, but which is incapable of explanation.

If your hostess does not offer her hand when she rises to receive you, simply bow as you pay your compliments, and take the seat she designates or that the servant places for you. When there are other ladies of the same family present, speak to each in succession, according to the age or other precedence, before you seat yourself. If there are ladies in the room whom you do not know, bow slightly to them also, and if you are introduced after you have assumed a seat, rise and bow to them. When men are introduced they mutually advance and shake hands.

Some tact is necessary in deciding your movements when you find yourself preceded by other visitors in making a call. If you have no special reason, such as a message to deliver, or an appointment to make, for lingering, and discover that you are interrupting a circle, or when you are in the midst of strangers where the conversation does not at once become general upon your making one of them, address a few polite phrases to your hostess, if you can do so with ease and propriety from your position with regard to her, and take

Cameron sahib asked [Karan] Singhjee only a few questions by which he quite cleared [two other cadets] and laid the whole blame on [Anantpur] durbar and [Karan] Singhjee. Now [the Indian guardian] was anxious about saving [Anantpur] but there was no way open. It was very much feared that [Anantpur] would be forever disqualified for getting any powers as a ruling maharaja.

The original letters with the cross examination of [Karan] Singhjee by Capt. Cameron were forwarded to the . . . foreign office with the result that an order was sent to the commandant to dismiss [Karan] Singhjee from the Imperial Cadet Corps within an hour's notice. . . .

Now came another scene. [Karan] Singhjee was called . . . and the durbar from [Anantpur]. . . . There was the political agent of [Anantpur]. . . . For three days these unfortunate culprits were questioned by . . . two officials separately but nothing could be arrived as the final result. [The Indian guardian] was very anxious to clear [Anantpur] durbar and luckily found a way. One morning he had gone out to walk . . . when he met Pistumjee, who was the man under whose charge [Karan] Singhjee had come. Now this Pistumjee . . . knows [the Indian guardian] well. They were fast and old acquaintances. [The Indian guardian] explained the whole situation and advised Pistumjee to tell [Karan] Singhjee that on the morrow, when the trial begins, he must say that [Anantpur] and [Sevpura, Karan Singh's state], being Ganayats can joke and always do so. [Among Rajputs, *Ganayat* designates a person from a lineage other than one's own, and into which one may marry.] It is the universal custom among the Rajpoots. They don't get angry by such jokes and they are not considered abusive. Having given full directions [the Indian guardian] came home.

Fortune favoured these miserable fellows and so, on this very day, the [Anantpur] durbar explained his position to [the Indian guardian] and asked his opinion. [The Indian guardian] told him exactly the same words that he had to Pistumjee for [Karan] Singhjee's direction. [This clever tactic takes advantage of British punctiliousness about respecting "native customs," however curious. On the other hand, the Political Department may have chosen to accept the Ganayat ploy in order to avoid confronting the question of whether or not to deprive [Anantpur] of his powers.]

The trial came in due course and, when questioned, both the culprits said the same thing, though they were in separate rooms and had not seen one another since a long time before. The [Anantpur] resident . . . was very anxious, and so was [the guardian] to clear the durbar, as [the Indian guardian] had impressed on them that any harm done to the durbar would give them a bad name as they were the guardians and were responsible. When they heard these words from the mouths of the culprits they at once knew that it was not the boys that were speaking but it was [the Indian guardian]. They both came out and congratulated [him] who made himself look in such a manner as if he knew nothing of the thing.

The Agent [to the] Governor General (A.G.G.), when giving the final decision, cleared both the fellows from the charge that had been put against them. . . . So the next day, when the A.G.G. proclaimed him "not guilty," [Karan] Singh said that he had been given a bad name for nothing and the only way to regain it and prove his innocence was that he may be sent back in the cadet corps. Hearing this the A. G. G. got furious and said that who was he? That there were several fellows like him, and who cared for them. He ought to be ashamed for giving such a big chief a bad name. Poor [Karan] Singh was badly scolded. I hear he is still trying to get back in this corps but this is all mere idle fancy. . . . These are the results of sodomy. Beware those who practise it.

3

"Too Proud and Haughty"?
Third Term in the Imperial Cadet Corps

[The "Rough Riding Sergeant Major" gets his comeuppance. Captain Cameron opens Amar Singh's third term by roundly chastising him for his imperious attitude toward fellow cadets and his insolent conduct toward the officers. Taking Cameron's criticisms to heart, he resolves to change his ways. And so he does, aided, it should be noted, by the departure of the Nawab of Jaora, his rival for leadership of the cadets.

A new shadow appears: doubts about the future. Lord Curzon fails to convince the Balfour cabinet that cadets who successfully complete the course at the ICC should receive king's commissions. Lord Kitchener, the hero of Khartoum and of the Boer War, who, soon after taking command of the Indian Army, challenges Curzon's authority, adamantly opposes king's commissions for Imperial Cadets. Amar Singh has to face up to the racism evident in the opposition. If Curzon fails to secure commissions that distinguish them from VCOs, his time at the Cadet Corps will have been wasted.

With some form of king's commission, successful cadets might be able to serve with princely state Imperial Service Forces. However, unlike cadets who can expect such appointments in their home state, there seems little likelihood that Amar Singh's maharaja, Madho Singh of Jaipur, will do anything for him. The alternative, serving as a lone Indian staff officer with British officers in an Indian Army command seems unlikely as well as unattractive. Will Amar Singh's time at the Cadet Corps have been for naught?]

Dehra Doon, Wednesday, 22nd October, 1902

What Capt. Cameron Talked to Me the Other Day. *While I was sitting in my room the captain sahib came and very kindly gave me a lecture for about an hour.[1]* The talk . . . was all concerning me but the conversation was so long and mixed up that for a writer like me it is out of question to describe fully and that well too. However I will try my best.

Cameron sahib had come to warn me as well as advise that during the last term I had got a very bad name and had displeased him as well as the major sahib. The chief fault found in me was that I was considered too proud and haughty and that I had been treating the others rather roughly as they were not experienced. Sahib said that there were several who were afraid to talk to me. Then he said that I did not mix among them so much as I ought to have done and as an instance I was told that why did I not talk to the Raja Sahib of Rutlam who was quite a good man . . . that I had not been good at saluting and obeying orders and taking advice. Besides this that I had offended both the commandant and the adjutant on more than one occasion.

Capt. Cameron told me that as I was the son of his greatest friend,[2] he wanted me to get a good name. . . . I must join each and every game with the keenest interest even if I did not like the things. . . . Now what I said in answer to each and every question I shall write here with all the explanations as far as I know and these explanations are exactly true in my opinion or rather conscience.

The first thing, that I had been too proud, is absolutely unfounded and to this sahib agreed as well, but at the same time he said that though he knew it well the others were too inexperienced to notice it. Why I was considered proud is simply this, that I never used to go to nawab sahib's [Jaora] room as most of the others did and flatter. That is one bad point about me. I cannot flatter and don't want to do it even now. Not going [to this room] gradually [led] to less talking, and the more he and his friends began to look coldly on me, the less I joined them. Then to add to this, polo spoiled everything. . . . If we played against each other, I used to go straight at him because he used to look upon himself as the overlord of all. These and other petty things gave me the title of proud. . . .

Added to all this were the hot words that passed between Deep Singhjee and myself when he [complained] about [me] inquiring into the mess accounts on the suspicion that some of the money had been embezzled. The result of those hard words was that I discontinued staying in the mess after dinner.

Another thing was that I never used to attend to the [religious] lectures of Pundit Nathu Lalljee. I find that some four or five times I had not attended music when all the others were there. . . .

I had no occasion to quarrel with anyone. Whenever I used to go out it [was] with either Kishengarh durbar or Akhai Singhjee; but this was because I did not enjoy the company of others. Now as regards my treating the others roughly, there is no ground except this, that I am rather in the habit of speaking loudly and forcibly, which sometimes shows that what I say I mean and mean to be obeyed as well. . . .

As regards the boys being afraid of talking to me I cannot understand. I have never been rude to anyone. Of course Deep Singhjee, Khuman Singhjee, Samandar Singhjee, Pratap Singhjee, and Rai Singhjee are a bit afraid of talking, but this is not the case with me only. These fellows are shy and don't mix up with any others but among themselves. I have been told by some others that I appear rather awe inspiring and that is why the others don't approach me. This may be true but I never meant to frighten anyone. . . .

As regards my not saluting, it is all bosh. I return the salute of the syces [grooms] as well as sweepers and as regards doing it first I have never missed doing it. We in Jodhpore are not in the habit of saluting much and I may have missed the thing but surely not intentionally. As regards obeying orders the only fault that can be found is that I may have not been able to keep step in marching or keeping a military seat on horseback. Mostly I was in for not keeping my legs steady but this was not a thing I did intentionally. It was and is a long set habit which is not at all easy to do away with. . . . Besides this I can find no disobedience.

Now as regards taking advice it has all to do with Capt. Cameron who used to interfere with my horse management Sometimes I used to take off my ponies' shoes which was quite against his principle. Then my ponies were a bit too thin and I was done in for not keeping them in good condition. I was sometimes told to keep polo boots or putties on my ponies' legs when I played but I never used to have them. . . . These things of course gave me a bad name and I deserved [it] . . . because I have no right to do anything against the order, advice, or wish of my officers.

As regards offending the commandant I do not know in the least though Cameron told me that the major sahib told him that he [Watson] was going to jump on me before the whole class and not let me do it any more. Now what the thing was, I . . . neither know nor can guess. I asked Capt. Cameron but he too could not remember it.

Of course I had given occasion for offence to Cameron sahib once and this he told me plainly. It was this, that one day I told him plainly that I was not going to play polo if I was made to play as a No. 1. . . . Sahib told me that I am not of the proper age to talk like this or pass opinions, that I must be willing to play anywhere. . . .

As regards my not taking any interest in other games than polo . . . I don't care for them. . . . I used to grumble at cricket which I ought not to have done. . . . I was well advised that if any one had a pony that did not behave well I must tell him what would be the right thing to do and not laugh at his inexperience. As an instance I was told that my father has probably forgotten more than I shall ever learn but he never brags about anything. He listens to all what one has to say and then, when he has himself to say anything, he always says in a very mild way. Cameron sahib said that my father always looked upon him as a youth and let him brag as much as ever he liked. He never takes offence and never gives one to anyone. These are the virtues I was advised to learn. . . .

This term I am determined to keep all the others pleased if I can. I have asked the sahib to warn me off on the slightest thing he finds wrong with me, and he has promised to do so. I am going to mix and I am going to flatter with everyone. I was advised to go and call on the commandant when he arrived and lend him ponies to play on and ride which both things I have done. I pray God to get me out of this corps with credit as soon as possible. . . .

Thursday, 23rd October, 1902

Major Watson came to me at about one o'clock to enquire whether we would object to dine on the same table with a Maharaja of high birth, as one from Kolhapore[3] was trying to join the corps. I said that we could have no objection whatever unless it was the Jats who might make a fuss.

Sunday, 26th October, 1902

Last night we . . . had to discuss some matters connected with the mess. . . . Khuman Singhjee, Deo Singhjee and Pratap Singhjee objected to dining with Mohammedans and one of them was so particular that he would eat nothing if a Mohammedan came on the carpet. Then there was Samandar Singhjee who would have nothing to do with us. He would not sit on the same table with us or eat anything that was cooked by anyone else but his own man. [Samander Singh, a Jat, hailed from a small thikana in Bharatpur. Along with Dholpur, Bharatpur is one of the two Jat-ruled states among the twenty-two princely states of Rajputana. Apparently Rajputs, who considered themselves ritually and socially superior, had no objections to dining with Samander Singh but he was more particular. The other Jat cadet, Ram Singh, Rana of Dholpur, apparently had no problems with the new mess arrangements.]

There was a mess meeting again at noon and Major Watson presided over it. It was settled that now we must have English food though there are some inconveniences to be encountered. . . .

Monday, 27th October, 1902

Samandar Singhjee's man came and asked me if I would arrange . . . separate plates for his master as he would not use any China materials out of which to eat. Now this was a great problem and I sent for Zorawar Singhjee, Akhai Singhjee and Samandar Singhjee. [Among ritually particular Indians concerned about pollution, the kaccha or unglazed clay pottery utensils available from the village potter are considered polluting if used more than once. Samander Singh seems to be equating English China with kaccha village pottery.] The final result of the whole discussion was that Samandar Singhjee would not mind electroplated things but only those that were wholly China made. Then was the question that he would not eat if any of us touched the food, and for this it was settled that the dish would not be passed to him but that he would get a plate ready served for him from the kitchen. Good God, what a foolish prejudice all this is? What is the difference between electroplated and China dishes? Absolutely nothing. . . .

Tuesday, 28th October, 1902

Last night we had dinner in the English manner. The food was English and was eaten in the same manner. This is the first day that the Rajpoot mess has done it. From today the dinners are always to be in English and lunch in deshi [of the country] fashion. Samandar Singhjee was seated on a separate table as he objected to dining with us.

Friday, 31st October, 1902

In the evening we went to polo. I played six chukkers of which the four fast ones were with the cadet corps team. . . . Major Watson was quite pleased with my playing and I wanted nothing more. . . .

Sunday, 2nd November, 1902

There was lots of talking about going to Somaliland where there is some fighting going on and for which Jodhpore durbar has volunteered. When I heard of this I wrote a letter to H.H. Idar asking him not to forget his old private secretary of the China campaign in case he himself went there. Then I asked Jodhpore durbar to try and take me with him if it could be done. He has promised to do so though I don't put much faith in his promises.

PHOTO IV-5   Cadets in full-dress uniforms practicing for the Delhi *durbar*. Lord Curzon's 1903 extravaganza celebrated Edward VII's coronation as King-Emperor. Like the *durbar* Lord Lytton staged in 1877 when Victoria became empress of India, it "copied the Mughals." The cadets were given a prominent role as the royal horse guard to the viceroy. Choreographed as an imperial ensemble, the *durbar* featured the princes of India as feudatories enacting their loyalty to the crown. Sir Pratap, honorary commandant of the Imperial Cadet Corps (left), Major W.A. Watson, commandant (right). Amar Singh is fifth from the left. Amar Singh's photo albums.

PHOTO IV-6 The State Entry at what became known as the Curzonation. "Lord Kitchener led the way with some cavalry regiments. Behind them was the bodyguard followed by the Imperial Cadet Corps. Then came the elephants in double file. H.E. the Viceroy was leading, followed by his Royal Highness, the duke of Connaught, after whom were all the chiefs on their elephants in their proper place." Amar Singh's photo albums.

Now while at the dinner table, Deep Singhjee said that if Amar Singh is taken why should he [Deep Singhji] not be taken. Jodhpore durbar who is a fickle-minded man said at once that here is a barrier for Amar Singh. I was disgusted with such a silly excuse but all the same I said that this cannot be so, as I had a better claim. Hearing this Deep Singhjee said that my claim lay with Jaipore and that he was nearer to the durbar if the genealogical table was to be considered. [Both men are Rathores, the ruling clan at Jodhpur, but Deep Singh may be of a branch closer to the ruling lineage].

I laughed at this silliness and said that my dear sir, this is not a case of adoption, that you are taking . . . clans in consideration. My claim does not lie thus. It is because I have served the [Jodhpur] state and specially the regiment for the last eight years and had only left it when I came to this corps. . . . I had been brought up in that state and had been a constant companion to the durbar. . . . Who else can have a better claim? Hearing this Deep Singhjee kept quiet and so did the durbar. . . .

Monday, 3rd November, 1902

I gave Ormonde to Vali Uddeen just for a trial. Cameron advises me to sell the pony for thirteen hundred but I am now sticking to fourteen. The worst of it is that he does not like my selling the animal to anyone outside the corps. What a nuisance! I cannot play this princely game. I must get some money if I can. We will see what happens. . . .

[The cadets leave for Delhi, to act as the viceroy's escort in the coronation durbar. The rituals occupy almost two weeks, from December 29, 1902, to January 10, 1903, after which the cadets return to Meerut.]

Meerut, Thursday, 12th February, 1903

I put on my full dress turban, turrah [filigree cockade] and breeches but not the coat and belt as the horse was not yet ready. I whiled [away] that time with Kishengarh durbar. When the horse [Sarkar's English black charger Fitzgerald] got ready I wore my full kit and went to Thomas A. Rust, the photographer. I had three photos taken. (See photo IV.7.) Sergeant Chapman was with me and helped a good deal in making the horse stand properly. . . .

Sunday, 15th February, 1903

I had breakfast in my tent with Akhai Singhjee. This over, I drove to the railway station to bid good-bye to the Nawab of Jaora who is going on leave for his marriage. He is not coming back but is leaving the corps for good. . . .

Friday, 20th March, 1903

Last night we had a big dinner in honour of Rutlam durbar's leaving the corps. At the end of it I rose and spoke a few words. I commenced by saying that we were pleased the durbar was going and that we ought to congratulate him. Jodhpore durbar was about to say something because I had said that we were glad because Rutlam was going. I knew what was to follow and hastened to say that of course we were sorry to lose the company of Rutlam, but all the same we must congratulate him at his departure because that is the goal for which we are all striving and, it is our duty to congratulate those who reach there first. This explanation quietened all tongues. I ended by saying that nearly all the members knew that Rutlam durbar has promised to present a thousand to buy plates and other things for the mess. Then we thanked the durbar. In conclusion I said that we would have gladly drunk to Durbar's health but there was no wine allowed in mess and to drink health with water was unlucky.

. . . Just before leaving Rutlam came round to the tent of every cadet to take leave. How good of him. . . . The time having arrived when the train was about to start, the durbar embraced (according to Rajpoot custom) every cadet and so did Bharat Singhjee [who] too has left the corps, and so we have lost three cadets who have gone after finishing their time though not the whole course. Just as the train was about to start I proposed cheering the durbar and said "Hip, Hip, Hoorah." The others followed and I repeated thrice.

Sunday, 22nd March, 1903

Last night I had heard privately from Capt. Cameron that there was going to be an examination on Monday and told about it to Zorawar Singhjee and Akhai Singhjee after they had promised me not to reveal it to anyone else. . . . The sahib has got a book which is a translation of some Hindi love songs. I asked him to let me have a look at it but was denied on the objection that it concerned love matters. I told the sahib that never mind, I can read them in my own language. Fancy his denying me a book on the ground that it has love songs, when I am already a father. How ridiculous. . . .

Thursday, 26th March, 1903

At eleven we went to school where there was examination in arithmetic. The questions were quite easy ones but unfortunately they all proved too much for my limited knowledge, and the result is that I am not right in a single sum. That is damn bad indeed.

Dehra Doon, Saturday, 16th May, 1903

Notes About My Third Term in the Cadet Corps.

III. Lessons

We were taught *Forty-One Years in India* by Field Marshal Lord Roberts [also taught in the second term].[4] The book was only taught in portions where the account was about the Indian mutiny of 1857. Every day we had reading and sometimes arithmetic and sometimes dictation. The time was about two hours and a half. There was not much stress laid upon studies this time. . . .

IX. Driving

Of this I had enough. The Maharaja Sahib of Kishengarh and I used to go out nearly every day, when not out hunting or shooting. His company was quite agreeable and I used to give him lectures on several subjects which have been fully described at those proper dates. [The lectures appear in Part V.] The durbar's trap is very light and beautiful and our pony was quite fast and handsome enough to compete among the best ones in the station. But I used to have a dull time while lecturing because the durbar used to cross-question me next to never and seemed as if he was sometimes inattentive, which very much dulls a lecturer. I always want someone with me who knows more than I do, is of a cheerful and talkative temper, and an intimate friend competent to talk on every subject. Such a man is Ram Nathjee, but unfortunately he is not a good horseman. . . .

XII. The Mess

. . . It is next to impossible to find good Hindoo cooks whereas any number of Mohammedans can be obtained. This was a great drawback to us. As regards the Rajpoot mess, though it was not quite so neat and orderly [as the Mohammedan mess], there was no discontent. We had to pay fifty rupees of which ten was the mess subscription and forty went for food. Living on English food is much more expensive than living on our Indian food, though the latter is considered more wholesome by many. As for me, one is just as good as the other, provided it be the best of its sort . . .

XIII. Examinations

. . . At arithmetic I am hopelessly bad and am left miles behind. . . . I don't think I shall now again have a chance of standing first or second in examinations as arithmetic is increasing. . . .

XIV. The Officers

There was not much cursing done this time here in Meerut against us and especially towards me.

(a) Major Watson. This term I had nothing to complain of. He got angry with me only once and that was at polo. I cannot quite say whether I was to blame or not, but as I am not quite sure I think and acknowledge that I must have done something wrong. He had by this time begun to realise that I was not a bad horseman, and as a proof he always used to make me ride his mare at riding school and was quite pleased with the good result that was obtained. . . .

(b) Captain Cameron. This officer has always liked me but it was the beastly Nawab of Jaora who stood in my way and gave me such a bad name. So long as the nawab was here Capt. Cameron was tied to him; but as soon as he went away we all felt relief . . . [Cameron] always used to give his horses to me to train and ask my advice. There was no ill-feeling this time. . . .

XV. Cadets

There were altogether twenty-three cadets during this term. . . . Zorawar Singhjee, H.H. the Raja Sahib of Rutlam, H.H. the Maharaja Sahib of Kishengarh, Akhai Singhjee, Vali Uddeen Khan, Aga Kasim Shah and Bharat Singhjee. . . .

These fellows were in the foremost rank of the society but at the same time all of them thorough gentlemen. I liked them all.

Zorawar Singhjee is very clever and well learned. The officers like him very much and so do the cadets except a few Mohammedans. Zorawar Singhjee is of a very mild disposition and good character. The mess members like him very much. H.H. Rutlam was very good. Before he was rather reserved but after the nawab [of Jaora] had gone the durbar mixed amongst us and we found how good he was. There was no pride near him and he was very obliging with a mild temper. . . . Vali Uddeen Khan [scion of Hyderabad's diwan family, educated at Eton] is more of an Englishman than a native. Some of the cadets like him and some not. He is a sort of fellow who leads his own free life like a prince. . . . Kasim Shah [whom Amar Singh describes as heir to the Agha Khan, leader of 20 million Ismaili Khojas, a sect of Shi'ite Muslims] never mixes much among the Hindoos though he is always laughing and joking amongst his own creed. He has a very good character and never offends anyone. I like him very much. . . .

The durbar [Maharaja of Jodhpur] considers the corps nothing more than a prison for him. Well, this is not good. The imperial cadet corps should not be turned into a sort of prison for . . . ruling chiefs, as they now think it to be, owing to Jodhpore durbar being kept here against his own will. If the government does not want him to live at his capital there are several other places where he may be sent.

XVIII. How I Enjoyed Myself

I think I enjoyed myself thoroughly well. . . . The Nawab of Jaora having left the corps there was no one to stir the officers against me. All these things combined made me lead a pretty happy and joyful life. . . .

XXI. The Future of the Corps

[Because official opinion in Britain, particularly in the cabinet and the war office, is hostile, and because Lord Kitchener, commander in chief in India since the previous year, is opposed to king's commissions for Indians, Viceroy Lord Curzon expects considerable difficulty in finding suitable careers for the cadets in the Indian Army.

Earlier, when the ICC was first sanctioned, Lord Salisbury, then prime minister, and Queen Victoria (died January 22, 1901) seem not to have shared the exclusionary views prevalent in official circles and in the Indian Army, which now fuel the opposition to Curzon. Sending graduates to princely states with Imperial Service Forces offered a face-saving way out, but it was distinctly second best. In 1903, Curzon seems to be trying for a better outcome.]

[The future of the Corps] is a question which everyone is anxious to know. . . . Nearly every Englishman who knows me has asked as to what is to be done with us at the end of the course. They do not know and we do not know. Whenever I ask Capt. Cameron he says he does not know anything about it. One thing is certain and that is that we are not going to get any commission in the British or

PHOTO IV-7   "When Sir Pratap's English black charger Fitzgerald got ready, I wore my full kit and went to Thomas A. Rust, the photographer . . ." Amar Singh's photo albums.

native army because Capt. Cameron himself told me so. The reason is that no Britisher would ever like to be under a native's command at present. It will require some generations before this feeling of the conquerors and the conquered, the ruler and the ruled, and of blacks and whites would fall away. At present it is impossible.

. . . One thing is certain, that if we are not going to have real commissions, we are not going to join the service on the same rank as jamadars or rissaldars [terms for native officers in the infantry and cavalry]; at least I am not going to do so. Then, if we are not to be given commissions, why the devil are they teaching us military work? This is a thing that bothers me most. . . .

My ambition is to get some good post in the Jaipore state. It is no good my getting a commission even, because I am a jagirdar's eldest son and must remain at home. Be that as it may, I am not going to try and leave the course unfinished as most of them want to do. I will see [it] through [to] the end. If some good comes out for me then my younger brother [Sheo Nath Singh] will come here, otherwise not.

[We have omitted Amar Singh's fourth term, much of which repeats the themes of his earlier experiences. When Amar Singh returns to Dehra Dun for his fourth term, his initial pride and excitement about being at the Corps fade as he worries about his future. Four princes who entered with Amar Singh do not stay the course. Kishengarh, who will depart in the fifth term, is preceded by the Nawab of Jaora, the Maharaja of Jodhpur, and the Maharaja of Rutlam. The departure of the princes compromises the Corps' chances of becoming a prestigious military academy whose native graduates can serve as officers in the Indian Army. On the other hand, six new cadets have joined up, two of them from princely families.

The princely departures reveal some unresolved questions about the aims of the Cadet Corps. Is the object to make achieving aristocrats out of princes, that is, to make them part of a professional service? Is it to add a bit of military polish to a prince's aura, or give him some experience of having to cope in the everyday world by becoming, for a time, one of the fellows? Or is it, as some declare, a disciplinary colony for problematic princes—such as the Maharaja of Jodhpur? "[The Maharaja Sahib] was not allowed to take his uniform with him. This was taken away from him, which is one of the signs that he has lost the opinion of his superiors and will most probably never get his powers."[5] Amar Singh gets intimations that the Corps may not yield the good career for which he is hoping:

[One evening] the commandant . . . rose and said a few words. Unfortunately I was not present at that time because I had just got stomachache. This speech . . . said that according to some one author the greatest peril to Englishmen would be on that day when Indian youths would not stick to their own religion and adopt Western ideas. . . . The major said that whatever the British government did was meant in good earnest and with good intentions though some of them turn out to be failures and possibly this [the cadet corps] is one of diem. This allusion to the corps was done hastily and with a dropping voice.

The cadets are a lot of idiots who, instead of attending to what was being said, were thinking of either their beds or homes. It was Zorawar Singh, who is an exception to the common rule, that caught the meaning of the speech and told me. I wish I was present on that occasion. . . . This clearly shows that we have not much to expect from the corps. . . . [6]

We resume the account with the fifth term.]

4

"To Command Europeans"?:
Fifth Term in the Imperial Cadet Corps

[The fifth term at the Cadet Corps marks the end of the course for those un-likely to qualify for commissions. Four of the most promising cadets, Amar Singh, Zorawar Singh, Aga Kasim Shah, and Vali Uddeen Khan are selected for two additional terms at training. Lord Curzon still cannot overcome the opposi-tion to making them KCOs. It is equally apparent that the cadets selected for a third year of training will not accept VCO ranks such as subedar major or rissal-dar, then the top ranks open to Indians. There is talk of establishing a new ser-vice and of founding an imperial regiment in which commissioned cadets would serve as officers.

A new service, variously styled as the Indian Native Land Forces (INLF) or Na-tive Land Forces (NLF), is eventually brought into existence, but not an imperial regiment. Instead, NLF officers are offered appointments in the princely states, usually in the ones from which they hail and which maintain imperial service units—not a likely solution for Amar Singh. Commissions in the NLF, like king's commissions in the Indian Army held by Englishmen, are to be signed by Edward VII. But the royal signature on NLF commissions is a subterfuge designed to mask the continued inferiority of Indian to British officers. The command au-thority of KCOs in the NLF is confined to "native officers, soldiers and other per-sons belonging to the said Native Land Forces;" they are not authorized to com-mand British Other Ranks (BORs) or British officers.[1]

Amar Singh loses his constant companion, the Maharaja of Kishengarh dur-ing this term. As a result, his friendship with Zorawar Singh, the most talented of the cadets, grows. Even though Zorawar Singh is not a good rider, he is a better conversationalist than Kishengarh.]

Meerut, Friday, 8th January, 1904

. . . I went out sketching on to the hills where we [cadets] had been before. *I am now beginning to understand this surveying business a little.[2] *This time the com-mandant taught us slowly and did not hurry up as he had done last [time]. . . .

After my return I bought some sixty books from a hawker, Anwar Ali. These books, though second hand, are almost new and I have got them for a quarter their value. . . .

Tuesday, 12 January, 1904

[Meerut cantomnent, the base for the ICC, is the preserve of English officers' families; this creates problems for the Corps.] . . . I must say we are awfully un-comfortable or at least the servants are, who cannot go on "the Mall," the Brooks street, or the Church road. These three are the roads that encompass us. When we go to polo we have a lot of bother. The trouble happened thus.

Kureem, the riding boy of Capt. Pinney [the officer who substituted for Cameron when the latter was on leave for six months], was one day seeing the performances of the Kunjurnis [female tricksters and street performers]. These women pick up a paysa [coin] with their female organ. I have never seen one do it, but this is a fact. This happened on the Brooks street and was noticed by one of the artillery officers who told all about it to his colonel who in his turn wrote a very strong letter to Major Watson. *Those fellows said they would have none of us on their side of the road and that we had better make a six feet wall all round our camp.³* The result was that the going of the syces was stopped on that road. *Every morning when the ponies used to be taken out for a walk there were a couple of sweepers walking behind to clean the road, because the people would not have us spoiling that road.⁴*

The Europeans here in Meerut are . . . envious of us and do not like to see the Indians moving about on better horses or beating them at polo or the other sports. In Australia and South Africa the feeling is greater and I shall write all about it on some other occasion. There are no signs of unity as yet.

Sunday, 17th January, 1904

[H.H. Kishengarh is about to leave the Cadet Corps.] . . . I had dinner with Kishengarh durbar as he had gone to ask the commandant whether . . . Akhai Singhjee and I would be allowed to get leave for his marriage.

Monday, 18th January, 1904

Last night we had a big dinner given to Kishengarh durbar as he was to go the next day. . . .

Stables over, we went to lessons and had arithmetic. After the first hour we were told that we could go away to see Kishengarh durbar off, which we did with the greatest pleasure. . . .

I am feeling awfully dull after Kishengarh durbar has gone. . . .

Saturday, 30th January, 1904

Last night after dinner . . . Zorawar Singhjee and I talked for a long time. He related to me all his history in the Raj Kanwar College at Rajkot. This history was all about his mischievous conduct. . . .

[From February 7 to 13 Amar Singh attends the marriage of H.H. Kishengarh to the daughter of the Maharana of Udaipur. His account of it is included in Part VI.]

Wednesday, 17th February 1904

. . . I read a little and after[wards] took some headings to write my notes about Kishengarh durbar's marriage. This occupied me for nearly an hour. I had got these headings before but now had to arrange the order in which I am going to write them in my book. . . . [Kishengarh's wedding, one of the seven marriage essays written during the first seven years, is organized under thirty-five Roman numeral headings. See Part VI.]

Saturday, 20th February 1904

. . . Most of this time I was at my table writing my notes about Kishengarh durbar's marriage. This subject was quite pleasing and I was writing at my very best.

Tuesday, 23rd February, 1904

Last night after dinner I wrote and finished my notes about Kishengarh durbar's marriage. It was about ten when I went to bed.

Saturday, 27th February, 1904

[Amar Singh enters a riding competition organized by the Corps] . . . The first event was chargers, which was won by Sarkar's horse Fitzgerald who had won last year as well. Then there were the ladies hacks. For the light weight hunters and hacks I rode the Rana of Dholpore's bay waler mare Sweetheart and got the first prize. . . . The show was over at ten and we went away to breakfast . . . I was not feeling well. I was a bit excited as I have to ride [again]. . . . It is always so with me. Whenever I go in for any competition I get very excited. When I could not read I tried to sleep but this too I could not manage and so wrote a fair copy of my notes that I am given at lessons.

Having washed and shaved myself I went to the horse show at three. The first event over and the second over, I went in for the third, which was the jumping competition for horses. I had two, Ghatotguch and Soodarsan, in for this show. I had great hopes from Soodarsan but he disappointed me very much . . . the first time he knocked some bricks from the wall jump, and the next time he dashed through the first jump, which looked simple enough but was in reality not so because it was a firmly fixed post and rail with grass all round. I had a violent knock, but luckily no harm was done. I did not expect much from Ghatotguch, but the gallant old fellow went beautifully over the thing and I won the first prize. . . .

Sunday, 28th February, 1904

. . . While I was coming back I met an officer of the 10th Hussars . . . on Ghatotguch. He is trying him. He told me that he liked the horse very much but doubted whether he would be in perfect condition for the Kadir Cup. . . . While I was at the meal, Cameron came and told me that the 10th Hussar man was not going to buy Ghatotguch. I said that . . . there was another man who wanted him. To this Cameron objected, because he does not want this particular man to buy Ghatotguch, as that man is a first class pigsticker, and if he had Ghatotguch under him he would have any chance of beating Cameron [who had won the Kadir Cup the previous year]. The latter wanted to buy the horse for himself but I did not advise him to do so because he only wants to give me Rs 800 whereas I shall get a thousand from anyone else.

Monday, February 29th, 1904

My Talk with Major Watson.   The other day I had a talk with Major Watson as to our future prospects. *This time while I was at Meerut I heard that the fauj bukshi [military commander] Mansoor Ali Khan, had died at Jaipore. I asked my officers to try and get me that post. The commandant did write but I was told in the end that the resident was out in camp at that time and by the time he returned the post was filled.5* . . .

It was after this [effort failed] that Watson asked me why I did not like to take service in government. I said that . . . I being the eldest son of my father [and hence heir to the Kanota title and estate], could not afford to live away from home, because if I did do so I would be losing more than I would be earning. . . .

Then Watson said that suppose I became the bukshi today, what I would do? There would be no other ambition for me. Would I be bukshi the whole of my lifetime? I said that it was not so. I could be a member of the council, and if luck was on my side, I would become a prime minister, in which case I would be getting some two thousand rupees a month, which would be quite enough. Hearing this, the commandant said that this would be alright.

Then he said that if I was in the state I might get kicked out any time the maharaja did not want me. I replied that he could and would do so if he himself employed me, but if I went through the political officers I would be quite safe. The durbar could not turn me out unless I did something very bad; and if the durbar did want to turn me out, then the government would find some sort of place for me. To this the major agreed.

Then I in my turn asked him what we had to hope for in the future. . . . Though he did not tell me I know what the suggestion is. Cameron had once told me that they are proposing to raise a royal or imperial regiment at Ajmere, which would be officered by Indians of high birth, and only the commandant, second in command and the adjutant would be Britishers. The Maharaja of Idar would be the honorary commandant. . . .

I said that before the viceroy goes away, I hope he would do something for us. The major . . . thinks that if there was any change in the government in England and the radicals came in force and a viceroy of that party came, he might want to give us commissions which would enable us to take command over Europeans . . . at present. . . . If we got that sort of commissions, there would be a lot of discontent which he thought ought to be avoided. He said that we are the beginning of the institution which would finally end in giving posts to Indians that would enable them to command Europeans.

. . . It is this very thing that stops me to accept a commission. Suppose I did get a commission, I would not like to serve under a man who would be my junior. My ideas are not [those] of a cringing man. Even here I hate [it] when I have to show undue respect to these officers. There are orders that we must salute every officer we meet on the road if he is wearing his uniform. This is all nonsense. I do not want to go saluting each and every Englishman I come across. . . .

[Major Watson] told me that he would keep some five of us whom he thought good enough for one more year and then he was certain of doing something for us. . . . [Amar Singh and eight other former imperial cadets receive regular King's commissions on August 25, 1917 (see Introduction to this Part).]

Wednesday, 2nd March, 1904

. . . while at polo I met Capt. Guest who is going to buy Ghatotguch. . . .

Friday, 4th March, 1904

. . . The whole day was cloudy. I have handed over Ghatotguch to Guest for a thousand rupees. . . . Before writing anything about my real motive [in] . . . selling Ghatotguch, I shall write a short history of the horse. This horse was bought by His Highness the Maharaja of Jodhpore for Rs 1500 in lot with some others, one of whom was the race horse Forest. Ghatotguch used to buck jump, and was not at all handsome, and was consequently sent for the Sardar Rissala, but Sarkar took a fancy to him and kept [him] for his own use. He had him for about a couple of months when I got him .

. . . When Sarkar gave me this animal he praised his qualities a great deal, but I was quite dissatisfied and never used to ride him unless I had to. However, the horse was good in itself, and began to show his . . . qualities. He turned out an excellent jumper and being a sensible horse soon began to learn what was taught [to] him.

When I had pig-sticking and bearsticking on him at Sewari, I was quite pleased and he gradually came in my favour. When I went to China, this horse was with me and won the International Steeple Chase . . . he won me a cup as the best pig-sticker in the [Cadet Corps] horse show of 1902 and I had a splendid ride on him at the Kadir [Cup competition of 1902]. . . . My father took him away to Alwar and he had some pig-sticking. It was there that the horse got spoiled. . . . He began to pull. This time when I was out pig-sticking at Nethari I could hardly hold him.

It was because he was pulling and getting down in years that I sold him. My father had told me to sell him even for eight hundred, for after a year's time no one would have him, and now we had many other big horses. . . . This horse served me very well. . . . He was with me at all the places wherever I have won a thing or got a name for myself. The only defect [was] that he had rather an ugly nose, and so people used to say, what an ugly horse! But what did I care. "Handsome is that handsome does," is the best principle, and I follow it. I was quite sorry to part with this honest and faithful beast.

Saturday, 12th March, 1904

Last night after dinner there was a lecture in the mess by a man of Sanathan Dharm.[6] The lecture was good but I did not hear much of it as I began to doze and was cursing the man the whole time because he would not finish. Watson and Cameron were both of them present . . .

Monday, 14th March, 1904

. . . Cameron sent for me to the polo ground to train his pony Sans Reproche to stick and ball. . . .

Tuesday, 15th March, 1904

. . . At about four I went out with Cameron to train the horses. . . . Cameron nowadays takes my advice and listens to it. . . .

Wednesday, 16th March, 1904

> 1. True pleasure is to be found from the back of a horse and the heart of a woman.
>
> Arab Proverb. From Capt. D.H. Cameron.

I went out for a ride with Cameron. We went to Mr Norton of the 15th Hussars. At that gentleman's house there were some other people and we spent a very nice half hour with them. These are the people who know how to enjoy life. Indian mode of life is absolutely rotten when compared to theirs. . . .

Jaipore Tuesday, 5th April, 1904

Notes About My Fifth Term in the Imperial Cadet Corps

VIII. Riding

. . . Akhai Singhjee and I used to go together and [eat] plums in the jungle. During these rides I never had a companion whose company I [relished a] great deal because Kishengarh durbar and Akhai Singhjee are not conversant on many points. They have their own limited subjects and one soon gets tired of monotony. Zorawar Singh was the only man with whom I would have enjoyed conversation, but he is not a good rider and never came out with me. . . . After Cameron's coming [from England] I had some good riding because we used to have long talks on various subjects which shall be written in their proper places. He was very fond of my company and always took me out with him. . . .

XIV. Theatres

I had seen several theatres before but never liked them. Those that I had seen were native [plays] and I was always able to see through the disguise. . . . Indians are not sufficiently educated to [write] life-like dramas, and if the English works are copied they lose their taste. Then the life of the Indians and Europeans differ so much that nothing can be satisfactorily done. . . .

This time at Meerut I was so much taken by these shows that I never missed a day so far as I was able to. The actors were all amateurs but . . . they were quite good enough. The other reason of my liking them is that I often read English novels and consequently the habits of those people I have come to know very well. There cannot possibly be much love shown in Indian dramas because the male and female sexes are so much apart. English [acting] is so much life like that there can be nothing more pleasing than to go and watch them. . . . Zorawar Singh and I always sat together. There were several things that I did not understand properly but he often managed to help me. . . .

XV. Field Days

This term we were taken out on manoeuvres. . . . There were four patrols made, and their commanders were H.H. Kishengarh, H.H. Dholpore, Rajjee [Maharaj Kanwar of Cooch Behar] and Zorawar Singh. . . . However, when the durbar went away I was given the command of that post . . . I had no idea that the commandant had such a good opinion of me. . . . The practical work is more pleasant and easy than work indoors. . . . I shall always remember [these days] with the happiest recollections.

XIX. Mess

The new china and the new lamp, the presents of H.H. Ratlam and H.H. Jaipore respectively, had come and our mess was looking quite decent. . . . There was only one new rule of some importance passed and it was very much against the will of the whole members. We had not been paying the mess subscription for the time that we were away on leave, i.e. vacations, and now we will have to. . . . In fact it was more of an order than a voluntary vote. I was writing down the notes for that meeting when the commandant after passing the rule asked me to put down that it was carried unanimously. This made me smile because there was no one for it except the Rana of Dholpore or the major. Seeing me smiling he said that I may put it anyway [I wanted], and I think that I wrote down that it was carried by the casting vote of the president.

Messing together is a good thing. Even now I am feeling the good effects of it and do not enjoy my food when I have to eat it all alone by myself in my tent. Besides this, we all see so much of one another and become friendly. Then we get into the habit of giving out our own and receiving the thoughts of other people. . . .

XXVI. The Cadets

[There follows a list of twenty-three names. . . . Of these the following three, in addition to Amar Singh, are recommended for further training and eventually for commissions.]

1. Zorawar Singh is a boy who is very good at lessons indeed. He has the record of being first in every examination up to the present. He is very handsome, tall, and well built. Besides this, he has a very good character and is liked by all the officers and cadets except the few from the latter who are jealous. The only drawback for Zorawar Singh is that he is not a good horseman. However he tries his best which is the best that a man can do. . . .

VIII. Aga Kasim Shah is a . . . good man and . . . nephew of H.H. Aga Khan.

XII. Nawab Vali Uddeen Khan is the second son of a Hyderabad noble who had a jagir of some thirteen lakhs. This boy was educated in England at Eton and is a good man. However, his English education has done him more harm than good. He does not know the Indian customs and hates Indian food, dress, living and people. I wonder if he would like to marry an Indian wife. He is not much good at any of the games. . . .

XXVII. The Officers

. . . I. I had always been having a good opinion of Watson but since then [have] been awakened of my mistake. I can say this much, that he is an honest, hard-working and strict officer, but at the same time he is a great politician, which means that he would not scruple to deceive people. . . . He favours those most who have got any influence, whether they deserve the favour or not. To me he has been more kind than ever before he was. . . . Most of the cadets . . . and the office baboo . . . say that he never exerts his influence in favour of the boys. . . . In my case, about getting the fauj bukshi post of Jaipore, he would certainly have succeeded if he and the resident had tried earnestly. . . .

II. Capt. Pinney was with us while Cameron was out in England on six months' leave. . . . Pinney is a thorough gentleman in the truest sense of the word. . . . Unlike Major Watson, and like Capt. Cameron, Pinney has . . . tried to help the boys with their home affairs. . . .

III. Capt. Cameron has always been represented as not a very good man in my diary. This was because of the Nawab of Jaora, for whom he had a great liking and partiality. Now I have come to know, and quite believe it too, that Cameron is a thorough gentleman. . . . Cameron being a great horseman has a natural liking for people of his own kind, and so I get the advantage. He loves me a good deal and [is] always asking advice how to train ponies. This he has begun doing after his return from England, where he rode some of my trained ponies. . . .

XXVIII. Those Who Have Left

He [Kishengarh durbar] left the corps . . . because his minister wanted him at home to teach the state work which is more important than doing foot drill and riding school. . . .

XXX. The Giving of Leave

The commandant delivered a short speech in which he said that he had called us to bid good-bye to the nine of us who were now allowed to retire from the corps after finishing their two years' course. He said that it was no shame to go now, as it was quite an honourable thing to go after having worked with credit. Those of the very best were kept for a prolonged stay of one more year, for they were to get some extra education. Those that were leaving need not be sorry that they were not selected. . . . God gives some longer brains than the others, and this is not their fault. So long as a man tries to do his best he is all right and cannot be blamed. . . .

The great thing in this world is to work hard and not be idle. He hoped that after leading this active [life] we would not return to the usual indolent habits of the Indians. . . .

As for those who stop three years, the government of India will provide something good. . . . We were always to remember that we had been imperial cadets and behave like that. . . .

XXXIV. Personal Friends

I shall now write who my personal friends in the corps were. The first and fore-most was Kishengarh durbar. We had become very intimate and I used to spend most of my time in his company. . . . I only regret that the durbar did not feel the same love towards me that I did towards him. I always looked upon him as my younger brother or son. So long as he was in the corps I hardly did any work be-cause I often used to go to him and talk on all sorts of things. There were two or three occasions when there was some ill feeling but this was merely for a short time. . . . The [Hindi] proverb says . . . that when earthen or brass utensils are stored together they will knock into each other. . . .

Zorawar Singh is daily becoming a fast friend. . . . I can now count on him as a very staunch friend and I hope the intimacy will continue to grow. . . . He trusts . . . me more than anyone in the corps and I do the same to him. We always tell one another our views and news. His friend Sardar Mohammed had become a friend of mine too because "things that are equal to the same thing are equal to one another." . . .

XXXV. The Examination

. . . I was second and Zorawar Singh first. I would never have stood so high as this had it not been Zorawar Singh who helped me a great deal. I did not of course copy him but I asked several questions where I was in doubt or did not know. . . .

XXXVI. The Return journey

[On his return from the ICC to Jaipur, Amar Singh breaks journey at Delhi.] At Delhi I went out for a walk in the Queen's Gardens, where I again went to Victo-ria's statue. My purpose was to copy the words that were written on it. When I had gone to Kishengarh durbar's marriage I had regretted not having paper and pencil to write the thing down. Here it is word by word:

> In their prosperity will be our strength,
> In their contentment our security
> And in their gratitude our best reward.
> And may the God of all power
> Grant to us, and to those in
> Authority under us, Strength
> To carry out these our wishes
> For the good of our people.

These were the words for the Indian people on this statue. They are carried out to some degree, but even if they are not actually carried out, they are noble sentiments and such as no other people in India has ever expressed. The Mo-hammedans had their watch word, "Death to the Kafirs." They had no idea what suffering is and lived a life of ease and luxury. Even the native ruling chiefs never think of having such high ideas. They want to enjoy themselves, and never care one hang whether their subjects are contented or otherwise. Their idea of their subjects is that these people are like coolies, who are bound to earn money for them to squander in whatever way they think or like best.

There is no doubt that the British are the best rulers that have ever come to India. . . . It was this very Delhi during Moghul times when no one was safe with his life or his property. Now people move freely in those very streets where murders were committed during the day-time without any fear. People enjoy tennis and other innocent games where it was dangerous to go unarmed. . . .

XXXIX. Talks with Cameron

This term I had several talks with Cameron. . . . One day I asked him as to why he did not marry to which he said that he could not find anything up to his taste. I said he ought to search to which he replied that it was no use searching for a good wife when one could not even get a good pony. I said that he had several ponies that were of the best sort and as an example I mentioned his favourite Musketeer. On hearing this he said that he had one pony to his satisfaction but that was after searching for a very long time. I said that if he kept his eyes open he was sure to find a good woman but if he did not he would never succeed. Then he said that suppose he did choose a woman who did not after all turn out to his satisfaction what was he to do. . . . He has an idea that married lives are never happy. The other thing he thinks over is that he would have to reduce his stable if he married. . . .

Another day Cameron asked me whether Akhai Singh had any children, to which I said that he had none. On this he said that this was owing to our people marrying without seeing. I said that here was the commandant married years ago but he has no children, though he has married after seeing a good lot of his wife. I said that no one in the world could tell whether a woman was to bear children or not unless it was by medical examination. . . . When he heard this he changed the subject and said that it was owing to our marrying unseen girls that our people did not lead peaceful lives. I said that I could show more disaffected pairs among the Europeans than he could among the Indians. He agreed to it. . . .

I knew of a good answer but could not say as he was my officer and I was not quite so familiar. The answer would have been that if one was to eat the same thing, or drink the same wine, or ride the same horse or play the same game, or wear the same suit of clothes he would soon get tired of it and that it applied exactly in the same manner to women. . . . The best thing under the circumstances is to be satisfied and be content . . . This principle was described to me by Ram Nathjee and it has taken firm root in my head. . . .

One afternoon while we were going to train our ponies Cameron asked me what I thought of satee [the Hindu custom of a widow's immolation on her husband's funeral pyre].[7] I said that it was a very good thing indeed so far as it was done willingly.

Cameron's meaning was whether I liked the idea of the British having put a stop to it. I said that it was good where the unwilling satees who on several instances have been burned forcibly [were saved] but as regards willing satees, it was a cruel thing to stop them. He said that it was a cruel thing to be burned alive. I said that it must be so, but the satees never seem to feel it. The satee dresses herself in her best robes and does not show any sign of being afflicted. On the contrary, she is always cheerful. . . .

Then there is an instance that one of the Kishengarh princesses became a satee even before she was married. She had been only betrothed, and when she heard of her espoused's death she prepared to bum herself. Her parents remonstrated with her but she would not listen. Her answer to all this was that she had thought of one man as her husband whom she had already acknowledged in her mind. . . . Since then a Kishengarh princess is not betrothed. . . .

The best is the wife of the late and mother of the present Maharaj Rana of Dholpore who, after her husband's death, sent for her children, caressed them, and told them to go and play. After this she slept with her husband's body and was found dead. God only knows whether she committed suicide or she died of her will.

After I had given all these instances, the sahib began to look at it in another sense. He asked me what I would say or think if my mother was to become a satee. I said that I would never raise a single finger to prevent her but would feel proud. After this answer the matter dropped, Cameron saying that it was all right to become a satee if one wanted to become, but why not do it by some other method that would not be quite so cruel.

As to the question why the women do not want to become satees so much in these days as in former ones. The answer is that during those times it was one of their first lessons to become a satee. Just as people are taught other things now, the girls were given the idea of becoming satees, which was the best work she could do towards the good of her future life. Now it has fallen into disuse, and that is why women do not become satees.

I also described to Cameron that Indian ladies had much better become satees than lead a life which is absolutely miserable. The widows do not dress in any coloured garments and wear no ornaments. They do not touch meat or wine and the food is coarse and of the worst kind. It is hell for them to live in a widowed state on this earth. . . .

After a time he told me that Englishmen will never forgive one thing. When I asked as to what it was he said it was the act of sodomy. If it is proved, a man is sent for seven years penal servitude, and with hard labour too. This is a practice which demoralises a people. If an influential man is suspected and the thing is about to be made public, he runs away to France or some other people and never returns to England. All this may be true according to the law, and we too in India have the same law, but the practice is universal in India as well as in England. The great thing is to get the thing proved.

There are all the colleges where the thing is prevalent. Cameron must have played the fool himself in his school days. He told me that it was [for] the want of education that people did these things. On the contrary, it is the education which is the foundation of it. These things begin at the colleges, where it is practised to the utmost. In Rajpootana and specially in the outlying districts of Marwar, Jaisalmere and Bikanere people do not even understand such things. It is only when they come to big cities when they learn such things. Cameron said that he hoped there was not a single boy in the corps who did the thing. I laughed in my mind though I did not say anything but passed the matter by saying "I hope not." . . .

XLV. Conclusion

I must thank God that I have been so lucky to pass my time during this term with credit and have pleased the commandant to some extent. Another thing to be thankful to God is that I have been . . . selected for a three years' course. The commandant had openly said that the very best had been picked and that we were sure to get some service, which is a great thing. Coming out so well in the examination was another bit of luck. I hope I shall be able to keep up a good name. . . . Now that we have become a bit more sure of our future prospects we shall work with a better zeal. . . .

5

"The Big Swells were Gone": Sixth Term in the Imperial Cadet Corps

[Amar Singh has two kinds of "work," the Cadet Corps and the diary. His essays are becoming longer; his ethnographic eye is becoming sharper. Planning and arranging the headings, in a Roman and Arabic numbered outline, is a major production, worked out over several days. An instance is the Kishengarh marriage with its thirty-five sub-headings. The diary provides Amar Singh with meaningful activity, by contrast with "these jonnies [who] have no work to do." It is a more constant companion for him than all except the most stimulating friend.

The Corps' strength is waning, with sixteen cadets as against the twenty-six which marked its high point "There were more Mohammedans than Hindoos, the latter being only four." Yet the small company is congenial.]

Dehra Doon, Thursday, 28th April, 1904

The meal over, I wrote my notes about my last vacations and would have done a lot of work had not Deep Singhjee and Amanat Ullah Khan come in. [Amar Singh writes regular "Notes About My Last Vacation," some of which are included in Part V.] These jonnies have no work to do and will take up other people's time. There I was cursing them from the very bottom of my heart but they were quite pleased with themselves because they did not think what I was suffering. Etiquette forbade me from telling them to go away because I had such a lot of work to do. At last when they did go I wrote a few more of my notes.

. . . Major Watson . . . had this morning returned from Simla after settling that we cadets were to get real commissions if we passed the final test examination.

Friday, 29th April, 1904

. . . I think they are going to give us regular commissions with all the pay, promotion and privileges of a British officer though we shall never be made to command them. The great thing that they are aiming at is that they will put us in the Imperial Service Troops and this much has been hinted in the newspapers too.

Sunday, 1st May, 1904

Breakfast over I again wrote my notes. . . . Deep Singhjee came twice. . . . However I showed such an indifference to talking that he went away. He must have felt something but to me he only said that he thought I was busy. He was very anxious to know what I was writing and when I said it was my diary he doubted because he naturally thought I do not write twenty pages a day. I did not like to tell him that I was writing my notes because then his curiosity might have increased and he would have wanted to see it . . .

Monday, 2nd May, 1904

Lessons over, I wrote and finished my notes about my last vacations. It was a great load on my mind and now that I have finished it I am quite pleased with myself This time I have written a good lot. . . .

Friday, 6th May, 1904

A Satee Story Comparatively Modern. . . . In Kishengarh maharaja's marriage time, I was driving alone with Ram Nathjee. I heard the following story from him. Sooraj Malljee, the great poet who has written *Vans Bhaskar*,[1] had gone somewhere and on his way happened to stop at Bhinai in Ajmere district as the guest of the thakoor sahib. As is the custom in our country, charans are treated with great honour and respect as they are bards. Some people really honour them and some fear that they may compose some poetry of ill fame to their name. . . .

When the time for dinner came, a man brought the great bard his food, and as he was putting it down said that the thookrani sahiba [wife of the thakur] had asked the barathjee to eat well, as she herself had cooked the dishes for him. Sooraj Malljee was a man of quite peculiar ideas. He pushed the plate aside and sent word that this was nothing extraordinary she had done. It is the custom of the Rajpoot ladies to prepare food for the charans, but if she wanted him to compose some lines in her praise, she should promise to become satee on the death of her husband.

On our side it is considered as very bad form and an evil omen too if any one speaks about the probable death of a living man. The ladies are particularly annoyed if there are such things spoken in their presence about their near and dear. As it was, no one could say the message and they all began to curse the great author.

After a lot of bother the thookrani managed to find out what the matter was and sent back word to her guest that, "There have been satees among the Rajpoots and he need not feel anxious about her but have his meal." Sooraj Mall stuck to his point and said that he would not eat her bread until she had promised to become a satee. The lady sent back word that she would become satee when she became a widow but that the barathjee had better take his food. Next day Sooraj Malljee went away and the thing was quite forgotten until some years after, when the great author heard that the Thakoor of Bhinai had died and his wife had become satee. Sooraj Malljee was in the habit of drinking wine before his meals and had finished the thing and was to eat. He however remembered his promise that when he heard of the lady's becoming satee he would not even eat until he had sung her praises. He kept his promise. The dish was removed and I hear that he composed such poetry as only he could compose. . . .

Sooraj Malljee was a great man indeed. He has written a book which can be excelled by no other in Hindi literature. . . . [He] lived during the times of the late Maharaja Ram Singhjee of Boondi. I am sorry to say the book was not finished because the author and his master disagreed on some points which related to the book. The fact is that Ram Singhjee asked him not to write about scandals, to which Sooraj Malljee would not agree. The result was that the book was left unfinished. After his death, his sons were ordered to finish it, which they did but not in the same style as that of their father. . . .

Saturday, 14th May, 1904

Last night there were very few of us at mess because Deep Singhjee and the Rana of Dholpore had gone out to dine with Major Watson. The rana sahib was always very particular about not eating with Mohammedans or Europeans while he was here. I have now found that this was all hypocrisy. He had been eating with all sorts of people even before joining the corps and had kept the thing a secret. I don't see what point he had in view. . . .

Friday, 20th May, 1904

Talk with Captain Cameron.   In the evening when I went out for a drive with Cameron the talk turned upon the merits of the new cadets. I told my companion that I could not understand why Ghosh [Ghaus] Mohammed Khan [from Bhopal] had been chosen. I said that he has no knowledge of English and could not ride at all. *His conversation in Urdu is not very pleasing too. He is the sort of fellow who will always be under the influence of his servants. . . . There is a lack of spirit and energy in his body.[2]* Besides this, he was not at all a good looking man. . . . He said that if all the cadets were good ones and likely fit to get commissions, there won't be any room. This then was the reason.

   . . . Well, this is rather a disappointing news. My idea was that they would always be selecting the best boys they would be able to get. . . . The selection of this year is not at all satisfactory, because Fateh Deen Khan and Ebrahim Khan will never accept commissions while Ghosh Mohammed is not fit. . . .

   Then I said that there were no Rajpoots taken this term and at the end of the year there will be only one man left, that is Prithee Singh, because Zorawar Singh and I will be going away. Cameron said he was sorry but he could not help because the Rajpoots would not come. He said that he had sent for Ram Kishan Singh of Bikanere but he would not join. . . . I told Zorawar Singh all this and he told me that while selecting new boys the commandant had asked him about certain Kathiawar boys and he found that he [Watson] cared for boys with money and nothing else.

Sunday, 22nd May, 1904

Last night after dinner I talked with Zorawar Singh for half an hour. We both of us walked between the lines. The best place to talk secret things is [in] the open. Our talk was about the future of the corps, and we were both determined that when we left we would try and send in as many Rajpoots as we possibly will be able to. Zorawar Singh told me that . . . Cameron said that there were lots of uneducated Rajpoots willing to come in the corps but he would not take them as during the present times we don't want mere fighting people, but we want something that is both a soldier and an educated man as well. . . .

   Then Zorawar Singh and I planned that we must try and see that the Mohammedans do not beat us at any game whatever. Zorawar Singh would never be beaten by any of them so far as studies were concerned, while I would hold my own in riding. . . . Our one ambition is that a Mohammedan should not win the point-to-point race. . . .

Sunday, 29th May, 1904

TABLE 4.3   Result of the Spring Examination 1903

Names	English Paper I	English Paper II	English Paper III	Arith-metic I	Arith-metic II	Total
Total Marks	200	200	200	200	200	1000
Zorawar Singh	190	175	185	200	200	950
Mohammed Akbar	194	145	145	185	190	859
Amanat Ullah	174	150	160	168	165	817
Basant Singh	172	135	140	155	190	792
Vali Uddeen Khan	180	145	155	198	70	748
Amar Singh	183	200	175	93	93	741
Kasim Shah	154	140	157	150	140	741
Sardar Mohammed	126	140	110	200	120	696
Talee Mohammed	126	130	90	160	140	650
Samander Singh	137	75	90	190	140	632
Pertap Singh	137	100	100	138	80	555
Deo Singh	116	90	75	110	80	471
Akhai Singh	133	120	absent	145	absent	398
Rai Singh	116	60	70	108	40	394
Rana of Dholphore	139	75	95	35	40	384
Gopal Singh	47	10	20	15	0	92

By some mistake I had not been able to write the result of the last three examinations at the proper place. I now remembered my mistake and have written on the principle "better late than never." . . .

TABLE 4.4   Result of the Summer Examination 1903, Senior Class

Names	Survey I	Survey II	Forti-fication	Drill & Equitation	Arith-metic	English History I	English History II
Full Marks	200	200	200	200	200	200	200
Zorawar Singh	188	153	100	195	180	195	140
Amanat Ullah	188	133	172	198	138	136	110
Mohammed Akbar	165	141	154	183	125	138	125
Basant Singh	180	161	159	147	145	128	85
Vali Uddeen Khan	93	121	183	172	110	104	115
Amar Singh	47	121	193	150	55	170	150
Kasim Shah	165	49	120	158	100	104	100
Raj Rajendra Narain	30	78	180	173	35	85	105
Rana of Dholpore	83	105	120	145	0	106	85
Pratap Singh	105	58	120	45	85	82	75

TABLE 4.5   Result of the Spring Examination 1904

Names	Tactics Paper I	Tactics Paper II	Topo-graphy Paper I	Topo-graphy Paper II	Forti-fication Paper I	Forti-fication Paper II	English
Full Marks	200	200	200	200	200	200	200
Zorawar Singh	195	171	185	200	198	160	175
Amar Singh	175	147	113	146	167	138	120
Amanat Ullah	128	167	122	145	158	106	80
Mohammed Akbar	98	182	72	90	116	121	140
Val Uddeen Khan	160	112	93	135	139	86	10
Kasim Shah	45	55	65	75	114	66	50

Friday, 10th June, 1904

. . . At three o'clock, Bala Sahib [Daphle] and I rode up to Rajpore, from whence we hired ponies and went up to Mussooree [the hill station above Dehra Dun]. We reached safely in good time and did a little of shopping. After this we engaged a room at Woodville Hotel, where we put up for the night. . . .

Saturday, 11th June, 1904

Last night we were awfully uncomfortable. We could get only one room between us two and there was one bed only which too was not wide enough. For a long time we could not get sleep because for myself I was awfully nervous the whole time, as I have not slept with anyone but my wife, and in sleep God knows what indecent thing might have happened. Poor Bala Sahib was labouring under the same difficulty and could not sleep. At last he said he would sleep on the floor, but I insisted that I would leave the bed. The result was that Bala Sahib slept on a high parapet which was covered with a thick bedding. . . .

As we were put up in Landour,[3] I purchased a few pens and pencils at Framjee and then went to see Mr Durand who is a dentist. I had some of my teeth rasped as they were very sharply pointed and my wife often complains of them. . . .

Sunday, 12th June, 1904

. . . Having come to my room I read and finished *The Three Musketeers*, by Alexandre Dumas. This is a good book indeed. In fact it is about the best novel that I have read. At ten I went to breakfast. The meal over I read a little of *Kanak Sundar*, which is a book written in Marwari by Shiv Chander Bharatia. It was interesting as well as instructive. I read a good deal of it.

Cameron asked me whether I would like to serve with the Imperial Cadet Corps in place of Deep Singhjee [as adjutant of the Cadet Corps]. I said I could not answer him until I had seen my father.

Tuesday, 14th June, 1904

. . . At six we had practical fortification and were taught how to make a gabion [a cylinder of wickerwork or iron bars filled with earth or stones and used in building field fortifications]. This work was rather amusing. . . . while we were making this gabion we had some coolies digging a trench. It is awfully hot nowadays and so the commandant very kindly gets some other people to dig for us. . . . Amanat Ullah Khan took a photo in which we sat on the fascine choker and put the gabion on Khan's body. [A fascine choker is a long bundle of sticks of wood bound together and used for such purposes as filling ditches and making parapets.] The photo will be an awfully funny one.

Monday, 20th June, 1904

. . . Kaloo [Amar Singh's servant for many years] and I had some disagreement today. I was buying the uniform boots worth Rs 85 for Rs 20 and he began to quibble. I got very much annoyed and did not buy.

Thursday, 14th July, 1904

[I] went out for a ride along the canal and the Chakrata Road. Sergeant major [Chapman] was with me. I asked him whether I would pass the examination, and he said that they would give us very easy questions because they want us all to pass, for they think that if we people don't get anything, there will be no more cadets coming. . . .

PHOTO IV-8 "Amanat Ullah Khan took a photo in which we sat on the fascine choker and put the gabion on Khan's body." Both contraptions are elements in constructing fortifications. From left, Amar Singh, his friend Zorawar Singh, Aga Kasim Shah, unidentified cadet, Mohammed Akbar Khan. Amar Singh's photo albums.

Thursday, 28th July, 1904

. . . I went to Zorawar Singh and while we were talking the conversation turned on poetry and he showed me his collection. There were some good dohas and other poetry and I took a fancy to them. . . . He read them over while I wrote [them on] a rough paper. . . .

Wednesday, 3rd August, 1904

Last night we had dinner in the Mohammedan mess. There were a lot of speeches and jokes. It was quite a nice party we had. This is the first time that all the members of the corps have dined together. . . . just before mess we had some tea in Zorawar Singh's room. It is a pleasant business to collect and talk.

Jaipore, Thursday, 25th August 1904

Notes About My Sixth Term In The Cadet Corps.

I. Lessons

This term we learned a lot. . . . The surveying work as well as the combined training were finished. . . . We were taught how to lay out schemes on maps . . . [and] how to make a sketch with a prismatic compass. . . .

III. The Point to Point Races

I was very much afraid that a Mohammedan cadet might win, but fortunately Bala Sahib kept up the prestige of the Rajpoots. I always used to tell him how to ride and what to do. . . .

VI. Reading

. . . It is much better reading histories, historical novels and biographies than novels. The latter are quite interesting but there is nothing to be gained except that it helps to kill time. If one was to look at the moral he might find one, but it is not worth the bother. . . . The books that I found very interesting were *How to Be Happy though Married*, *The Heart of Asia*, *The Story of Nations*, and *Military Adventures of Hindustan*.

XIV. Mess

. . . When we had turned out two of the cooks Bhoora began the cooking and all of a sudden we got the best food that we ever had in the mess. This proved to me that though this boy was the best cook, Chogjee, the storekeeper, would not let him work through jealousy. This boy comes from my village and I had put him there to learn the work.

Though we were few we were very intimate with one another and at table there was always some joke. Dinner over we used to sit ourselves on comfortable chairs and then commenced either stories, jokes or songs. The singing was [what we] most enjoyed. Even I used to follow the songs, though I knew my voice was making a mess of the whole thing. Our mess was like a small family whose members were very intimate with one another. The leading members were Zorawar Singh and myself, but the others too were always happy and there was no diversity of opinion. . . . The plates, the linen, the lamps and everything was perfect. . . .

XVII. The Servants Inspection

These were held at the end of each month. There was the usual question of keeping old and not young servants. At the first inspection the thing was merely suggested, but the next time the commandant got annoyed and ordered that he did not want to see the young ones any more and that they were to go away as soon as possible. [The same subject, apparently in connection with the interest in controlling "sodomy," was raised the previous term.]

XVIII. The Officers

. . . Major Watson was much [more] kindly disposed towards me this term than he has ever before been. I do not know the real cause. It may be that I have now been made a corporal, or perhaps he thinks I have improved. . . . Whenever he talked to me he kept a smiling countenance instead of the never-changing frown that used to greet me. . . .

Capt. Cameron as usual was very kind to me. He mixes more with me than anyone else. . . . If a pony does not do a thing properly he is handed over to me. . . . We were free with one another. I am a man of rather a hot temper. Sometimes when Cameron used to say something not up to my taste, I used at once to show him my disapproval of it and then there was the discord, but fortunately for me Cameron has a very good heart and never took the thing seriously. . . . We soon got reconciled to one another and the old things were forgotten. . . .

There was once a talk about selling ponies. Cameron told me that I sold at the best profit. The situation became rather critical when I told him that he could sell almost any sort of horse and as an example I said that he had just sold Sanctuary, for which no one would ever have given me more than a couple of hundred rupees, whereas God only knows for how much he had sold him. This was indeed too much. He said something very much against my saying so and I found out that he was offended. I did not think it proper to agree with him and he too knew that I had got offended. The result was that when I did not talk well, but went on saying yes to everything he said, he too got quiet and as soon as someone else came I slunk away. Even after all this argument he was quite himself a couple of hours afterwards. I always have in mind that my interest lay in keeping him pleased. . . .

XIX. The Sergeant Major [Sgt Chapman]

This chap, though not an officer, is quite an important person in the corps. He was on good terms with us all and he always takes the part of such cadets as are quiet and whom the officers tease. . . .

XX. The Cadets

There were very few cadets this term. . . . The whole strength would have been sixteen, but we were never so many. . . . The real show of the corps had fled. It is now a mere shadow and I am afraid it will grow fainter and fainter as people do not come unless they have to. There were more Mohammedans than Hindoos, the latter being only four. However, we four were all good ones, while there were a lot of rotters in the other lot. . . . [There follows a list of cadets, and comments on each.]

1. Zorawar Singh is the cleverest boy of the whole lot that have come up to the present. . . . This term we became very intimate. This boy never offended anyone except Akbar Khan. The latter [who has a strong record in examinations] is very jealous because the former always stands first in the examinations. . . . He helped me all through the studies and even at the examination. . . . He was fond of singing and I used to make him sing a lot either when he went out for a ride or was at mess. . . . He, being about the most fair or even white coloured, some of the boys tried to spoil him. . . . He was however too good and clever to be caught by them. He did not offend the wretches and yet escaped.

2. Is myself and I need not write because I can't. . . .

XXVIII. Facts

[Events concerning] this naughty fellow, [Rais (a pseudonym)] Singh. One day we were sitting in the verandah as it was raining. There was only one easy chair and he and Zorawar Singh were both of them sitting on it and were very much pinched up for space. There were the jokes going on. I was standing at the back of the chair and, catching hold of Zorawar Singh's hands, told [Rais] Singh to have a good bite at Zorawar Singh's cheeks. These were all jokes indeed. [Rais] Singh began trying to kiss and Zorawar Singh tried all he could to escape but could not succeed as I was holding his hands. I never knew that [Rais] Singh would actually kiss. These were the usual jokes and I knew that he was only joking but I was quite surprised when [Rais] Singh, like a fool, actually kissed. I knew the mischief was done.

Now the boy wanted to run but Zorawar Singh held him tight and when I let go his hands [Rais] Singh got two or three good slaps. He, however, apologised. Luckily there was no mischief done. It was indeed very bad of the boy to kiss. Jokes are one thing and to put them in practice is another. I too was very sorry because I had been an innocent partisan in this business. I am glad there were no reports about it to the officers. This was because there was nobody else to see except Bala Sahib Daphle and that boy is too good.

XXIX. The Return Journey

I have only to say this much, that from Dehra I got into the through carriage for Delhi and was quite comfortable. An English couple were travelling with me but they were quiet people and I had no bother with them.

Now I shall write about that Indian lady who travelled with us from Riawalla to Delhi. When she came in she sat on the middle seat, and as she had no bedding I made her comfortable on my rugs and gave her a seat on my berth. At first I was very reserved, but we soon began to talk, and after a time got quite familiar. Her mother was a Rajpoot but had married a Christian. Now this girl has married a Mohammedan who had one wife before and married a third. This last marriage put some ill-feeling between this couple, and since then this lady lives by herself and does not see her husband who lives at Saharanpore. The other ladies are in purdha [purdah] but this one is not. The father and daughter are not on good terms because the girl had married against her parents' wish.

I must here write to my everlasting shame that I was quite tempted by this woman. We talked until late in the night, and I several times touched her cheeks, pressed her hand which I held in mine, and had my legs [against] her while sitting. She did not object to any. It was only when I touched her breast that she told me not to do it. God only knows what would have happened if the other pair had not been with us. I was thinking in my mind that I would not do anything but was merely tempting her. I am afraid the temptation would have been too much for me.

I have never been to any other woman but my wife up till now. I would have looked down upon myself a great deal if I had fallen. There is of course no doubt of it but God protects us everywhere. I have a sort of vow never to go to another woman, but I do not know whether I shall be able to carry it out to the end of my life. May it please God that I do so. It is all right while you don't have the temptation. But it is quite a different thing when you get a chance. I am sure I would never do such a thing so long as I have my wife near me, but I may be tempted while away from [her] and specially if the separation has been of a long duration. I really don't know what I would have told my wife and [whether I could have] looked her in the face as if I was the same true and honest Amar Singh.

I would of course have been cheating her, because to tell the truth would have been out of the question. Then suppose she had some disease and I had contracted it. This would have been the worst thing possible. The whole house would have known it and how ashamed I would have been.

What must my father have said and thought, for he is a very, very chaste man. In fact, he is the only one that I know to be a really chaste man. It is not only I who says so but the whole of Jaipore and everyone who knows my father intimately will say the same thing. When I think of all these things my hairs stand on their ends.

In future I shall always try to avoid the company of women if possible. . . . This page of my diary shall always remind me of my temptation and it will be a page that will make me look a bit ashamed.

XXXI. How I Liked

. . . The officers were more pleased with me and the boys too were more friendly than they had been before. . . . Perhaps the officers were pleased because all the big swells were gone and the boys were pleased because we were so few. . . .

XXXII. How I Enjoyed

There is not the slightest doubt when I say that I enjoyed myself thoroughly this term. In the foregoing terms I had some friends and I had to adapt myself to their will. . . . Though there were several advantages in Kishengarh Durbar's company there were some disadvantages too. The latter was that he being a big man I had several times to do things that he wanted. . . . It was a sort of work. This time I was quite free to go where I wanted and do what I liked. . . .

In concluding the notes I have simply to say . . . that this was the best and happiest term that I had passed. . . .

6

"Good-bye, My Dear Corps": Seventh Term in the Imperial Cadet Corps

[The last term at the ICC ends with a reception at Agra where the viceroy, Lord Curzon, personally congratulates the first four cadets to graduate and be commissioned. Keeping Amar Singh's "hand in his for more than a couple of minutes," the viceroy tells the cadets that he looks upon the Corps as his "dear child" whose future depends more on "us four" than on the viceroy, whoever he may be. Like generals and viceroys, cadets have to go on learning.

The departure has its moments of sadness. Amar Singh will lose the companionship of his admirable and talented classmate, Zorawar Singh, the only cadet smart enough to provide Amar Singh with the stimulating conversation he craves, and with a poetry collection. And he must part from Captain Cameron, officer and now friend. Their earlier antagonism has given way to an intimate and rewarding friendship, full of companionable sessions of Shakespeare reading.

It is a critical moment in Amar Singh's career. Lord Curzon's efforts to arrange regular king's commissions for the cadets have failed for the moment. The viceroy secures a tepid second best, a commission signed by King Edward, to be sure, but not in the Indian Army. They will be officers of the Indian Native Land Forces (INLF), a service whose very title announces its restriction. INLF officers will have a more elevated status than VCOs but they are barred from commanding British troops and officers. There is a big question mark over their role.

Curzon's best hope is to secure posts for the newly commissioned cadets in the Imperial Service Forces of their respective princely states. Such an outcome would be quite congenial to Amar Singh, who could be near his wife and keep an eye on the *thikana* (estate) and family affairs in Jaipur even while pursuing his chosen profession. But it is not to be.

Amar Singh mobilizes all possible voices on his behalf: the former British resident at Jaipur, Colonel Pears; the new British resident, Mr Herbert; his officer at Jodhpur and in China days, Captain Hughes, who is serving as liaison with the Jaipur Imperial Service Forces. But he fails to arrange an audience with the Maharaja of Jaipur, Madho Singh, to remind him of his promise of an appointment in Jaipur. None, not even the viceroy, can move Madho Singh, who remains adamant about not giving an appointment to the son of his enemy, Narain Singh of Kanota. The maharaja's resistance also rests on fiscal objections: raising a cavalry regiment for imperial service from scratch would be very costly for Jaipur. Such a regiment is finally raised in the 1920s, after Madho Singh's death. Amar Singh—retired from the Indian Army—commands it.

The diarist leaves the Corps to take up the first of a series of staff positions he will occupy over the next fourteen years. Because staff officers are not in the line of command, they do not raise the vexed question of a "black commanding a white." Amar Singh's first and longest assignment, from 1905 to 1914, is as ADC to General O'Moore Creagh, general officer commanding, Fifth Division, Western Army Corps, Indian Army, at the Mhow cantonment in central India. Amar Singh is the only Indian in the officers' mess. From there, he proceeds to Europe in 1914, to join the Indian Army on the Western front, seeing active duty in France and Mesopotamia on the personal staff of general officers commanding the Sirhind Brigade of the Lahore Division. In 1916, he joins the personal staff of General Knight at Bombay; in Waziristan in 1920 and 1921, he commands troops in the Third Afghan War.

The list of cadets studying with him during his seventh and last term contains historic names, some hitherto unnoticed, of the eight former cadets who, on August 25, 1917, become with Amar Singh the first Indians to receive regular king's commissions in the Indian Army.]

Dehra Doon, Thursday, 13th October, 1904

. . . Coming to my room I wrote my notes about [the marriage of my sister-in-law at] Satheen [a large celebration in the western desert of Jodhpur which Amar Singh has attended]. I kept myself pretty busy at them and only rested for a little when Zorawar Singh came and began to talk. That was all right because I was in want of a little rest too. . . .

Monday, 17th October, 1904

. . . I wrote my notes about my last visit to Satheen and at a quarter to three went to polo. . . . A black waler came down with me. I did not feel any pain then but I am doing so now. . . .

Tuesday, 18th October, 1904

. . . When the Sergeant Major moved us I could not keep up the step [because of the pain] and was allowed to fall out. A short time after this Cameron came and said that I may go and change and he would be coming with some medicine that he will himself apply. I did as was wanted and wrote my "Notes About My Last Visit to Satheen." He came in after eight and applied the medicine. It is a black stuff like tar and he used it for his horses. This is called the Parsee's medicine. After this he went away and told me to lie down. If I wanted to write I had better do so on my bed. . . .

Wednesday, 19th October 1904

. . . The pain in my ankle [is much better]. This is really a wonderful medicine that Capt. Cameron . . . tried on me. . . . I again sat down to write my "Notes about My Last Visit to Satheen" and I am glad to say I have at last finished them. I wrote one hundred and twenty-nine pages of this diary, which means more than four months' extra diary pages. What a lot. After this I selected the headings for my "Notes About My Last Vacations." . . .

After Cameron had gone I . . . again wrote my notes. . . .

PHOTO IV-9   Amar Singh shooting birds, probably in 1909. His attire expresses his cultural stance: Jodhpur *sapha* (turban); English shirt, tie, and well-cut gentleman's sport coat; "Jodhpur" breeches. Amar Singh's photo albums.

Tuesday, 1st November, 1904

. . . At half past six Zorawar Singh and I went out sketching. We wanted to give the others a slip. . . . The boys knew well that they could not do anything without Zorawar Singh, and were soon on our tracks. . . . When we had crossed the Tons [river] and wanted to sketch the bank . . . we had a hard time of it. We could not see the points to resect[1] ourselves and besides this, it was dreadful walking just on the top of the precipices through the tall dal [lentil] cultivation. However, we had to make the best of what we could. Zorawar Singh was the only man who was doing real work. The rest were copying him. Some of the boys could not even resect their points. . . .

[With the coming of the cold weather, the corps shifts from the cool hills of Dehra Dun to the warmer plains at Meerut.]

Meerut, Monday, 7th November, 1904

. . . I went out shopping. . . . I bought some collars and neckties. We then went to another shop, where I bought some shirts and ordered some suits. I am afraid I shall have to dress in collars and cuffs and trousers [if the assignment is as a staff officer in the Indian Army. If Amar Singh were to serve in princely India, he could make different choices.] . . .

Tuesday, 8th November, 1904

. . . I came to my room and changed. I had an awful lot of trouble to wear new collars and neckties which I have begun using from today. I have commenced these because I was told to do so. [Subsequently, when Amar Singh wears English dress, he accompanies it with a sapha, a Jodhpur-style turban, and, in the photos we have, Jodhpur-style breeches.]

Saturday, 12th November, 1904

Last night after dinner I wrote my diary and arranged the question papers with my examination papers of the last term, as I am going to send them to Colonel Pears, the resident at Jaipore [in the hope that the resident will use his influence to secure a post from the Maharaja of Jaipur]. . . .

Sunday, 27th November, 1904

. . . while out hunting, Cameron told me that he was going to marry Miss Pilkington.

Monday, 28th November, 1904

Last night after the hunting I rode back with Mrs Barrett and talked to her the whole time. She is a very good lady. She is the sister of Lord Kensington. This morning, Cameron told me that Mrs Barrett was praising me a great deal, and he was pleased to hear it. . . .

Thursday, 1st December, 1904

Last night after dinner we stopped in the mess for some time and after coming to my tent I found myself so much out of spirits by what I had been told by the Capt. Sahib about the commandant's getting angry *with me for not being able to do that simple sum[2]* that I could not even write my diary. . . .

[Today] I went to some shops though I did not buy anything. I find that I have already spent over three hundred rupees on clothes after coming to Meerut. This is too much, but then I have had to get quite a new outfit for myself as the other things are considered unbecoming by the officers.

Sunday, 4th December, 1904

. . . Capt. Cameron was not here. He has gone to Delhi for one day and is busy making love to Miss Pilkington, with whom he is going to marry very soon.

Monday, 5th December, 1904

. . . In the morning I . . . went out and worked my ponies. I saw Capt. Cameron and asked him whether he had a good time at Delhi. He said "Yes, thank you" at first, and then smiled and said "Big joker!" He understood that I was joking about his engagement. . . .

Wednesday, 7th December, 1904

. . . Polo over I came home and went to Capt. Cameron. We had several talks on different subjects, and I am glad he has taken a good idea of me. There are some boys whom he does not like and he told me so. He showed me his genealogical table and I find that he is descended from the Scottish kings.

Saturday, 17th December, 1904

. . . In the evening the rain stopped though it was very cloudy still. Captain Cameron and I went out for a ride. He gave me one of his ponies to ride. The evening was very nice and cool and reminded one of home. . . . He is getting very friendly with me indeed. After our return I went and talked to him and he read me out a little of Shakespeare. It was about King Richard II. He can read very well indeed. I understood every word of what he read and the beauty of it was that while he read he changed his feelings according to the sentiments of the book. I wish he would read me the whole of Shakespeare in this manner. It would do me a world of good indeed. . . .

Sunday, 29th January, 1905

. . . I went to Capt. Cameron, who was talking with Miss Pilkington. They called me in and I talked to the lady for a short time. This over, I went to Zorawar Singh, and we read a little of *Combined Training*. I then came to my tent and wrote a letter to Umaid Ramjee asking him to get half a dozen gold buttons, with blue enamel, made and sent at once. I want to make a present of them to Miss Pilkington on her marriage. . . .

Wednesday , 1st February, 1905

. . . Today I got a letter from Thakoor Ram Nath Singhjee of Peepla congratulating me on the appointment of commander in chief of the Jaipore Imperial Service Troops. Here is the exact copy of the letter:

> My dear Bhanwarjee,
>   I am highly pleased to hear the welcome news of your appointment as the Commander-in-Chief in the Imperial Service at Jaipore, which is to be in force from April next. Though it has been known to me privately, yet I could not restrain myself not to communicate this happy news to you. Nothing could have given me more pleasure than such news concerning our dearest friends. Please accept my most hearty congratulations for the same. Congratulating you again.
>
>   I remain, Yours most affectionately,
>   Sd/- [Signed]
>   Thakoor Ram Nath Singh of Peepla.

I do not know how much of this will come true. I would not put much faith in such idle gossip, but there is just a slight chance of its being true. The first is the wording "which is to be in force from April next." I do not know the thing at all, but what I think is this, that the Jaipore Durbar had gone to Calcutta and the viceroy must have suggested to him to have a cavalry regiment. Now if they want to raise a regiment, there is every chance of my getting the job. . . . What I am afraid of is that there might be some one fooling me. However, let us see the result. [There seems to be no follow-up on this letter. It is likely to have been a hoax.]

Saturday, 4th February, 1905

. . . At eight we had practical fortification. We were to dig a trench. I was so stiff with the pain in my back that I could not even stoop down to dig. When the commandant knew that I was not well he told me to put on my coat and watch the sand-bag revetments that we were building. While we were at work, I told Kasim Shah that one of the sand-bags that he had laid was not correct. Upon this Rajjee [the Maharaj Kanwar of Cooch Behar] said something to the effect that why did I not do it. I said that I could do just as well as he could but this morning was not well. I then told Rajjee that I had never spoken a word to him and he had no business to quarrel with me in this manner. The argument stopped there because I was afraid of our quarrel reaching the commandant, who used to think that I was a proud and conceited fellow, and if he now heard something of this quarrel, he might think that I am still what I used to be, and this might come in my future career, as we are just about to get something. Therefore, I thought silence the best thing, and acted upon it accordingly. . . .

Sunday, 5th February, 1905

Last night there was a big dinner in our mess. In fact it was the polo dinner given by my mess to the Mohammedans. I did not attend. I was well enough to go if I wanted but I thought I had better not, as Rajjee and I had had some hot words in the morning and we might clash again, which would result in my disfavour, because the officers would think I was [unheeding]. Besides this, that fellow is a swell, and has been brought up in England, and consequently has everything in his favour. . . .

Saturday, 11th February, 1905

. . . At the [polo] ground we bid good-bye to Capt. Cameron, who is gone to Muttra, and will be married there on the 16th instant. Capt. Capper will work in his place.

Monday, 13th February, 1905

. . . Capt. Cameron having gone away, I feel as if I was quite lonely. . . .

Wednesday, 22nd February, 1905

. . . We were told by the commandant that . . . he was going to commence the examination tomorrow. . . . I don't know why, but somehow or other I felt sorry when I realised that this was the last day he will lecture us. He was very kind indeed. . . .

Monday, 13th March, 1905

. . . After school Zorawar Singh and I asked for leave for a few days as our examination was now over. After a little hesitation the major granted it [and] Zorawar Singh and I had a jolly good gallop [to] the train. . . .

Kanota, Monday, 10th April, 1905

Notes About My Ten Days Leave. [Amar Singh makes a final effort to get a military appointment at Jaipur, a possibility that is contingent on the Jaipur maharaja creating a cavalry regiment.]

V. The Durbar

I had sent word to the maharaja sahib [of Jaipur] requesting that I may be given the honour of coming and paying my respects. The durbar sent back word that he was not feeling well but that he would send for me before I went away.

What I wanted to see the durbar about was that he had promised to employ me in the state after I had finished my course. This promise was made at Dehra Doon, and I wanted to find out whether the maharaja sahib would keep his word. I am sure he never would do such a thing, but all the same I wanted to try. I might perhaps have been allowed to go and see him but, the plague having broken out with some force, I went away to Kanota and never again thought of the matter. My grandfather of course told me that it was no use trying, because the durbar will never be pleased with us in his life. . . .

XIII. Capt. Hughes

Capt. E.M. Hughes of the 14th Hodson's Horse who is the inspecting officer [for Imperial Service Forces] in Jaipore is my great friend and I told him all about my affairs and he promised to speak to the resident, Col. Herbert, who is a new man here. [Hughes had served with the Jodhpur Lancers on their China expedition, where he and Amar Singh were associates.] The result was that I went to see Herbert twice. The first day he was so busy that I had to wait for nearly two hours and even then he came and apologised that he could not talk to me just then as it was his luncheon time. He asked me to come the next day. I did as was desired. I did not talk to him about my affairs, because I knew he would not do anything for me, as he had told Hughes that nothing could be done for Amar Singh in this place as the maharaja is so much against Narain Singhjee. . . .

Hughes advised me to serve outside in government. He even asked me to breakfast and I would have gone but Bheem Singhjee advised me not to do so [because of the maharaja's opposition to interdining with Europeans]. . . . Hughes lent me his ponies to play polo and altogether he was very good to me. . . .

Meerut, Friday, 24th March, 1905

. . . In the morning I . . . went to Capt. Cameron and gave him the tusks of his pigs, and six gold enamelled buttons, which are a present from me to Mrs

Cameron. It is rather a pity I could not see him for long and his wife not at all because I had to come to parade. . . .

The commandant showed us the result of our practical examination in which Zorawar Singh is first, I second, Vali Uddeen third, and Kasim Shah fourth.

Dehra Doon, Sunday, 2nd April, 1905

. . . The commandant told us that he had just heard the result of our written examination. In the morning he had told me that we had all of us passed, but now he told us the order in which we stood. Zorawar Singh was first, Kasim Shah second, Vali Uddeen Khan third, and I last. This was a great surprise not only to me but even to the commandant. This Kasim Shah was the greatest blockhead, and I had always beaten him and Vali Uddeen at all the test papers and it was only at the last moment that he beat me. This was rather curious. . . .

Mount Abu, Saturday, 27th May, 1905

Notes About My Seventh Term in the Cadet Corps.

XIV. Mess

This time we had quite a jolly mess. We were only four of us for most of the time. . . . If there were no messes, the boys would hardly have become familiar to one another. It was at mess that we used to express our opinion and heard the others comment upon our ideas. . . .

I am much in favour of eating in the European fashion rather than the Indian. The former is much more neat and clean, and has the advantage of the dishes coming one by one and at intervals. This helps conversation and one gets his food hot. As regards Indian custom, the food comes all at once and while you eat one thing the other gets cold. Then it is a much dirtier way. People may say what they like but truth is truth after all.

. . . Well cooked English food is just as much to my taste as the Indian. I might say that if there is Indian food and one has to eat with knives and forks then there is no fun. In the same way if there is English food and one has to eat it without knives and forks then it loses the enjoyment.

XV. Studies

I did all my work well except those subjects in which there was arithmetic or calculations to make. I was so bad at it that the commandant used to get very angry indeed. . . . After we had been selected for the third year I knew I would pass all right and hence I did not take much trouble. . . .

After having gone through this course I think what an ignorant fellow I had been before, yet I used to think that I was just as good and clever an officer as any other when I was out in China. . . . Zorawar Singh was a great help to me in all the work . . . but then I always used to tell the commandant that I had taken help. . . .

I am an awful man at marching. The sergeant major used to say that I never did nor ever will march. I was extra cautious when the officers were watching, but it was no use. I was always out of step.

XVII. The Officers

The commandant Major W.A. Watson . . . plays polo just as well and just as hard as the best of us and when out sketching he used to be on his . . . feet all the time and never seemed tired. He used to climb up hill at Dehra Doon before most of us. . . . He knows how to teach and is very very patient at it. I am sure there are very few men who could have patience to teach me surveying. Watson used to get very angry and sometimes even swore but was alright afterwards. His knowledge is very great and he knows a lot about religion. . . . He was very polite and kind this term. . . .

Capt. D.H. Cameron too is a perfect gentleman. It was only during the last days that I saw his descent. He comes from the royal house of Scotland and his great-grandfather was an earl. He mixes up with people of big families. There had been arising a great friendship, or I may safely say love between us. During the latter days he used to call me to his room and talk to me for hours and read Shakespeare to me. He used to take and value my advice too. Of all the cadets he liked . . . me best. . . .

There was a time when he used to shun the society of women, but when he was about to be married, he one day asked me whether a few ladies among gentlemen out hunting did not look pretty. This made me smile, though I did not express my opinion or remind him of his old ideas. There is no doubt women look pretty when out hunting, but formerly he did not like to go out with them. I had got so familiar with him that on several occasions I used to crack jokes at him about his running away on every holiday [to see Miss Pilkington].

He had just married, and though he did not accept any present from any other cadet he accepted mine and afterwards that of Zorawar Singh. . . . Mrs Cameron is a nice lady though not very handsome. She is of a good family and by this marriage Capt. Cameron has got related to some big swells. His father-in-law is Pilkington, who is a very rich esquire in England and is fond of keeping and breeding hounds. . . . Even now [Captain Cameron] writes to me very often and is very intimate. . . .

XVIII. Cadets

The following are the cadets that we had during the last term. The first seven are the old ones and they have been corporals. Out of them the first four were given commissions:

+1. Thakoor Zorawar Singh of Bhavnagar.[3]
+2. Bhanwar Amar Singh of Kanota, Jaipore.[4]
+3. Aga Kasim Shah of Bombay [nephew of H.H. Aga Khan].[5]
 4. Nawab Vali-Uddeen Khan of Hyderabad.[6]

+5. Khan Mohamed Akbar Khan of Hod Mardan.7
 6. Raj Rajendra Narain, Maharaj Kanwar of Cooch Behar.
 7. Sahibzada Amanat Ullah Khan of Tonk.
+8. Banwar Prithee Singh of Kotah.[8]
+9. Bala Sahib Daphle of Juth Kolhapur.[9]
10. Nawabzada Kuli Khan of Cambay.
11. Nawab Ibrahim Khan of Sachin.
12. Nawab Fateh Deen Khan of Manawadar.
+13. Malik Mumtaz Mohamed Khan of Shahpur.[10]
14. Nasar Khan.
15. Ghaus Mohammed Khan of Bhopal.
16. Buldeo Singh of Murshan.

[+ Cadets who received king's commissions on August 25, 1917.]

2. I am writing about myself now. I too was one of the successful candidates and stood second in one and fourth in the other final examination. I was made a corporal.

At one time I managed to have a squint at our long roll and the first remarks about me entered there are "Champawat Rathore of Kanota. Jaipore, Born in 1881.[11] Date of joining 3/1/1902. Educated at Nobles School, Jodhpore, for six years. Then Rissaldar in Jodhpore I.S. [Imperial Service] Cavalry. China Medal 1900. First class horseman. Education good. Son of Narain Singh of Kanota."

6. Raj Rajendra Narain, Maharaj Kanwar of Cooch Behar, had joined the corps late and then was away for one whole term to England.[12] He was made a corporal because he was a big man. He was good at all his work and all the games. I don't think the boys liked him much because this boy had been brought up in England and looked down upon Indians as mere animals. I am always against bringing up boys in England. This makes them used to English life and they always afterwards hanker to go there. They get English ideas and like English food, dress and women. I don't think they would care to marry Indian ladies. What a great mistake. . . .

7. Sahibzada Amanat Ullah Khan was one of those that had been selected for a third year's course and was made a corporal. He was very spendthrifty and the officers noticed it and asked him several times but he always said that he was not in debt except for a couple of hundreds. To these officers he used to say this while to his political officer at Tonk he used to say that he had to spend a lot of money to keep his position as all the others were spending a lot of money.

. . . The political officer enquired about it from Major Watson who said that the boy, who keeps one pony, can easily maintain himself on Rs 160. It was then that the resident wrote and said that the boy was in debt some Rs 20,000 at Tonk and Jaipore and he suspected him owing money to some people at Delhi. On this, enquiries were made, and then the curtain was drawn aside. The boy was in debt to nearly every big European firm in India. At Delhi he bought some five thousand rupees worth of jewellery from one man and the very next day he sold it for Rs 800. This buying was merely a means of getting money. He used to get money by saying that he was a member of the Imperial Cadet Corps and that on his word of honour he would pay. Gradually there came in complaints from all the shops and the whole thing burst up.

On this Amanat Ullah was degraded from the rank of corporal and the following was the order that appeared in our order book, "Imperial Cadet Amanat Ullah Khan is deprived of his rank as Corporal for conduct unbecoming an Imperial Cadet and for disobedience of orders." . . . Lord Curzon . . . said that a boy who had deliberately told a lie and tried his level best to cheat his officers was not deserving of a commission. . . .

16. Now I come to the last of the cadets, Kanwar Buldeo Singh of Murshan. He joined about the middle of last term. He is a Jat and his elder brother is the Chief of Murshan. He is very obstinate and thinks that he knows all . . . about horses and talks a lot about pigsticking. The boys rag him a lot and the officers too don't like him. Buldeo Singh is so very obstinate that he will never do what he is told. One day it took Zorawar Singh more than half an hour to convince him that it was better to eat with a European gentleman than with a Hindoo sweeper. Buldeo Singh held out that, though a sweeper, the man was after all a Hindoo while a European was a Christian and not worth eating with. His education too is not much. He can hardly talk English and his pronunciation is horrible. The officers don't like him and I think he too will never get a commission. . . .

XIX. The Sergeant Major

Sergeant Major Chapman of the XVth Hussars was our instructor during the whole of the three years. . . . He was a very good man taken all round. He knew his work very well and had the knack of teaching too.

. . . I did not associate with him because he was a soldier and if he did not mix with the officers why should he do so with me. Even at home I did not mix with him because he had habits like a tommy[13] and not an officer. . . .

When I left the corps I made him a present of Rs 50. Zorawar Singh most probably did the same but I don't know what the others paid.

XX. The Office Baboos

There were three baboos in the office, viz., Harsooram Dass, Heera Lall and Sasti Chander Chatterjee.

1. Harsooram was a short and thin chap and a clever one too. He was the senior of the baboos and did all the responsible work. . . . I don't think the baboo is worth confiding secrets with, because when he used to tell us the corps secrets he would certainly have no scruple to disclose other peoples' secrets. Besides this, his ideas are not at all high. He always told us that Englishmen were not worth trusting and that they would do nothing whatever for us. I used to get bored by his arguments. He thought India could drive the English out if all the native states united. This he said because he does not know what a lot of difference there is between the training of Indian and English officers. The soldiers are just as brave but it is the officers who win battles nowadays.

XXIII. Visit to Agra

We four successful cadets, Zorawar Singh, Kasim Shah, Vali Uddeen and myself were taken to Agra to the viceroy for interview . . . where we put up at Laurie's Hotel. . . . The viceroy . . . wanted to see us at once. . . . We were ordered to wear our long coat khakee uniform. I had not worn it for some time past and so the belt had become very tight.

[At] the circuit house . . . we had to wait in the drawing room . . . about three quarters of an hour and that time was spent most uncomfortably because of the belt which was awfully tight. I could hardly breathe.

At last we were called to the presence of the viceroy who shook hands with us and then gave us a short lecture in which he said he was very pleased to see us all pass and that we must now be satisfied that we will get commissions, and that the government of India had all along been intending to give commissions to the deserving few and that the talk in the newspapers about the cadet corps "tottering to its fall" was all humbug and that we will now know that our time and money had not been wasted but was used for the best possible purpose. The future of the corps depended more on us four who have passed than [on] the viceroy. If we did good work and were liked by everyone, then there will be more commissions given, otherwise it will have to be put a stop to. He had always looked upon the corps and treated it as his dear child and that he will continue to look upon it in the same light and he had no doubt that his successors would do the same.

Then he [advised us] that wherever we go we ought not to think that our work is done and we know everything. On the contrary, we have just begun learning. . . . Even the generals and the viceroys have to learn. We ought never to give airs of conceitedness . . . [but] show ourselves to be eager to learn. Our behaviour ought always to be modest and civil.

This sort of lecture lasted for a few minutes after which the viceroy asked how we stood in examination. Major Watson said that Zorawar Singh was first in both exams but he did not know about the others, as there is a little changing in the results of the exams if taken separately.

Then the viceroy asked whether we would have to go to our states eventually. On this the major pointed me out and said that when this boy becomes a thakoor he would have to go. The viceroy then asked me whether my father was a member of the council. I said that my grandfather is in the council and my father is guardian to H.H. Alwar. On this he said that he remembered my father. The viceroy then asked me about my medals and was glad that I had seen war service. He told us that he did not know for certain where he would send us, but one was going to the imperial service and that he was communicating with the military authorities about us. . . .

When the conversation was over the viceroy shook hands with me. He kept my hand in his for more than a couple of minutes and all that time he was expressing his pleasure and happiness. Then he shook hands with the others. . . . This over, we took our leave and came away. . . . We took leave of the commandant and his wife who are going to England on six months leave. . . .

XXIX. "After the Ball"

"After the Ball" was a chestnut entire pony that I bought from the Alwar Durbar for Rs 600. . . . Major Watson . . . sold him for me to Major Vaughan for Rs 1000. 1 would have sold him for about 12 to 15 hundred rupees had the brute not gone lame.

My object in writing this is that Major Watson gave me a lecture on it one day. He said that horse dealing was not at all a good thing and people often cheat others by sticking them with bad animals for long prices. He said that if I bought a trained pony simply for the sake of making money it would not look well. People would look upon me in the light of a dealer and consequently I would fall down in their estimation and lose that respect which they would otherwise give me. He advised me to be very careful about it. Even among Englishmen people such things are noticed and if I did so I would be noticed much more so because I, being an Indian, and having obtained a commission, I would be more noticeable. I promised him that I would not sell any bad pony and that was the reason of my selling "After the Ball" so cheap.

XXXIII. Conclusion

Now I have come to the conclusion of my labours. This is my last term in the cadet corps and I am glad to write that I have gone through it with credit and am one of the few who have been lucky enough to get commissions. Another great point is that I have nothing but the happiest of recollections for the three years and three months spent there. I learned a lot. When I joined I thought I knew all. Now I think I am just beginning to learn and am very ignorant. . . .

Good-bye, my dear corps, I shall ever remember thee with gratitude and love.

PART V:
PRIVATE LIVES IN PATRIARCHAL SPACE: AMAR SINGH AT HOME IN PRINCELY INDIA

"For a long time historians, like bourgeois Victorians, hesitated on the threshold of private life, held back by modesty, incompetence, and respect for a system of values according to which public figures were the heroes and makers of the only history worth recounting: the grand history of states, economies, and societies."[1] So say the French authors of the monumental five-volume *The History of Private Life*. The historical conventions they deplore, which privilege large structures, élites, and the public, have been breached in the last several decades. The private realm has come to rival states, economies and societies. Private arenas, we are told, nurture categories and practices that shape constellations of power. To retrieve these practices and categories, the micro-chronicles of the dining table, the kitchen, the bedroom, the study, and the salon emerge as history worth having and knowing.

The History of Private Life emphasizes the complex agency implicit in objects of everyday use and in customs and practices of intimate living. The escritoire in the boudoir, like the desk in the library, marks the art of letter writing and related forms of sociability; seating patterns at the farmer's table buttress patriarchy; solitary reading of novels feeds the inner world of imaginative truth; consulting and winding clocks on the mantle and in the hall inscribe linear time and the metrical calibration of life; gazing into a mirror reveals a previously unsuspected individual self and promotes self-regard; proliferating undergarments enhance and suppress sensuality. Diaries themselves—who wrote them, when, and under what circumstances—are important; in Alain Corbin's phrase, they become a means to realize "understanding and self control."[2]

The concept "private" has thereby gathered considerable theoretical and empirical baggage, serving to celebrate the unraveling of the individual from communities, corporate structures and authorities, patriarchs and masters, the family, the church, and the locality. Part V contains Amar Singh's account of private life in the haveli—the 100-person "big house" in Jaipur city where his extended family and its retainers, staff, and servants live and work. We have tried to attend to private life in the context of the complex society of the *haveli* (mansion), rather than confine our attention to contextless individuals.[3]

What can and should be said about the private lives of individuals in a Jaipur haveli? If the extended family's daily life in the big house under the patriarchal sway of Thakur Zorawar Singh creates and celebrates community and corporately defined persons, how does the solitary vocation of the diarist come into being in the same haveli? Can Amar Singh write about his and others' "private lives" where this practice is forbidden, where seeking privacy—insulating the self—is viewed as self-regarding and presumptuous?

The diary, written in secret for "understanding and self-control," is itself a challenge to patriarchal authority, communal living, and corporate self-definition. A diary is like a mirror which allows a person, accustomed to seeing the self through the eyes of others, to do so through the eyes of the self. Amar Singh's diary allows him to experience a self provisionally extricated from the demands of others, to commune with himself. It allows him to examine, evade or contest the judgments and commands of those who shape and govern his life, his immediate and extended family, his Champawat lineage, his Rajput status order.

The diary reveals selves constituted by communitarian and corporate living. Identity and conduct are subject to the ever-present eyes, ears, and admonitions of others. The collective interest has multiple agents and objects: Amar Singh's grandfather Zorawar Singh, the dominant geriatric force; Narain Singh, Amar Singh's much admired father, painstakingly obedient to his father; his mother, apparently weak and aggrieved, who constrains her sons through her power over daughters-in-law; the Greek chorus of aunts, surprisingly effective even when widowed; his uncle Roop Singh, the Naila thakur, the richest and most powerful of the three Champawat[4] houses, upholder of the lineage's status as measured by lavish expenditures; the cousins, Bhoj Raj Singh (Gondher) and Pratap Singh (Naila), Amar Singh's peers, suffering "generational subalterns," victims of the project of corporate solidarity.

The gaze of the elders approves and shames, sanctions and forbids. Respect for elders mandates self-effacement. Eyes should be demurely lowered. Laughter is suspect. Smoking or drinking show disrespect by exhibiting self-regard. All actors collaborate in an elaborate theater of denial, suppressing public display of affection. On stage, Amar Singh acknowledges neither his wife nor his daughter. He must not be seen at midnight ascending the back stairs of the haveli on the way to his wife's room. Affect and sexuality are seen as threatening to generational hierarchy. Flaunting the autonomy of individuals or the bonds of a nuclear family represents a danger to corporate life. The communitarian society licenses and regulates the sentiments and emotions of its members, especially the young and the female.

The diary violates this solidarity. It reveals the surreptitious strategies of circumvention that actors can employ. It expresses and affirms the individuality and autonomy of sentiments that bind Amar Singh to his wife, daughter, cousins. It records that the generational "underclasses" feel oppressed. The very idea of a self-searching diary, which entails probing for a more authentic self beyond the conventional self, is subversive. The imperative not only to enact but also to feel deeply the requisite sentiments of respect is so stringent that entertaining unlicensed sentiments even in the privacy of one's own conscience is dangerous. The *Rajasthan Patrika*, a widely distributed regional daily, in the mid-1980s serialized Hindi translations of the diary that revealed Amar Singh's criticisms of his master, mentor, and patron, Sir Pratap Singh, regent of Jodhpur. Irate readers wrote to the editor to upbraid the diarist for allowing himself even in secret to have such thoughts.[5]

The diary reveals the asymmetries built into the communitarian structure. The patriarch, Zorawar Singh, controls the community and selectively empowers and disempowers its members. His domination is revealed in both generational and gender relations. His approval is required for every expenditure, every trip, every important family interaction, every extra-familial enterprise. Amar Singh becomes adept at circumventing Zorawar Singh's licensing process and confides to the diary his increasingly critical view of his grandfather's policies and actions.

He and his father, Narain Singh, heirs to the title and estate, obey because obedience to Zorawar Singh seems to them legitimate, the keystone of the extended family edifice and, more broadly, their way of life. They are prepared to contest Zorawar Singh's patriarchal rule covertly and by evasion but not directly. Amar Singh sums up his ambivalence by asking, "At what costs must elders be obeyed?"

The hierarchical system of the joint family produces a radical democracy among the generational and gendered subalterns, enforced by daily mutual supervision. "I am even afraid of getting clothes made for [my wife]," Amar Singh tells in the diary, "because the other ladies don't like the idea . . . If they can't have something, why should others?

Is "private" then an impermissible epistemological import, not applicable to any part of the diary? The word "private" seems to have relevance only in one sense: the *zenana*, the women's quarters in the haveli, appears to be "private" space, in contrast to the "public" space of the *mardana*, the men's quarters. Visitors from the world outside the lineage find admittance only in the mardana. Yet what is private about a life lived under the authoritative scrutiny of elders and betters? Is not the entire life of the joint family by definition "public," that is, a sphere in which there is no space for a private self? Private and public, it would seem, are fluid categories, situated in history and practice. They vary with time and place; they remain under constant review.

In organizing the diary into parts and sections, we have tried to follow Amar Singh's sense of the distinction between two realms. For him the "public" world, its culture and morality, lies beyond "home," beyond the havelis of his immediate, joint and extended families, beyond the Champawat connection—the Kanota, Naila, Gondher and Peelva households. It is a marker of Amar Singh's liminal existence that the public-private distinction coincides roughly with English and Indian, raj and Rajput. Our division of the diary into parts mirrors the emerging dichotomization of private and public spheres that is a hallmark of the "modern," coeval with, though not restricted to, the British empire. Amar Singh himself makes the same distinction when he writes of the Imperial Cadet Corps (ICC) experience in a compact essay "My Second Term in the Imperial Cadet Corps," while separately reporting on "My Last Vacations at Jaipore."

Families look different when viewed from outside than from inside. Viewed from an external perspective, they become unified actors in public space, and are so seen. The three families descended from a common ancestor at Peelva thikana in Jodhpur, are often referred to, in Jaipur, by their sub-clan aspect as "the Champawats," a branch of the Rathore ruling clan of Jodhpur state. This characterization lends them a solidarity which does indeed sometimes appear in their public actions. In the project of using marriages to enhance the families' status, a strenuous enterprise requiring skill, money, and a capacity to stage ceremonial theater, they often collaborate and profit from each other's successes. For Maharaja Madho Singh, who doubt their loyalty, and tries to confiscate their estates, the Champawats at Jaipur appear as a corporate entity. For the several branches of the family, Kanota, Naila, and Gondher, on the other hand, each house of the Jaipur Champawats has a distinct identity. Much of the diary is about the sometimes acerbic internal politics of particular joint families, and conflicts among the three houses that make up the extended lineage network.

Amar Singh's life is framed by Kanota haveli. The large house on Mani Ram ki Kothi ka Rasta, the street of Mani Ram's house, inside the walled city of Jaipur, was built by Zorawar Singh in 1874, three years after he was granted the jagir of Kanota for service as a senior minister at court.[6] Mohan Singh calculates that the house accommodated something like a 100 persons, including some who slept elsewhere: the accountants, the family priest, and resident artisans and craftsmen. Three generations of Kanota men and their families lived there: grandfather (who was widowed); father, with his wife and children and father's brothers with their wives and children; and father's sons with their wives and children.

The numbers are increased by a large complement of servants. They sleep on the verandahs of the house to be available around the clock: Amar Singh's wife brings five maid servants from her home estate of Satheen; other women of the family have variable numbers of maid servants; father's brothers each have several men to look after their needs. Amar Singh too has several men, even at the Cadet Corps, where the number is restricted to two. Among them is Kaloo, the influential head servant and guardian of family honor and dignity, who advises him how to conduct himself at the thikana of Satheen. We have photographs only of the men servants, not the maids, even as we have no photographs of the Kanota *thakuranis*, the wives of the thakurs.

The three-story haveli is wide and spacious, with many open courtyards as well as closed chambers. It teems with people. It is an *oikos*, a self-contained economy, as well as a place to live. On the ground floor are spacious storerooms for supplies—grains, oil, pulses—brought in from the lands around Kanota village; there are sheds for cattle who produce fresh milk for the household, and stables for nine or more horses. At the front are rooms for the accountants who keep records of the common expenditures of the joint family, tailors and craftsmen who cater to the household's needs, and a puja room where rituals to the *kul devis* (household goddesses) are performed.

Space is strictly gendered. The zenana, women's quarters, are separated from mardana, men's quarters. Traffic is one way—from mardana to zenana. Special walls are built, visible on the floor plan, to shelter the women from the public gaze. Space marks generational status: lower and larger rooms are better. Until her death, the senior thakur's wife holds the prime space on the ground floor shown as, "Zorawar Singh's wife" in the floor plan. One can follow the progress of the women who marry into the household. They start out on the "second floor"—a third floor by American concepts—and gradually move to the first. As they acquire sons, age, and importance, they descend and expand. Amar Singh's mother, as the wife of the heir apparent ("Narain Singh's wife"), should have first claim in the room lottery: she moves from her original quarters on the second floor to several quarters on the first floor, until she reaches the most desirable space at the center of the first floor, overlooking an open terrace on one side and the floor below on the other. For the sheltered women behind the zenana grillwork, that space was most precious which allowed them to observe the comings

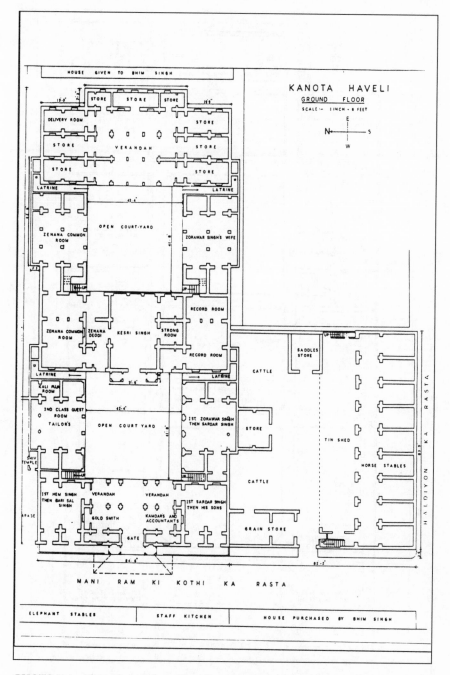

PHOTO V-1   Floor plan of Kanota haveli at Mani Ram ki Kothi ka Rasta, Jaipur city. The plan shows *mardana* (men's space), *zenana* (women's space), horse and elephant stables, g storage, and offices for accountants and stewards. The *haveli* (mansion) accommodated some 100 persons, including four generations of the family and personal servants.

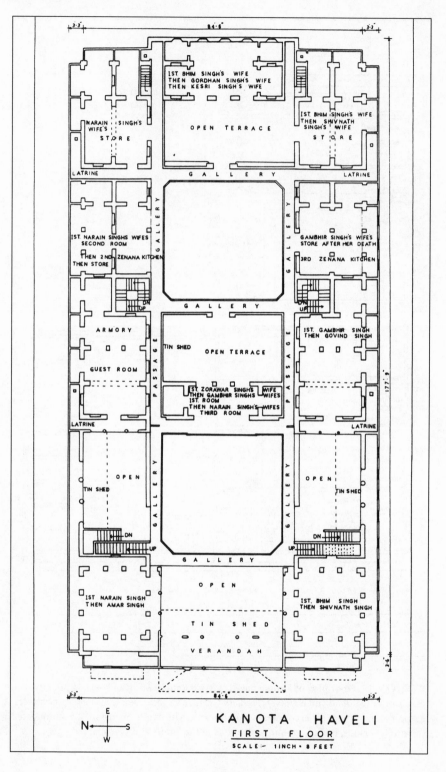

1ST BHIM SINGH'S WIFE
THEN GORDHAN SINGH'S WIFE
THEN KESRI SINGH'S WIFE

OPEN TERRACE

NARAIN SINGH'S
WIFE'S STORE

1ST BHIM SINGH'S WIFE
THEN SHIVNATH
SINGH'S WIFE
STORE

LATRINE

GALLERY

LATRINE

1ST NARAIN SINGHS WIFES
SECOND ROOM

THEN 2ND ZENANA KITCHEN
THEN STORE

GALLERY

GALLERY

GAMBHIR SINGH'S WIFES
STORE AFTER HER DEATH

3RD ZENANA KITCHEN

GALLERY

DN
UP

DN
UP

ARMORY

TIN SHED

OPEN TERRACE

1ST GAMBHIR SINGH
THEN GOVIND SINGH

GUEST ROOM

PASSAGE

PASSAGE

1ST ZORAWAR SINGHS WIFE
THEN GAMBHIR SINGHS WIFES
1ST ROOM
THEN NARAIN SINGH'S WIFES
THIRD ROOM

LATRINE

LATRINE

OPEN

TIN SHED

GALLERY

GALLERY

OPEN

TIN SHED

DN
UP

DN
UP

GALLERY

OPEN

1ST NARAIN SINGH
THEN AMAR SINGH

1ST BHIM SINGH
THEN SHIVNATH SINGH

TIN SHED

VERANDAH

N E S W

177' 9"

84' 6"

3' 3"

3' 3"

84' 6"

3' 3"

3' 3"

KANOTA HAVELI
FIRST FLOOR
SCALE:- 1 INCH = 8 FEET

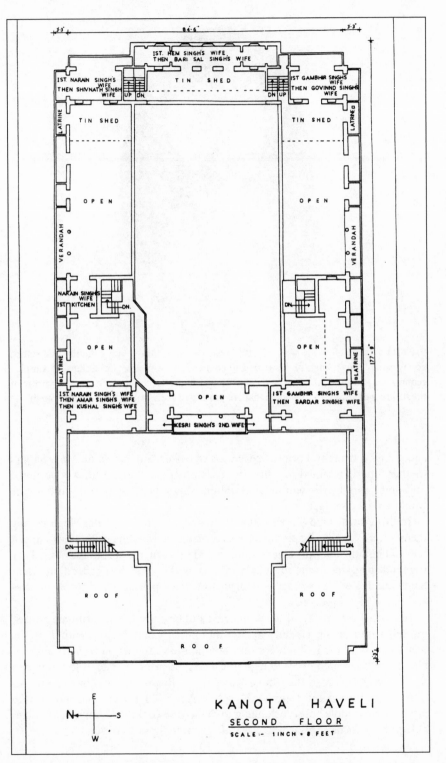

KANOTA HAVELI

SECOND FLOOR

SCALE :- 1 INCH = 8 FEET

PHOTO V-2   "Kaloo, my servant" (1907) worries about the family's dignity and status, accompanies Amar Singh on his trips and advises him in matters of conduct at complex ceremonial and mundane events, e.g. to bring along an adequate retinue, as is worthy of the future *thakur*; not to buy boots that are too expensive. Photograph by Amar Singh.

and goings outside and below. Space wars were frequent and acrid. Amar Singh's mother bitterly resented that the prime chamber she yearned for was occupied for some years by the widow of Gambhir Singh, Narain Singh's brother. She would not be dislodged.

In this crowded, busy arena, those who sought privacy—Amar Singh among them—were usually disappointed. Everyone knew everyone else's affairs, and if they did not, the omnipresent servants would find out and spread the news. They were indispensable to the social control exercised by the older generation. Amar Singh and his wife nevertheless struggle to make a private world for themselves and sometimes do succeed.

In Part III, we saw Amar Singh married and beginning to incorporate himself into his Jaipur family. He does so after more than a decade spent entirely in the men's society of the Jodhpur Lancers, among the young Rajput princes and nobles in the household of Sir Pratap,[7] regent of the princely state of Jodhpur, and the soldierly society of the China War. When a Rajput marries, the wife moves into the groom's parents' house. Now that Amar Singh's wife has moved into *bichli haveli*, middle house, belonging to the second of three Champawat families at Jaipur, the focus of his private life shifts from Jodhpur to Jaipur.

The transition is eased by changes in his family and career. Sir Pratap, his guardian and master, has left Jodhpur, first for the China campaign, then to become Maharaja of Idar. Amar Singh's professional life has moved from the Jodhpur Lancers to the ICC, and from the princely setting of Jodhpur to the more British one of Meerut and Dehra Dun, the winter and summer locations of the Corps. The old Jodhpur men's society, revolving around Sir Pratap, has virtually disappeared.

Many of the long essays in this part are called "Notes About My Last Vacations at Jaipur." They signal the realm of the household, of women's affairs, Marwari speech, and Rajput etiquette, as distinct from the professional, English, and men's society of the ICC. Amar Singh undergoes an apprenticeship in the rules and practices of what he calls "Hindu family life," observances meant to foster harmony and protect and improve the family's status.

He begins to recognize himself as a family man. He begets a daughter and becomes attuned to his identity as a father, husband, householder. Amar Singh is expected to perform important ceremonial and ritual functions in connection with lifecycle events, such as his first visit to his wife's family. He is initiated into the legal position of the thikana, which is threatened by the maharaja's enmity. At the age of twenty-four, he begins to know the father who has been a virtual stranger to him during the years he lived with Sir Pratap, and begins to experience the authority of the seventy-five-year-old Kanota family patriarch, grandfather Zorawar Singh.

This "private life" is lived in the vacations that are sandwiched between terms. Amar Singh keeps daily entries, but also writes extended essays on his experiences, often after he has returned to the ICC. We have again shaped Amar Singh's account into a more coherent form than the diary naturally offers, gathering entries around a dominant theme, and allowing the reader to see particular practices more intensively.

1

Diplomacy of Everyday Life: "This Damned Etiquette"

Dramatis Personae

Thakur Zorawar Singh of Kanota, chief of the thikana of Kanota in Jaipur state. Grandfather of Amar Singh.

Kanwar Narain Singh of Kanota, eldest son and heir of Zorawar Singh. Father of Amar Singh.

Banwar[1] Amar Singh of Kanota, the diarist. Eldest son and heir of Narain Singh.

Thakur Roop Singh of Naila, uncle of Amar Singh.

Mehtab Singh, estate steward (*kamdar*) of Naila, cousin and favorite of Roop Singh.

Umaidjee Purohit, Kanota family priest and intermediary.

"My Wife" [Giving her name would be "out of etiquette"].

"My Sister."

"My Daughter."

Thakur Kishore Singh of Satheen, chief of the thikana of Satheen in Jodhpur, brother of Amar Singh's wife.

Thakur Sultan Singh of Peelva, chief of the estate in Jodhpur from which Amar Singh is descended.

Kaloo, "my servant."

Moti Singh, servant of the Thakur of Satheen.

H.V. Cobb, British resident at Jaipur.

Barath Ram Nathji, Amar Singh's teacher and friend.

[Amar Singh, having become a father, arrives in Jodhpur on a short leave from his studies at the ICC. His object is to fetch home the wife he has not seen for nine months. As is common in north India, she had returned to her family's estate, Satheen, for the birth of a daughter in the last week of July. Since it is "out of etiquette" to acknowledge his interest in bringing her home from Jodhpur to Jaipur, Amar Singh establishes a good and dutiful reason with which to extract the required permission from his grandfather to travel to Jodhpur: the delivery to the Maharaja and Maharani of Jodhpur, head of the Rathore clan, of the invitation to his sister's wedding. Such eminent persons are supposed to receive invitations by hand. Not mentioned in his application for permission is his eagerness to see his wife and to arrange her return to Jaipur.]

Dehra Doon, Friday, 8th August, 1902

I Become a Father.   Yesterday I received a letter from Jaipore, written by Umaidjee, in which he informs me that my wife has given birth to a girl on . . . the July 30 last. All my family were expecting a son and so was I. It is rather a disappointment to them all. As regards myself I do not much care whether the child is a male or is female. What I most care is for my grandfather. What a disappointment it must have been to him. If he had seen a great grandson he would have been very much pleased. He has already a lot of them but this one would have been the one that would have caused the greatest happiness, as he would have been the direct heir to the thikana.

Then my mother would have liked to see one very much and so would my father. However, what is done is done. Hope to have better luck next time. . . .

[Amar Singh, as eldest son of the eldest son, Narain Singh, is heir to Kanota. Failure of male issue entails adoption, which may cause conflict within the family. In the event, Amar Singh has six daughters but no sons. Only one daughter survives.[2]]

Jaipore, Saturday, 6th September, 1902

Notes About My Visit to Satheen.

I. The Beginning

My wife had gone to Satheen in the middle or end of January last. . . . She was there even when these vacations commenced, though she had given birth to a daughter who was yet only twenty days old. My grandfather had written to Thakoor Kishore Singhjee to send my wife [back to Jaipore] as my sister's marriage was to take place [a time at which younger women are needed to help with the ceremonies], but my brother-in-law wrote back saying his sister was too weak to undertake the journey and so the matter was dropped. . . .

[Amar Singh lays plans to visit his wife's home thikana to bring her back to Jaipur. Such a visit is a weighty matter. Beginning with his own wedding, and across the years covered by this volume, Amar Singh aspires to become an authority on ceremonial matters and an exemplary Rajput like his father, Narain Singh. His ethnographic proclivities conspire with his concern to become one to whom others turn for guidance in matters of ceremony and other aspects of culture. The careful observations of major rites of passage, such as this first visit to his wife's house in the honored status of son-in-law, or the many accounts of weddings are fruits of this ambition.[3]

The bridegroom's first visit to the *sasural* (in-laws) poses delicate problems of interpretation. Amar Singh is on his own for the first time and his moves illustrate the contested and ambiguous nature of conventions. He is beset, on the one hand, by conventional expectations about how such an event "should" be conducted—with much *eclat* requiring careful preparation, an escort of many men, and a long and expensive stay. The event should emphasize the superiority of the groom and his family. On the other hand, Amar Singh has come to share his guardian Sir Pratap's opposition to bankrupting expenditure and conspicuous consumption in Rajput ceremonial events. Amar Singh's servant, Kaloo, speaks for the view that only an ostentatious visit is worthy of Kanota's future thakur. So too does the head of Amar Singh's lineage, Thakur Sultan Singh of Peelva. The debt-ridden Thakur of Satheen musters thirty men for his retinue when he receives Amar Singh—who comes with fewer.

On such visits the bridgeroom may conduct himself as an imperious and demanding figure. Amar Singh is reluctant to do so. He is torn by the contrary pulls, his wish to visit Satheen and his unwillingness to play the conventional role of churlishly demanding son-in-law. He tells us that "one should do unto others as one would be done by."]

When I came to Jaipore . . . I was in a fix. . . . My mother and sister were very keen that my wife should come. They always used to tell me at least half a dozen times whenever I used to go in to see them. Matters having come to this crisis, I told Umaidjee to tell my grandfather from my mother's side to send some men to Satheen to call my wife. [Propriety demands that his mother, not Amar Singh, display an interest in the wife's return.] And to make the matter easy, I sent a telegram to my brother-in-law [Thakur of Satheen] to come and meet me at the station [on the way to Jodhpur] as I was leaving for Jodhpore that very night [to deliver the *nota* (invitation) to the Jodhpur ruler]. My intention was to tell the Satheen Thakoor Sahib to send his sister as soon as possible because my mother and sister were very keen on the matter.

II. Unexpected Order

[On my return from Polo] Umaidjee told me that my grandfather had ordered that if the Satheen Thakoor Sahib was to ask me to stop at his house I would do so and if my wife was allright I could bring her along with me. What more could I want? My arrangements were all ready. I was given two hundred rupees for the expenses. I took two servants and told Umaidjee to send Madho Singhjee [a Rajput member of the household staff] tomorrow as I would want some men. How little did my grandfather know about my plans. He had told Umaidjee that on my way to Jodhpore the thakoor sahib [of Satheen] would not know of my passing but after I had reached there the Satheen vakil [the thikana's agent at the Jodhpur court] would inform his master who would ask me to break my journey for at least a couple of days. I was laughing [up] my sleeve. How naughty of me! . . .

IV. My Uncle Sooltan Singhjee's Views

[Sultan Singh, the head of Amar Singh's sub-lineage, resides at Jodhpur. He is Thakur of Peelva, the small Jodhpur estate from which Amar Singh's grandfather and two granduncles had left for Jaipur to seek their fortunes in the mid-nineteenth century. Amar Singh stays at his uncle's town house while in Jodhpur, and is told to consult him as the expert on local conduct.]

I kept very quiet and did not inform my uncle [about the proposed visit to Satheen]. I told Kaloo and the other servant to keep the matter quite secret. At last, when Madho Singhjee came the next day, he advised me to let my uncle be informed and take his advice [about the visit to Satheen]. Sooltan Singhjee Sahib arranged for some of the things that would be required and was rather against my going [due to the sparse preparations] but when he heard that it was my grandfather's wish nothing was done to prevent me. The following were the men that accompanied me: Kaloo, Sundio and Mego as servants, Madho Singhjee and Morjee Kuramsot as thakoor log [that is, Rajputs, equals in status whose presence would add weight and dignity to the party], and Baloo Darjee as the family bard or charan.

V. Kaloo's Views

My servant Kaloo was quite against my going. His arguments were that this was the first time that I was going after my marriage and according to the usual customs I must go with at least twenty men and have all sorts of deshi clothes and ornaments [of the native costume]. Further on he said that when I was married nothing was done owing to the presence of Sarkar [Sir Pratap, Amar Singh's guardian, who insisted on simplicity][4] and so this time something must be done. His arguments were quite good enough and had such a force on me that I once wavered and had half a mind to postpone my going. This was, however, put off by Mod Singhjee [servant at Satheen] who had come from Satheen to invite me.

VI. My Talk with Moti Singhjee

Kaloo's arguments had so much divided my mind that I flatly refused to go when Moti Singhjee asked me but that fellow had his orders from his master and pressed me so much that I had to agree at last. What I argued was that I had no clothes with me that were befitting the occasion and as regarded ornaments I had practically none at all. Then I had no men that would be suitable. The last though not the least point was that my sister's marriage was so very near which would not permit me to stop for more than one day.

Moti Singhjee said that there was no need either of clothes or ornaments as all the people knew me so well. As regarded men, he said that all those in Satheen were at my service. Then the point of my sister's marriage was settled by his promising not to keep me more than three days. . . . [I kept] the matter secret from my uncle Sooltan Singhjee Sahib.

VII. The Journey from Jodhpore

. . . In the train I had a little talk with Kaloo who was still against my going. I explained the whole matter to him and then he agreed that I must go if the matter stood as I represented. . . .

At the Pipar Road Station [which is a day's camel journey from Satheen thikana] some men [from Satheen] with horses and camels had come to receive me. . . . In the way [to Satheen] I had some shots at a chinkara [gazelle] and wounded him. I fired at a bustard [cranelike bird] but missed. During the whole of the way I was [persuading] Moti Singhjee to try and get me leave by tomorrow noon. My arguments were as follows. First of all my sister's marriage was so near and there was so much work to be done. My grandfather was too old and my uncle Bheem Singhjee too weak to do all this. Then my father had not come from Alwar yet. Besides this I told him to think whether he himself or his master would go to see his wife at her paternal home when there was work to be done at home. The last though not the least argument was that the Thakoor Sahib of Satheen would always wish my good and not bad name. If this was true then I must go as that would give me great credit, whereas if I stayed they would all laugh at and crack jokes at my expense.

I was talking with so much force that Mod Singhjee agreed to try his best in my behalf. . . . To do to others as you would want them to do to yourself," I said, was the best way of doing and settling such things. This sort of talk whiled away our time. . . .

VIII. The Meeting

About a mile and a half from Satheen, Thakoor Kishore Singhjee came to receive me. He was driving in a phaeton carriage to which were harnessed a pair of heavy Australian horses. One elderly gentleman was with the thakoor sahib holding the hooka [pipe] which they were both of them smoking. Behind them were from twenty-five to thirty horsemen as an escort. As soon as we met we got off our different conveyances and embraced each other. The thakoor sahib did my nichrawal and I did his. [This is a ritual to honor a person; the person honoring rotates rupee notes around the head of the person being honored and then throws them on the ground as a gift to servants, singers, dancers.] He asked me to smoke but I declined. After this the usual formalities of inquiring after each other's health were observed.

This over I was asked to ride on and stop at the temple of Matajee [the lineage deity, a mother goddess] while my brother-in-law followed. . . .

IX. Waiting at the Temple

I had to wait at this temple until after sunset as the rules required that a janwai [son-in-law] should not reach his sasra [in-laws] before nightfall. . . . I was made to sit on a bed and on a mattress spread on the ground. All the others [were] seated. These fellows were all the notables in Satheen. The hooka was circulated all round. . . .

X. Entry in Procession

At the temple I had put on decent deshi clothes [the elaborate ceremonial dress that he had managed to avoid at the wedding, when his ascetic guardian, Sir Pratap, was in charge.] I had on an achkan [long, fitted coat] of silk richly worked in gold and a gold work turban with the picture of Sarkar on it. Round my neck I had some ornaments. My brother-in-law had sent a white mare which had a deshi saddle richly worked in gold. On this I mounted and started for the koat [fort]. The village people had thronged the streets and were all looking eagerly at me. Mid-way some of the Brahmans came and made a tilak [mark of a red paste] on my forehead. Some women came with brass vessels in [which] were put some neem leaves. This was the Kalas [pitcher] ceremony and is observed on joyful occasions while welcoming someone near and dear. I reached the koat where Kishore Singhjee was waiting to receive me.

XI. I Sit in Durbar

Immediately after my alighting from the mare I was conducted by Kishore Singhjee to the chowki khana which is a sort of platform with a stone railing. Carpets had been spread on it and in the middle was a thicker one with a great big round pillow where I was made to sit. All the people [were] seated round me and began to talk and smoke. Opium was circulated but stopped very soon as none of us would take it. The thakoor sahib is a sensible man and so did not argue at all. If there had been someone else with the silly notions of Rajpoot customs, he would have forced us at least to taste a bit of opium. I talked very little but quite enough for the occasion. Some of the bards came and recited a few welcome stanzas. The dholees [female musicians] were singing and playing on their guitars. It was all rejoicing in the house. . . .

XII. I Go into the Zenana

At about nine o'clock some women came singing. This was the invitation for me to go in. . . . I was taken before the room of my dadeer sasoo, that is to say the wife of my brother-in-law's father's uncle who is now dead [the senior woman in the thikana]. Having taken her aasees, that is to say blessings, I was taken to the upper apartment where I used to be taken when I was married. The women stood in the door and said that it was barred and I must open it. This is a Rajpoot custom. To enter I must recite a verse of poetry which must be to the point of asking their permission to let me go in. I did not know and so walked in without saying anything. The women had to give way and so I walked in and sat on the padded carpet in spite of the women telling me that it was barred. I simply said that nothing was barred to me in this house as they were all opened when I last came here. Hearing this they all laughed.

Now the room was overcrowded by the women who pressed over one another. It was hot and they made it doubly so. At last they brought my wife in [and] asked me to get up and conduct her to the seat near my side. I refused to do so, saying that it could not be done every time, but it was no use denying. They had their own way and I had to get up and just touch the arm of my wife who now came and sat near me. This over, the women began to ask me to give them something for the welcome news of my daughter's birth. I could not say anything and kept quiet. At last the curtain was put up and both the wives of Kishore Singhjee and both his sisters came and sat behind it. They now began to ask me questions which were all out of my understanding as they were a sort of riddle [such riddles are often *risque*]. I continued saying that I did not know anything, to which they said that if I did not know anything, then how was the child born. Such sort of thing continued for a long time.

I got up and gave wine to them and they to me. I could not of course see them as the curtain was between us. I had to lift it to pass my hand and tumbler under it. At last dinner came. I now asked them to send my sister-in-law (the sister of my wife) to join us which they refused to do. I said that I would not dine unless they did so. The argument continued for a long time, they denying and I insisting. The women said that she had gone to bed but I said that it was all humbug as she was just here and that the excitement of the moment was enough to keep her up all night. At last, after a long time, they did send her. As soon as she came in she did the moojra [a low bow with folded hands]. I got up to receive her and conducted her to my right. She had no veil over her face as she is younger than my wife and consequently a sort of sister. I made her drink wine which she returned to me. We kept talking for a long time even amidst this noise.

During this interval I put a gold mohur [coin] in my salee's [wife's sister] hand and the conversation was full of jokes. We three, that is to say my wife, her sister and myself, had dinner together. The meal over, my sister-in-law brought my daughter and asked me to take her in my arms. I could not do so as it was against etiquette, but my salee chased me all round the carpet. I used to move to one corner when she used to come there and try to put the child in my lap. At last I gave her an oath which put a stop to this joke which was being enacted at my expense.

It was now past midnight and all the women retired and I was left to talk to my wife. She was very weak though looking quite healthy. I now had a look at my daughter. She is quite a handsome babe though it is too difficult to judge her beauty at this early age.

XIII. Talk with Kishore Singhjee

Next morning after I had washed and bathed myself my brother-in-law came to me and talked for some time in private. The subject of conversation was my going. [Persuading a guest to stay on is thought generous, and allowing him to go early is thought stingy.] I gave him all the reasons that I had [given] to Moti Singhjee on the way. When I explained to him the principle of "to do to others as you would want them to do to yourself," he found my necessity and agreed that I may leave at two p.m. What more could I want?

XIV. I Go in to Breakfast

. . . I sent for my sister-in-law. . . . She asked me to give her something for the welcome news of my daughter's birth, to which I replied that I would find her a very good husband. When she heard this she kept quiet as there was no answer to it. This sort of jokes continued for a long time. She told me not to take away her sister and my daughter as she was so very fond of them both. I told her that if she liked them to such an extent she had better go along with them and if she was willing I would make arrangements. This question kept her quiet, because she can not go to my house unless she marries me, and marrying is a word out of etiquette for her to speak in my presence.

I got very fond of her, as she is a very good looking girl with gentle and noble features. Her disposition and her talk are very mild. She is well built and taken all round a very good woman. All the same she is like a younger sister to me and I will try my best to get her a good husband. I went out as it was time to leave Satheen which is such a dear place to me.

XV. I Leave Satheen

Having put off the achkan I changed myself into my riding clothes and went to take leave of my brother-in-law. The Brahman came and put a tilak on my forehead. The siropaos [set of clothes given at a ceremonial departure] were shown. Not only I but the men with me were given as well. On mine there were one hundred and fifty one rupees, a couple of gold mohurs, and some other clothes. One mare was given. This being done I took leave and started. . . . Madho Singhjee and Kaloo were left behind to accompany my wife. This is how I visited my sasra the first time after my marriage. I hope to go there many more times.

XVI. The Mare

The mare that Kishore Singhjee showed to me was a brown one. There was red cloth put on her and so I could not see whether she was a good or a bad one. Even if she had been a bad one I would not have spoken a word. My principle is that whatever he gives with pleasure I consider as best and don't desire anything better. The next day, after I had gone, Madho Singhjee [the accompanying staff member from the Jaipur house, left behind to bring Amar Singh's wife] just dropped a hint that this was not quite a nice mare. Hearing of this, the thakoor sahib told him to have his pick out of his whole stable. Madho Singhjee chose a bay filly which was at once given with the greatest pleasure. When I heard of this I told Madho Singhjee that there was no need of his doing such a thing. I did not like this at all and wrote a letter to my brother-in-law in which I asked his pardon for any trouble or inconvenience that may have been caused to him by this incident. Just imagine how you yourself would have liked if Karan Singhjee [Amar Singh's sister's bridegroom] had said that he would have Ghatotguch or some such horse. How annoyed were our family when the Thakoor of Achrol made this fuss [when Amar Singh's cousin was married to him]. "Do to others what you would like them to do to yourself," is my principle.

XVII. How I was Received

I was received very warmly indeed. . . . we wanted nothing. The food arrangements for my men were excellent. . . . Though we were only a few of us, we were supplied with fresh meat for which one big goat was killed every day. One of these goats would have been sufficient for a whole bridal party of three hundred men if used economically. . . .

XVIII. Concluding Remarks and Comments

. . . The clothes and ornaments that have been given to my wife this time are quite good and enough. They are much more than any member of our family has got yet. Of course this is the biggest thikana. . . .

[Amar Singh returns from Jodhpur with his wife to the family haveli at Jaipur.]

Jaipore, Saturday, 23rd August, 1902

. . . Having taken a slight breakfast I went to see my aunts who began to taunt me about my going to see my wife on the way [to Jodhpur]. . . .

Monday, 25th August, 1902

At about six a.m. Sheonath Singh and Gordhan Singh [cousin] went to the railway station to receive and bring home my wife who had arrived in the early morning by the mail train from her brother's house at Satheen. . . . After coming from there I had breakfast and then sent in word to my sister if I could come in and see her. So long as my wife was not here I was quite free to go in whenever I wanted but things are now changed and I have to take great care.

My sister asked me to come in but when I went she brought forward my daughter and so I had to come out again. Etiquette requires that I must not touch my daughter before other people. My sister had no great need of me as she was busy talking to my wife who has come after a long time.

["Etiquette" routinizes and naturalizes conventional proprieties that express social hierarchies and enact social distance. The severe sanctions on public displays of affection Amar Singh reports between husband and wife, father and child, are not unique to north Indian Rajputs at the turn of the century, although they may vary among castes. Such inhibited behavior may be interpreted in various ways: A Freudian would suggest that the young are obliged to deny their sexuality which challenges or competes with the sexuality of seniors; the functionalist would say that these practices protect against exploitation of women in a joint household where a range of senior and junior males live in close proximity with young women not their wives, or alternatively, that these practices protect the commonality of the joint family against the challenge of intense emotional ties among married pairs and their nuclear family; the feminist would perhaps suggest that the power structure of a patriarchal household represses all energy and vigor that may compete with the senior patriarch; and the Indologist, that these practices demonstrate the control of passion and desire as a cultural value in Hindu society.]

Tuesday, 26th August, 1902

Last night we had dinner at a late hour and at about midnight I went in [to my wife's quarters]. I had a great difficulty in doing so as I had to take every care not to be seen by either of my aunts or my mother. . . .

Thursday, 16th October, 1902

At about twelve o'clock I went in the zenana to my mother where I stopped for a while and then went over to my wife in whose company I passed my time from half past twelve fill three o'clock. We chatted and we talked all about our affairs and love. I instructed her to always keep my mother, aunts and all the others pleased for this is the only way she can hope to please me forever. Then there came my daughter who is all healthy and blooming. I fondled her about for a while and then came out . . .

Tuesday, 2nd December, 1902⁵

Notes About My Last Trip to Get Ponies.

I. My First Idea

[Having successfully schemed to see his wife at Satheen in August and Jaipur in October on his last leave from the ICC, Amar Singh soon plots another trip to see her, this time at home. The problem is how to do so while feigning an appropriate disinterest, especially before his father.]

While at Dehra Doon [winter quarters of the Cadet Corps] it one day occurred to me that I may get leave for about a week on pretence of going to Jaipore to try the ponies there and get some for the corps as we were wanting for the tournament. . . . This might prove enough excuse to get leave. When I had thought the scheme over in my mind I spoke about it to Akhai Singhjee who began to joke me. All the same he approved of my plan. . . . Without my first opening the subject, Capt. Cameron one day told me that he would grant me leave to go to Jaipore and bring some ponies . . . I did not want anything better and so the telegram was sent and worded as follows: "May I send Amar Singh for pony Bandabust?"⁶ That very night there came an answer saying "Send Amar Singh at once." . . .

I started for Alwar. The only fear that I now had was whether I would be allowed to go to Jaipore. I could not ask of my father straight off whether I could go home, as I am now a married man and etiquette demands that I must not let my father know that I am keen on going home to see my wife, which is the idea that all the people at home have whenever I go there. . . .

IV. Talk with My Father [at Alwar]

. . . My father asked me as to how many day's leave I had. I said that it was up to the 29th and I was to be present at parade on Monday morning. My father then said that I must run up to Jaipore and see the ponies there. How pleased was I! My grandfather thought that I had come on leave and did not trouble. He thought I would get ashamed if he showed any suspicion that I had come to see my wife. Thus the matter got quietly off. Most people [were] thinking that I was now a married man and taking every opportunity of coming home even for the shortest time possible.

PHOTO V-3   The family coach and four on the Agra road, heading for the country estate at Kanota. Photograph by Amar Singh.

. . . The talk drifted towards the sickness of my sister . . . married [three months ago to Karan Singh of] Gurhi. My father had been [at Garhi] on the occasion of the marriage of Karan Singhjee's sister. My father had a painful story to relate to me. *While describing the scene [he] was speaking in rather a husky voice. My sister gets fits and becomes unconscious for hours together. The Gurhi people think that this is no sickness but that some she-devil (Bhootnee) [spirit, ghost] has got hold of her. My father puts no belief in such silly stories.[7]* . . . He had gone in the zenana to see my sister who at that time was lying senseless and with [clenched] teeth. The women had to force them open. My father's tone began to falter while he described this. I wish he was an author because he can so well picture . . . a scene. . . .

However, my father could not have any talk at that time as the fits last for hours together. Next day when he went in the zenana again my sister was better. She clung to his neck and began weeping. She could hardly talk and begged my father to carry her home and blamed him for having sent her in such a strange place. Well, this is a customary thing. Women of India always do this. In most cases this is looked upon as etiquette and girls have to do it.

The people of Gurhi are under the impression that a bhootnee has got hold of my sister and all manner of cruelties are perpetrated to drive her off. One of these is the putting of chillies in my sister's eyes. Just think of it! My father made my sister understand that there are no such beings as bhootnees and as she was the daughter of such a noble house it did not become her to say bhootnees took hold of her. She ought to keep up the name of her family.

My father's conclusion was that my sister is pregnant, and while under this condition women often get sick, and these sicknesses are of all sorts and this present sickness is one of them, though a rare one. This was not a matter that my father could say personally to his daughter. Now the difficulty was how to let her know. He sent for the slave girls[8] that had come from Jaipore but there too was the block. Two of them are the ones that had come from Satheen in my wife's dowry[9] and these cannot talk to my father. [Women who marry into a Rajput household and their servant girls observe purdah, seclusion, with men in that household, and therefore do not communicate.] The other two had just been purchased and married when my sister's dowry was given. These were quite strangers to my father but they were the only ones in Gurhi [to] whom my father could talk and who could answer back. [Belonging to the Kanota household, they could speak with the men of that household.] To one of these my father explained the matter and told her to advise my sister to keep a good heart.

All this trouble arises through this Rajpootana etiquette. Englishmen talk straight off to their daughters and sisters. However good the latter may be I am not in its favour. I like my own country's customs. . . .

Concluding Remarks

My wife was indeed glad that I had come and it was to see her that I had done all this. I used to spend some hours of the daytime in her company as well. This custom is not prevalent in our house, but I do it sometimes. *I got two Hindi books and advised my better half to read them. She had promised to do so.[10]* We had a jolly time together, which was much more brightened when we had our little daughter smiling between us both. The little child is all rosy and healthy. I am now beginning to appreciate or rather notice what a maternal love means. . . .

Delhi, Tuesday, 23rd December, 1902[11]

[Amar Singh comes home during the Imperial Cadet Corps' Christmas vacation.] *Notes About My Last Vacations of Two Months.*

IV. I Go to Kanota

[Construction of Kanota fort, 13 kilometers from Jaipur on the Agra Road, began probably in the 1870s after Maharaja Ram Singh granted Zorawar Singh, then one of his ministers, several revenue-paying villages of which Kanota was the principal one. At the time of Amar Singh's visit, its massive earthen walls are half completed and an older haveli is the main residence. A more massive two-story

PHOTO V-4   Amar Singh and his fox terrier on the terrace of the *durbar* hall at Kanota fort. The three black bucks were "my bag at Kanota in five minutes," 1910. Amar Singh's photo albums.

haveli with a large durbar hall and other rooms was under construction. Like other nobles' houses, these buildings replicate functional and architectural features of the maharaja's palaces. So long as thrifty Zorawar Singh lives, the son and grandson are not allowed to spend much money on completing the fort or the new haveli. After his death in 1908, Narain Singh completes the wall and develops the garden, stables, and durbar hall.[12]]

To my village Kanota I only went twice and that for a very short time too. . . . The horny and woollen things are being eaten up by the moths while the wooden ones are being treated in the same manner by the white ants. There is no man to take care of them. *I . . . went and had a look at the armoury which, I am sorry to write, was in the most ruinous state possible. The beautiful rifles were all full of rust and going to pots. . . . I had some of the very best ones taken out and well cleaned.[13]* . . . Those that live there don't care whether the things are looked after or not. No one even brooms the place. In corners there are piles of stones lying just as they were when the building was stopped. More than half the fort has been completed but there still remains a lot to be done. I love the place very much. There used to be a garden but that has been removed owing to too much expense.

If I lived there I would put to rights several things that are rotting about and would make the place look much nicer without increasing the expenditure. . . . My father does not go there and my grandfather is too old to look to everything.

PHOTO V-5   Sitting room of *durbar* hall at Kanota fort. Amar Singh, a committed host and gourmet, gave elaborate dinner parties at the fort, drawing on the many books of recipes and food lore he assembled over the years. Photograph by Robin von Breton, 1971.

VIII. Games

[Both at Jodhpur and Jaipur, much of the social life between English and Indians revolves around sport—which transcends both linguistic and, to an extent, cultural boundaries.] . . . Polo is not very popular. It is only my uncle Roop Singhjee [Naila] who is carrying it along. It is he who keeps lots of ponies and players. Of the outsiders there is only Mr Stothard [C.E. Stothard, acting executive engineer, public works department[14]] or some of the inspecting officers of the transport corps. . . . There are several others who would like to play this game but they stand in awful awe of the maharaja sahib who hates manly games and sports. Mr Stothard looks after the polo club arrangements and they are very well kept. All the Englishmen of rank are members of the club. I did not enjoy the games very much as they don't play very fast here and . . . there is too much flattery going on. No one ever dares to ride off my uncles Roop Singhjee and Mehtab Singhjee. Mr Stothard is looked upon as a great big swell and no one must touch him. . . .

Next comes racquets. This game has been recently started by Mr Cobb [the British resident] who is very keen on it and plays beautifully well. Even those who are not fond of it come and play simply to flatter the political agent. . . . Thrice a week there are parties at the residency, the doctor's house and Colonel Jacob's.[15] Those of the Sardars and nearly all the Englishmen go to play. At the residency they too go who do not play. . . .

The last is badminton which is not much [of] consequence. . . . It is only the ladies who join it as a rule. . . .

I found out from Paonaskarjee that Mr Cobb, the resident at Jaipore, has a very good opinion of me, though he took me for a bit of headstrongness. All the same he thinks that this headstrongness is backed up by a great force of moral courage and character. I am proud to have such a good opinion from a resident.[16] . . .

XII. Conclusion

Some people say that after marriage one should stop at home. My experience says that come home as often as you can but remain at a distance. I think this increases love between the pair. . . .

Meerut, Thursday, 29th January, 1903

Notes About My Last Visit to Jaipore.

V. My Garden

[Amar Singh, who on the vacation reported above visited the village and fort at Kanota and complained of the upkeep, now reports on the Kanota family's other suburban property, the "garden" located in the outskirts of the walled city. At the turn of the century, it became fashionable for thikanas to build pleasure gardens near the Rambagh, the maharaja's suburban pleasure palace.[17]]

Here I used to go nearly every morning. Whenever I went inside and saw all the nice trees ruining it cut my heart but there was no help. My father had planted some three thousand mango trees of which there are hardly fifty left and even these are drying up and getting eaten by cattle. These come from all sides, as the walls are of mud and broken in several places. There is only one man looking after the garden but he is too old to work and too indifferent to care for the waste. . . . *Last year the garden was given to a contractor for one year for 250 rupees and this year for forty rupees only. Just think of the ruination. In former years it used to be leased up to 700 rupees.[18]* . . .

VIII. Some Ideas of Our People

One of the greatest causes of the fall of Rajpoots, or I might say of the whole of India, is selfishness.[19] Besides selfishness my family, with a few exceptions, is noted for miserly habits. I shall now write what harm this miserliness does. We don't keep good servants because we have to pay them higher wages. They spoil the work which costs us much more than the wages that we would have to pay good servants that would take care and not let things [get] spoiled. Then there is no end to dirtiness. No one cares to look after our guests and I don't know what they say after they have gone. . . .

This is all because my grandfather either does not care or cannot see [to] the things himself though at this advanced age he is wonderfully active. . . .

XI. Roop Singhjee

[The Nalia family, which is both richer and more inclined to spend than Kanota, gives Amar Singh ideas about how to spend gracefully.]

This uncle of mine is alright in some respects such as cleanliness and treatment of guests, but he has got some faults that put everything in the dark. His garden is well kept and so are his havelis. He has got quite enough servants and horses. The latter and the carriages are well kept and in very good order. But for all this my uncle's temper and habits are not good. . . . He is always finding faults with other people. . . .

XIII. My Brothers

We are seven brothers. I live with the Imperial Cadet Corps, the [next] younger two, Sheonath Singh and Sardar Singh, are at the Mayo College, my father keeps with him at Alwar the younger two, Bari Sal and Kaisar Singh, and the youngest two, Govind Singh and Isri Singh remain at home with our mother.[20] [Mayo Princes and Nobles College at Ajmer was established by Lord Mayo in 1875. Modeled on the English public school, its medium of instruction was English. Since most students were destined to be princes or thakurs, revenue, accounts and law were taught in addition to its mainstay, general education subjects.[21]]

. . . [The brothers] all have a great love for me but at the same time are in great awe of me. My father and myself are the greatest awe inspiring [persons] in the whole of our family.

Amongst us four brothers we have got only one sister. She was recently married. She is a very quiet and a very good girl. She is awfully fond of me. [Apparently, Amar Singh's sister has returned home for a visit. There is no further mention of the fits she suffered, reported two months earlier, after her marriage at Garhi in Alwar.] To make our family and home ties more loving I always call her in whenever I go to my wife who on her part has got strict orders to keep my sister pleased. If my wife and sister are on very good terms my mother is sure to like my wife, whereas if the latter either quarrelled or was indifferent to my sister the result would be very bad. . . . For all that, I know my family are living very harmoniously. May God always keep it as it is forever.

XIV. Ram Nathjee

Though not a family member, this gentleman always finds himself room in my book. [He was Amar Singh's tutor at Jodhpur.] He is much more dear to me than most of my family members. His lectures have made me quite a different man. He came to my house once and I showed him the library. He was very much pleased with some of the books that I have got. He wanted to take some but I would not let him. *I had, of course, made him a present of *Marcus Aurelius*.[22]* He loves me nearly as much as he would his own child. . . . Whenever I write about him I fear of overdoing and spoiling the whole. It is he who clears all my ideas and gives explanations on subjects that no one else can. Though I have so

PHOTO V-6   Estate servants: Moolji Champawat and Soorji Bhati. Photograph by Amar Singh.

much respect for him I am so very familiar that we exchange our most private thoughts freely.

XVIII. How I Passed My Days

. . . From twelve till two I used to be with my wife. During the first few days I used to read *Kaisar Bilas* to her. *This is a good book indeed. The beginning of the play is very interesting but the end is not quite so exciting. This is the first book that I have seen written in Marwari language. A book written in one's own tongue and full of everyday occurrences must be interesting. Anyway I liked this book awfully.[23*] I made one mistake and this was that I used to read for long periods at one time, and this rather made her tired and did me as well. The result of all this was that whenever I began reading she feared I would spend the whole of the time with the book and not talk at all.

. . . The nights were the most pleasant. I used to talk to my wife and sister until ten when the latter used to retire. My wife and myself are quite contented with one another. She has never given me any opportunity to get displeased and I on my side have always tried to keep her as much satisfied as I can. I think she wants nothing better. For all the love she has she stands in an awe of me.

Playing with my daughter was one of the things I did at night whenever she woke. Twice I had great singing [by my wife and my sister]. *I am now beginning to understand this a little and hence I take so much interest in this subject. Besides this, the songs being in Marwari interest me much more than those that are sung in phonographs or by professionals.[24*] . . .

[On the night I was leaving for the Imperial Cadet Corps,] our intention was not to sleep for the whole of the night but the temptation of sleep was too much. It came gradually and irresistably. However, I woke up at four and took leave of my wife. It was a painful moment but there was no help. Having washed and dressed I took leave of my mother and sister. This too was a painful event However, all passed off well because I assured them that I would be coming on leave in April.[25]

2

Lectures to the Maharaja of Kishengarh: "How to Promote Love" and "The Abuses of Youth"

Dramatis Personae

Amar Singh of Kanota, age twenty four.

Maharaja Madan Singh of Kishengarh, age seventeen.

[The prospect that his dear friend and "pupil," the minor Maharaja of Kishengarh, is to be married to a daughter of the Udaipur maharana provides Amar Singh with an occasion to summarize his ideas on the subject of marriage and intimacy. He has thought intensely on this subject over the two years since his own marriage. His "lectures" to the seventeen-year-old assemble what he has learned from Ram Nathji, his friend and tutor, and from Dr George Drysdale, author of the moral and sexual guidebook, *Elements of the Social Sciences: Or Physical, Sexual and Natural Religion. An Exposition of the True Cause and Only Cure of the Three Primary Evils—Poverty, Prostitution and Celibacy,*[1] an essential text for him at the time of his marriage. He also draws on what experience has taught him. ("This I have never heard any man say he knew and have neither read about it in any book."[2]) The "lectures" are delivered when the two friends go out on their daily ride at the ICC in Meerut.]

Meerut, Monday, 2nd February, 1903

Polo over Kishengarh durbar and myself went out for a drive [in his trap]. It was a very pleasant time for conversation and I lectured him on the duties of a husband. My chief points were that the durbar must never marry more than one wife, that he must be quite content with her, that he must never engage any mistress, which is a common rule among the chiefs of the present time, and that he should never trouble his maharani. The explanations were rather lengthy and cannot be written here. However, I will give a point or two of each.

Marrying more than one wife would be very troublesome and would prove the ruination of one's enjoyment in life. In a house where there are two wives, the result can never be any other than quarrelling. Besides this, it is not right by the laws of nature, and one man can never satisfy more than one woman. The next thing [is] that he must be quite content with her, in order that he need not wander out in quest [of] debaucheries as this is a very mean thing. It is the source of all sorts of diseases. Besides this, if a man is not satisfied with one, he will never be with two, three or any number. He will always be hungering for new ones. . . .

At the time of marriage the man makes several promises whose witnesses are all the relatives and the gods. Of course these promises are made in Sanskrit and are not intelligible to common people. The priests know them, but they don't take the trouble to translate. They simply recite what the slokas [sacred verses] are. I myself knew of it when my sister was married. What could be more sinful than breaking such promises?

The next question [is] that he must never engage a mistress which is usually done. I said that it was better to marry a second wife than engage a mistress. Here for the first time the durbar differed [with] me. He said that an engaged mistress would always remain submissive to the maharani and this would save quarrels. I said that he was mistaken. After a time these become just as quarrelsome and sometimes even more. That you can never get a chaste one. Besides this, their progeny would be mere golas [slaves], whereas if he had a wife her sons would be Rajpoots. Durbar being quite inexperienced said that it could easily be managed by keeping a Rajpootni mistress. This made me burst out laughing, and it took me some time to explain him fully that this has never before been done, cannot be done and must not be done. [Amar Singh thinks no respectable Rajput woman would serve as a concubine.] Fancy maharajas having such ideas.

Some nine months ago he had asked me a similar question when he [asked] whether a Rathore man can marry a Rathore woman. Simply think of his ignorance. [The conventions of Rajasthan Rajputs of princely or noble status dictate that they marry outside the lineage to which they belong.] . . .

I said that there cannot be real pleasure without love between husband and wife. This must be promoted with the greatest care. A wife must always know that her husband never goes to any other woman, that he considers her the most beautiful and the most charming one in the world and so on. . . . Bhagwan Manu says "that those houses in which women are honoured are the most peaceful. Those houses in which women are happy are the most prosperous and wealthy. And those houses where women are not honoured and kept happy are always in disunited states and everything is ruined by their curse." [Amar Singh is citing Manu, legendary author of an influential *Dharmasastra*, classical rules of proper cultural conduct, thought to have been composed in the third century of the common era.[3]] These lines have a great and deep meaning. . . . A woman leaves her parental home in the hope of finding another one more comfortable and welcome. If she is disappointed how severe the blow must be. . . .

I made the durbar thoroughly understand the doha [couplet],

> If you have disciplined desire
> Why become a celibate holy man?
> You can experience both human love
> and divine devotion, Berya.

This is one of the dohas whose principle I follow. The Durbar got so much interested that he gave me the reins [of the horses pulling the trap] and listened attentively the whole time. . . .

Tuesday, 3rd February, 1903

[In the previous remarks, Amar Singh provides advice with respect to family issues that are for the most part particular to Rajput society, and draws on his own insight. In the accounts that follow, the influence of Ram Nathji, who appears to have thoroughly absorbed Drysdale's views, and of Drysdale himself, becomes more evident. Amar Singh has learned from Drysdale and Ram Nathji to speak in a matter-of-fact manner about intimate sexual subjects. Drysdale's defensive strategy in a prudish climate, like Freud's, was to adopt a hygienic tone of voice: moderate sex is healthy. He employs the metaphors of science, urging the study of the laws of the body and obedience to them.[4] The metaphors of religion, he says, have obscured insight. According to him, Christianity has led humans away from an understanding of the body.[5]

Drysdale's main object is to liberate people from "rosewater mentality;" and he would have found much of Freud congenial. "One of the greatest causes of all irregularities in the sexual appetites is the destructive checks, obstacles, and degradations, to which they are exposed in their normal course. This has been shown to be the chief cause of masturbation, and so it is of these unnatural practices."[6] He favors "a moderate amount of sexual indulgence,"[7] which he regards as the promoter of strength, vigor, and normalcy; he believes it healthy that women be sexually satisfied. Female hysteria is due to repression of women's need for sex and meaningful work. But he shares the views of his era with respect to "sodomy," understood as "intercourse of two persons of the same sex."[8]]

I had a discussion with [Kishengarh] durbar in which I fully described to him the evils of masturbation and sodomy and a little of the heartlessness of prostitutes. In describing masturbation, I told Durbar that somehow or other young boys learn it even though they are looked after with the greatest care. I am now becoming very free with the durbar and told him that when a man gets fond of or takes a liking to masturbation or sodomy he does not much enjoy intercourse with a woman for some time and this makes him think that the latter is nothing when compared with the former. Some become so shy that they fear to go near a woman. Some do not get an erection at all with a woman. . . .

These points on which I am able to talk and lecture a little are . . . almost the repetition of what had been told to me by Ram Nathjee. Of course some few examples are of mine own and a little knowledge acquired from books is also used here. . . .

Wednesday, 4th February, 1903

. . . After polo Kishengarh durbar and myself went out for a drive to the lines of the Third Bengal Cavalry to tell Zalim Singhjee that we would be coming tomorrow morning at about eight to hunt. During this drive, which was a long one, we had a discussion. The first question was "Smoking" and the second "How to Promote Love"? In order that we may not lack conversation and I may not forget to tell these things that I want to say, I have now taken to write notes on all the things I want to lecture, with a few examples as they occur. Today I gave a copy to Durbar for choosing a subject out of those that I had got written there. . . .

As regards smoking I had not much to say. In the first place I explained that this is a habit which does harm and not a single good can be found in it . . . The bad points about it are that in the first place a smoker's mouth begins to smell [of] tobacco which is not an inviting thing to non-smokers. . . . The second bad thing is that it spoils the liver, which soon gets blotched by smoke, just as the teeth and lips are after some time. Besides this, smoking leads to drinking, which is the worst that a man can do.

. . . Our Rajpoot people spend or rather waste most of their time over this. They wait for a hooqa for some time, and when the thing comes in they all sit round it and smoke by turns. . . . [Amar Singh in his later years becomes an inveterate hookah smoker. A cartoon that once hung in the office of the commander, 61st Cavalry, Jaipur,[9] shows him with a book in one pocket and a small hookah in the other pocket.]

Now to take to the other subject, "How to Promote Love." I had to speak a lot before I could make any impression on the Durbar's mind . . . to promote love . . . is not an easy thing. . . . One must be careful never to use harsh words as their effect is not quickly wiped off. The more tender you will be the more love you will gain. . . . As far as possible one should read amusing books together. . . .

Towards the end the conversation drifted towards the abuses of youth. . . . [What if] one man married two, three or twenty wives. It is the law of nature and a true one too, that no one man must or can satisfy more than one woman as regards sexual enjoyment. If this is true . . . then the rest of the women, besides the one who becomes favourite, suffer from want of intercourse. Nature's wants must be satisfied in some way or the other. It is then that the women either see other men if they can manage otherwise they practise masturbation or sodomy. . . . When women once take to sodomy they do not care for men. . . . Even the prostitutes who are in this habit practise it, though they can get as many men as they like.

Then, just as we were nearing our camp, I said that to enjoy real and full intercourse which would satisfy both parties it was desirable to have simultaneous discharge. This I have never heard a man say he knew and have neither read about it in any book. I did not explain it as this is too indecent and I would have to be more free than I think I ought to. I told the durbar that this one point I will describe when he gets married as it would be rather out of his comprehension. . . . I wish the durbar spoke a bit as well. . . .

Saturday, 7th February, 1903

In the beginning I explained to the durbar the vices of drinking and other intoxications. To take the subject of wine, I said that there was not a single good in this. [Amar Singh uses wine as a generic term for alcoholic beverages, including both the liquors made in Rajasthan, e.g. asha, and English hard liquor.] That as soon as he [Kishengarh] came of age the courtiers and flatterers would gather round him and make him drink. They would say that God made these things for the maharajas and if they did not enjoy them would it be the poor? The aim of the courtiers would be to draw him into the snare, because they know it well that once a chief is addicted to this habit he is no good anymore. He can't work, he can't think, he can't ride or walk, in fact he can't do anything at all, except lying on a bed, talking nonsense and filling the pockets of the flatterers.... [The Maharaja of Kishengarh dies relatively young, in his forties. The oral tradition in the Kanota family has it that drink was a contributing factor.]

Some people think and say that when a man is drunk he enjoys sexual intercourse very much. Now this is a very wrong idea. Alcohol stimulates the mind so much that a man does not enjoy well.... Some say that when drunk a man stays for a longer period during the intercourse. Now this too is wrong....

Now we started the subject as to when children are born and what are the causes of their being males and females. To explain this required a long time. I began by saying that each of the testicles was made of a long tube which has been formed into a round ball. The semen is collected in these. Now when a man has intercourse the semen is discharged from one of the testicles and not from both. Even according to our Hindoo ideas as well as by English doctors it is proved that the semen in the right testicle contains male and the left female germs. For a woman to be pregnant the semen of both the man and the woman ought to be from the same testicles, that is to say, a woman can only be pregnant when both the male and the female discharge take place from the same, that is to say either right or left, testicles. Besides this the discharge must be simultaneous and not one after the other. Because if so, the germs die very soon, and nothing can be done. Besides this, if on any occasion the discharge takes place from all four testicles, the result is impotence, that is to say, they are hermaphrodites or men who are no good for sexual purposes. We call them Napunsak.

Now to have pregnancy one must try and control the discharge, which can be done if anyone knows the way. I have found the way myself though I have never yet seen it written anywhere or heard about it from anyone. This I did not explain to the durbar as it would have been too indecent and obliged me to use words I have not yet done. Then I said that women have the same sort of testicles and penis as men, only theirs are inside. The discharge takes place by both the penises rubbing against one another.

The next subject was when the education of the child begins. This I said begins the very day a woman gets pregnant.... She must think of God and good and virtuous deeds. She must never let a bad idea enter her head. Just the same ideas appear in the child as the mother had during pregnancy....

Further on I said that in our country, and specially among the big families, it is a custom very much prevalent that the mother does not suck her baby. One special woman is employed for this work. Now this is a very bad custom. That woman who does this office is not always a good character and the milk formed in her body has very bad effects upon the future of the unconscious baby. In my opinion it is much better to bring [up] babies with goat's or sow's milk than of other women.... [Our ladies] have a sort of idea that if a woman sucks a baby she loses her beauty which, if true, would be very hard and specially with us people because whenever one of us finds no taste in one wife he goes and marries another....

The last question was as to when a man must marry. . . . Some people have this idea that if people are married at an early age they stop from growing strong and their children are not strong. This is quite wrong. Nature is always right and never in the wrong. . . . So in my opinion one must marry as soon as he becomes of age. That sexual enjoyment which one gets from nineteen till twenty-five can never be obtained in after life. . . .

One can produce children so long as his semen is not spoiled. One drop of semen contains over a hundred and fifty tiny germs and the more a man abuses himself the lesser these get. The lowest number is forty, after which there is no hope of pregnancy from that semen. . . .

Sunday, 8th February, 1903

Kishengarh durbar and myself went out for a drive. Our object was to have a quiet conversation . . . and this we had. . . . Now to take to the first [topic], that is to say dristant [what is seen or heard at the time of intercourse]. I explained that if a woman sees a bad man or a bad picture at the time of intercourse she is quite liable to produce children like that. In our country when a mare is covered, we always keep one very fine horse in her view, so that she may bear a good colt. This point I had to say because the durbar had once told me that there were many nude pictures kept in the zenana palaces . . . they always keep a woman's mind full of the thoughts of intercourse and never let her think of God. . . .

I said that in the zenana there ought to be pictures only of the best Rajpoot characters. . . . There ought to be several pictures of . . . the durbar himself, because nothing so much pleases a father as to see . . . children of his likeness. In some instances fathers begin to suspect the virtues of their wives when children are born resembling others. . . .

The third subject was that I told Durbar that according to his own words some of these babas [natural sons of the maharaja, usually by a kept woman, sometimes by a servant girl] go in the zenana. I advised him to discontinue their going as they are doing no good there. According to Manu Bhagwan no man ought to be in company with even his mother, sister or daughter when alone. The reason is that sexual desires are very difficult to be controlled. . . .

[Amar Singh is arguing that the illegitimate sons of the master are especially dangerous morally and must be excluded from the zenana access allowed to the legitimate sons.] These babas [inherit] . . . the bad character and licentiousness both on the part of the father as well as the mother and mostly the latter, who is never a chaste woman. What can be expected of children born of them? The mother's influence will never go. It must appear in the child. . . . At Kishengarh the babas can go in the zenana at any time and may pass the night there if they want. What a bad custom.

Now I shall come to the last question. Durbar asked me that when a man gets married his wife and mother are always quarrelling. What was the cause of this? The mother puts a lock to prevent her son from seeing his wife, why was [that] so? and what was the best way to prevent these troubles? Then the durbar said that his mother does not like that he should marry at Odeypore, what was the cause of this? I told the durbar that I had quite grasped his question and I was really pleased to hear such an intelligent question from him. Besides this it was a very useful one.

The first question as to why a bride and her mother-in-law are always quarrelling. I said that this is all owing to their both of them being not educated. The mother-in-law thinks that if she kept the new bride under her thumb from the very beginning she would always be obedient. To do this they perform all sorts of cruelties on the poor girls who are quite defenceless. Their husbands as a rule can not help them as etiquette demands their silence.

As regards putting a lock to prevent the husband from seeing his wife [it] is a very bad practice, though it is unfortunately too often used. . . . In smaller houses [this] is done because the mother thinks that if she became so strict and always said that the girl's parents did not give sufficient dowry they (the parents) would send some more things.[10] In bigger families it is used to worry the poor harmless girl. In most cases the mother herself has been treated in the same manner by her own mother-in-law and now tries [it] on her daughter-in-law. This is indeed not [only] very bad but cruel and base.

Then the durbar's question as to why his mother does not want him to marry at Odeypore. [Udaipur is most senior of the four largest princely states in Rajputana, larger and more important than Kishengarh. The Kishengarh maharaja is to marry the daughter of the Maharana of Udaipur.] The reason is that she comes from Sirohi which is a very small place in comparison with Odeypore which is the biggest and proudest Rajpoot house in India. The mother thinks that a girl coming from that family would not care much for her and hence her not liking to marry at that place. [He eventually does marry the Udaipur princess.]

Now comes the question as to how to prevent these troubles. The best and only one for the durbar was to impress on his wife's mind that if she wanted to gain the favour and love of her husband she must never displease her mother-in-law. . . . Besides this, she . . . must be enjoined to wait on her mother-in-law. She must not do anything without permission. She must go and touch her feet every night before taking leave for the night.

Hearing this the durbar laughed out saying he had never heard such a thing. I explained that throughout all Rajpootana this was a custom, that a bride goes and touches the feet of her mother-in-law. . . . Durbar said there was no such custom in Kishengarh. . . . The durbar must insist that his wife not speak as far as she could help and then very little. It is good in this way. If she begins talking she is sure to answer some day when any cross words are spoken to her. The result would be bad. So it is much better not to speak. . . .

Monday, 9th February, 1903

Polo over, Kishengarh durbar and I went out driving. We had our usual conversation. . . .

The durbar told me that there were some hundred women kept in the zenana and all these are virgins and not allowed to marry. These are supposed to be kept for the maharaja's enjoyment. These poor women cannot even go out of the zenana walls, except on certain occasions to worship a god. But this privilege is granted to a very few. I said that this was a very bad custom. . . . There is no hope for any enjoyment to them. If a man or woman had any hopes of being able to get enjoyment after a certain period, he or she may pass that time in chastity; but if, on the other hand, they not only know but are certain that they can never marry, and the only enjoyment they can ever hope to get was from the durbar . . . this is a hopeless business. . . . The result is that they practise all sorts of things to gratify their desire.

Now what ought to be done? . . . I said that when the durbar got married and had got his powers he ought to allow them all to marry. . . . The durbar has promised to do it. . . .

The last though not the least question was the durbar asked me whether I was in favour of exercising our ladies or not? If I was, then how should it be managed? I said that I was in favour of exercising them. Why our big people are not active is that our women are not allowed to [go] out and exercise. They lead an idle life and this tells on their children. A just retribution from heaven for our cruelty to the fair sex. . . .

Now, how should it be given? I said that the only means was through ping pong, lawn tennis, badminton and billiards. These are the only games that can be managed in the zenana and in which the ladies can partake. Durbar said as to what I thought about teaching them to cycle. He said he could get a road closed to other people and reserve it for this purpose. I said that I did not like this idea. I would be the first man to vote for the abolition of the purdah[11] and commencing widow marriage but I would not advise the durbar to take such steps. These would give him a bad name as they did to Jodhpore durbar. So long as we have the purdah we must observe it strictly. . . . I said that it would be alright if he took his maharani sahiba to any place in Kishengarh, but as regards taking them outside to such places as Calcutta, Bombay, Simla, etc. I was quite against. So long as we have the purdah we must not do such things. . . .

3

Women at Home: "What Real Difficulties There Are in a Rajput Family Life"

Dramatis Personae

Kanwar Bhoj Raj Singh of Gondher, Amar Singh's cousin and friend, eldest son and heir to Gondher thikana.

"*My Bhabee*," wife of Bhoj Raj Singh.

"*Mother-in-Law*," the Thakurani of Gondher, Bhoj Raj Singh's mother.

"*My Wife*."

"*My Mother*."

"*My Father*."

"*My Grandfather*."

Thakur Roop Singh of Naila, Amar Singh's uncle.

Mehtab Singh, estate steward of Naila.

[Amar Singh becomes enmeshed in his joint family.[1] Grandfather Zorawar Singh asks him to start mastering thikana affairs; his father Narain Singh and Ram Nathji chastise him for "boyishness;" his mother tries to broaden her control; the invidious comparisons offered by women relatives and servants get to him and his wife. "I am now just beginning to taste of [family life] and I don't like it."

If he begins to find his mother's regime oppressive, his Gondher cousin, Bhoj Raj Singh, finds his mother's even worse. Amar Singh and his wife frequently meet for a companionable evening with Bhoj Raj Singh and his wife. "My bhabee" [elder brother's wife, here cousin's wife] suffers at the hand of Amar Singh's aunt, the Thakurani of Gondher. Amar Singh reassures himself and his wife that his mother would never be so severe.]

Delhi, Friday, 27th March, 1903

I found that a letter had come to me. This was from my father and contained the news that . . . my grandaunt had died. . . . I had my head and moustaches shaved in token of the mourning and took leave of the major sahib to go home. It was of course granted. . . . [She had been the senior surviving woman in the three thikanas, wife of the late Thakur Sahib Fateh Singhjee of Naila, ex-prime minister of Jaipur state.[2]]

Jaipore, Sunday, 13th April, 1902

* ... My grandfather ... told me all about the decision of our case. The villages that had been granted [to us] before [by the maharaja] are to be kept [by us] and those given afterwards are to be exchanged. [The case concerned the attempt by Maharaja Madho Singh of Jaipur to confiscate the estates of the three related Champawat families at Jaipur, Gondher, Kanota, and Naila, on the grounds they had been fraudulently acquired. The families contest the case with mixed success. The settlement provides that the villages given by Maharaja Ram Singh of Jaipur to the three related thikanas in the 1870s, which constitute more than half the holdings of Kanota and Gondher, were to be exchanged for others. Jaipur state argued that these, unlike the villages given to the family in the 1860s, had been fraudulently acquired.[3] The case went up to the highest levels of the raj, where the viceroy's legal advisers declared the Jaipur state's case untenable. H.V. Cobb, the British resident[4] in 1900–1902, apparently supported that outcome. But Amar Singh discovers that subsequently an agreement has been reached which partially supports the claims of Jaipur state by mandating an exchange of the 1870 villages for others. This may have been an effort by the Political Department of the Government of India to save the face of Maharaja Madho Singh. Amar Singh later has bitter words for Cobb.[5]*]

Sunday, 29th March, 1903

I went and talked to my grandfather who showed me a paper in which there was a copy of the orders that have been issued by the Jaipore Durbar for changing our jagir villages and [requiring] a few extra horses for state service. . . .

Monday, 30th March, 1903

. . . I . . . went to the Noara [stables] where two thousand men were being fed, as it is the twelfth day from my grand[aunt's] death. [Lavish death feasts were thought to be a mark of status.] This is the last day of mourning. . . . In the evening at about five the Jaipore sardars began to come and pay their condolence visits which took the whole of the evening.

Wednesday, 1st April, 1903

At three my grandfather sent for me and ordered [me] to read an account of our case. He wishes that I may become thoroughly acquainted with [it]. From this work I got leave at four. . . .

Friday, 17th April, 1903

> How strange a thing is this love of woman, that is so small in its beginning and in its ends so great! See, at the first it is as the little spring of water welling from a mountain's heart. And at the last what is it? It is a mighty river that floats argosies of joy and makes wide lands to smile. . . . She is shy slave, yet holds thee captive; at her touch honour withers . . . barriers fall.

> Book II, Chapter IV, *Cleopatra*
> By H. Rider Haggard

Wednesday, 22nd April, 1903

. . . [I and] Major Commeline [inspecting officer, Imperial Service Troops, Rajputana] went out riding towards Khatipura. I had breakfast with Commeline sahib. This is the second time I have eaten with a European in Jaipore. . . . [This is a matter of some concern, because the Hindu orthodox maharaja, Madho Singh, frowns on interdining between Hindus and non-Hindus.]

Friday, 24th April, 1903

I learned that the late Thakoor of Doondlod [an important Jaipur nobleman] had a pretend son, that is to say, he had no son born to him but he borrowed someone else's and said he was his own. There was a commission set on it and it was proved that the son was really a pretend one and so he has been set aside. [In case of a failure of issue, a nobleman may adopt a child, usually from a related lineage, to succeed him. Because such a succession often moves control of the property from one branch to another of a large joint family, it may become a matter of sharp controversy and fraud.] Now remains the adoption which will be [decided] in favour of Thakoor Chatar Singhjee, the younger brother of Thakoor Bhoor Singhjee of Malsisar. Chatar Singhjee had promised to pay 50,000 rupees [to the maharaja, who must approve the adoption] if his son would be adopted and is willing to pay just as much more if he himself is adopted. I think he will be; but what an everlasting shame to the durbar who accepts bribes!

*The Idea of Bribes

This is a thing prevalent all over the world, but I fear nowhere so much as in . . . the native states of Rajpootana where all the officials, from the maharaja to the lowest state servant who has got any occasion for it, take bribes. . . . Of all the places that I know of, Jodhpore is about the worst. . . . In Jaipore the Maharaja Sahib himself and his Maharani Jaddonjee[6] take bribes. The state posts are given to those who can pay for them.

Fortunately this curse was not and is not so much prevalent in our family. . . . [The] two brothers Shambhoo Singhjee [the Gondher granduncle] and Zorawar Singhjee never went near them. . . . Now comes my family or rather house in particular. I know it for certain that neither my grandfather nor my father or uncles have done it up to the present. My grandfather . . . was giving me a lesson on this head and said that, "Suppose I squeeze some hundred rupees out of some one, you will some day throw them away to a musician. It was I who committed the crime and to what purpose? Simply to spoil my name both in this as well as in the other world. I shall have to suffer for that wrong." These were his very words. He is not a spendthrift, far from it; he is more of a miser, but his money is all honest labour and nothing else. He is always preaching the same lesson to his sons.[7*] . . .

Sunday, 3rd May, 1903

I learned from my wife that the slave girl Bhoori had absconded. It happened thus. My mother had given some wheat to that girl for grinding. On the flour being weighed it was found short of two seers. On this my mother punished the girl who confessed that she had hidden it and went to bring the quantity back. To be on the safe side my mother sent [with her] one of the servant girls belonging to my wife. This girl soon returned and gave the information that Bhoori had gone away and would not come. On being asked to tell everything, she said that after getting out of the haveli the girl walked fast and of this (the guardian) girl's remonstrating she took no heed. The poor guardian, instead of following or bringing back the culprit, returned to give the information. Men were sent to search all round but no trace was found.

My mother put the whole blame on my wife's servant and said that it was the latter who had purposely made the girl either run away or sold [her] to someone else. I, for myself, do not believe this for a single minute. My belief is that the girl has run away for fear that she might be beaten again. As regards my wife's servant, I think her quite innocent. There are several points in her favour and none against. In the first place she is not an inhabitant of this place but comes from miles and miles away. Then she has had no opportunities of leaving the haveli except sometimes at night when she goes to see her husband. Then there seems no premeditated scheme because she went when ordered and not of her own will. If the thing had been planned beforehand she would not have taken this opportunity.

Be that as it may, my mother fully believes that she has been sold. All the same, whether the girl is guilty or not the whole brunt has fallen on my wife who, poor fellow, is quite innocent. I cannot think how she can be blamed; but whether or not, my mother is very angry with the poor fellow. This wretched business does not even leave me quite free. My mother thinks that I obey my wife more than I do her. God only knows how much I obey my mother. Now enough of this.

Tuesday, 5th May, 1903

I was ordered to sit and get some copies of our case papers written out. This took the whole of the morning time and I could not go out. . . . After breakfast I read and finished *Thrift*. This is a very good and useful book written by Samuel Smiles. . . . I read a little of *Maharaj Shivajee* which is a Hindi book. . . .

Saturday, 9th May, 1903

Last night after dinner I read some papers connected with our case. I was so much engrossed in them that it was eleven o'clock by the time I thought of going to bed. In the morning I woke early and after washing myself was thinking whether to go out or not when Bhoj Raj Singhjee came and told me that I was to accompany him to my uncle Roop Singhjee's garden and show [him] the petitions [contesting the maharaja's actions in exchanging the family's revenue villages for others] that we had prepared yesterday. The object in sending me was to bring back [his opinion on it]. [Roop Singh is a judicial officer of Jaipur state, and has some expertise in these matters.] . . .

My uncle was of opinion that this was all useless and that nothing would come out of it. My grandfather on hearing this got very angry. This shall however be written at length some other time. . . . [Amar Singh never does report the details. He finds the subject "altogether too complicated for one to understand in one hour or one day.''[8] The Kanota family archive has a number of undated petitions from Zorawar Singh on behalf of the three thikanas indicating the losses involved in the exchanges and remonstrating against them. It is not clear whether the petitions were submitted or, if so, had any consequence. Kanota family tradition has it that Roop Singh, still in favor at court, was pusillanimous about fighting the case.]

Delhi, Wednesday, 20th May, 1903

Notes About My Last Summer Vacation[9].

III. Delhi

There is one incident worth noting that happened here during the short time I had to wait until the train for Alwar started. I had no servant with me and was travelling quite quietly. Having written my diary in the waiting room I was eating oranges when two persons came in. They were both of them Eurasians. I fell in conversation with them and found that one of them was in some relation to the Director of Gas Works at Jaipore. When that fellow found out who I was and from whence I had come he became free with me and asked several questions about the Imperial Cadet Corps.

The fellow . . . began telling me that we ought not to have gone to the cadet corps and done escort duty. He was dead against the Indian government and abused it freely. He said that the officers in the British and native army were not gentlemen. This fellow said that there was sure to be a mutiny some day and that he would be the first man to rise against the British government [which] was no good but full of politics. He told me that the government was doing a good thing in teaching us military work as this will enable us to turn the Britishers out quicker. . . .

Both these fellows complained of the government for not enlisting a regiment of Eurasians and cursed Lord Curzon like anything. They said that the government feared to enlist them but he said that they (the Eurasians) were multiplying by thousands every year and that the government would have to yield in the end. When I did not agree with him about rising against the government he said that I was too loyal at present as I had been taught all this in the cadet corps. However, he said that [while] I may not agree with him at present it would be all right in the end when I came to see things in the same light as he did. Such sort of conversation lasted for a long time. I do not know what the fellow really meant. Whether he was a detective or whether he said all this in earnest is still a mystery to me. The other fellow in his company was of the same opinion.

V. My Grand-Aunt

It was mourning period and for twelve days the ladies from my haveli used to go [to Naila house] everyday and weep. What a nasty custom. Whether any lady is sorry or not she has to weep and that very loudly too. I learned from my wife that she and the wives of Bhoj Raj Singhjee, Hem Singhjee, and Prithi Singhjee [the younger generation, Amar Singh's cousins] instead of weeping, used to hit one another with their elbows and talk and joke. They were not sorry, but to show to the foolish world and society, they had to cry as if their hearts were about to burst These are Indian customs. . . . Custom forbids us [at mourning time] to eat meat and sleep on beds and do some such sort of things. I am not much in their favour. . . .

VIII. My Mother

My mother is very fond of me and, I think, loves me more than any of my other brothers. I, on my part, always try to keep her pleased and glad. This is the first injunction that I have given my wife, to keep my mother pleased. I am very particular on this subject. My wife has been obeying me very well up to the present. If ever there is anything that my mother wants I supply her with it. . . . In spite of all this my mother sometimes says that I am more obedient to my wife than to her. This is not at all right but there is no help. She never says so before me. I love my mother and I love my wife too but their grades of love are different. . . . I love my mother just as a dutiful and sensible Rajpoot ought. . . .

IX. My Wife

One great thing is that my mother always grumbles at her for no purpose whatever. It is no fault of my wife if her brother [the Thakur of Satheen] does not send her a certain thing and so on. It is no fault of my wife if I love her. Mothers ought rather to be pleased to see their sons and the sons' wives love each other. This is not the case in Rajpootana but I must be satisfied that my case is much better than most other people's. . . .

X. My Father

I had occasion to live with him for a very few days. He is always pleased and satisfied with me. He never gets angry with me. In fact I never do anything that would offend him. I think he has great pleasure to see me moving so well and in such good and high society. Once while in Jaipore he got angry with me [and said] . . . that some of my habits are rather too boyish. He admonished me for a long time but in such a manner as not to offend my feelings. He is too careful about these things. I want to live with him for some time if I can and learn the many things that he knows. Unfortunately I have never had any occasion. . . .

XI. My Grandfather

My grandfather too is very kind and glad with me. Up to the present I have never done anything that would offend him. Of course he is more severe than my father. . . . My grandfather is very strong though so old. He attends the [Jaipur state] council regularly and sits there longer than any of the other members. . . .

XVI. The Resident

. . . I had very little to do with Colonel Pears, the resident who succeeded Mr Cobb. I used to go to the residency for tennis, but that was not much of an acquaintance. . . . I am only [writing about these residents] because of an incident that happened. One day Major Commeline said as to what was my future object and aim. I said that perhaps I may be sent here in Jaipore [Amar Singh hopes for a position in the military forces of Jaipur state]. On this Commeline said why did I not point out [a post I might want]. I said that Hari Singhjee had two [Posts] . . . and I could quite easily manage one of them.[10] On this I was [told] that this was the way . . . to make out an opening. . . .

Now it so happened that Major Commeline had driven with the resident that evening to [Lt.] Col. Pank's house [Philip Durrell Pank, the residency surgeon] where we were all assembled for tennis. This led all to think that it was most probably the resident [who] wanted to know as to what I wanted. *I went to my grandfather and told him all about my conversation with Major Commeline, who had dropped me some hints about my applying for some post in Jaipore. My grandfather said that the other posts would be too difficult for me owing to my not knowing Persian[11] and want of personal experience. He recommended [four] posts—viz. the commander-in-chiefship, the commander of the forts [comman-der of the transport corps], and the jagir bakshi [who supervises the *jagirs*, es-tates, of the Jaipur nobles]. In these [four] posts there is not much hard work to do. [Under Maharaja Ram Singh family members had held the command of forts and the jagir bakshi. Amar Singh's Cadet Corps training might in time qualify him for the first mentioned. Indeed, he ends his career in the 1930s as comman-der of the Jaipur State Forces.][12*] . . . The matter was dropped for some time un-til the resident expressed his wish to see me before I left Jaipore. This incident further gave me hopes. . . . At last, when I went to see Col. Pears, there was no such talk as to what I would like to have. . . .

XVII. Arguments at Polo

These are one of the greatest nuisances at this game. Mehtab Singhjee and Mr Stothard [the acting executive engineer] are the men who always contend on this subject [Mehtab Singh is Thakur Roop Singh's cousin, steward and favorite]. . . . One evening there happened the following incident. Mr Stothard and Bukhtawarjee [a Naila retainer subordinate to Mehtab Singh] were on one side while Mehtab Singhjee was on the other. It so happened that one of Mehtab Singhjee's partners was going at the ball when the former shouted "leave it." The fellow obeyed but he was followed by Bukhtawarjee who too in his turn did not hit the ball. This made Mr Stothard very angry with Mehtab Singhjee. The former said that it was not fair to order people of the other side to leave [the ball] for him and that the game could never be a decent one unless it were all gentlemen that played. By gentlemen he meant independent people who did not [have to obey] one another.

There was a great argument and Bukhtawarjee was called to give an explana-tion. The poor fellow said that he did not hit because his pony would not go near the ball and as a proof he said that anyone doubting may try the animal. Mehtab Singhjee said that he never meant Bukhtawar to leave the ball but had called to his own partner. At first there was a great discontent and both the gentlemen got angry, but Devi Singhjee [Thakur of Chomu] mended the whole thing. Mr Stothard came and apologised himself and shook hands with my uncle.

Now came the worst thing. At next polo Mehtab Singhjee did not play but simply watched the game. I asked him the reason and he said that there was no particular reason but he was not playing. When polo was over I drove Mr Stothard to his house and on the way he told me that in their society, when one apologises and hands are shaken, the bygones are forgotten as if they had never happened. He said that he had never given the matter a single thought and considered it very childish of Mehtab Singhjee to think so. I said that it would be all right and I will tell Mehtab Singh not to do so again. On this Mr Stothard told me not to do so and said that he would play his game and did not care at all whether Mehtab Singhjee played or not.

Now what I feared most was that Mr Stothard would surely tell all about it to the other Europeans and the result would be that our family would fall down in their estimation, and specially as Mehtab Singhjee was very popular in this society. So next morning I told the whole story to Ram Nathjee while we were travelling together in the train, and urged him to impress it upon the mind of my uncle that it was very childish of him to do, and specially when we had this case of ours for whose sake we are trying so hard to win the good opinion of these Britishers. Ram Nath promised to do his best and I hope he has proved successful. . . . Such a small incident, though we don't much think of it, sometimes throws a lasting effect, and specially on Europeans. . . .

XXII. Reading and Writing

. . . I had a great mind to teach my wife to read but there was no time and then I found the business to be quite hopeless just for the present and postponed it. . . .

XXI. How I Enjoyed Myself

I tried to enjoy myself as much as I was able to but unfortunately did not succeed as much as I had anticipated. . . . The family circumstances had become so much complicated that I did not think it advisable to go in the zenana during the daytime. The thing was this, that my mother had begun saying that we, the youngsters, were too obedient to our wives, whom we did not leave even during the day-time. . . . My father never used to do such things. This and many other hints forbade me from going in the zenana during the day.

I am of a habit of having things decently put up and arranged to my taste. This made the others envious and was another source of trouble. . . . Besides this my grandfather used, during the latter days [to] make me do some of our case work. This was too tiresome as I was quite unfit for it Out of all this there was one thing that I enjoyed thoroughly. This was the company of my brothers and sister. We were always cheerful when we were all of us gathered together. Oh! how pleasant it was.

XXXII. My Experiences

. . . It is now gradually dawning upon me as to what real difficulties there are in a Hindoo and specially a Rajpoot family life. I am now just beginning to taste of it and I don't like it. I am determined to follow my father in his principle of obeying his parents. Of this I have the greatest possible consideration. At the same time, other members of my family, and specially my wife, deserve my consideration. . . . I am in duty bound to regard them, and at the same time common sense makes it quite clear that she requires mine and only mine support. . . .

Indian mothers-in-law are really very cruel. For my own mother I have no complaint whatever, except a few trifling things which are nothing of importance. I will here give an instance of Bhoj Raj Singhjee. It is now nearly twelve years when he was married. Ever since he has not known a single night or day of comfort so far as married life is concerned. His wife is truly noble. I not only cannot find fault in her but I admire her conduct. Bhoj Raj Singhjee has a great love for her, which she well deserves. The unfortunate part comes in here. The mother of Bhoj Raj Singhjee first of all got angry with her daughter-in-law because the parents of the latter did not give enough dowry. This was no fault of the poor girl. She can not ask her parents or brothers to give anything at all. Besides this, our family is rich whereas hers is not. I am perfectly sure that she herself (Bhoj Raj Singhjee's mother) did not bring more than that. This anger continued for some years.

Now comes the second calamity. The younger of Bhoj Raj Singhjee's cousins got sons and daughters but he did not. The mother now gets angry why her son [does not] have any child. The anger falls on the poor daughter-in-law and she is threatened that either she must have a son or her husband must marry a second wife.[13] This too is no fault of the oppressed. She would be only too glad to have a child . . . if God gave her one. Now Bhoj Raj Singhjee is not only asked but forced to marry another wife. To this he absolutely refuses, and the anger of the mother falls on the poor daughter-in-law, who is accused of having used some enchantment on her husband. There is nothing but abuses for the poor girl who is the best of women.

She can do nothing but weep the whole day. Constant care and sorrow has thinned her very much. Bhoj Raj Singhjee himself told me that it was no use going in the zenana to his wife because there is nothing but tales of sorrow and oppression to be heard with weeping eyes. What a damn shame! What a wretched life. To add to all these miseries, Bhoj Raj Singhjee's wife is given jao, barley bread with no ghee [clarified butter], and very little of anything else to eat. *It went to such a length that at night my aunt used to lock the door in order not to let the husband and wife meet.[14]* Simply think of this cruelty. She is given clothes of the rottenest sort to wear. It makes me ashamed to write any more.

My poor wife trembles when she hears all these things. All what I have written about Bhoj Raj Singhjee has been related to me by his own lips, and the feeding on barley was told by my wife. I told my wife that she must be thankful to God that she has not these troubles. To this she said that wait a few days and all these will happen. I have impressed, or at least tried my best to do so, that she is able to keep my mother pleased whatever be the troubles. She should never care for clothes or ornaments, as I shall get her as many of these as she requires.

To tell the truth, I am even afraid of getting clothes made for her because the other ladies don't like the idea . . . their idea is that if they can't have [some] thing, why should the others. This has now become a common talk in our houses, that the Marwar ladies are not good. I don't agree to this. In my opinion the [Bhatianis] are the quietest and noblest among the Rajpoots [Amar Singh's wife is of the Bhati clan].

4

Joint-Family Responsibilities: "My One Aim Is to Secure Peace at Home"

[Amar Singh, on various vacations from the Imperial Cadet Corps in 1903, begins to experience joint-family responsibilities. He tries to understand the politics of women, their power, and the effect of their conflicts on the men. Although unhappy with the interference and harassment entailed by joint-family life, he nevertheless resists the idea of partitioning the family by dividing the property. "Union is strength" he says, not an unreasonable thought for the future thakur, for whom being able to command a significant number of men is almost as important as being able to command land. His language begins to reflect his identification with the family's corporate identity: "It is a great mistake *we* are doing," or "May God help *us*" meet the challenge.]

Jaipore, Sunday, 23rd August, 1903

I . . . went to my grandfather who told me all about our case and then told me to think over and give my opinion whether my younger brothers should be given land in Kanota itself or in the other villages. [Convention has it that younger brothers, who, under the prevailing system of primogeniture, do not share in the inheritance, should be allotted a living. Zorawar Singh is consulting the eldest son of the eldest son, in his role as future thakur.]

Wednesday, 7th October, 1903

Last night before dinner I read and finished *The Elementary Text Book Of Hindu Religion and Ethics*. This is a very good book indeed. I took it in the zenana with me to read some parts of it to my wife as this book speaks about women and their duties as written in our vedas.

Saturday, 10th October, 1903

. . . As soon as I came out of the zenana, I learned that my bhabee, Pratap Singh-jee's wife, had died in the night at about half past one.[1] She had just given birth to a daughter. What a sad news it was indeed. She was not much sick and there was no fear of her dying until all at once the fever increased to 106 and she died even before anyone considered her to be dangerously sick. Such is life to which we all cling so tenaciously. . . . I went to the choti haveli where I waited for some time.

When the proper time came we went in the zenana and brought out the dead body. When I went in the zenana I found that my bhabee was lying on the ground and was fully dressed in yellow garments.[2] We took the coffin in and placed the body in it.[3] Then a cloth was laid over and tied with a string. This over, we brothers and cousins brought the coffin out on our shoulders and handed it over to the Brahmans when once we were out of the haveli. All along the way to the funeral ground we followed together with our uncles. We stopped twice on the road where some ceremonies were performed and reached the cremating place where we made a pile of wood and placed the coffin on it and again piled logs on it. . . . *Before placing the body on the pyre we took it once all round in Parikrama[4] but care was taken that the head was always leading.[5]*

Care was taken that the logs were heavy because when the corpse begins to burn the sinews and tendons shorten and the body begins to bend, with the result that the light wood is knocked aside and the body gets erect in a sitting posture, or gets thrown out of the fire. . . . When the funeral pyre was ready it was lighted and it blazed off. The wood used was peepul and about half a dozen small bits of sandalwood were placed near the face. These were very, very small and served only as an excuse that sandalwood was used.[6]

While piling up the wood I had to touch the body in order to take the bedding out. I shall never forget that touch. I had several times read of cold bodies but never imagined what it really was. It was as cold as ice. While the cremation was going on I sat watching. I wanted to know how everything is done. The Kapal Krya [breaking of the skull so its contents may be consumed by the flames] was performed by Umaidjee Purohit [the family priest]. Duleep Singh [younger brother of the widowed Pratap Singh] was doing all the ceremonies. . . . A long bamboo was split at one end and a coconut was placed in it. This nut was secured by a string. Then this nut was broken at one end and some ghee had been poured in it. Now with this coconut the skull was touched and the string having got burned the nut dropped on the head where it burned. . . . When only a very small portion was left we piled the burning embers . . . round it and came away. Each of us threw some cow-dung Chanas [cakes] into it as we went past.

The cremation over we went to a neighbouring garden, bathed ourselves and performed the Tilanjali [giving water to the dead persons's soul by pouring it on a peepal tree]. . . .

My Feelings.   I am just writing a few lines in order to explain my real sentiments. . . . In the morning when I heard the news I was very sorry but there was nothing of that sort of sorrow that I had felt when once my mother was very sick. . . . While at the choti haveli [Naila House, my] feelings . . . changed. . . . My mind ran to the day when we [first] brought over bhabee . . . from Khatoli [her home thikana] and what rejoicings we had. . . .

When we went in the zenana and put the corpse in the coffin my ideas ran to the ladies and women that were weeping. They must have been all of them sorry, but alas, how few of them to that degree as they were expressing. Some . . . must have been cursing the dead one for putting them all to this bother. Some of them must have been talking to the others on different subjects. I know that none of them talked gaily or on pleasant subjects so long as the corpse was in view. . . . After a couple of days no one talks about the departed one but converses secretly on private subjects and even jokes with one another. . . .

While we were carrying the body to the funeral, my ideas were changed and I was thinking about what Shree Krishen has preached to Arjun in Bhagawat Gita.[7] Sometimes my ideas went to Syam Sunder Lal [a Brahman counselor of the

Maharaja of Kishengarh] and the book that he had given me to read, . . . *An Elementary Textbook on Hindu Religion and Ethics*. These ideas . . . occurred to me while the cremation was going on. While I had [ordinary thoughts]. . . . I was sorry, but as soon as I thought of these books and what they teach, sorrow ran away. . . . The thing seemed inevitable and I looked on it as an everyday business. Then the ideas of Buddha came to me from the book, *The Light of Asia*.[8] These were very consoling indeed. I felt as if there was no sorrow for me.

While we were piling the heavy logs of timber I thought . . . that but yesterday we would . . . have defended this body at all hazards. This was the body too tender for the lightest weight. . . . Today it lay unconscious of the heavy loads and the burning fire that was roaring all round . . . consuming it. . . . What passed through my mind . . . [was] of the other forms that this soul must be now undergoing, or, in love of the body, hovering round.

I am now quite confident that if a man knew the Hindu religion perfectly well there is no wonder if he becomes a yogi. . . . leaves home and disregards all the worries and pains of this world. I do not know how far this reading has changed me. Let me see what happens when one really dear dies. May God postpone the day for a very long time.

Thursday, 15th October, 1903

I read and finished *Kusum Kunwari*. This is a novel written by Baboo Deoki Nandan Khatri.[9] I do not think much of it. The language is plain and easy but the plan of the story is not up to much. . . . Specially the love scenes are not much good. English books describe these very well indeed.

Dehra Doon, Thursday, 20th October, 1903

Notes About My Last Vacation[10].

IV. Kanota

[Amar Singh once again surveys Kanota fort, but also those belonging to the related thikanas and makes comparisons unfavorable to Kanota.]

. . . I had some things taken out of the saddle room. There were sixteen saddles . . . but at present there is not one to be found. . . . I brought away all the English leather things and put them away in boxes at the haveli. Nearly everything is getting spoiled. . . .

V. Naila[11]

I went to this place [uncle Roop Singh's estate] twice, once when we went out pigsticking in the Patias [grass farm] and the next time when we went for panther shooting. This place is very well looked after. The arms, the saddles, the houses, the horses, the camels, in fact everything is in good order. . . . My uncle is building a new gate just on the road where it enters the village and he is intending to build another gate and a wall round the village. [The village was in fact laid out on quadrants, like Jaipur city.] This will of course cost him a good lot of money. There is a garden, a fort, a haveli and a bund [artificial pond] in this village.

VI. Gondher

. . . There are raj men [servants of the Jaipur state] in this village but the haveli is still in my uncle Mookend Singhjee's possession. [Under the settlement of the maharaja's case against the three Champawat families, Gondher has been seized by Jaipur state. Eventually, Mukend Singh is given the lesser village of Santha, 70 miles away from Jaipur, for his chief revenue village, and loses the Gondher village and haveli.] Unlike Kanota this place was much cleaner and there was nothing out of order. All the things that there were, were lying in their proper places. There were enough men to look after the house and horses. . . .

PHOTO V-7   Mukend Singh, Thakur of Gondher, head of one of the three Champawat families at Jaipur. As the senior branch, the Gondher joint family lives in *badi* (big) *haveli*, Kanota in *bichli* (middle) *haveli* and Naila in *choti* (little) *haveli*. He and the Thakurani of Gondher struggle to force Bhoj Raj Singh, Amar Singh's cousin and dear friend, into a second marriage. Mukend is wearing traditional court dress. Amar Singh's photo albums.

PHOTO V-8   Cousin Bhoj Raj Singh (Gondher) is protagonist in the diary's most poignant connubial drama. He is under severe pressure to marry a second time because his first marriage has not produced the male heir needed to ensure that the Gondher title and estate remain in the family. Amar Singh's photo albums.

XVIII. Bhoj Raj Singhjee

Whenever I go home I always hear of some sort of wrong done to this cousin of mine who is the best and noblest of us all. The more wonder is that this wrong is done him by his own parents. . . .

My aunt always says that when she will get a second wife for her son she will treat her as the lady of the house and the former will be kept as her slave. My aunt has several times spread this report that her son is not a good character and has some secret connection with certain women. This is all to stir up disaffection. My uncle Mookend Singhjee is quite under the influence of his wife and so remains angry with his son whom he calls a "Kapoot," which is about the worst word possible for a Rajpoot son to hear from his parent. I am glad to write that this word is quite undeserved.

My uncle opens the letters of my bhabee, reads them, and hands them over to his wife, who too reads but never passes to her [to] whom they are addressed. . . . However, Bhoj Raj Singhjee and my bhabee have never yet complained to any one. . . . [The lack of an heir is a threat to the family. Were Bhoj Raj Singh to die without an heir, as indeed he does in 1928, the title and estate of Gondher would—and did—pass to the collateral line of a cousin, Kalyan Singh, leaving the surviving women without a powerful son or husband.]

At last, after all this tormenting, Bhoj Raj Singhjee did agree to marry a second time, but he said that what guarantee had he that peace will then reign. Now my aunt won't marry him because she says that her son agrees because he is forced to it. Suppose she got him married but he did not treat the second wife as he is treating the first one, then it was of no use her getting him married. . . .

I am about the happiest in the three houses. I am blessed with a calm and quiet wife who does not quarrel with anyone. My mother too does not bother her daughter-in-law much. Then I am blessed with the best of fathers such as very few people have the luck to possess. . . . He told my mother that she should keep her daughter-in-law with great care and love and should never cause her sorrow or even annoyance as it was her duty to look after her well-being and comfort.

I fear I shall be running into too much praise . . . of my father, and I fear this praise will look a bit odd after I have written so much against my uncles. . . . Up to the present I have never had any occasion to complain against my father even in the slightest matter. He always treats me in such a manner that I have the greatest love as well as the greatest fear of him. . . .

XIX. My Brothers

. . . Sheonath Singh and Sardar Singh study at the Mayo College. They had come here for seventeen days. They too have a great love for me and I think I reciprocate it just as much or even a bit more. I gave a Mauser pistol to Sheonath Singh while we were at Kishengarh, and he was very much pleased with the present. . . . It is my duty to supply them with whatever they want and so win their love and esteem. By doing this I shall win the greatest possible peace at home and good name abroad, just as my father has done, . . . [and] win the love and esteem of my parents. I am glad to write that at present my brothers have a great love for me but at the same time they stand in great awe, always taking care not to displease me.

My one aim is to secure peace at home in every possible way. . . .

XX. How I Passed My Days

. . . In the morning I used to rise pretty early [4 to 5 a.m.] and so soon as I had finished my dundh and Indian club exercise, Bhoj Raj Singhjee used to come. . . . So soon as I was dressed we used to go to my garden where we used to train our polo ponies and go out in the jungle. Then I had to do my walking exercise and by the time I returned from that we had shooting. All this occupied the time until about ten, at which time I used to get to my haveli. There was the teacher of Urdu ready and I used to study with him until breakfast was announced. The meal

PHOTO V-9   "Picture taken at my haveli by an American globetrotter"—1906. Amar Singh with walking stick; his second brother and heir, Sheo Nath Singh, to his right. Amar Singh's photo albums.

over, I used to write my letters or go in the zenana if my mother sent for me. Then I used to go to bed at twelve [noon] and wake at three.

I was hardly washed, shaved and dressed before I found a man calling me to the bari haveli [Bhoj Raj Singh's haveli], from whence I used to drive down either to polo or tennis as the case was. Soon after my return from the games I used to write my diary and have my bath. Then I used to go in the zenana again, but this time to my wife. We used to be up till twelve as a rule but sometimes it went so late as one or even two. While in company with my wife I used either to read myself if I was alone or we both used to talk. Sometimes I used to make my wife read a couple of pages from *Kaisar Bilas*. This reading business she used to hate but I used to persuade her to read.

Sometimes we used to take a little wine, but this was never more than an ounce and a half between us both. The wine was always one of the sweet liquours, which are of course expensive things. In the beginning, my wife had no taste for these English wines, but now she can not drink deshi. In fact she is not fond of drinking like me. . . . Say during these two months we drank a bottle and a half between us. . . .

Jaipore, Friday, 4th December, 1903

[Amar Singh returns from the Cadet Corps for a brief vacation to receive bad news.] Last night after dinner I went in the zenana and found my wife to be unusually calm and silent. The room too looked as if there was something missing. I told my wife to get wine and then to take off her veil but none of my wishes were carried out. In addition to the usual odni [head scarf] she had a thick shawl which prevented my seeing her face. She was not talking up to her usual form and I found it the most difficult thing to get a word out of her. At last I asked where my daughter was and how she was getting on. Instead of an answer there was silence and my wife fell in my lap and began to sob. I guessed what the matter was but still, to make myself sure, I questioned her and when there was no answer I knew the thing and asked her when the poor child had died. She said on the last nomi[12] that is to say, five days ago. This was sad news indeed but there is no alternative but to sit down and console ourselves with the words, "God's will be done."

In spite of my sorrow I had to look after my wife. After a time I succeeded in making her calm. . . . I wanted to talk but this could not be done and so we went to bed. I tried all I could and recited several things out of the Bhagawat Gita to assure her that we must not be sorry for things that can't be averted, and besides this, what is life and what is death. These are all inquiry things.

The poor child had been suffering from nearly eight months. The sickness started with smallpox over which she got all right and there were no marks of it left. But fever followed and of it there was no getting away. Besides this, there was no good medical arrangement, as my mother does not like the treatment of English doctors. The girl had got so thin and was looking so bad that I never had the heart to look at her and touching was quite out of the question. Before her sickness she was all hale and hearty and I used to put her on my stomach and she used to play about and laugh and suck my nose. That was a happy time. The world is full of ups and downs, sorrows and happinesses. I shall write no more about my daughter because "let the dead past bury its dead."

Monday, 7th December, 1903

Last night before dinner I went to my mother and talked to her for about half an hour. The talk was about the killing of girls when they are born. This subject I will treat at length some other time. I had dinner in the zenana with my wife. I must say, one enjoys his food best when he eats it with one most dear to him. The relation of being dear is of course different when one has to consider the difference between a parent and a wife. . . .

Meerut, Wednesday, 16th December, 1903

Notes About My Last Leave of Thirteen Days.   [Amar Singh, returned to the Cadet Corps, reflects at leisure on the events of the leave.]

XXXVII. My Wife

. . . My wife had been very sick indeed just the day before her daughter died. I now find that this sickness of hers is owing to her being pregnant again. This is at least what is believed to be the reason. . . . I found that her stomach is increasing a bit and there are all the other signs of pregnancy to be seen.

She was awfully grieved at the loss of our daughter, but there was no help to it. I did not enjoy much of home life this time because I could never even ask about my daughter's sickness, as my wife used to begin weeping no sooner I put her that question. This time I dined with my wife twice and this is quite a novel thing because I don't often do it unless I am pressed. This time I had to do it simply to drive away the cares of my wife and keep her cheerful as she had recently lost her child. I was just as sorry to lose that girl, but a mother's love is ten or I may safely say a thousand times more than that of a father.

XXXVIII. My Daughter

. . . My grandfather felt this death awfully, as he used to love his great-grand-child very much, and used to speak about her to all his friends. [When] my sister used to take my daughter to my grandfather the latter used to clasp his hands and say "where have you come from," and "where had you been waiting for us." These two were the terms he often used to use, and then he would take the child in his arms and fondle about. The little thing used to go without any shyness. When she died my grandfather told his friends that he had never loved either his sons or grandsons but his great-grandchild whom God has to-day removed.

He was so fond of her that from this very early age he had arranged a betrothal with the son of Devi Singhjee of Chomu. This match was not formally done but my grandfather had expressed his wish to the Thakoor of Chomu who had agreed to it with pleasure. . . . Though I was so sorry I was not supposed to show it, as it would have been bad form. I kept a cool front as if nothing had happened. . . . I hope to have better luck next time. . . . [Amar Singh has five other daughters, only one of whom survives.]

XXXI. Life with Father[13]

[This and other entries provide the appealing sight of Amar Singh, at twenty-five, talking to his father, whom he is just beginning to know. Amar Singh, who is easily bored, as with Sir Pratap or some of his ICC comrades, is never bored with father's "talk which was both amusing and instructing."]

It is sometime [since] . . . I have lived with my father for so many days. In fact, I may say this to be the first time after my growing up. I was with him some few years ago but then I was too young. The time that I spent was very pleasant. I was never tired talking to him or even of sitting there. There was always some talk which was both amusing and instructing. He always treats me as if I were a friend. He used to tell me all that happened in the whole day and on some occasions used to ask my opinion.

PHOTO V-10   Narain Singh, Amar Singh's father, heir to the Kanota title and estate (second from left), seen with assorted companions after a polo match. In disfavor with Jaipur Maharaja Madho Singh, he serves in Alwar as native guardian to the maharaja and later as minister. The Alwar service is a sort of exile. Amar Singh's photo albums.

The only places where formality was observed was when it came to the zenana. On that subject no one touched. I was very anxious to go to Jaipore [to see my wife] and was devising means to ask him but there was no use of it. He himself told me that there was nothing particular going on at that time and so I had best go to Jaipore for four or five days. I wanted nothing more and away I sped. I had a mind to tell him once that I was the luckiest of all in having such parents because all my cousins are suffering in one way or another except me. . . .

I feel the greatest possible love for my father and at the same time fear him most of all my family, though he has never got angry, much less beaten me. . . . *I pray to God to give me a parent like him ever and ever after in my next generations.[14]*

Delhi, Friday, 6th November, 1903[15]

Notes About My Cousin's Marriage[16].   [Marriages in Rajputana were matters of dynastic and family status and fortune, not sentiment, the subject of complex calculations and strategies. Amar Singh's grandfather Zorawar Singh controls the Kanota extended family finances and determines the strategies. Amar Singh calls him a miser. Zorawar Singh's thrift is in tension with the family's striving for status and honor via hypergamous marriages. If one wants to marry one's daughters up, that is, into richer, higher status thikanas, and Kanota does, one has to keep up with the Joneses with plentiful and conspicuous consumption and display.[17] A *sine qua non* is a substantial dowry. Because political power is an element in social standing, the Champawat lineage, with some family members still in service as ministers, can to a degree substitute influence via court and government for the size of the dowry. Zorawar Singh as a member of the state council can take advantage of this trade-off. Even so, Amar Singh reports that the family has spent Rs 75,000 on the marriage of his sister and two cousins, a sum more than three times the stated annual income of the Kanota estate.[18]

Zorawar Singh started his entrepreneurial career at Peelva, the family's home thikana in Jodhpur, by "futures trading" that yielded a share of the estate. His hardy thriftiness and entrepreneurial spirit yielded significant income in Jaipur through loan operations. The same thrift made him reluctant to spend more than necessary on marriages. Commenting on the recent marriage of his cousin, Amar Singh remarks: "This time our arrangements were not quite satisfactory . . . we did not spend much money . . . it was because my grandfather had an eye on everything."

Amar Singh's uncle Roop Singh is thakur of the prosperous and elegant Naila thikana; the first Thakur of Naila, Fateh Singh, as prime minister under Maharaja Ram Singh, had accumulated a small fortune.[19] Roop Singh is more concerned with social respectability than thrift. He complains that the Kanota branch of the Champawat connection is letting down the side with insufficient dowries and display. While Zorawar Singh consents to prestigious marriages for all his granddaughters, he refuses to spend as much money as Roop Singh thinks he should.]

I. The Idea

It had long been the wish [of] all the family members to marry this cousin of mine as soon as possible. My grandfather wished to see all his granddaughters married before his eyes, whereas my father and I and my mother wanted that the marriage take place during the lifetime of my grandfather, because if it was done afterwards [when we cease to have political influence,] we would have to spend twice the amount of money and still get no credit for it. . . .

[The cousin is the daughter of Amar Singh's uncle Gambhir Singh, a younger brother of Narain Singh. With her mother, she is resident in the Kanota joint family haveli. Gambhir Singh has died. This is not the first marriage in the family. One cousin was married to Achrol, one of Jaipur's largest and most influential thikanas, and Amar Singh's sister to Garhi in Alwar which, though deeply indebted and only an eight-village thikana, is that small state's most important estate. So long as Zorawar Singh lives, the cousin "is" the granddaughter of the Thakur of Kanota, a member of the Jaipur state council. When he dies, she becomes the daughter of a deceased younger son. The dowry required for a prestigious marriage would then be substantially higher. Not to pay a large dowry would expose Zorawar Singh's heir, Narain Singh, to an accusation that he was saving money at the expense of his deceased brother's daughter.]

Then my cousin is getting older. This marriage would have been performed long before but the thing was this: the boy to whom my cousin was betrothed was to be adopted in the Nawalgarh house and if the raj people knew that we had connection there then they would raise all sorts of objections against the adoption. . . . [Nawalgarh was a major Shekhawati thikana. Because the Kanota family was out of favor, it was feared Maharaja Madho Singh's government might block the adoption.]

V. The Bridegroom

His appearance shows him to be rather a dull sort of fellow. My father and grandfather were very sorry when they saw him. The strangest thing was that no member of our family had seen him except my grandfather, but that was some fifteen years ago. They were very sorry for the mistake, but there was no help. Luckily the ladies of our family have taken a liking to him. . . .

My grandfather asked me what I thought of the bridegroom and I said that he was all right except for his colour. To this my grandfather said that the darker the colour the braver a man is supposed to be. I agreed with him. I have my conviction that those who are of a very light and white colour are always delicate, whereas those that are darker are more hardy. . . . Our janwaijee [brother-in-law] when he went in the zenana the next day after his marriage, was teased by the ladies who asked him all sorts of riddles. He was clever enough, or I should rather say lazy enough, to bring a manuscript book which contained all the answers. This was a source of immense amusement [unlike Amar Singh's marriage, where he "failed" the marriage riddling (see Part III, 1)].

VIII. The Marriage Ceremony

. . . Towards the end, the story of Shiv and Parvatijee was related [the mutual vows of this divine couple]. . . . Unfortunately I do not remember them all. . . . They were awfully good ones but no one now cares for them. If there is any nation that acts up to them it is Englishmen, or I may say Europeans. We people have trampled down on the rights of women. We look upon them in the light of mere playthings. . . .

XIX. My Aunt

This time I am writing about my aunt who is the first wife of my uncle Roop Singh. . . . She began by telling me how badly she had been treated by her mother-in-law. She said that the servant girls used to scold her and that as if she was an animal. No one ever cared if she ate anything or not. No decent clothes were given her and of money there was nothing to be seen except the little she got from her parents.

Then she told me with what difficulty my mother had brought me up. . . . How the slave girls used to snatch me out of my mother's hands and throw [me] aside, how my mother had to keep quiet for fear of my grandmother, how my mother had suffered for want of servants and how badly she was treated by my grandmother. . . . All these stories hurt me to the quick. My aunt told me that I ought to follow her advice and always help my wife if she wanted anything in the shape of money, clothes, etc. She said that we bring in wives from big thikanas but don't treat them properly. . . .

XXIV. The Kaman Threads

Our ladies have a great belief in Kaman (magical) things. My aunt is one of those who believes these things and knows how to avert them. Personally I have no be-lief in magic. This time it so happened that my aunt sent some coloured cotton threads which were tied in the way on which the bridegroom and party were to pass. . . . My father noticed and as soon as he came to the kotri [big house] he sent Sheonath Singh in the zenana and through him had my aunt scolded in his (my father's) name. . . .

My father got awfully angry and ended by saying that if she could do anything by her magic she had best try on him (my father), so that he would be always pre-sent in Jaipore and carry out her orders and wishes. He further said that what had happened had happened, but if he was to hear of another such nonsense, he would be awfully angry.

The belief was not on our side only. The Nawalgarh women who had come with the bridegroom were very careful that our ladies did not do any magic on their master. The meaning of this magic being that my [aunt] was trying that her daughter may have control of her husband, while the Nawalgarh women took care that their master had his upper hand over his wife. What rubbish and nonsense. . . .

XXVI. Talk with My Father

. . . I was . . . advised to be thrifty, as money was the only thing that nowadays helps people to get along in the world. I think my father has an idea that I am a bit of a spendthrift, which I surely am in comparison to most of the other family members. I was told that only a few years ago my grandfather had practically no money, that is to say, he had about six or seven thousand only in reserve. People think us to be fabulously rich, but they are mistaken. We are not in debt but rather in affluent circumstances. However, we are not rich enough not to serve or try to earn [as Narain Singh earns at Alwar and Amar Singh at the Cadet Corps] because if we don't try we won't have anything.

Some seventy-five thousand rupees have been spent for the marriages of my sister and two cousins [The cousins to Achrol and Nawalgarh and the sister to Garhi]. This amount is not a small one. Then the house and fort at Kanota has cost a good lot. It was only through the strenuous economical ways of my grand-father that we are keeping up our appearances. . . . If our family were to take bribes it would be otherwise. Then we could amass immense treasures, but fortu-nately our family has been free of this curse. . . .

The third topic was that my grandfather had before determined that my cousins should be married by my uncles [at their own expense], as they had been given their different shares [that is, taken off the joint family accounts, given a regular allowance, and expected to manage their own expenses.[20]] However, my father suggested that my grandfather should do these marriages as all the three were his granddaughters. It was thus that the marriages came to be performed at the expense of the thikana.

It is a great mistake we are doing in marrying the daughters of our chut bhais [younger brothers, who have lower incomes] to such big thikanas as Achrol, Mandawa and Nawalgarh. Not only this, but my uncle Roop Singhjee has contracted a bethrothal for Mehtab Singhjee's daughter with the Thakur of Danta whose revenue is nearly a lakh [100,000] of rupees. Bheem Singhjee, Chhiman Singhjee and Gumbheer Singhjee [the Kanota uncles and a cousin with marriage connections to "big houses"] have got about five thousand rupees of income, but Mehtab Singhjee has hardly two hundred annually.[21] . . . If the same system continues, our thikanas would be ruined because a marriage with such thikanas means at least twenty-five thousand rupees. Let us wait and see the result. . . .

XXXII. Conclusion

. . . In concluding, I say that one burden from the back of the thikana [the cousin's marriage] is over. This was about the heaviest, as my uncle Gumbheer Singhjee is dead. I must call myself and my father very fortunate that this marriage has come off during my grandfather's time, otherwise it would have cost us much more. . . . There now remains one event to be performed, and that is the marriage of Tikam Singh, son of Gumbheer Singhjee. May God help us to pass that satisfactorily.

[Having written one set of "Notes About My Cousin's Marriage," Amar Singh finds out a few weeks later from cousin Bhoj Raj Singh that there is grumbling at Jaipur. . . . He feels compelled to write a second set of "Notes About My Cousin's Marriage."]

Meerut, Wednesday, 16th December, 1903

XXXIII. Notes About My Cousin's Marriage

I. Roop Singhjee

I had thought that the marriage [of Gambhir Singh's daughter] had passed satisfactorily and we had nothing to be anxious for. I did not know all the particulars at that time but this is a story that Bhoj Raj Singhjee told me. . . .

They had gone to Naila for panther shooting and while sitting in the Odi [shooting box] Roop Singhjee, looking all round, said that now that no outsider was present, he would say something about the marriage which was performed very unsatisfactorily. The particulars being that the bridegroom's party were given leave the very next day, which is not at all good as the poorest man stops them for at least three days. The next thing was that the horses given were very bad. Two of them were the rotten ones that had come from Satheen [Amar Singh's wife's thikana], one that had been given from Dego and the fourth had been caught from the kharra [salt marshes] which means was running loose with no one to look after him, and given away. . . . The fourth point was that an elephant was not given and the fifth that no siropaos [sets of clothes] were given to the kamdars [estate agents of the groom].

In that assembly no one dared to contradict my uncle, but Bhoj Raj Singhjee, who said that these were all false things, and I will answer for all of them. As regards the first point of giving leave the very next day, we were not to be blamed because those fellows [were] very keen on it and their reason was quite sound. They said that the thakoor sahib's [Nawalgarh's] sister's marriage was very shortly to come off and they will have no time left to make preparations for it [the same reason for Amar Singh's spending less than the conventional time at his wife's thikana in the opening section of this Part]. We were not foolish to argue against a good and sound excuse. . . .

As regards horses, we gave them what we had. The two of Satheen were given us on an occasion of this very kind and we passed them on. The one from Dego had just been given and we forwarded it. As regards the one that had been caught from the Kharra, he was one of our colts by a very nice mare. We gave them the best we had. Of course no one gives horses worth a thousand rupees. We gave what is usually given on such occasions. . . .

An elephant was not given because it had not been done so when my cousin was married at Achrol and sister at Gurhi. If one was given now the others would have got angry, which we did not want to do. If we did not give the elephant we gave them a necklace which was worth more than that beast.

As regards the fifth and last argument, it is quite groundless, because we did give siropaos to them and attached their names on them. . . . That Mahabux [estate agent at Nawalgarh] is the fellow who often comes to my uncle and says these things because he knows my uncle gets pleased. . . .

When Roop Singhjee found no answer, he said that he was not present on the occasion but had only heard this from other people. To this Bhoj Raj Singhjee answered that he had better believe those of his own family than outsiders. When Roop Singhjee found that he could not argue on that subject he changed it and said that we want to have connections with big thikanas but don't want to spend money. We do want connections with big families but at the same time don't want to waste our money which is earned with great labour. My uncle then said that he was going to marry Mehtab Singhjee's daughter at Danta and it was his intention that this marriage shall be celebrated with more pomp than any of the previous ones. Now this is a mistake. Mehtab Singhjee is not big enough to have connection with Danta. The poet says:

> Like blood, like goods, like ages,
> Make the happiest marriages.

I quite agree with him.

[Mehtab Singh, the impecunious cousin of Roop Singh of Naila, is the fourth son of the Thakur of Peelva, the small ancestral thikana at Jodhpur of the Champawat families at Jaipur. (See *Appendix, Genealogical Charts I and II*). During the famine years after 1898 Mehtab Singh was one of two *chut bhais*, younger brothers of the Peelva thakur, who came to make their living at Jaipur by taking service under their more fortunate cousin, Roop Singh of Naila. Handsome and clever, Mehtab Singh soon became Roop Singh's favorite and his estate manager, treated as well as or better than his own sons. "My uncle Roop Singhjee is so very fond of Mehtab Singhjee that the former treats him in exactly the same manner as Sarkar used to [treat] Hurjee."[22]]

Danta's income is over a hundred thousand rupees whereas Mehtab Singhjee has hardly two hundred. . . . The difference is too much. . . . According to my idea they made a great mistake. If my younger brothers will want to marry their daughters in such big thikanas they would be ruined. At present the people don't ask money of us because we are influential but we can not continue so for ever. . . . This is sowing the seeds of jealousy, hatred and disunion between Mehtab Singhjee and Pratap Singhjee [Roop Singh's eldest son]. . . .

PHOTO V-11   Thakur Roop Singh of Naila. He thinks Amar Singh is too opinionated, and the Kanota family too parsimonious. He spends the wealth which his father, Fateh Singh, accumulated during his term as prime minister of Jaipur, on an elaborate fort (now used to shoot films), gardens and *havelis*. The building program is the envy of his relatives, and spurs Amar Singh's renovations. Amar Singh's photo albums.

Wednesday, 6th January, 1904[23]

IX. My Uncle Roop Singhjee

Roop Singhjee has betrothed [Basant Kanwar, Mehtab Singh's daughter] to the Thakoor of Danta and has agreed to pay twenty thousand rupees [in dowry, an amount approximating the annual income of Naila thikana]. Just think of this. Besides this amount he has paid several minor sums to the kamdars and go-betweens in this betrothal. Roop Singhjee intends to celebrate this marriage at Naila with much greater pomp than any of the marriages of my sister or aunts. *I told all this account to my father who said that "Roop Singhjee will do anything that Mehtab Singhjee will want," and the other remark was that "this marriage won't make Mehtab the Thakoor of Naila."[24]*

[Roop Singh] was rather reserved with me this time. When I met Ram Nathjee he was telling me that my uncle was talking very much against me. He went even so far as to say that I was the greatest kapoot [abusive word for a Rajput son] in the latter generation of our family. Roop Singhjee has always been kind to me. I do not know what the real cause of this displeasure is. I can only think of the following. . . . Mehtab Singhjee . . . thinks me proud and a likely enemy who might one day incite Pratap Singhjee [Roop Singh's son] to protest against this unaccountable expenditure. However, let us see what comes out in the end.

PHOTO V-12   The lavishly furnished Victorian sitting room in the Naila country house built by Roop Singh in the suburbs of Jaipur city. Photographed in 1971, courtesy of Robin von Breton.

Meerut, Wednesday, 16th December, 1903

Notes About My Last Leave of Thirteen Days.   (*cont.*)

[When Amar Singh's mother is discovered making off with a pot of *ghee* (clarified butter) from the joint-family stores, he is made aware of the internal economy, especially the women's economy, of the haveli, the large, 100-person joint-family household. Amar Singh reflects on the desirability of allocating expenditures between the collective and private sectors of the household.

Joint-family households often established a common thikana account for the nuclear families spread over three or four generations living in the big house's common space. Zorawar Singh's sons and grandsons are expected to deposit their salaries with him. From time to time, they request funds for special expenditures, although there seem to have been variations in this pattern. Zorawar Singh's younger sons have been given "shares." As a result, they are expected to pay their own and their family's personal expenses, such as food not eaten out of the joint-family kitchen, and gifts and clothing. As Amar Singh reveals in the discussion of marriages, the thikana nevertheless undertook the expense of marrying the daughters of these brothers to large and prestigious houses. Also, Amar Singh appears to be free to dispose of funds of his own—his salary from the ICC.

PHOTO V-13   Cosmopolitan gathering at the gate of Naila country house, showing family members with assorted English visitors wearing garlands. Amar Singh's numbers: 1) Mehtab Singh; 2) Thakur Mukend Singh (Gondher); 3) unknown; 4) Jawahar Singh (Peelva); 5) Thakur Roop Singh (Naila); 6) Bhoj Raj Singh (Gondher); 7) Pratap Singh (Naila); 8) Inder Singh (Peelva). Amar Singh's photo albums.

Zorawar Singh controls the finances, including expenditures for the household's food and supplies. Unlike wives from wealthy thikanas, who may have their own income from land, older women in the Kanota haveli don't have independent sources of income. As a result, they have to request money for every single expenditure.[25]

The household is fed from two kitchens, a public one for guests and visitors, and a zenana-kitchen that serves the family and their maid servants. Both kitchens draw rations from a common store. An accountant closely monitors the store by entering all transactions in record books. Amounts withdrawn are fixed by status in the household. An important guest would warrant more and better rations—more ghee, for example—than an ordinary guest, and the families of senior males would warrant more than the families of junior males. Fixed rations generally exceeded requirements; a clever housewife without independent means, like Amar Singh's mother, might try to make a little pocket money by sequestering the surplus and selling it to the only market to which she has access—maid servants.[26]

The death of Amar Singh's two-year-old daughter and the conduct of three costly marriages leads to renewed ruminations on the moral and fiscal economy of women. Amar Singh recognizes that the immense expense associated with marrying off Rajput daughters to richer and higher status households can contribute to the practice of female infanticide.]

XXXV. My Mother

As regards my mother I have to write only two incidents. She is awfully fond of me and I think loves me most of all her children up to the present. These two incidents are one concerning herself and the other about the killing of daughters. As regards the first one it is this. On her last visit to Kanota, when my cousin was married, she used to prepare food for her janwai [son-in-law] the Thakoor Sahib of Gurhi. For this food the supplies used to come from the thikana stores. As a rule, women are very economical and my mother is one of them. She saved some ghee which she did not return to the stores but brought away with her to Jaipore. As ill-luck would have it the utensil in which it was brought got upset and spoiled the carpet in the rath [the bullock-drawn, covered carriage in which zenana women ride]. This led to enquiries and my uncle Bheem Singhjee found the real thing and so did my grandfather. The latter, as usual, got angry with my mother, but the former told all about it to my father, who got very angry with my mother, who was very much afraid as to when her husband would get pleased again.

I can quite see that this work of bringing the ghee was not at all a high minded and noble one and this was why my father got so angry. . . . All this sounds very good but only to those who know the one side [of the story]. In the first place my mother brought her own property, as whatever the thikana has is hers. Then, if one says that it was not at all creditable in the way in which she brought it, for this defence I will say that she is forced to it and I don't blame her in the least. My father does not give her a single pice [coin] for her private expenses which are very great. The reason why he does not give is that he is too good and obedient a son, who does not want to hurt the feelings of his father in the least [by implying that father is being miserly in his support]. I fear he is doing a great injustice to his wife whom he owes some duties. His idea is that his father will do everything in this direction but when [he] does not do then it is his duty to find some way out.

When . . . my grandfather does not give, then there must be some other way . . . and this is what she had at last to find. Women are very particular about keeping the dignity of the house and looking to the treatment of guests. People who come from Bhootera, Kochore, Satheen and such other places [connected to Kanota by marriage] are taken care of and fed by my mother because the food in the [common] kitchen is simply disgraceful. Then my father, my brothers, and myself always get our food from our mother because we can't eat what is cooked in the [common] kitchen. This feeding requires some money, but where is it to come from?

My nanaira, i.e. the parental house of my [mother] is not rich enough to supply her with money. . . . My grandfather's idea is that if he supplied to my mother he would have to do the same to my aunts [who live in the joint family], and this would be doing an injustice to my father, as my uncles have been given their share [an income share of the thikana] and must support themselves. This is all very well and sounds pretty, but life is short and if we suffer in the midst of plenty we cannot have any greater misfortune. My mother eats the coarsest food, yet keeps good for us her children, her husband and the guests. I admire her as will anybody else. . . .

[My grandfather] should boldly say that as my uncles have got their shares they must supply to their wives and he was going to do it only for his eldest son's wife. . . .

Besides this, my grandfather never supplied her with servants, and I know there was a time when she was sick with no one to look after her. There was not even anyone to bring her the food from the kitchen. My sister used to bring water from the tap, which was luckily going on at that time in the zenana, and my brother Sheonath Singh, who was the only one of age to do any slight work, used to bring the food. . . . She had to brush the very floor with a broom as there was no one to do it all. Through all this miserable life my grandfather never arranged anything at all, and my father had at last to employ some women.

Of what use is the money, the dignity and the jagir we possess when we ourselves cannot enjoy. My heart burns and I am very nearly bursting out with tears while writing these lines, which make me remember those miserable days when my own mother suffered while all others around her enjoyed.

Thank God she does not have to undergo all this now. I have asked her to employ even a dozen servants if she wanted and spend as much as she wanted as I have both the money and the courage to help her. . . .

One day, during this last leave, I was talking to her and the wife of Rawat Singhjee, who is the Mama [maternal uncle] of Gumbheer Singhjee. The talk turned on the killing of infant daughters. It was a horrible subject to talk about but I wanted to know the mysteries as much as I could. To our eternal shame I am writing that several such cases have occurred. . . . One of these is that there was a daughter born to [Mahadev] Singhjee. [Mahadev] Singhjee's mother insisted on having that innocent girl murdered, but her [the infant's] mother would not do that deed. The old lady got so angry [she] swore that she would never ascend the steps of the upper story until the deed was done. The poor mother had to yield and so a murder was done. . . .

. . . [Another girl] was killed, though after she had grown up. She was unfortunately dumb and deaf. I am not quite sure whether she was killed or died a natural death, which thing had happened at her nanaira. These things, so far as I know, have been done by the ladies without the permission of their husbands. My mother was saying that she can never stand these things and though she has lost a daughter and a granddaughter they have both of them died natural deaths. If something is not done to facilitate the marriage business, the evil will never cease. One daughter means the ruin of a house whose income is small and dignity great. . . .

Jaipore, Sunday, 27th December, 1903

The Incident About the Dinner of the Night Before Last. I have a few remarks to make about this incident which . . . depicts the life that we Hindoos, and specially the Rajpoots, lead daily. The night when I arrived here I took my meal with my wife and the next day I ordered the same thing. My idea being that the more pleased I kept my wife the better it will be for the child that she is bearing at present [a second pregnancy].

Indian ladies think a great deal [of dining] . . . with their husbands. This may sound very odd to the Europeans who daily dine with their wives, but it is not so with us, and particularly in our family, where the etiquette is strictly observed. My wife and my bhabee [Bhoj Raj Singhji's wife] always tell me that in this family we have got a peculiar custom of enjoying ourselves in old age. . . . They daily see my uncles Mookend Singhjee and Bheem Singhjee dining in the zenana. My grandfather and granduncle Shambhoo Singhjee used to do the same thing. . . . The only exception to this rule is my father who never did and I fear never will do this sort of thing. . . .

To resume my account, the dinner on the first night passed off very well, but the next time, when my food from the kitchen was sent in the zenana, my mother understood what it meant and began to say in a roundabout way that the present generation was getting quite shameless. Even my devar [her husband's younger brother], meaning Bheem Singhjee, keeps more etiquette than my sons who are keeping their wives over their heads. When such complaints began to be poured out, my wife could not bear [it] and so sent my dinner outside.

[When] I was about to go in the zenana I found that my wife had had no dinner simply because she had got out of . . . humour. . . . I could not make her talk to me. She was even shedding tears. Thus came out the result of my dinner. It rather proved a nuisance than a blessing. . . . All the same, I know perfectly well that I am the happiest man in my family, and specially among my cousins and brothers, because my father is a model parent and never hinders me from enjoying myself. My mother too is about the best of all the other mothers. . . .

I heard my account of expenses from Umaid Ramjee. I don't think I am a spendthrift but still, the money that goes out of my hand is quite enough. It slips quite unconsciously. . . .

Meerut, Wednesday, 6th January, 1904

Notes About the Christmas Leave[27].

VIII. My Grandfather

The day that I reached Jaipore he was at Kanota and when he came the next morning I went to him. I found him unusually cold, but thought that he wanted to go to bed and not to talk at this moment. I was just going when Umaidjee told my grandfather that Amar Singh had come. Hearing this my grandfather said "What of that, he will kill some more foxes." I at once knew the cause of his anger and wanted to go away, but he began to tell me that why I had killed so many animals and birds when I could have just shot a black buck. I came away at that time but in the afternoon he sent Umaid Ramjee to explain the cause of his anger. It was because I had killed foxes which were of no use to me.

The next day when I went to him, he gave me two examples, one was of his own self . . . When he himself was a boy he used to go out shooting and the people once told his father, my great-grandfather, that Zorawar Singh was such a good shot that he never missed. Hearing this the thakoor sahib said "Ask him how much punh (charity) he does in a day." His purport was that he was doing a lot of sin and not a single good deed. . . . I was told that I could shoot those things that were useful but never indiscriminately. Further on I was told that when too much sin is committed by killing animals, the result is bad. If sin is committed at all there ought to be good deeds side by side to balance it. He gave me this lecture for about an hour. . . .

TABLE 5.1   Register of Shikar in the Year 1903

Name	Jan	Feb	Mar	Apr	May	June	Jul	Aug	Sep	Oct	Nov	Dec	Total
Hares	1	7	9	0	0	0	0	1	0	0	0	4	22
Foxes	5	2	1	0	0	0	1	0	0	0	0	4	13
Jackals	10	7	2	0	0	0	0	0	0	0	0	1	20
Pigs	7	0	0	4	0	0	0	1	3	2	0	6	23
Partridges	8	1	1	1	0	0	0	1	0	0	1	7	20
Quails	1	0	2	1	1	0	0	0	2	0	58	0	83
Lavas	2	0	0	0	0	0	0	0	0	0	3	0	5
Green Pigeons	3	0	0	2	1	1	0	0	0	0	3	8	15
Black Buck	0	0	0	0	1	0	0	0	0	0	0	1	2
Chinkara	1	0	0	0	0	0	0	0	0	0	0	1	2
Sand Grouse	2	0	1	0	0	0	0	4	0	0	0	0	7
Conrries Plover	0	0	1	0	0	0	0	0	0	0	0	0	1
Hyena	0	0	0	0	0	0	0	0	0	1	0	0	1
Jungle Fowl	0	0	0	0	0	0	0	0	0	0	1	0	1
Dhanvair[a]	0	0	0	0	0	0	1	0	0	0	0	2	3
Total	49	19	26	7	2	1	2	7	5	3	63	33	217

[a]This Dhanvair was shot under ignorance. I did not know what bird it was and so have not given it any name. It was afterwards when I shot the others that I found that the one shot at Dehra Doon was also a Dhanvair. In English Dhanvair is called the Rhinocerous bird.

TABLE 5.2   Books that I have Read in the Year 1903

No.	Names of books	Authors	Remarks
January 1903			
1.	[Kesar Bil Natak][a]	[Shiv Chandra Pita Baldevjee]	Very good indeed
2.	[Smitri Prakash]	Nihal Chandra	Good collection
February 1903			
3.	Count Hannibal	Stanley J. Weyman	Very interesting
4.	The Idle Thoughts of an Idle Fellow	Jerome K. Jerome	Good essays
March 1903			
5.	The Hound of the Baskervilles	A. Conan Doyle	Very interesting
6.	Maiwa's Revenge	H. Rider Haggard	Not much good
7.	At Delhi	Lovat Fraser	Good description
8.	The Coronation Durbar at Delhi	Printed at the Pioneer Press	Fairly good
April 1903			
9.	Anna Lombard	Victoria Cross	Very good
10.	The Long Exile and Other Stories for Children	Count Tolstoy	Not much good
11.	Cleopatra	H. Rider Haggard	Very good
12.	Minor Hints	S.T. Madhav Rao	Well worth reading
13.	[Sikh Yudh][b]	[Sri Kewal Ram]	Very good
May 1903			
14.	The Subaltern	Damfool Smith Sahib	Very amusing
15.	Phroso	Anthony Hope	Good
June 1903			
16.	Allan Quatermain	H. Rider Haggard	Very good
17.	King Solomon's Mines	H. Rider Haggard	Very good
18.	She	H. Rider Haggard	Splendid
July 1903			
19.	The Adventures of Sherlock Holmes	A. Conan Doyle	Very good
20.	[Chittor Chatiki][c]		Full of rot and lies
21.	The Memoirs of Sherlock Holmes	A. Conan Doyle	Very good

(continued)

TABLE 5.2   *(continued)*

No.	Names of books	Authors	Remarks

August 1903

22.	Seekers after God	Rev. F.W. Farrar	Very good indeed
23.	Illa	Kartick Prasad	Fair
24.	Mr and Mrs Brown at Home	John Brown	Amusing
25.	The Life of Abdur Rahman Ameer of Kabul, vol. 1	Mir Munshi Sultan Mohammed Khan	Good

September 1903

26.	The Life of Adbur Rahman, vol. 2	Sultan Mahomed	
27.	Kamla's Letter to Her Husband	Venkata Subha Rao	Good
28.	[Maharaja Shivaji]	[Pritam Bhag]d	Very good
29.	[Sarojini Natak]e	[Kesab Prasad Misra]	Fair
30.	The Festival of the Passions; or Voluptuous Miscellany	Philo Cunnus	Very indecent and rotten
31.	The Light of Asia	Sir Edwin Arnold	Very good

October 1903

32.	[Dhanjay Vijay]	[Sri Harish Chander]	Fair
33.	[Maharana Pratap Singh [Itihasik Natak]f	[Sr. Radha Krishanjee]	Good
34.	An Elementary Text Book of Hindu Religion and Ethics	Printed by the Board of Central Hindu College	Very Good
35.	The Sign of Four	A. Conan Doyle	Good
36.	[Hamir Hat]	[Pandit Chander Shekar Bajpaee]	Not much good
37.	[Kusum Kumari]	[Babu Devki Nandan Khatri]	Fair
38.	[Maharani Padmawati]	[Babu Devki Nandan Khatri]	Rot
39.	[Chander Kanta]	[Babu Devki Nandan Khatri]	

November 1903

40.	A Queen of Atlantis	Frank Aubrey	Fair
41.	The Bhagavad Gita	Annie Besant (Trans.)	Very Good
42.	[Uttam Acharan Shiksha]g	[Sushila Tal Ram]	Good
43.	The Murder of Delicia	Marie Corelli	Very good

The End

aKesar Belas; Play. Items in brackets are Romanized and or translated from the Devanagri.
b"The Sikh War"
c"Some Stories of Chittor"
dMaharaja Shivaji: First Volume
ePlay of Sarojini
fHistorical Play : Maharana Pratap
g"The Teaching of Good Manners"

Thursday, 18th February, 1904

[Amar Singh goes on leave from the Cadet Corps to attend the wedding of the Maharaja of Kishengarh. As usual, he takes advantage of every opportunity for a little side trip home.]

III. Jaipore

It was not quite necessary for me to stop at Jaipore but I did so just to see my relations. Imagine my disappointment when I could not sleep in the zenana on the very night that I reached. I had sent Boodh Singh on to arrange for a carriage to be sent at the station and to inform that I was coming. All the arrangements were ready but my wife's room was locked. I was simply furious but there was no help. When I went in and asked her the reason she said that she could not sleep there unless her mother-in-law ordered. It is this damned etiquette that makes most of the Hindoo lives miserable. . . .

1. Bhoj Raj Singh

This unfortunate cousin of mine has always some sort of trouble. . . . The latest news is this. All the family were forcing him to marry a second wife on the ground that he has no children, and in that case there was fear of the thikana being confiscated under the mori sala system, which means that only the [direct] descendants of [the founder of the thikana] can succeed to this thikana. Now he, Bhoj Rajjee, is the only son to his father [Mukend Singh], and [his father's brother, the other direct descendant] had no son. Now, by the grace of God [his father's brother] has got a son during the last fortnight, and that anxiety has been put off apparently.

Unfortunately, it is not so for poor Bhoj Raj Singhjee. He is pressed more than ever because. . . . Mookend Singhjee and [his brother] are not on the best of terms. [The family therefore is opposed to the succession going to the brother's son]. . . .

In this particular case, the couple is so much bothered that they have said that a second marriage may be performed. Now comes this difficulty. The mother says that suppose she married her son a second time but the latter did not go to see the new wife? . . . At present this is the point on which the poor couple are tormented. . . .

Bhoj Rajjee and his wife both love me a great deal, and they both tell me freely of their sorrows, because I sympathise with them. . . . While at home I often send wine at night because they are not allowed this luxury. . . . I fear I have written a bit too much of our secret history and will so stop my pen and take another subject.

5

Men in the World:
Estate Management, Horses and Books

Dramatis Personae

Zorawar Singh, grandfather.

Roop Singh, uncle, Thakur of Naila.

Narain Singh, "my father," in his role as horse trader.

Mehtab Singh, estate steward of Naila.

[Amar Singh's grandfather Zorawar Singh begins to initiate him, the future Thakur of Kanota, into the division of family resources. How shall the estate's income be distributed within the joint family, specifically to the brothers of Amar Singh's father and to their sons, Amar Singh's cousins? All of them are entitled to some maintenance by the thikana. Just how much is uncertain. There are no fixed rules.

Younger sons and their offspring do not always live on allowances from the thikana. Sometimes they take jobs. Narain Singh's brothers were or are in service to the Jaipur state, Bhim Singh as deputy inspector general of police and Gambhir Singh in the Jaipur cavalry. Amar Singh's brothers, Sheo Nath, Kesri and Bari Sal take service in princely states such as Kashmir and Gwalior. But even where a *chut bhai*, a younger brother, has a salaried job, the allowance from the thikana is a matter of great importance.

Relations between jagirdars and their sons or chut bhais were often troubled. Discontented or aggrieved younger brothers might turn to the maharaja, who had formal authority in lineage matters. A jagirdar's reputation among his peers could be affected by the generosity or miserliness of family settlements. Discontented siblings could make life hell in the close quarters of the joint family.

The issue of shares for Narain Singh's brothers arises now because of the outcome of the maharaja's case against the Champawat families. Although the related families have been cleared of the charge that they acquired villages fraudulently, a face-saving arrangement has been invented by the resident in favor of Maharaja Madho Singh: the disputed villages granted in 1873 were to be exchanged for new ones. How should the new villages be allocated among the claimants inside the family?]

Meerut, Thursday, 18th February, 1904

4. My Grandfather.[1]

About this parent I shall write only . . . about the short talk he had with me when I was leaving Jaipore. He told me that I was to think over and tell him as to

PHOTO V-14   "Damodar, my accountant" who keeps the complex account books of the joint-family household. Photograph by Amar Singh.

how much share should be given to my uncles and how much to my brothers and whether this share ought to be given in Kanota [village] itself or in the other villages. The advantages and disadvantages of giving in Kanota itself are as follows. The advantages are that if given in Kanota [the principal village, which yields the most revenue and is the site of the fort], the younger branch can never separate themselves and so throw off the authority of the thikana, and the disadvantages are that if we all lived together we would be constantly quarrelling.

The second [question] was that the villages of my cousins have been confiscated and some other ones will have to be given them instead. [These villages were granted to the uncles and cousins of the Kanota branch for their maintenance, and would have reverted to the thikana at their deaths.] Now which [should] these villages . . . be and how much worth ought they to be. . . .

The thikana has suffered too much and cannot afford to give [them] so much as it had before. But then the difficulty will be that if my uncle [Bhim Singh] refused to accept [the offered settlement because it is too little], or my aunt [Gambhir Singh's widow] presented a petition to the durbar [for the same reason], there

PHOTO V-15 "The Kanota Patels," estate servants who collected revenue from the villages of the estate, *circa* 1912. Amar Singh's photo albums.

would be a lot of trouble, as the maharaja sahib wants to find some opportunity to spread disunion in our family.

I was to think all these matters over and give my own opinion. Besides this I was to tell my father and ask him to answer the questions when he met my grandfather who is very anxious to settle as much work as he can in his lifetime *because no one can stop him or even blame if he gives less, whereas it will be very difficult for my father and still more so for me [as neither commands such patriarchal authority]2* . . . have spoken about it to Ram Nathjee. . . . His advice is that both my uncles [Bhim Singh and the deceased Gambhir Singh's family] should be given about five hundred rupees income each, and this should be settled [and] that they shall not have to keep up the two horses of their share with which we serve the state. [Until 1935, Jaipur state required feudal levies from all its nobles in the form of mounted horses that could be called up for use in time of trouble.]

This arrangement will be beneficial to both parties. My uncles will have to suffer some little harm because instead of thirteen hundred and seven hundred they will have to take only five hundred. Then their income was a good deal but now it would be very much reduced. However, it would be all right if they consoled themselves with the idea that they do not have to keep up the horses, and the thikana has suffered a lot. Then it would be well as it would set an example to the later generation. . . .

My father's opinion about giving shares to younger brothers is that they ought to be given very little so that the power of the thikana may not be broken, but he, being the eldest, cannot express his ideas as it would look as if he was selfish. My ideas are the same as his. I fear I go a little . . . further. I like the English system, by which the eldest receives all the estates and titles and the younger has to earn his own living. . . .

[Conversations with his grandfather have alerted Amar Singh to problems of family financial arrangements. He makes notes of a conversation with his friend and fellow cadet Akhai Singh about how the Raoti family, a branch of the Jodhpur ruling family, handles thikana finance.]

Jaipore, Tuesday, 5th April, 1904

A Family Talk[3]. One day at Meerut, Akhai Singhjee and I had gone out for a ride and the conversation turned on family subjects. Here I shall write about what I learned from him [about] how the Raoti family is supported [a branch of the Jodhpur ruling house]. Maharaj Fateh Singhjee [elder brother of Akhai Singh] is the head and does all the work.[4] . . . Fateh Singhjee's wife [as senior woman in the zenana] receives Rs 150 a month for her pocket expenses and Simrath Singhjee's, Ratan Singhjee's. . . . Inder Singhjee's and Akhai Singhjee's wives [as wives of the younger brothers] receive Rs 100 each per month. Achal Singhjee, Ajeet Singhjee and the third bastard receive Rs 50 each. The last three get for their own as well as their wives' supports this sum, but those mentioned first get this amount for their pocket expenses while food and clothing, to some extent, are supplied by the thikana This is a very generous arrangement. . . .

Fateh Singhjee . . . spends well. . . . My family have about the same or say just a little less income but our ladies do not get anything at all. Formerly they used to have Rs 80 per year for their clothes but now even that is stopped and the ladies have a hard time of it . . . This fixed allowance is a good thing. It prevents constant quarrelling and ill feeling.

The two younger sons [of Fateh Singh], Indar Singhjee and Ratan Singhjee, have been given a certain fixed amount which they get every month. This money is with their father who deposits it in their name and interest is got. This has already made a good fortune for the boys and this will go on increasing until the time when the boys will be given separate homes when they will have plenty to carry on their business. This is a good plan, because the thikana does not get burdened by being obliged to give too much all at once. . . .

Dehra Doon, Tuesday, 26th April, 1904

[In the following entries, the family falls out over acquiring horses. The quarrel with Roop Singh comes on top of tensions between Kanota and Naila over the cost of marriages and over nephew Amar Singh's uppity ways.

If Americans love cars, Rajputs loved horses; they were virtual centaurs. Horse stories abound. Chetak, Rana Pratap's faithful steed, carried him to safety in 1576 after the great battle with the Mughal army at Haldighati; Chetak's death scene recurs in postcards and folk art. Ballooji Champawat's horse leapt over the ramparts of Agra's red fort to save its rider. Of some 600 photographic glass plates prepared by Amar Singh, nearly 300 portray horses. His diary also includes many passages concerning horse sense: how to measure a big horse in such a manner—splayed legs; no feed for two days—so that it can be certified as small enough to be a polo pony; brooding over the price of a horse; enthusiasm about the splendid qualities of the latest purchase (not included in this selection). Amar Singh's eulogy to Ghatotguch, who saw him through the Boxer Rebellion, and won him many prizes, can be found in Part IV.

Polo, hunting, pig-sticking, sports that claim about a third of Amar Singh's waking hours, depend as much on the quality of the mount as on skill. His father, Narain Singh, was a widely reputed horseman and connoisseur of horseflesh. So too was his master and mentor, Sir Pratap. Amar Singh follows in their footsteps. Later in life, buying, selling, and training horses become a critical part of his military career.]

Notes About My Last Vacation.

I. The New Ponies

This time the lot of new horses was very good indeed. [Some time ago,] my father [had] bought twenty ponies of which two were for Devi Singhjee [Thakur of Chomu], two for Mr Stothard, four for Bhoj Raj Singhjee, one for Roop Singhjee of Kalwar, three for me, four for my uncle Roop Singhjee and four for himself. Now when all these animals came at Jaipore my uncle [Roop Singh], as usual, wanted to have all the good ones for himself . . . Roop Singh took all the ponies that my father had brought for his own use and wrote a letter to my parent saying that as all his lot had been taken, he had now better buy for himself as no one wanted any animals at Jaipore. . . .

When my father got this letter he waited for a couple of weeks more and bought seventeen Waler ponies newly arrived from Australia. . . . When the ponies arrived, Bhoj Raj Singh took two of the new ones because they had been brought for him and one was taken by my uncle Bheem Singhjee. The remainder of the lot remained for my father. . . .

[Though] my uncle Roop Singhjee had written to my father telling that he . . . did not want any and my father was to buy for himself . . . When he saw these new ones, he wanted to choose from these the best and give back what he had taken before. This my father would not listen to and the result was that my uncle became awfully angry.

Roop Singhjee was so much put out that he stopped talking either to Bhoj Raj Singhjee, my father, or myself. The anger with my cousin was that he had chosen and got the best lot. The displeasure to me was that I had selected the best ones without first offering him and with my father because he would not say that he could select what pleased him best. . . . My uncle Bheem Singhjee always tells my father not to do this business as there was sure to be some ill feeling some day. His prophecy has come to be true.

Fancy Roop Singhjee wanted to take the best of my father's Waler ponies for Mehtab Singhjee. He ought to have considered that he was just as good, if not better, a brother as Mehtabjee. . . .

XII. The Kala Gora

[Mehtab Singh] said "good morning" to Bhoj Raj Singh, who did not hear as he was looking the other way. Mehtab Singhjee then came up closer and said that if the uncles were worthy of nothing else they were at least worth being bid good morning. My cousin said that he was looking the other way and did not see him. It was here that Roop Singhjee interfered but not for anything good. He said that he [Bhoj Raj Singh] was having the company of Kala Gora [the black white man]. This was an allusion to me. What Roop Singhjee meant was that this disrespect was the result of Bhoj Raj Singhjee's keeping me company. There is a proverb in our language which means that if a white one keeps the company of a black one he may not pick up the colour but will certainly pick up the habits of the latter. I do not know what I have done to deserve such a remark unless it was that I took away the ponies that he wanted to have for himself . . .

Meerut, Thursday, 14th January, 1900[5]

[On his way to the Maharaja of Kishengarh's wedding in February of 1904, Amar Singh chances to meet the Indian woman author, Sushila Tahl Ram, whose works—*Cosmopolitan Hinduani* and *Uttam Acharan Shiksha* (The Teaching of Good Manners)—he has read and admired.[6] "She is," he writes, "an Indian lady brought up in England. She writes beautiful Hindi and the book [Shiksha] too is a good one."[7] He first encounters her books at the Cadet Corps.]

. . . *Cosmopolitan Hinduani* . . . is a very nice book indeed. The author is an Indian lady, but her style of writing English is just as good as that of most of the Englishmen. The stories are very good and there is one that is exceptionally real and lifelike. This is about a man being married to a young girl and afterwards of their great love and the jealousy of the mother-in-law. That is simply a charming story. . . .

[After the brief meeting, and back at the Cadet Corps, Amar Singh finds himself the object of much attention from the author's husband, who appears to live in Meerut. Tahl Ram comes to Amar Singh's tent at the Cadet Corps.]

Tuesday, 16th February, 1904

* . . . At Kishengarh station I met Sushila Tahl Ram who is that Indian lady that has been writing some books. I was very much pleased to form her acquaintance. Doctor Dal Jung Singhjee introduced us. I am sorry I could talk to her only for a few minutes.[8]* . . . Tahl Ram came and asked me whether I would attend the dinner party of his friend, to which I had to decline as I was sick. He brought me three books written by his wife. These books are for sale. . . .

Thursday, 18th February, 1904

. . . Tahl Ram came and I had a talk with him. I am beginning to [wonder] . . . whether he is a gentleman or a rascal. Anyway, I don't want to see him anymore if I can help. He talks of things he does not seem to understand. . . .

Friday, 19th February, 1904

. . . Tahl Ram came to me and I had a talk with him. I am now getting sick of him but not he of me. I have now introduced him to Pratap Singhjee and Brijander

Cosmopolitan Hinduani

Depicting Muhammedan

and

Hindu Life and Thought

In Story Form,

BY

SUSILA TAHL RAM.

Lahore:

PRINTED AT THE CIVIL AND MILITARY GAZETTE PRESS.

1902.

"Spell of black eyes!"

"Remember, British prestige!"

"Love!"

"Confound you!" thundered the General, and thus the duet subsided.

Honri-soro the Captain rushed from the stormy atmosphere to his tranquil home, fragrant with the sunny smiles of his Floweret, whose sweet breath soothed his ruffled spirit, and tender kisses healed the wound. Lulled in loving arms, as he passed into dreamland, he consolingly whispered to his heart, "Oh, if there is bliss; if there be an Elysium on earth; it is this, it is this.'" The repose having calmed him down, he arose in good humour and attended the Mess. After dinner when he got among his particular set he ordered champagne and with glasses sparkling and merrily clinking; amidst mirth and laughter breaking in between Whist, he sang with great gusto, "Two Black Eyes," while his comrades returned the compliment that Green was a "Jolly Good Fellow." A year after when with great pride he showed them his Rose-bud, a pearl of a baby, the hearts of his brother Officers melted, and they forgave merry Green, 'the spell of the eyes,' and his indiscretion. But before Rose could toddle the mother passed away to bloom in another Sphere, and hence she was nurtured by her widowed aunt, Gulzár, whose husband had met with an untimely death at a shooting party, when he had been severely mauled by a tigor. Until Diláwar's marriage had been solemnized and he had joined a Battalion of the Irregulars stationed at Shahpur, he was the constant companion of his pretty cousin; and the young knight, notwithstanding his mother having pledged him to another, constantly declared she was his rose-bud bride. The loss of the young wife was irreparable to the gay, humorous Captain Green. It seemed as if sunshine had departed from his home, and he never recovered his spirits, but gradually because gloomy and morose. When he retired from service, he settled down at Nasimábad, and on his death-bed

Kishor and he is now coming round to get his money for his books out of them. . . .

Saturday, 20th February, 1904

. . . Tahl Ram once came but I was cool to him. He asked me whether I was too busy to talk, and I said I was. He said he had come simply to inquire after my health, and I said that I was much better.

[Then, in April, Amar Singh goes to Jaipur on vacation where once again he meets the author.]

Jaipore, Tuesday, 19th April, 1904

. . . In the evening I went to Doctor Dal Jung Singh's house to see Mrs Sushila Tahl Ram who had come this morning from Kishengarh. I talked to her for a short time and went out for a ride in the jungle on Jhalana road.

Thursday, 21st April, 1904

. . . [I] went out with Bhoj Raj Singhjee to the Ram Niwas where we called upon Mrs Sushila Tahl Ram and talked to her for about a quarter of an hour. . . .

Dehra Doon, Tuesday, 26th April, 1904[9]

XXII. Mrs Sushila Tahl Ram

This lady had come from Kishengarh and was putting up with doctor Dal Jung Singh. I went to see her twice. I did not ask her to come to my house because my family members would not have liked to see me in the company of an Indian lady, however good she may be. Once I took Lichman Singh and the other time Bhoj Raj Singhjee to introduce to her. She was telling me that she will now go to England and try to learn how to write books. There are people who have made it their special study . . . and they can teach you how to write. I asked her what her new book is that she is writing. She said I had better not ask her the name as yet.

She asked me about her husband for she had heard that I had met him. I had to tell her that he was quite undeserving of her. The poor woman was quite sorry and told me that she had tried all she could, but he would not live properly. He would not dress in a gentlemanly manner, wash or keep himself clean. She had to look after him as after a small baby. It was of no use. All the money that he had he spent away in fooling about or giving to the Arya Samaj [the influential Hindu reform society which was also patronized by Amar Singh's master, Sir Pratap]. It is all right to give a little but don't overdo it. The poor lady wants to stick to Hindu laws, otherwise she can obtain a divorce. She was telling me that if her husband gave her even Rs 50 a month, she would be quite content.

I asked her as to why she does not settle down somewhere and take employment in one of the states where they will be glad to employ her for teaching the maharanees. She said that she has been offered this sort of post several times but has refused. She says "Keep me as a guest while I am with you, but don't employ me." . . . Once she takes service she cannot be independent. She had been presented to the late Queen Victoria and if she wanted to be presented again after taking the employment she could not. She won't be able to join the same society, as the post of a tutor or governess is not looked [upon] in a high sense while that of an author is. Such sort of talks we had.

Tuesday, 26th April, 1904[10]

[Amar Singh, as usual, reports on the Jaipur vacations.]

VII. Company

. . . At night I had the company of my wife which was always the sweetest and pleasantest of all the other companies. We used never to go to bed before half past eleven or twelve. The talk was of course all love, because our ladies are not conversant on any other subjects.

So long as my father was at Jaipore I was in his company as much as I was able to get. There is not a single man's company that I like so much as that of my father. I could not get so much as I wanted. This is the company I had, besides that of the authors whose books I read.

X. My Wife's Ideas

. . . My present purpose of writing this [concerns] her ideas of her coming pregnancy. . . . Someone had told her, even before our marriage, that I was going to have two wives. She knows well that I am not going to marry [while] she is alive, but she believes that she will die before long and I shall have another wife. The recent death of Pratap Singhjee's wife has upset her a great deal, and she has very little hopes of surviving child birth. . . . Even when I was taking leave of her she seemed as if she did not expect to see me any more. . . . I assured her that we were going to meet and that she need not feel anxious. My words had not the desired effect, because the prophecy is deeply rooted in.

. . . Several people have told me, by looking at my hand, that I was going to have two wives . . . The other day when talking to a pundit of Peepla . . . I asked him how many wives I was going to have. At first he would not speak but after looking at my hand he mentioned two. I said that I was determined to prove his prophecy a false one. . . . I also asked him whether I was going to have two wives at a time or one after the death of the other. When I pressed him this much he told me that all these questions had been asked before and that had it not been for Sarkar [who does not credit palmistry and other prophesies] I would not have been married at Satheen. I asked the reason and he said that he had seen by his science that this girl that was to be married had not a long life. He had predicted to my father and repeated to me that after giving birth to two daughters and one son she will die. I would have been married at Barwara had it not been for Sarkar.

. . . I do not expect to get a better wife than the one I have at present. It is a dreadful thing to think over such matters but one cannot help. . . . All this is of course nonsense and I don't put much faith in [it]. [Amar Singh does not marry again, despite the fact that he and his wife never have a son, and the family presses him to remarry. Amar Singh's wife, who dies in 1945, survives him by three years, though paralyzed by a stroke in 1940 or 1941.] . . .

XIII. Dinners

Nowadays it has come a little in fashion to give dinners. Now, the dinners are often given by Devi Singhjee of Chomu, Rajajee of Khandela or sometimes by Kesri Singhjee of Achrol [all leading noblemen of Jaipur state] and my uncle Roop Singhjee. . . . [These] . . . three gentlemen have a dinner almost every week. I do not say it is a bad thing. Far from it. I am of the opinion that to start dinners and meet one another as often as we can is about the best way [to] promote our education and welfare, but at the same time I must say that these dinners are a step in the wrong direction. Common prostitutes[11] are sent for for singing and much money is squandered. The other day Devi Singhjee gave a dinner to Roop Singhjee when the prostitute Doorga was sent for. This woman has Rs 100 (one hundred) as her fees for one night's singing.

To add to this, these prostitutes come up with a cup of wine and give manwar [a gift of food among equals] with their own hands. This is too absurd. . . . It started at Naila when Pratap Singhjee was lately married. Then my uncle Roop Singhjee had manwars given to all his nephews.

Manwar is a very sacred thing. Only one's dearest friends or relations give it. When it comes from the hands of common prostitutes it degrades the man as well as the manwar. There is no saying where it might end. A pretty girl giving you manwar with her hands and looking at you full in the face and that at a time when your head is turned with wine is a temptation that few young men can withstand. If dinners were started on the English principle, when there was no fooling and no unnecessary expense, I would be the first man to back them up. . . .

XXVI. The New Villages

This time I went to see two of my villages, Khori and Sindoli. [These are the villages that the Jaipur maharaja has given the Kanota family in exchange for those taken over as part of a compromise after Jaipur state's unsuccessful suit against the Kanota family.] The former has been given to us for Rs 1,100 eleven hundred a year and the latter Rs 2,500. [These are the formal valuations of the villages' income earning capacity, usually based on twenty-year averages.] Khori has quite a [nice] small house, but the land under it is not much. However, the little that there is is all very productive. You can make nearly [two] crops in it if you take the trouble. We already get Rs 1,900 for it and there is every hope of our getting twice as much. . . .

What I like best in this village was the hill under which is the village of Khori on one side and Rophara on the other. I climbed to the highest top and from it there was an awfully good view to be seen. I wished that I had a small house built there and lived quietly with my wife. For the whole family it would not be enough. When I came to Jaipore I told my wife about this idea of mine and she began to laugh and said that first I had better build a house. . . .

My grandfather has already begun building some kaccha [rough] wells, and when a bund is made there will be plenty of water in the wells. We are trying to get some new men to come and settle. There will be plenty of them coming when once the wells turn out a success. These are the villages [given] to us in exchange for those that have been taken.

6

Harmony and Dissidence in the Joint Family: "Show Sympathy and You Will Earn Confidence"

Dramatis Personae

Roop Singh, Thakur of Naila, Amar Singh's uncle.

Pratap Singh, Roop Singh's eldest son, Amar Singh's cousin, harassed by Mehtab Singh.

Mehtab Singh, impecunious cousin, favorite of Roop Singh and estate agent of Naila.

Mukend Singh, Thakur of Gondher, and head of the now impoverished estate of Gondher.

Mukend Singh's wife, the Thakurani of Gondher, in the role of mother-in-law.

Bhoj Raj Singh, Gondher's eldest son, cousin and close friend of Amar Singh.

"My Wife."

"*My Bhabee*" (Bhoj Raj Singh's wife), in the role of oppressed daughter-in-law.

[Amar Singh becomes ever more preoccupied with the problems of his male cousins. He empathizes with the difficulties they experience in their relations with wives, fathers, and mothers, but reassures himself, somewhat nervously, that his lot is better than theirs. Bhoj Raj Singh and his wife are not the only sufferers.

In earlier entries, Amar Singh reported that Roop Singh's eldest son, Pratap Singh, has cause for complaint over the lavish expenditures his father, the Thakur of Naila, has vowed to incur on the forthcoming wedding of the daughter of Mehtab Singh. Mehtab Singh is *kamdar* (estate manager) of Naila and executor of major and lavish improvements which eventually inspire Narain Singh and Amar Singh to similar improvements at Kanota. Amar Singh is outraged that this propertyless chut bhai of a related family is being treated as well or better than his cousin Pratap Singh, Roop Singh's son and heir. Amar Singh's overt support for Pratap exacerbates his poor relations with his uncle Roop Singh.]

Dehra Doon, 26 April, 1904[1] (cont.)

XIV. Pratap Singhjee

This is one of my cousins, son of Roop Singhjee, who is leading a most miserable life. His father is spending all that his grandfather had collected and is quite careless as regards his sons and wife. All that Roop Singhjee cares [for] is Mehtab Singhjee and his wife and daughter. Matters have reached to such a crisis that I am afraid there will be something very disagreeable one of these days. Pratap Singhjee and his brother are treated very unfairly by their father and still more by Mehtab Singhjee, whose sole idea is to . . . keep Pratap Singhjee as much broken in spirit as he can so that he may not raise his head and insist on his having the Naila work [that is, the management of the thikana, which is now Mehtab Singh's responsibility]. Now I shall write the present existing state of things in the Naila family.

Roop Singhjee . . . is so much in the hands of his cousin Mehtab Singhjee that he dares not raise his head even when the latter does things against the former's will. Roop Singhjee's wives are quite neglected. No one cares for them except their son Pratap Singh, but the poor fellow has nothing in his hands. The boys too [a sixteen-year-old brother of Pratap Singh and his four-year-old son] are neglected except Raghunath Singh [the four-year-old son] who is being spoiled by over love. It is now time he was being taught something, but he is not done so. The result will be that he will be without any education. . . .

. . . I shall begin by giving a little account of [Pratap Singh's] third and last marriage. . . . [The first and second wives had died, each leaving a child, a son and a daughter respectively. In consequence, it was difficult to contract a third marriage. The Naila family was willing to settle for a girl from an impoverished but respectable Rawalot family on the look-out for an hypergamous match.]

Some Rawalot Bhatees [a Rajput lineage from western Rajputana] had a daughter and had brought her from Jaisalmere to marry her to some Raja but, having failed in that, they have married her to Pratap Singhjee. . . . There was not much fuss made this time. . . .

Pratap Singhjee told me on several occasions that he would never have married this time if he could have foreseen the troubles. There is the trouble of Mehtab Singhjee and Roop Singhjee and his mothers and all that. Now to add to all this has arisen the trouble of this new marriage. . . . This new girl has come from a poor house where her parents did not have so many ornaments, clothes and things. She does not know the methods of big houses and the etiquette and all that. When I went to pay my respects I noticed the poor thing was quite ignorant even up to the manner of keeping her face veiled; but all this is not her fault. Her mother-in-law abuses her every morning and calls her all sorts of names because she is from poorer parents. The poor girl feels it, and at night tells all the things to her husband, who too in his turn gets annoyed, but what can he do. Indian mode of life is miserable in some ways. It is not the poor girl's fault that she is poor, or still more that she is married in this house. If the mother-in-law wanted a better wife for her son, why did she not get another girl? . . .

Poor Pratap Singhjee is so much annoyed by these things that he does not want to sleep in the zenana much, but then there comes the trouble. If he goes regularly to his wife, Roop Singhjee says that he is now getting under the influence of the lady, and if he does not go, then he says what can the present generation do when they cannot even go to their wives regularly. They are afraid of them. No man ought to be forced to such things. It must be left to Pratap Singh-jee's choice as to when he goes in and when he does not. Roop Singhjee would soon know what a difficult thing it is to do if he was made to go to his wife regularly whether he wanted or not . . .

The natural consequence of all this trouble is anxiety and the result of that is sickness. My cousin is now very much broken in health. All of medicines are given but they are to no purpose. The only medicine that can cure him is to get rid of Mehtab Singhjee. This can't be done and he can't be cured. I will quote a poetry.

> [Why are you putting sandal paste on your body?
> Why are you pouring rose water on your body?
> Why are you making garlands of blossoms for your neck?
> Why are you collecting wealth?
> These are no remedies.
> Why are you asking the Brahmans and Sadhus for cures?
> My question is, can anyone show me my Beloved?]

This is a sawaia [a poetic form] from Prabin Sagur. On one occasion Prabin is said to have been very sick for want of seeing her lover and people thought that she was sick and tried all sorts of medicines. It is supposed to have been recited by her then. However it exactly fits Pratap Singhjee. . . .

When [Mehtab Singhjee's] son was alive he used to get the best education and his slightest wish was gratified at a moment's notice while poor Duleep Singhjee [Pratap's younger brother] is still being left uncared for. There is no one who teaches him or gives him any advice. Roop Singhjee is always swearing at him and says that he is the servant of his nephew [refers possibly to Mehtab Singh]. This will have a bad consequence. The English proverb says, "Tell a man he is a dog and you will make him one." . . .

One day at polo Pratap Singhjee was looking about for some one to walk with him to his home. There being none present I suggested Duleep, on which he said quietly, "Don't mention his name." I asked the reason and he said that people will think why these two brothers went together and what they talked in the way. By the people he meant his father and Mehtab Singhjee. The father is always afraid of Pratap Singhjee revolting against his brother ["cousin-brother" Mehtab Singh]. . . .

XV. Bhoj Raj Singhjee

[The fate of this branch of the Champawat lineage from Peelva has worsened as a result of the exchange of villages. Most serious was the loss of its *kotri* (fort) village, Gondher, with its substantial revenue and recently constructed palace.]

. . . Bhoj Raj Singhjee has always been bothered about a second marriage. . . . Arrangements are being now made for the second marriage, and the Punditjee of Peepla is examining horoscopes to find out the best girl that will bear a child. Some three have been selected, but I do not know who is to be married in the end. . . .

When Bhoj Rajjee told his wife about it, she sent for me and begged me to tell my father in her name that he ought to settle this marriage before he goes to Alwar, otherwise she is having a very bad time of it . . . I have never heard of a wife asking her husband to get another wife but in this instance, and this will show what must be the sufferings and privations that she is made to undergo. . . .

While I was coming back [from tennis at the residency] Bhoj Raj Singhjee told me that his wife was sick. . . . I went to see her and it was with the greatest difficulty that I could persuade her to lie down while I sat. I gave her a little advice which was somewhat of a gyan [aphorism; words of wisdom]. She got so pleased that she caressed me with both her hands. What I said was that she ought to forget her troubles, which could best be done by remembering God.[2]

[With the confiscation of the main village and its fort, Mukend Singh's family has nowhere to keep the animals.] As I have written enough about (my aunt) I shall now take her husband in hand. . . . [Mukend Singh's] horses are at my garden. The dung of these animals has collected and formed a huge hill. Every effort has been made to sell it but without success. Bhoj Raj Singhjee suggested that it looks very bad and as no one buys it had better be thrown in the field where it will serve the purpose of manure. To this [Mukend Singh] would not consent because it belongs to him and should not be used for our profit. . . . The gate near the place where his horses are tied has broken to pieces and so has the pillar. The son suggested that these might be repaired, but he would not consent. Why should he repair? The garden does not belong to him but to us and we ought to do it. . . .

At present he has got some twelve or thirteen horses but there are only three or four syces there. These poor beggars are kept pretty busy the whole day. They have to bring a couple of horses and the carriage pair every morning. Then some of the ponies require exercise. At polo there is required a pair of horses to take the party to the ground and a couple of syces to take the polo ponies there. How can three syces do all this work. . . .

Who will serve on these conditions for Rs 2 [fr ½] a month? Then even this is not given at the proper time. It is never earlier than six months before which they get their pay, and then it is found that they have overdrawn . . . from time to time to get something to support themselves with. The result of all this is that no syce will come to serve. They say that you don't pay us properly. When these fellows don't get their pay they naturally steal to support themselves. It was only the other day when they were caught [because they] *had stolen some few things and grain. They were being tied preparatory to being beaten [by agents of Mukend Singh] when I came away, because I can not stand such sights. This comes out of having cheap servants. They must steal if only to have enough to eat. If well paid people steal then they are to blame.[3]* Then their pay was cut as a fine. Fancy cutting the whole pay and expecting them to serve. They of course went away.

There is no one who will serve here, but two unfortunate human beings are caught from those villages that belong to Mookend Singhjee, and if they want to . . . leave service they are caught and imprisoned at the village. It does not end here only. Sometimes they are tortured and have to come. The torturing machine is quite a simple one. It is a long wooden log with holes in it all along at intervals.

These holes are large enough to let a man's foot in and the log is sawed into two long halves. The prisoners' legs are put into the holes and the logs are bolted and locked together. This keeps them in sitting or lying positions. For torturing purposes the legs are put far apart in the holes. It must be awfully painful but the system is prevalent all over Rajpootana and is called the khora.

Mookend Singhjee buys things and never wants to pay for them. The Bunyas [merchants] have now got clever. They know that they won't be paid until six months and so they charge interest too when making the bill. . . . When Bhoj Rajjee wants clothes, the sanction is given after a long time, and then the things are sewn by such bad tailors that they are not worth wearing. His father wants him to move in the best society but will not pay for clothes. People surely laugh when they see a shabbily dressed fellow among them, and specially Europeans who hate the very sight of unclean or unfitting dresses. . . .

I am tired of abusing my relations and I think I will now take to something else pleasanter. . . .

XXIV. Talk with My Father

The particular talk that I am going to write about is that he one day asked me . . . on what terms Bhoj Raj Singhjee, Pratap Singhjee, and I were. I said that we were on just as intimate and friendly terms as we possibly could. Roop Singhjee may feel what he likes, but his son does not. It was after this that he asked me about Pratap Singhjee, and said that he had better be removed from the house, otherwise there would be something awful one of these days. Pratap Singhjee gets so much annoyed that sometimes he thinks of ridding himself by committing suicide. I then asked my father to take him away to Alwar with him. He promised and even spoke about it but there being plague at present he could not do anything. I hope he will call him soon. I was asked about his illness and replied that it was nothing but Mehtab Singhjee.

XXXII. Experiences

I learned [a] great secret: . . . show sympathy and you will earn confidence and friendship. There is Bhoj Raj Singh and his wife . . . who thoroughly believe in me and will tell their greatest secrets. . . . The two . . . are very intimate. I only once had occasion to talk with Pratap Singhjee and he told me all about his secret things. Then there is the example of Ram Nathjee or my father, who always manage to get people's secrets out. It is sympathy and costs nothing more but a few kind words.

Jaipore, Sunday, 18th September, 1904

In the morning I woke early and . . . went to my grandfather who had sent for me. He asked me about my expenses and the servants' wages that I have to give. His orders were to show him all the accounts, but luckily Kaloo said he had not the account books with him. I then went and read him my own book which was written in English and as I myself was reading out there was no fear. I read out what I liked and omitted the rest. As luck would have it Roop Singhjee came and I found an opportunity to slip away. . . .

Wednesday, 21st September, 1904

Last night I went in the zenana to sleep. I must here say that there is nothing in this world that can equal a truly loving wife. We love one another, I suppose, as much as a husband and wife can love. . . . I quite forgot my fever as soon as I was in her company, and we talked and joked until eleven when I took medicine and went to bed. . . .

Saturday, 8th October, 1904

. . . In the morning . . . we went out to the Rev Trail's house where his daughter was waiting for us. My father went to see the resident and we stopped at Trail's house for a few minutes. I must say that that little house is a paradise compared to our homes. It was so neat and clean. . . .

Tuesday, 11th October, 1904

. . . I . . . went to my grandfather who kept me with him for about a couple of hours telling all kinds of old stories. He showed me the genealogical table of the Rathores, Kachhawas and Seesodias [the ruling clans of Jodhpur, Jaipur, and Udaipur respectively. Amar Singh is a Rathore.] . . .

Dehra Doon, Friday, 21st October, 1904

Notes About My Last Vacations.

I. Reading

I did not do much of it because I was away at Satheen most of the time . . . . However, the few books that I read are as follows: 1. *The Childerbridge Mystery*, 2. *Shree Bharathari Shatak*, 3. *Recollections of Westminster and India*, 4. *Love Made Manifest*, 5. *A Mad Love: or the Abbe and his Court*, 6. *A Bid for Fortune*, 7. *Lying Prophets*, 8. *The Exploits of Brigadier Gerard*, and 9. *The Marriage of Esther*. Of all this lot there is only one book which gives advice and that is *Shree Bharathari Shatak*. The rest was light reading and helped to beguile the time. . . .

X. Roop Singhjee

This uncle of mine . . . is angry with me, he is angry with my father and he is angry even with my grandfather [in consequence of the dispute over horses]. . . . I as well as my father often went to him and spent hours in his company. He was never moved but was always the same cold man towards us. . . . He then found another means of finding fault. . . . He began to say that boys who have learned English are irrevocably spoiled. At polo he said that these English-educated children know the following: to beat a horse without any cause, to saunter about with a cigar or cigarette in their mouths thinking that there is no one wiser than themselves in the world, and to have no idea about their elders or relations. . . .

. . . Next time there was tennis at the residency we went for the drinks on the platform near the house. There was a durree [cotton rug] spread out and round it were chairs. All the chairs were occupied except the one near the resident [Lieutenant Colonel T. C. Pears] and so I went and sat on it. Now Roop Singhjee has a habit of monopolising the resident. . . . He does not want anyone to talk with the resident while he is there. In this case too it happened that the resident began to talk to me. First he asked me when I was going [to the Cadet Corps], and then . . . he began to ask me about the Kishengarh [state polo] team as I had told him that I had just been there. . . . I then said that really good ponies cost a lot and polo is therefore becoming a very expensive game. To this he said that if you train your own ponies and buy them new it won't be so expensive. I agreed to this and said that one can make a bit of money too if he managed things in this manner.

It was as much as Roop Singhjee could bear. He interrupted our talk and began saying that it was not his opinion that these chiefs should be . . . allowed to play polo. Then he began counting all the faults in the training of a chief . . . He said that a chief should not be given English training as he gets spoiled by it; . . . that he should not be allowed to travel, because by this they lose their love of home and become fickle minded. One day they want to go to Ceylon and the next day to England. This was the worst that Roop Singhjee could have said. In the first place he had said that chiefs get spoiled by English education and the next was that . . . they get spoiled by going to Ceylon and England. . . . I don't know what the resident thought of it. . . . Roop Singhjee goes on babbling unconsciously without thinking what he is saying. . . .

To add to all this he told Ram Nathjee, a week or so afterwards, that Amar Singh does not know manners. While he (Roop Singhjee) was sitting he (Amar) began to talk in English with the resident. [The implication is that Roop Singh, a Hindi speaker, felt excluded.] I said to Ram Nathjee that it was not my fault when Pears began the talk in English; I had to answer him in the same tongue. . . . I have written every word with the greatest impartiality. I have neither exaggerated nor minimised matters. Let the reader judge for himself how far I am correct in my ideas. People say that the peace of the house must be kept at any cost. Is it possible to keep the peace under these conditions? . . .

. . . One day there was tennis at the residency and when it was over all of them decided to go and have drinks at the Rajajee of Khandela's (junior branch) house and afterwards have a dinner too. Devi Singh of Chomu and the Rajajee asked my father to come but he excused himself . . . My father told Bhoj Raj Singhjee and me that these are bad things that have started. . . . It would be all right if there was a quiet and homely dinner. . . . He had noticed these three gentlemen talking at the polo club and did not in the least like their mode of conversation, because they used very common and low words. The result in the end will be a bad one. They have one nearly every other day and a day's feast means at least fifty rupees. When they have dancing and singing then it reaches nearly two hundred rupees. Just think of the expenses. . . .

XVI. My Mother

[Wars over space in the haveli can be most bitter. Amar Singh's mother is the senior woman in bichli haveli. But she does not have good rooms. For historical reasons, the best are already occupied by the widow of Narain Singh's younger brother, Gambhir Singh. The reasons are these. Grandfather Zorawar Singh married twice. The first wife bore Narain Singh and Bhim Singh, the second Gambhir Singh. When the second wife died, she was occupying the best rooms. Rather than passing them on to the next senior woman, who was married to her stepson, Narain Singh, she passed them on to her son, Gambhir Singh's wife. When Gambhir Singh died, his widow continued to occupy the best rooms. Amar Singh's mother feels she has been deprived of her claims as the future thakurani.

In the course of these struggles, Amar Singh learns something about the situation of widows. While widows, often regarded as a burden and inauspicious, are sometimes badly treated, his widowed aunt skillfully turns the tables on the family. Her steady complaint, that now that her husband is dead she and her children will not receive proper treatment, becomes an effective weapon.]

. . . Here again I am to repeat what I said before, that if you treat a man according to his position he does not feel it, but when you treat him below his position then he feels it and very acutely too. My grandfather treats my mother in the same way as he treats my aunts, and this the former resents because she considers herself the mistress of the house, as she really is, because I have no grandmother. She has had no proper room and the good one that she had she gave to my wife. [Presumably the family's interest in the succession lends great importance to the eldest son and his wife having a private room.] Now she had been living in a sort of a verandah which is very uncomfortable. . . .

My aunts had the best of rooms and they enjoyed themselves better than my mother. . . . Ladies always want to have a place from whence they can observe what is passing outside the house. Now, my mother's rooms do not overlook the outside houses and so she was rather uncomfortable while my second aunt was the possessor of the best room in the whole house . . . and "possession is nine points [of] the law," as the saying is. When my father comes home at the same time as I am there, he has a great bother because he has no room to sleep in the zenana and specially in the hot weather.

It was for this purpose that my grandfather ordered my aunt to vacate her room for my mother, and live in one of her other rooms. She made a bit of fuss but she knows that when my grandfather wants a thing done there is no refusing. He must have his own way and so he had. . . .

Why is all this? Simply because my grandfather would insist on keeping the whole family together. . . . Instead of bringing any good, it will breed ill feeling between the family members. . . . We are crowded up. There are no doubt enough rooms, but we must have separate ways to go in the zenana at night. There are only five doors to the zenana houses, but the ground floor door is no use, as no one can live there with any comfort. This leaves us only four doors. Now, if we all remain at home, i.e. my father, my uncle, (my cousin) Hem Singh-jee and myself, we would have enough ways, but when the other [brothers] get married there will be trouble and inconvenience. Well, let us see what happens. Another botheration is that when my father [upon his succession] will have to separate his brother [from the household] there will be some trouble, but if my grandfather does it then there will be neither trouble nor ill-feeling. . . .

XXII. Colonel Pears

I went to call upon Colonel Pears, the resident of Jaipore, twice and he received me very kindly. . . . He asked me several things about the Corps and my prospects. Then he asked me what we were taught here. I showed the question papers of the last examination and he was quite pleased to see them and said that they were just what the British officers have to learn at Sandhurst or Woolwich. I do not know exactly what opinion this man has of me but I am sure it is not a bad one. This officer has not got such a strong will as Mr Cobb, the former resident. . . . I always liked Col. Pears, and I hope he will help me when I shall require a post after leaving the cadet corps. . . . He was very good to my father too, whereas Cobb was very angry. I always hated the very sight of Cobb because he looked like a man whom you could not trust or put faith in. [Cobb devised the damaging scheme of exchanging the Champawat families' revenue villages for others].

XXIII. Ram Nathjee

. . . He was very anxious to meet me and my desire was just the same. He advised me to patch up a peace with my uncle Roop Singh, because my uncle had told him that he had a talk with the resident, who is bent on doing three things. . . . [One] is that he is going to organize the state troops, which are in a miserable condition. . . . It was owing to this army reform business that Ram Nathjee advised me to patch up a peace, for he said that perhaps Roop Singhjee might say that I am too young or not clever enough or something of the sort to the resident and thus stop my getting that post.[4] . . .

XXVI. Some Anecdotes

. . . I got a letter from the private secretary of the Maharaja Sahib of Idar [Sir Pratap, Amar Singh's former guardian] asking me to send my China diary to help the people who are writing the biography of Maharaja Sir Pratap Singhjee. This was a surprise and a blow to me. I cannot possibly send the diary to any man, and Sarkar would be the very last man to whom I would send the thing, because there are pages and pages written that would reveal the inner life of the man. I am sure he would never speak to me if he once heard my diary.

I took Ram Nathjee's advice, who said that I must certainly not send the book. . . . I have not answered the letter and when I shall receive another letter I shall pretend that I never received the first letter. This is no doubt a lie but there is no help. If I am pressed too much, I shall have to say that the book is lost, and finally, if the thing becomes too pressing, would rather destroy the book with my own hands than send it to him. To destroy my diary would cut me to the heart, as this is a thing I have written with great delight and interest. Then it is my ambition to keep on writing so long as I live in order that people can have an idea of what sort of a life I led and what my ideas were. . . .

XI. My Father[5]

[Amar Singh, whom we have found inveighing against hypergamous marriages in his own family when his cousin was married to the wealthy Shekhawati thikana of Nawalgarh, now criticizes the practices of the Rawalot Bhatis and the Shekhawats. Both communities insist on marrying their daughters to ruling chiefs. The practice, according to Amar Singh, makes for unhappy marriages because ruling chiefs have many wives and the girls are exploited by their mothers-in-law because of their inferior social status.

Amar Singh vacillates between justifying and damning the social conventions he describes: "The English idea is quite the best, to respect and protect women. . . . English education will, I am sure, do something to make us change our ideas in this line."[6] But: "We must abide by the laws and rules that have been put down by our ancestors and specially if those laws are good,"[7] or yet again: "Custom is custom and will ruin all Rajpoots in the end."[8]

Much of Amar Singh's reaction has to do with the possibilities of happy marriages. But there is also a status issue at stake. When the parents of a Rajput girl reject the boy's family's offer of marriage, they may be suggesting that the boy's family is of insufficiently high status. The Kanota and Naila families have already once broken "this silly custom," which denigrates the Champawats, by arranging for Pratap Singh to marry a Rawalot Bhati. Rawalots are a Rajput lineage that, impoverished though it is, ordinarily tries to marry ruling chiefs.[9] Now Zorawar Singh wants to marry a son to another Rawalot Bhati. This is the second time the Kanota family has launched a campaign to ally with a lineage that has a history of shunning marriages with Jaipur Champawats. Earlier, Narain Singh used his influence and standing as a favorite of Maharaja Ram Singh and as Nazim of Jhunjhunu, Jaipur state's principal administrator in Shekhawati, to persuade Shekhawati thakurs to marry their daughters to Jaipur Champawats.[10]]

XI. My Father (*cont.*)

. . . My father said that . . . Mookend Singhjee [should have] listened to my grandfather's advice and married Bhoj Raj Singhjee to the daughter of Arjun Singhjee Bhatee. . . . Arjun Singhjee is a Rawalot Bhatee, which is a clan who says that they do not marry their girls to the Champawats, but their sons marry Champawat girls. This I must say is a silly notion, but custom is custom. There is no instance of a Rawalot Bhatee girl being married to a Champawat except the quite recent one when my cousin Pratap Singhjee was married. This sort of thing shows that the Bhatees of Rawalot clan look down upon the Champawats. It was to break this silly custom that my grandfather had tried. Unfortunately it did not succeed. . . .

My father . . . said that . . . Arjun Singhjee won't marry his daughter to any of the younger brothers [of Amar Singh because they will not succeed to the thikana], otherwise he would arrange the matter. After a little thought he said that he would not mind marrying Amar Singh a second time. [As Amar Singh is heir to the thikana, Arjun Singh might consider the match.] I am afraid this expression of his mind might be true because he once hinted about it before me. . . .

I do not in the least want to marry, because I know what the troubles will be in the end. Besides this, I sincerely love my wife and do not want to hurt her feelings. A second marriage . . . will hurt her happiness as well as mine and no one knows it better than me. The will of parents will be obeyed but at what a cost? . . .

The mere idea of it makes me sick. My happiness will be shattered forever and there is no doubt of it. All that I shall do, when the last moment arrives will be that I shall send word to my parents that I do not want this thing, but if they want me to I will do their bidding and bid good-bye to happiness forever. My duty as a husband will bind me to keep both wives equal. . . .

. . . The Shekawats never used to marry their daughters to Champawats. The first instance is when my father was married at Kochore. The second is when Thakoor Kesri Singhjee [of Khatu] was married. The third is my uncle Bheem Singhjee's marriage at Dhanota. Now there are Sheonath Singh, Indar Singh and Duleep Singh engaged with Shekawat girls, and so the coast is all clear in this direction.

There were several objections when my father was married, but at that time the late durbar Ram Singh was living and it was his wish that this marriage should take place and the custom break. In the Khatoo marriage there was a great row, but it was my father's will, and he was backed up by the late Rajajee of Khetri [a leading Shekhawati thakur], who was a very well-educated and wise man. Just as this has succeeded, I hope the matter with the Bhatees will succeed also. At present there can be found Bhatee girls of forty to fifty years and they are maidens. Why are they maidens? Because their parents want ruling chiefs for their janwais [sons-in-law] and the chiefs do not marry them. What a brutal custom. . . .

In spite of the strict prohibition against infanticide, there are people among these Rawalot Bhatees who kill their daughters at the very birth for fear of not getting them married in after life. What a cruel and horrible custom. It is brutal, it is savage, it is anything but human . . . no living thing would ever kill its own offspring. It is only man who can do it-and why does he do it? Because of being ashamed among his fellow-men. It is not only so in Rajpootana. . . . In England, in America, in fact, in every country, maidens and widows kill their [illegitimate] children. Why do they do it? It is the same old word, shame . . . all the other animal life . . . don't have any such things. Why does man do it? Because he has what he calls sense. . . .

XIX. Khandela

. . . The present Rajajee . . . has got a daughter. This girl is the handsomest that I have ever seen. Whenever I see her I take her in my lap and pet her as if she was my own daughter. . . . This jewel of a girl is now to be sacrificed to some damn ruling chief . . . Just fancy, they are trying to marry her to the Maha Rao of Kotah, who is old enough to be her . . . father. . . . They have tried Bikanere, but the maharaja has refused. The Rajajee is ready to give . . . lakhs of rupees to any chief he can get . . . The Rajajee . . . ought to look out for a fine, well-educated boy with a moderate income. Then his daughter will have a good home and a good husband. . . . If she is married to a chief, she will have to spend her days in the greatest wretchedness. . . .

The late Maharaja of Jodhpore had about half a dozen wives and just as many mistresses. He very seldom went to anyone. They were . . . sort of state prisoners. They had plenty to eat and wear, but this is not all what a woman desires. . . . Another instance is the present Maharaja of Jaipore, who has got about a dozen or more wives and mistresses, but he likes only one of them and passes his time in her company. . . . The Maharanas of Odeypore used to marry their daughters to their chief nobles, and there was no trouble. . . .

XXVI. Some Anecdotes

. . . It is a custom that two sinjaras [presents] are sent to a daughter or sister every year after she is married. These sinjaras are costly things in the beginning, but after a few years they come down to only a few rupees. These two sinjaras are sent at the gingore and the teej [festivals].[11] My grandfather had sent some to my cousin married at Achrol [a very substantial thikana in Jaipur], but since my sister was married he stopped the rule and said that he will send only one sinjara and no more. . . . My aunt [Gambhir Singh's widow, mother of the woman married to Nawalgarh and living in Kanota haveli], when she heard this got very much annoyed, for women are very particular about such things, and devised a plan.

A servant had gone to Nawalgarh [where her daughter was married] and she had just returned from that place. My aunt sent her to my uncle Bheem Singhjee to say that her [daughter] had sent word that she had never known her father was dead because all the other relatives were as parents to her. Now if the sinjara came to her she would think that her father was alive, otherwise she will think that her father is dead, and there is no one to take care of her. Such words are very very seldom uttered among us, and only on occasions of the greatest emergency. My uncle knew at once and said so afterwards that he was very very angry, and it was all he could do to restrain his anger. He knew that the poor girl would never send such a message. If it had been any other lady, Bheem Singh would have got angry, but widows are always considered, because we think they have enough sorrows even without scoldings. The greatest possible care is taken not to hurt their feelings. . . . A weaker-willed man than my grandfather would have been induced to send the sinjara, but my grandfather never changes his will.

Here I shall say that these troubles are because we want to marry at big places. If my cousin had been married to the second [son] of a thakoor, he would not have expected all these things, but big people want big arrangements which we cannot afford. . . . Nawalgarh and Achrol are much too big thikanas for the daughters of Gumbheer Singhjee and Bheem Singh. The only good and equal match done in our family up to the present is that of my sister and the Thakoor of Gurhee. The rest are all humbug and nonsense.

XII. Bhoj Raj Singhjee[12]

[Cousin Bhoj Raj Singh, having resisted the idea of a second marriage for some years, finally gives in to his mother's persistent campaign.]

. . . I have said before that there are great preparations made for this second marriage. That dress which was prepared when this present wife was married about thirteen years ago was never given for a single day to this unfortunate lady [to wear]. Of course she wore it at the time of marriage but not after coming to Jaipore. During this time the lace has got all spoiled and so it was taken off and exchanged a few days ago and new dresses are being prepared for the new bride.

Such dresses as these new ones the poor first wife had never been allowed to wear. Then there is a new room being furnished for the new bride. The furnishing is done on a very large scale and the [servant] women often tell this first wife to go and see whether she likes it This is all taunting her and so she refuses to go and see. . . . The retribution will fall, sooner or later, on those that are responsible for all this. The poet says

> Don't harass the weak
> For the sorrows coming from their hearts have great weight before God
> Even as a dead sheepskin bellows burns metal.

There is not the slightest doubt about it. . . .

In Indian houses a son and his wife are not counted for much. I am afraid it is the cursings of these unfortunate and wrongly-used girls that has ruined the Rajpoot race . . . The English idea is quite the best, to respect and protect women. Our people do just the opposite. They never respect their wives and look upon them as slippers. When one pair gets worn you chuck it away and get another one. What a difference of opinion and ideas. English education will, I am sure, do something to make us change our ideas in this line. . . .

When [Bhoj Raj Singhji's wife] went to her parents' home, my aunt sent a couple of women from Jaipore . . . with my bhabee. These women never allowed my bhabee a moment's freedom. They were present everywhere and the mother and daughter could not have a single minute's private conversation. . . .

XIV. Pratap Singhjee

This . . . unfortunate cousin [son of Roop Singh] . . . has troubles all round him. . . . His constitution is broken and so is his health. He wants or rather it is imperative for him to have a change but it's absolutely out of the question. . . . Mehtab Singhjee is the cause of all this. . . . *Now the unfortunate Roop Singh has not only to support Mehtab Singh and his wife, but [Mehtab's brother] Jawahar Singhjee and his family too.[13]* Mehtab Singh . . . will eventually be the ruin, if not of all the three, of this one house. . . . There is a separate house built for these fellows and its expense is greater than that of either the bari or bichli havelis [the Gondher and Kanota city palaces]. Where does it come from? Roop Singhjee's pocket. Mehtab Singhjee has got such an influence over his cousin. . . .

. . . To be free from these daily troubles Pratap Singhjee asked permission to live at the thikana village. This was granted. The poor boy was not allowed to stop there for more than a week. However, it did him a lot of good, because when he weighed he found that in that week he had put up a weight of two pounds. . . .

. . . His mother too is not backward in giving trouble. . . . She is very badly treated, and wants to take revenge on someone. When she cannot do anything against her husband she tortures her son and his wife. . . .

> When the potter cannot master his wife
> He twists the ears of the (she) donkey.

It is exactly what is happening here. . . .

[The mother] is proud and has got a very bad temper. The first two wives [now deceased] of Pratap Singhjee had a hard time. The present one [the Rawalot Bhati girl] is quite ignorant of what a life in big families is, because she is of poor parents. She is so ignorant that she does not yet understand how to dress properly, because the poor girl had never seen all these ornaments at her parents' home. Now when she is taunted with all this humbug she naturally feels it.

The great cause of all this trouble is the female servants, who always want to breed discontent between the ladies so that they might have an easy time. . . . They do not let Pratap Singhjee's wife do any work in the kitchen and snatch the things from her hands if she wants to cook. . . . When her mother-in-law comes the women say that this lady does not do anything with a will and spoils the things. The elder lady on this begins her cursings and so the younger feels it and goes away. . . .

I am the luckiest in the four houses of our family among my cousins. I have no bother. I have a little money of my own which I can spend as I like. Then my father and grandfather do not even so much as tell me not to do a thing. They let me enjoy as best I can. . . . My mother too is very kind to me and to my wife too, considering the others. . . . If my father or I take any good things home, she shares them with my wife and sister. A fair division is made, while in the other two houses this is not the case and hence all the troubles. . . .

Meerut, Wednesday, 4th January, 1905

Notes About My Christmas Vacation.

XIX. Thakoor Kishore Singhjee [of Satheen]

. . . *[When still at the Cadet Corps] I . . . heard of my brother-in-law, the Thakoor Sahib Kishore Singhjee's death [Amar Singh's wife's twenty-seven-year-old brother]. . . .

I am really very much bereaved at Kishore Singhjee's death, but I must say it was a good thing for him personally, as he was lingering between life and death, and the coming of the latter has relieved him of suffering. Even when I was there I knew he would not live long.[14]* . . . Who I am really very sorry about are the two wives of my brother-in-law. They are quite young and will have to drag a miserable life henceforth, according to us. People in Marwar are more strict on widows than they are on Jaipore side. There, at Satheen, a widow never goes up to the first floor even. She must be on the ground floor for the remainder of her time. Those ladies have not enjoyed much life, as their husband was sick for some time past, and even when he was well he used to be drunk most of the time. . . .

. . . When the late thakoor [Kishore Singh's father] died he had left three lakhs of rupees [Rs 300,000] in cash and ornaments of exactly the same value. All that has been squandered by Kishore Singhjee. I hear that at present there are no costly ornaments left with his wives. They have all been pawned or sold. Besides this money there was some other treasure. . . .

In spite of squandering all the hoarded money, my brother-in-law was about a lakh of rupees [Rs 100,000] in debt, and all this within the few years that he was his own master. He has not built a single house or done anything to perpetuate his name or memory. He supported a good many people during the last great famine, but he could not have spent much money then. . . . His favourites had spoiled him, and now they will find to their cost the results of their evil doing. . . .

I may here say that there is no more sasra enjoyment for me . . . the charm has fled with the departed soul. There is no one now for whom I would care to go to Satheen. . . . The two ladies [Kishore Singhji's wives] who had got so familiar to me are widows and will never again come to joke at me. Satheen will now be for me a place of pleasant memories. . . .

I shall now write about the death scene. Kishore Singh was under the treatment of several people. There was one hospital assistant or compounder who treated him for some time. He was kicked out, and there were some Marwari physicians. The last of these . . . treated him for some months and at last, when he found that death was very near, bolted away. . . .

He was conscious up to the last, and knew very well that he was dying. He retained his senses and the faculty of speech. . . . When he was very near dying he made a noise and sign with his fingers (which meant that he must now be taken to the ground). [This is a common practice at the death of Rajputs.] Immediately after this had been done he passed peacefully away. . . .

I am sorry I have to remember all this and put on paper, for each word as I write gives me pain. However, I have one consolation and that is that I am immortalising his memory for me. Years after, when I may open and read this account, I shall see that my brother-in-law had no fault except that he was a spendthrift and this of course spoiled all his life and thikana.

VI. My Father

. . . My father is very particular about the feelings of the people, which my grandfather is not. As an instance I shall give the recent case of my brother-in-law's death. The general rule is that when there is a death like this, one of our family members from my grandfather to any of the minor ones ought to go, and . . . if this could not be done, then we ought to send someone else. My father, as soon as he heard this, sent Mehtab Singhjee Bhattee privately, but my grandfather has not as yet sent anyone.

Again my grandfather would not send me or my wife. We ought to have gone and my father thrice sent word to his parent that we ought to be sent, but my grandfather would not give his permission. All that he said was that my wife would be sent after I had gone away to Meerut. His idea was that I come so seldom that I must enjoy myself and not run about. This is all very well in a way, but this was an exceptional case and he ought to have allowed us to go.

When my grandfather refused the third time my father too got a bit annoyed, as I could plainly see by his countenance. All that he said to Umaid Ramjee [the family priest] was that "I have done what I could and tell them (meaning me and my wife) that my vakilat [representation]—has been unsuccessful."

I really don't know how much grateful I am to him for his taking so much bother. It is on very rare occasions that he repeats his request a second or third time to my grandfather. It is this consideration of his for the feelings of other people that has won for him the love and esteem of everyone that he comes across. . . . [Grandfather ultimately relents and sends Amar Singh's wife to Satheen with two of Amar Singh's brothers.]

XX. Capt. E. M. Hughes

He is the inspecting officer of the Imperial Service Troops of Rajpootana and a great friend of mine [from China]. . . . We met at the residency and there, in the course of conversation, he asked me whether the Maharaja of Jaipore would raise a cavalry regiment. . . . I explained to him that it would be the best thing if he could be induced to do so. He then asked me who could induce him. I said that if the [British] resident [at Jaipur] or the A.G.G. [the agent to the governor general, senior British officer with jurisdiction over the twenty-two princely states of Rajputana] strongly suggested, he would do [it]. . . . Hughes . . . said that he did not know that and now he was going to speak about the matter to Colonel Pears [the British resident at Jaipur]. He said that General Beatson[15] and he were both thinking of raising a regiment here.

I said that it would be best to do away with the transport corps, but he said that the government would not like to do that. Their idea is that if Jodhpore and Alwar can afford two regiments each, why can't Jaipore, which is a bigger and richer state. Hughes promised to give me the post of the commandant if they raised that regiment. . . .

XVI. Basant Kanwar's Marriage[16]

[Roop Singh of Naila has been taking in as family members the younger sons of the Peelva thikana in Jodhpur, the senior branch from which the three Champawat families at Jaipur are descended. (See Peelva genealogy later in this chapter.) The adverse effects of the 1898–1902 famine conditions on this modest thikana compared to the prosperity at Naila help to explain why and how Roop Singh can support his Peelva relatives. Kanota's many sons and Gondher's relative impecuniousness make these two thikanas less likely candidates for the role of employer and sustainer.

Jawahar and Mehtab, the chut bhais of the current Peelva thakur, live in the ample house constructed for them by Roop Singh. Mehtab Singh is the Naila estate manager and Roop Singh's favorite. Roop Singh treats them like close family. The expensive and prestigious marriage arranged by Roop Singh for Basant Kanwar, Mehtab Singh's daughter, has been the subject of continuous commentary in the family. Inder Singh and Boor Singh, the sons of Jawahar Singh, are being well educated in Jaipur. Amar Singh alleges they are favored at the expense of Roop Singh's own children, particularly his second son Dalip, who is not being educated as are the Peelva cousins.[17] Amar Singh's source for Naila happenings is Roop Singh's eldest son, the future thakur, who feels marginalized.]

Basant Kanwar is Mehtab Singhjee's daughter. She has been recently married to the Thakoor of Danta. The latter is [worth] about a hundred thousand rupees a year, while Mehtab Singhjee is only worth about two hundred a year. This marriage had been done through the influence of Roop Singhjee, who has undergone all the expenses.

The Thakoor of Danta is very tall and thin. He is black . . . and he has a face full of small pox marks. The boys at Roop Singhjee's garden used to call him hyena-man. I have never seen him but this is the description that I have heard. Then there is a great difference in age. The girl is hardly thirteen, while the boy is about twenty-seven. All these things show that there is no possibility of there being a good and contented married life between the couple.

Roop Singhjee has spent more money on this marriage than we have done on any girl in our family. It was his boast that he will do this marriage on a grander scale than of any others. . . . Pratap Singhjee was the only man who felt all this expense, but the poor boy is helpless. On some occasions he spoke a little but very mildly. . . .

Roop Singhjee . . . wanted to seat a maid servant in the rath when the bride and bridegroom were going away to the latter's place after the marriage. To this the maid servants of the bridegroom objected and so too the bridegroom. . . .

Roop Singhjee wanted to seat the maid servant because Basant Kanwar was too young. If she was so young, why the devil was she married at all? After a lot of bother, the maid servant was allowed to sit and they went away, but then the Danta thakoor said that he won't send his wife back that night. Even then there was a lot of bother and swearing. Well, the girl was sent after all, but the bridegroom got so annoyed that he refused to have his dinner. This was another bother. It was after every one of my cousins had gone and begged him to eat that he did so, and even then with a very bad grace. These are the results when you want to marry in places above your position. . . .

I hear that there has been spent nearly twice the amount of money than in any of the former marriages in our family. . . . I will conclude by saying that this marriage will always have very bad results. After Roop Singhjee is no more, or after he ceases to care for Mehtab Singhjee, as he has done for his former favourites, who is going to stand all the expenses that are bound to occur now and then? Besides this, the new couple will never command respect or love for one another. . . .

IX. Sooltan Singhjee [Thakur of Peelva]

[When Sultan Singh, uncle of the bride, comes to town for the wedding of Basant Kanwar, the Peelva thikana suddenly appears on everybody's horizon as a possible target of opportunity. It is the senior lineage, settled at Jodhpur, from which the three Champawat families at Jaipur are descended. Sultan Singh has "no issue" (meaning no sons) and must decide on whom to adopt as his successor. The three Champawat families at Jaipur, related to Peelva, are within the possible circle of adoption. Roop Singh of Naila, as patron of one set of candidates, and Narain Singh of Kanota, as favorite cousin of Thakur Sultan Singh of Peelva and hence a possible competitor, clash over the succession. Among Rajputs, adoption

Peelva Succession[†]

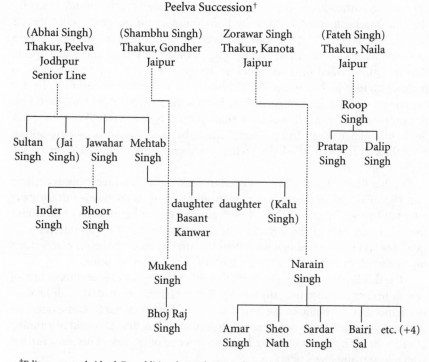

†Editors entry, abridged. For additional genealogies and particular entries, see Appendix. This chart is selective, mainly omitting women and some other "irrelevant" players. Parentheses mark deceased persons.

is normally from a collateral branch of the family. Convention favors the male nearest to the main branch, but the rule is variable. In this case the nearest is Sultan's Singh's nephew, Inder Singh, the son of Jawahar Singh, nephew of Mehtab Singh. The Gondher, Kanota, and Naila branches of the family are descended from younger brothers of Sultan Singh's father and have some claim, though a more distant one. (See Genealogical Chart I, appendix, for an overview of the four families.)

The Gondher branch has no great interest in raising such a claim, because it has only one son to provide for, Bhoj Raj Singh, and he will succeed to Gondher. Naila too has no interest in raising a claim, as it has two sons, and a very valuable estate that will accommodate them. But Kanota has seven sons, too many for the estate to easily support. Roop Singh believes that Narain Singh is lobbying the Peelva thakur, who likes him, on behalf of his sons, in preference to Jawahar Singh's sons. Narain Singh is being disingenuous when he says below that he cannot "remember" who is being mentioned for adoption.]

This uncle of mine [Sultan Singh], has a great love for me and a great respect for my father. He had come to Jaipore since the last few weeks. He is the

man who commands respect in our family just or nearly just as much as my fa-
ther. He had been asked to come by Roop Singhjee on the occasion of Basant
Kanwar's marriage. . . . My father had been to Jodhpore on his way back from
Bombay, where he went last to buy some horses. When he came to Jaipore,
Roop Singhjee asked him, in rather an angry tone, as to why he had gone to
Jodhpore and if he had gone why did he not let him know about it . . . To this
my parent said that he had gone there because Sooltan Singhjee had asked him
to come and see him. It was now that Roop Singhjee said, "Why does not
Sooltan Singhjee adopt Indar Singh?" My father said, "What is there to adopt,
he is the son and will be adopted whenever there is any necessity. Where is the
hurry at present?"

On this Roop Singhjee said that Indar Singh's grandmother is always telling
him [Roop Singh] to marry Indar Singh, and so long as the boy is not formally
adopted by the Thakoor Sahib of Peelva, none of the big thikanas would give
their daughter to him [because there is no guarantee that he will inherit an es-
tate]. My father answered that what does it matter whether the boy is married at a
big or a small thikana. It won't make any difference in his adoption.

After this Roop Singhjee asked whether Sooltan Singh had ever spoken to him
(my father) about adopting anyone. My father said that he had, though he does
not remember the name of the boy. It was now that my father took the offensive
and told him that he was not a man with such low ideas that he would be running
after Sooltan Singhjee and asking him to adopt one of his sons. This put a further
stop to Roop Singhjee's talk.

This is all the doings of Mehtab Singhjee, who is now damn keen that Indar
Singh be adopted, though a few years ago he was trying his best to have his own
son Kaloo Singh adopted. That boy is now dead. My father then told me that
Sooltan Singhjee had once expressed his desire to adopt me. I told my father that
I heard that he (Sooltan) wanted to adopt Sheonath Singh [Narain Singh's second
son]. On this my father said that he might have changed his mind afterwards, but
at first he wanted to adopt you.

I might here say that I do not much fancy leaving Kanota and going to Peelva.
In the second place it would be an injustice on poor Indar Singh. I for one have
no desire to be adopted anywhere.

This much I know, that there is bound to be some disturbance about the succession of Peelva, because Sooltan Singhjee will never adopt either of his brothers' sons.[18] I know he wants to adopt one of my brothers. My grandfather once
wanted him to sign that no one was to adopt anyone from the other houses while
there were children in his own house. To make my meaning clear, he wanted his
sons and nephews to sign that no one was to be adopted in Peelva while there was
any of Abhai Singhjee's grandsons living. In the same manner, no one was to be
adopted at Gondher while there was one of Shambhoo Singhjee's grand or great-
grandsons living. To this they all agreed and signed except Sooltan Singhjee and
Chhiman Singhjee.[19] The latter began to weep when he was asked to sign the paper, but still he would not sign.

Before concluding this account, I shall say that once Thakoor Fateh Singhjee [of Naila, father of Roop Singh], after his return from Jodhpore, said to my grandfather that he had a talk with Maharaja [Sir] Pratap Singhjee and it was agreed that Lichman Singh [Fateh Singh's grandson through his second son, Guman Singh] be adopted at Peelva in case Sooltan Singhjee got no son. My grandfather, when he heard this, said that he ought not to have done this, because there are several grandsons of Abhai Singhjee living and they have a better right. Fateh Singhjee wanted to pass the matter off, but my grandfather said that he ought to have consulted before doing such a thing, and further said that if there was no one to fight among Abhai Singhjee's descendants, he would fight, as he had a better right to send his grandsons than Fateh Singhjee. This was because there was no one that could be adopted from Shambhoo Singhjee's house,[20] and therefore Fateh Singh's line comes third, and he [Zorawar Singh, whose line comes second] has several grandsons to spare. Fateh Singhjee kept quiet because he could not answer and knew that he was wrong. . . .

XII. Mookend Singhjee [Gondher][21]

[Bhoj Raj Singh has to resign himself to living with two wives.] . . . The new arrangement now is that Bhoj Raj Singhjee's new wife is not allowed [by her mother-in-law, Mukend Singh's wife] to speak to any of the other ladies. I might here say that a new bride does not speak to her elder relations for some time, but she always speaks to the ladies of her own age. The new girl cannot talk even to my wife. This is to prevent her from being spoilt by anyone. . . .

XIII. Bhoj Raj Singhjee

. . . Nowadays he is leading a miserable life. He has two wives and has to go to them by turns. This is alright, but the worst of it is that his mother keeps her maid servants constantly at the doors of the room and every morning they report exactly what happened during the night. One ought to consider that one of the wives has been married some thirteen years since, while the other is married hardly thirteen weeks. . . . These marriages are not contracted on love but merely on the choice of a family, and therefore there ought to elapse some time before the couple can know anything of one another and have some love. . . .

. . . The new wife is treated as if she was the daughter of my aunt, while the old one is treated as if she was a maid servant or even lower than that. There were times when Bhoj Raj Singhjee could never get anything to drink. Now there are dinners in the zenana regularly and the best of wines are ordered. I went to see my bhabees. The old one was just as familiar though the new one never spoke a single word to me. . . .

My father had told Bhoj Raj Singhjee not to look so sorry because he had been married against his will. . . . [He] told me to tell Bhoj Raj Singhjee that this cannot be helped and he advised him to bear as much as he could and never let his parents know that he can bear no more. Then the other thing that he must be careful about is that he must treat both his wives equally well, because the second one too has now just as much a right as his first one. . . .

Bhoj Raj Singh says that all men as well as birds and beasts feel happy after their labours, and look forward with pleasure to the idea of going home. In this case it was quite the reverse. He is happy while he is away from home, but as soon as he gets there his tortures begin, which go on increasing and only end when sleep comes to his rescue. . . . Ah! what a wretched life. . . .

XIV. Pratap Singhjee [Naila]

. . . Pratap Singhjee is by nature a very jolly fellow but he is sworn at so much that he cannot do anything. . . . Even his servants are not allowed to be what he wants. He must have servants whom Mehtab Singhjee appoints and the latter takes care to appoint those who are sort of spies on the boy. Thus he cannot tell what he feels to anyone. . . . As an instance I shall say that this time we began to talk at polo. We were sitting rather away from the others. As soon as my cousin noticed this he said that we had better go and sit with the others because he was afraid Mehtab Singhjee might think we were having some private talk. Can there be anything more degrading? . . .

Mount Abu, Friday, 16th June, 1905

Notes About My Last Stay At Kanota.

XXIV. A Talk with My Grandfather

[The earlier account of disputes over the Peelva adoption makes it clear that the politics of inheritance in the extended family can be complex and acrimonious. These two accounts provide a report on lineage contests as seen by a participant. Here grandfather Zorawar Singh recalls a dispute he himself precipitated about the conventional rights of an eldest son, his brother Abhai Singh, Thakur of Peelva, then head of the senior lineage of the Champawat families. The story illustrates the entrepreneurial spirit of Zorawar Singh who, with a little luck, went from being an impecunious chut bhai to becoming the most prosperous of the brothers while they were at Peelva.]

One day we were alone together when [grandfather] told me that his [step] grandmother who was of the Inda tribe[22] [and who had no son of her own] wanted to adopt someone and asked Thakur Jivraj Singhjee of Peelva [her step-son] to recommend one of his sons. On this Shambhoo Singhjee was recommended but Indajee said that she would have Jora, i.e. Zorawar Singh. Thakur Sahib Jivraj Singhjee smiled and said that this boy will not serve her properly but will spend his time killing the chinkaras. Indajee's mind was made up and my grandfather was adopted. [These events date to the 1850s.[23] Practices in the Punjab in that period may be some guide to what follows. In much of northwest India, it was customary to endow a widow, for maintenance in her lifetime, with lands from her husband's share in the joint family property. These reverted to the joint family at her death. The Indajee, who is widowed, is looking for someone

The Peelva Family[†]

Thakur Madan Singh—First Wife: The "Indajee"

Thakur Jivraj Singh (step son of Indajee)—Wife

Thakur Abhai Singh (Peelva)	Shambhu Singh (Gondher)	Zorawar Singh (Kanota)	Fateh Singh (Naila)
Thakur Abhai Sultan Singh	Mukend Singh	Narain Singh	Roop Singh
		Amar Singh	

[†]Table by the editors.

who can manage her lands. This seems to be regarded as a possible threat to the joint family's residuary rights.[24]]

Now this lady wanted my grandfather to go and plough the fields and he did it. This was objected to by my great grandmother [who may have feared the land would slip out of the control of her husband, Thakur Jivraj Singh], but Indajee said that she would eat the grain cultivated by her [step-grand] son. In due course the corn grew and now coolies were required to clear the field of the undergrowth, but where was the couple of rupees to come from to pay them. These were, after some bother, borrowed, and at last the corn was cut and put in the house. Abhai Singhjee, the eldest brother, made a great row about this corn and said that it was his [as the eldest son and future thakur] and that his brother had no right to it. After a time all these disputes were settled and the corn was sold and with that money my grandfather began his [loan] business, which was so prosperous that he lived in plenty while there was no corn in the thikana several times. [Zorawar Singh carried on this loan business after he migrated to Jaipur.[25] There he was well placed to collect because the family usually held a high post in the police and could enforce collection.[26]]

Th[ere] is a common saying in most of the thikanas in Marwar, where the people are too poor . . . that the kitchen is closed and the people had better go to bed. Such was the condition of Peelva when my grandfather lived in plenty. . . .

The Indajee who had adopted my grandfather married him to her own niece. I have often heard her [the niece's] praise. My grandfather, when he was married, one day said to her that he would have rumjol [broad heavy silver anklets with pendants which jingle] made for her exactly as those that his mother had. When the corn, about which I have written before, was sold, my parent fulfilled his promise. It was then that my grandmother said that when she was first told about them she had laughed, because she thought it was merely a false promise, because they had no money to make them with. . . .

When the Indajee, my grandfather's grandmother, was about to die, she sent for her adopted [grand]son and embraced him very endearingly and said that it was through his hands she hoped for her future salvation. . . . It was his hand that will supply her with water in heaven were her actual words.

When my great-grandfather [Jivraj Singh] was dead and the four brothers separated from one another the eldest, Abhai Singhjee, began giving shares of land. In Peelva the younger brothers got a hundred beegas[27] of land as their share. Shambhoo Singhjee and Fateh Singhjee accepted their shares and when it came to Zorawar Singhjee's turn he said that he had nothing to do with these shares. He had [already] separated from his grandfather [Madan Singh] and did not want shares from his brother. [The implication is that he already has a share, that is, the land of the Indajee.] On this Abhai Singhjee began to weep and said that he ought to leave his rights to that adoption as it would be a very bad precedent for the later generations [if a younger son could establish rights independent of the shares allocated to him by the eldest who became thakur]. My grandfather agreed to this arrangement but on the condition that he would have those [choice] fields which were being cultivated by the thikana. This was agreed and so our share of the patrimony is about the best and richest.

PART VI:
PRINCELY COURTS IN IMPERIAL SPACE

Fifty years after the end of princely rule in India[1] and the shrinking of the Rajput nobility by land reform, academic studies are still being written as though an account of Rajput rulers exhausted the story of Rajputana/Rajasthan.[2] Only recently have other social categories—religious sects; occupational guilds; merchant and craft castes; agrarian classes—received some attention. Even so the cultural hold of Rajput identity persists. Rajput princes and aristocrats have followed the example of British baronial classes by commercializing their ornate historic real estate. Their success has shaped foreign and domestic perceptions of Rajasthan.[3] Tourist departments of semi-socialist Indian governments cultivate aristocratic images of a superceded nobility. Hindu nationalists in search of heroes impose twentieth-century religious nationalist motives on seventeenth-century rajas. Commerce and politics conspire to give Rajput-oriented history continuing hegemony.[4]

Amar Singh's diary does not undo Rajput-centered history, a history of kings and heroes. But it provides what many such historical accounts do not, a quotidian perspective, a view from clerk's offices, mail pouches, *zenana deorhi* (women's quarters), the horse stables, the drawing rooms and dining tables. It is the account of a critical insider, whose work ethic, monogamy, and respect for discipline are offended by self-indulgence, idleness, and promiscuity, traits often displayed by the Rajput nobility of his time.

Amar Singh describes what Norbert Elias calls "Court Society," a concept that parallels the more familiar "industrial society" and "agrarian society." "The princely court and the society belonging to it," Elias tells us, "are specific figurations of people that are no less in need of elucidation than cities or factories." "At a certain point in the development of European society individuals are bound together in the form of courts."[5] Elias' court society concept is useful in theorizing and explaining a good bit of what Amar Singh is writing about in the diary entries included in Part VI.

Amar Singh tells us about court society in India when he speaks about the durbar, a usage inherited from Mughal/Persian discourse. Its double meaning is instructive. It refers at once to the person of the ruler, as in "Durbar was not feeling well" and to the formal assemblage of notables who constitute the ruler's social and political circle, as in "Maharana Fateh Singh held a durbar on the occasion of his daughter's wedding." Person and institution merge.

Amar Singh details the personal equations of court society: the enactment of status; rituals of honor; the struggle for office. The court commands a variety of resources—wealth, status, power—and these are to an extent fungible: power can yield honor; wealth can yield power; power can yield wealth. When the Maharaja of Jodhpur arranges for the wife of the British viceroy, most lordly representative of the raj in India, to dine with his modestly born favorite, Ogumji, we witness an effort to magnify Ogumji's status.[6] Power yields honor. When Sir Sukhdeo Prasad, an English-educated Kashmiri Brahman, displaces Sir Pratap Singh, a Rajput who is better at riding a horse than reading a newspaper, as the prime minister of Jodhpur, we witness change in the qualification for office in Rajasthan's version of court society.

Amar Singh's accounts of life at princely courts and in imperial space portray late nineteenth-century constructions of the Indian "prince" and of court society. The two-fifths of British India "ruled" by Indian princes[7] is framed by the sovereignty discourse and practice of "imperial monarchy," and "paramountcy," metaphors and stereotypes created by late raj hegemony.[8] In Amar Singh's time and in the words of his diary they appear as natural, as the ways things are.

But such terms had not been heard of at the time of the Battle of Plassey in 1757, when the British East India Company staked its claim as a major military presence on the subcontinent. For the next 100 years the Company, the representative of British interest in India, vacillated between working for profit as a trading company or for power as a hegemon and forerunner of empire. In 1817, Company armies defeated the Marathas, until then the Company's rival for succeeding Mughal hegemony on the subcontinent. In 1818, when Rajput kingdoms, weakened by Maratha depredations and extractions and by internecine wars, signed treaties of subsidiary alliance with the Company, they began to be perceived and treated in Company discourse and practice as tributary states.[9] These treaties laid the foundation of the imperial narrative of a "paramountcy" relationship over "princely" states. But in 1818, no one spoke of paramountcy or its interpretive gloss, "subordinate cooperation."

A traumatic event, the bloody revolt of 1857, forced the Company to rethink its strategy of establishing territorial and cultural hegemony in India. The revolt was in large measure a reaction against conquest of territory by annexation[10] and against conquest of consciousness by cultural intervention. It forcefully reminded British imperialists that India could not be ruled by force alone. Legitimacy too was required. Repudiating conquest by annexation, Queen Victoria's 1858 proclamation replacing Company with crown rule sought legitimacy by pledging to recognize and preserve the sovereignty of the Indian rulers and to respect Indian religions and cultures. Kings and rajas and chiefs would not be eradicated. They would be ordered and disciplined. Crown legitimacy was consolidated and enhanced when Victoria was declared Queen Empress of India in 1877 at Lord Lytton's grandiose spectacular, the Delhi Durbar.[11] The durbar launched an era of reconstruction of Indian ranks and titles along lines both Mughal and medieval. The bewildering medley of kings, little kings and chiefs began to be rationalized into a single order, certified by British recognition, designated by heraldry and ranked by a graded table of precedence and gun salutes. Imperial monarchy featured the Queen Empress' loyal vassals, India's newly minted "princes," performing Anglo-Mughal acts of ritual submission and assuming knightly obligations. They carried unwieldy standards bearing royal coats of arms which simulated familiar British models, newly invented for the occasion by heraldic specialists.

To arrive at Amar Singh's naturalized language of "princes" and "paramountcy," post-1858 Englishmen had to retell Company history: the military rivals of the 1820s became the feudal vassals of the post-1877 imperial monarchy; the "subsidiary alliances" spawned by the Company's precarious victories in 1818 became post-1877 paramountcy's routinized "subordinate cooperation."

"Princes" and "paramountcy" were constructions that showed the Company as the successor of a Mughal empire in "decline" after Aurangzeb's death in 1707. Contrary to more recent post-colonial accounts, colonial narratives saw the eighteenth century as a time of troubles: anarchic, lawless, and violent. The Company's final victory over the Marathas in 1817, in what history books now designate as the third Anglo-Maratha War, was depicted in these narratives as the event that saved the subcontinent from further despoliation by barbaric marauders.[12] In the Company's telling, this victory justified its claim to be the legitimate successor of the Mughal empire.

At the British 1858 trial of Bahadur Shah, the last of the Mughal emperors, the 1857 revolt was characterized as a challenge to British sovereignty in India. The Judge Advocate General purported to show that the deposed emperor was "a subject of the British Government of India" who disregarded "the duty of his allegiance" when "on 11 May 1857 or thereabouts, as a traitor against the state [he did] proclaim and declare himself the reigning King and Sovereign of India. . . ."[13] Since the late eighteenth century the Company had, *inter alia*, conducted trade, war, and diplomacy as the *diwan* (minister, sometimes first minister) of the emperor's Bengal *Subah* (province), that is, as an agent of Mughal sovereignty. By charging Bahadur Shah with treason and rebellion, a Government of India called into existence that very year by Queen Victoria's 1858 proclamation was claiming that it rather than the Mughal emperors in whose name the Company exercised authority *had been* the sovereign power in the preceding century.[14] This remarkable retelling laid the basis for the British claim of paramountcy, filling a suzerainty slot left vacant by Bahadur Shah's exile.

The world Amar Singh portrays in the entries included in this part presents particular princes and their courts not from the rationalizing point of view of the annual administrative reports, but from the more patrimonial perspective of everyday local observers. It portrays Sir Pratap Singh and Maharaja Sardar Singh of Jodhpur; Maharana Fateh Singh of Udaipur; Maharaja Jai Singh of Alwar; Maharaja Madan Singh of Kishengarh; and their greater and lesser thakurs, holders of landed estates, titles, places at court and ministerial office. It also presents the princes' and thakurs' imperial counterplayers, the viceroy and his entourage; the agent to the governor general (AGG) residents; and political agents; emissaries of the Government of India's (GOI's) political service[15]; and British officials serving in princely states.

The princes' counterplayers who conducted the British crown's "diplomacy" with the princely states belonged to the Political Department, GOI's foreign office. Officers on leave or deputation from other raj services, especially the army, served as senior administrators or in technical positions. In principle they were responsible to the ruling princes who appointed them. In fact, the reverse was often true. The political service was styled a diplomatic service because it conducted the GOI's relations with ambiguously sovereign political entities. These included not only the states of princely India but also the political entities in what the GOI regarded as its spheres of influence, those located on the litoral of the Arabian Sea, the Persian Gulf and the Bay of Bengal, and in Central, Western and South-East Asia. With help from the Indian Army, the political service pursued the GOI's political and security interests in an arc defined by the approaches to India, particularly Afghanistan and central Asia, and the territory surrounding the Suez Canal, Persia, British protectorates in the Persian Gulf and East and South Africa.

We have used the term "Princely Courts" in Part VI to avoid the misleading force of the usage, princely "states." In a twentieth century dominated by realist and neo-realist doctrines, "state" evokes a political entity that makes monopoly claims to sovereignty within a defined territory and the freedom to act as it pleases. By contrast, paramountcy limited the autonomy of the kingdoms that populated princely India through an asymmetrical sharing of sovereignty between the raj and the princes.[16] Paramountcy concretized aspects of the ambiguous and fluid relationships among levels of sovereignty that characterized earlier empires on the subcontinent, not least that of Britain's immediate predecessor, the Mughal empire.[17] The raj studiously protected the ambiguity of "paramountcy" which allowed it to exercise hegemonic control when necessary but freed it from responsibility for conditions in the princely states.[18] Such indirect rule also minimized claims on the raj purse.

The nineteenth century witnessed the naturalization of the modem state form in Europe, and its export by colonial rulers to far flung empires in Asia and Africa. The result was something we know retrospectively as the colonial state. When late imperial administrators in India encountered the many varieties of statehood on display on the subcontinent their response was to apply the state template with which they were familiar: revenues and expenditures based on regulations, formal administrative procedures and budgets, a government of laws, a professional civil service. Rajputana's twenty-two kingdoms in north-west India were also designated to receive the modern state. But intervention to concretize British conceptions of statehood was fraught with difficulties.

By treaties and Victoria's 1858 and Edward VII's 1902 proclamations, raj authority was supposed to be limited to external matters, for instance, foreign affairs, defense, communications and coinage, leaving India's princes in charge of domestic or internal authority. But domestic autonomy was compromised by the viceroy's *de facto* discretion in recognizing successors and granting them their full powers; deposing rulers for crimes or "gross misrule"; overseeing the administration of states during minorities; appointing English guardians to supervise the education of minor maharajas; and offering "authoritative advice."[19]

These modifications provided an ambiguous space for intercession by the Political Department officers deputed to Rajputana. A senior political service officer exercised oversight over twenty-two princely states as AGG from Ajmer, an imperial enclave which had also been used by the Mughals to monitor their Rajput allies. The AGG stood above the "residents," who served as envoys to major princely states or to several smaller states and their "agents." They were prohibited from offering "authoritative advice" not only by the spirit and letter of crown proclamations barring intervention and interference in the domestic affairs of princely states but also by viceregal policy. The ambiguous spirit was epitomized by Curzon's successor, Lord Minto, in a 1909 speech in Udaipur: ". . . Our policy," Minto told the notoriously foot-dragging Maharana Fateh Singh,

> is with rare exceptions one of non-interference in the internal affairs of Native States. But in guaranteeing their internal independence . . . it naturally follows that the Imperial Government has assumed a certain degree of responsibility for the general soundness of their administration and could not consent to incur the reproach of being an indirect instrument of misrule.[20]

Minorities made it possible for British officers to become guardians to young princes. They would shelter the minor prince from what was presumed to be the malign influence of the zenana, the women's quarter where the queen mother held sway among a bevy of lesser queens and concubines. After Mayo College, a public school for princes and nobles, opened its doors in 1875 considerable effort was made to have minor princes educated there. The Imperial Cadet Corps was another agent for the discipline considered suitable for princes (see Part IV).

Administrations that took over due to "misgovernment" or to supervise minor princes were also regarded as windows of opportunity to put princely state administration right. Colonel Eden, the Mewar resident, assured the AGG in his report for 1865–1866 that "reforms and progress [were] made during the few [minority] years [of Maharana Shambhu Singh] in which the administration was under our supervision."[21] Between five and eight of the twenty-two states of Rajputana were normally under such supervision.[22] The long minorities of Maharaja Ganga Singh at Bikaner and Maharaja Man Singh at Jaipur, when Sardar K.M. Panikkar and Sir Beauchamp St John respectively took charge, help account for these states developing the most formally bureaucratic administrations in twentieth-century Rajputana.[23]

The links of local English officers, residents and agents to the higher authorities in Calcutta and Simla engendered an active informal politics. It provided opportunities for princes, nobles and high state officers embedded in princely state factional networks to leverage personal relations with English officers in ways that protected or enhanced their interests. Amar Singh's family would not have survived the displeasure of Jaipur Maharaja Madho Singh without the help and protection of a political network that reached across princely state lines and across princely state—British lines. Political officers who believed that a good man—Amar Singh's father, Narain Singh, a subject of Jaipur state—had been done an injustice, were mobilized by Narain Singh himself and by Amar Singh's patron, Sir Pratap of Jodhpur. Sir Pratap Singh, for many years regent or first minister of Jodhpur, would not have survived the enmity of Jodhpur court factions, the Jodhpur maharaja, and even Viceroy Lord Curzon, without his friend and protector, Sir Walter Lawrence, Lord Curzon's personal secretary. By 1900, "Court Society" is not limited to princes, nobility, and state officials. It includes *British* officials deputed to the states as well as local notables. It is this extended version of court society, the Jodhpur-Delhi-Simla network as well as the factions that constitute the local balance of power, that is the particular subject of Amar Singh's interest.

1

Court Society at Jodhpur:
The Struggle for the Maharaja's Person

[Amar Singh's story about Jodhpur court politics[1] starts in 1899, soon after Maharaja Sardar Singh is granted his powers, and when Amar Singh is still learning how to write a diary. The maharaja's writ runs, and indifferently at that, in the *khalsa* (crown lands) of this underpopulated and resource-poor desert state. Control of the greater, though not the most lucrative, part of the state's revenue-paying lands[2] is wielded by the great magnates or landed aristocrats, the sardars and thakurs, mostly the maharaja's lineage brethren. In the diary's early years, Jodhpur, an arid state, has been devastated by the 1898–1899 famine. A million and a half animals have died, 150,000 of the state's 2 million population have migrated, and an undetermined number have died.[3]

The princes who rule Jodhpur consider themselves as belonging to the Rathore lineage. From Rao Rinmal's rule (1427–1459) the Rathores have been organized into eponymous sub-lineages known by the names of Rinmal's many sons.[4] Jodha, Rinmal's second son who had re-conquered Marwat from Mewar's Sisodias, founded the city of Jodhpur and gave the kingdom its modern name. Amar Singh is bound to Jodhpur by his identity as a Champawat, a descendant of Rinmal's third son, Champa.

PHOTO VI-1   Sir Pratap Singh, Amar Singh's patron, served intermittently for fifty years, between 1873 and 1922, as first minister of Jodhpur state or as regent during the minorities of his nephews, Maharajas Sardar Singh, Sumer Singh and Umaid Singh. For a short time he also served reluctantly as Maharaja of Idar/Ahmednagar, a minor impoverished state in Gujarat. Celebrated by the raj as a soldier and sportsman and for his loyalty and probity, he was often defeated in factional struggles by cleverer court bureaucrats. Amar Singh's photo albums.

The diarist's special competence with respect to events and persons at Jodhpur arises from his relationship to Sir Pratap Singh, younger brother of the late Maharaja Jaswant Singh of Jodhpur. Sir Pratap serves intermittently as his brother's first minister from 1873, when Jaswant Singh succeeds to the throne until his death in 1895, and as regent during the minority of Jaswant Singh's successors. He is Amar Singh's mentor and patron throughout the diary years presented in this volume.[5] Amar Singh lives as his protege at Jodhpur from 1888 to 1901, when he marries and changes residence to his family's house at Jaipur.

It was fashionable in the raj establishment to admire Sir Pratap. A favorite of Queen Victoria, he was celebrated for his bluff manner, his eccentricities, his skill as a soldier, his sportsmanship and his fine polo skills.[6] According to the official narrative of the Jodhpur state administrative reports, when Pratap Singh first became regent in the 1880s, the state was "disorganized, life and property were insecure, the finances were in a bad condition, and debts had accumulated." After he adopted what might be called the full restructuring and reform package recommended to the princely states by the GOI, administration in Jodhpur was said to have markedly improved. As the AGG told a large audience at Jodhpur in 1897: "So ably was the administration conducted, that law and order were restored; large sums expended on railway construction and irrigation works; the revenue nearly doubled; and the whole state was placed in a prosperous condition."[7] There is an alternative view of Sir Pratap; he is quaint, pompous and ineffectual, a view entertained by the viceroy, Lord Curzon, but not by his private secretary, Sir Walter Lawrence, who was among Sir Pratap's ardent admirers.[8]

When Amar Singh's commentary picks up the story in 1899, denizens of Jodhpur court society, like planets of a dual solar system, orbit two suns, Sir Pratap Singh, until recently regent, and his young nephew, Maharaja Sardar Singh. Their conflicting gravitational pulls affect the movements of local players. Pratap, the rough and ready illiterate soldier and polo player is being jostled not only by his nephew, the maharaja, but also by an "outsider," Sukhdeo Prasad, a talented Kashmiri bureaucrat with good command of English and finance.

On February 14, 1898, six months before the diary begins, Sardar Singh at eighteen is invested with his powers. The regency council of 1895, headed by Sir Pratap, which governed during Sardar Singh's minority, is dissolved. Sir Pratap becomes *musahib ala*, first minister, but the title is little more than a face-saving device. The epicenter of court society shifts from Sir Pratap's bungalow and polo ground to Sardar Singh's palace. As "durbar"—ruler, court—Sardar Singh is now master of "Sarkar," that is, government, as Sir Pratap is known to the diary.

The capable Kashmiri pandit Sukhdeo Prasad is not only distinguished by what was at that time a rare accomplishment in princely India, a university degree (B.A.) and fluency in English, but has also held senior administrative posts at Jodhpur for a decade. He has won the approbation of the raj's Political Department by his work on the Famine Commission and the revenue settlement of Jodhpur state. Sir Pratap detests him. Sukhdeo (later Sir Sukhdeo) and Percy Powlett,[9] resident in Jodhpur between 1880 and 1892, are the instruments of the administrative reforms for which Sir Pratap is celebrated.[10]

As adolescents, both Sardar Singh and Amar Singh lived under Sir Pratap's strict regime and were educated by Ram Nathji, court poet-turned-schoolmaster. Sardar Singh proved a disappointing student. Described in the diary as fickle, fun-loving, extravagant and sickly, Sardar Singh does not measure up to Sir Pratap's or the raj's standards for an Indian prince.[11] But after Maharaja Sardar Singh's investiture, sharing his pastimes or emulating his manners rather than those of his ascetic uncle becomes the path to favor and advancement in Jodhpur's court society. While Amar Singh remains loyal to Sir Pratap's faction, he also maintains surreptitious friendships with classmates and others attached to the maharaja's coterie.

Amar Singh's and Sir Pratap's outbursts against scandalous behavior at court do not always distinguish the felony of dissolute action from the misdemeanor of liberalizing Rajput social customs, especially those relating to women. Amar Singh sees Sardar Singh's drinking and his willingness to let the maharani appear in public as vices arising from the same flawed character.

In 1903, the Government of India's Political Department deprives Sardar Singh of his powers, then restores them with restrictions in 1905, and fully in 1908. Three years later, in 1911, Sardar Singh dies at 31. Sir Pratap, still a raj favorite, again becomes regent to Sardar Singh's son and heir, the twelve-year-old Sumer Singh.[12]]

Dramatis Personae

"*Durbar*" (court), the young Maharaja Sardar Singh of Jodhpur, invested with ruling powers in 1898.

"*Sarkar*" (government), Sir Pratap Singh, until recently regent of Jodhpur; now prime minister.

Sir Sukhdeo Prasad, minister at Jodhpur and Sir Pratap's rival for the prime minister's position.

Ogumji, Maharaja Sardar Singh's controversial favorite.

The Maharani Sahiba, Sardar Singh's bold wife, a princess of Bundi.

Jodhpore, Wednesday, 1st February, 1899

. . . This was also the . . . [first] "birth day" of the maharaj kanwar sahib [Maharaja Sardar Singh's first son and heir apparent, Sumer Singh, who succeeds in 1911]. The rejoicings and feast were held at Chhitar house. None of us who live with Sarkar went to tender our presents, for we had no orders. [The Hindi for "orders" and "permission" is the same. Amar Singh's English does not distinguish the two.] These little things are the causes of the big disputes between Durbar and Sarkar. . . .

Monday, 23rd October, 1899

. . . Thakoor Sardar Singhjee of Rama who is an intimate friend of mine came to see me. . . . When he learned that Sarkar was here he stopped in the kitchen and sent for me there because he did not like to let Sarkar know that he had come to see me. It would have been nothing to him but a great harm for me. Sarkar does not like that we should meet or talk with any of durbar's favourites. Instead of doing any good it engenders hatred.

Durbar himself with whom I was brought up is not quite pleased with me. This is all on account of the feud between Durbar and Sarkar. This feud has gone so far that it has spoiled the management of the state. . . .

Tuesday, 24th October 1899

. . . I think I must write a little more about my last night's visits to my old friends. I had gone there to pay back the visit of Sardar Singhjee [Thakur of Rama], who was my school fellow for a long time [at Jodhpur at the Powlett Nobles School]. At times we used to be the most intimate friends and at others the most implacable enemies, which was always his fault. . . . The first time we became close friends we changed turbans and became brothers which is a Rajpoot custom and is called a "Pagri buddal Bhai." He is a great favourite with Durbar but is not proud like the others. . . .

I went very quietly to them and saluted but they could not recognise me until I was very near for they had not the remotest idea of my visiting them. But when they did know me they were both very much pleased and Sardar Singhjee embraced me. They were . . . drinking soda and whiskey and forced me to join them. I was received and treated very nicely, just as I had expected and one would wish. I also took my dinner with them. Except once when I was at Dadai in company with Bukhtawar Singhjee this is the only time I have tasted liquor or wine of any sort since coming from Jaipore in January 1898. . . .

Sunday, 5th November, 1899

. . . In the evening we had polo. Jiverajjee has not played since yesterday when Hurjee told him to do something. He gave an unfitting answer and so [Hurjee] gave him a good boxing on the nose and face. Jiveraj is such a fool that he takes it too much . . . [to] heart and does not even come out of his room. [Thakur Hari Singh, Hurjee is one of Jodhpur's greatest polo players as well as Sir Pratap Singh's close companion.]

Monday, 6th November, 1899

. . . Jiverajjee . . . has basely deserted Hurjee. . . . his brother-in-law [Jiveraj's sister was married to Hurjee], and Sarkar, who had brought him up. From a long time past he had been trying privately to go to Durbar who is also a good deal pleased with him. Durbar himself is very fickle-minded. Once he loved Jiveraj so much that he took him away from Sarkar and afterwards turned him out. Now he is again pleased with him and had promised him that in a very few days he would ask Sarkar to send him to his house.

The dispute about his displeasure arose on this. Hurjee had sent for some sowars [soldiers] and syces [grooms] from the stables to clean the house. Jiveraj sent very few. Hurjee sent two more men to get some more but he [Jiveraj] did not send [them]. Hurjee got angry, went himself, and brought all except a very few. Jiveraj who is always in the habit of grumbling [asked] . . . who will now saddle the polo ponies. Hurjee said that he himself and Bharjee will have to do it. Jiveraj grumbled that he could not spare enough time to saddle his own polo ponies. Hurjee who was in a bad mood [replied] . . . that he was [not] . . . very fond of arguing for no purpose, and as a chastisement he beat him on his face with his fists until his face was a swollen. Now Jiveraj got angry and did not come for polo.

The other day he did not come out of his room and today he has gone to Daulat Singhjee's house from whence in a day or two he will go to Durbar. He has gone there even without asking Sarkar. . . . Hurjee was saying that he . . . beat him [only because] he considered him as his relative. While Hurjee had . . . a point . . . Jiveraj took it ill . . . [to desert Sarkar] is a sure sign of . . . [his] narrow-mindedness.

Jaipore, Friday, 20th April, 1900

Comments Upon Maharaj Dheeraj Sardar Singhjee [Of Jodhpur].   [Influenced by his reading of *Plutarch's Lives*, Amar Singh started a similar account early in the diary but excised it for fear of discovery (see Part I, 1). In Jaipur, away from Jodhpur and the possibility of prying eyes, he resumes it]

Maharaja Sardar Singh Bahadur of Jodhpore, who is the only son of the late Maharaja Jaswant Singhjee, is of middle stature.[13] He is thinly made. In his boyhood he was rather fine looking. . . . No one who saw him before he ascended his paternal throne ever thought that this boy who looked so promising would in the long run turn out . . . profligate. He has dishonoured Sarkar's training which is at the present considered the best procurable for a Rajpoot prince. Sarkar is also to blame a little in this matter, for as long as he kept him under his personal supervision he guarded him very strictly . . . so soon as Capt. Mayne was appointed guardian he left off scolding him. Capt. Mayne was himself a very mild man and next to never rebuked him.

A man kept under restraint for a long time and then at once let loose is sure to get bad unless he is perfectly well experienced. . . . He was never kind to me and I hope never shall be. We had passed the whole of our boyhood together . . . Being too familiar [I] could never please him.

He is very fickle-minded. He never talks with learned and able, or experienced older men but is seen continually to be talking to one of his favourites who are a disgrace to him and the Rathores.[14] . . . They envy one another for a kind word or look. His favourites have been innumerable and nearly all of them of the same type. They have been alternately changing, for one knocks the other down as soon as his charms captivate Durbar's heart. They are like so many mistresses who always envy one another and try to pull each other down. . . .

He is very fond of horses and has many very good ones. He buys too rashly and the result is that he often gets broken down and bad horses. Horse dealers rob him too much: just imagine a horse that he has bought for forty thousand rupees and is not worthy for even a trooper. This horse was bought for racing. It

PHOTO VI-2   Maharaja Sardar Singh of Jodhpur, 1880–1911. Seventeen months younger than Amar Singh, the maharaja, like Amar Singh, lives with assorted princely nephews under Sir Pratap's severe discipline. Invested with full powers at eighteen in 1898, he immediately frees himself from his uncle's supervision. Sent to the Imperial Cadet Corps in the hope that its discipline would improve him, he is asked to leave under shadowy circumstances. Sickly, self-indulgent and at the center of court intrigue, he has trouble carrying the responsibilities of his office and is periodically deprived of his powers. Amar Singh's photo albums.

was disliked and sent in the rissala [state forces] after a short time. Major Turner did not like it and so it was sent to Ajmere and auctioned there where I hope he is now dragging some hired carriage. . . .

He is very fond of dogs which are kept in the number of two hundred at the least. He pays very high prices for them though they are of no use to him. A man cannot enjoy two hundred dogs even though they be packs of fox hounds. Dogs of every sort are to be found with him. . . .

He is very fearful of his wife. . . . Some of his favourites were dismissed through her anger. Though Durbar likes to keep them yet he was obliged to part with them by her order. *One time when Buchanjee and I were talking . . . he told me that she keeps the carriage door open in the way. I told him that we shall see when she comes back from the fort. An hour afterwards she came back from the fort She was driving in a closed borough [he possibly means a brougham] and a cloth was thrown over it. But she had thrown aside the cloth from the middle windows and even the glass panes were drawn aside. Her hands were even seen from a distance of two hundred yards. How shameful for the Rathores.[15]* This is too bad. I don't say the purdah . . . system is very good, yet when it is observed among us it should be fully observed or not at all . . . [Throughout the diary Amar Singh opposes *purdah*—the seclusion of women—"in principle" but holds that as long as it is the custom among Rajputs, purdah should be strictly observed.] At night time she goes out for a drive with Durbar in dogcarts with one of the favourites with them. Riding is also practised on moon light nights when nearly all the great favourites join. Once when a panther was let loose she fired her rifle with Durbar and Ogumjee [the maharaja's favorite] from the elephant's back. The panther being not hurt it was chased by some horsemen. There was a great crowd. Major Turner too was one of the spectators. All the while she was sitting openly with Durbar. A hundred instances may be written like this.

Reports proclaim her to be very beautiful. . . . [At the maharaja's social gatherings] husbands and wives sit and eat together before their elders, quite contrary to the Rajpoot custom. . . . Sarkar alone never goes or allows his wives or daughter to join these festivals though often sent for.

Jodhpore, Monday, 14th May, 1900

A Table Talk.   I think it will be interesting and worth remembering a few remarks of last night's table talk. At first Sarkar [Sir Pratap] sat silently and seemed not at all inclined to talk. We all too sat mute, looking at each other. Not a word passed. No one knew why Sarkar was so much out of temper. . . . Gradually his moroseness faded and he began talking.

The first talk . . . [was] about the state of Jodhpore and its royal family. He was very sorry for the frivolous conduct of the Jodhpore durbar. He said that of all the Rajpootana states Jodhpore had gone very high but is now gradually falling down. From the first it has become the last. . . . Self-interested persons have done it all. For their own interest they have spoiled Durbar, ruined the state and are and will be ruined themselves.

He was quite right. If one was to throw a glance at the recently passed affairs all will be seen as plain as if seen on a mirror. How many persons have tried, succeeded, and were again hurled down from Durbar's favours by the envy of some mischievous and plotting rival. Look at Durbar's favourites . . . in the past four years. The first were Bunjee, Chhimanjee, Bhoorjee, Paboodanjee, Mobjee, Daulat Singhjee, Sawai Singhjee, Arjon Singhjee. Next came a horde of Mohammedans such as Hafiz, Bikdoo, Gubbo. . . . There were many more. . . . If on an average each one has at least taught two vices, the number of vices goes too high. . . .

Next [Sir Pratap] said that the police was to be taken [away] by the [British] government, which will be a terrible blow to the administration or rather power of the durbar.[16]

. . . Then he said that he often wondered at his own royal family the members of which are quite degraded . . . Why [are] the sons not like their fathers? . . . Of

PHOTO VI-3   The Jodhpur fort. Rao Jodha, the Rathore founder of Jodhpur state, began its construction in 1459. It is one of the sites of factional struggles between Sir Pratap, regent or first minister, and his nephew, the youthful Maharaja Sardar Singh. Photo courtesy of Jack Davis.

the twenty sons of Maharaja Takhat Singhjee [Sir Pratap's father][17] half were natural ones. The eldest who succeeded . . . him was Maharaja Jaswant Singhjee. . . . [He] often occasioned great troubles to his father. In his old[er] days [Jaswant Singh] was a model raja, but . . . licentiousness had its firm hold until his death. . . . Among his sons is the present durbar [Sardar Singh] . . . I wish his son Maharaj Kanwar Sumer Singhjee[18] would turn out a better ruler than his father.

There are also two [of ten] natural sons, Sawai Singhjee and Tej Singhjee, who are . . . not worth talking to. [A detailed discussion of Takhat Singh's sons and their descendants follows.][19] Maharaj Madho Singhjee, Bahadoor Singhjee and Mohabat Singhjee [seventh, eighth, and ninth sons of Takhat Singh] all died in the prime of their life by excess of drinking and diseases.[20] The first and third of them died without any issue at all. The second had two sons, but one of them is a natural one. . . . The real son is affected very badly with leprosy. He is about to die. He has squandered all his father's fortune and now starves.

Maharaj Zalim Singhjee [tenth son of Takhat Singh], who is the youngest of all is the only one of the ten brothers who stands erect with no blemish. . . . He is truly a model maharaj and the only one that was or is properly educated . . .

[A year and a half intervenes between this lugubrious account of regal decline at Jodhpur and the next entry, which makes it clear that Sir Pratap is about to fall victim to a cabal formed by the senior minister, Sir Sukhdeo Prasad, and the

British resident, with the maharani and the favorites playing supporting roles. The competition between Pratap Singh and Sukhdeo Prasad is not unique in the court politics of Rajput states.[21] Maharajas and political officers often welcomed competition among court factions because it gave them a way of controlling powerful and entrenched administrators. "Outsiders," for example, Bengalis and Kashmiris not tied to local interests and factions, were more dependent upon the ruler for their survival. The Jodhpur first ministerial post alternates between Sir Pratap and Sir Sukhdeo over a twenty-five-year period.][22]

Saturday, 23rd November, 1901

Today I want to give a little account of the present existing state of affairs in Marwar, which unfortunately [is] not at all good. . . . The poor people are dying by hundreds of starvation but nobody seems to care for them. Everyone looks after his own business. The durbar is quite satisfied as long as he can spend some few thousand a month in buying horses or dogs. No one listens to Sarkar. I know he has not the full capacity for state affairs and he himself does not work. Sukhdeo Prasad, who is nowadays the moving figure, is . . . always inciting Durbar against Sarkar, and as these two persons vie with each other, he gets his business [done]. Sarkar is bent on ridding him [Sukhdeo] from the state but he is too clever and Sarkar too simple. . . .

Sukhdeojee always arranges matters [in ways] that throw discredit on Sarkar and breed disunion between him and the durbar. The latter is a puppet in . . . [Sukhdeo's] hands and does not understand the tremendous mischief that is being done to him and his state. He is in turn ruled by his favourite Ogumjee who in his turn is a lamb before Sukhdeojee. . . .

Just fancy, they [Sukhdeo and Ogumji] have arranged matters to such a height that Durbar has not seen his wife the maharani sahiba [who is perhaps a political influence] since his return from Europe. They had arranged that Durbar should put himself up in the Rai ka Bagh so that they [husband and wife] may not have the chance of seeing one another. To add to this, they devised a plan that the maharanijee sahiba should be called here to the Rai ka Bagh and then, instead of bringing her there, she was to be driven up to the fort and there kept . . . with no chance whatever of her being able to see Durbar or interfere with him. But she was too clever for this plot and absolutely refused to leave her house . . . which of course no one could force her to do. Now the matter stands exactly the same. Durbar does not dare to go to that house. No, not even to play polo in that polo ground. . . .

Sukhdeo Prasadjee and Sarkar are the two competitors for this post of prime ministership. The latter, who now holds it, is gradually losing ground and the former is advancing and there is every probability of his succeeding. The other day, I have heard, it was arranged that as the durbar is going to the Imperial Cadet Corps for one year, Sarkar will be acting for him. . . . Then after the return of Durbar he is to take charge of his own work and Sarkar to resign.

There is this great famine here even this year, yet nobody in Jodhpore seems to care for it except the poor people. There is the same buying of horses and the same playing of polo. I, sitting here in this room, have at present no idea of what a famine is like. I get the same food, same clothing and the same horses and enjoyments and I care for nothing more. But it is really a man who suffers that can know what is it like. . . .

The thakoors who are the nobles and have a right to speak in state affairs are looked down [upon]. . . . They do not understand these matters, and even if they do, they dare not speak for fear of the state officials. It is the policy of the state officials to keep down and suppress their spirits so that they may not some day be able to interfere in state affairs. These nobles nowadays do nothing else but . . . drink to excess and pass their time in illicit love. With a few exceptions they are all of them hopelessly in debt with no idea of paying it back.

. . . The high posts in the state are held either by Brahmans or Bunias [merchant caste] but of recent years the Kashmiris are increasing. There is not a single Rajpoot who holds a high or responsible post. They are all deemed unworthy. Sarkar for all his love for the Rajpoots never promoted them to this high standard. He never arranged for their education but once, when he opened the Elgin Rajpoot School.[23] Unluckily it is all gone to pots now. . . .

Sarkar can neither do . . . things nor would he allow anyone to do them. . . . Even the work of the regiments [the princely state forces which fought in China in 1900] is getting worse and worse every day. Not one of the officers is allowed to look into the accounts. Sarkar Lall, who is the clerk, is doing what he likes, knowing full well that Sarkar does not understand these things and no one else will ever dare to ask any question.

Nowadays it is the policy of the state to increase . . . [its] fiscal property, not by the right and justifiable way, but by putting a stop to adoption [thereby forcing the property to escheat to the state]. This is indeed very unjust.

There is a new law started called the mori sala which treats . . . these adoption customs. . . . There is unfortunately no courage in the Rajpoots to make a union and put a stop to this once and forever. [As has been noted above, more than two-thirds of Jodhpur's land was held by jagirdars, limiting the revenues of the maharaja's government. Application of the mori sala rule would expand the maharaja's revenue lands at the expense of the thakurs.

In 1895 the mori sala rule was codified by a committee including some leading Jodhpur jagirdars. The code specified that adoption to a jagir must be from the lineal male descendants of the original grantee. This rule did not ban adoption, as had Lord Dalhousie's doctrine of lapse in the mid-nineteenth century, often cited as a cause of the rebellion of 1857, but did restrict Rajput adoption from distant branches. In default of a direct lineal descendant, a thakur's estate could escheat to the khalsa.[24]]

Even Englishmen are now becoming aware of the mismanagement of the state, and I hear that the government is now proposing to send four English officers to look after four of the chief departments.[25] Durbar is being sent to the Imperial Cadet Corps which I know he must be hating like poison. I also hear that he is trying to avoid it if possible but I doubt very much he will ever succeed. . . .

[Amar Singh too is about to leave for the ICC; he views it as an opportunity rather than as a restraint. The ICC objective is "the better and effective training of the scions of the Indian aristocracy."[26] General Sir O'Moore Creagh, who succeeded Lord Kitchener as commander in chief of the Indian Army, takes a different view:

> The Cadet Corps, I believe, originally included, and was intended only to include, embryo Ruling Chiefs, heirs of Ruling Chiefs, or scions of Ruling Chief families. Its particular object was to remove youths destined for ruling powers from the evil Court influences at an impressionable age, and give them a sound moral [cum-military] training. . . .
>
> It was common talk, whether if true or not I am unable to say, that the Cadet Corps was used by the Political Department as a penal settlement [for problematic rulers].[27] . . .

O'Moore Creagh's characterization of the ICC may have been influenced by Amar Singh who served as his trusted ADC at Mhow between 1905 and 1909. Amar Singh's diary accounts of Sardar Singh at the ICC (included in Part IV) make it clear that the young maharaja does think of his life there as a form of exile and imprisonment. The effort to reform Sardar Singh through military discipline ends in disaster; he is dismissed from the Corps and deprived of his powers.]

Jodhpore, Thursday, 18th September, 1902

Notes About My Last Visit To Jodhpore.   [One year after the previous account, Amar Singh, who was married in 1901 and whose home is now his family's haveli at Jaipur, goes to Jodhpur personally to present to the maharaja, Sardar Singh, an invitation to the marriage of his sister. As head of the Rathore lineage, the maharaja is entitled to be informed of the marriage alliances of his lineage brothers. The *nota*, invitation, is presented on a salver with *gur*, unrefined brown sugar; it is conventional for the recipient to give a nominal gift of money upon such a notification.

Amar Singh last saw Jodhpur at the time of his marriage a year earlier. Sir Pratap, having lost his position as prime minister, has departed to become the Maharaja of Idar, a succession he claims by virtue of his Rathore lineage. Maharaja Sardar Singh spends most of his time in forced probation at the ICC. The desolation Amar Singh describes reflects not only the devastating effects of the 1899 famine but also the absence of Sir Pratap's active government and Sardar Singh's indifference to affairs of state.]

IV. Sarkar's House

This is the place I love most of all. . . . It was all closed now. There were no men and no horses. Only the Thakoor Sahib of Jakurn was there guarding the zenana deorhi. I sent my respects to both the sirdars who were glad to see me here [Sir Pratap's wives, left behind at Jodhpur after his departure to Idar]. The bara sirdar, that is to say, the eldest wife, began to joke about my newly born daughter. Of course I could not answer to such a question as she is as respected to me as my mother. . . .

V. Durbar's House

The durbar [Maharaja Sardar Singh] being here his house was full of people. I found him breaking some horses to harness. This is how he wastes his time instead of doing any work. I showed him the goor and was ordered to hand it over to Ogumjee's man. . . . I asked permission if I could send the goor in to the maharani sahib and I was allowed to do. I took leave from both the places and was allowed to go. . . . At the durbar's house I have several friends but none of [them] expressed . . . much warmth.

VIII. Polo

Such of the players as now live here have formed a club which is under the superintendence of Mr Todd [English manager of the Jodhpur Railway]. Some of these people are so stingy that they do not pay any subscription. What a shame. Maharaj Arjun Singhjee absolutely refuses to do so and Maharaj Ratan Singhjee has left the game simply for this reason. Just fancy this. This game has much fallen down since Sarkar and Durbar are not living here. Jodhpore is not [as] advanced in civilization as Jaipore where a club flourishes in spite of the durbar's being dead against it. I played a game with the Raoti people. At present they have no good horses. They have not even decent saddles, bridles, or sticks. . . .

IX. How Jodhpore Looked

To me it looked as if I had come to some deserted place, somewhat like the cenotaphs outside the ghat gate [near a cremation ground] in Jaipore where there are any number of tombs but no man is seen. Jodhpore has as many houses as one can imagine but there was no life in them. There were a few men at the railway station but further on there was nothing at all. The courts of justice, though open, were not full], at least there were no men seen outside. The lines round it were empty and the cabins [offices for touts and scribes] were full of stones and all sorts of filth. In some there were donkeys and in some dogs sheltering themselves from the rays of the burning sun. The garden of Paota is nothing more than a waste. There was no green grass and sand had accumulated in [the] corners. The trees were all dead.

The Rai ka Bagh [royal garden] with all its palaces and stables make the sight still more dreadful. Who can imagine that there was a time when every stall had a horse in it and every room its occupants. The Jodha Squadron lines [of the princely state forces] are going to ruins, and in a few years time will be the home for jackals. The Shekawatjee ka Talao lines are without life. The mess and the quarter guard has six men apiece and as many besides to look after the stores, etc. Fancy, this place used to have nearly a thousand men and over a thousand animals. . . .

The durbar's house has the same peculiarity. In one corner where he himself may be sitting or standing there is a small crowd, but even that is not so much as we used to have at Sarkar's house when he was prime minister. The two stables of His Highness are a good deal more than half empty. There is practically no one seen on the roads. Old houses are crumbling and [no] new ones are being built. There was no green grass to be seen, though it was the season when there ought to have been green grass all round. . . . The places where there used to be very thick trees are now absolute plains, as all the wood has been cut down by poor people who do it by stealth for their livelihood. In Jodhpore there seemed to be no one living, in fact there seemed to be no life. I . . . [could] not think where and to whom to go. Just fancy what a difference there is between this place and Jaipore, where there are gardens all round and the place is full of life. . . .

Abu, Monday, 19th June, 1905[28]
Notes About My Last Visit To Ahmednagar.

XIV. Talks with Daulat Singhjee

Under this heading I have got to write a great deal. The first thing that I shall now attempt to write is the Jodhpore story as described by this man. I don't really know how much of it is true. [We have inserted this account out of sequence because it is a retrospect on events at Jodhpur in 1902. It reflects the point of view of Sir Pratap's party at the Jodhpur court. Amar Singh's age-mate, Daulat Singh was adopted by Sir Pratap as his heir when in 1902 he became Maharaja of Idar. Daulat Singh takes it for granted that Sir Sukhdeo Prasad, then the Jodhpur prime minister, has evil designs and could, often with British inspiration or help, move royal personages like pieces on a chessboard.]

[In 1902] the durbar [Maharaja Sardar Singh] had his full powers and was doing all sorts of nasty things. The state had got in debt [because of the maharaja's extravagances, especially horses] and there was no end of complaints from all sources against the maharaja sahib. Now to put matters right, it was arranged that the durbar should be set aside and the work be given to Sarkar for one year, after which he was to give in his resignation.

The government sent this letter to Sarkar who was . . . thinking whether to accept it or not. Some of his friends advised him to accept while others stopped him from doing so. Each one had his own arguments in support. Those who advised acceptance said that this was a good chance of showing his merits. Afterwards the government might reconsider the matter and he may be kept for a longer period. Those of the opposite opinion urged that nothing can possibly be done in one year and the whole result in the end will be his resignation with a bad name, and that after earning the disaffection of the durbar and most of the other people. It was best to decline the offer. . . . This was going on when the posthumous son of the Maharaja Kesri Singhjee of Idar died and Sarkar was adopted there [as maharaja].

In the meantime, arrangements were being made to put the Jodhpore durbar aside and have the work done by a council. General Beatson [commander of the Imperial Service Forces], who is a personal friend of the durbar, did not like the news. To make the best of a bad bargain he came to Jodhpore . . . [where he] advised the durbar to send in an application desiring to enlist in the [Imperial] Cadet Corps.

The durbar listened to this advice . . . [then] went to the station and sent a telegram. It was not very long before he changed his mind and there was some trouble to persuade him to go.

Well, when he [Sarkar] went [to Idar] the work was handed over to Sukhdeo Prasadjee. The durbar had always liked this man; on this occasion there was some trouble. Up till now [Sukhdeo] was out of the way. Sarkar being the prime minister [Sukhdeo] used to throw all the blame on [Sarkar] and remain himself free. Now when Sarkar went away, Sukhdeojee had to work. . . . [When] the responsibility fell on his shoulders . . . he had to check the durbar. . . . The result was that [the durbar] began to complain against [Sukhdeo].

The chief cause of disagreement was that the durbar issued an order granting Busalpore village to Ogumjee. Sukhdeojee remonstrated against it, and finally had to go and tell the resident. Ogumjee was very angry at this interference and said that he would have Sukhdeojee removed from the work. The durbar was absolutely in the hands of this boy who persuaded him to write a long letter of complaints to the government of India against Sukhdeojee.

[Pandit] Sukhdeojee was always careful. Before this he had got a letter, complimentary to himself, written by the durbar in which [Durbar] had written that Sukhdeojee was the best man and he [Durbar] could rely on him. Another thing of cleverness was that Sukhdeojee told Sheonath Singhjee of Bera [Sir Pratap's son-in-law] to get him a letter of recommendation from Sarkar who was just then leaving for Idar. . . . That letter . . . was framed by [Sukhdeo] himself and . . . went so far as to say that all the writer's [Sir Pratap's] work was done through the bearer [Sukhdeo Prasad]. Possessed of these recommendations, Sukhdeojee felt quite secure.

The durbar, when he [temporarily] returned from Meerut [the ICC base], wrote a very strong letter to the Government of India in which he said that he had been duped by this pandit fellow and that [the pandit] was the cause of the disagreement between him and his uncle. . . . He [Durbar] was quite reconciled to Sarkar and wanted [Sarkar] to work for him [Durbar] for five months while he was with the cadet corps. Further on [Durbar] wanted to kick out not only Sukhdeojee but the whole lot of Kashmiris. There was every chance of this letter being accepted, but the question arose as to who was to work if Sukhdeojee was kicked out.

The durbar said that the Maharaja of Idar would [work] for five months after which he himself would do the work. The resident and the AGG both said that the durbar could not himself work and it was no use giving the work to one man for five months only. If, however, the durbar would give the work for five years to Sarkar the matter may be reconsidered. The durbar was firm in his resolution because he had been tutored by Ogumjee who wanted to become a minister himself. There was Maharaj Zalim Singhjee who wanted to become a minister and he advised the durbar to call Sarkar for five months only, and after that to give the work to him [Zalim]. [Zalim Singh was a brother of Sir Pratap's, and a competent officer according to Amar Singh's earlier opinion.] He [Zalim] said that he would be a minister only in name while he would let Ogumjee do all the work for him. . . .

Sukhdeojee was not idle in the meantime. He told the resident that the Maharaja of Idar was instigating the durbar [against him], and he could not work while this man [Sarkar] was here. The result of this was that Sarkar had to go away to Idar and was not to come [to Jodhpur] without sanction. . . . That letter of the durbar complaining against Sukhdeojee had no effect, because only a couple of months ago he had written a very complimentary letter for Sukhdeojee, and now he was writing against him in spite of his being away at the time and not having seen the work.

Now the viceroy [Lord Curzon] came to Jodhpore. Sukhdeojee arranged to have the durbar made a fool of. Lady Curzon had come a couple of days before, and the durbar and all his staff dined with her the first day. Next morning Mrs Erskine [wife of the resident] . . . told Lady Curzon that Ogumjee and the lot were not worth shaking hands with and [that] she had made a great mistake in dining with them. Next time she had her meal alone on the plea that she was not feeling well and said that they may dine with her staff. The latter [Lady Curzon's staff] said that the durbar can come and join them if he liked but they won't have his staff [Ogumji and his friends]. On this they all went away.

When Lord Curzon came, his wife got very angry with him . . . Why had she not been informed of all this before? On this the viceroy got angry with his private secretary, Mr [Walter] Lawrence.[29] . . . He asked as to who had been complaining. . . . On being told the name of Mrs Erskine . . . [Lawrence] said that she had better be made a private secretary [to the viceroy]. The viceroy and his secretary were angry with one another. . . . The latter never went out while they stayed at Jodhpore. . . .

Major Erskine [the resident] had been complaining against Ogumjee and the durbar for some time. . . . When the viceroy came to Jodhpore and got out of his carriage he could not recognize who the durbar was. The durbar had on a plain silk achkan and a plain turban and perhaps a string of pearls round his neck. . . . Behind him stood Ogumjee who had on very fine clothes and was wearing the very best and richest ornaments of the state. Besides this, Ogumjee is a much handsomer man than the durbar. Had it not been for the resident, who . . . [quickly] introduced the durbar, the viceroy might have shaken hands with Ogumjee. When Lord Curzon asked as to who that man was, Major Erskine said that he was not worth shaking hands with and he would speak about him afterwards.

Then there was the occasion of the durbar [court ceremonial]. . . . Sukhdeojee made up his mind to get the maharaja sahib and Ogumjee into further trouble. [At durbars seats are assigned by hereditary status but ambiguities or anomalies can lead to contestation. In the hope of eliminating conflicts the Political Department tried over the years to codify durbar seating arrangements. Like the GOI's warrants of precedence and censuses, its codification of durbar seating arrangements attempted to freeze hitherto fluid relationships. We find, for example, in the sixth edition of the GOI's *Rajputana and Ajmer: List of Ruling Princes, Chiefs and Leading Personages*[30] a "rule" for seating at the Jodhpur durbar:

> . . . in the arrangement of seats two rows are provided in the Durbar—one on the right and the other on the left of the throne. On the right are seated descendants of the Princes who preceded Rao Jodhaji [founder of Jodhpur]. The prominent clans of this line are the Champawats and the Kumpawats. Among the former, Pokran and Auwa are the Sarayats [nobles of the first rank] and among the latter, Asop. If two or more Sarayats of the same line attend the Durbar, the first seat is occupied by turn.

Ogumjee, while a Kumpawat, does not figure in this status ordering; he is not from a *sarayat* (first rank) lineage and held no estate until given the village which became a source of dispute between the maharaja and Sukhdeo Prasad. The Thakur of Pokaran, whose place Ogumji tries to occupy, is Jodhpur's premier noble, a Champawat of the first rank, master of Jodhpur's largest estate, and hereditary *pradhan* (minister).]

The Durbar sent word to the Thakoor of Pokaran that he should sit below Ogumjee, and said that the first seat belonged to the Thakoor of Asope. . . . As he [Asope] was not present any other Kumpawat [such as Ogumji] might sit there. The Pokaran Thakoor said that it was only he [Maharaja Sardar Singh] who had made Asope Thakoor sit above him, otherwise this had never before been done. . . . This could not be done as Ogumjee was practically nobody. . . . On the other hand he [Pokaran] would get a bad name and that was why he would not sit below [Ogumji]. Foiled in this, the durbar succeeded in persuading the Bera Thakoor [Sheonath Singh, Sir Pratap's son-in-law] to sit below Ogumjee. Sheonath Singhjee would not have agreed to it but Sukhdeojee told him to accept it. . . .

The resident told the . . . [viceroy, Lord Curzon] that the boy sitting next to Pokaran had no right to that place and he was sitting above the son-in-law of the Maharaja of Idar. The viceroy even asked who that man was because he was wearing a lot of jewels of the best kind. . . . When the viceroy went to see the fort, he went to the highest place . . . and was shown all the houses. . . . Particularly pointed out [was] the new house built by the durbar for Ogumjee. This building was conspicuous because it is built of red sand-stone [a material usually reserved for state buildings].

The people did not stop here. They . . . wanted to give a bad name to the maharani sahib. They told the [viceroy's] people that she would meet Lady Curzon at the fort and [then] sent rumours to [the maharani] that if she once went up to the fort she would not be allowed to come down again. On this she refused to go up. . . . It was at the eleventh hour that she was persuaded to go up. There was only one conveyance to go up [to the fort] and in this mahdol [large palanquin] she went. As ill-luck would have it, and as the rascals had arranged, Lady Curzon arrived and asked for her conveyance to go up. She was told that the maharani sahib had just come and had taken what was intended for [the vicereine] and that she would have to wait for its return and she did it.

When Lady Curzon went in the zenana, the maharani sahib ought to have met her at the threshold, instead of which she did not finish her toilet [until] some time after her guest had come. . . . Lady Curzon complained a lot about this treatment to her husband. . . .

. . . It had been arranged that Sarkar would be given the Jodhpore work, but here again the chance was lost through his own folly. The viceroy and Mr Lawrence [who were] arranging to send Sarkar to Jodhpore . . . were thinking of doing so through the recommendation of Mr Martindale, the A.G.G. Sarkar heard . . . [this] news at Simla. . . . On his way to Idar [he] stopped at Jaipore, where he told everyone that he was again going to Jodhpore. [When] this news reached Mr Martindale at Abu [the Rajputana hill station] he said that Sarkar was spreading reports of his going to become a prime minister and that he had made all the arrangement with the people at Simla. These sorts of talks were undermining the authority of the A.G.G. . . . If Sarkar is to be sent without his recommendation, he was going to resign. It was owing to this that there were rumours of the A.G.G. going to resign owing to sickness. The argument of this government official [Martindale] prevailed and Sarkar lost his chance. . . .

Now I shall write [about] some other talks. . . . I asked [Daulat Singh] whether the maharani sahib used to go out. He told me that they often used to go riding at night. The maharani sahib . . . [rode] a horse with a deshi [native] saddle and wore the dress of a man. Several times they used to come quite near Sarkar's house and considered it an act of boldness. Out in camp the maharanijee used to go out riding too. Daulat Singhjee said that he was of opinion that the ladies ought to go out though privately. It was not long before I convinced him that it would be an act of the greatest folly when we did away with the purdah system. I gave him several instances and in the end he believed what I had said. . . .

Meerut, Thursday, 12th March, 1903[31]

The Present State Of Affairs In Jodhpore.

I. Dismissal of Ogumjee

. . . Jodhpore is in a very unsettled state of mind. Col. Jennings, the resident [for the period 1903–1906], is a man of very fiery temper. From what I could make out from Jiverajjee's talk, I find that this resident has been purposely sent to clear Jodhpore from all the mismanagement. The most prominent feature is the dismissal of Ogumjee. When the maharaj kanwar sahib [Sumer Singh, son and heir of Maharaja Sardar Singh] went to call on the resident, the latter had sent word that if Ogumjee accompanied him, the resident would not see the maharaj kanwar.

At last one day Ogumjee was sent for by Col. Jennings and questioned whether he, Ogumjee, was the son of the late durbar Jaswant Singhjee. [Sardar Singh often referred to Ogumji as *bhai* (brother). The resident's implication is that Ogumji made himself out to be a natural son of Maharaja Jaswant Singh, who would have a certain standing at Jodhpur, as well as a natural brother of Maharaja Sardar Singh]. The poor fellow was frightened out of life and said that he was merely a servant of the durbar.

Col. Jennings would hear nothing . . . [further from Ogumji]. He [told Ogumji that he] had strict orders to turn him out. He dismissed Ogumjee with the orders that he was to clear out of Jodhpore within twenty-four hours' time. The miscreant said that he might be allowed to serve Maharaj Arjon Singhjee [one of Sir Pratap's nephews] but the resident only grew more furious and said that he was not to do so. He was not even to see or correspond with the durbar and if he did so and the news came to the residency, he, Ogumjee, would be sent to the Andaman Islands, which is a place of exile for the worst of Indian criminals. [Presumably this was an attempt to intimidate Ogumji; there was no legal ground for such a threat.] For the future Ogumjee is to live at his village, Chandalao, and not go out anywhere without the sanction of the khas mahakma [secretariat]. It is a sort of imprisonment for the poor fellow. But all the same he richly deserves it.

II. How Ogumjee Left Durbar's House

This I hear was a very bad scene. When Ogumjee returned from the residency he broke the fatal news to all his favourites and well-wishers. It was very hard for these poor fellows who were getting their livelihood by the favour of this fellow. Now, they gathered in a room, shut the doors, began drinking wine and weeping. The last was the worst of all for I hear that they wept as Indian women do when some near relation of theirs dies. . . .

IV. My Ideas of the Present and Near Future of Jodhpore

The present idea of the political officials, as far as I can guess, is that the durbar be kept as far away from the state as possible and the work . . . conducted by the resident and Pandit Sukhdeo Prasadjee. I fear Durbar will never get his powers. Most probably he will be kept in this corps for some years to come and if he does not improve may forever be disqualified, and the maharaja kanwar be installed on the gaddi [throne, literally, cushion, upon which the ruler is seated].

The only chance for the durbar is to make friends with Sukhdeo Prasadjee and turn a new leaf in his life. He ought to leave off racing altogether, in which he is still indulging himself in spite of the wishes of the political officers. This horde of useless favourites will be broken up, work will be done by one steady and capable hand instead of being hindered by fools and favourites. The names of useless pay drawers will be struck off the pay lists, men worthy of the posts will be employed and then and only then can we hope for some peace in Jodhpore.

X. The Character of Ogumjee

To begin with, Ogumjee was not at all a big man. He was of course a Rajpoot of the Kumpawat clan of Rathores. He was body-servant to Gumanjee Kheechee for some time. When the durbar began to live apart [from Sir Pratap] and Gumanjee was sent there, this boy of course went with his master. He attracted Durbar's notice, rose into favour and became one of the leading miscreants who spoiled Durbar forever.

He is a handsome looking fellow. . . . Durbar always calls Ogumjee his brother and Ogumjee's wife is mentioned as Baijee Lall [daughter of the maharaja, a kinship usage which assimilates both husband and wife to the royal family]. . . . Though merely a poor boy in the beginning, he was adopted by the late Thakoor of Chandalao and has consequently become a thakoor. . . . This fellow tried his utmost to get Sarkar out of the state and give that place to Sukhdeo Prasadjee who, I am glad to write, has turned the actual culprit out . . .

Saturday, 14th March, 1903

The Holi Dinner.   The Holi dinner [being] of the ordinary type there was nothing extraordinary that would have required a separate description but for the change that was so strikingly manifest in Jodhpore durbar. Now this maharaja is in the habit of talking at great length and always dwells on subjects concerning himself . . .

That night, as usual, he was giving descriptions of his hunts and tigershoots by moon light. While doing so he repeatedly mentioned the name of Sher Singhjee but not of the third person. . . . On former occasions whenever this shooting was spoken of the name of Ogumjee was the first to be mentioned. That night he was very near mentioning it through constant habit but by some effort checked himself. This shows a clear sign that the durbar has received orders to have nothing to do with Ogumjee.

Three of four times I was very near questioning him as to the name of the third shikaree [hunter] but checked my tongue with the thought that nothing good would come out of it. Either the Durbar will keep quiet or say something which might draw me into an unpleasant quarrel. I am glad I did not speak. . . . Durbar is looking a little beaten and crestfallen. The air of bravado has passed and he looks a bit sensible. . . .

Jaipore, Saturday, 29th August, 1903

Notes About My Fourth Term In The Imperial Cadet Corps.

XXII. Those Who Have Left the Corps

Only two cadets have left the corps this term, that is to say, they will not return any more. They are under officer H.H. Maharaja Sardar Singhjee of Jodhpore and Sahibzada Talee Mohammed Khan of Palanpore. As these two have left the corps for ever I must give a detailed account of them.

Jodhpore durbar led a most miserable life in the corps. He was practically never at either parade or lessons. He was most of the time on the sick list and preferred to be in his room to going out. . . . Durbar never got well. He had been trying hard to go to Jodhpore but never succeeded. He has tried his best to recall his friend and favourite Ogumjee but with no success. . . .

He preserved his good name for some time in the corps until just before our march to Delhi, on which day he got drunk. From that day onward he was pressed harder and harder. He was not allowed to spend money of his own will. Capt. Pinney was appointed his private secretary though he was in fact a guardian, and not a pice [coin] could be spent until sanctioned by him. The durbar was not allowed to go to Jodhpore after the end of the term but was sent straight off to Pachmurree [a hill station in Madhya Pradesh] where he is to stop for two years. If he does not improve himself he will never be allowed to go to Jodhpore but will have to abdicate in favour of his son. . . .

While in the corps I thought of an idea. . . . As the Alwar durbar was about to get his powers [as a prince], my father [his guardian] would be wanting a post. It would not be a bad idea if he got into the council at Jodhpore. I commenced the subject once with the durbar who jumped at the idea and asked me to write and enquire from my father if he would like to come to Jodhpore. I had told the durbar that if he could get my father in the state council it would be much better, otherwise he could get him as his own guardian, in either of which cases he would be able to help the durbar to get his powers very soon. . . . I said he would of course be able to give more help if he was in the council.

The durbar approved my idea and asked me to write and enquire if my father would like to come. The answer, as I expected, was in the affirmative, but there was some sort of delay as the durbar wanted to settle the matter verbally with the resident before allowing my father to try on his own behalf. What I think is this, that he must have consulted with his favourites, who must have advised him not to call in such a formidable man and the matter slackened. . . .

He was not allowed to take his uniform with him. This was taken away from him, which is one of the signs that he has lost the opinion of his superiors and will most probably never get his powers. This taking of his uniform is a very bad thing indeed. Uniforms have not been allowed to those only who have either been turned out or been not thought good enough to wear it. . . .[32]

2

Court Society at Kishengarh and Idar: Replicating Marks of Sovereignty

[Amar Singh's first view of serious political rituals and symbols is the Delhi durbar of January 1903 celebrating the coronation of Edward VII.[1] He remarks that
"it is more or less copying the Mughals." Lord Curzon, the viceroy who choreographed the affair, had closely followed his predecessor Lord Lytton's arrangements for the 1877 durbar that proclaimed Queen Victoria empress of India. Lytton expected to enhance the loyalty of Britain's colonial subjects, especially its
princes, by basing "the Queen's authority upon the ancient throne of the Moguls,
with which the imagination and tradition of [our] Indian subjects associate the
splendour of supreme power."[2]

Bernard Cohn in "Representing Authority in India" links "copying the
Mughals" with attempts to enhance the raj's ritual sovereignty. Drawing on We-
ber's concept of "typification," Stanley Tambiah sees "replication" of a "center" as
a mode of diffusing ritual sovereignty in the galactic polities of South and South-
East Asia.[3] Rajput kingdoms from the sixteenth century onward had assimilated
Mughal political rituals, symbolism and architecture to advance their status and
legitimize their rule. In the twentieth century, they emulated British variants of
Mughal public performances.

When Amar Singh visits Alwar in April 1902 at the time of Jai Singh's installation as maharaja, he encounters reduced versions of the political rituals and symbols employed by Lytton in 1877 and recapitulated by Curzon in 1903. Other
princely state courts that he visits in 1902 reproduce Mughal cultural forms on a
progressively diminishing scale.

At both Kishengarh and Idar, minor states[4] with limited revenues, Amar
Singh finds lesser versions of Jodhpur's public space, for example, a fort, a city
palace, an armory, a wardrobe, a *jawaharkhana* (jewelry office), a library, and
royal practices such as hunting. Indeed, thikanas too replicate in descending
order Delhi, Jodhpur, and Idar: in the 1870s, Amar Singh's grandfather, Zorawar Singh, having been made the Thakur of Kanota, built a durbar hall and,
in an era when artillery had rendered it obsolete, a fort with moat, ramparts
and battlements.

Like the proliferation of small *Kurfursten* states in imperial Germany,[5] court
societies in Rajputana were as much family as state affairs, expanded households
so to speak. Were it not for the British classification, it would be hard to distinguish small "states" from large "estates," for example, to distinguish Idar and
Kishengarh, the 15-gun-salute "states" from large thikanas such as Sikar and
Khetri in Jaipur or Pokran in Jodhpur.]

Dramatis Personae

The Maharaja of Kishengarh, Madan Singh, Amar Singh's dear friend from the Imperial Cadet Corps.

The Maharaja of Idar, a new incarnation of Sir Pratap, ex-regent of Jodhpur; "Sarkar," or "the durbar."

Daulat Singh, Pratap Singh's adopted son and heir to the *gaddi*, the ruling seat, at Idar.

Ram Nathji, Amar Singh's close friend and former teacher at Jodhpur, now a minister at Idar.

Jaipore, Wednesday, 2nd April, 1902
I received a telegraph from Syam Sunder Lalljee [prime minister] of Kishengarh. He invited me and informed [me] that Sarkar was at Idar. This settled all my plans. . . . [Kishengarh is about an hour and a half by train from Jaipur. The rail line continues southwest through Sirohi to Idar. Amar Singh visits Kishengarh for two days, Idar for three.]

Idar, Wednesday, 9th April, 1902

[We have disturbed the sequence of entries to preserve the continuity of the narrative.]
  Notes About My Stay At Kishengarh. . . . Kishengarh is a very small state [858 square miles; with a population of 86,000 in 1931, compared to Jaipur, 15,590 square miles, population 2,631,000 and Jodhpur, 36,021 square miles, population 2,125,0001 but in point of honour and consequence it is more prominent than other states of comparable size [for instance, it is a 15-gun-salute state; Jaipur and Jodhpur are 17-gun-salute states]The ruling family is of the Rathore Rajpoot clan [the same as Jodhpur]. . . .

City and Surroundings

[The fort] is quite a nice little place. The view from the top is very charming. The houses are few and small. The durbar hall is quite a big one. . . . The battlements and the gates are all good though some of them require a few repairs. . . . For modern warfare this fort is not much good. The hills round about are quite close and high; a gun planted on any one of them would give the fort a bad time. There are good stables for horses and quarters for men on the fort.

  The maharaja sahib . . . goes up to the fort to worship in the temple twice a day so long as he is in Kishengarh and in good health. There is quite a steep ascent and the road is paved with stones that are . . . slippery. Added to this there are many sharp turns at the gates but the present maharaja sahib always drives in his tum tum [a one-horse conveyance]. He took me with him. When I wondered he told me that he has driven a pair and a four in hand as well up here. I was rather surprised.

H.H. The Maharaja Sahib

The present maharaja is Madan Singhjee [See Part IV] He is a nice looking little boy of seventeen years of age. He is short in stature and is thinly built. Though quite a boy, and with no experience of the world, he is far better than most of the native princes. His habits are all good though sometimes he looks indifferent to what is told or explained to him. . . . His ideas are good and high. There is no meanness near him. . . . His education is not much. He knows a little English and can write and talk better than he can read. . . .

My Treatment

For the two days that I was there, I experienced the warmest welcome. The maharaja sahib was always with me and used to go out hunting or pigsticking simply for my own entertainment. On Egaris [eleventh day of the moon] a day on which he does not even eat meat, far less go and kill anything, he went out for shooting and pigsticking only because I was going away so soon. . . .

Idar, Sunday, 6th April, 1902

[Amar Singh's next stop is another mini-state, Idar, size 1,669 square miles, 1931 population 260,000, like Kishengarh, a 15-gun-salute state. Sir Pratap, having been removed as prime minister of Jodhpur by Lord Curzon, has become the maharaja of this poor, backward little kingdom in present-day Gujarat state which abuts Rajasthan on the southwest. Like Kishengarh, Idar is ruled by a branch of Jodhpur's ruling clan, the Rathores, and thus eligible for adoption to the Jodhpur gaddi. In the middle of the nineteenth century, Takhat Singh, Sir Pratap's father and a junior member of the Idar royal family, became Maharaja of Jodhpur by adoption. In 1902, in the next generation, Sir Pratap is adopted at Idar.

Idar includes Ahmednagar, the abandoned seventeenth-century capital of the Sultans of Ahmednagar. The famine of 1899–1900 has reduced Idar's population to 168,557, half its size in 1891. Its revenue, Rs 450,000 annually, is dwarfed by Jodhpur's five million.[6] Poverty and mismanagement have led to a debt of one million rupees,[7] twice the size of the state's annual revenue. Despite Idar's financial condition, Sir Pratap, shortly after his installation as maharaja in 1902, travels to England for four months with six companions for Edward VII's coronation.

For an empire celebrity like Sir Pratap, Idar is small beer. "You have placed my head in the heavens, my feet in the mud," he writes to Sir Walter Lawrence, private secretary to Lord Curzon.[8] Idar is ignored by viceroys and inspectors of the Imperial Service Forces, not to speak of the Prince of Wales.

Sir Pratap's installation to the gaddi is a casual affair; unlike at Jai Singh's installation at Alwar, the viceroy, Lord Curzon, absents himself. The political agent for western Gujarat does the honors, reading a carefully composed letter from the governor of Bombay, who, like the viceroy, does not bother to attend.

The Idar adoption provides the raj with a heaven-sent opportunity to clear the air at Jodhpur. Lord Curzon is willing to have Sir Pratap occupy harmless ceremonial positions such as honorary commander of the ICC but does not think well enough of his talents to weigh in on his side in Jodhpur. His "exile" is, in fact, deliberate. "To Idar I have sent him, and in Idar he shall remain."[9]

In his Gujarati Siberia, Sir Pratap has gathered around him various familiar faces. Bukhtawar Singh, who, like Amar Singh, had served on Sir Pratap's staff in China in 1901 during the Boxer Rebellion, becomes military secretary and commander of Idar's motley army. Ram Nathji, Amar Singh's much admired former teacher, serves as a minister.]

We started [from Ahmednagar station] at eight [by tonga] and reached Idar at a quarter past eleven. The road is in a very broken state and makes the journey quite an unpleasant one. [Because] . . . these fellows do not change [the ponies] . . . the same ponies have to travel the whole distance of eighteen miles.

At Idar I went to the garden where I met Ram Nathjee, Bukhtawar Singhjee and several others. I had breakfast in the mess and afterwards . . . talked with Ram Nathjee for the whole of the day time. He is indeed very kind to me. This very morning [he] walked about four miles and a half to [meet] me on the road. I came too late and so he walked back. . . .

Monday, 7th April, 1902

At about seven Ram Nathjee and myself walked to the palace in the city. There I was shown the library where there is a collection of some very nice books. I admired it very much. In course of time I hope to have a collection just as nice and big.[10]

Then we went [to see] . . . the other rooms and the big durbar hall. Here I saw a silver [canopy] in which there used to be an image which was worshipped by H.H. Kesri Singhjee, the late maharaja. Sarkar has now taken this [image] . . . out . . . [and] sent [it] to some other temple. . . . A picture of the late Queen Victoria has taken the place of the idol. . . . A fresh garland of flowers is placed round it every day. Sarkar, whenever he goes there, bows to it. How very foolish. At least I hate it. The singashans [thrones of deities] and several other silver things that were once sacred are placed round . . . [the Victoria shrine]. I am too sorry for Sarkar.

[Committed to Swami Dayanand's reformist Arya Samaj, Sarkar opposed "idol worship." It is not clear whether Amar Singh disapproves of Sir Pratap's "worship" at a Victoria "shrine," the removal of the late maharaja's sacred objects, or both. Sir Pratap's attentiveness to Queen Victoria has a history. Sir Walter Lawrence, private secretary to the viceroy and a friend and admirer of Sir Pratap, tells this story about Sir Pratap's relationship with Queen Victoria:

> In 1905 Sir Pertab was Chief of the Indian Staff attached to the present king [George V], and at one place a statue of Queen Victoria was to be unveiled. The day before the ceremony I was going to church, as it was Sunday, and I asked Sir Pertab what he would like to do. "I going church too," he said. "I going Queen Sahib's statue." I explained that the statue was veiled but this did not impede Sir Pertab, and he sat like a statue himself in silent meditation for two hours."[11]]

After this we went to Sarkar. He talked to me the whole of the day time. He was asking a thing over and over again and quite tired me out. Anyway, he was very kind and quite pleased to see me. I had a long talk [too] with Maharaj Kanwar Daulat Singhjee [Sir Pratap's nephew whom he has adopted to succeed him as Maharaja of Idar].

Tuesday, 8th April, 1902

We saw the polo ground. . . . Nearly a thousand rupees have been spent on it yet it is not a quarter ready. Again I am surprised at Sarkar's doing. One of his English guests had given him Rs 1500 . . . for the poor and deserving people of Idar. Now that sum has been spent on this ground. What a shame. I can write no more.

After . . . [watching the horses being groomed] we went to the city palace. First the saddlery and then the wardrobe and armoury were inspected. . . . From the wardrobe I got a picture of Sarkar which had been sent for me from England as my China medal.[12] . . . From the armoury I got a 577 bore double barrel rifle for tiger shooting. . . .

Meerut, Thursday, 10th April, 1902

Notes About My Stay At Idar.

My Object of Going

The sole and only idea of my going to Idar was to see the durbar sahib to whom I am deeply indebted. This was the first opportunity I had of going and paying my respects and presenting the nuzzar [ceremonial gift to a ruler]. The durbar had quite recently made me a present of Cockchafer (which is really a very fine horse) and heaped kindness over kindness ever since I was a child. All these things combined together drew me to Idar. People may think that I went only because my wife was not at Jaipore but this is all false. It was my full will to go. Even if she had been at Jaipore, I would have gone just the same. . . .

III. The Idar City

Idar is quite a small city but it is as neat and clean as a city can possibly be in India. I have never seen a cleaner one before anywhere. The houses are small and mostly of the old fashion. It is situated under a hill on which stands the fort. There is a wall round it though it requires repairs. There are not many roads. Idar has a nice little school where English is taught. Besides this there are Gujarati schools and a girls' school as well. Then there is a small hospital well looked after.

VI. The "Jawaharkhana"

This contains very few ornaments. Those things that have been brought over by the durbar and maharaj kanwar [Daulat Singh] are more costly and numerous than those found in the treasury. There is not a single big thing worth admiring. I saw the mardana [men's quarters] ornaments but not the zenana [women's quarters]. From what I heard from the maharaj kanwar there is not much in that as well. The durbar intends taking all this jewellery to England and selling it there. This will sell at about a lakh and a half rupees [Rs 150,000] which will [help pay off] the debt. This is a good policy. By this the state will save interest and jewellery can be bought afterwards again.

VIII. The Fort

It is situated on the top of a hill which has three peaks at three corners and in [the] middle is a plateau. . . . The few quarters for men that were there have been pulled down by Sarkar and the place turned into a maidan [an open ground]. In olden days there was severe fighting on this fort and the places where the blood of the warriors fell is still marked by oil and sindoor [red mercury oxide]. . . . On the highest peak there is a small room, known as roothi-rani-romalio. This when translated means, "The room of the Rani who was displeased and lived apart."[13] . . . The ascent is very steep.

XIII. The State Officials

Chief among these is the dewan. Sarkar does not like [him] but dares not turn him out. He talks a good deal of doing so but has not enough energy or will power. He can turn out the poor and weak but funks the strong one. The dewan does not care much about him, and, I fear, will turn out a second Sukhdeo Prasad [Sir Pratap's rival at Jodhpur]. He is very clever and wily. Bukhtawar Singhjee is appointed the military secretary and his brother Kishore Singhjee superintendent of police.[14] Ram Nathjee was to be made the foreign secretary [in charge of relations with the raj via the Political Department] but the dewan does not send him the English papers and Sarkar dares not to force him [to do so]. Kishorjee Bhattee of Vikamkore is made the chief judge. These are the chief officials and I am sorry to write here that most of them are good names but bad presences.

XIV. Finances

The state is in a very bad financial state. Since the great famine, the population is decreased by half, and the product [revenue] is only two lakhs; [Rs 200,000]. Before that the revenue used to be four.[15] Now as long as the population does not increase there are no hopes of the increase of the revenue. Then the state is head and ears in debt. It amounts to over Rs 1,500,000, fifteen lakhs. Seeing the financial state it cannot be paid off before twenty or thirty years and that only if the greatest care is taken and there are no more famines. Sarkar is rather in an unenviable state now. His going to England for the coronation [of Edward VII] and the Delhi durbar [January 1903] will again put the state under an increased debt.

XVI. The People

The people of this part of India are ugly looking and as a rule weak. They resemble the Bunyas [merchant castes]. They don't at all look like soldiers. Even the Rajpoots are of the same type. When placed side by side with one of their brothers from Marwar they look like miserable beggars. Most of them have big stomachs and their [facial] expression . . . is cowardly and poorly. The complexions are quite different from the Marwaris. Those people who had migrated [here] have quite degenerated. I, for myself, would not like to come and settle here.

I like the desert and the desert is my home. I feel very sorry and ashamed when it occurs to my mind that I was myself born in the city of Jaipore. I wish I had seen the light in the desert at Peelva where my forefathers were born. This is the cause of my being weak and not one-tenth so strong as either my father or grandfather. Thank God I was brought up in Jodhpore by Sarkar. That is one great consolation. What small spirit that I think I have in me is owing to that. Otherwise I would have been a real Jaipooree, which means a chicken-hearted fellow when compared to a Jodhpooree. Of course the Gujarat people are better educated, but that does not stand too high in my opinion when I see them degenerated in body and vigour. However, enough of it for the present.

XVIII. The Matrimonial Alliances

Now this is something secret and private, though as most other secrets of Sarkar, it is an open secret. The Idar State being at present hopelessly in debt, something should be done to pay it off. But where is the money to come from? Here is a way. The sister of the Maharaja of Rewah is, according to what I have heard, over thirty years of age. She is also said to be somewhat deformed and having spots of leprosy.[16] People knowing this do not like to marry her. The Rewah people were hankering after the Maharaja of Kishengarh to marry her but he absolutely refused. The Rewah durbar is ready to give eight or nine lakhs of rupees to any of the chiefs who would marry, but no one apparently cares for her. Now Sarkar has sent Ram Nathjee to arrange about this alliance and get the money to pay off his debts.

Sarkar will either marry her himself or to Daulat Singhjee, just as the Maharaja of Rewah will agree to.[17] He wants the money and neither a wife nor a daughter-in-law. If this thing is settled everything will be alright. I don't at all blame Sarkar, for whom there is no other way, but I do blame the Rewah durbar, who is throwing his sister blindly away, knowing full well that her life would be a wretched one. She will never enjoy a married life. Why does he not marry her to one of his nobles or any Rajpoot [other than] a ruling chief, so that the poor girl may enjoy a married life even so late in life? According to the silly notions of the Rajpoots she must be married to a chief and sacrificed. What a pity. . . . [Amar Singh throughout the volumes of his diary firmly opposes the practice of hypergamy, marrying a girl to superiors, widely practiced in Rajputana[18] (see Part V).]

The other place is Khandela, a subordinate noble of Jaipore, who has a daughter. There is no fault with her. She is quite handsome. Her only fault is that she was born in the house of Khandela and so must be sacrificed [by being married to a ruling chief]. The rajajee, as the Khandela chief is known, never dreams of marrying her to anyone but a ruling chief. Ruling chiefs are few and girls like these are more. It would be far better if Khandela married her to some noble of good moral character and education. Then the girl would be always happy and bless her father. If she is married to a ruling chief, he is almost sure to get at least a couple [of wives] more, and then, if any one of them attracts his fancy most, the others may go to the devil. These troubles of the poor and innocent girls are not considered. She must have a ruling chief and none else.

She [the Khandela daughter] is at present about eight years old. Her father is ready to pay a lakh and a half of rupees in cash if any ruling chief would marry her. They tried at Kishengarh but did not succeed. Now they are trying at Idar and most probably the poor and innocent girl will be tied to Daulat Singhjee for all her life. She is too young [for] . . . Daulat Singhjee [who] . . . is over twenty-six. He is not worthy of having such a young girl. It has not yet been settled but will, I think, be done very soon. In this way Idar will pay off its debts and two Rajpoot girls will be sacrificed. Shame on the Rajpoot nation.

I admire the courage and high ideas of Sarkar who married his daughter to Thakoor Sheonath Singhjee of Bera [not a hypergamous marriage]. That is one of the few Rajpoot daughters of the big swells who is enjoying a real life. Both the husband and wife are on good terms and each loves the other with unbounded affection. The daughter of Kishore Singhjee maharaj [member of the royal family] was married to the Boondi chief, against Sarkar's wishes, and I am sorry to write is suffering the common lot that falls to most wives in her position. The Boondi chief is a great drunkard and has some three other wives besides her.[19]

XX. An Anecdote

. . . The other day the durbar sent the maharaj kanwar sahib [heir apparent Daulat Singh] to the resident. Among other things [he] directed him to ask the resident to send on the English papers connected to the state business to his own (durbar's) address direct and not through the dewan. The maharaj kanwar did as he was ordered to. Now as a private friend and also as a courtesy the resident wrote a private letter to the dewan informing him of the durbar's intentions and his working up to it. Naturally the dewan, when he saw the durbar, told him that he had received a private letter to this effect. Sarkar had not the moral courage to own what he had done. He straight away said that he did not want this and he was to continue getting the papers as usual. The dewan wrote back to the resident that it was all a mistake. The durbar does not want any change . . . and the letters are to be sent as usual to the dewan.

Next time, when the durbar saw the resident, the latter said that Daulat Singhjee had told him to send the letters to the durbar but he has now found out through the dewan that it is all a mistake. Sarkar was quite confused and could not explain the matter. There was nothing to explain.

This incident throws a bad light either on Sarkar as an unsettled and fickle man or on the maharaj kanwar as a liar or intriguer. Sarkar wants to do a thing and babbles about but never dares to say so face to face. This is how he lost all his power at Jodhpore. He used to say something to the officials and [then] deny [it] when Sukhdeo Prasadjee asked. He was too afraid of him [Sukhdeo] and never dared to rebuke him face to face, though I have often heard him complaining before the Europeans. I fear the same results here in Idar with the present dewan whom he fears and hates. . . .

Mount Abu, Monday, 19th June, 1905[20]

Notes About My Last Visit to Ahmednagar.

I. The Idea

Once, while my father and I were sitting in the stables, a telegram came to my father from H.H. the Maharaja Pratap Singhjee of Idar as follows: "Is your son Bhanwar Amar Singh at Abu. If so send him here for one day." . . .

[The Maharaja of Idar has now shifted his capital from Idar to Ahmednagar. It lies on the bank of a river and is thought to be a more salubrious site.[21] The city was built by Ahmed Shah, Sultan of Gujarat, in the fifteenth century.[22] When Sir Pratap's father, Takhat Singh, was adopted from Idar to become maharaja at Jodhpur he provoked much anger and jealousy by giving plum patronage jobs to relatives and dependents from Idar. The shoe is now on the other foot: Sir Pratap has brought along a platoon of Jodhpur relatives, none of whom speak Gujarati, to administer the state of Idar.]

IV. Ahmednagar

This is not that Ahmednagar where there is a big [government] horse depot . . . and which is a very well-known place; this is called Idar-Ahmednagar. At one time it was a very big city, though now it is merely a small village. There is a huge wall built all round what used to be an old city.[23] This wall is very high and built of great big solid blocks of stones cemented with lime. There are some gates and any number of bastions. The northern side of the wall has the river Hutmutee flowing under it and thus forms a natural obstacle. Now the wall is broken or down and so are the gates. People bring the stones of this wall to build their houses. The new palace and fort of the maharaja [Sir Pratap] has been built from the stones of this wall. . . . The new polo ground is inside the city walls and so is the race course.

X. Jagat Singh

This boy is the second son of Hurjee [Sir Pratap's dear deceased friend. See Parts I and I]. His elder son, Dalpat Singh, is at present in England where he is being educated. This younger boy lives at Idar with the durbar.

XI. Himmat Singhjee

Himmat Singhjee is the son of Daulat Singhjee [nephew of Sir Pratap and adopted by him as his successor]. This is a very handsome and good looking boy. He has all the qualities of a good man at present and his very face shows him of mild character and gentlemanly habits. Even before there was any talk about this adoption of Idar and this boy was the son of the plain Maharaj Daulat Singhjee I used to love him a great deal. I used to take him in my arms or play polo with him on foot. Now he has become, by adoption, my master and benefactor's grandson and I have every reason to love him.

I am afraid he will be utterly ruined because the durbar keeps him and Jagat Singh together. These two boys live together, eat together, sleep together and play together. I told the maharaj to keep [Himmat Singh] separate but this cannot be done. The durbar [Sir Pratap] . . . says that the others have got to serve to become A.D.C.'s while this boy [Jagat Singh] has done his service, meaning that even if he does not serve, he is entitled to love and gratitude as his father [Hurjee] had done good service. I advised the maharaj kanwar to send Jagat Singh to England with his brother. He had this idea even before [I suggested it] . . . and has been trying to do so but something or other has prevented him up to the present from going.

These boys are made to live with too much restraint. [The regime described is characteristic of Sir Pratap's ascetic principles of childrearing.] They are allowed soup and very little meat with bread and one vegetable. Fruits are allowed but in very small quantities, while there is no allowance of sweetmeats, and milk is given in very small quantities. These boys are allowed only two tolas of water in the whole day and the poor fellows, when they get thirsty, have recourse to the bathroom tub. I asked Jagat Singh whether he ever drank out of the tub and he said he did when he got thirsty. Such is the manner in which the boy is brought up. He is made to wear khaki dress and [is] not allowed to go and see his mother for fear she may feed the boy . . . some luxury. It is this strictness of . . . manner in which boys are brought up and this manner has proved a failure in most cases.[24]

XII. The Jamadars

There are six jamadars [junior commissioned officers who can command mounted troops] and all these have come with the maharaja sahib from Jodhpore. They are Girdhari Singh, Bachan Singh, Banai Singh, Chotu Singh, Zorawar Singh, and Kishore Singh. The first three of these are Jodha Rathores and the fourth a Mertia Rathore. The fifth is a Shekawat and the sixth a Bhatee [Rajput lineages]. They were all of them daffadars [non-commissioned officers] in the Jodhpore Lancers and the durbar has made them jamadars. These jamadars have no sowars [soldiers] to command. There are going to be thirty dispatch riders, and for these thirty men we have six jamadars. The durbar has great bother to control them.

Girdhari Singh lives with the durbar and is the head of them all. Through him they obtain appointments and through him their doings, good as well as bad, are reported. Whoever wants a change of post or any recommendation goes and flatters . . . Girdhari Singh. This fellow is hated by the maharaj kanwar [Daulat Singh]. The jamadars are a great nuisance because they are always quarrelling with one another. These fellows are sent on these appointments by turns. Whoever is appointed becomes the object of envy for the others and then there is great jealousy. They are such fools that [none wishes] . . . to see any one of them in a better position than that of the common lot. . . .

At present Chotu Singh is the superintendent of the district police, while Banai Singh is his assistant. Bachan Singh is looking after the horses and cattle and Kishore Singh after the garden. Zorawar Singh is without any appointment—and is waiting for Girdhari Singh (who is on leave) to come, when he will try to induce him to get some one deposed and get himself put in his place. I hear that these jamadars are taking bribes from the banyas [traders] who supply the gram and from the village people when they go out as police officers. . . .

The jamadars get Rs 40 a month. Sometimes the durbar feeds them at his table and sometimes they feed themselves. These fellows wear solar hats [pith helmets, a British form of dress] and so do some other boys too. This is a great fashion. Some of the Idar people have taken to it and the khaki dress too. . . .

XIII. The Maharaj Kanwar

. . . Daulat Singhjee is in good health and is looking very well. He is supposed to be doing all the work [administering the state] though he does not do it. He used to live in the new house but the durbar worried him too much. [Sir Pratap] . . . put Girdhari Singh in the next room to him. Every hour someone used to come on some pretence or another but with the object of seeing what the maharaj kanwar was doing and who he was talking with. . . .

The maharaj kanwar now spends most of his time in the zenana quarters where there are no spies and botherers. People think him to be in the zenana though in reality he is not in there the whole time. He comes out in the morning and works a horse or two and then goes in the zenana quarters and again comes at breakfast time. . . . He has given the zenana house the name of Fort William and used to joke that once in there, he was safe from all bother.

He does not read or write but spends his time by joking and talking either with his own private men or with his wife. The durbar is not happy there and neither is Daulat Singhjee. They both require company.

XIV. Talks with Daulat Singh

. . . Daulat Singhjee managed to get all the chiefs at Abu to come to Jodhpore house and dine with the late Rajajee Sahib Ajeet Singhjee of Khetri. . . . If Daulat Singhjee did that then I must say that he did a very good thing indeed. Sukhdeo Prasadjee [the present chief minister of Jodhpur] and Babu Kanti Chander [Mukerjee, the late chief minister of Jaipur][25] were of one opinion and were always helping one another. *The babu had been trying his best to excommunicate Khetri Rajajee because he went to England. He could not say so openly and so they blamed him for keeping a Mohammedan concubine mistress.[26]* Had the real intention been known, Sukhdeo would surely have tried to stop the dinner and most probably some of the chiefs would have refused to come.

[The dinner indicates that leading chiefs in Rajputana continue to regard the Raja of Khetri, Ajit Singh, master of Jaipur's second largest thikana, a fellow Rajput, that is, worthy of commensality. It seems likely that the Jaipur maharaja, Madho Singh, not only disapproves of the raja's social practices[27] but also suspects him of ambitions for greater autonomy. When Narain Singh, Amar Singh's father, was Nazim in Shekhawati where Khetri is located, he was charged with conspiring with Khetri's desire for greater autonomy.]

The last though not the least important conversation was that Daulat Singhjee, like me, does not care much about these empty honours and medals of the

British government. We were talking one day and he gave me his photo in uniform. It was then that I told him that I [preferred] . . . one of him [in] native dress and did not at all care for photos in uniforms. It was then that he expressed to me his ideas.

. . . Just one more thing I remembered at the eleventh hour. . . . When Daulat Singhjee was married, he was given a couple of girls to serve his wife. One of them was pretty young but the other a mere girl. Both of them are beautiful. In the beginning there was trouble with the elder girl, who had to be turned away, because Daulat Singhjee began looking with favour on her. There was a great row about that between husband and wife. Now for the younger one, who has just become mature, Daulat Singhjee's wife has begun suspecting and is pressing to have the girl married to someone. They have found a man who is willing to marry her. Daulat Singhjee promises to his wife to arrange this marriage and gives her every assurance. . . .

XV. The Durbar

The durbar [Sir Pratap] is lonely in the midst of a state. He is still spending where he ought not to spend and saving where he ought not to save. Most of the people complain of sickness owing to bad water and climate but this does not seem to affect the maharaja sahib. The work of the state is all going to pot. [Nevertheless Amar Singh was able to praise the cleanliness and orderliness of Ahmednagar.] No one seems to care for it. The durbar has left it on the maharaj kanwar who in his turn evades it by going in the zenana and so the people rot. . . . There is no dewan [indicating that Sir Pratap, contrary to Amar Singh's expectations in 1902, managed to rid himself of "another Sukhdeo Prasad"]. The maharaj kanwar is supposed to be doing that but he does not fulfill his duties. In the same manner the other posts are changed and the work spoiled.

The durbar wanted to confiscate the lands of several people. They appealed to the government of India, who, of course, gave justice. This was a blow to the durbar. He thinks he can do what he likes, and used to do at Jodhpore, but he ought to know that Gujarat is an educated and civilised country. The people know the laws, and he cannot have all things his own way. He has now begun to realise it. . . .

XVII. Leave Giving

When I was about to come away the durbar ordered to arrange for ghora siropao [a horse and set of clothing given to honored visitors]. I said that this ought not to be done as I was like one of his own private servants and besides this I had not come officially. After some arguing he told me that I was to obey and not argue with him. I did accept it. This ghora siropao was sent to me afterwards because at that time the treasury was closed. The ghora siropao sent to me was Rs 150. Other presents besides this were some photos, a pair of spurs, a couple of Idar-bred grey hounds and, last though not least, two books, *Annals and Antiquities of Rajasthan*, by Col. James Tod and *Ras Mala* by Col. Forbes.[28] The former is a very expensive book and cannot be got for even a thousand rupees. It was very kind of the durbar and maharaj kanwar to let me have these books.

Ram Nathjee, when I wrote to him about these, said that I had robbed Idar of two of its best jewels. He is quite right, but these jewels were not appreciated there at present. . . .

3

H.H. Kishengarh Marries at Udaipur:
The Ceremonial Enactment of Inferiority

[Until Queen Victoria's 1858 proclamation ending East India Company rule, Rajput marriages were more a matter of political alliance and dynastic aggrandizement than of social mobility and financial advantage. The Pax Britannica that followed crown rule in 1858 eliminated the security concerns that had fueled political alliances, and, by freezing the status quo, reduced the importance of dynastic ambition in marriage calculations. In the second half of the nineteenth century marriages increasingly became matters of honor and wealth, an arena for the pursuit of social status and economic advantage.

In the seven years of the diary covered in this volume, Amar Singh writes ethnographic accounts of five marriages of which we reproduce only two, his own (see Part III) and that of the Maharaja of Kishengarh.[1] Amar Singh attends the wedding of Maharaja Madan Singh of Kishengarh as a guest of the groom, and as a member of the party from Alwar state; Kishengarh's sister is married to the maharaja of that state. He accompanies his father, Narain Singh, Kanwar of Kanota and a senior minister at Alwar. Maharaja Madan Singh, four years junior to Amar Singh, has been a fellow cadet for two years at the ICC and Amar Singh's most intimate friend at the Corps (See Part IV).

Kishengarh is being married to the daughter of the Maharana of Udaipur (Mewar), "the proudest house in Rajpootana." The marriage is remarkable for its inversion of the hypergamy that Amar Singh has frequently deplored.[2] By the hypergamous standard which leads Rajputs to marry their daughters to superior houses, the Udaipur-Kishengarh alliance is an anomaly. Kishengarh is a lesser state with limited revenue and little wealth, Udaipur, also known as Mewar, the most prestigious kingdom of Rajputana with substantial revenue and considerable wealth. The maharana's daughter is marrying "down." But Udaipur, like the later Mughals, was peculiarly positioned with respect to marrying its daughters.

The practice of hypergamy by houses like the Mughals and Mewar that see themselves as superior to others raises in acute form the question of how to marry off their daughters.[3] From Rana Pratap's time Udaipur limited its choices by rejecting marriages with Mughal emperors and their sons, the obvious candidates for a hypergamous marriage. Other Rajput rulers saw the matter differently; Frances Taft documents twenty-seven Mughal-Rajput "royal" marriages and tells us that the Mughal emperor Jahangir's mother may have been the sister of the Amber [later Jaipur] Raja Bharmal.[4] Obliged to accept Mughal over-lordship in 1614, Udaipur maharanas continued to interpret marriage alliances with Mughals as "bowing the head," a mark not only of subordination and inferiority but also, from Rana Raj Singh's reign (1652–1680) as a violation of Hindu

PHOTO VI-4   Amar Singh [right] with Maharaja Madan Singh of Kishengarh, a small princely state near Ajmer in the center of Rajasthan. They are steady companions at the Imperial Cadet Corps. Seven years his senior, Amar Singh finds the maharaja "a nice little boy with good manners . . . " "for whom I have a sort of paternal love. He had been practically put under my charge by his prime minister." Amar Singh and his father, Narain Singh, are key members of Madan Singh's wedding party when he marries the daughter of the Maharana of Udaipur. The maharana, conscious of his standing as the premier Rajput prince, misses no chance to remind Kishengarh of his inferior status. Amar Singh's photo albums.

dharma. In consequence, it seems to be the case that from Pratap Singh (1540–1597) to Raj Singh (1652–1680) Udaipur rulers also shunned exchange (equal) marriages with Rajput kingdoms that married daughters to Mughal rulers or princes. Thereafter there seem to have been Udaipur marriages with Rajput houses that had given daughters to the Mughals.[5] Nevertheless, after Colonel Tod's canonical Udaipur-centric reading of Rajput history in his *Annals and Antiquities of Rajasthan* (1829, 1832), extensive evidence of the use of political marriages by Mughal and Rajput rulers was ignored and suppressed by Indian and British historians of the princely states.[6] Udaipur's tradition of upholding Rajput honor, independence and "purity" by not making hypergamous marriages with daughters of Mughal ruling families and by avoiding exchange marriages with Rajput kingdoms which engaged in such marriages became the dominant view in raj and nationalist historiography.[7]

The implication of this history for the Kishengarh-Udaipur wedding is that since there are no obvious "superiors" to Udaipur, the rulers have shown willingness to marry daughters to "inferiors," including its own nobles and modest princely houses of good blood, like Kishengarh.

In the late nineteenth and early twentieth centuries Udaipur's claim to superior standing was fed by British romantic[8] and Hindu nationalist historiography (See Introduction, 1)[9] and by a medievalist mentality[10] that put a premium on Mewar's ancient pedigree.[11] In the present account, Mewar's maharana, Fateh Singh, is father of the bride. Little is known about her, but a great deal is known about him.[12] His conservative outlook, Hindu orthopraxy, and aversion to innovation led him to oppose British-inspired administrative reforms and British cultural influences and to adhere to a stringent standard of ceremonial punctiliousness.

Under Fateh Singh's rule the tiny complement of metalled roads in Udaipur fell from 270 to 257 miles and he long resisted the extension of the railway line from the famous fort city of Chitor to Udaipur. Because his idea of personal rule was to concentrate all functions and all paperwork in his own person, and because he feared a prime minister might become a British tool, he refused to appoint one.[13] Administrative and judicial activity of the sort valued by Political Department rationalizers languished. Efficiency reigned however in projects which the maharana favored: he restored the historic Kumbhalgarh fort and meticulously preserved the extensive royal hunting lands.

The Kishengarh wedding party is treated with haughtiness by the Udaipur rana, reversing the conventional role of a bride-giver. The rana chooses to ignore the relationship he bears to Kishengarh as father of the bride—which places him in a supplicant posture—and instead stresses his position as a ruler, which places Udaipur and its nobles in a superior role. Amar Singh responds to the rana's ostentatious ceremonial profanations with characteristic impatience to such status games: "If Odeypore is so big, why the devil does he give his daughter to Kishengarh?"]

Dramatis Personae

Madan Singh, Maharaja of Kishengarh, the groom.

Shishodianiji, the bride, woman of the Shishodia lineage, daughter of Maharana Fateh Singh of Udaipur [off stage, invisible, and unreported].

Narain Singh, Amar Singh's father, a leading guest.

Syam Sunder Lall, Prime Minister of Kishengarh.

Maharana Fateh Singh of Udaipur, father of the bride.

The Baraat, the groom's wedding party.

Meerut, Thursday, 18th February, 1904

Notes About Kishengarh Durbar's Marriage.

V. Journey [to Udaipur] in the Special

[Wedding journeys include elaborate travel arrangements to convey the groom's party, the baarat, to the bride's home. Amar Singh boards the train carrying the Kishengarh baraat, consisting mostly of men from Alwar state.] The train was rather overcrowded. There were thirty-seven carriages in it, and this is the limit of carriages that the railway people put in a special. There was not much room for all. Syam Sunder Lalljee [the Kishengarh prime minister] had made good arrangements [by posting] . . . cardboards on each carriage on which the names of the would-be occupants were written. This arrangement was all spoiled by our people, who are not only ignorant but fools and . . . [spoilers] of other people's works. These guests were asked to send in a list of their servants that they would take with them in the special train. This work the worthies declined; I do not know from what motives. The result was that they brought more men than they were expected to or there was room for in the train. This naturally caused a great inconvenience. . . . The people who were given first and second class tickets wanted to have their servants in the same carriage. I will give the instance of my own carriage. There were to be Rao Raja Amar Singhjee, the Raojee of Banarwara, Joshi Ash Karanjee, and myself in it. . . . The Raojee of Banarwara had two of his servants and Ash Karanjee about four of his menials in the first class, in which there were only four seats. The raojee had told to the baboojee that he would prefer travelling even third class if he could have his servants with him in the same compartment. To this Syam Sundar Lalljee said that it was too low for his dignity . . . [but] he could do it if he liked. . . . When these fellows travel by themselves they buy third or intermediate tickets, but on such occasions they want first class carriages . . . reserved to themselves.

Besides the above mentioned difficulties . . . we travelled happily and had a good time of it. Just one station before Debari the train stopped for one hour for us to dress. All the people were in good spirits and decking themselves in their best apparel. The durbar [Madan Singh, Maharaja of Kishengarh] was travelling in the Jodhpore saloon carriage [an elegantly fitted bogie borrowed from his more prosperous Rathore lineage brother, Sardar Singh, Maharaja of Jodhpur].

We reached Odeypore without any further event worth noticing. At the station I had expected to find the maharana sahib [Fateh Singh] but he was not there—no, not even any big sardar was sent to receive us. We were still to learn what was in store for us and what was the idea of the maharana sahib. There was no decoration on the railway station [usual when welcoming a wedding party]. Everything was as usual except that there was a good collection of carriages and other conveniences which were of course our own. The Odeypore people had nothing to do with it.

V. Reception[14]

... There was neither the maharana sahib nor any of his sardars at the station. We got out of our [railway] carriages and went out of the station. There was some half an hour spent in the usual formal questions and inquiries as to where the reception was to be. At last we got into our carriages. The durbar had Syam Sunder Lalljee and my father with him in the state carriage which was a really handsome one drawn by four big grey Walers. The whole of this suite had been borrowed from Jodhpore. There was a great rush for carriages. It was exactly the same thing as before. People took their servants with them and thus occupied all the seats. It was only a place for rowdy beggars. Gentlemen were badly handicapped.

The reception itself was not much. . . . There was this argument, that Kishengarh durbar should do the nichrawal [an act of recognition and respect[15]] of the maharana sahib but not the latter of the former. It was to be done from the maharana sahib's side by one of his nobles. Then the nobles of Odeypore were to meet Kishengarh durbar but the Kishengarh sardars were not to meet the maharana sahib. This was too ridiculous. . . . [Instead] both the chiefs met, and, as there were only Odeypore sardars present at that very moment, they did the nichrawal ceremony and thus the thing was patched up. These formal things [that is, the nobles meeting with the rulers] were postponed for a regular durbar [court assemblage].

This meeting [of the two rulers] took place at a bridge on the river about a quarter of a mile from the city gate. After this the maharana sahib got in our durbar's carriage and drove up to the city gate from whence he took leave and went to his palace in his own carriage. There was not much fun on this occasion. . . . The Kishengarh people were not at all pleased at this reception. They were made to succumb at every point, which was not good on the part of the maharana sahib. . . .

VI. The Camp

Our camp had been beautifully planned and laid out by Poorkha who had come from Jodhpore. [*Poorkha* is a Jodhpur specialist at camp-making, a highly developed art in the princely states, whose large hunting and marriage parties were accommodated in tents]. All the tents had been borrowed from that state. The entrance was a gate of bamboo work, covered with red cloth. In the centre was a road with two oval grass plots and roads running on both sides of them and in between them as well. In the front was the big shamiana [a flat tent-roof, usually with sides] which was for the usual dances. Behind it was the reception room and then the drawing room tent. Further on were the zenana tents, protected with big kanats [screens].

On both sides of the drawing room [tent] were two tents, one of which was prepared for the durbar and the other was occupied by my father and myself [who were evidently the most honored guests in the Kishengarh party]. Then there were two lines of tents on both sides which met at the red gate. In the middle of the side line of tents there were two small squares in which there were big tents. These were meant to increase the number of tents as well as the beauty of the camp. The roads were well laid out and made of red gravel, which was marked by the green doob [turf] and white stones. To add to all this charm was the flagstaff and the water spout, which was working the whole time.

In my opinion the camp was very well laid out indeed and there was room for twice as many men as we had with us but unfortunately there was no room for gentlemen. People made a rush for tents and secured the biggest they could lay hands on. For instance Ash Karanjee secured a double-poled tent quite for himself and would not take another man with him. . . . I have often to mention his name but this is not because I have any ill feeling for him. It is simply because he was the prominent mischief maker. I wonder why such a wretched fellow was invited.

Syam Sunder Lall could not find room for Ram Nathjee and Nathu Lalljee, brought them to our tent and asked my father if he would take them in. My father was only too glad and said if there was inconvenience more could be sent, as he did not mind company. It would have been best if names had been put on the tents beforehand but this again could not be done. Sunder Lalljee wanted to do it but could not because nobody was sure until the very last minute as to who will accompany and who will not. Such are the comforts and enjoyments of camp life in marriage parties in Rajpootana. The gentlemen starve while the rowdy fellows are comfortable.

VII. Procession to the Toran

Up to the last moment it was not settled as to when, i.e. at what exact time, the ceremony would take place. There were two times [Presumably set by the astrologers]. One was just when the sun was setting . . . and the other four o'clock in the morning. Everyone was in favour of the former and so the ceremonies that come before were hastily gone through. These were the tika [cash and jewels given by the girl's family at the time of the engagement or just before the marriage] from the Odeypore side and the pudhla [clothes and ornaments sent by the bridegroom for his bride-to-be] from ours. The maharana sahib gave one elephant and nine horses on this occasion. The latter were good animals. I had two occasions to observe what sort of horses were given. The first was when the maharaj kanwar sahib, the present durbar of Jodhpore [Sardar Singh], was married. On that occasion the horses given by Boondi were absolutely rotten animals. The other occasion was when the Maharao of Boondi was married at Jodhpore. On the latter occasion I well remember Sarkar sent for all the casters [cast-offs] from the regiment and gave the worst of even that lot. On this, the Odeypore occasion, the animals were all of them good ones and one was an Arab.

At about four in the evening the [groom's] procession started. First of all went the usual thing i.e. the lead horses, the kettle drums, the colours, etc. Then there were eight big sardars [noblemen] on horses and my father was the leading figure of the lot. I am not only glad but proud to say that he was looking the best man in the whole procession. He was riding my horse Soodarsan and had a plain saddle which made him still more conspicuous. He was about three feet higher than anyone on horseback there. The horse was doing justice to the rider and the rider to the horse. . . .

After these horsemen was the elephant of the durbar who was dressed in purple clothes. Thakoor Bharat Singhjee was occupying the back of the howdah [seat]. There were more elephants, one on each side of the durbar. . . . Behind the elephants were the carriages which were occupied by those people who were big men but not yet quite big enough to ride horses. . . . We were most of us in . . . [carriages]. The rest of the people walked. I fear it did not make an impressive show because everything became short and compact.

Each carriage held some five gentlemen. As usual there was a rush for carriages. Ash Karan occupied a four-in-hand carriage quite by himself and his wretched servants. I was to have my seat in that carriage and when I went there Ash Karan offered me the front [coachman's] seat. I had half a mind to throw him out of the carriage but it would have been bad form on this occasion. . . .

This is the first time I have seen the people going in conveyances when following a bridegroom [instead of walking]. The bridegroom is given the place of a king for the time being. He is the only one who is either on an elephant, a horse or a palanquin. The rest must . . . follow. When my father and uncles were married, Jaipore durbar Ram Singhjee walked. When I myself was married, Sarkar walked by my side. The bridegroom is called beend raja and so he is treated. Way is always made for him. . . .

. . . Close to the chief gate . . . the toran was ready [a ceremonial plaque hung over the gateway to the bride's quarters. The groom, mounted on an elephant or horse, touches it with a sword or staff]. I had never seen such a big toran. It was a huge thing . . . [with] any number of wooden models of women on it. . . . The durbar [touched] it with his sword. Having alighted from the elephant the ceremony was done. . . . [Then] near relations of the bride come and make the bridegroom sit and perform some ceremonies. . . . We all went away because the maharana sahib was not there and none of his nobles were present. . . .

After I had my dinner my father told me to go to the palace and come back with the durbar [H.H. Kishengarh, after the marriage ceremony conducted in the bride's home] as it would look nice. . . . I had a mind of going and cracking some jokes at the durbar but Ram Nath kept me back as there were several women walking around the mahdol [covered palanquin in which the couple is carried].

Arrived at our camp the mahdol [carrying the bride] was taken in the zenana tent. We came out [of our tent] when I saw people gathering to show their nuzzars [a ceremonial offering from an inferior to a superior]. I slunk away because I cannot show nuzzar and if I did not do so while all the others did it would look . . . odd.

[The reasons for this slinking away become clear from an earlier entry:] *I asked my father whether I ought to show nuzzar to Kishengarh durbar on his birthday. My father said that we have never done so and ought not to as there is ground for an objection from the Jaipore durbar. The reason is that between big states the sardars of one state show nuzzar to the maharaja of the other state. . . . This custom has never been observed with [the small state of] Kishengarh either in Jaipore or Jodhpore. I was told that if an occasion arose I was to explain my position to the durbar and ask his pardon. My father personally has no objection as the durbar is treating us in such a friendly manner. Of course the late maharaja [of Kishengarh] used to look upon us as inferior beings and never used to dine with us, I mean my father. The result was that my father had, on two or three occasions, to show them rudeness for which he is now sorry but all the same they deserved all that. . . . [16*]

VIII. The Illumination

I think the best sight . . . was this function. The palace, the bank of the Pichola, Jugmandir, Jugnewas and several other palaces in or about the lake were lit with lamps. Such a fine show as this I have never before seen though I have had the luck to witness such sights in several other states. The lake was the one thing that added charm to the show. The two places, Jugmandir and Jugnewas, in the middle of the lake, looked as if they had been built of fire. We got into boats. When we got midway, the scene became awfully charming. At the end of the show they let off some fire works.

The reason of my not stopping was that the best boats had been reserved for Europeans and I did not like to crowd in the big boat with the whole of the other lot . . .

IX. Dinner to Europeans

On the same night that the illumination took place there was a big dinner given to the European guests. [Apparently many of the political officers deputed to the Rajput states attended, including the chief British officer in Rajputana, the AGG.] There was this arrangement. After the dinner was over the Agent [to the] Governor General would propose the health of the bride and the bridegroom, then Kishengarh durbar would get up and thank all the people for their kindness in drinking the health. . . . [Before this could happen] . . . the . . . maharana sahib sent the durbar in the zenana on pretence of performing some ceremonies and he did not come out again until next morning. . . . I learned afterwards that Colonel Pears, the resident of Jaipore, answered the toast instead of the durbar. I cannot understand why the maharana sahib did not want the durbar to say a few words personally. [Again the implication is that honoring Kishengarh would be an act of lèse majesté on the part of Udaipur.]

. . . Look at the ideas of these people. The Europeans take their boats [to] the palace but we natives are not allowed. How ridiculous. In the same manner, no Indian is allowed to shoot or fish in the Pichola, but Europeans may do. These are the ways of the world.

X. The Reciting of Poetry

There was one occasion when there was a sort of a durbar in the [Kishengarh] camp. The maharaja sahib [of Kishengarh] sat on a chair and such fellows as waited [on him] came and showed their nuzzars. After this ceremony was over, the charans [bards] and some pundits [learned men, Brahmans] began to recite the poetry that they had themselves composed in praise of the durbar and the occasion. As a rule such things are nonsense. I like the poetry when it praises or criticizes a man according to his merits. Unfortunately our bards don't follow this rule. . . . This has become a sort of profession for flattering big people. On this particular occasion the poetry was nothing more than humbug. What was the good or the exceptional that the durbar had done? He was married, as all the other people are married. He was just as handsome as most of the boys in the camp or the city. It is these false praises that swell the brains of the big people and bring about their ruin. . . .

XI. At Home

One day the [Udaipur] durbar and his party were "at home." All the European guests came to tea. There was dancing and some photographs were taken as well. The maharana sahib had sent for some Highlanders and their playing upon their pipes was excellent. Then there was a band from Alwar and some dancing girls from Jodhpore. The shamiana in which the gathering took place was beautifully furnished with old arms and coats of mail and rich carpets, some of which were the gold embroidered elephant jhools [covers]. There were very few people whom I knew and even these were engaged in talking to others.

We Indians cut a ridiculous figure everywhere. For instance, on this particular occasion, the Europeans were standing, talking and enjoying themselves while our people stood in two rows near the entrance like mummies. It was Durbar's intention to call only a few of us who could talk English or understand etiquette but our people [did] . . . not listen . . . They must all come whether they cut a good or a bad figure.

After the photographic business was over all the good horses of the durbar and those that were given in the tika were brought and made to walk in a circle. This over, we had some jumping. There were my two good horses, Soodarsan and Kingfisher. First I jumped the former and then the latter. Kingfisher jumped some twenty-two feet. . . . I am sorry they did not measure the leap that my horse took. The jump was a sheet of white cloth. . . . For Kingfisher the jump was only long, but for Soodarsan it was both long and high. After the jumping was over I showed the people how quick the horse could turn in spite of his great bulk. People admired my horses and my riding a great deal. My father told me afterwards that I did very well except that I was leaning a bit forward instead of backward when going over a jump. Soodarsan has become quite a famous horse by this jumping. . . .

XII. I Go to See the Maharana Sahib

I had a mind of going to see the maharana sahib and had spoken to Fateh Karan-jee [an influential charan at court and a friend of Amar Singh's father] about it . . . Word was sent if Narain Singhjee and his son had leisure and wanted to come, the maharana sahib would like to see them, but at the same time we need not come if there was any inconvenience. . . .

The others had their pugrees on but I had my safa [*pugree* is the tight small turban worn at Udaipur; *sapha* the larger, looser turban of Jodhpur]. The dress was a silk achkan [long, fitted knee-length coat with a high collar] shoes, etc. The maharana sahib was sitting on a chair [with] . . . two rows of chairs on each side. The right row was occupied by about seven of his nobles. . . . The row on the left was reserved for us. Some dancing girls . . . were singing. As soon as we came in the maharana sahib rose and we showed our nuzzars. First was Simrath Singhjee, then Akhai Singhjee and after myself. The nuzzars of the first two were accepted but not mine. I protested that it ought to be taken, but he continued saying "no it is all right." He of course touched.[17] . . . I asked why my nuzzar was not accepted, to which Fateh Karanjee said that [it was] because I was a boy. This put me on the false scent, and I withdrew after touching the skirts of the maharana sahib's achkan. . . .

[Exchanges in court settings can be complex games of one-upmanship. Narain Singh's reputation rests partly on the adroitness of his repartee on his own behalf and on behalf of those he serves. In the conversation during the meeting with the Udaipur ruler the maharana seems to have implied that people at Kishengarh or Jaipur were willing to eat things or wear things that would not be eaten or worn at Udaipur.] At one time the maharana sahib wanted to turn the talk on eating and dressing with a purpose to mock us, but my father was quick to the moment. He took the conversation in his own hands. He began by saying that whatever is aleen [not fit to be eaten] can never be made leen [fit to be eaten]. [It] does not matter how you cook it. At the same time whatever is leen can never be aleen. Now remains the question of cooking, which can be done to anyone's particular taste. Then he began the talk of dressing. . . . The dress should be worn as best suited to the occasion; for instance, at the present moment there ought to be achkans and jewels and such like things while there was durbar being held, but this won't answer the purpose of shooting, for on that occasion we ought to have a strong cloth and coats, otherwise the long skirts of the achkans would get entangled in the thorny bushes. The maharana sahib did not speak a single word in contradiction.

My father had said these things because the other day when we had gone out shooting the maharana sahib and his followers were wearing achkans. There were occasions on which two servants used to come up and hold the skirts of the maharana sahib's achkan. . . .

After we had sat down, the maharana sahib ordered the wine to be brought in. I of course refused. [Amar Singh does not drink in the presence of his father, and possibly of other elders.] First it was brandy and soda water, and afterwards some deshi wine [local wine, possibly the famous Udaipur asha]. I noticed one peculiar thing. The maharana sahib was sitting on a chair . . . [with] about half a dozen men standing behind him. Whenever anyone came to whisper anything, he either put his hand or his handkerchief, whichever was handy, to his face before speaking. It amused me awfully to see them do this.

There was one special man who had the charge of the maharana sahib's wine glass. Whenever the maharana sahib wanted to have a sip, he lifted his hand and the glass was handed over by this particular man. After the sip had been taken and the glass returned, a small handkerchief was handed over, by which the maharana sahib wiped his lips. This process was repeated every time that a sip was taken.[18]

This I have seen and so can quite believe another story which I have heard. . . . Whenever there is a big dinner and a pantia [dining cross-legged seated on the floor in rows] the maharana sahib picks something out of the plate, puts it into his mouth [then] raises his hand . . . a servant, who is specially told off for this duty, carefully wipes off every finger. When another mouthful is taken, the same process is gone through, and this does not stop until the meal is over. . . .

On this occasion the maharana sahib was dressed in a tight green silk angarkhi [fitted coat with round cut-out front] with a thin line of silver embroidery at the edges. The turban was quite simple. The maharana sahib is about forty-five years of age and is a fine looking man. He is rather thin, and his tone is mild and sweet. I have heard that he is very obstinate and self-satisfied. He is a real orthodox Hindoo. He is very fond of shooting and spends days and days in the jungle. All the hills have small odis [shooting boxes] built on every possible place where there is the chance of any animals going. I hear he is very fond of riding, but his stables are not worth much. The horses there are simply as fat as bulls. . . .

After our return home my father told me something about the nuzzar. The reason why the maharana did not accept mine was because I had shown [it] at a time while he was standing. Nowhere in the state [is] this honour paid to kanwars and banwars [sons and grandsons of thakurs]. Another thing that he did not like was that I touched his feet. My father was afraid that he [the maharana] might . . . jump aside to avoid my touching his feet. The reason is that touching the feet is considered equivalent to embracing. . . . I did not know any of these rules. I had several times shown nuzzar to [the] Jaipore and Jodhpore durbars and [they had] been accepted standing and sitting both. . . . My idea was that a son of a tazimi sardar [one honored by the maharaja by being allowed to wear gold anklets] was entitled to it . . .

XIV. The Shikar [Hunt]

There is plenty of shikar in Odeypore and this is of all sorts. There is small game as well as big. . . . Each hill has got its odi and there are narrow roads cut to walk from one odi to the other so that there is not much trouble. . . . What I liked best about shikar in Odeypore was the arrangement of beating [to drive the animals toward the hunters]. There are some eight hundred Bheels [a "tribal" people subjugated by the early rulers of Mewar] employed for this very work. They wear a khaki uniform and work by words of command as well as trumpet call. Their beating is the most perfect thing, because they have one man looking after them who brings them along in perfect order.

. . . This system saves the poor people of Odeypore from a lot of jhulum [injustice]. I know of instances where the poor villagers are collected [like] herds of cattle [to do the beating]. No consideration is given to age or work. Old men are brought out and sometimes even [the] sick. Farmers are dragged who are looking after their crops. The result is that their fields are laid waste by cattle in their absence. . . .

Another jhulum connected with shikar is when a kill is arranged for tigers. On these occasions the shikarees . . . catch a young . . . buffalo that is giving milk. They would prefer a young cow to a young bull because the former is more valuable to the poor husbandman. These rascals even go so far as to catch big buffaloes that are giving milk. The price given by the state is very little—a good buffalo is worth at least fifty rupees. If that animal is taken away . . . the poor man's family must starve because there is no more milk to be had. The state empowers these ruffians to take by force young buffaloes because [it] knows people don't like to sell animals . . . to be used as kills. This [permission to take animals by force] applies to young bull buffaloes, not to full grown and milking ones [which the shikaris are not supposed to take]. All this is done to tease the poor man who gives a couple of rupees to these shikarees, who in turn leave him and find someone else with whom they play the same game. . . .

XX. The City

The city is situated below the Pichola tank. . . . The palace commands a good view of . . . [Pichola]. . . . The city has no municipality committee but the police do their duty and do it creditably. There is no bad smell even in the narrowest lanes; at least I never felt [one in] those that I passed through and some of them were very narrow . . . The principal streets are lighted and most of them have good pukka [concrete] roads. The cleanest city that I had seen was Idar, and Odeypore is second only to that. . . . There is nothing of prettiness about the place. The wall round the city[19] is in good order and there is a ditch too. The city gates are small and narrow and nothing like Jaipore. . . .

XXI. Roads

There are plenty of roads and they are all of them in very good order. . . . I had never expected to find Odeypore in such an advanced state. My idea of Odeypore was that this place would be something like Boondi was when I saw the latter at the Jodhpore durbar's marriage.[20] . . . The roads . . . the city . . . are all lighted by oil lamps, which is a poor contrivance but I now see that the palace is being fitted out with electric light and hope the city roads will also be allowed to have this beneficial system. . . .

XXIV. Allowing People in the Zenana

This is a question that the [Kishengarh] durbar had discussed with me several times and with Ram Nathjee as well. I had advised him never to allow any man, how ever near he may be, in the zenana. Not only men but even boys ought not to be allowed, as these things are not good in the end. . . . I went even so far as to stop the going in of strange women and European ladies. Why should they be allowed to go in? Some of them write diaries and some . . . stories in the magazines. When they have seen our zenanas they go and describe them to the public, which is a thing we don't want . . .

In my own family neither my grandfather nor my father ever allow anyone to go in. I am still more strict and I don't even let boys go in whenever I am there. These boys are the sons of the women who serve in the zenana. . . . I know none of the ladies approve, and even say that all the three, meaning my grandfather, my father and myself, are alike. I am glad they think so.

XXVI. Father's Advice

Of course there was advice in every word that my father spoke to me. However, I shall narrate the particular episode on which some serious advice was given. One night, after everyone had gone to bed, Govind Singhjee came and woke me. He asked me to come and join the party that [they] were having, some drinking and singing, in Akhai Singhjee's room. I refused for some time but Govind Singhjee persisted so much that I had to give in. . . . I was advised to come away stealthily by the drawing room, but this I refused, and went by my father's [room] even speaking loudly that he may hear and know that I was not doing a thing with the intention of hiding it.

The singing was all rotten. It might have been very good but I am no judge for these things. There was some drinking and I was forced to take a few sips. What was most annoying to me was when one of the singing girls came up and, taking the tumbler, volunteered to give me her manwar [an exchange of food among equals, here a gesture of intimacy]. This I refused to accept and never took, even though the others forced me. Amar Singhjee [from Alwar] was the man who accepted these every time that one of the girls came up.

I remember the fascinating manner in which the girl spoke to me [about] why I was so unkind to the patars, meaning prostitutes. I said I was not unkind but would not drink. These words still haunt me and I sometimes dream of them, though I honestly write that I had not the slightest desire towards her. I don't wonder that these girls are the ruin of several people. They are not to be blamed for it. It is their profession.

However, to take to my story. I took leave at midnight. They wanted to stop me . . . but I said that if they forced me too much this time I would not come again. I went straight to bed. The first thing I did in the morning was [to tell] . . . Ram Nathjee to acquaint my father with the story. . . . If he hears of it from any other source he would not like my conduct, and besides this, I did not want anything to be hidden from him. . . . When Ram Nathjee had heard (my story) . . . he said I ought not to have gone [to the party]. However, what was done was done .

. . . On the night after our return from the visit to the maharana sahib, my father stood outside our tent and began to lecture me on this subject. He said that he was surprised to hear that I had gone stealthily from him and that the whole time we were out he was feeling the matter very much, that his son was trying to play hide and seek with him. At the same time he was sure that his sons won't do any mischief He gave a long lecture, depicting horrors of all sorts. . . . He said that I had still to form my character. If people even saw me with such company, they would begin thinking badly of me. . . . He gave several instances as he alone could give. . . . He was thankful that [Ram Nathji] . . . had expressed his disapproval to me even without his [Narain Singh's] asking him to do so.

After all this was said I informed my father that Ram Nathjee knew nothing of the matter until I told him [about it] in the morning, and that I had particularly asked him to inform [him] all about it. . . . I told (my father) . . . that I had not followed the advice of going stealthily but had gone by the front door talking loudly [and that] I had been warned by Kaloo [Amar Singh's servant] that I was committing a chor ["theft"]. I had answered that the very first thing in the morning will be the confession by my own lips. When my father heard this he was quite pleased. . . .

This incident has given a proof to my father that I will not do such things and even if I do I will never hide [them] from him. He told me that "Amar Singhjee and the other lot from Alwar were the worst possible fellows." Had I refused and said . . . I would not come I would have been a great man in their estimation. . . . My refusing to go would have displeased them for a time but would have been good for [my reputation].

That very night, after this explanation, there was a great talk between Ram Nathjee and my father. I was hearing it while writing my diary and found that everything was in my favour by the grace of God.

XXIX. How We were Treated

. . . This I fear was not at all satisfactory. . . . Wherever there is a marriage in Rajpootana the bride's father comes forward and shows his humbleness [to the groom], but here the matter was quite different. The maharana was showing indifference time after time.

The first thing was that he did not come to the station. The second was not doing the nichrawal of Kishengarh durbar. People will say that this is because Odeypore [as a state] does not do this for Kishengarh. This may hold good when state visits are paid, but this was a quite different occasion. At the present moment [on the occasion of a marriage] all that possibly can be done [for the groom] ought to be done. . . . If Odeypore is so big why the devil does he give his daughter to Kishengarh. . . . This was the occasion when the maharana ought to have met each of the Kishengarh nobles and enquired after their health, which would have raised him in [their] esteem. These are the ideas that never pass the heads of our people. They think that true greatness comes in . . . slighting other people.

I cannot help giving an instance of true greatness here. While the American president George Washington was walking with a friend in the streets of one of the great cities, a Negro passing by raised his hat to them. Washington raised his still higher in return. The friend remonstrated that the fellow was merely a Negro, to which Washington replied that he did not want to be beaten by a Negro in politeness. Now this is real greatness. . . .

In the same manner our ruling chiefs and big men do not return the salaam of the poorer people thinking it below their dignity. . . . Then the maharana never came to our camp even . . . once. This was showing downright insult. He never called the bridal party to a dinner . . . in his palace, which is another mistake. This shows that either he was too proud to eat with us or did not think us pure enough. No entertainments were prepared for us [and] . . . the shikar arrangements were not made. This too showed indifference.

. . . The boats were ever ready for the European guests, but those from the [Kishengarh] camp may wander about and still never get anything. The Europeans had good shooting but we fellows had none. What was given in the dowry I have no idea. I wanted very much to see it so but could not. . . . To sum up, our treatment at Odeypore was not [as] warm as one could expect on such occasions. . . .

XVII. My Talks with Ram Nathjee[21]*

I had several talks with Ram Nathjee . . . he told me that the maharana sahib of Odeypore has given a very good dowry to his daughter [when she married the Maharaja of Kishengarh]. They did not show the things at Odeypore. People began to suspect that they don't want to show because they have not given enough. Those that came from Odeypore had orders that they may show the things if Kishengarh people wanted to see [them], otherwise there was no necessity. At first the [Kishengarh] dewan and other people did not show [the dowry] but after a time . . . the things were laid out in the zenana. . . . The durbar [Kishengarh] called a select few to see [the dowry] and Ram Nathjee was one of them.

[Ram Nathji told] . . . me that there was one complete set [of ornaments] with diamonds and another one with pearls. Besides this, there were two sets in plain gold. In addition to all these there were some extra ornaments too. There was no counting the other gold and silver utensils and clothes. . . . He estimated the things at over Rs 300,000. In addition . . . there were thirty-five horses and five elephants. What can people want? I have forgotten to mention the rifle which too is a very good one. The durbar [Kishengarh] was telling me that it was not really so much. Ram Nathjee's opinion was that either the durbar does not know the value of these things or he does not want to say so. However, be that as it may, it is a handsome dowry and such as this state has probably never had. . . .

XXXII. The Return Journey

We had a hard time of it at the very beginning. At Chittor junction the waiting room was a small one. There was only one table which had a looking glass on it. I found some trouble to write [the diary]. I went to the ladies' [waiting] room. That place had a table in the middle but there was no chair that could be used with it. They were all easy chairs. What a nuisance it was to me. . . .

The only good thing in this journey was the company of [a doctor, Dal Jung] who was jovial and never tired of talking. He is very keen on having political change in India. What was the most exciting was the breaking out of the war between Japan and Russia, and the point still more exciting was that the former had been successful in sinking and disabling some of the Russian war ships. It was a good beginning for Japan and our sympathies were with that nation which is the only hope of Asia. . . .

XXXV. Experiences

The people [of Udaipur] are good; they never use harsh words. Their accent is soft and sounds sweet to the listener. They don't use low words so far as I have heard. I never saw anyone who was really strong of physique. They look weak rather than strong, but all the same they have performed wonderful deeds in past history. The Mohammedans here wear white dress. There was no abusing heard.

Some of our people were complaining that these fellows don't understand jokes. It is better they don't. If it had been Jaipore, then there would have been some indecent words heard. . . .

These people here stick to their old custom. . . . Everyone who attends on the durbar and even the other people wear achkans and tie something over it as waistband. They all wear pugrees; no safas are to be seen. No boots are allowed in the palaces. The women wear such clothes that it is often difficult to distinguish a widow from one whose . . . husband is living. . . .

Besides [learning] these customs, I have known what it is to be with ruling chiefs when they go to marry. The more a man sees the more he learns. The other thing is that I have had experience of how princely marriages are done. If ever I have to go with another chief I may be useful in several ways. . . . I had [my first] experience of being present at a durbar. I know now what sort of talk is done on such occasions. This of course was due to my father for he was the only one that was talking in that assembly. . . .

4

Imperial Ritual at Alwar: Lord Curzon Invests Jai Singh with Full Powers

Dramatis Personae

Jai Singh, being invested as Maharaja of Alwar [off stage].[1]

Narain Singh of Kanota, Amar Singh's father, "native" guardian to Jai Singh during his minority, becomes a minister in his government.

[Amar Singh goes "on his own" to Alwar where Lord Curzon, the viceroy, is to invest Jai Singh with restricted powers as maharaja. Despite some reservations,[2] the viceroy and the Political Department have high hopes that Jai Singh will prove to be the kind of maharaja they need and want: loyal, manly and responsible. Alwar is a modest state; at 3,000 square miles and a population of 800,000 it is about a fourth the size of Jaipur—and receives a salute of 15 guns compared to Jaipur's 17.[3] British hopes and attention can be measured by comparing the quality and size of the company in attendance at Alwar with the British turnout for Sir Pratap's installation as Maharaja of Idar. On that occasion, the governor of Bombay sent a lone representative. At Alwar, not only is the viceroy present to do the honors but also the AGG and a bevy of senior Political Department officers attend, including William Curzon-Wyllie, soon to be political ADC to secretary of state for India, John Morley.[4]

Although not invited to the investiture, Amar Singh comes to Alwar anyway to be with his father, Jai Singh's "native" guardian. Jai Singh has figured prominently in Amar Singh's accounts of polo matches (see Part I, 7). On two memorable occasions the Alwar team with Jai Singh in a starring role defeats Sir Pratap's Jodhpur team. Amar Singh's accounts of the matches credit Jai Singh's brilliance as a polo player even while remarking on his haughtiness, arrogance and bad language.

In 1903, at the time of his investiture, the young Alwar, handsome, intelligent, a talented sportsman, and a Mayo College graduate, seems to be realizing British aspirations about the education of princes.[5] There are hopes in the Political Department that he would set a standard.[6] These hopes remain intact for about twenty years. During these years Jai Singh places Alwar state forces at the disposal of the empire in World War I and during the Third Afghan War (1919).

The British shower him with raj honors: K.C.S.I. (Knight Commander of the Star of India) in 1909; K.C.I.E. (Knight Commander of the Indian Empire) in 1911; G.C.I.E. (Grand Commander of the Indian Empire) in 1919, G.C.S.I. (Grand Commander of the Star of India) in 1924. In 1923, he attends an Imperial Conference as a representative of India, plays a leading role in the Chamber of Princes after its inception at the time of the Montagu-Chelmsford reforms in

1919,[7] and in 1930 is elected by his fellow rulers as the Chamber's pro-Chancellor.[8] But this story of a potential model prince does not have a happy ending.

In the early 1920s he begins styling himself raj rishi (kingly sage), becomes a patron of orthodox Hindu learning and an early advocate of Hindu nationalism in national politics. Having started his career as a reforming ruler as concerned with the welfare of his Muslim Urdu-speaking subjects as his Hindu, Hindi-speaking ones, he ends it by promoting and exacerbating Muslim-Hindu differences. His language and agrarian policies alienate and oppress the Meos [or Mevs], syncretic Muslims and cultivators who constitute about 25 percent of Alwar's population.[9] After ten years of mounting tension, the Meos revolt in 1933. Jai Singh has to request British military intervention to deal with a civil war. Having restored order, the British send Jai Singh into an exile from which he does not return.[10]

PHOTO VI-5   Maharaja Jai Singh of Alwar, *circa* 1905. Age mates and rivals, the young maharaja and Amar Singh compete in polo tournaments. Narain Singh, Amar Singh's father, is Jai Singh's "native" guardian. Brilliant, handsome and learned, he inspires great hopes in the *raj* that he would be an exemplary, loyal prince. He becomes a leader in the Chamber of Princes and a prominent patron of Hindu learning and causes. But stories of sadism and cruelty cloud his reputation. In 1933 his impoverished Muslim subjects rebel, provoked by his Hindu extremism and oppressive agricultural and educational policies. Deposed and exiled, he dies in Paris in 1937. Amar Singh's photo albums.

There was a dark side to Jai Singh's personality. The confidential records of the raj suggest that he was deposed and exiled as much for "depravity"[11] as for gross misrule. He acquired a reputation for cruelty, sadism and violence. It was said for example that he tortured horses that failed to do his bidding and that his junior maharani's[12] death by suicide in 1919—the official account says she "shot herself in the head with a revolver"—occurred under suspicious circumstances.[13] Jai Singh's youthful Muslim aide's death in London by stab wounds in the groin remained unresolved. On May 19, 1933, Jai Singh was told to quit Alwar within forty-eight hours and not to return to India for two years.[14] He died in Paris in 1937 under ambiguous circumstances; was he pushed, did he throw himself, or did he fall down the stairs at whose foot his body was found?

Amar Singh's father, Narain Singh, reads his vocation as Jai Singh's guardian to include loyal service to him whose salt he eats. Loyal service includes not only keeping him out of trouble but also getting him out of trouble should it arise. While having no illusions about Jai Singh's character he finds himself having to balance the expectations of the Political Department about his obligations as "native" guardian against his own sense as a Rajput of his obligations to his master. We find Amar Singh, who greatly admires his father's character and skills, having qualms about how Narain Singh handles this delicate balancing act.

Jai Singh's investiture provides an occasion for the British raj to practice the kind of ritual sovereignty that it derived from its Mughal precursors. Both used recognition of lesser rulers to buttress and legitimize their hegemony. Under the British, investitures as political rituals recognized princes' sovereignty even as they affirmed princely loyalty and fealty to the King Emperor. After 1857 "the princes" became an important part of the imperial monarchy that came to characterize the Victorian and Edwardian eras in India.

We find Amar Singh noting the parallels between the Mughal-style rituals concocted by Viceroy Lord Curzon for the January 1903 Delhi durbar declaring Edward VII King Emperor of India and those used when Jai Singh is granted his powers as Maharaja of Alwar in December.]

Meerut, Wednesday, 16th December, 1903[15]

Notes About My Last Leave of Thirteen Days.

III. My Invitation

The Maharaja of Alwar had not invited me but I had gone on my own. I several times hinted as much to some of his favourites when they asked me to come and stop in the visitor's camp. I never went [to the camp]. . . . I never went to the durbar. The maharaja thinks himself too proud. He invited Sher Singhjee and Dhokaljee from Jodhpore, Kalyan Singhjee from Jaipore and Akhai Singhjee from the cadet corps but left my name out. I don't feel for it but he ought to have thought that I was the son of his best well-wisher and benefactor through whose untiring work he was that day getting his powers. I think it hurt my father's feelings, though he never told me. . . .

XI. The Camp

The camp was beautifully laid out and the arrangement was something like that at the Delhi durbar though, of course, on a much smaller scale. There was an enquiry office and everything that can be imagined. There was green grass and beautiful roads laid out. The guests were in one circle while close at hand was the camp of the viceroy. All these camps were near the residency. . . . The principal street, through which the guests were to pass, and the fort high up over the city, were lighted with the common Indian lamps which were quite simple. The light on the hills looked very pretty. . . .

XIII. The Guests

There were chiefly the [English] political people who had been invited, including the viceroy and his staff, the Agent to the Governor General for Rajpootana, and the residents of Jaipore and Jodhpore.[16] Besides this there were the former [English] guardians and regents in addition to the polo players and some other special guests who had been invited. Among the natives were the Maharajas of Kishengarh and Bikaner, the uncle of the former and representatives from other states where invitations had been sent . . . The camps for the natives and for the Europeans were separate which, I think, was a good thing.

XV. The City Palace

The palace in the city is a grand thing indeed. It was the first time that I saw it. It being night, the whole thing was brilliantly lighted. I was quite struck with amazement. . . . There was no one to be seen except the sentry. . . . It is not at all an exaggeration when I say that I thought . . . I was moving in a fairyland. . . .

The central hall of the big room is not so big as it is high. . . . In one corner . . . was a very fine and big glass candle lamp. The lamp is really a big one and beautiful too. It is too heavy to be [hung from] a roof so is set up on the floor. . . .

The man who showed [the lamp] . . . to me said that the grandfather of the present maharaja, when he went to Calcutta, visited a shop [whose] owner . . . told him that several chiefs had been there but had not been able to buy anything. This aroused the maharaja's vanity. He asked the man the price of his whole shop which amounted to I don't know how many lakhs of rupees. The maharaja told the man to get out, had the shop locked and paid the sum that was asked. So much furniture is said to have been in the place that it is still coming. . . .

XXIX. Future Prospects

[With Jai Singh's investiture on 16 December 1903, Alwar's minority administration, including Narain Singh's post of native guardian, ends.] There are different men for different works. I do not know what prospects there are for my father in the future. I hope the [Alwar] durbar will do something for him. I don't know what that something will be but he has been promising to do it for some time. . . .

[Narain Singh is made a minister in the Maharaja of Alwar's government.[17] A prudent counselor, Narain Singh knows what kinds of explanations and justifications to use with Political Department officers when his master's welfare or security is at stake. "My father is a man who keeps the high principles of the old Rajpoot school and having eaten the salt of the Maharaja of Alwar he will always try and serve him to the best of his ability."[18]]

Jaipore, Thursday, 25th August, 1904

[Six months later Amar Singh returns to Alwar and reports on changes since the installation of the maharaja.]
Notes About My Sixth Term in the Cadet Corps.

XXX. The Maharaja of Alwar

Though I stopped for a very short time at Alwar I learned a few things about the durbar. These cannot be wrong because they have been told to me by my father [now a minister]. In the first place I must say that the ideas of the maharaja sahib have quite changed. In the former days he was very fond of eating food cooked by Mohammedans. Nowadays he has turned out the Mohammedan cooks and has become an orthodox Hindoo.

He has begun washing his hands if touched by an Englishman. . . . One day . . . Capt. Ricketts came to bid good-night and, after he had shaken hands, went away. The durbar and the raj kanwar Umaid Singhjee of Shahpura were at dinner. The durbar got up, washed his hands, and again began eating. The guest had to do the same thing as his host had done.

My father who was watching said that he wanted to ask them a question. Umaid Singhjee said that he was not clever enough to answer but the durbar was ever ready. Then my father asked them the reason of their washing their hands the answer was that they had shaken hands with Capt. Ricketts. On this my father said that it was very foolish on their part. They were eating food cooked and served by Mohammedans. . . . Englishmen were much better than the Mohammedans. The latter are the enemies of our religion and try to spoil it if they can, while Englishmen respect all religions. . . . I have written this story to give an idea what the change was.

Now listen to the present account. The durbar has become a really religious man. He does the Syndhya every day and has taken the sacred thread. [*Sandhya*, morning and evening worship, as prescribed in Vedic texts, includes the recitation of the *Gayatri Mantra*, a sacred verse.] The Ramayana is read every day and all the favourites are ordered to come and listen. This time when he went to Calcutta he stopped at all the sacred places.

The thing does not stop here. The Durbar has learned just a few of the preliminary things and thinks that he has become a great and learned man. He gives lectures to his favourites and state officials [of whom] none . . . can contradict him. One day he began to argue with my father. The latter did not speak at first. When pressed he began [requesting] that he may not be asked these things. Then in private he told the maharaja sahib that he was [a] boy, and having learned a few things thinks that he knows all, but that he was greatly mistaken. He ought to know that these talks don't become him. People don't say so, but they don't believe that the durbar knows anything because he is too young [Jai Singh had turned twenty-three in June] for such things. My father reprimanded him so severely that the durbar left the arguments for some time. . . .

5

Paramountcy and Corruption:
Talks with Political Officers

Dramatis Personae

Captain A.D'A.G. Bannerman, former guardian to Maharaja Sardar Singh of Jodhpur.

Lt. Col. W.H. Curzon-Wyllie, a senior officer in the Political Department; after 1906, ADC to the secretary of state for India, John Morley; assassinated in London by a terrorist's bomb in April 1909, in an attempt on Morley's life.

Lt. Colonel T.C. Pears, resident at Jaipur.

Meerut, Wednesday, 16th December, 1903 (cont.)

XIX. Talk with Bannerman

One day I went to call on Capt. [A.D'A.G.] Bannerman of the 31st Lancers. He had been an assistant inspecting officer for the Rajpootana imperial service troops and was guardian to Jodhpore durbar [Sardar Singh]. He is a friend of our family. . . . [Bannerman served as resident at Jaipur in 1881, where he was active in an embezzlement case brought against Amar Singh's granduncle, Thakur Fateh Singh of Naila, who, until Maharaja Ram Singh's death in 1880, had been prime minister of Jaipur state.[1]]

. . . The subject [turned to] the relations between the Rajpoots and the political officers. He, Bannerman, was telling me that the political fellows do not like those who get friendly with the Rajpoots. . . . As instances he gave his own name and that of Major Mayne. He said that they, the politicals, do not like these guardians to accept any present from wards. Bannerman said that he had given two ponies to the Jodhpore durbar and had kept him as guest at his house in England and had taken nothing from him.

All the same I know the durbar gave him those twenty thousand rupees that Sarkar had sent for him quite privately, through me, by the name of "Bucking Horse." This story is written at full length in my diary of August or September 1901.

[Bannerman's assertions of injured innocence trigger Amar Singh's recollections of events two years earlier when elaborate precautions were taken to keep secret a transfer of funds intended for Bannerman. Sir Pratap, then prime minister of Jodhpur, colludes with Maharaja Sardar Singh in this transaction. He screens the transaction from the ever curious eyes of his office babus by sending Amar Singh on a mysterious errand.]

Jodhpore, Wednesday, 14th August, 1901[2]

. . . My cousin . . . arrived from Jaipore.[3] He had come with a hoondi [letter of credit] worth thirty thousand rupees. This is the money for which Sarkar had written to his sisters [the wives of the late Maharaja Ram Singh of Jaipur] to send at their earliest convenience. . . . That letter of Sarkar's to his sisters had been enclosed in that to my uncle Roop Singhjee but there were great precautions to be taken before it could be sent to its destination [the sisters] without its causing suspicion.

My family, even before sending the letter [on to the sisters], sent my [cousin] with a hoondi to that amount to save unnecessary delay. This was very good of them indeed and Sarkar seemed very pleased with it After ordering me to write a receipt for the amount he instructed my cousin that he was to start off tonight and take me with him. . . . If anyone asked him as to the purpose of his coming here he was to say that he had come to take me to Jaipore owing to my marriage which is to take place very soon. . . .

He instructed me privately that I was to go . . . to Ajmere and get the hoondi cashed at the bank of Omed Mulljee and thence proceed on to Bombay and send twenty thousand of that sum to Durbar [Maharaja Sardar Singh] in England through King, King & Co. All this was to be done very privately and I was not to see any friend or acquaintance but live in utter seclusion. The money was to be sent by the name of Bucking Horse. No one was to know anything about it, not even my family. . . . [Rs 20,000 is a very large sum, more than the annual income of Amar Singh's Kanota family or its allied thikanas, equivalent to the annual salary of the viceroy of India. It is surprising that the family should have the money available in ready cash. That they should turn it over so expeditiously is a comment on their very intimate relationship with Sir Pratap.]

Friday, 16th August, 1901

. . . Sarkar came and took me aside and said that I was to go to Bombay tonight secretly [rather than to Ajmer].

Bombay, Sunday, 18th August, 1901

. . . The train having reached Bombay at the Grant Road Station I got out and taking a carriage went to the Esplanade Hotel which I had heard was the best and most respectable. . . .

Tuesday, 20th August, 1901

. . . In the morning I awoke early and, after washing myself, shaved and then had my bath. I then applied myself to the *Ramayana* and read the few remaining extra pages which have been annexed afterwards. This is a *Tulsi Krit Ramayana* [the epic as recounted by Tulsi Das in Avadhi, a precursor of modern Hindi] and has been translated in plain Hindi [that commonly spoken in north India] by Pandit Rameswar Bhutt. . . . The more I read this book the more I like it. I love the way in which it has been written. In some parts the poem is very lovely either to read or hear. The only drawback being that I do not know the proper rhyme in which I should read or sing and had to read the translations to understand the full meaning. . . .[4]

Wednesday, 21st August, 1901

. . . [I] went to see the manager of Seth Samir Mulljee. Their branch here is known by the name of Gadh Mull Goman Mull. They had received a telegram in answer to their letter saying that the money was to be given at either Jodhpore or Ajmere [thus not authorizing payment at Bombay]. However they are expecting a letter in answer tomorrow and advised me to stop for one more day. . . .

Thursday, 22nd August, 1901

. . . At half past nine [I] went to see the gomasta [commercial agent] of Seth Samir Mulljee. They all know me by the name of Himmat Singh of Bharatpore of the Jat clan, except the gomasta [to] whom unfortunately I had introduced myself thinking him to be the son or near relation of Omed Mulljee [a banker at Ajmer known to Sir Pratap].

Friday, 23rd August, 1901

. . . It being now half past eleven I ordered my carriage and went to see the gomasta. . . . The reply of the gomasta was that no letter had been received and consequently nothing could be done. To my mind the situation is this. The gomasta having written from here to his seth he must be making enquiries there from my uncle and Sarkar. . . .

Saturday, 24th August, 1901

Last night after dinner I received the answer of my telegram (which I had sent to Seth Govind Mulljee at Ajmere asking him to inform his gomasta to give me over thirty thousand rupees) which ran as follows: "Gadh Mull Goman Mull informed, take money." Seeing this I was quite delighted and saw the end of this troublesome business. . . .

I went to the office of Gadh Mull Goman Mull. The attitude of the gomasta was quite cold but what had I to do with him. I knew that he will have to pay me now and my work was over. However, the cashier was not there and had gone to some temple and was paying his devotions there while here I was cursing him. The brute of a gomasta did not care a hang for me but sat bare-bodied reading an occasional letter or chatting. At length the cashier came and I got the money. . . .

I had to receipt the hoondi and while I was going through this ordeal the gomasta came to me and said that as I was having the hoondi cashed here instead of at Jodhpore I ought to give some commission which he named hoondan. This sum was meant as a sort of bribery or present which was to go to his pocket . . . I understood it but feigned unintelligence and said that I had got him one telegram and if he wanted anything more would get another. He took the hint and so went away and I was not molested any more. Just fancy giving him a hoondan after all the slight and indifference he had shown me.

When everything was done, the cashier asked me to pay for the one anna stamp used on the receipt. Well, it was quite too mean. The smallest English firm will never think of it. But as the cashier can earn an anna in some way or the other why should he not do it? He is a mean fellow and thinks of his anna and not the firm he is serving. I however gave the pice which luckily I had. The rogues were all staring at me maliciously. . . . Putting on my boots [I] went out without even saying a word of thanks because they did not deserve any. . . . The gomasta was too proud to look at me because he got no hoondan. . . .

I had my breakfast and after that dressed myself to call on King, King and Co. [who was to forward the mysterious sum to the Maharaja of Jodhpur in England.] To make . . . unrecognizable . . . that I had come from Jodhpore I put on a peculiar dress. The turban I put on in quite a fantastic manner with curls all round. The coat I put on was not of the English cut but old Indian approaching up to my knees. It was of black silk richly worked in gold. . . . It was given to Sheonath Singh (my brother) by my grand uncle Sooltan Singhjee when the former went to join in the marriage ceremony of the latter. Instead of breeches I put on a dhoti [ankle-length breech cloth] . . . [with] black socks and pagurkhi [pointed Indian shoes].

[As] this was quite a strange dress . . . I put on my waterproof coat which reached down to my very ankles. . . . It served to hide this fancy dress of mine at which I was myself smiling in the mirror. . . . I rather felt ashamed to get out of the hotel in this manner. . . . I shuffled along as best I could looking all round [to see] if . . . people were laughing at me or not. At last I came to the office and went up to it. I took off my waterproof . . . and then went in. I sent in my name as "Bucking Horse" and was asked to come in.

The manager asked my business and I told him. There were no unnecessary questions. We joked a little about the name of "Bucking Horse." . . . In less than five minutes I got my receipt for the Rs 20,000 in the name of Bucking Horse even without their knowing whence I had come. I thanked them most heartily for their quickness. There were no charges to be paid for the one anna stamp on the receipt. There were thank-yous exchanged on both sides and everything was over.

Down below the steps of the office I met Colonel Beauchamp of the 20th Hussars. He recognized me inspite of my waterproof and we talked for a few minutes. . . .

[Returning now to the events of 1903:]

Meerut, Wednesday, 16th December, 1903

Talk with Bannerman (*cont.*)

As regards Major Mayne, [Bannerman] said that it has just leaked out that the above mentioned officer took Rs 30,000 from Kotah durbar. It recently came to light when the accounts of the late Seth Samir Mull were examined by [the] government . . . [it was] found that this sum was given to the Maha Rao of Kotah. . . . On it was a pencil mark saying that it was for Major Mayne. The Kotah durbar would have hushed the matter, but inquiries were made even before he was aware. . . . I was told that Major Mayne has got orders to resign. It will be awfully hard for him as he has not saved a single rupee and is very liberal hearted. Bannerman was saying that his pension will be about Rs 150 a month, on which he won't be able to support himself.[5] He would most probably commit suicide.

As an illustration of Mayne's generosity I said that when the present maharaj kanwar was born at Jodhpore he gave one thousand rupees to the man who had given him the news first of all. This is a sum that none else, except the durbar, gave on this occasion. This sort of talk continued for some time.

Bannerman was too familiar with the [Jodhpur] durbar [whose guardian he had been] and that is why he was kicked out of the imperial service. He used to defend the durbar against Sukhdeo Prasadjee [first minister at Jodhpur] and even the resident and this is the reward he got. He has no chance of going to any state so long as Lord Curzon is viceroy in India [who was notoriously stern about corruption]. . . .

[Two years after these conversations at Alwar, Amar Singh hears additional stories that suggest the "politicals" are vulnerable to temptation. Several are told to him by General O'Moore Creagh, commander of the Fifth Division and the Western Command at Mhow (later commander in chief of the Indian Army, after Lord Kitchener), whom Amar Singh serves as a staff officer after his graduation from the ICC and commissioning in the Indian Land Forces in April 1905. O'Moore Creagh tells Amar Singh about his distrust and dislike for what he calls "the politicals," British officers from the Political Department serving as residents in princely states or on deputation to them as guardians, council members or ministers.]

Mhow, Monday, 31st July, 1905[6]

The general [O'Moore Creagh] is always against the politicals. Now when he went to Alwar [to raise Imperial Service Forces] the maharaja sent him his daily food allowance which consisted of about a bottle of whiskey and a bottle of brandy and a bottle of champagne and God only knows what amount of meat and cakes and fruit and such like things. The general told the durbar that he could not possibly eat all this which would be more than enough for ten men. The maharaja replied that he sent this allowance to the political agent and there was no reason why he should not send him. On this the general said that he would try and get the politicals in trouble.

He therefore wrote a letter to the foreign office people at Simla and said that he was sent this much food every day and when he refused to have it the maharaja said that it was what he sends to the political officer daily and therefore he too must accept it.

The general enquired what he was to do. An answer came by wire telling him to accept the allowance. The foreign office people must have had a friend in that particular officer or they were afraid of starting this question.

Politicals

Creagh . . . said that these politicals were a great nuisance. They bother the chiefs a great deal. He was very pleased when he heard that Lord Curzon had ordered that the residents were to have their own conveyances and not borrow from the states. If they had to borrow on any occasion they were to write to the higher authority that they had to do it because they could not get any conveyance anywhere else. The politicals are awfully sick about it. There is one political agent at Alwar who wrote to the maharaja to send him a dozen bottles of champagne when he was going away. Is this not very mean?

Talking of politicals [O'Moore Creagh] one day said that he was once reading the London *Times* when he read that Sir [William] Palmer [acting commander in chief of the Indian Army, 1900–1902] when he died left £3000 for his family. In that same paper [there was a story] about the death of Col. Beynon [political agent at Jaipur from 1877 to 1881] who had left £218,000.[7] Both these men had about the same length of service and pay but just think of the difference of money between them. Beynon was a political officer and . . . was at Jaipore for a some time after the late Maharaja Ram Singhjee's death [in 1880]. He was a greedy fellow and took bribes openly.

[Reverting to conversations at Alwar about the relations between the princely states and the raj:]

Meerut, Wednesday, December 16, 1903 (cont.)

XX. My Talk with Colonel Sir Curzon-Wyllie

[The Kanota family fortunes are still suffering from the consequences of a case brought by Maharaja Madho Singh of Jaipur and Babu Kanti Chander Mukerjee, his prime minister, against the Champawat connection in Jaipur, the three related houses of Kanota, Gondher and Naila.

Having "won" the case and staved off confiscation, the families find that the maharaja has persuaded the resident, who presumably speaks with the backing of higher authority, to support a face-saving compromise: the disputed villages, alleged to have been fraudulently acquired, will be exchanged for other less desirable villages. We find Amar Singh discussing the case with Lt. Col. W.H. Curzon-Wyllie in the larger context of governance under paramountcy. A prominent member of the political service, Curzon-Wyllie has served as resident at Jodhpur and Udaipur and will soon become political ADC to John Morley, secretary of state for India in the 1906 Liberal government and coauthor of the historic Morley-Minto reforms.[8]]

When I went to Jaipore from Alwar I found that Col. Wyllie had come to India on a visit. He was formerly resident at Jodhpore and afterwards acting Agent to the Governor General for Rajpootana. Sarkar had once introduced me to him and I know that he was very well acquainted with my family. My grandfather had told me that I must enquire after an officer who has come here and was formerly the A.G.G. and had helped us in our case.

[As AGG, Sir Curzon–Wyllie visited Jaipur in 1900 at the height of the conflict between Maharaja Madho Singh and his prime minister on the one hand and the Champawat families on the other. Curzon-Wyllie asked prime minister Kanti Chander to meet him in his private railway car where they discussed the Jaipur

PHOTO VI-6   Jaipur court, *circa* 1903, including the *solah* [sixteen] premier nobles and the *tazimi* [gold anklet] *sardars*, at the time of Lord Curzon's visit, Amar Singh's photo albums.

state's efforts to seize Champawat villages. In the exchange of letters that followed, the raj shows its rhetorical teeth.

Curzon-Wyllie begins by implying that the maharaja's very generous gift to the famine relief fund of 1901 was meant in part to gain the Government of India's support for his decision to seize the three Champawat thikanas. Kanti Chander, obviously offended on behalf of his master, says he has told the maharaja of the accusation. In a tart letter that exhibits some talent in the rhetoric of resistance he adds:

> If I have reported your message to His Highness correctly then you need not reply . . . but if any part of it is incorrect then I shall expect a reply from you. His Highness will write you soon on further consideration of the matter in hand.

Curzon-Wyllie, not about to be pulled up by a clever Bengali babu, retorts in the language of command:

> In conclusion I bring to your notice that the penultimate paragraph of your letter . . . is in its abruptness of expression lacking in the courtesy with which the Governor General's Agent is to be addressed. I take the trouble to mention this to you, in order that you may not fall into similar error in future correspondence.[9]

When I went to see this Wyllie at Alwar he was quite pleased. . . . At first the talk was quite general and about our prospects in the Corps. He was saying that he would be very much pleased if something would be done for us. . . . Wyllie said

PHOTO VI-7   Maharaja Madho Singh of Jaipur receiving an unidentified royal person, probably the Prince of Wales, later George V, at the railway station in 1905. Madho Singh is accompanied by his nobles and attended by Amar Singh in the uniform of the Imperial Cadet Corps. Amar Singh's photo albums.

that we can't get commissions in the army as the native officers would not like us to supersede them. I said that this may be but at the same time the British officers would never like to be under us. To this he said that it would be another difficulty. [Note that Wyllie suggests the obstacle is Indian objections to serving under Indian officers, while Amar Singh suggests British officers are the problem.]

After this the talk changed and he said that he was so glad we had got out of our case so well. He never expected this much. I said that we had suffered a great loss and much more than we ever thought. Then arose an argument. He said that we were lucky to escape so lightly, and I said that we had lost a great deal. He asked me the losses . . . I said that the [Jaipur] raj has paid us for our house in one village and not for those in others which was quite unjust. Then I said that I alone had lost an income of Rs 10,000 annually. He asked me the reason . . . I said that the raj says that they have given us villages of the same income [as the ones they have taken] but they have not. Those [former villages] were given on the average income of ten years whilst those that we got now are on the highest income that has ever come out of them.

[In the face-saving "compromise" of 1902, Kanota and Gondher did not fare as well as Naila. Even so the three thikanas join in a petition against the settlement. In the petition they show that the three thikanas had increased the income of the villages given to them in 1873—Gondher from Rs 8,872 to Rs 10,530; Kanota from Rs 6,872 to Rs 17,490; and Naila from Rs 6,995 to Rs 13,689. These

PHOTO VI-8   Elephant chariot passing the *Hawa Mahal*, Palace of the Winds, built by Maharaja Sawai Pratap Singh of Jaipur (1778–1803). Amar Singh's photo albums.

increases, they say, were not recognized in the exchange of villages offered to Kanota and Gondher. Roop Singh of Naila, Amar Singh's uncle, agrees to the exchange of villages because those he is offered are perceived to be of equivalent value. The petition also charges that Jaipur state is compensating the thikanas for the cost of buildings in Gondher village only, but not for the cost of buildings in other villages.[10]]

Besides this, the income of all villages has increased in the whole of the state, and so we cannot increase their income even if we tried for twenty years. Wyllie said that he never knew about it and even Col. Pears [resident at Jodhpur in 1898 and at Jaipur in 1903–1904] did not say so. However, he promised to speak to the resident about it.

The argument was still the same;. . . he said that we were lucky for what we had got I said that it was not at all so, because we never expected so much injustice. Wyllie said that the maharaja can take what he gives. I said that he can't. Then he said that our villages were given only because he was pleased and not because any of our ancestors had been killed in battle.[11] I said that whether they were given for this or that reason they cannot be confiscated. On this Wyllie said that he would show me several instances where villages have been taken away and never returned. I said that I would show several on which villages have been restored by the pressing of the political officers. He said that this is not done always. I said that of course not in those cases where the people cannot reach the politicals and lay their grievances [before them].

[In the argument that follows, Curzon-Wyllie interprets the raj's paramountcy relationship to mean that the British should follow a "natural" Rajput political constitution that allowed maharajas to seize a thikana. He implies that intervention to block such seizures would violate the princely prerogatives that the raj's paramountcy relationship required it to protect. Amar Singh insists that jagirdars have rights and that the protection of those rights is part of the raj's duties under paramountcy.]

He asked me what we would do if our villages were not given back. I said that in former days we used to fight and force the durbar to give us back but now the government does not allow this but has taken the responsibility on their shoulders that no injustice shall be done. This was too much and he said that this showed we did not look upon the durbar as our lord. I said that we do look upon him as our lord but if he robs us we must make headway and specially when we are wronged. Wyllie said that the government cannot interfere with the management of the state too much. I replied that it has done so several times.

Seeing that the contest was growing a bit hot I said that I had not come to talk on this matter, but simply to pay my respects and would not have touched on this subject but it was he himself who started it. Then I further added that I was merely a boy doing my work in the corps and was not acquainted with the case. Whether we were right or wrong was best known to him as he had helped us so much. . . .

. . . I regret . . . that I did not give him one answer which unfortunately occurred to me a bit later. He was saying that our villages were given simply for favour's sake and not for moond kuti, i.e. for getting killed in battle. The colonel was thinking that only those that are given for getting killed are considered permanent and the rest may be taken away. I quite missed the point. I ought to have said that "What is moond kuti?" It is also a sort of favour. In one battle there are some five or six hundred men killed but all the sons and successors of those killed do not get villages. It is only a select few, who are favoured, that get a jagir. This would have put a stop to arguments like this.

There was another question like this which the baboo [Kanti Chander] used to tell to the political officers, and that was that these Rathores [the Jodhpur ruling lineage to which Amar Singh's family is related] had no right to get a jagir in Jaipore and if any be granted it can be confiscated at any time. [This assertion echoes the co-conquership theory (the collective act of a founding lineage) of Rajput polities by implying that only families belonging to the ruling clan of the state have secure jagirs, for example, that in Jaipur only Kachhawa estates are secure. Historical precedents suggest that this is a dubious claim; ganayats ("outside" or non-royal lineages) in Udaipur and Jodhpur as well as in Jaipur were as secure and honored as "home" clans.[12]]

Wyllie and Mr Lawrence used these very words [about the confiscation of ganayats] before my father at Simla to which he got a good reply. My father answered that you don't know these things and listen [to] only one side's version, and that this is simply a false excuse which the people have been trying to impress on you. He further said that there is not a single state in Rajpootana where the ganayats don't enjoy the same rights and honours though they are comparatively few in number. This calmed Mr Lawrence a bit.

Such was my talk with Curzon-Wyllie, and I took his leave after thanking him to take such an interest in our case. He promised to speak to Col. Pears about our annual loss of Rs 10,000 which he was not aware of. I told my father all about it. . . . [After] he had listened [he] said that it is all right. Wyllie has always taken a great interest in our case and his purpose was to find out if we had any answer left.

He then told an instance of his own. When Kanti Chander died, Wyllie asked my father what he would now say when the baboo was dead. . . . Up to that time we were saying that the maharaja sahib had nothing to do [with it] and that it was all the baboo's doing. To this my father said that the durbar has got into a trap out of which he cannot escape. The baboo has impressed on his mind that if he does not vigorously carry on the case he would be the laughing stock of all. . . . Consequently the durbar is not going to leave the matter so easily. Wyllie was very much pleased with this answer.

XXI. My Father's Talk with Colonel Pears

[T.C.] Pears is the present political agent at Jaipore. My father went to see him. . . . After a few ordinary words the talk turned on our case. It has been our aim to find out what are the government orders about our case but we have been unable to do so. On that day it leaked out of Pears' mouth. My father thinks that they are to the effect that our villages be given back to us, or if not those, then others of the same value. My father explained that the durbar, after having done us the greatest injury, tells you [Lieutenant Colonel Pears] that he has done what [the] government [of India] wanted and that he has given other villages. These other villages do not bring even that amount for which they are granted and there is no hope of their ever increasing. My father said that he wanted nothing more than what [the] government had decided. . . . This can only be done when the durbar either returns our original villages or grants others that are equal in value to what our confiscated villages' yield at present.

Pears then said that Roop Singh [of Naila, one of the three related estates] says it is all right and Mr Cobb had settled everything. My father then further explained that Roop Singh is a mere boy and does what he is ordered to do. It was he himself [Narain Singh] who was the guiding spirit of all.

[Roop Singh is six years junior to the fifty-three-year-old Narain Singh. Kanota family tradition has it that Narain Singh had taken the lead in the conflict, traveling to Simla to speak with the relevant officers, and, with the help of the Jodhpur regent, Sir Pratap, carrying it to an apparently successful conclusion.

The Government of India found Jaipur state's allegations of fraud in the original grant of villages implausible.[13] It seems that Roop Singh, without consulting with Narain Singh, took it upon himself to negotiate an exchange of villages with the resident, Col. Cobb. The exchange of villages simultaneously saved face for the maharaja and advanced Roop Singh's reputation as a compliant thakur but was disadvantageous to the interests of Gondher and Kanota. In the wake of the case, Roop Singh becomes a judicial officer at the Jaipur court, while Narain Singh remains in disfavor.]

My father's talk has thrown a good impression on the resident and he has promised to make enquiries in the case. . . .

XLI. Conclusion

Even in our own homes we Indians are excluded from European society. Here at Alwar the Englishmen [sat] . . . on the best of chairs and sofas in the middle while the Indians [stood] . . . most of the time, or if they sat, it was outside the pavilion and on the rude common chairs. Even the ruling chiefs were not at home amongst these European swells. God only knows what is going to be our dignity in a few year's time. Ruling chiefs are considered nothing more than puppets in the hands of the political people. I wish God would show a day to me when we Indians would be a free nation moving about at our own free will and ranked as a nationality on the same footing as England, France or Russia. I fear I shall never see it . . .

NOTES

INTRODUCTION

Introduction

1. See, for example, one of the best known of the modern European diaries, *The Diary of Samuel Pepys*, Robert Latham and William Matthews, editors (Berkeley: University of California Press, 1970–1983), 11 vols. The diary covers the years 1659 to 1669.

2. The term Rajputana was used before Independence to characterize the twenty-two princely states in northwest India. After the princely states were integrated into independent India in 1947 and subsequently merged into a state of the federal union the territory occupied by the former twenty-two princely states was designated Rajasthan. The usage eliminated the reference to the Rajput social order while preserving the regal significance by combining "Raja" (king) with "sthan" (land of).

1: Provenance: Making a Self at the Jodhpur Court

1. The British crown from 1858 exercised direct rule over "British India" comprising three-fifths of the subcontinent and indirect rule over "princely India" made up of 565 states of varying size whose rulers exercised limited sovereignty and owed allegiance to the British crown through the viceroy. For a more nuanced account of a complex and interesting relationship, see Part VI.

2. Sir Pratap's regency ends temporarily in 1898 when Maharaja Sardar Singh, his nephew and heir to the throne after the death of Maharaja Jaswant Singh in 1895, is invested with full powers. The balance of activity among palaces and bungalows shifts accordingly. When Sardar Singh dies in 1911, Sir Pratap becomes regent again during the minority of Sardar Singh's son, Sumer Singh. The details of these shifting arrangements and a reasonably frank account of the Jodhpur royal family in Sir Pratap Singh's time can be found in Dhananajaya Singh, *The House of Marwar* (New Delhi: Roli Books/Lotus Collection, 1994), chapter entitled "Of Boy Kings and a Grand Old Man," 129–158.For further particulars of nineteenth-century Jodhpur history see R.P. Vyas, *Role of Nobility in Marwar* (New Delhi: Jain Brothers, 1969); Lt. Col. Archibald Adams, *The Western Rajputana States: A Medico Topographical and General Account of Marwar, Sirohi, Jaisalmer* (London: Junior Army and Navy Stores, 1889); N.K. Acharya, "Administration of the Jodhpur State, 1800–1947," (Ph.D. dissertation, University of Rajasthan, 1961), and annual editions of *Report on the Political Administration of the Rajputana States* (hereafter *AGG Report*). Such annual reports consisted of the report of the Agent to the Governor General (AGG), who represented British suzerainty over all of Rajputana, and of the reports rendered to him by the British residents and agents in particular states. These reports begin in 1865 and are variously published by the Government of India at Bombay (1865–1867) and Calcutta (1867–1907).

3. Takhat Singh ruled from 1843 until 1872. He was succeeded by Maharaja Jaswant Singh (1873–1895), Takhat Singh's eldest son. Sir Pratap Singh is Takhat Singh's third son.

4. See Sidney Toy, *The Fortified Cities of India* (London: Heinemann, 1965) for photographs and the history of Jodhpur fort. Before Rao Jodha refounded the Rathore kingdom in 1459, it was known as Marwar. To this day, it is often so referred to.

5. See, for example, Michael N. Pearson, *Merchants and Rulers in Gujarat: The Response to the Portuguese in the Sixteenth Century* (Berkeley: University of California Press, 1976);

Holden Furber, *Rival Empires of Trade in the Orient, 1600–1800* (Minneapolis: University of Minnesota Press, 1976); K.N. Chaudhuri, *The Trading World of Asia and the East India Company, 1660–1760* (Cambridge: Cambridge University Press, 1978); Surendra Gopal, *Commerce and Craft in Gujarat, 16th and 17th Centuries* (New Delhi: People's Publishing House, 1975). Ferdinand Braudel's *Wheels of Commerce*, vol. I in the three-volume series, *Capitalism and Material Life* (New York: Harper and Row, 1973), provides accounts of Europe's trade with India in the sixteenth and seventeenth centuries. For an earlier period, from the rise of Islam through the twelfth century, see Andre Wink, *Al Hind* (New Delhi: Oxford University Press, 1992).

6. Marwari refers to people from Marwar, Jodhpur's ancient name. Marwar is sometimes translated as "land of death." Today's Marwaris are among India's most prominent business communities. Active in commerce, finance, and industry, these early traders and financiers until recently epitomized independent India's business community. The Birlas, a Marwari family from Shekhawati, Jhunjhunu district, Rajasthan, continue to rival the Tatas, a Parsi family from Bombay, for preeminence in today's rapidly changing business climate. See Thomas A. Timberg, *The Marwaris: From Traders to Industrialists* (Delhi: Vikas, 1978).

7. Ram Nathji's assignments included *dohas* (couplets, in this case in Marwari), Plutarch, Daniel Defoe, Samuel Smiles, Indian classics (the *Mahabharata, Ramayana*, and *Bhagavad Gita*), novels (Rider Haggard, Mary Corelli, and *Mysteries of London*), histories, and biographies.

8. R.B. van Wart, *The Life of Lieutenant-General H.H. Sir Pratap Singh* (London: Humphrey Milford for Oxford University Press, 1926), 180–182. Sir Pratap also wrote an autobiography: *Maharaja Sir Pratapsinghji Sahib ka Swalikhit Jivan-Charitr*, Shriman Radhakrishan, editor (Mori Gate, Lahore: Vir Milap Press-Khushalchandji "Khursand," 1939).

9. See Frances H. Taft, "Honor and Alliance: Reconsidering Mughal-Rajput Marriages," in Karine Schomer, Joan L. Erdman, Deryck O. Lodrick, Lloyd I. Rudolph, editors, *The Idea of Rajasthan: Explorations in Regional Identity*, 2 vols (Columbia, MO: South Asia Publications, 1994). As a result, in part, of Mughal-Rajput marriages, by the end of Akbar's reign, "Raja Mansingh of Amber was perhaps the single most powerful figure in the empire after the emperor himself, and the rajas of Bikaner and Jodhpur had become prominent as well." The Jodhpur princess Manbhavati had married Sultan Salim (later the emperor Jahangir, himself the son of an Amber princess), and their child, Sultan Khurram, became the emperor Shahjahan. "Shahjahan . . . favored his Jodhpur relatives." For an extended discussion of Jodhpur-Mughal relations, including marriages, see Dhananajaya Singh, *The House of Marwar*, 75–77.Taft tells us that the literature on Mughal-Rajput marriages is "not large" and that such marriages "have been virtually ignored in the *khyats* (traditional histories) and in modern histories" because of "Rajput prejudices." After Tod (see later note) and particularly after the rise of nationalist and communal history, many Rajputs viewed such marriages as "dishonorable" or "shameful," 217, 229, 230, and *passim*.

10. The phrase is used in *The India We Served* by Sir Walter Lawrence, secretary to Lord Curzon while Curzon served as viceroy, to characterize his own and his circle's opinion of Sir Pratap. (London: Cassell and Co., 1928). Lawrence was regarded by Sir Pratap and via him, by Amar Singh's family, as a friend and patron (1899–1905). Later, Lawrence became a confidant of the young George V. See James Pope-Hennessay, *Lord Crewe, 1858–1945: The Likeness of a Liberal* (London: Arnold Constable, 1955), 94.

11. The British adapted from the practice of Mughal and other Indian courts in holding celebratory events. The 1877 Durbar celebrated Victoria's being declared Empress of India; 1903 Edward's coronation as King Emperor; 1911 George V's coronation as Emperor.

The principal jubilees at London were Victoria's silver and gold in 1887 and 1897 respectively. For a detailed and intimate evocation of the milieu and mentality of Edwardian England at home and in India, see Francis G. Hutchins, *The Illusion of Permanence* (Princeton: Princeton University Press, 1967); Allen J. Greenberger, *The British Image of India: A Study in the Literature Of Imperialism, 1880–1960* (London: Oxford University Press, 1969); and Benita Parry, *Delusions and Discoveries: Studies on India in the British Imagination, 1880–1930* (Berkeley: University of California Press, 1972).

12. Pratap Singh was knighted in 1885, awarded an honorary LL.D. by Cambridge University on his 1897 visit and created a Grand Commander of the Star of India (G.C.S.I.). In 1901, he became the only Indian Military Knight Commander (K.C.B.).

13. Maud Diver, *Royal India: A Description and Historical Study of India's Fifteen Principal States and Their Rulers* (New York: D. Appleton-Century Company, 1942),46. We are grateful to Ian J. Barrow for bringing to our attention Maud Diver's reference to this scene. It was later at this meeting that Sir Pratap presented Victoria with his sirpesh. Rather than "touch and remit" as was usually done with a *nazar* (gift), she took it and subsequently often wore it. According to the account attributed to Sir Pratap by Maud Diver, "She was pleased to call me near her, and to say that, as I had presented my nazar with my heart's esteem and affection, she was wearing it in the same spirit" (46). We learn from Amar Singh's diary that Sir Pratap often garlanded a photograph of Victoria and meditated before her statue. (See Part VI, Chapter 2.)"Pratap Singh's imaginative improvisation and fusion of 'Indian' and 'English' courtly elements . . . suddenly and unexpectedly elevates him to being in control of the proceedings and [of] his lady Sovereign, and begins to suggest . . . the erotics of feudal relations and the potential for ironic subversion. Pratap Singh certainly captivated his Sovereign and prompted her to improvise." Ian J. Barrow, "Towards New Histories of the Princely States," unpublished paper, South Asia Seminar, University of Chicago, March 1993, 37.

14. Van Wart, *Sir Pratap Singh*, 11, 49.

15. In the words of Ram Nath Ratnu, Amar Singh's teacher, who served several states and found most princes disappointing, Ram Singh was "the ablest, wisest and the most cultured prince that any State in Rajputana has had in recent times." *A Brief Account of the Life of His Highness The Maharaja, Col. Sir Pratap Singh of Idar, K.C.B., G.C.S.I., LL.D., Maharaj-Dhiraj of Jodhpur and Aide-De-Camp to His Majesty the King-Emperor Edward VII* (Bombay: Times of India Press, 1902), 3. The biography lists no author, but is regarded in the Kanota family, who knew Ram Nathji well, as having been written by him.

16. Van Wart, *Sir Pratap Singh*, notes that Pratap was paid from the private purse of Maharaja Ram Singh, 43. Van Wart also reports that the difficulties that drove Pratap to Jaipur had to do with Faiz Ullah Khan, who became one of the Jodhpur maharaja's "most trusted advisers" (41).

17. In English official eyes, he did not initially succeed. "It was not to be expected that Maharaj Pratap Singh, who had no previous experience in the work of managing a state, could undertake with perfect success a task in which so many had failed." "Marwar Agency Report," in *AGG Report, 1878–1879*, 67. But he was well thought of even then: "No one charges him with taking advantage of his position to amass money . . . and perhaps he is the only Marwar minister of whom this can be said." Lt. Col. Percy W. Powlett, in "Resident's Report" in *AGG Report, 1881–1882*, 118–119.

18. *Jeth Budhi* 11 (Hindu calendar), no year. Letter in Kanota Family Archive.

19. See our "A Bureaucratic Lineage in Princely India: Elite Formation and Conflict in a Patrimonial System," in *Essays on Rajputana: Reflections on History, Culture and Administration* (New Delhi: Concept Publishing House, 1984), 81–140.

20. Letter from G.R. Irwin, resident at Jaipur, to Babu Kanti Chander Mukerjee, September 25, 1899. Copy in Kanota Family Archive, Box 23, item 1286. For the maharaja's reaction to this event see Memo 1, annexure to letter from Maharaja Madho Singh of Jaipur to A.H.T. Martindale, AGG, August 4, 1900, Kanota Family Archive.

21. See the comprehensive genealogical study of the Champawats, the three-volume work by Amar Singh's nephew and heir, Mohan Singh of Kanota, *Champawaton ka Itihas*, 3 vols (Jaipur: Ranbankura Prakashan, 1990, 1991).

22. Rathore history in what became known as Jodhpur state begins with Chonda's conquest of Mandor in 1394. Mandor lies on the outskirts of contemporary Jodhpur city. Jodha, who founded Jodhpur city in 1459, is the second son of Rao Rinmal, an important figure in Rajputana history. Champa was the third of Rao Jodha's 26 brothers. See Vishranath Reu, *Marwar Ka Ithas* (Jodhpur: Jodhpur Government Press, 1938) 80.

23. For particulars, see our "A Bureaucratic Lineage in Princely India" in *Essays on Rajputana*, 81–140.

24. The social ideology of varna appears in *Rig Veda, The Laws of Manu* and other Brahmanical texts and was accepted until recently as authoritative by "Indologists" from Max Muller to Max Weber to Louis Dumont. Varna social ideology depicted "caste" in terms of *brahmans* (priests), *kshatriyas* (warrior rulers), *vaisyas* (merchants), and *sudras* (manual workers, including peasants and artisans). Beyond varna were untouchables (*mlechchas* or "foreigners"; conquered people or *dasas*; those outside the caste system including latter day "unclean" or "impure" "untouchables" whom the British, and after Independence, the Government of India, designated "Scheduled Castes"). Recent scholarship has denaturalized varna and caste, depicting them not as timeless and fixed but as historically constructed and subject to continuous change. See, for example, Romila Thapar, *Ancient Indian Social History: Some Interpretations* (New Delhi: Orient Longman, 1978); our *The Modernity of Tradition: Political Development in India* (Chicago: University of Chicago, 1967 and subsequent editions), Part I, "Traditional Structures and Modern Politics: Caste," 15–154; Nicholas Dirks, *The Hollow Crown: Ethnohistory of an Indian Kingdom* (New York: Cambridge University Press, 1987).

25. We will cite the relatively accessible *Annals and Antiquities of Rajasthan or, The Central and Western Rajpoot States of India*, two volumes in one, preface by Douglas Sladen (London: Routledge and Kegan Paul, 1914), reprinted in 1923 and 1950.The drawings for the engravings were made by Captain Waugh, Tod's cousin who accompanied him on most of his many travels while an agent in Mewar. The originals and remakes can be seen at the Royal Asiatic Society, London. Tod's construction of Rajput identity relied heavily on what he took to be, as it turned out wrongly, an authentic late twelfth century text, the Chand Bardai *Prithvi Raj Raso*, the story of "the last Hindu king of Delhi." ". . . every noble family of Rajasthan will find some record of their ancestors *in Prithviraj Raso* . . . " "It is accordingly treasured amongst the archives of each race having any pretensions to the name of Rajpoot," Tod, *Rajasthan*, vol. I, p. 206, note 2. For Tod and for Rajputs of his time and since, the *Prithviraj Raso* ". . . validated Rajput claims to elite status by 'proving' that various Rajput lineages were both ancient and worthy." Cynthia Talbot, "*The Prithviraj Raso* in the Making of Tod's Annals," paper presented at the Annual Conference on South Asia, Madison, WI, October 15, 1999, p. 4. Talbot using different evidence follows Kavi Raj Shymaldas' "The Antiquity, Authenticity and Genuineness of the Epic called *The Prthi Raj Rasa*, and commonly ascribed to Chand Bardai," *Journal of the Asiatic Society of Bengal*, vol. LV, Part I, 1886, in arguing that the Chand Bardai text was a late sixteenth or early seventeenth century creation.

26. See our *The Modernity of Tradition* for the historical circumstances and moral and psychological grounding of British racial ideology about martial and non-martial races: "Within twenty years of the deliberate exclusion of United Province Brahmans from the Bengal Army because of their leading role in the rebellion of 1857, the idea that Brahmans lacked fighting qualities had become prevailing opinion. . . . [I]n English minds at the end of the century, the distinction [between martial and non-martial] was stressed as much for its instrumental utility in the imperialist theory as for its academic interest as a description of caste or regional character. The 'martial' races for the most part adhered to the British raj, not because they were martial . . . but for political considerations, the Rajputs because they were the princes of states whose autonomy was threatened by a self governing India, the Muslims because they feared a Hindu majority in independent India. . . . Those described as the non-martial races produced nationalism" (165–167).

27. See Chapter XIV, "The Martial Classes" of Philip Mason's *A Matter of Honour: An Account of the Indian Army, Its Officers and Men* (London: Papermac, 1986), 341–361, particularly "2. Lord Roberts and his Views," 345–350.

28. The mass of the people of India," MacMunn averred, "have neither martial aptitude nor physical courage." Of India's 350 million people only 35 million qualified as martial races and of these only 3 million were males between twenty and thirty-five years of age. Mason adds that "the idea that some people will make soldiers and some will not is of course much older than the British. It is implicit in the Hindu caste system; no raja would have the money-lender or the trader castes to bear arms. But it was the British, after the Mutiny, step by step, who formulated and codified the principle, turning what had been a matter of practical choice into a dogma proclaimed with theological rancour." Mason, *A Matter of Honour*, 348–349.

29. Rudyard Kipling's *Kim* introduced the English-speaking world to the great game. See Lloyd I. Rudolph, "The Great Game in Asia: Revisited and Revised", *Crossroads: An International Socio-Political Journal* 16 (1985): 1–46.

30. For a 1990s account of Rana Pratap that melds bardic skills with objectivist historical method, see Kesri Singh, *The Hero of Haldighati* (Jodhpur: Book Treasure, 1996).

31. Norman Ziegler's study of the Khyat of Nainsi, a seventeenth-century Jodhpur administrator, shows how Mughal administrative categories and practices were assimilated into Rajput political ideas and practices. It also suggests the creation of a more complex and hierarchical status order on analogies with Mughal court society. Ziegler's study of fifteenth-century Rajput folksongs and tales is a striking report on the absence in them of the florid literary and cultural embellishments characterizing later bardic accounts, and suggests that Kolff's characterizations of Rajputs, as plain fighting men of diverse origins may apply to Rajputs in Rajputana as well as in other parts of north India. "The Seventeenth Century Chronicles of Marvara: A Study in the Evolution and use of Oral Traditions in Western India," *History in Africa* 3 (1976): 127–153; "Marvari Historical Chronicles: Sources for the Social and Cultural History of Rajasthan," *Indian Economic and Social History Review* 13 (1976): 219–250. Nicholas Dirks, in *The Hollow Crown*, argues that the political processes associated with kingship rather than canonical texts or Brahmanic understandings determined social preference and standing, including caste identity and privileges. South Indian kings, he argues, used symbolic and material resources under their control to reshape or constitute status orders and castes.

32. "During the sixteenth and seventeenth centuries, the top layer of Rajputs [in Rajputana], encouraged by the openings presented by the Mughal state and helped by the expertise of their bards, tended to . . . articulate new norms of Rajput behavior. Bards had always encouraged their Rajput employers to assume aristocratic self-images closely linked

with myths of origin that established their status as *kshatriyas* and traced back their genealogies to, for instance, the great dynasties of ancient Indian history. . . . The tendency to interpret Rajput history in genealogical terms was later inherited by Tod and other British administrators. . . . [S]omething like a new Rajput Great Tradition emerged [in the seventeenth and eighteenth centuries] which could recognize little else than unilineal kin bodies as the elements of which genuine Rajput history ought to be made up." Dirk H.A. Kolff, *Naukar, Rajput and Sepoy: The Ethnohistory of the Military Labour Market in Hindustan, 1450–1850* (Cambridge: Cambridge University Press, 1990), 72–73. Kolff sees the "original Rajputs" as an open status group which, as late as the nineteenth century, included "errant soldier, migrant labourer, or pack-animal trader." This interpretation is not accepted by many contemporary Rajputs who hold that Rajputs are descended from a historical Ram or from his sons. For a debate about Rajput status a generation ago, see Rushton Coulborn, editor, *Feudalism in History* (Princeton: Princeton University Press, 1956) and the debate that followed about "feudalism" as a universal category. For example, did it exist as a "stage" of development in India and Japan? The debate at that time about whether Rajputs in India were a feudal status category or class was innocent of the understanding that Tod, who established the term for India, used Henry Hallam's reading of medieval feudalism as the core of his historiographical construction of feudalism in India.

33. Aspects of these perceptions and attitudes can be gleaned from E.M. Forster's *A Passage to India* and Paul Scott's four-volume *The Jewel in the Crown*. Philip Woodruff's (Philip Mason), *The Men Who Ruled India*, 2 vols (London: Jonathan Cape, 1953–1954), traces the evolution of East India Company and Indian Civil Service (ICS) mentalities and is itself a document reflecting those mentalities. Clive Dewey's recent *Anglo-Indian Attitudes: The Mind of the Indian Civil Service* (London: Humbledon Press, 1993), shows the complexity of culture, provenance, motive, and intention among several prominent late nineteenth-century ICS officers.

34. Fifty years later, in 1879, the romance of the ancient, freedom-loving Rajputs was still alive and well in Sir Alfred Lyall's authoritative historical note to the first *Gazetteer of Rajputana*. "We may describe Rajputana," Lyall wrote "as the region within which the pure-blooded Rajput States have maintained their independence under their own chieftains, and have kept together their primitive societies ever since their principal dynasties in Northern India were cast down and swept away by the Mussalman irruption. Of the States of Rajputana, eighteen belong to the first rank in the Empire, being under treaty with the Imperial Government." The quotation is from the historical introduction to *Rajputana and Ajmer: List of Ruling Princes, Chiefs and Leading Personages* (Calcutta: Government of India, Central Publication Branch, 1931). This is the sixth edition of a "work projected in 1890 by Colonel G.H. Trevor, C.S.I., Agent to the Governor General for Rajputana . . . and put together by C.S. Bayley, C.S., then Political Agent, Bikaner," Preface. Some parts of the account in the historical introduction were written as early as 1879. Discourse about "primitive" is insightfully explored in Marianna Torgovnick's *Gone Primitive: Savage Intellects, Modern Lives* (Chicago: University of Chicago Press, 1990). "[P]rimitive societies" such as the Rajput States invoked by Lyall, become "a place to project our feelings about the present and to draw blue-prints of the future . . . " (244).

35. Lawrence, *The India We Served*, 56. Lawrence's reference to "chivalrous gentlemen" invokes discourse generated in English public schools that blended reverence for ancient Greece and medieval chivalry. We deal with the concept of "native gentleman" in Part IV. Here we see how "Rajput" took on gentlemanly overtones. For narratives, histories, and tropes of "gentleman", see Rupert Wilkinson, *Gentlemanly Power* (New York: Oxford University Press, 1964).

2: Liminality: Making a Self Between Two Cultures

1. When Amar Singh arrives at Mhow in 1905 it is a divisional and command headquarters. At that time there were three Army Commands covering India, the Eastern, Southern and Western. Mhow is the headquarters of the Western Command. Amar Singh is ADC to General O'Moore Creagh, general officer commanding in chief for the Western Command. Each of three GOCCs ". . . is responsible for the command, administration, training and efficiency of the troops located in his area. Each Command contains a certain number of districts which in turn contain a certain number of brigade areas; the boundaries of the Command and districts being as far as possible formed to correspond with those of definite civil administrations." A fourth Command, the Northern, was added on November 1, 1920. L.F. Rushbrook Williams, *India in the Year 1920* (Calcutta: Superintendent of Government Printing, 1921), 20.

2. Major General Sir Wyndham (Charles) Knight, K.C.I.E. He served on the North-West Frontier of India in 1897; served the Mohmand Expedition as road commandant; Tirah, 1897–1898; South African War, 1900–1902; D.A.A.G., 8th division in India, 1904–1908; brigade commander and embarkation commandant, Bombay 1915–1918; in command of Bombay District 1917–1919; major general in charge of Administration, Southern Command, 1919–1922.

3. "Curzon to Dawkins," in David Dilks, *Curzon in India: I, Achievement* (New York: Taplinger, 1970), 240.

4. "No. 2012 Secretary of State to Viceroy, Telegram P., November 18, 1915, 7 p.m. (rcd. 19th, 10 a.m.)," Hardinge Papers, vol. 103, Correspondence re European War, Part I, Cambridge University Library. On July 20, 1917, Edwin Montagu, the new secretary of state for India, endorsed Chamberlain's views and forwarded to the cabinet Chamberlain's note recommending that "nine officers holding commissions in the Indian land forces [be selected for king's commissions] as captains and lieutenants in recognition of their services in the present war . . ." In that letter Chamberlain spoke of "the right of the Indian gentleman to take his place beside his white fellow subjects in the King's Army," and of the importance of conceding "the principle of giving Indians command over Europeans." In an earlier letter he had spoken of the negative "effect on recruiting of the racial bar." Letter from India Office to War Office (M. 19105), Dated June 1, 1917, India Office Library and Records, L/mil/7/19013, Secret, Indian Reforms, Grant of Commission to Indians.

5. From the diary entry *Kohat, Tuesday, 31st May, 1921* (continued), "Notes About My Last Leave of Fourteen Days", 1. The Idea. The initial version of the conversation is reported in the entry *Tank, Saturday, 2nd April, 1921*: "Now I had some hot words with the Colonel [Mears] as he had not given me a good report this year."

6. Minority administration refers to the government of a princely state while the maharaja is a minor. See Robert Stern, *The Cat and the Lion: Jaipur State in the British Raj* (Leiden: E.J. Brill, 1988), Chapter 6, "The Chain of European Control," particularly 230–255. "For the first two decades of Sawai Man Singh's reign," Stern observes, "Jaipur's administration advanced under the direction of British officers" (235).

7. Liminality has more than one meaning arising from its basic Latin derivation, *limes*, the boundary. One variant can be found in narratives of rites of passage, from a boy to a man, a girl to a woman—the kind of life-stage passages that Victor Turner invoked in defining liminality. Meanings that defined the self in a known, predictable context evaporate in a miasma of uncertainty that precedes the new, prefigured identity. See his *The Forest of Symbols: Aspects of Ndembu Ritual* (Ithaca: Cornell University Press, 1967), Chapter 4. Turner's is not the variant of liminality we have in mind, though his subsequent treatment of "liminoid" phenomena somewhat resembles it. See Victor Turner,

Process, Performance, and Pilgrimage: A Study in Comparative Symbology (New Delhi: Concept Publishing House, 1979), 53. Another kind of liminality—again, one that we do not have in mind-arises from socially relevant incongruity, from enactments of what Goffman calls profanations, roles, and status "violations" that dramatize disrespect and invert power asymmetries by defying or reversing established conventions. See Erving Goffman, "The Nature of Deference and Demeanor," *American Anthropologist* 58 (1956), especially 493 ff. Persons who find themselves located in a no-man's land between unfamiliar, alien or incommensurable forms of life experience another kind of liminality, the one we do have in mind. Its chaos is the chaos of uncertainty or ambiguity—generated by unknown expectations and unpredictable responses. Talking or acting in absence of the familiar or the prescribed poses dangers, runs risks, arouses fears even as it raises hopes and offers opportunities to become and be someone else and to constitute and experience another form of life.

8. *Mount Abu, Saturday, 27th May, 1905.*

3: How We Encountered the Diary

1. See endnote 26.

2. See C.A. Bayly, *Rulers, Townsmen and Bazaars: North Indian Society in the Age of British Expansion, 1770–1870* (Cambridge: Cambridge University Press, 1983) and Muzaffar Alam, *The Crisis of Empire in Mughal North India: Awadh and the Punjab, 1707–1748* (Delhi: Oxford University Press, 1986).

3. The late Ashim Kumar Roy's *History of the City of Jaipur* (Delhi: Manohar, 1978), particularly Chapter 1, "Jai Singh II, The Founder of the City," and Chapter 2, "Planning of The Jaipur City," provide fairly detailed accounts of Jai Singh's political activities and ambitions, and of the astronomical and religious concerns and commitments that shaped Jaipur's founding and early development. A wide (108 feet) two-mile-long avenue connecting the Chand Pol (Moon Gate) on the west to Suraj Pol (Sun Gate), on the east initially divided the city into four rectangular blocks, now grown into seven, one of which is occupied by the city palace and its buildings, park, and temple environs.The foundation-laying ceremony took place on November 29, 1727, and the city was officially recognized by the Mughal Emperor Muhammad Shah as a capital city in 1733. By Jai Singh's death in 1743, Jaipur had grown into a prosperous, beautiful city. Today's tourists know Jaipur as the "pink city"—a comment on the rose-colored building stone and matching wash that from Maharaja Ram Singh's time (1835–1880) characterized the walled city's shops, houses, temples, and public buildings.We follow Joan L. Erdman's "Jaipur; City Planning in 18th Century India," in A. Dallapicolli, editor, *The Shastric Tradition in Indian Arts* (Heidelberg: University of Heidelberg Press, 1990), 219–235, in our interpretation of Jaipur as a planned city. As she makes clear, its origins were *de novo* as a capital; it did not grow out of a commercial, military or religious site. Erdman's article is particularly rich with respect to ritual and symbolic influences on Jaipur's conception, planning, and construction.

4. Nobles carried a variety of titles inherited from different historical moments.

5. For an account of princely rule and post-Independence land reform in Rajasthan see, "Rajputana Under British Paramountcy" and "The Political Modernization of an Indian Feudal Order: An Analysis of Rajput Adaptation In Rajasthan" in our *Essays on Rajputana*; the latter includes an account of the civil war waged by the "small" Rajputs against the devastating economic effects of simultaneously losing—usually to Jat tenants—their small holdings and their service jobs with big thakurs and princely courts and governments. A Police Memorial at the roundabout near Kanota House is meant to honor those who lost their lives trying to maintain order while implementing land reform.

6. Princess Prem Kumari and the heir apparent Bhawani Singh, now known as the Maharaja of Jaipur. See Quentin Crewe's biography of Man Singh, *The Last Maharaja: A Biography of Sawai Man Singh II, Maharaja of Jaipur* (London: Michael Joseph, 1985), for a more detailed account.

7. In a brief typescript autobiography, Colonel Kesri Singh reports that at various times in Jaipur he held charge of the *Shikarkhana* (Hunting department), and the Forest, and Police departments. His *The Tiger of Rajasthan* was published by Robert Hale in England, by Dodd Mead in America, and by Paul Perry in West Germany. His other books were *Hunting with Horse and Spear* (Delhi: Hindustan Times Press, 1964), *Hints on Tiger Shooting; Pocket Encyclopaedia of Shikar* (Delhi: Hindustan Times Press, 1970), and *What is not Prose is All Poetry*. (No place, no publisher, 1952). Stylistically, he drew on Kipling's ballad format. A good example is a ballad reproduced in his autobiography about how little Kesri outwitted a horse-dealer who had fooled his older brothers. See for details "Colonel Kesri Singh of Kanota," typescript (no place, no date, *circa* 1970s), in Kanota Family Archive.

8. Refer to our introduction to Part VI for an extended explanation of these terms.

9. For more on the meaning and consequences of this pregnant phrase, see the essays in Ashis Nandy's *The Intimate Enemy: Loss and Recovery of Self Under Colonialism* (Delhi: Oxford University Press, 1983).

10. Honorifics showing respect were widely prevalent in princely as in British India. Amar Singh, for example, when he refers to contemporaries often adds the suffix "jee"— which we spell as "ji." Amar Singh is usually referred to in contemporary accounts as General. He was promoted, at the time of his retirement from Jaipur state service in 1936, to the rank of Major General of the Jaipur Forces by Maharaja Man Singh, to whom, as an elder statesman of the realm, he was a friend and confidant. This relationship can be seen in the biography of Man Singh by Quentin Crewe, *The Last Maharaja*.

11. See Mohan Singh, *History of the Champawats* (title in English). His genealogical history, to our knowledge, was the first to include women (wives and daughters) identifying them by the names of their lineage or estate but not by their given names. Champawat is a live social category; in 1992, for example, a major gathering was held of Champawats in former Jodhpur state with hundreds in attendance. Mohan Singh delivered the chief address.

12. Devi Singh is the author of several historical studies. See Devi Singh Mandawa, *Shardul Singhji Shekhawat*, published by the author (Jhunjhunu: 1979). He was editor of a scholarly journal, *Rambankura*.

13. "Sir Pratap Benam Amar Sinha," *Rajasthan Patrika*, May 22, 1983.

4: Reconstructing the Text

1. See earlier endnotes.

2. As Avron Fleishman argues with respect to autobiographies, diaries should not be read as "a self-written biography designed and required to impart verifiable information about the historical subject" but as telling "a truth only [the autobiographer or diarist] . . . can know, the report of how his experience looked or felt from an inside view." "[S]elf-writing" provides "subjective truth or, more properly, a true account of subjectivity." *Figures of Autobiography: The Language of Self- Writing in Victorian and Modern England* (Berkeley: University of California Press, 1982), 7, 8. For thoughtful conceptualizations about and comparisons of autobiography and diaries, and analyses and examples of their practice, see James Olney, editor, *Studies in Autobiography* (New York: Oxford University Press, 1988), and Ronald Blythe, editor, *The Pleasures of Diaries: Four Centuries of Private Writing* (New York: Pantheon Books, 1989). Felicity A. Nussbaum's

"Toward Conceptualizing Diary" which we have found particularly insightful and use elsewhere, appears in the Olney volume, 128–140.

3. Docudrama in print or film may have become the dominant genre of our time. Docudrama blends imaginative and positive truth, fact and fiction, archival sources, and imaginative representations. We may learn more about the truths of Caribbean history and society from Gabriel Garcia Marquez's *One Hundred Years of Solitude* (New York: Harper and Row, 1970) or about Lady Hamilton and Horatio Nelson from Susan Sontag's *The Volcano Lover* (New York: Farrar Strauss Giroux, 1992) than from scholars writing "disciplined" history based on archival sources. We find it hard to choose between Simon Schama's call for disciplined imaginative reconstruction when archival sources are not available to answer important historical questions and Gordon Wood's injunctions to historians to avoid at all costs the slippery slope of the selective use of imaginative truth. The choice is difficult because of recent developments on the docudrama front: Joe McGinniss's docudrama biography of Ted Kennedy; Oliver Stone's docudrama film about President Kennedy's assassination; or Janet Malcolm's articles and book, *In the Freud Archives* (New York: Knopf, 1984), about Jeffrey Masson. For a view that assimilates Malcolm's journalistic practice to an undesirable version of docudrama, see Fred Friendly's review of Janet Malcolm's *The Journalist and the Murderer, The New York Times Book Review*, February 15, 1990.

4. Our ideas about authenticity have been shaped by Henry Louis Gates Jr.'s thought that "like it or not, all writers are 'cultural impersonators.'" See his "'Authenticity,' or the Lesson of Little Tree," *The New York Times Book Review*, November 24, 1991.Written by one Forrest Carter, the initially much celebrated *Education of Little Tree* (New York: Delacorte Press, E. Friede, 1976), presented itself as the autobiography of a Cherokee Indian of that name. Orphaned at the age of ten, he learns the ways of Indians from his Cherokee grandparents in Tennessee. (A critic said it captured a unique vision of native American culture and professors of literature assigned it as supplementary reading on Native American literature.) Then Forrest Carter was "unmasked" as a pseudonym for the late Asa Earl Carter, who Dan Carter, the unmasker, said was "a Ku Klux Klan terrorist, right-wing radio announcer, home-grown American fascist and anti-Semite, rabble rousing demagogue and secret author of the famous 1963 speech by Governor George Wallace of Alabama: 'Segregation now . . . Segregation tomorrow . . . Segregation forever.'"Among the morals of this story, according to Gates, is that "Death of the author types (read Derrida) cannot come to grips with the fact that a book is a cultural event; authorial identity, mystified or not, can be part of that event. What the ideologues of authenticity cannot come to grips with is that fact and fiction have always exerted a reciprocal effect on each other, However truthful you set out to be, your autobiography is never unmediated by literary structures of expression" (1 ff.).

5. The full text of the diary is accessible in two places. In 1976, at Mohan Singh's initiative, the diary, whose physical condition concerned him and us, was microfilmed by the Nehru Memorial Museum and Library. It can be consulted there and in the Regenstein Library of the University of Chicago on written request by *bona fide* scholars. Decisions are taken jointly by the three of us.

5: An Indian Diary in English?

1. This section draws on a paper prepared by us for the Conference on the Preservation of Culture and the Environment in Rajasthan, University of Rajasthan, Jaipur, December 14–17, 1987, and subsequently published as "Becoming a Diarist," in *The Indian Economic and Social History Review* 25:2 (1988): 113–132.

2. *The Rhetoric of English India* (Chicago: University of Chicago Press, 1992), 4.

3. *The Location of Culture* (London: Routledge and Sons, 1994), 7.

4. *Jodhpore, Thursday, 29th August, 1901.*

5. From the entry of January 10, 1916.

6. The second part of the nineteenth century saw a movement for education in the princely states. The British spawned schools on the public school model at Rajkot, Indore, Ajmer and Murree among others. Rulers of the larger states sometimes sponsored schools for the nobles at their courts. Jaipur Nobles School was an example. The philosophy of the British-style public school for princes and nobles is epitomized in a speech given in 1890 by Viceroy Lord Lansdowne, in which he spoke of engrafting upon the old aristocratic society "a form of education adapted to the requirements of that society but to a large extent derived from and inspired by the education at the great public schools of England." Cited in letter of October 24, 1997, from The Mayo Heritage Society, New Delhi, to the Rudolphs. See also Herbert Sherring, *The Mayo College, "The Eton of India," A Record of Twenty Years, 1875–1897*, 2 vols (Calcutta: Thacker, Spink and Co., 1897).

7. For a more extended discussion of Rajput identities, see Chapter 1 of this Part.

8. Philippe Lejeune's phrase in *L'Autobiographie en France* (Paris: 1971), 47, cited in Fleishman, *Figures of Autobiography*, 16. For an overview of the diary as *genre*, see Blythe, *The Pleasure of Diaries*. For a critical theory of diary writing, see Nussbaum, "Toward Conceptualizing Diary," in Olney, *Studies in Autobiography*.

9. See Alain Corbin, "Backstage" and "The Secret of the Individual" in vol. IV, *From the Fires of Revolution to the Great War*, in Philippe Aries and Georges Duby, general editors, *A History of Private Life* (Cambridge, MA: Harvard-Belknap Press, 1990).

10. Crewe, *The Last Maharaja*, xiv.

11. "Timeless Symbols: Images as Icons: Royal Portraits from Rajasthan, 17th-19th Centuries," in Karine Schomer et al., *The Idea of Rajasthan*.

12. See the account by Harbans Mukhia, *History and Historiography During the Reign of Akbar* (New Delhi: Vikas, 1976), 17 ff., 126, 103–104.

13. For details of the text and its translation, see Wheeler M. Thackston's "Translator's Preface" in his *The Baburnama: Memoirs of Babur, Prince and Emperor* (New York and Oxford: Oxford University Press, 1996). After comparing Babur's memoirs to the *Confessions* of St Augustine and Rousseau, and the *Memoirs* of Gibbon and Newton, Thackston tells us that they "are the first—and until relatively recent times, the only—true autobiography in Islamic [sic] literature. Although the biographical sketch had long been an integral part of the literary legacy, and biographical dictionaries for various classes and professions abounded, the autobiography as we know it was unheard of when Babur decided to keep a written record of his life" (9). For an account of subsequent "royal memoirs" see note 4 (10–11). Here is what Babur has to say about his extraordinary autobiographical subjectivity: "I have not written all this to complain: I have simply written the truth. I do not intend by what I have written to compliment myself. I have simply set down exactly what happened. Since I have made it a point in this history to write the truth of every matter and to set down no more than the reality of every event, as a consequence I have reported every good and evil I have seen of father and brother and set down the actuality of every fault and virtue of relative and stranger. May the reader excuse me; may the listener take me not to task." *Baburnama*, folio 201, as quoted by Thackston, 10. For more on Babur and his context, see Stephen Frederic Dale, "Steppe Humanism: The Autobiographical Writings of Zahur Al-Din Muhammed Babur, 1483–1530," in Mariola Offredi, editor, *Literature, Language and the Media in India* (New Delhi: Manohar Publishers, 1992), 3–33.

14. Another remarkable autobiographical work is Ananda Ranga Pillai's diary for the years 1736–1761 which details the military struggle between Britain and France for hegemony

on the Indian subcontinent. Pillai was a scion of the leading commercial family of the Carnatic and for some years first minister to Joseph Francis Dupleix, the French governor of Pondicherry. *The Private Diary of Ananda Ranga Pillai*, 12 vols, Rev J. Frederick Price, editor, K. Rangachari, translator (vols 1–4) and H. Dodwell, translator (vols 5–12) (Madras: Superintendent, Government Press, 1904) and republished (New Delhi: Asian Educational Service, 1985). Also see the recently rehabilitated first-person account by Dean Mahomet of his life in eighteenth-century India, Ireland, and England. See Michael Fisher, *The Travels of Dean Mahomet: An Eighteenth-Century Journey through India* (Berkeley: University of California Press, 1997). Yet another early first-person travel journal is Mohan Lal, *Travels in the Punjab, Afghanistan and Turkestan to Balk, Bokhara, and Herat and a Visit to Great Britain and Germany* (London: Allen and Co., 1846).

15. *Ardhakathanaka* (Jaipur: Prakrit Bharati Sansthan, 1981), viii.

16. Ibid., xx. It might be argued that the epistemological influence of *smriti* (written texts) and *sruti* (orally transmitted knowledge that is heard) influenced the tendency toward anonymity. For example, the vedas, the alleged source of "original" Hinduism, were regarded as authorless versions of cosmological knowledge. Both forms of knowledge lack agents; what was read and heard was said to have existed from time immemorial. The knowledge resembled revealed truth but, unlike revealed truth, there was no source, no son of God or prophet, to tell the world what God or Allah willed or thought. At a more mundane level, those who spoke or created art, e.g. sculptors, musicians, etc. were instruments of anonymous truth or beauty.

17. Ibid., x and xiv. Lath critiques the widely-held view that artistic creations, e.g., sculpture and architecture, like literary texts, were produced anonymously by citing considerable evidence to the contrary.

18. Ibid., x-xxi, where Lath examines the evidence, e.g. playwrights such as Kalidas, authors of Sanskrit texts such as Dandin and Bana, and authors of *katha* ("novels" or romances) and *akhyanika* (accounts of everyday experiences) as well as musicians, painters, sculptors, and architects. Milo Beach in his essay on "The Artists of the Padshahnama," makes clear that individual artists were known, recognized, and, within the confines of a hierarchical court culture, celebrated. He quotes the emperor Jahangir: "I derive such enjoyment from painting and have such expertise in judging it that no work of past or present masters can be shown to me, without the name being mentioned, that I do not instantly recognize who did it." Milo Cleveland Beach and Ebba Koch, editors, with new translations by Wheeler Thackston, *King of the World: The Padshahnama, An Imperial Mughal Manuscript from the Royal Library, Windsor Castle* (London: Aximuth Editions/Sackler Gallery, 1997), 212.

19. There are, for example, a number of brief autobiographical writings by Bengali widows: Rajasundari Dasi, *Amarajibana* (Kalikatu: Kalija Strita Pabalikesana, 1987) with 128 pages; Nistarini Debi, *Sekeleg Kathai* with fifty pages; Sharasundari Debi (the latter two are discussed and cited in Malavika Karlekar, *Indian Book Review* 20:12 [1997]); and the accounts of a turn-of-the-century Christian convert family, Lakshmibai Tilak, *Agadi: Step by Step* (Nasik: M.A. Tilak, 1968) and *I Follow After: An Autobiography* (London: Geoffrey Cumberleage/Oxford University Press, 1950). D.D. Karve (with the editorial assistance of Ellen E. McDonald) provides autobiographical accounts of "what it was like to grow up in an awakening India sixty years ago" in *The New Brahmans: Five Maharastrian Families* (Berkeley: University of California Press, 1963). Leslie A. Fleming provides an insightful account of three autobiographical texts by Krupabai Sattianadhan, Cornelia Sorabji and Pandita Ramabai in "Between Two Worlds: Self-Construction and Self-Identity in the Writings of Three Nineteenth-Century Indian Christian Women," paper presented at the

Association for Asian Studies, March 1988. Fleming mentions in passing autobiographical works in English by élite non-Christian women: Sunity Devee, Maharani of Cooch Behar, *The Autobiography of an Indian Princess* (London: John Murray, 1921); Dr S. Muthulakshmi Reddy, *Autobiography* (Madras: MLJ Press, 1964); Vijaya Raje Scindia, .*The Lost Maharani of Gwalior* (Albany, NY: SUNY Press, 1987); and Gayatri Devi of Jaipur (and Santha Rama Rau), *A Princess Remembers: The Memoirs of the Maharani of Jaipur* (New Delhi: Vikas, 1984), 5th edition. See also Barbara Ramusack, "Fairy Tales, Soap Operas, or Expressions of Individuality: Autobiographies of Indian Princesses," unpublished Ms., National Humanities Center, 1986–1987.

20. Cited in Fleishman, *Figures of Autobiography*, 15.

21. The list for 1898–1899, when he is just getting going, is modest in length and literary merit: it includes three books by that great proponent of self-help in the Victorian era, Samuel Smiles—*Character, Duty*, and *Heroines of India*; the somewhat salacious four-volume *Mysteries of London*, by G.W. Reynolds; *Sports in Many Lands*, by "The Old Shikarry"; three books in praise of empire, W.H. Filchett's *Fight for the Flag* and *Deeds that Won the Empire*, and C.W. Stevens' *With Kitchener to Khartoum*, and, as befits a Jodhpur Lancer, General Sir Evelyn Wood's *Achievements of Cavalry*.

22. John and Lawrence Langhorne, translators; published by Ward, Lock, Bowden, and Co. Amar Singh's library also contains a 1910 printing of a ten-volume edition of the first (1577) English translation of Plutarch by Sir Thomas North, W.H.D. Rouse, editor (London: J.M. Dent). North's translation was a turning point in cultural history because it introduced Plutarch to the English reader and to Shakespeare in particular. The translation was based on Amyot's 1559 French rendering of the Greek text first published in 1517. Amyots translation too was a critical event for the Renaissance in France.

23. Alain Corbin, "The Secret of the Individual," in Aries and Duby, *A History of Private Life*, 501. Corbin cites Maine de Birand, *Journal*, 3 vols (Paris: Vrin, 1995).

24. *Jaipur, Friday, 7th July, 1905*, "Notes About My Last Visit to Mount Abu."

25. *Shanhai Kwan, 18th December, 1900.*

26. *Jaipur, Friday, 7th July, 1905*, "Notes About My Last Visit to Mount Abu."

27. Ibid.

28. Ibid.

6: Reversing the Gaze

1. M.N. Srinivas, "Indian Anthropologists and the Study of Indian Culture," *Economic and Political Weekly*. March 16 (1996): 657.

2. For a theoretical justification of what we have in mind here, see Richard Shweder's chapter on "Cultural Psychology: What Is It?" in *Thinking Through Culture: Expeditions in Cultural Psychology* (Cambridge, MA: Harvard University Press, 1991), where he remarks, "[p]syche refers to the intentional person. Culture refers to the intentional world. Intentional persons and intentional worlds are interdependent things that get dialectically constituted and reconstituted through the intentional activities and practices that are their products, yet make them up" (101).

3. We say "resemble" because Amar Singh was not a professionally trained anthropologist. We return to the question of non-professional ethnography later.

4. See Renato Resaldo on "Cultural Visibility and Invisibility" in his *Culture and Truth: The Remaking of Social Analysis* (Boston: Beacon Press, 1989), 198–204. "[T]he more power one has, the less culture one enjoys, and the more culture one has, the less power one wields."

5. See, for example, Lloyd Warner's studies of Newburyport, Massachusetts in his "Yankee City Series," *Yankee City*, abridged edition (New Haven: Yale University Press, 1963);

Robert S. and Helen Merrill Lynd's studies of "Middletown" (Muncie, Indiana) *Middletown: A Study of Contemporary American Culture* (New York: Harcourt Brace, 1929) and *Middletown in Transition: A Study in Cultural Conflicts* (New York: Harcourt Brace, 1937) and Wilkinson's *Gentlemanly Power* for early studies of downwardly mobile élites in America and Britain. David Riesman, in reference to the Lynds' studies of "Middletown," regularly spoke of "anthropology coming home." Lecture, American Society and Social Structure, Harvard, *circa* 1962. Lloyd Warner's "Yankee City Series" and John P. Marquand's novel, *Point of No Return* (Boston: Little Brown, 1949) are among the earliest reflexive studies of "us" by "us." The humanistic perspective is meant to show how little Warner's behavioral explanations can explain. Both the Lynds and Warner studied downwardly mobile WASPs whose culture, as Resaldo suggests in *Culture and Truth*, became more visible as their power decreased.

6. James Clifford's "On Ethnographic Allegory" tells the story of a student of African ethnohistory who prepares for his fieldwork in Gabon among the Mpongwe by consulting an early twentieth-century work of a pioneering ethnographer, Raponda-Walker. His interview with a Mpongwe chief proceeds well until the chief has trouble with a particular word. "'Just a moment,' he says cheerfully, and disappears into his house to return with a copy of Raponda-Walker's compendium. For the rest of the interview the book lies open on his lap." James Clifford and George E. Marcus, editors, *Writing Culture: The Poetics and Politics of Ethnography* (Berkeley: University of California Press, 1986), 116.

7. For an account and rebuttal of authenticity's epistemological and ontological claim that it takes a native, including a native American or African American, to know and tell about a native, see Gates, Jr., "'Authenticity,' or the Lesson of little Tree." An early ironic, perhaps satiric account of the claim that in order to study a witch you have to be—or become—a witch can be found in Allison Lurie's novel, *Imaginary Friends* (New York: Coward-McCann, 1967), an account of two Cornell sociologists trying to study an upstate New York religious sect whose members believe in the existence and power of extraterrestrial beings/persons with whom they communicate and whose presence among them they anticipate.

8. In Andre Beteille and T.N. Madan, editors, *Encounter and Experience: Personal Accounts of Field Work* (Delhi: Vikas Publishing House, 1975). Madan is one of the earliest reflexive "others" among Indian anthropologists; he makes no special claims in the name of "authenticity." At the same time he sees himself as an anomaly when he remarks that "social anthropology took a very long time to realize the potential of "studying one's own society" (153). He cites two of Bronislaw Malinowski's students, Jomo Kenyatta, "an African tribal chief," and Fei Hsiao-Tung, "a Chinese Mandarin," whose studies were published in 1938 and 1939, as earlier examples of reflexive "natives" writing their own ethnography. He cites Malinowski's observation that writing anthropologies "of one's own people . . . [is] the most arduous, but also the most valuable achievement of a field worker," from Malinowski's Foreword to Fei's *Peasant Life in China*.

9. "On Critical Self-awareness," in *Pathways: Approaches to the Study of Society in India* (Delhi: Oxford University Press, 1994), 159–160.

10. These themes are developed in "On Critical Self-awareness" from accounts of the work of Levi-Strauss and Louis Dumont.

11. See the "Introduction" to Michael Young, *The Ethnography of Malinowski* (London: Routledge & Kegan Paul, 1979), 1–20.

12. "It is clear," Clifford Geertz tells us in *Works and Lives: The Anthropologist as Author* (Stanford, CA: Stanford University Press, 1988), "that in . . . [Foucauldian] terms, anthropology is pretty much entirely on the side of 'literary' discourses rather than 'scientific'

ones.... [E]thnographies tend to look at least as much like romances as they do like lab reports..." (8). Geertz further dismantles the claims of anthropology to be a human science in *After the Fact: Two Countries, Four Decades, One Anthropologist* (Cambridge, MA: Harvard University Press, 1995). See also Michael M.J. Fisher, "Working through the Other: The Jewish, Spanish, Turkish, Iranian, Ukrainian, Lithuanian, German Unconscious of Polish Culture-or-One Hand Clapping: Dialogue, Silences, and the Mourning of Polish Romanticism," in George E. Marcus, editor, *Perilous States: Conversations on Culture, Politics, and Nation* (Chicago: University of Chicago Press, 1993), 187.

13. Geertz, *Works and Lives*, 4–5.

14. Diarists wrote, Felicity Nussbaum tells us, on "the perplexing boundary between the private and public worlds.... [I]t is in that privatization of self, that division between public and private self, that journal is born.... Before diaries were published, they provided a way to keep the truth about oneself out of the tangled skein of power. Nussbaum, "Toward Conceptualizing Diary," 134–135.

15. When early in the diary's history his father, writing to him at the Jodhpur court from the Jaipur court, tells Amar Singh to destroy his letter, Amar Singh goes further. He cuts out several pages of his diary about his age-mate, Jodhpur maharaja, Sardar Singh, for fear of the consequences if their contents became known. His father's injunction to destroy his letter makes him aware that speaking his mind in the diary could, if its secrecy was breached, bring dangerous knowledge to light. (A few months later, his confidence restored, he writes another essay assessing Sardar Singh's character.) Some years later, his patron and mentor, Sir Pratap Singh, formerly regent at Jodhpur but now Maharaja of Idar, is arranging to have his biography written. He asks Amar Singh to help by making his diary available. Amar Singh declares himself ready to destroy his diary rather than have it fall into Sir Pratap's hands. He evades and procrastinates long enough to scuttle the request.

16. Clifford, *Writing Culture*, 14.

PART I - GETTING STARTED

1: About the Diary

1. Amar Singh suffered seriously from boils all his life. Family tradition has it that in his later years he showed signs of being diabetic, a condition that correlates with boils.

2. Translation from Rajasthani by Mohan Singh.

3. Here and below the translations of dohas from Hindi and Marwari are adapted by Mohan Singh and us from those prepared by Professor Shambhu Singh, University of Rajasthan, Jaipur.

4. When Amar Singh sources a doha, he sometimes means the author, but more often the person from whom he got the doha.

5. There is a tradition that Hamir Chauhan resisted an attempt by the Afghan Alauddin Khilji to seize Ranthambor fort. Hamir died in battle and the women of the court performed *johur*, self-immolation. Hamir refused to yield up Mohammed Shah Mongol, a rebel against Alauddin who had sought asylum in the fort. See, for example, R.V. Somani, *History of Mewar* (Jaipur: Champalal Ranka, 1976), 89, 90, 94. A woman's head is anointed with oil at her wedding.

6. Agunta, a friend of the Kanota family, had turned dacoit when his estate was confiscated. Subsequently he was rehabilitated, then brought into Jaipur state service as a deputy superintendent of police.

7. Ram Nathji's diary is in the possession of Kesri Singh, collateral descendant of Ram Nathji and himself a poet and author. Kesri Singh has shared Ram Nathji's 1894 diary with

us.We have no direct evidence for why Ram Nathji kept a diary but we infer that his involvement with things British included an awareness of English public school practices, which included making students keep diaries, and of the diary habits of the upper classes. For example, Stanley Weintraub's 1988 biography of Queen Victoria, *Victoria* (New York: Truman Talley-Dutton, 1988), is replete with references to late nineteenth-century diaries. Their prevalence is confirmed in Michelle Perrot's section, "The Secret of the Individual," Philippe Aries and Georges Duby, general editors, *A History of Private Life, IV: From the Fires of Revolution to the Great War*, Michelle Perrot, editor, Arthur Goldhamer, translator (Cambridge, MA: Harvard-Belknap Press, 1990), 457–547, where the rise and practice of diary writing is insightfully reviewed.

8. ". . . I read the Memoir of Major Leveson' from the *Sport in Many Lands* and 'The Life of Plutarch' from *Plutarch's Lives* and also wrote some dohas from Kishenjee's copy book." *Wednesday, 5th October, 1898.* Plutarch does not appear to have written a life of himself, but the North and Dryden versions of *Plutarch's Lives* include introductions that recount the life of Plutarch. An annotated copy of the Langhorne edition of North's 1579 translation [John and Lawrence Langhorne, translators, *Plutarch's Lives* (Ward, Lock, Bowden and Co., 1889)] in the Amar Singh library at Kanota is inscribed by him on September 22,1898. His library also contains an edition "Englished by Sir Thomas North" (London: J.M. Dent and Sons, 1910). Amar Singh begins "The Diary" on September 3, 1898. We have no positive evidence that he saw or read *Plutarch's Lives* before he began "The Diary." He probably had access to a copy if, as we suppose, Ram Nathji lent him his copy. In any case it is evident from Amar Singh's epigraphic use of Plutarch passages that reading Plutarch played an important part in establishing, shaping and sustaining his diary habit.

9. English officers posted to Rajputana repaired in the hot weather to Mount Abu, Rajputana's hill station in the southwest on the Gujarat border. Sarkar was calling on the Agent to the Governor General (AGG), the senior raj official responsible for Britain's indirect rule (paramountcy) over the twenty-two princely states of Rajputana. Like the Mughal subedars (provincial governors) who preceded him, the AGG normally resided at Ajmer, at the center of Rajputana. From there he supervised the British officers of the Political Department, the raj's foreign service, who served, depending on the importance of the state in question, as "agents" or "residents." For an account of the service, see Sir Terence Creagh Coen, *The Indian Political Service: A Study in Indirect Rule* (London: Chatto and Windus, 1971).

10. Peelva, the small estate in Jodhpur from which two of Amar Singh's great-uncles (Fateh Singh and Shambhu Singh) and his grandfather (Zorawar Singh) left for service in Jaipur in 1854 and 1861 respectively. See our "A Bureaucratic Lineage in Princely India" in *Essays on Rajputana, Reflections on History, Culture and Administration* (New Delhi: Concept Publishing House, 1984), 90 *passim*.The reference seems to be to the house maintained by the family in Jodhpur city, not the haveli at the Peelva country estate.

11. *Jaipore, Saturday, 8th July, 1905.*

12. *Jaipore, Friday, 7th July, 1905,* "Notes About My Last Visit to Mount Abu," continued on July 11.

13. *Mount Abu, Monday, 12th June, 1905.*

14. *Jaipore, Friday, 7th July, 1905,* "notes".

15. *Sevari, Wednesday, 12th October, 1898.*

16. *Jaipur, Thursday, 5th April, 1900.*

17. *Meerut, Tuesday, 5th January, 1904.*

18. *Jodhpore, Thursday, 22nd March, 1990.*

19. *Jadhpore, Monday, 19th February, 1900,* "Comments on My Trip to Heeradeosar and Birai."

20. *Jaipore, Wednesday, 5th October, 1904.*

21. *Jaipore, Thursday, 6th October, 1904.*

22. *Plutarch's Lives* became a key Renaissance text only after 1517 when it was first published in a Greek version. In 1559 Jacques Amyot translated the Greek text into French and in 1579 North translated Amyot's French text into English. North's published translation introduced Plutarch to the English-speaking world of Shakespeare's time. The Lives' moral assessment of persons, narrative, and drama, which did so much to shape Shakespeare's literary imagination and the characters and morality of his Roman tragedies, apparently contributes to Amar Singh's temporarily aborted decision of September 18, 1898, "to depict if possible the features and manners of any man I come across who interests me."

23. Sir William Napier, a literary giant of his time, was said by Samuel Smiles to have garnered from a lifelong devotion to Plutarch "a passionate admiration for the great heroes of antiquity," *Duty* (London: John Murray, 1883), 276. His brother, Charles Napier, conqueror of Sind in 1843 and himself a devoted reader of Plutarch and an important literary as well as military contributor to the heroism of empire, is "immortalized" by statues in Trafalgar Square and St Paul's Cathedral.

24. Samuel Smiles, *Character* (New York: A.L. Burt, c. 1888), 277.

25. See Part VI, Chapter 1, *Jaipore, Friday, 20th April, 1900,* "Family Politics at the Jodhpore Court."

26. Amar Singh's use of the word "heard" here is not an awkwardness. Sir Pratap, whose English was indifferent, usually had material in English read to him.

27. *Dehra Dun, Friday, 21st October, 1904.* Notes About My Last Vacation, XXVI, "Some Anecdotes." See *Maharaja Sir Pratapsinghji Sahib ka Swalikhit Jivan-Charitr,* Shriman Radhakrishan, editor (Mori Gate, Lahore: Vir Milap Press-Khushalchandji "Khursand," 1939).

28. *Jaipore, 9th, 12th, 14th, 16th, 19th October, 1904.* "Notes About My Last Visit to Satheen," 27. Epilogue.

29. In a sense, Amar Singh delivers on this commitment when, in several long essays, he gives the gist of his "talks" with the Maharaja of Kishengarh, Madan Singh, his younger friend who is about to be married to a princess of Udaipur. See Part V, Chapter 2.

30. *Jodhpore, Thursday, 29th August, 1901.*

31. *Jaipore, Saturday, 6th September, 1902.* "Notes About My Visit to Satheen," VII. Journey from Jodhpore.

32. *Jaipore, Saturday, 6th September, 1902.*

33. Sheo Nath Singh's diary is in the possession of Mohan Singh, his son and heir. Sardar Singh's diary is in the possession of his son, Gulab Singh.

34. *Jodhpore, Saturday, 7th October, 1899.*

2: Education of a Diarist

1. One hundred years after its publication in 1898 Oxford University Press declared Corelli's *The Sorrows of Satan* "an influential *Fin-de-Siecle* text" and republished it as an Oxford World's Classic. See E.S. Turner's review of Teresa Ransom's *The Mysterious Marie Corelli: Queen of the Victorian Bestsellers,* in *London Review of Books,* July 29, 1999, pp. 30–31. See G.S. Fowler, *Creative and Sexual Science, or Manhood, Womanhood and their Mutual Interrelations* (London: Fowler and Wells, 1875) and George Drysdale, *The Elements of Social Science: Physical, Sexual and Natural Religion . . . Containing an Exposition of the True Cause and only Cure of the Three Primary Social Evils—Poverty, Prostitution and*

Celibacy. First edition, 1855, entitled *Physical, Sexual and Natural Religion*, last edition 1905. *Elements* ran into thirty-five editions over fifty years, sold 90,000 copies, was translated into eleven languages and influenced Margaret Sanger's feminism and campaign for birth control. A neo-Malthusian, Drysdale read his era's grinding poverty and low wages, its mental and physical sexual disease, and female oppression and wretchedness as curable by a preventive check beyond Malthus' celibacy and late marriage: "preventive intercourse" using contraception. Drysdale's *Elements* made a case for total revision of sexual and social attitudes. Contraception and free and autonomous sexual relations were his answer to not only the Malthusian dilemma but also to sexual repression, prostitution, and venereal disease. J. Miriam Benn tells us in her comprehensive account of Drysdale's neo-Malthusian political economy and cultural resistance, that "In England," *Elements* "was the most notorious [book] of its age, read in the guiltiest secrecy." *The Predicaments of Love* (London: Pluto Press, 1992), 10.

2. We infer his year of entry as 1888, when Sir Pratap brought him and his brother Sheo Nath Singh from Jaipur. In 1889–1890 he is reported in class III. *Administrative Report of the Jodhpur State, 1889–1890* (Jodhpur: Jodhpur State, 1891, hereafter JoAR). He is reported leaving in 1896 (*JoAR, 1895–1896*), 124. Administrative reports of Jodhpur state begin in 1884–1885, and are published variously at Calcutta (1884–1885); Madras (1885–1886); Jodhpur (1886–1918); Ajmer (*Report on the Administration of the Marwar State, 1918 to 1920–1921*); Jodhpur (1921–1922 to 1946).

3. Herbert Sherring, *The Mayo College, "The Eton of India": A Record of Twenty Years, 1875–1895*, 2 vols (Calcutta: Thacker, Spink and Co., 1897).

4. *JoAR*, 1889–1890, 14–4.

5. *JoAR*, 1885–1886, 130.

6. Sir Walter R. Lawrence, *The India We Served* (London: Cassell, 1928), 205.

7. *Jaipore, Friday, 7th July, 1905* (continued July 11). "Notes About My Visit to Mount Abu," XXX, Oria.

8. Ibid.

9. *Jodhpore, Sunday, 18th December, 1898*. Chittaranjan Dutt, principal of the Landour Language School, Mussoorie, UP, was consulted on the translation.

10. We have heard two traditions about the dohas attributed to Rajya. 1) A conference of *darogas* (a community of persons who were servants in Rajput households) claimed that Rajya was a daroga. Born in 1769 at Khuchaman near Makrana, Rajya's proper name was Raja Ram; 2) Rajya is part of the formal literary tradition of Rajputana. The author of Rajya dohas was Charan Kiriya Kirpa Ram, born in village Dani, in Shekhawati, in 1795. Kirpa Ram is said to have fallen sick. Nursed back to health by his servant Rajya, he immortalized him in his couplets.We are indebted to Kesri Singh for these accounts.

11. The first doha is one of fifty of Rajya's dohas Amar Singh enters at *Jodhpore, Wednesday, 1st March, 1899*; the second is from a retrospective account about a visit to Alwar entered at *Jodhpore, Tuesday, 14th August, 1900*.

12. For example, in Rabindranath Tagore's *Katha* (first published in 1880, then edited and republished in 1894 by Mohitchandra Sen and subsequently included in a Tagore collection brought out by the Indian Publishing House), Tagore tells us that "[t]he Rajput stories were retrieved from Tod's *Rajasthan* . . . " where, for example, the Prithvi Raj poem about Rana Pratap discussed below appears in Tod's translation from the Dingal [for which he apologizes]. We are indebted to Sujit Mukherjee for the bibliographic references to Tagore's tales and poems about Rajasthan. For a recent overview of early nationalism in Bengal, see Sudipta Kaviraj, *The Unhappy Consciousness: Bankimchandra Chattopadhyay*

and the Formation of Nationalist Discourse in India (New Delhi: Oxford University Press, 1995).

13. A new translation with comparisons to and commentary on Tod's translation, and an account of the circumstances under which Prithvi Raj is said to have written the doha, is given in Kesri Singh, *The Hero of Haldighati* (Jodhpur: Books Treasure—Maharana—Mewar Publications Trust, 1996).

14. See Kesri Singh, *The Hero of Haldighati*, 104.

15. In this translation we have drawn on versions from Mohan Singh (personal consultation), Dr Shambhu Singh (personal consultation), and Kesri Singh, *The Hero of Haldighati*, 107. Most of the dohas Amar Singh records are in Rajasthani, and not readily accessible to Hindi speakers by virtue of differences in vocabulary and syntax.

16. Samuel Smiles wrote more than twenty books. Of these, *Self Help*, the first, made his reputation, selling 20,000 copies in the first year, 150,000 by 1889. Asa Briggs, "Samuel Smiles and the Gospel of Work," *The Cambridge Journal* 2:9 (1949): 553. It was translated into Dutch, French, Danish, German, Italian, Japanese, Arabic, Turkish, and several Indian languages. For an analysis of Smiles and the creation of what Bruce Bell calls a mid-nineteenth-century "business ideology," see his "The Business Ideology of Samuel Smiles," (Master's thesis, University of Chicago, 1972), 5.

17. As an adept of the science of phrenology, Fowler presented conventional morality as science derived from observation of the species rather than as religion: "Males are the natural protectors of females and offspring. . . . Threatened swine instantly form with their pigs in the centre, sows next outside, and boars outside of all, heads to the front, fierce in defence of both. . . ." (119). *Creative and Sexual Science* was widely prescribed at the collegiate level. The late Irene Gilbert's work on Aligarh Anglo-Indian College suggests that it was in use there and in other élite collegiate institutions in India in the second half of the nineteenth century (Personal communication from Irene Gilbert, 1973).In their time Fowler and his brother were widely respected for their development of the science of phrenology, a "science" based on meticulously controlled observations. Phrenologists claimed that they could generate theories about character and personality on the basis of physique and physiognomy: "The highest type of manhood unites both forms [of two types of physique] by being both broad, from shoulder to shoulder and deep from sternum to scapula. Of this form, George Washington, Thomas Jefferson, John Hancock and Daniel Webster, formed perfect types," *Creative and Sexual Science*, 118. Another Fowler volume is entitled *Human Science of Phrenology* (Philadelphia: National Publishing Company and San Francisco: A.L. Bancroft and Co., 1873). Henry Bauer, in *Scientific History and the Myth of the Scientific Method* (Champaign: University of Illinois Press, 1993), uses Fowler to critique the pretensions of scientific method by arguing that phrenology like astrology and other now discredited sciences, used "scientific methods" and claimed verifiable results but lost the ability to attract respectable validating paradigm communities. Phrenology is sometimes read as a forerunner of various "scientific" schools of psychology.

18. Amar Singh followed him in this practice. At his death in 1942, his library contained some 2,300 volumes, a good many runs of journals, and ninety bound volumes of recipes and culinary lore, many taken from magazines and newspapers, that he collected and organized. Amar Singh's library has been preserved and cataloged and is housed at Kanota fort.

19. Taking the life of a charan, like taking the life of a Brahman, was regarded as a particularly heinous crime because its *karmic* consequences were severe, e.g. reincarnation in the lowest form of life. As a result, charans were often employed to accompany and "guard"

trade caravans, a lucrative occupation that connected charans to the traders and merchants among the Oswal and Jain communities as well as to Rajput warrior rulers whom they served in the other capacities noted in the text. According to British ethnographic sources, charans at Jodhpur performed sacred legitimating functions that elsewhere were performed by Brahmans, e.g. the barath of the village invoked the blessings at the wedding and installation of the ruler and, in return for his service, received from the durbar (crown), a robe of honor and an elephant. *Rajputana and Ajmer: List of Ruling Princes, Chiefs and Leading Personages,* sixth edition (Calcutta: Government of India Central Publication Branch, 1931), p. 105.

20. Kaviraj (Court Poet) Shyamaldas' four-volume *Vir Vinod* (Hero's Delight) is probably the most important "modern" history of Rajputana in Hindi. It did not shape pre-Independence historiography or language because, at its printing in 1894 (on folio-size, non-acid paper and with beautiful fonts), it was suppressed by the then-Udaipur maharaja, Fateh Singh, a policy continued by his successor, Bhupal Singh. The volume is available in a reprint by Motilal Banarsidas (Delhi: 1986).

21. Our knowledge of Ram Nathji's pathbreaking European tour is based on the diary he kept during his time abroad.

22. With the fading of the unselfconscious favoring of positivist and Rankian history and the renewed attention to myth, epic, and storytelling traditions as valid sources for historical reconstruction, Ram Nath Ratnu's standing as an early, if not the first, published "modern" historian of Rajasthan becomes less striking than might have been the case in the 1970s. He was a participant in a late nineteenth-century movement to create histories that, by combining post-Rankian positivist historiography with Carlyle-like heroic moral drama, prided itself on being liberated from the *hukumvad* (at the command of) historiography of bardic literature. Ram Nathji's competitors for an inaugural role in modern Rajasthan history are: Shyamaldas, *Vir Vinod*; Jwala Sahaie, *Waquaya Rajpootana*, 3 vols (Agra: Mufid-aum Press, 1878–1879); Maulvi Mohammad Oobeyudulla Farhati, *Tarikh Tuhf-i-Rajasthan* (Udaipur: Sajjan Yantralaya, 1889), Hindi and Urdu; and Munshi Devi Prasad, *History of the Castes and Communities of a Marwar* (no place, no date available—mentioned in *Kshatra Dharma*, November 1939; the editor of a recent republication of one of Prasad's works says it was published between 1881 and 1894); *Solahavi Sadi me Rajasthan athva Munshi Devi Prasad Krt 'Aitihasik Caritra-Mala* (Ajmer: Manohar Prakash, 1977).

23. *The Mysteries of London,* by George W.M. Reynolds, appears to have been frequently republished in the nineteenth century. Three volumes were published by George Vickers (London: 1845). The volumes appear to be collections of free standing articles that may have been published separately. *The Mysteries of the Court of London* were published by John Dicks at London (no date). Amar Singh's library has eight volumes.

24. For the context of Ram Nathji's *History of Rajasthan,* see note 56.

25. Published in London between 1894 and 1946.

26. Published at Allahabad, the *Pioneer* was the widest circulating newspaper in north India. In the 1880s it became the vehicle of Kipling's earliest writing. See Martin Fido, *Rudyard Kipling* (London: Hamlyn, 1974), 35 and 52.

27. J.T. Headley, 1813–1897, a prolific (thirty books) "popular" historian and biographer.

3: Sarkar

1. See "Introduction, 1, for a discussion of Sir Pratap's relationship with Queen Victoria.

2. Lawrence, *India*, 203. Encomiums to Sir Pratap lingered on, a measure of the powerful image of the perfect prince—soldier, sportsman, and gentleman—which pervaded Amar

Singh's youth. A 1989 book on the Indian Army, *Armies of the Raj*, by Byron Farwell (New York: Norton) devotes two pages to Sir Pratap, "the most famous of the Indian commanders of Imperial Service Troops" (230–231).

3. Philip Mason in 1974 presented Sir Pratap this way: "It is extraordinary how often the name recurs of Sir Partab Singh . . . 'a man whose name spells chivalry and all that is highest and noblest in the human race.' Thus wrote General Sir Horace Smith-Dorrien in *Memories of Forty-Eight Years' Service* who adds that all Englishmen admired 'his bravery, his adroitness at every form of sport and especially pigsticking and polo and his wonderful stories, so modestly and picturesquely told.' Indeed, Sir Partab summed up the Englishman's idea of what an Indian should be: brave, courageous, dignified, handsome, manly— and devoted to Queen Victoria." *A Matter of Honour: An Account of the Indian Army, Its Officers and Men* (London: Papermac, 1986), 389.

4. Akhai Singh, a grandson of Maharaja Takhat Singh of Jodhpur, has lived for some years with Amar Singh at Ratanada Palace, Sir Pratap's residence. They become fast friends in China and remain so at the Imperial Cadet Corps. To avoid confusion we have edited Amar Singh's text to use the title maharaja for rulers only and maharaj for a ruler's brothers or sons. The *baboo* is office secretary, and the munshi may also be office staff.

5. For an extended discussion of Sir Pratap's views on religion, see R.B. van Wart, *The Life of Lieut.-General H.H. Sir Pratap Singh* (London: Oxford University Press, 1926), 191–199. See also Daya Krishna, "The Vedic Corpus: Some Questions," *Indian Philosophy: A Counter Perspective* (Delhi: Oxford University Press, 1991), 63–94, where he challenges Arya Samaj and other "vedantic" claims about the "original" nature of the four *Vedas* and questions their validity as texts.

6. The *Ramayana* tells the story of Rama's virtue as son, brother, and husband, his war with Ravana, exile and return as king of Ayodhya. The *Mahabharata*'s 100,000 verses include Krishna's view of *karma* (the *Bhagavat Gita*) in the larger context of the war between the related Pandava and Kaurava lineages for possession of the ancient kingdom of Bharat.The ethics of the much longer, complex, and sophisticated *Mahabharata* are ambiguous and skeptical. The two epics' heroes and demons, stories and events, furnish the moral imagination and mundane vocabulary of Indian literary and village discourse, somewhat like the Bible and Shakespeare's plays do for western consciousness, metaphor, and vocabulary. They are recreated in folk theater and the oral tradition. See Philip Lutgendorf, *The Life of a Text: Performing the Ramcaritmanas of Tulsidas* (Berkeley: University of California Press, 1991), Paula Richman, editor, *Many Ramayanas: The Diversity of a Narrative Tradition in South Asia* (Berkeley: University of California Press, 1991), and Lloyd I. Rudolph, "Cultural Politics in India," in Harold Gould and Sumit Ganguly, editors, *India Votes: Alliance Politics and Minority Governments in the 9th and 10th General Elections* (Boulder: Westview Press, 1993), for contemporary accounts of the *Ramayana*'s place in literary and popular discourse. Recent translations and interpretations of the *Mahabharata* include Hans Van Buitenen, editor and translator, *Mahabharata* (Chicago: University of Chicago Press, 1973), incomplete in five volumes.

7. The most honored and celebrated of Marwar's folk heroes, Pabuji is said to have been a forebear of Rao Jodha, founder of Jodhpur. He is said to have died while fighting against robbers who were stealing the cows of some charan women (source: Mohan Singh). *Bhopas* (wandering balladeers) perform episodes from Pabuji's life in song and verse, music and dance, before a *padh* (a scrim-like colorful backdrop painting on cloth of the Pabuji legend).

8. No doubt a British characterization, drawing on the currently fashionable classical analogies, and comparing the now retired regent to the Greeks' wise old counselor at Troy.

4: Hurjee

1. Sir Pratap, as commander of Jodhpur's Imperial Service Forces, manages to have a small contingent accompany Indian Army units in campaigns at Mohmand, Tirah, and Black Mountain. Imperial Service Forces' participation in these campaigns paves the way for the Jodhpur Lancers to be sent to China during the Boxer Rebellion as part of the Allied Expeditionary Force. See Part II. Beginning in the 1890s, the British, in order to counter what they perceived as a renewed Russian threat to Afghanistan, built roads, bridges, and railways to strengthen control over the frontier generally and in relation to particular passes leading into Afghanistan. "[B]y 1897, the whole tribal area was simmering with discontent that often erupted into open rebellion. . . . In all 75,000 troops were engaged for three years in checking uprisings and pacifying the area." Parshotam Mehra, *A Dictionary of Modern Indian History, 1707–1947* (Delhi: Oxford University Press, 1985), 521. See also Ram Nath Ratnu, *Idar*, 12, and Charles Chevenix Trench, *The Indian Army and the King's Enemies, 1900–1947* (New York: Thames and Hudson, 1988), 122–126.

2. R.B. van Wart reports this *contretemps* in his *Sir Pratap Singh*, 97. "A new departure was made by housing [the Marquis of Lansdowne] at the bungalow of Thakur Hari Singh at Ratanada, instead of at Paota, where distinguished visitors had previously been lodged."

3. "Rajput" is not a self-evident category, although it so appears to upper-class Rajputs in Rajputana. There are several stories about the "origins" and making of the category, some discussed in Introduction, 1. The theories advanced by Dirk Kolff and Nicholas Dirks do not coincide with those of local Rajput historians who assert that Rajputs are the descendants of the Vedic Kshatriyas, not occupants of social categories created in recent historical time. Thus, they hold, the Maharaja of Jaipur is a direct descendant of Ram, as the Maharaja of Karauli is a direct descendant of Krishna, and both can trace their genealogical tables to the Vedic period. For more on genealogies, notably those of the Jodhpur lineages, see Thakur Mohan Singh Kanota, *Champawaton Ka Itihas*, 3 vols (Jaipur: Ranbankura, 1991).Dirk Kolff argues that in the fluid social landscape of the sixteenth and seventeenth centuries "Rajput" was an "open" status category used for fighting men recruited from local "milit-ary labor markets" for mobile fighting units. Conquering chiefs of various provenances also could manage to become Rajput rulers through the practice of "Hindu" rituals and the acquisition of suitable genealogies. Kolff believes that during the Mughal era, when Rajput rulers in Rajasthan allied with and fought for the Mughal emperors, joined their court societies, and married their daughters to Mughal emperors, "Rajput" tended to become a closed or exclusive category. At the village level among Rajputs of small means it probably continued to resemble practice in the Gangetic plain where status remained more fluid and relatively open. Dirk Kolff, *Naukar, Rajput, Sepoy: The Ethnohistory of the Military Labour Market in Hindustan, 1450–1850* (Cambridge: Cambridge University Press, 1990). Sir Pratap struggles to win recognition for Hurjee in the context of Rajput exclusivity. His effort illustrates the limits on how far kings can manipulate the caste structure. For an argument about the political nature of the process by which caste status is created and changed, see Nicholas Dirks, *The Hollow Crown: Ethnohistory Of an Indian Kingdom* (New York: Cambridge University Press, 1987). For the role of bards in the process of assimilation, see A.M. Shah and R.G. Shroff, "The Vahivanca Barots of Gujarat: A Caste of Genealogists and Mythographers," in Milton Singer, editor, *Traditional India: Structure and Change* (Philadelphia: American Folklore Society, 1959), 55 and 62. For the constitution of Rajput identities in the seventeenth century, see Norman P. Ziegler, "The Seventeenth Century Chronicles of Marvara: A Study in the Evolution and Use of Oral Traditions in Western India," *History in Africa* 3 (1976): 127–153; "Marvari Historical Chronicles: Sources for the Social and Cultural History

of Rajasthan," *Indian Economic and Social History Review* 13 (1976): 219–250; See also Richard G. Fox, *Realm and Region in the Anthropology of Complex Society* (paper prepared for conference, "Formal Models for the Study of Regional Social Structure," University of New Mexico, October 18–20, 1973).

4. Dalpat Singh is celebrated as a heroin the *teen murti* (three images) monument, a three-sided cenotaph that gives an important New Delhi roundabout its name. His is one of the three full-sized figures depicted on the cenotaph. The teen murti provides the address for the Nehru Memorial Museum and library, site of Prime Minister Jawaharlal Nehru's residence and, before Independence, the residence of the commander in chief of the Indian Army. Dalpat Singh is commemorated on Haifa Day, an event celebrated by the 61st Cavalry on the grounds at Jaipur which Amar Singh built for the Jaipur Lancers, the princely state cavalry he commanded in the 1920s. *Times of India*, September 25, 1991. For a detailed, critical account of the war in the Middle East during World War I, including the role of Indian forces at Haifa and elsewhere, see A.J. Barker, *The Neglected War: Mesopotamia 1914–1918* (London: Faber and Faber, 1967).

5. Amar Singh's generous if critical retrospective assessment of Hurjee is given in an "obituary" in Part II, 4.

5: The Apprentice

1. Lieutenant Colonel Archibald Adams, who served as administrative medical officer in Rajputana, reports that the Lancers, "locally known as the Sardar Risala" after the minor Maharaja Sardar Singh, were first raised ten years before these events, in 1889. Ten years later, in 1899, the Lancers had two regiments. Each regiment had eight squadron officers, of whom Amar Singh was one. In addition, each regiment had eight Jamadars, eight Kote Daffadars, ninety-six Daffadars, and 1,058 Sowars. The squadrons, Adams says, were organized by "clan" — Jodhas, Khichis, Mertias, Gogades and Kaimkhanis. He does not tell us whether this principle of organization springs from local inspiration or is driven by a British understanding of Indian society. See Adams' *The Western Rajputana States: A Medico-Topographical and General Account of Marwar, Sirohi, Jaisalmer* (London: Junior Army and Navy Stores, 1899), 109.

2. This disastrous population decline occurs between the census of 1891 and 1901. Its causes include famine and emigration. Over the decade from 1891–1901, Jodhpur's population drops from 2,528,178 to 1,935,565. To judge from the export of hides, 1,400,000 cattle died. For details see *JoAR* for 1898–1899, 11 and 22, and for 1899–1900, 6.

3. "No one who had the privilege of knowing Sir Pratap will ever forget the wonderful language which he ultimately evolved for himself. His constant associations with Europeans for the rest of life [during and after his visit to England for Queen Victoria's golden jubilee in 1887] should have enabled him to speak English both well and fluently, had he so wished; but his knack of summing up the situation in a most apposite and original phrase of broken English proved so entertaining to his hearers that he clung to it throughout his life. "Those who should know best tell me that he was never a scholar, and could not have improved his English. One wonders!" van Wart, *Sir Pratap Singh*, 80.

4. The three essays in Kesri Singh's *The Hero of Haldighati* including translations of bardic poetry in Dingal about Rana Pratap, provide a detailed critical reconstruction of the battle of Haldighati and critique the historiography about it.

5. The Boer War is being waged in the Transvaal and other provinces with large "native" (African) populations. Amar Singh's remark makes clear that he expected the Jodhpur Lancers might be sent to fight in the Transvaal. According to Philip Mason, his expectation proved incorrect because British military commanders and senior administrators and

politicians feared sending "native" troops to fight the Boers in areas with such native concentrations. Doing so ". . . might have showed [natives] . . . the way to fight the British too; it was agreed it should be a 'white man's war,'" *A Matter of Honour*, 305.

6. The allied Boer states of Transvaal and the Orange Free State had declared war on Britain on October 12, 1899. Their initial successes included the capture of Mafeking and sieges of Kimberly and Ladysmith. By 1900 heavy reinforcements under the commands of Generals F.S. Roberts and Lord Kitchener turned the tide of battle, including the relief of Ladysmith, the occasion for Col. Wyllie's celebratory party. For reasons mentioned in note 5, Jodhpur sent only a notional transport unit to participate in the Boer War. As becomes apparent in Part II, the main body of its forces, the Lancers, was dispatched in 1900 to China where they became part of an Allied Expeditionary Force whose initial mission was to relieve the Boxer's siege of the foreign legations in Beijing.

6: Manners and Mores

1. Maharaj Fateh Singh's father, Maharaj Zorawar Singh, was Maharaja Takhat Singh's (1843–1872) second son, Sir Pratap Singh his third. Royal descendants were usually granted estates.

7: A Mania for Polo

1. The matter between asterisks has been advanced from the essay of June 17 which follows below.

2. Our account is drawn *inter alia* from the following sources: Earl of Suffolk and Berkshire, *The Encyclopedia of Sport and Games*, vol. 3 (London: William Heinemann, 1911), 352–370; *Encyclopaedia Britannica*, 11th edition, vol. 22 (1911), 11–12 and 19th edition, vol. 14, 760–762; Frank G. Menke, *The Encyclopedia of Sports*, 5th revised edition (New York: A.S. Barnes and Co., 1976), 808–820.

3. Abu al-Fadhl Ibn Mubarak, al-Hindi, *Ain-i-Akbari*, edited and translated by Henry Blochman (Calcutta: Asiatic Society of Bengal, 1873).

4. The scheme of Imperial Service, that is, forces raised in and paid for by some princely states, was inaugurated in the viceroyalty of Lord Dufferin (1884–1888) as part of an effort to lower Government of India (GOI) military expenditures. Sir Pratap, Jodhpur's regent, immediately joined, but Jaipur's Maharaja Madho Singh held back. By the mid–1880s, GOI military expenditures accounted for 40 to 50 percent of its annual revenue. Reducing military expenditure became one of the first demands of the Indian National Congress at its founding in 1885. Stanley Wolpert, *A New History of India* (New York: Oxford University Press, 1977), 259. The effort to organize the Jodhpur Lancers began in 1889 but was not "completed" until 1896 when "irregulars" had been disbanded and the program for European style training fully established. Acharya, *JoAR*, 150.

5. The Challenge Cup tournament took place at Poona, where Jodhpur defeated the 7th Hussars by eight goals to love. Van Wart, *Sir Pratap Singh*, 103.

6. Quentin Crewe's *The Last Maharaja: A Biography of Sawai Man Singh II, Maharaja of Jaipur* (London: Michael Joseph, 1985), elaborates on Man Singh's distinguished career in polo.

7. J.N.D. La Touche, executive engineer in the Indian public works department, was on deputation to Jodhpur.

8. The young maharaja, Jai Singh, who is about Amar Singh's age, has two guardians, one English, Major Kettlewell, the other Amar Singh's father, Narain Singh, who is referred to as his Indian, native or assistant guardian. Jai Singh has not yet been granted his powers and so remains under tutelage. Educating this prince proved an enormous

challenge and, in time, an enormous disappointment to raj administrators. Brilliant, charismatic, and willful, he was cast in the role of a leader like Sir Pratap of Jodhpur and, after him, Ganga Singh of Bikaner. Instead, his life ended in exile where, in 1937, he died in Paris as the result of a mysterious accident. Jai Singh became a patron of Hindu learning and nationalism and a figure in the Hindu revival of the 1920s, a revival that laid the groundwork for and spawned some of the leaders of the post-Independence Hindu nationalist politics of the Bharatiya Janata Party (BJP). Shail Mayaram's *Resisting Regimes: Myth, Memory and the Shaping of Muslim Identity* (Delhi: Oxford University Press, 1997) provides a powerful, innovative interpretation of Alwar and Jai Singh. Anne Norton is working on a treatment of Jai Singh in her work on the education of Indian princes.

9. Cantonment near Ajmer. After Independence, Nasirabad remained a cantonment, serving as the headquarters of the Rajput Rifles.

8: Blood and Other Sports

1. Sir Swinton is responsible for several of Jaipur's most famous buildings, including the Indo-Saracenic Prince Albert Museum in Ram Niwas garden and for Ramgarh Lake, for many years the source of Jaipur's water supply. He served from about 1874 to 1903. For more on Sir Swinton Jacob's career and legacy in Rajputana, see Thomas R. Metcalf, *An Imperial Vision: Indian Architecture and Britain's Raj* (Berkeley: University of California Press, 1989), and Vikramaditya Prakash, "Productions of Identity in (Post) Colonial 'Indian' Architecture: Hegemony and Its Discontents in Jaipur" (Ph.D. dissertation, Cornell University, 1993).

9: My Family

1. Women in cultivated Rajput society in Rajasthan were known by the name of their lineages: thus, the Shishodianiji, the woman of Shishodia lineage, the ruling lineage of Mewar-Udaipur. Some interpreters see this usage as a mark of respect and sheltering, others as form of subordination and erasure. See below, Part V, for more on women's lives as seen through Amar Singh's often empathetic vision. For aspects of Rajput womens' lives in Rajasthan, see Varsha Joshi, *Polygamy and Purdah: Women and Society among Rajputs* (Jaipur: Rawat Publications, 1995), and Rama Mehta, *In the Haveli* (New Delhi: Arnold Heineman, 1977).

2. *Jodhpore, Monday, 14th May, 1900.*

3. Amar Singh, according to the Kanota Family Archive, states that the property was of 60 *bighas* (one bigha is half to 2/3 acre depending on a provisional standard).

4. The Rambagh palace and its gardens were converted, in the 1960s, into Jaipur's premier five-star hotel. In the late 1970s Mohan Singh, Amar Singh's nephew and heir, converted the Kanota gardenhouse into Narain Niwas Palace Hotel, named after Amar Singh's father Narain Singh.

5. See Thomas Metcalf, *An Imperial Vision*, Chapter II, for Madho Singh's tactics in resisting British architectural incursions, even as he resisted for some time raising imperial service troops. Madho Singh took *ganga jal* (Ganges water) in three large, handsome copper urns with him when he crossed the "black waters" to England in 1902 to attend the coronation of King Edward.

6. Urdu, i.e. use of the Persian script, was introduced as Jaipur's official language soon after 1864 when Nawab Faiz Ali Khan, who had served in the North-West Province of British India, became first minister and commander in chief of its army—such as it was. Faiz Ali Khan hailed from an area in Uttar Pradesh that continued the elegant and elaborate

cultural and political traditions of the Mughal court. He may have imagined that by introducing Urdu he was providing the state with a linguistic vehicle of a more learned and elegant court society, even as the British imagined they were introducing a more advanced civilization through English. Official language, which means here the script in which it is written, is one thing; spoken language is another. As is usually the case with respect to language, the situation was fluid. What was beginning to be called Hindustani, a language whose lexicon and syntax were heavily Urduized and which could be written in Devanagri or Persian script, was increasingly understood throughout northern India. Shymaldas, Udaipur-Mewar poet laureate as well as its erstwhile prime minister, wrote his *Vir Vinod*, a classic of this era, in Hindustani with Devanagri script. Among Rajputana's princely states, regional "dialects" (e.g., Dingal) distinct from but akin to Hindustani, dominated speech and literature, including the doha that Amar Singh loved.Few in Jaipur knew Urdu in the sense of commanding Persian script. According to the Rajputana Census Report for 1901, only 2,000 persons in Jaipur state "knew" Urdu. Urdu remained the official language of Jaipur state until Independence, partition, and the integration of the princely states in 1947. An agitation on behalf of Hindi in 1943 led to both Hindi and Urdu being declared official languages. See A.K. Roy, *History of the Jaipur City* (New Delhi: Manohar Publishers, 1978), 82–83, 128, *passim*.

7. Sir Pratap's arrangement of Amar Singh's education by Ram Nathji seems to indicate that he favors Amar Singh continuing to perfect his English. Sir Pratap is said, by Sir Walter Lawrence, to have held strong anti-Muslim feelings, which may have translated into opposition to Urdu, associated as it was with the culture of the Mughal court and of north Indian *nawabs* (kings) (Lawrence, *The India We Served*, 209). Sir Pratap is said to have reorganized Jodhpur's military forces to exclude Muslims. Major Stuart Beatson, reporting in January 1890, as inspector of the Jodhpur Lancers, writes that Sir Pratap remembered the 1857–1858 rebellion against British rule when Jodhpur Mohammedan soldiers went to Delhi to attack British forces. Like some Rajputs and other Hindus in northern India, they had supported the restoration of the Mughal emperor instead of remaining loyal to the British (East India Company) cause. Their response to the rebellion is said to have influenced Sir Pratap's efforts to exclude Muslims from Jodhpur state forces and to recruit only Marwar Rajputs. Acharya, *JoAR*, 150. In 1894, however, Archibald Adams reports the presence of a Kaimkhani squadron in the Jodhpur Lancers. *The Western Rajput States*, 109. Kaimkhanis are "Muslim Rajputs." Their conversion is usually placed in Mughal times. Amar Singh mentions a Kaimkhani squadron in his account of the Jodhpur Lancers in China during the Boxer Rebellion. Sir Pratap's "hatred" for Muslims was inconsistent. It can be interpreted in light of the fact that his brother, Maharaja Jaswant Singh, refused to appoint him as a minister in his government, but made "Pratap Singh's old enemy, Faizulla Khan. . . . Prime Minister, with practically the entire charge of affairs," van Wart, *Sir Pratap Singh*, 49. Faiz Ullah Khan held the coveted post of prime minister, and all its patronage, for some years, accounting for Sir Pratap's years of residence at the Jaipur court of his brother-in-law, Maharaja Ram Singh. He was a professional civil servant from the British-Indian state of Uttar Pradesh and brought other UP civil servants and administrative conventions, including Urdu, to Jodhpur. When Sir Pratap eventually returned to become prime minister, he thoroughly, not to say ruthlessly, purged Faizulla Khan appointees and relatives. On the other hand, when Sir Pratap was himself in charge earlier of his brother's administration of Jalore district, he appointed a pupil of his old Muslim riding master, Sheik Karim Buksh, head of the Jalore troops and later rissaldar of the Jodhpur state troops (34).

Part II - The Jodhpur Lancers in China:

Introduction

1. Fearing Colonial Secretary Joseph Chamberlain's designs on Transvaal's gold and anticipating German help, the president of the Boer Republic of the Transvaal, Paulus Kruger, in October 1899 launched preemptive attacks against the Cape Colony and Natal.

2. "At the time of the Boxer movement, Britain was engaged in an aggressive war to conquer the Boers in South Africa. Except for a number of warships and some army troops from India, it was unable to send much support to China." Hu Bin, "Contradictions and Conflicts Among the Imperialist Powers in China at the Time of the Boxer Movement," in David D. Buck, editor, "Recent Chinese Studies of the Boxer Movement," *Chinese Studies in History* 20: 3–4 (1987): 160. For a recent authoritative account of the Boxer uprising and its relationship to international politics, see Joseph W. Esherick's concluding chapter (10), "Prairie Fire" in *The Origins of the Boxer Rebellion* (Berkeley: University of California Press, 1987).

3. For a longer description of Sir Pratap, see Introduction, 1, and Part I, 3.

4. *Yihetuan*, practitioners of martial arts like those known today as Tai-chi. The Boxers were a social movement whose ". . . link to popular culture was even more obvious than the Taiping's. . . . [T]he Boxers were not a reactivated and reoriented branch of the White Lotus sect, but a new ritual complex that was easily learned and spread rapidly across the north China plain. To argue that the Spirit Boxers were created *de novo* is not to say that they arose *ex nihilo*. The crucial elements of Boxer ritual were put together from a repertoire of martial arts and folk religious practices that were familiar to most north China peasants. . . . The notion of invulnerability had been present in such martial groups as the Armor of the Golden Bell, at least since the eighteenth century." Esherick, *Boxer Rebellion*, 327.

5. Esherick tells us that "the 450,000,000 tael indemnity stands out for its enormous size—more than four times the annual revenue of the Beijing government. . . . It was to be paid over thirty-nine years at 4 percent annual interest, the annual payments representing about one-fifth of the national budget." Esherick, *Boxer Rebellion*, 311.

6. For a discussion of *Water Margin* in the context of the Boxer Rebellion, see Esherick, *Boxer Rebellion*, 329, and Suzuki Chusei, *Chugokushi ni okero kakumei to shukyo* (Tokyo: Tokyo University Press, 1974), 1–47, cited in *Boxer Rebellion*, 355, note 2.

7. Tarak Barkawi is exploring "The Constitution of Force Beyond Borders" by the major European powers in the colonial era. (Abstract submitted to the Committee on International Peace and Security in a Changing World, SSRC-MacArthur post-doctoral fellowship competition, endnote 1.) For a discussion of the Indian context, see F.W. Perry, *The Commonwealth Armies* (Manchester: Manchester University Press, 1988); J. Lee Ready, *Forgotten Allies*, 2 vols (Jefferson, NC: MacFarland and Co., 1985), and Chandar S. Sundaran, "A Grudging Concession; The Origins of the Indianization of the Indian Armies' Officer Corps, 1817–1917" (Ph.D. dissertation, McGill University, 1996).

8. See Philip Mason, *A Matter of Honor: An Account of the Indian Army, Its Officers and Men* (London: Jonathan Cape, 1974) and Byron Farwell, *Armies of the Raj* (New York: Norton, 1989).

9. The agreement can be found in *India, Foreign and Political Department: A Collection of Treaties, Engagements and Sanads Relating to India and Neighbouring Countries*, revised and continued up to the June 1, 1906, compiled by Charles U. Aitchison, vol. 3 (Calcutta: Superintendent of Government Printing, 1909), 180–181.

10. The full text of the note is "affixed" by Amar Singh at the end of an essay of August 31, 1900, "Comments Upon My Stay at Mathura and the Journey Thence to Calcutta Until We Go on Board the *Mohawk*." (See Part II, 1) Note, in Part II, 5, that Captain Hughes'

punishment of Jasji, the "native" commandant, for drinking on duty does not adhere to the terms of this document.

11. For an extended account of the issues of status and power as they confronted Amar Singh and other military officers, see Susanne Hoeber Rudolph and Lloyd I. Rudolph, "Setting the Table: Amar Singh Aboard the *S.S. Mohawk*," *Common Knowledge* 3:1 (1994): 158–177.

12. From the entry *Jaipore, Sunday, August 29 to September 13, 1903*, "Notes About My Fourth Term in the Imperial Cadet Corps."

13. Henry Hamilton Fyers Turner served with the Indian Army from 1887. He was a squadron commander in the 2nd Bengal Lancers (Gardener's Horse) from 1899, was promoted to major in 1905 and lieutenant colonel in 1913, when he became second-in-command of the regiment. On December 2, 1915, he returned to the regiment from staff employment and assumed command. Turner was mentioned in dispatches in 1916, and was killed in action during the Second Battle of Cambrai on December 1, 1917. (We are grateful to Dr Mark Nicholls, Department of Archives, Film and Sound, National Army Museum, London, for these particulars of Henry Turner's military career.) We find Henry Turner in Jodhpur when the diary begins in 1898. He is the officer assigned to "advise" the Jodhpur Lancers on training and to "inspect" the unit with a view to its fitness for active duty. According to Amar Singh's diary account, Turner held the acting rank of major while serving in Jodhpur and while accompanying the Lancers for duty with the British Expeditionary Force.

14. Matter between asterisks is from *Jodhpore, Friday, 17th August, 1900*.

1: Getting There

1. Stuart Beatson, later Major General Sir Stuart Beatson, collaborated with Sir Pratap in the 1880s to make Jodhpur the "home of polo" and to raise the Jodhpur Lancers.

2. George Nathaniel Curzon, *Problems of the Far East: Japan, Korea, China* (London: Longmans, 1894). Curzon was a leading theorist, ideologue, and practitioner of imperialism in its heyday.

3. Cloth fixed at the doors and stairs leading below deck to catch the breezes and direct them into the lower reaches of the ship. Functions like a fan.

4. See reference to Aitchison's *Treaties* in endnote 9.

5. Marina Warner, *The Dragon Empress* (New York: Atheneum, 1986), 213–215.

6. This sentence is advanced from later in the same entry.

7. Roberts also compared the Jodhpur forces favorably to those in other Rajput states; Jaipur and Udaipur he found wholly ineffectual. Frederick S.R. Roberts, *Forty-One Years in India, from Subaltern to Commander-in-Chief*, 30th edition (London: Macmillan, 1898), 431.

8. K.M. Panikkar, *His Highness the Maharaja of Bikaner* (London: University Press, 1937). Panikkar, a Malayalee, served as prime minister to Ganga Singh. He was one of the group of distinguished Indians who took service in princely state administration in the 1930s and 1940s.

2: Tensions in the China Garrison

1. Kaimkhanis are a Rajput lineage converted to Islam.

2. The wall, parts of which date from the second century BC, was built to deter invasions from the nomadic steppe peoples who continually harrassed the Chinese borders. It was built by large forcible levees of labor. The brutality of the construction work is memorialized in Chinese folk literature, and the wonders of its extent—from east to west across most of northern China—have been admired as an extraordinary feat of early engineering.

It was, however, frequently overrun. "No linear frontier between China and Inner Asia could be permanently held and kept clean and clear by either the pastoral society of the steppe or the agricultural society of China." Owen Lattimore, *Inner Asian Frontiers of China* (Oxford: Oxford University Press, 1988), 511.

3. The entry of October 25 has been advanced to preserve the unity of the Wong Kun Ying account.

4. This is a *doha* (couplet) translated from Marwari into English by Mohan Singh.

5. The matter between asterisks is included from a previous paragraph of the November 10 entry.

6. For a full account of the case, see our "A Bureaucratic Lineage in Princely India: Elite Formation and Conflict in a Patrimonial System," in *Journal of Asian Studies* 34:2 (1975): 717–753 (with Mohan Singh) and reproduced in Susanne Hoeber Rudolph and Lloyd I. Rudolph, *Essays on Rajputana: Reflections on History, Culture and Administration* (New Delhi: Concept Publishing House, 1984), 81–140.

3: Under Fire at Lijapoo

1. Matter between asterisks has been moved from the entry of *Tuesday, 15th January, 1901*.

2. R.B. van Wart, *The Life of Lieut.-General H.H. Sir Pratap Singh* (London: Humphrey Milford for Oxford University Press, 1926), 125–126.

3. The entries of January 15 and January 21 overlap and have been merged.

4. The compensation was in the shape of remission of tribute. After 1857, Jodhpur state was under obligation to pay Rs 108,000 to the British Government of India, plus Rs 98,000 for the Erinpura Irregular Force. It was subsequently given a remission in tribute of Rs 10,000 "in consideration of the cession (No. LVI) to the British Government of the rights of Jodhpur to the district and fort of Umarkot." Aitchison, *Treaties*, 131.

5. See Sir Walter R. Lawrence, *The India We Served* (London: Cassell and Co., 1928), 202 ff. While Lord Curzon himself took a dim view of Sir Pratap, Lawrence was most positively inclined.

6. Sir Griffith offered a rather cavalier two-page review of the decision of the Jaipur court: "The conclusion is so startling and violently improbable that it would lead an ordinary mind at once to the conclusion that there must be something wrong about the inference which led to that conclusion. . . . Nothwithstanding the admiration one feels for the ability and ingenuity of this judgement, it wholly fails to produce in my mind the feeling that any frauds were in fact committed." "Opinion of Sir Griffith Evans, February 12, 1901," Copy in Kanota Family Archive. Cited in our "A Bureaucratic Lineage in Princely India," in *Essays in Rajputana*, 116.

7. For an account of the Idar claim, see van Wart, *Sir Pratap Singh*, 131–133.

8. Lawrence, *The India We Served*, 207.

4: Thinking it Over

1. Matter between asterisks is from *Aboard the Transport Ship Kai Fong, Wednesday, 3rd July, 1901*. The volume is probably *Mixing in Society: A Complete Manual of Manners by the Right Hon. the Countess of ******** (London: Routledge and Sons, 1870).

2. Early portions of this account are included in Part I, 1.

3. *The Golden Oriole* (New York: Viking, 1987), 180.

4. Lawrence, *The India We Served*, 207.

5. This passage is difficult to interpret. Maharaj kanwar is used for the heir apparent. The heir apparent at this time, Sumer Singh, is three-years-old, and it seems curious that he should be brought to Kuchaman Road in the middle of the night.

6. Maharaja Sardar Singh had been sent away from the state by the British on the claim that he was suffering from ill health and that under him the state suffered mismanagement.

7. Matter between the asterisks is from *Jodhpore, Saturday, 3rd August, 1901*.

8. Matter between asterisks has been brought here from the long essay of the same day.

9. These notes are continued on March 11.

10. The significance of this term is contested. Darogas say that they originated as Rajputs. Shortly after Independence and while the memory of royal and noble status was still fresh, high-ranking Rajput nobles tended to deny that claim. In recent years in both Gujarat and Rajasthan, Rajput nobility have begun to honor such claims and set about creating a large, inclusive category which functions as a political resource. (Interview with Devi Singh Mandawa, then chairman of the Rajasthan Rajput Sabha, Jaipur, November 1992). For the Gujarat variant of such inclusive Rajput associations in politics, see Myron Weiner's discussion of Kaira District in *Party Building in a New Nation* (Chicago: University of Chicago Press, 1967). For a general discussion of Rajput and Kshatriya labels in the social mobility process and in the electoral arena, see our discussion of caste and politics in *The Modernity of Tradition: Political Development in India* (Chicago: University of Chicago Press, 1967 and 1996). Historically the term was used in Rajasthan by ruling and noble Rajputs to designate supervisors of government departments (Daroga of the *zenana deorhi*) on the one hand, and domestic servants on the other. Such servants, referred to as *chakars* or *golas*, both male and female, were attached to a family and transferred with the dowry of a married daughter. "These people accepted a modified form of slavery in exchange for a permanent position and guarantee of their basic livelihood." Varsha Joshi, *Polygamy and Purdah: Women and Society among Rajputs* (Jaipur: Rawat Publishers, 1995), 155. G.S. Sharma asserts that they originated from destitutes purchased especially in times of famine; from Rajputs marrying a low-caste woman or, in Udaipur, a Bhil woman; from the illegitimate progeny of the ruler. "Das Pratha Ka Swarup" (Forms of the Institution of Slavery), *Shodh Patrika* 30 (July-September 1970), cited in Joshi, 179. See also Part I, 4. See the account of darogas by the nationalist-activist-scholar Har Bilas Sarda, *Speeches and Writings* (Ajmer: Vedic Yantralaya, 1935), 436 ff.

11. As we noted in Part I, when the viceroy, the Marquis of Lansdowne, visited Jodhpur in 1892, "a new departure was made by housing him at the bungalow of Thakur Hari Singh at Ratanada, instead of at Paota, where distinguished visitors had previously been lodged." Van Wart, *Sir Pratap Singh*, 97.

12. Sir Pratap's *chattri* (cenotaph) was placed at his death in 1922 by the side of Hurjee's. Van Wart, *Sir Pratap Singh*, 226.

PART III - TRANSGRESSION AND RECONCILIATION

Introduction

1. Amar Singh writes seven lengthy accounts of marriages in the early years of the diary. The longest account is the one of the marriage of his wife's sister at Satheen in 1905, which occupies 129 folio pages. It is not included among these selections. Another, that of the Maharaja of Kishengarh at Udaipur, is reported in Part VI.

2. For a critique of Colonel Walter and the reform movement, see M.S. Jain, *A Concise History of Modern Rajasthan* (New Delhi: Wishwa Prakashan, 1993), 121–26. Jain argues that certain of the "abuses"—such as large dowries—were a means of correcting the imbalance between girls and boys created at different levels of the social structure by the practice of hypergamy among Rajputs. He accuses the reformers of not having an adequate sense

for the social consequences of their acts, for instance, that without such side payments the "market" would not be "cleared" of girls or boys, whichever is in "excess" supply. The critique is curiously *ad hominem*: "[Walter] therefore decided to promote a scheme of social reform which could enable him to secure extension in period of service and better pensionary benefits"; the historian Shyamaldas "deliberately avoided mentioning details [of an earlier reform association] in Vir Vinod [his history] probably because by doing so he might have brought down the value of the contribution of Walter" (122–23).

3. Department which provided tents, rugs, furniture, and other supplies for the movable camps in which maharajas and their households lived when traveling.

1: An Uncommon Wedding

1. The events surrounding the marriage take place between September 3 and 9. Amar Singh writes the essay between September 17 and October 1.

2. The matter between asterisks is from *Jodhpore, Tuesday, 3rd September, 1901*.

3. The picture of Sarkar was worn by Man Singh, Kanwar of Kanota, at the marriage of his brother, Prithvi Singh Kanota in February 1996.

4. A *purdait* is a woman in purdah (seclusion); in this case, she is the mother of Sir Pratap's natural sons. He had none by his wives. Concubines who lived in seclusion and veiled themselves were distinguished in social standing from women who were seen in public and considered generally available, such as actresses, singers, dancers. Note that the purdait is present, though she does not perform, at these ceremonies.

5. The matter between asterisks is from *Bisalpore, Thursday, 5th September, 1901*.

6. Maharaj Sher Singh, grandson of Maharaja Takhat Singh of Jodhpur, nephew of Sir Pratap; Sardar Singh of Bhadrajoon, son to the lord of a large thikana in Jodhpur state; Maharaj Akhai Singh, brother of Sher Singh, later Amar Singh's close friend at the Imperial Cadet Corps; and Thakur Jawar Singh of Malgurh, another thikana in Jodhpur.

7. The matter between asterisks is transferred from later in the same entry.

8. The thikanas of Satheen, Khejarla, and Kharia were held by three brothers of the Bhati clan.

9. Nephew of Sir Pratap, he is eventually adopted at Idar state and becomes its maharaja.

10. It was considered disrespectful to smoke or drink in the presence of elders.

11. The matter between asterisks is transferred from previous paragraph.

12. The meanings have been supplied from conversations with Rajput friends and colleagues. See also Karine Schomer, "Rajasthani Marriage Riddling: Cultural Affirmation through Competition," in Karine Schomer, Joan L. Erdman, Deryck O. Lodrick, and Lloyd I. Rudolph, editors, *The Idea of Rajasthan: Explorations in Regional Identity* (Glen Dale, MD: Riverdale, 1992 and Delhi: Manohar Publishers, 1992).

13. Since all pictures of Amar Singh, including his wedding picture, show him in Jodhpuri *sapha* (turban) we assume that is what is meant here.

14. See Susanne Hoeber Rudolph and Lloyd I. Rudolph, *Essays on Rajputana; Reflections on History, Culture and Administration* (New Delhi: Concept Publishing House, 1984), 91.

15. *Rekh* here refers to the official valuation of the thikana, as distinguished from its actual income. But the amounts overstate the financial condition of Satheen, which is deeply in debt.

16. See note 1.

2: Becoming a Householder

1. Bari haveli was given to the three brothers in 1864, and they occupied it jointly. With growing prosperity, status, and power, the two younger brothers built havelis at adjoining

locations, transferring bari haveli to the eldest. The patta of bari haveli, now Santha house, was issued Asos Budi 6th Bikram Samvat 1929 (1864–46). Kanota Family Archive, box 20, document 1160. (The Kanota Family Archive at Jaipur is a collection of papers dealing with thikana and state affairs, collected and arranged by Mohan Singh. It consists of 34 boxes and 3,500 items.)

2. Thakur Fateh Singh of Naila built the Naila garden house in the 1870s. The Kanota garden also dates from that time, but the house was not built by Amar Singh until the 1930s. The Santha (Gondher) garden house dates from the 1940s. Interviews with Daulat Singh of Naila and Sheo Nath Singh of Kanota, 1975. Having asked Maharaja Ram Singh for some grazing land on which to build the garden, Narain Singh, Amar's father found that the prime minister, his uncle Fateh Singh, was blocking the legal transfer. An appeal to the maharaja broke the log jam. Kanota family oral tradition.

3. See, for example, Quentin Crewe, *The Last Maharaja: a Biography of Sawai Man Singh II, Maharaja of Jaipur* (London: Michael Joseph, 1985), Chapter 2.

4. Madho Singh's desire to carve out a non-European space for himself led him to use architecture for the purpose. See Thomas R. Metcalfe, *An Imperial Vision: Indian Architecture and Britain's Raj* (Berkeley: University of California Press, 1989), 137.

5. His ministers were Indian. The members of council were drawn from the major nobility of the state, while his prime ministers were mostly Bengalis, notably Kanti Chander Mukerjee, his son Ishan Chander, and Sanser Chander Sen. See *Annual Reports on the Administration of the Jaipur State*. Printed versions of the *Annual Report* became available via the Rajputana Agency Press at Abu after 1907. Appointments before that can be followed in the *Report on the Political Administration of the Rajputana State*, compiled by the A.G.G. in Rajputana, beginning in 1865 and published at Bombay (1865–67) and Calcutta (1867–1907). Toward the end of Madho Singh's life access to him was regulated by "Kawasji," Khawas Bala Bux, who had no formal standing and was regarded with fear and snobbery by the court Rajputs, who asserted he descended from the tailoring caste.

6. Earlier discussions of the confiscation case brought against the three Champawat families by Jaipur state may be found in Part II, 2. A full-length account is provided in our "A Bureaucratic Lineage in Princely India: Elite Formation and Conflict in a Patrimonial System," in *Journal of Asian Studies* 34 (1975): 717–53. The hostility continues well after the years covered in these pages. After Narain Singh becomes the Thakur of Kanota, upon the death of Zorawar Singh in 1908, he is subject to the rule that all jagirdars must take permission from the maharaja whenever they leave the state. When Madho Singh dallies over giving Narain Singh permission to leave the state to continue his service at Alwar, Narain Singh departs without permission. As punishment, the maharaja confiscates one village, which is not restored to the family until 1936, when Maharaja Man Singh returns it to Amar Singh.

7. The entry between asterisks is transferred from *Jaipore, Tuesday, 17th September to October 1, 1901*, "Notes About My Marriage."

8. The *Jaipur Pocket Directory* of 1936 reports thirty Europeans at Jaipur, including the governess to the palace nursery; the nurse and the undernurse to the same; Sergeant Major W. Well, instructor of the Sawai Man Guards; Mr K. Leech, the superintendent of the kennels; Mr E.G. Ross, chauffeur to the maharaja; Father Polycarp, "Church of Rome"; and numerous others in official and unofficial positions. Published under the orders of the council of state (Jaipur: State Press, 1936), 103–106.

9. Michael Mason, review of J. Miriam Benn, *The Predicaments of Love* (London: Pluto, 1992), in *London Review of Books*, October 22, 1992.

10. "A moderate amount of sexual indulgence braces and ennobles body and mind, and heightens the virtue of each, but to be always thinking on amatory subjects . . . has a very bad effect on both men and women." *The Elements of Social Science: Or Physical, Sexual and Natural Religion. An Exposition of the True Cause and Only Cure of the Three Primary Evils—Poverty, Prostitution and Celibacy*, 31st edition (London: privately published, *circa* 1880), 187. J. Miriam Benn's fascinating biography deals with Drysdale and his relations, all of them reformers on medico-social issues—prostitution, women's medical training and treatment, and birth control. Benn reveals that Drysdale's account is probably driven by painful personal suffering and nervous breakdown before he himself took up "regulated sexual exercise." *Predicaments*, cited in Mason, *London Review*.

PART IV - SOLDIER FOR THE RAJ?

Introduction

1. Lord Curzon uttered these words in the early stages of a protracted and ultimately unsuccessful effort to have regular king's commissions given to graduates of the Imperial Cadet Corps. From "Curzon to Dawkins," cited in David Dilks, *Curzon in India, I. Achievement* (New York: Taplinger, 1970), 240.

2. This view of the outlook and perception of the British officers who staff the Indian Army is developed in Ch. XV, "Her Majesty's Servants," "1. A Military Order," in *A Matter Of Honour.—An Account of the Indian Army, Its Officers and Men* (London: Papermac, 1986), 362–371 (first published by Jonathan Cape, 1974).

3. L. F. Rushbrook-Williams, *India in the Years 1917–1918*, Government of India, Central Bureau of Information (Calcutta: Superintendent of Government Printing, 1919), 13, footnote 36.

4. The term is misleading. True, the recently installed Afghan Amir, Amanullah "sent his regular army across the Indian border in May 1919." But the Afghan regulars were soon "bundled back into their own country. . . . But the tribes in Waziristan and north Baluchistan rose; . . . nearly all the Wazirs and most of the Afridis in the Waziristan Militias defected, with their rifles; and by the end of the year the British were faced with a frontier war harder than any they had experienced." Charles Chenevix Trench, *The Indian Army and the King's Enemies 1900–1947* (New York: Thames and Hudson, 1988), who devotes Chapter 9 to the war, more properly titled as "Waziristan, 1919–1921," 104–114.

5. According to entries in his diary, Amar Singh, an acting major, assumed officiating command of the 16th Cavalry Regiment in Waziristan during the Third Afghan War on the following occasions: Dehra Ismail Khan, Tuesday, September 28, 1920, vice Hill; Tank, Thursday, March 10, 1921, vice Hutchinson; Tank, Tuesday, March 15, 1921, relieved by Col. Storey of the 113th Regiment.

6. The reference is to the anti-hero, Robert Merrick, in Paul Scott's four-volume *The Raj Quartet*, on the end of empire in India; the fourteen-part television series based on the novels fixated audiences in the UK and the USA, and was named after the first of the four volumes, *The Jewel in the Crown* (St Albans: Panther Books, 1977).

7. Amar Singh's formal date of retirement is July 4, 1923. From June 1921, he goes on long leave pending retirement. Here is Amar Singh's account of a farewell dinner that he and Col. Mears share two months after their "hot words."*Kohat, Monday, 6th June, 1921*. "Last night the regiment gave a dinner to Col. Mears and me. At the end when Mears' health was proposed and we had a drink to it, he got up and said a few words. Then my health was proposed but just then the rain came and thus saved me the trial of a speech."

8. See David Dilks, *Curzon in India*, 239–241, for the background to Curzon's decision.

9. James Morris, who says that Curzon was "cruelly immortalized" by these "famous verses" ascribes the first couplet to J.W. Mackail, later professor of poetry at Oxford, the second to Cecil Spring-Rice, later British ambassador to the United States. *Farewell the Trumpets: An Imperial Retreat* (San Diego: Harvest/HBJ, 1978), 108.

10. See Rupert Wilkinson, *Gentlemanly Power: British Leaders and the Public School Tradition: A Comparative Study in the Making of Rulers* (New York: Oxford University Press, 1965) (published in England as *The Prefects*) for how and with what effect England's public schools from Arnold's Rugby onward created a blend of aristocratic manners and middle-class muscular Christianity that dominated British public life until World War II.

11. The Curzon family were hereditary peers. Nayana Goradia, *Lord Curzon: The Last Of the British Moghuls* (Delhi: Oxford University Press, 1993), 24–25.

12. James Morris, *Farewell the Trumpets*, 108.

13. These charges against the upper classes are from Catherine Hall's "The Sweet Delights of Home," a section in "The Curtain Rises" by Lynn Hunt and Catherine Hall in Michelle Perot, editor, *A History of Private Life, IV: From the Fires of Revolution to the Great War*, translated by Arthur Goldhammer (Cambridge, MA: Harvard University Press, 1990). Hall argues that "The increase in economic, political and social power of the middle classes in the early nineteenth century was reflected in the adoption of practices . . . by their 'betters,' the aristocracy and gentry. . . . [B]y mid-century the upper classes had moved closer to the upper middle classes, the social gap between them had narrowed as the upper classes adjusted their image to make it acceptable to middle class morality" (88–89). We use the term "achieving aristocracy" in part to capture this macro-historical transformation.

14. R.B. van Wart, *The Life of Lieut.-General H.H. Sir Pratap Singh* (London: Oxford University Press, 1926), 149.

15. Our account of rituals of power follows Bernard S. Cohn's "Representing Authority in Victorian India," in his *An Anthropologist among the Historians and Other Essays* (Delhi: Oxford University Press, 1987). This essay appeared earlier in Eric Hobsbawm and Terence Ranger, editors, *The Invention of Tradition* (Cambridge: Cambridge University Press, 1983, 1984). Here is how Cohn describes the great moment of the event: "At noon on 1 January 1877, all was in readiness for the entry of the Viceroy into the amphitheatre. The princes and other notables were all seated in their sections, the spectators' grandstand filled, and thousands of Indian and European troops were drawn up in ranks. The Viceroy and his small party, including his wife, rode into the amphitheatre to the "March from Tannhauser." As they got down from the carriage six trumpeters, attired in medieval costume, blew a fanfare. The Viceroy then mounted to his throne to the strains of the national anthem. The chief herald, described as the tallest English officer in the Indian Army, read the queen's proclamation which announced that henceforth there would be the addition "Empress of India" to her royal styles and titles" (673). Val Prinsep, commissioned to paint a picture of the scene, was not amused. "Oh Horror! What have I to paint. A kind of thing that out does the Crystal Palace in hideosity." *Imperial India: An Artist's Journal* (London, 1879), as quoted in Cohn, *An Anthropologist*, 669.

16. It was a portrait of the empire like the painting of the "jewel in the crown," Victoria at the center, that Paul Scott has Barbie Batchelor puzzle over in *Towers of Silence*, vol. 3 in *The Raj Quartet*.

17. This is a gloss on Curzon from Cohn, *An Anthropologist*, 677.

18. The language is Sir Pratap Singh's as quoted in van Wart's admiring *Sir Pratap Singh*. A celebrated participant in the 1903 durbar as prince regent of Jodhpur and honorary commandant of the ICC, he rode at the head of the Corps wearing its uniform, "every inch

a Rajput and a soldier . . . with his flashing eyes that no detail escaped, clear-cut profile with a proud curl to the nostril, and a stern mouth with its touch of humour lurking in the corner" (van Wart, 146).

19. In practice it was only after the Aitchison Commission report of 1886 that Indians, who could get to London to sit for the examination, began to qualify in limited numbers.

20. Lord Curzon's memorandum on "Commissions for Indians," June 4, 1900, in C.H. Phillips, editor, *The Evolution of India and Pakistan, 1858 to 1947 Select Documents on the History of India and Pakistan*, vol. IV (London: Oxford University Press, 1962) 520–521.

21. Imperial Service Forces were maintained by some of the larger princely states, advised and inspected by English officers, seconded for such duty. For example, General Frederick Roberts inspected the Jodhpur Lancers in 1889. He "praised the smart appearance of both men and horses," van Wart, *Sir Pratap Singh*, 93. Captain Stuart Beatson, later inspector general of Imperial Service Forces, had been seconded to Jodhpur in the late 1880s. Later, in 1900, at the time of the Boxer Rebellion when the *S.S. Mohawk* sailed for China from Calcutta, Major H.H.F. Turner, who had been seconded to the Jodhpur Lancers at Jodhpur, accompanied them in a command position. See Part II.

22. See note 1.

23. For details of the controversy between Kitchener and Curzon, see Mason, *A Matter of Honour*.

24. See IV, 1 of this Part for details on the cadets.

25. Amar Singh's commission of July 4, 1905. Kanota Family Archive.

26. Report of the Committee on Government of India Proposals on Commissioning Indians, July 24, 1911, Appendices. "From His Excellency General Sir O'Moore Creagh, G.C.B., V.C., Commander in Chief of India," 64. We are indebted to Dewitt Ellinwood for the reference. General Sir O'Moore Creagh went further. He pressed, in the same report, for including Indians in regular officer appointments: "it is absolutely necessary to provide for the military aspirations of Indians of noble fighting families. We can no longer justify the opening of all appointments in civil life to Indians, while excluding them, except in subordinate positions, from a military career." India Office library and Records, L/nil/A/5/1750, Appendix with Report of Committee on Government of India Proposals on Commissioning Indians, December 7, 1911.

27. Mhow, located in central India near Indore, became a key army center after Kitchener, as commander in chief in India, reorganized the Indian Army. The only war anticipated was on the North-West Frontier. There were only two ways into Afghanistan, one by Peshawar and the Khyber, the other by Quetta and Kandahar. Divisions were placed near the two lines of communication, one from Calcutta through Lucknow to Peshawar, the other from Bombay through Mhow to Quetta. Each line made an army command, thus the (then) Northern and Southern Commands. See Mason, *A Matter of Honour*, 398.

28. A diary entry from St Vincent, dated March 1915 reads: "I was appointed ADC to the General Commanding the 9th Sirhind Brigade. . . . General Brunker, who was really its commander, was in officiating command of the 3rd Lahore Division. . . . General Watkins . . . would come and take command of the Division."

29. Mason, *A Matter of Honour*, 414.

30. As quoted in Mason, *A Matter of Honour*, 409.

31. Mason, *A Matter of Honour*, 413.

32. These locations are taken from Amar Singh's diary entries. There are many more, starting at Orleans in October 1914 and running through December 20, 1915, when he left from Toulon for Mesopotamia where he fought at Basra and Kut. The entry for Neuve Chapelle, for example, describes four days, March 10 to 14, 1915, when for the first time

the Indian Corps (under British command) took the offensive. The battle is described in Mason, *A Matter of Honour*, 419–421, where he concludes that "Neuve Chapelle proved that it was possible to take the first four lines of German trenches . . . [but that] the organization of a wave of fresh troops who could succeed in exploiting the first success remained a problem never solved, either by the Germans or ourselves" (421). Trench's account of Neuve Chapelle in *The Indian Army* can be found at 40–41. He concludes that "Neuve Chapelle was a strategic failure, the first of many such. There was no breakthrough" (41). A sentence from Amar Singh's diary entry on June 23, 1915, reads: "I find my name mentioned in the despatches . . . in today's *Times.*" The text of the dispatch can be found in the Kanota Family Archive.

33. The *Recessional* was written for Victoria's Diamond Jubilee in 1897. The phrase is mitigated by the stanza's warning against pride in empire that forgets God is even mightier: If, drunk with sight of power, we loose / Wild tongues that have not Thee in awe, / Such boastings as the Gentiles use, / Or lesser breeds without the Law— / Lord God of Hosts, be with us yet, / Lest we forget—lest we forget!

34. Cambridge University Library, Hardinge Papers, v: 1, 103. Correspondence re European war, Part I. Courtesy of Dewitt Ellinwood.

35. Rushbrook-Williams, *India in the Years 1917–1918*, 19.

36. Prithvi Singh, like Bala Sahib Daphle, from the Cadet Corps' second batch, served till 1926 while Aga Kasim Shah and Zorawar Singh, Amar Singh's batch fellows, retired in 1925. *Indian Army Lists*, 1921 through 1931, consulted at the United Services Center, New Delhi. The *Indian Army Lists* were published at Calcutta for various years, and are available at the National Army Museum in London and at the United Services Institute at New Delhi.The name of Lieutenant Rana Jodha Jang appears after those of Captain Amar Singh and Lieutenant Bala Sahib (Daphle) as among the three serving officers most fit for regular King's Commissions in Austen Chamberlain's telegram of November 18, 1915, to the viceroy, Lord Hardinge. Jang's name does not appear in the diary as an Imperial cadet until an entry of February 3, 1934, when Amar Singh refers to him as a former Imperial cadet and to his retirement. Amar Singh does not make clear when precisely this occurred but it could well have been in 1934. If this proves to be the case, it is likely that he was commissioned with the batch of August 25, 1917, and that he was the last to retire among those commissioned on that date. In the November 18 telegram of the secretary of state to the viceroy, Amar Singh and Bala Sahib Daphle are referred to as "not British subjects" (one being from Jaipur, the other from Kolhapur) while Rana Jodha Jang is said to have "a British Indian domicile origin." Interestingly, Chamberlain remarks, "I should have to consult the War Office as to their [Amar Singh's and Bala Sahib Daphle's] legal eligibility."

37. K.M. Carriappa's date of rank is given as July 17, 1921, date of first commission and date of appointment to the Indian Army as July 17, 1920, in the *Indian Army List April 1924*, 337. A.A. Rudra, second-most senior officer at Independence, entered service on July 17, 1920; his date of rank is July 17, 1921. *Indian Army List April 1924*, 1131.

38. Lieutenant General Nathu Singh of Gumanpura, Dungarpur, who was GOC Eastern Command at the time of Independence, told us in a 1957 interview that Prime Minister Jawaharlal Nehru discussed with him the possibility of his being appointed the first commander in chief of independent India's Army. He says that he discouraged the idea on the ground that it would be a very bad precedent to begin the Army's post-Independence career with a supercession. In April 1992, General Nathu Singh, now deceased, was 92.

39. For the story of the resistance to efforts to Indianize the Indian Army, including the racial attitudes and bureaucratic maneuvers involved, see Mason, *A Matter of Honour*, Chapter XVIII, Part 4, "The King's Commission," 453–466. Mason, in an otherwise

scrupulously researched book, seems to be unaware of the story being told here about ICC graduates receiving qualified king's commissions beginning in July 1905 in the Native Land Forces, nor does he report that on August 25, 1917, they are commissioned in the Indian Army as KCOs, nor that Amar Singh is acting commander of the 16th Cavalry Regiment in Waziristan during the Third Afghan War.

40. We do not know whether Zorawar Singh went to England "to work on [their] case" but we doubt that he did. His "memorial" may not have borne fruit either, unless it helped in rectifying the former cadets' pension provisions. From an examination of *Indian Army Lists* (IAL) it would seem that Zorawar Singh, the holder of an M.C. (Military Cross), resigned in protest (in the sense that he refused to serve with an Indian Army unit) but that the others did not. Having failed to convince the powers that be to go "whole hog" on the date of commissioning in the army, Zorawar Singh, according to the *Indian Army List 1918* was on duty as "Squadron Officer, Commandant, Bhavnagar Imperial Service Troops" *and* as "commissioned with 1st Lancers, Duke of York's Own Lancers (Skinner's Horse)." The *IAL 1922* lists him as "with Imperial Service Forces," *IAL 1924* as "unemployed in India, 1 May 21 to 31 July 23," and *IAL 1929* as on the "non-effective list" on retired pay as an ILF officer. In all, seven former cadets and two others were made KCOs in the Indian Army as of August 25, 1917. A Military Department office record of 1918 notes the arrival of a communication concerning the "matter of posting of the 9 Indian officers who have Kings Commissions to units," and reports: "The King has approved the admission of the undermentioned officers to the Indian Army. . . . Zorawar Singh, Kanwar Amar Singh, Kanwar Pirthi Singh, Bala Sahib Daphle, Raja Jodha Jang Bahadur, Kunwar Savai Singji." India Office Library and Records, L/min/7/19013, M2400, 1918, Military Department. We are grateful to Dewitt Ellinwood for the citations. Daphle, a Maratha from Kolhapur and younger brother of a jagirdar, served longest, retiring on January 1, 1929, after being on leave for two years pending retirement. Prithvi Singh served next longest. A Rajput from Kotah and a kanwar (eldest son and thus heir to title and estate), he went on two years leave pending retirement on April 9, 1926. Malik Mumtaz Mohammed Khan (listed in 1918 as [A.R.O.] Assistant Recruiting Officer, Campbellpore, an extra-regimental appointment), and Khan Mohammed Akbar Khan (listed as a Captain, C.I.E. and ADC in 1918) are not mentioned after 1921. Aga Kasim Shah—of the Aga Khan family—retired August 1, 1925. (Amar Singh's diary entry for January 5, 1934, reports him as in a "lunatic asylum" at Poona; "He had taken to drink.")Rana Jodha Jung, is mentioned by Amar Singh as an Imperial cadet in the diary entry of February 3, 1934. He may have been the last to retire, rather than Daphle.

41. See note 3 for the occasions. For the context of his command experience, see *The Third Afghan War, 1919: Official Account*, compiled in the General Staff Branch, Army Headquarters (Calcutta: Central Publications Branch, GOI, 1925), especially 55; H. de Watteville, *Waziristan 1919–1920: Campaigns and Their Lessons* (London: Constable, 1925); Lieutenant General G.N. Molesworth, *Afghanistan, 1919: An Account Of Operations in the Third Afghan War* (Bombay: Asia Publishing House, 1962).

42. Diary, entry of November 17, 1919.

43. Diary, entry of March 17, 1919.

44. Diary, entry of November 17, 1919.

45. The act was to replace the Defence of India Act, soon to expire. It authorized a police state to deal with future "dangerous activity" such as "subversion" and "terrorism." The Rowlatt Act vitiated the Government's declaration of August 20, 1917, to move toward responsible government and the Montagu-Chelmsford reforms that followed in 1919, by articulating and institutionalizing a counter-current of distrust, fear, and alienation.

46. For accounts of civil disobedience in Delhi during this period, see Ravinder Kumar, editor, *Essays on Gandhian Politics: The Rowlatt Satyagraha of 1919* (Delhi: Oxford University Press, 1971).

47. Diary, entry of June 28, 1919, "Some Thoughts About the Riots at Delhi."

48. General Lord Rawlinson, the commander in chief at the time, "reduced the military budget from Rs 82 crores [1 crore is 10,000,000] in 1921 to 56 in 1925; the number of British troops was reduced from 75,000 to 57,000 and the Indian Army from 159,000 to 140,000." Mason, *A Matter of Honour*, 456.

49. Lord Esher, a shadowy figure close to the royal household and influential members of David Lloyd George's coalition government used his committee's wide terms of reference to press for the consolidation of the imperial structures and authority established during the war. His goal of using the Indian Army for purposes of "imperial security" were opposed in the Indian Legislative Assembly, and his grandiose schemes for an imperial cabinet and general staff came to naught in the face of enhanced national feeling in the dominions and their reluctance to commit themselves to participation in future European wars or imperial security. See L.F. Rushbrook-Williams, *India in the Year 1920*, 16–18, and Appendix VI, for a summary of the Esher committee's recommendations on these points. The quote in the text is from page 261. See also Peter Fraser, *Lord Esher: A Political Biography* (London: Hart-Davis, McGibbon, 1973).

50. There was a Nawab of Tank, whom Amar Singh reports visiting. Two or more squadrons of the 16th Cavalry seem to have been stationed at Tank for much of the time the unit spent in the North-West Frontier, July 1919 through 1921.

51. Diary, entry of April 2, 1919.Two weeks later Amar Singh speaks to General Holman, whom he had known in France, when Holman and Lord Rawlinson, commander in chief of the Indian Army, inspect the troops at Tank. "He asked me what I wanted. . . . I told him that I wanted two years leave pending retirement. He made a note of it and told me that he would see what could be done." Diary, entry of April 17, 1921.

52. Under the "eight unit scheme" announced on February 17, 1923, Indian officers were formally given command at the lowest level in Indian Army units. There were by then sixty-six Indian officers holding regular king's commissions. They were encouraged to transfer to the designated units (two cavalry regiments and six infantry battalions) and no British officers were to be posted to them. The units, in effect, were to become segregated units. The eight unit scheme, Philip Mason tells us, was officially justified in terms of giving Indian officers "'a fair chance' to show that such units could be just as efficient as those with British officers. But there could be not doubt," he continues, that the eight units scheme "was primarily a solution of the difficulty of 'serving under natives.'" Mason, *A Matter of Honour*, 455.

53. Mason, *A Matter of Honour*, 511. Having started the war with just over 1,000 Indian officers, the Indian Army ended up with 15,740, three times the total peace time establishment, British and Indian, in the mid-1930s.

1: "An Example for Others"

1. As noted in the introduction, recruitment was by recommendation. Here the British resident to Jodhpur is the recommender, and turns to the reliable Sir Pratap for advice.

2. Sheo Nath Singh does eventually attend the ICC but not for the complete course. After passing out of the ICC in 1907 he joins Alwar's Mangal Lancers, an early imperial service unit.

3. Fellow of Arts, an intermediate degree, ordinarily two years post-matriculate. Zorawar Singh may have been the best educated among the first entering class. In the princely India of 1902, a university degree was rare, though Lord Curzon hoped cadets would have attended or graduated from one of the four chiefs' colleges, which aspired to equivalence

with an English public school. The princes and noblemen had to be constantly pressured and cajoled to send their sons, particularly the eldest son and heir, to the chiefs' colleges at Ajmer, Lahore, Indore and Kathiawar.

4. Madho Singh, the Jaipur maharaja, is known for his Hindu orthodoxy. Amar Singh has mentioned plans to establish a common mess at which all the cadets, regardless of caste and religion, would eat.

5. The other cadets presumably have some experience with mathematics. Amar Singh, who has had only six years of formal education, performs at or near the top of his class in English and history but barely scrapes through in mathematics, scales (metrics of surveying), and topography.

6. Uniforms were a key element in regimental identity and pride: "Each [regiment] cherished its own traditions; they were magnificently different in their full dress, apricot and yellow, blue and silver, blue and scarlet, scarlet and gold." Mason, *A Matter of Honour*, 379. Bernard Cohn has shown how such "Indian" regalia, a construction of British Orientalist imagination, became the real India for most Britishers and some Indians.

7. Published from Allahabad in the United Provinces, the *Pioneer* circulated widely from the 1870s in the Punjab as well. It published literary work including, in 1885–1890, the stories of the young Rudyard Kipling that established his initial reputation in London's literary circles.

8. Amar Singh here indicates his identification with the Rathore lineage. The Rathores rule at Jodhpur, the "original" and senior Rathore kingdom, and at Idar, Kishengarh, and Bikaner.

9. Amar Singh seems pleased with the prospect of educating a prince, of doing for the young Kishengarh what Sir Pratap and Barath Ram Nathji had tried to do for the Jodhpur prince, Sardar Singh, when he was a minor. These educational projects must be read in the context of the raj's developing patterns for the education of princes, influenced in turn by evolving English models. Thus Colonel C.K.M. Walter's *Bharatpur Agency Report, 1869*, calls for establishing "an Eton in India. . . . [A] college on an extensive scale" staffed by "thoroughly educated English gentlemen, not mere bookworms, but men fond of field sports and out-door exercise. . . . [W]e desire to raise the Chiefs of India to the standard which they must attain in order to keep pace with the ever-advancing spirit of the age." Cited in Herbert Sherring, *The Mayo College, 'The Eton of India': A Record of Twenty Years, 1875–1895* (Calcutta: Thacker, Spink and Co., 1897), 1–3. Sherring was Mayo's second headmaster.

10. Muslim rulers are usually styled Nawab.

11. Chaprassis are the omnipresent liveried attendants who populate Indian offices, carrying tea and messages, and announcing arrivals. The British often endowed them with gaudy liveries.

12. The official view, reflected in the Cadet Corps' "Rules" and in the practice of scheduling lectures by Hindu pandits, which Amar Singh regarded as too boring to attend, seemed to be that religious (and "caste") orthodoxy was a good thing for British rule.

13. The "other mess" signals the existence of a Muslim mess and the failure of the "hopeful" beginning, mentioned in the entry of January 4, of having a common mess. Many cadets may have wanted to have a common mess but it is unlikely that Watson and Cameron, the commandant and adjutant, would risk displeasing a leading orthodox prince such as Madho Singh of Jaipur whose patronage and support they sought. Amar Singh does not usually observe orthodox commensal rules.

14. Amar Singh's remark that singing, after all, is an "innocent amusement" reflects the changes wrought by his wife, who liked singing, and by the musically talented Zorawar

Singh, the classmate he most admires. He overcomes the suspicion that the road to hell is paved with song.

15. On the one hand, Deep Singh is the native adjutant of the ICC and in this sense a commanding officer who might require deferential seating. On the other hand, he is also an ordinary fellow Rajput, not, like Amar Singh, an old acquaintance of the maharaja, a classmate; nor is Deep Singh socially superior to Amar Singh. Amar Singh classifies the occasion as social, not official, and takes offense.

16. Sir Walter Lawrence, *The India We Served* (London: Cassell and Co., 1928), 213–215.

17. In 1905, Babu Sansar Chander Sen became head member of the maharaja's council, equivalent to prime minister. GOI, *Report on the Political Administration of the Rajputana States, 1905.* These reports began in 1865 and were variously published at Bombay (1865–1867) and Calcutta (1869–1907) by the Government of India.

18. Matter between the asterisks has been transferred from the entry *Meerut, Friday, 8th January, 1904.*

19. Transferred from the entry, *Dehra Doon, Monday, 21st April, 1902.*

20. Walers are large, rugged saddle horses, exported from New South Wales to India for military use.

21. Morris, *Pax Britannica*, 286. The *Hobson-Jobson* (1903) entry derives Kadir from *khadar*, "the recent alluvial bordering a large river. . . . The Khadir Cup," it continues, "is one of the chief racing trophies open to pig-stickers in upper India." William Crooke, editor, *Hobson-Jobson: A Glossary of Colloquial Anglo-Indian Words and Phrases*, by Colonel Henry Yule and A.C. Burnell (republished at Delhi: Munshiram Manohar Lal, no date), 478.

22. Pig-sticking helped members of the Indian Civil Service to "purge their lusts" while cavalry officers had the additional benefit of improving their horsemanship. Philip Mason, *The Men Who Ruled India, II. The Guardians* (London: Verso, 1954).

23. For example, Captain R.S.S. Baden-Powell, *Pigsticking or Hoghunting: A Complete Account for Sportsmen and Others* (London: Harrison and Sons, 1889).

24. Matter between these and the next set of asterisks has been taken from later on in the account.

25. The first such bodyguard, styled the Governor's Troop of Moguls, was formed in 1773 by the then governor general of India, Warren Hastings. When, during Lord Lytton's viceroyalty, Queen Victoria assumed the title of Empress of India in 1877, the bodyguard was styled officially as H.E. the Viceroy's Bodyguard. After Independence, in 1948, the unit was styled as the President's Bodyguard. *Mewar Polo* 16.6 (1990): 8.

26. A.R. Waller and A.W. Ward, editors, *The Cambridge History of English Literature*, vol. XIV, Part 3 (New York: Macmillan, 1937), 83–84.

27. Wordi major was the highest rank available to an Indian, serving in the specifically restricted rank of VCOs.

28. Sardar here designates a Sikh, noble or common.

29. In Rajputana, Kanwar refers to the son (and Banwar to the grandson) of a living Rajput but is also often used, as in this case, to designate the first son, heir to a thikana.

30. Raj Kanwar was often used to address the heir of a ruler, usually the eldest son. Because in Rajputana and Gujarat, especially the latter, there were many small princely states, titles such as Raj Kanwar were no guide to the political standing or wealth of a prince.

31. Maharaj indicates a prince of the blood or royal person.

32. A Thakur, it will be recalled, is the head of a Rajput family, that is, a Rajput whose father is deceased. Thakur in Rajasthan was also commonly used as a title of an estate holder, as in Thakur of Kanota.

33. Banwar in Amar Singh's case signals his being the eldest grandson and thus heir after his father, Narain Singh, to Thakur Zorawar Singh of Kanota.

34. Jaisalmer is the kingdom of the Bhati Rajputs. Kanwar here is probably used by reference to his thikana by adoption, Eta. Jawar Singh has a chance to succeed by adoption to the Jaisalmer throne because Eta is closely related to the royal line. Jawar Singh, son of Thakur Sardar Singh, was adopted in 1889 by Thakur Man Singh of Eta. On June 26, 1914, he succeeded to the Jaisalmer *gaddi* (throne).

35. Sahibzada designates the son of a living Muslim ruler or nobleman. Amanat Ullah was the son of the prime minister of Tonk, a small Muslim-ruled princely state in central Rajputana.

36. Ordinarily Nawab designates a Muslim ruler. Vali Uddeen is the second son of a nobleman of the Piagah family, Vicral Umrao, dewan or prime minister of Hyderabad, the largest princely state and not in or part of Madras Province.

37. By name and place we may take Akbar Khan to be a Pathan.

38. Major Watson, who is himself very religious—according to Amar Singh—takes very seriously the mandate to protect the religion of the Indians under his command. This means preserving the boundaries of the religions—Hindu, Muslim—in ways that erase the possible adaptability and fluidity of those boundaries.

39. One of the Jat cadets asks to eat at a separate table.

40. The inclusion in Hinduism would now be contested by many Sikhs.

2: "The Results of Sodomy"

1. "This position, usually assigned to the novice or weakest player on a team, is, in fact, one of the most difficult to play. Requiring great anticipation of the play, determination, and self-control, the Number One is theoretically responsible for scoring goals and neutralizing the opposing Number Four [defensive player]. He places himself to receive passes from his teammates and generally serves as an offensive spearhead." *Encyclopaedia Britannica*, 15th edition, vol. 14, 762.

2. Matter between the asterisks is from the entry of August 10, 1902.

3. From *Friday, 11th July, 1902*.

4. Italicized names are pseudonyms. The diary from time to time deals with what at the time was considered deviant sexual conduct. In a few instances, reputations of living persons or their immediate descendants cannot be protected by pseudonyms; such accounts have been omitted.

5. The Jodhpur maharaja is "acting" in Deep Singh's temporary absence, and this is regarded as a significant honor since wordi major is the highest rank available to an Indian.

6. Roman emperor, A.D. 161–180, Stoic.

7. The Foreign and Political Department of the Government of India (GOI) was staffed by the Political Service. It maintained a kind of diplomatic corps to the princely states—representatives were styled "political agents"—and to states on the periphery of India in Central, Western, and South-East Asia. See Part VI. Curzon toured the Gulf Emirates during his viceroyalty and sent the Younghusband expedition to Tibet. The GOI's geo-political calculation and foreign policy were sometimes at odds with Whitehall's (the foreign office), not least during Curzon's time.

8. We have included in this section matter from the entries of October 30 and 31, and November 1, 2, 3, and 13, 1902.

3: "Too Proud and Haughty?"

1. Matter between asterisks is from the entry *Dehra Doon, Sunday, 19th October 1902*.

2. Cameron and Narain Singh were colleagues in that both had served as guardians to maharajas who were minors—Cameron to the Nawab of Jaora, Narain Singh to the Maharaja of Alwar.

3. Kolhapur, a princely state in western India, was ruled by a Maratha prince. Rajputana Rajputs did not intermarry with the Maratha ruling families of western India; would they interdine? The young maharaja did not join the corps; the problem about eating arrangements therefore did not arise.

4. Field Marshall Lord Frederick Roberts of Khandahar, hero of the Second Afghan War (1878–1880), commander in chief of the Madras Army (1880) and the Bengal Army (1885), commander (after Redvers Buller was relieved) of Imperial Forces in the Boer War, October 1899-May 1902, and field marshall at his retirement before the outbreak of World War I, he began his military career as a subaltern in the Company's artillery in 1852. "He became a legend in the British and Indian Army alike," Philip Mason writes, "because he was direct, uncomplicated and brave and because he put his duty to . . . the men under his command before his own comfort and convenience," *A Matter of Honour,* 340. "It is really inescapable to go on quoting Roberts," Mason writes, "because he does so accurately represent the prevailing view" (347). Kipling knew and admired Roberts, and Roberts admired Kipling. Roberts, who knew that armies needed good coverage, talked to Kipling before leaving for South Africa to take command and saw to it that Kipling got to South Africa and to the front. Kipling made "Bobs" a household word. See Martin Fido, *Rudyard Kipling* (London: Hamlyn, 1974), 103, 129. When the second class of ICC cadets read the *Forty-One Years in India* in 1902, the book had been out for five years and was well on its way to becoming canonical. As is evident from ICC practice, it was frequently reprinted and made assigned reading for civilian and military officers.

5. *Dehra Doon, Saturday, 15th August, 1903,* "Notes About My Fourth Term in the Imperial Cadet Corps," XXII. Those Who Have Left the Corps.

6. *Jaipore, Saturday, 29th August, 1903.* "Notes About My Fourth Term in the Imperial Cadet Corps," XXV. Major Watson's Speech.

4: "To Command Europeans?"

1. The language is that of Amar Singh's commission of July 4, 1905. Kanota Family Archive.

2. Matter transferred from the entry *Meerut, Friday, 29th January, 1904.*

3. Matter transferred from the entry *Jaipore, Tuesday, 5th April, 1904,* "Notes About My Fifth Term in the Imperial Cadet Corps," XLI. Indecent Tricks.

4. Ibid.

5. Matter between the asterisks is from the entry *Jaipore, 5th April, 1902,* "Notes," XXV. Try for a Post.

6. A generic term for an 1870s movement organized initially by Pandit Din Dayal Sharma as the Sanatan Dharm Rakshini Sabha. Sanatan Dharm discourse gained momentum as a response to Swami Dayanand Saraswati's Hindu reformist Arya Samaj. "The adherent of Sanatan Dharm," Philip Lutgendorf writes, "might best be described in negative terms—as one who was not an Arya or Brahmo Samajist, not a Christian or Westernizer, and who did not advocate widow remarriage, the initiation of untouchables, or the abandonment of image worship." Lutgendorf, *The Life of a Text,* 363.

7. To latterday feminist critics, *satee* or *sati* represents an act of patriarchal coercion, and the idea of voluntary sati is an oxymoron. In the Rajput worldview this act went beyond the conventional understanding of it being an act of devotion to the departed husband. Because it is said to involve *sat* or truth, it is taken as an act of spiritual purity and heroism,

and the spirit of the sati is said to have great efficacy. For an interpretation of the contested meaning of sati, including the debate surrounding a *sati* in Rajasthan at Deorla in September 1987 that launched a national controversy, see Richard Shweder, *Thinking Through Cultures: Expeditions in Cultural Anthropology* (Cambridge, MA: Harvard University Press, 1991), 15–16. There is an extensive literature on sati. It begins when Governor General Lord William Bentinck (1828–1835) declared it barbaric and tried to stamp it out. Among the recent interpretations, see Ashis Nandy's "Sati: A Nineteenth Century Tale of Women, Violence and Protest," in V.C. Joshi, editor, *Rammohun Roy and the Process of Modernization in India* (Delhi: Vikas Publishing House, 1975); Lata Mani, "Contentious Traditions: The Debate on Sati in Colonial India," in Kumkum Sangari and Sudesh Vaid, editors, *Recasting Women: Essays in Colonial History* (New Brunswick: Rutgers University Press, 1990).

5: "The Big Swells Were Gone"

1. Surya Mal Mishran, 1815–1868. *Vans Bhaskar* is a historical epic, in Dingal, about the Hada Chauhans of Bundi and Kota. Edited by Ram Karan Asopa with commentary by Krishna Singh Barhat, cited without publisher and date in Vishnu Datt Sharma, editor, *Vans Bhaskar* (New Delhi: Sahitya Akademi, 1976).

2. The portion between asterisks is from the entry *Jaipore, 25th August, 1904*, "Notes on My Sixth Term in the Imperial Cadet Corps."

3. Much of our work on the diary was done in Landour—at Fernworth (1979–1980); Oakville Terrace (1983–1984); Stoneledge (1975–1976 and 1987–1988); and Oakville (1991–1992), where we stayed with Robert and Ellen Alter. The trip from Rajpur that Amar Singh accomplished by pony takes about one hour by car.

6: "Good-Bye, My Dear Corps"

1. Resecting is a method in surveying by which one determines a position on a map after it has been properly oriented by drawing lines from two or more distant objects through their plotted position on the map.

2. Matter between asterisks is from the entry *Meerut, Wednesday, 30th November, 1904.*

3. Date of first commission, NILF, July 4, 1905. Appointment and first commission, Indian Army (IA), August 25, 1917. Date of retirement, July 4, 1923; rank Captain, IA; Major, NILF.

4. Date of first commission, NILF, July 4, 1905. Appointment and first commission, IA, August 25, 1917. Date of retirement, July 4, 1923; rank Captain, IA; Major, NILF.

5. Date of first commission, NILF, July 4, 1905. Appointment and first commission, IA, August 25, 1917. Date of retirement, August 1, 1925; rank Captain, IA; Major, NILF.

6. While Amar Singh speaks of Nawab Vali Uddeen Khan as one of the commissioned cadets, he does not appear in the *Indian Amy List* for 1918 (the earliest we consulted) nor in the subsequent ones. We surmise that while Nawab Vali Uddeen Khan was first commissioned in the NILF on July 4, 1905, in the ceremony Amar Singh describes in the entry *Mount Abu, Saturday, 27th May, 1905*, XXIII. Visit to Agra, he left the service prior to World War I.

7. Date of first commission, NILF, July 4, 1905. Appointment and first commission, IA, August 25, 1917. The diary does not mention him among the first four to be commissioned, and he did not go to Agra to meet the viceroy. Amar Singh has a very negative image of Akbar Khan. "Khan Mohammed Akbar Khan was not at all a gentleman. No one liked him and he was hated by most. Capt. Cameron had a very bad opinion of him and the same may be said of Major Watson. He was a corporal and would have been one of the successful cadets had he not been sent with the Dane mission to Kabul. *Mount Abu, Saturday, 27th*

May, 1905, "Notes About My Seventh Term in the Cadet Corps," XVIII, The Cadets. This has to be balanced against the fact that Akbar Khan performed well in the examinations, ahead of Amar Singh in English, Arithmetic, Survey, and behind Amar Singh only in tactics, topography, fortification and history. (See examination results, *Dehra Doon, Sunday, 29th May, 1904*.) We find out further from the diary that Akbar Khan was sent on a special mission to Kabul, and that arrangements were made to assure him that he would not be disadvantaged because of this mission. Hoti Mardan is on the frontier. It seems plausible that his presence at Kabul was politically helpful to the British.

8. Date of first commission, NILF, January 1, 1907. Appointment and first commission, IA, August 25, 1917. Date of retirement, January 1, 1929. Major (NILF?).

9. Date of first commission, NILF, January 1, 1907. Appointment and first commission, IA, August 25, 1917. Date of retirement, January 1, 1929). Major (NILF?).

10. Date of first commission, NILF, probably January 1, 1907. Appointment and first commission, IA, August 25, 1917.

11. Amar Singh was born in 1878. It is probable that his age was differently reported to the Cadet Corps, whose formal record has his birth-date as 1881, in order to stay within the age limit for joining the ICC. The limit was twenty-one, and Amar Singh would have been twenty-three in 1902.

12. The Maharaja of Cooch Behar, Rajjee's father, attempted to enter his son at Sandhurst, but failed. The attendant discussions probably added to the urgency for setting up the ICC.

13. Colloquial designation for a soldier of the ordinary ranks. Not an officer.

PART V - PRIVATE LIVES IN PATRIARCHAL SPACE:

Introduction

1. Michelle Perrot, "Introduction," *From the Fires of Revolution to the Great War*, vol. IV of Philippe Aries and Georges Duby, general editors, *The History of Private Life* (Cambridge, MA: Harvard-Belknap Press, 1990), 1.

2. See particularly vol. IV of Aries and Duby, *The History of Private Life*, where Alain Corbin's account in "Backstage" and "The Secret of the Individual" speaks of diaries as a means of "understanding and self-control."

3. According to *The History of Private Life*, self and social recognition of the individual—of a private person in private space aware of private thoughts—mark an important transformation in the history of private life. Yet while we are often told that life in medieval Christian Europe displayed little awareness of or concern about privacy in court, castle, manor house, and cottage, like life in Rajasthan it had niches for a construction of privacy. The monastery and the convent, where God's presence mattered, had long since created its own form of privacy, the cell, an "observed" private space.

4. See Introduction, 1.

5. The selections were translated by "Nagrik," journalistic *nom de plume* of Nand Kishore Parikh between 1983 and 1985. The complaint may be found in Onkar Singh, "Sar Pratap Benaam Amarsingh," *Rajasthan Patrika*, May 22, 1983.

6. He was put in charge of "36 departments"—which actually turn out to be twenty two: horse stables, buggy garage, elephant stables, hunting department, *rath* garage (bullock carts), armory, camp equipment, dairy, carpentry, performing arts, religion and charity, food and supply, library and records, camel corps, gardens, guest house, electricity, personal kitchen of the maharaja, zenana deorhi, forest, mining, and grass farm. Kanota Family Archive.

7. See Introduction, Chapter 3.

1: Diplomacy of Everyday Life

1. *Banwar* is the grandson of the lord of a thikana, *kanwar* the son, and thakur the lord.

2. Amar Singh does not adopt in his lifetime. He seems to have been immobilized in the face of the conflicting claims of Sardar Singh, his third brother, and Sheo Nath Singh, the second brother. Sheo Nath Singh, the better educated senior brother, has had six daughters by his second wife, suggesting the line might come to an end, until October 2, 1937 when a son, Mohan Singh, was born. Amar Singh keeps postponing action. When he dies on November 1, 1942, a bitter contest ensues. Ultimately, the Kanota thikana is granted to Sheo Nath Singh, whose son, Mohan Singh, is an editor of this diary. Initially a Jaipur state court held for Sardar Singh, but its ruling was reversed by Maharaja Man Singh of Jaipur, partly on the basis of diary excerpts that convinced him that Amar Singh wanted Sheo Nath Singh to succeed. Sardar Singh, the third brother, for many years acted as Amar Singh's *kamdar* (estate manager). The family believes that Amar Singh's wife favored Sardar Singh because his son, Khushal Singh, the prospective heir, was married to her niece. The niece and her children shared Amar Singh's wife's quarters and seem to have provided her with the company of offspring she did not herself have. The account of the circumstances surrounding the succession is part of the Kanota family traditions as recounted by Mohan Singh.

3. We have excluded long accounts of three weddings from this volume, but have included Amar Singh's own (see Part III). They contain much characterological and ethnographic detail. The longest account, of the marriage of his wife's sister at Satheen, encompasses 129 pages; that of the Maharaja of Kishengarh to the Princess of Udaipur is also quite long (see Part VI).

4. Sir Pratap favored simplicity in Rajput marriage and death rituals, both expensive competitive social events that often created heavy debts for the thikanas. The state of Jodhpur under Sir Pratap tried to enforce the rules limiting such expenditure initiated by the Walter Krit Hitkarni Sabha, a Rajput reform association. See Part III.

5. Continued on December 4, 1902.

6. Literally, tying and binding. Any mode of regulation or settlement. Here, arrangement.

7. Passage between asterisks from *Alwar and Jaipore, Wednesday, 26 November, 1902.*

8. Prosperous Rajput households had tied servants who were transferred with a daughter when she was married. For a discussion of the *davris*, the tied female servants that are proprietary to households and are transferred with dowry, see Varsha Joshi, *Polygamy and Purdah: Women and Society among Rajputs* (Jaipur and Delhi: Rawat Publications, 1995), 153 ff. For those interested in the historical background of the practices discussed in this Part of the diary, Joshi's book is invaluable. A Jodhpur act of unknown dating says that "Rajputs who have Darogas born under their roof and have brought them up shall be entitled to give away the daughters of these Darogas in dowry along with their own daughters. Rajputs of the position shall be entitled to give away in dowry whole families of the Darogas." Cited by Joshi at p. 156 from B.S. Pathik, *What are the Indian States?* (Ajmer: Diamond Jubilee Press, 1928), 136.

9. Dowry transfers have a sort of chain effect. Servant girls transferred from Satheen to Kanota when Amar Singh gets married are recycled to Garhi when Amar Singh's sister marries there. Similarly horses given in Amar Singh's marriage are recycled in the marriages of his cousins which are described a little later in the diary.

10. Matter between asterisks from *Jaipore, Saturday, 29 November, 1902.*

11. These notes are continued on December 24, 25, 26, 1902.

12. See Amar Singh's Diary, volumes for 1915. Also Kanota family tradition.

13. Matter between asterisks from *Kanota, Thursday, 11th September, 1902.*

14. In 1905, he succeeds Sir Swinton Jacob, see below.

15. Colonel Sir Swinton Jacob, executive engineer of Jaipur, was architect of the Albert Hall Museum in Jaipur's Ram Niwas garden, an important and charming example of "Indo-Saracenic" architecture, as well as of the redesign, under Maharaja Madho Singh, of the Ram Bagh palace, originally built in 1850. He served in Jaipur for forty-five years, beginning in 1867. Thomas R. Metcalf, *An Imperial Vision: Indian Architecture and Britain's Raj* (Berkeley: University of California Press, 1989), 129–138.

16. Matter between asterisks from *Meerut, Wednesday, 11th March, 1903*. Paonoskar is first private tutor, then one of the ministers of Maharaja Madan Singh of Kishengarh, then teacher at Mayo College.

17. Now a well-known luxury hotel.

18. Matter between asterisks from *Jaipore, Sunday, 5th October, 1902*.

19. The kind of "decline and fall" language used in this passage, invoking major historical swings grounded in moral failing, is much in prominence in the English literary traditions of Amar Singh's time.

20. Of the brothers, Sheo Nath became the Thakur of Kanota after Amar Singh's death. Sardar Singh became estate manager of Kanota. Bari Sal Singh was born in 1890, and served over the course of his career at the princely courts of Kashmir, Idar, and Udaipur and died in 1964. Narain Singh and Zorawar Singh having held office in the courts of princely states, such service was considered a usual and proper family vocation. Kesri Singh was born in 1892 and educated at Mayo College and the Agriculture College, Poona. His early career was spent in service at Kashmir and Gwalior. Later he served in Jaipur as deputy inspector general of police, head of its *shikarkhana* (hunting department), and ADC to Maharaja Man Singh. He authored *Hunting with Horse and Spear; The Tiger of Rajasthan; The Encyclopedia of Shikar;* and other works on hunting and animals. As one of India's leading shikaris, he was in charge of the arrangements for Queen Elizabeth and Prince Philip when they visited Jaipur in 1961. Govind Singh "though nearly eight years old, cannot properly speak as yet." Isri Singh is weak and dies young.

21. See Herbert Sherring, *The Mayo College, "The Eton of India": A Record of Twenty Years, 1875–1895*, two vols (Calcutta: Thacker, Spink and Co., 1897). Sherring was headmaster.

22. Matter between asterisks from *Jaipore, Wednesday, 28th January, 1903*.

23. From *Jaipore, Sunday, 25th January, 1903. Kaisar Bilas Natak* was a play by Shiv Charan Pita. "Books that I Have Read in the Year 1903."

24. From *Meerut, Thursday, 29th January, 1903*.

25. Ibid.

2: Lectures to the Maharaja of Kishengarh

1. (London: E. Truelove, 1852). The book was in its 31st edition in 1895. See earlier discussions of the publishing and cultural history of this volume in Parts I and III.

2. Matter between asterisks from *Meerut, Wednesday, 4th February, 1903*.

3. See, for example, Georg Buhler, translator, *The Laws of Manu* (Oxford: Clarendon Press, 1886), or Wendy Doniger, translator, with Brian K. Smith, *The Laws of Manu* (New Delhi: Penguin, 1991).

4. Edition of 1885. For an extended discussion of Drysdale, see Miriam Benn, *Predicaments of Love* (London: Pluto Press, 1992). "In England the book was the most notorious of its age, read in the guiltiest secrecy" (10).

5. Edition of 1885, 5.

6. Ibid., 249.

7. Ibid., 187.

8. Ibid., 247.

9. He founded the Jaipur Lancers, forerunner of the 61st Cavalry.

10. Treating the wife as a hostage to extract resources from her parents is a feature of the "dowry deaths" that have become conspicuous in urban north India since the 1980s. This passage suggests similar practices are quite old.

11. Purdah is a veil; the word refers more broadly to female seclusion. See, for example, Doranne Jacobson, "Purdah and the Hindu Family in Central India," in Hanna Papanek and Gail Minault, *Separate Worlds: Studies of Purdah in South Asia* (Delhi: Chanakya Publishers, 1982).

3: Women at Home

1. For an early attempt to set this experience in the context of psycho-cultural theory, see Lloyd I. Rudolph and Susanne Hoeber Rudolph, "Rajput Adulthood: Reflections on the Amar Singh Diary," *Daedalus* Spring (1976). The essay is reprinted in Susanne Hoeber Rudolph and Lloyd I. Rudolph, *Essays on Rajputana: Reflections on History, Culture and Administration* (New Delhi: Concept Publishing House, 1984).

2. Fateh Singh of Naila served as first minister under Maharaja Ram Singh from 1873 until Ram Singh's death in 1880. He died in 1897.

3. "Memo Concerning the Jagir Case of the Thikanas of Gondher, Kanauta and Naila," (Kanota Family Archive, 1903?). The state charged that family members, due to their access as ministers, had slipped papers granting the estates into a pile of signatures the maharaja executed hastily before departing on a journey, and the grant was thus unwittingly made. The family argued that the maharaja himself had visited the newly granted estates, and therefore had to be knowledgeable about the grants.

4. The resident is agent of the British viceroy to the semi-autonomous princely states, in this case Jaipur state. He embodies the working of British "paramountcy," the loosely defined British suzerainty that overarches the autonomy the princely states are allowed in matters of domestic policy. For a more extended account of the workings of paramountcy, see Part VI.

5. Matter between asterisks is from *Jaipore, Sunday, 13th April, 1902.*

6. Maharani of the Jaddon clan. In ordinary speech among Rajputs, women's public identity took the form of their clan affiliations.

7. Matter between asterisks from *Meerut, Saturday, 9th January, 1904.*

8. Entry of *Jaipore, Thursday, 7th May, 1903.*

9. These notes are continued on May 21–23.

10. Hari Singh, Thakur of Khatu, a Shekhawati thikana. He was known as Hari Singh Ladkhana, his sub-clan. Seen in the family as a rival of Narain Singh, he succeeded him as superintendent of police, Jaipur. Amar Singh is taking advantage of the Rajasthan presumption that office was often, but not invariably, heritable. For an account of bureaucratic patterns in the princely states of Rajputana, see our "Oligopolistic Competition Among State Elites in Princely India," in George Marcus, editor, *Elites: Ethnographic Issues* (Albuquerque: University of New Mexico Press, 1983), republished in Rudolph and Rudolph, *Essays on Rajputana.*

11. Zorawar Singh is looking to the past in giving this estimate, even as he was when he attempted to educate Amar Singh in Urdu. English is being increasingly used as the language of high level administration in Jaipur, and is an important opportunity language.

12. Matter between asterisks from *Jaipore, Wednesday, 22nd April, 1903.*

13. That infertility, as well as determination of the child's sex, may be associated with the male partner was not part of the medical theories of the Rajputs in Amar Singh's family.

14. Matter between asterisks from *Dehra Doon, Thursday, 20th October, 1903.* XVIII. Bhoj Raj Singhjee.

4: Joint-Family Responsibilities

1. Cousin Pratap Singh is the eldest son of Thakur Roop Singh of Naila, Amar Singh's uncle. Bhabi is an elder brother's wife; in Indian discourse, where language sometimes assimilates more distant members of a joint family to near ones, cousins are often referred to as brothers, or cousin-brothers. Pratap Singh had married her in December of 1901, and Amar Singh had been part of the wedding party.

2. In Rajasthan, the dead are immediately placed on the floor, not a bed. A woman who dies in pregnancy or childbirth and prior to her husband is dressed in yellow or saffron garments.

3. It is unclear why Amar Singh speaks of a coffin, conveying the image of a wooden container not seen in Rajasthan. There it was usual to place bodies on a light litter, and the rest of the description coincides with that practice. The passage gives an idea about Amar Singh's imagined audience for this kind of ethnographic account.

4. Circling, as of a temple, or a fire, usually as part of a ritual.

5. Matter between asterisks from later in the same account.

6. Sandalwood emits a pleasant scent. It is also very expensive.

7. A long devotional poem, part of the epic *Mahabharata*, which examines the religious paths available to an observant Hindu.

8. Amar Singh refers to Sir Edwin Arnold's poetic rendering of Buddhist legend and doctrine (1879).

9. The babu wrote numerous books of which the most famous is *Chandra Kanto*. The figure he invented, Booth Nath, ghost's master, figures in several of the novels. Many consider these novels extremely gripping.

10. These notes are continued on October 22 and 25, 1903.

11. Located, like Kanota, to the east of Jaipur, Naila lies a few kilometers beyond Kanota on the northern side of the Jaipur-Agra road. From the battlements of Kanota fort one can see Naila fort to the north and Gondher fort to the south. It was the site of President Clinton's 2000 visit to Jaipur.

12. Ninth day of the moon calendar.

13. This entry is inserted here out of the essay sequence in order to keep together entries about the death of the daughter.

14. Matter between asterisks from *Alwar, Sunday, 13th December, 1903*. We surmise that Amar Singh's sentence refers to transmigration.

15. This entry is inserted out of sequence to group together matter relating to Amar Singh's "cousin's marriage."

16. Notes continued on November 13 and 15, 1903.

17. See, for example, Bernard S. Cohn, "Is there a New Indian History? Society and Social Change under the *Raj*" in *An Anthropologist among the Historians and Other Essays* (Delhi: Oxford University Press, 1987), 181–184. This essay, first written in 1970, when we were all still committed positivists, explores hypergamy while seeking to specify the objective determinants "causing" female infanticide. It is, therefore, rather light on the way practice and interpretation shape cultural givens. It relates infanticide to upward and downward social mobility, pursued via hypergamous marriages, and grounded in increases or decreases of land wealth. The Champawats are upwardly mobile on the basis of expanded landed wealth, but the ambition for status sometimes outruns the economic capacity to support it. Amar Singh steadily opposes hypergamy, even while interested in social status.

18. An undated memo in the Kanota Family Archive gives the 1875 and 1901 yields of the villages of each thikana in the year they were given and in the then-current year: Gondher, Rs 8,872 (1875) and 10,530 (1901); Kanota 6,872 (1875), 17,490 (1901); Naila,

6,995 (1875), 13,689 (1901). This memo was probably written as part of the negotiations to settle the case the maharaja had brought against the Champawat families.

19. Fateh Singh was also accused of having made off with a good cut of the state treasury when he left office at the death of Maharaja Ram Singh in 1880, although the case brought against him was not proven. This charge seems to have colored the other charges against the Champawats. Munshi Triloke Chand, private secretary to Thakur Fateh Singh of Naila translated and edited *Thakur Fateh Singh's Case* (Ajmer: Privately published, 1901), 1. Kanota Family Archive. The volume contains the following letter written by Fateh Singh: "One day in the beginning of July, 1881, Colonel Bannerman, the Resident, and Captain Talbot, after the General Meeting of the Council, had a private interview with H.H. the Maharaja [Madho Singh, ed.] at Chunder Mahal, and a short time after, sent for me. Colonel Bannerman asked me whether I had taken a number of Currency Notes worth Rs 175,000 from Kishen Lall Chella after the Late Highness' demise. . . . Then he told me that the Agent, Governor General, had written him to say that information had reached him that the notes above referred to (the property of His late Highness) had thus been taken away by me, and consequently the Agent, Governor General, was very much displeased with me." There follows a complex defense. When Fateh Singh died, he reportedly bequeathed Rs 100,000 and a great deal of jewelry to his second son, Guman Singh. Guman Singh's wife attempted to give the jewelry to charity, to the Kalyan temple, and was prevented from doing so by the maharaja's police, apparently on the request of Roop Singh of Naila and Zorawar Singh of Kanota. But the money was then confiscated to the state treasury and not returned, on the plea that Guman Singh and his wife were not responsible. This story is from the Kanota family oral tradition. For a more extended account of the family's finances, and how they compare to incomes by other wealthy persons in Jaipur and India, see our "A Bureaucratic Lineage in Princely India: Elite Formation and Conflict in a Patrimonial System," written with Mohan Singh, in our *Essays on Rajputana*, 100 ff. and endnotes.

20. Bhim Singh and Gambhir Singh, second and third brothers of Narain Singh, had been taken off the joint family accounts, given a regular allowance, and expected to manage their own expense—even though their families continued to live in the joint family haveli. Bhim Singh served in the body guard of Maharaja Ram Singh at Jaipur, and after Ram Singh's death as deputy inspector general of police, Jaipur. He represents one of the ways in which the Kanota family continues to be connected to court even when Amar Singh's father, Narain Singh, is "exiled" to Alwar. Gambhir Singh, the third son, served in the cavalry of Jaipur state prior to his death on October 3, 1900.

21. See Kanota genealogical table in the Appendix.

22. From *Delhi, Wednesday, 20th May, 1903.* "Notes About My Last Summer Vacation." XII. Mehtab Singhjee.

23. This entry is inserted out of sequence to be near related entries.

24. Matter between asterisks from later in the same account.

25. For an account of the zenana economy in princely and noble houses, see Varsha Joshi, *Polygamy.*

26. Information from Kanota Family Tradition.

27. Continued January 7, 1904.

5: Men in the World

1. This account is from Amar Singh's long essay, "Notes About Kishengarh Durbar's Marriage."

2. Matter between asterisks from later in the same account.

3. This is from "Notes About My Fifth Term in the Imperial Cadet Corps" (continued April 8, 14, 16, 18, and 20).

4. Fateh Singh is descended from the Jodhpur royal lineage. He is eldest son of Maharaj Zorawar Singh who is the second son of Maharaja Takhat Singh, who ruled Jodhpur. (We follow the Jodhpur convention of naming the rulers maharaja and members of the lineage maharaj.) Sir Pratap is the third son of Maharaja Takhat Singh. Fateh Singh had a jagir valued in 1931 at Rs 40,000, a substantial estate. The last estimate we have for Kanota is Rs 17,490 for 1901. "Memo concerning the jagir case of the thikanas of Gondher, Kanota and Naila" (Undated Memo, Kanota Family Archive).

5. The entries relating to Sushila Tahl Ram have been grouped together.

6. *Cosmopolitan Hinduani* (Lahore: Civil and Military Gazette Press, 1902). See "Books that I have Read in the Year 1903," Part V4.

7. *Alwar, Thursday, 10th December, 1903.*

8. Matter between asterisks from the essay written on February 18, 1904, "Notes About Kishengarh Durbar's Marriage," XXII. The Return Journey.

9. The title of the essay of this day is "Notes About My Last Vacation."

10. The heading of the essay of this date is "Notes About My Last Vacation."

11. Amar Singh's use of the Victorian word "prostitute" obscures a complex cultural phenomenon that includes the cultivation of music and dance forms through gharanas, usually eponymous "schools" based in whole or in part on family. His attitude is shaped by the spatial segregations of genders and the seclusion of women. Women in the respectable household may sing and dance, as on the occasion of weddings or other festivities, but do so only in the zenana, their segregated space. Women whose vocation is cultural performance, singing, dancing or music, are suspect because they appear before strangers, and are assumed to be available. There was an ambiguous relation between women of pleasure and those who were bearers and sometimes teachers of culture and manners. The word prostitute reduces to commodified sex an identity that included cultural virtuosity. Amar Singh's Rajput expectations are overlaid and compounded by the puritanical attitudes he acquired from his master and mentor, the Arya Samajist and Victorian Sir Pratap, censorious of the music and dance and liberal lifestyle associated with Maharaja Sardar Singh of Jodhpur. See, for example, Part I and elsewhere, where Amar Singh comments on the shocking behavior of the Jodhpur rani, who allows her hands to be seen when the royal carriage passes, or joins tiger hunts where she can be seen. See Joan Erdman, *Patrons and Performers in Rajasthan: The Subtle Tradition* (New Delhi: Chanakya Publishers, 1985), for a discussion of the performers at the Jaipur *gunijankhana*, performance department.

6: Harmony and Dissidence in the Joint Family

1. The essay of this date is entitled "Notes About My Last Vacation."

2. Matter between asterisks from Jaipore, Saturday, 16th April, 1904.

3. Matter between asterisks is transferred from *Jaipore, Saturday, 16th April, 1904.*

4. Amar Singh's opportunity does not come until 1923 when the Jaipur Army is reorganized. A military board recommends the recruitment of a regiment of cavalry and a battallion of infantry. The decision coincides with the death of Maharaja Madho Singh, who had resisted such a regiment and particularly the possibility that any of the Kanota clan would play a role in it. The cavalry is placed under the command of Lt. Colonel Amar Singh (Jaipur State Forces). The transport corps and the infantry are commanded by other officers. In 1931 Amar Singh is appointed commander of the Jaipur Corps, newly formed out of seven units of Jaipur forces.

5. Order of the subheads of the October 21 essay has been violated to bring together related matter.

6. From XII. Bhoj Raj Singhjee, of the same essay. These "notes" are continued on October 24, 27, and 31.

7. Ibid., XVII. My Aunt.

8. Ibid., XVIII. Mandawa.

9. There are other factors at work besides the hypergamy question. The Rawalot family is quite poor, and they are having trouble marrying their daughter to a dignified noble family. She is a person of significantly lower social standing than Pratap's previous wives. But finding a bride for a man twice widowed, whose deceased wives have both given him children, a son and a daughter, is difficult.

10. For an important empirical and theoretical account of the role of political power in defining status, see Nicholas Dirks, *The Hollow Crown: Ethnohistory of an Indian Kingdom* (Cambridge: Cambridge University Press, 1987), and, in shorter compass, his "The Original Caste: Power, History and Hierarchy in South Asia," in *Contributions to Indian Sociology* 23:1 (1989).

11. The Gangore festival is especially celebrated by girls wishing for a husband and women with living husbands. Teej is celebrated by married women on the third day of the bright half of the month of Shravan.

12. This subsection and the following one, inserted out of sequence, again deals with the problems of Amar Singh's cousins.

13. Matter between asterisks from omitted subsection XIII preceding the entry on Pratap Singh.

14. The matter between asterisks from *Meerut, Monday, 19th December, 1904.*

15. Major General Sir Stewart Beatson, inspector general, Imperial Service Troops and friend of Sir Pratap from his days at Jodhpur when the Jodhpur Lancers were raised. He and Sir Pratap were instrumental in formulating and popularizing modern polo in north India. He knows and is sympathetic to Amar Singh.

16. This, and the following subsection, inserted out of sequence, deal with related matter.

17. In the next generation only one of Dalip Singh's three sons is educated enough to have a professional career while all six sons of his Peelva cousins, Inder Singh and Boor Singh, become educated professionals.

18. Sultan Singh did adopt Inder Singh in 1910.

19. Chhiman Singh is the second son of Shambhu Singh of Gondher (See Appendix, Genealogical Chart II). Perhaps he had hopes of adoption at Peelva, since Shambhu Singh of Gondher was the nearest line to Peelva in the absence of a direct descendant of Abhai Singh. The failure of Sultan Singh to sign this document strongly suggests that he was considering not following the "rule." When it became apparent that Bhoj Raj Singh of Gondher would not have a male heir, Chhiman Singh's son Kalyan Singh was adopted there.

20. That is, Shambhu Singh had no sons or grandsons available for adoption.

21. Out-of-sequence insert.

22. A people ruling in Marwar (Jodhpur) before it was conquered by the Rathore Rajputs. The Indas are said to have married their daughters to Rathores. In particular, the Rajput chief Chunda, eponymous ancestor of the Chundawats, received in dowry Mandore, the first capital of the Rathores, when he married the daughter of an Inda chief. Today the tombs of the early Rathore maharajas can be seen at Mandore in a lovely garden setting.

23. Zorawar Singh was born February 24, 1827; he died February 2, 1908 (Kanota Family Archive). He migrated to Jaipur at the age of thirty-four, in 1861 (Mohan Singh memorandum on family dates, from Kanota Family Archive).

24. Among Jats, it was usual to marry a widow to her deceased husband's younger brother in order to prevent her from cultivating her share separately from that of the joint family. See Prem Chowdhry, "Customs in a Peasant Economy: Women in Colonial Haryana," in Kum Kum Sangari and Sudesh Vaid, editors, *Recasting Women: Essays in Indian Colonial History* (New Brunswick, NJ: Rutgers University Press, 1989), 302–307.

25. See Kanota Family Archive, Box 1, Documents 67 and 71, as examples of hundreds of loan documents reflecting Zorawar Singh's activities. Other examples are "The court decision about the loan given to Thakur Jaswant Singh of Akheypura" (Urdu, 1919, KFA Box 2, Document 133); "The Document about the loan given to Thakur Kalyan Singh of Mohanpura and the agreement of the important persons of the village" (Urdu, 1913, Box 2, Document 134). Kanota, presumably in the person of Narain Singh, continued to give loans after the death of Zorawar Singh in 1908. The Archive has documents recording seventeen major loans between 1910 and 1920.

26. Narain Singh was for many years nazim, in charge of law and order in Shekhawati. Bhim Singh was deputy inspector general of police at Jaipur.

27. A bigha is about five-eighths of an acre. The shares given to younger brothers are heritable until the younger brother's line expires.

PART VI - PRINCELY COURTS IN IMPERIAL SPACE

Introduction

1. For an account of the integration of the princely states into the Indian union at Independence in 1947, see V.P. Menon, *The Integration of the Princely States* (New York: Arno Press, 1972).

2. Rajputana is the name by which the area of twenty-two princely states and chiefships under the agent to the governor general (AGG) of Rajputana was known under the British. After independence its official name became Rajasthan. The basis for a different understanding that reaches beyond Rajputs is being laid by the Rajasthan Studies Group of the Association for Asian Studies and the Institute of Rajasthan Studies headquartered in Jaipur. Their publications include Karine Schomer, Joan L. Erdman, Deryck O. Loderick, and Lloyd I. Rudolph, editors, *The Idea of Rajasthan: Explorations in Regional Identity, I. Constructions, II. Institutions* (New Delhi: Manohar Publishers/American Institute of Indian Studies, 1994) and N.K. Singhi and Rajendra Joshi, editors, *Folk, Faith and Feudalism* (Jaipur: Rawat Publishers, 1995). Scholars working on accounts that avoid or supplement a Rajput-centric understanding of Rajasthan's history and society include: Dilbagh Singh, G.L. Devra, Shireen Moosvi, Lindsey Harlan, S.P. Gupta, Shail Mayaram, Dominique Sila Khan, Thomas R. Rosin, Ann Gold, Daniel Gold, Katherine Clementine-Ojha, Catherine Weinberger Thomas, Alan Babb, Michael Goldman, Joan Erdman, Caroline Humphrey, David McCurdy, Barry Michie, Hugh Plunkett, Richard Sisson, John Smith, Thomas Timberg and Pauline Kolenda. For a selected list of scholars working on Rajasthan, see Varsha Joshi, editor, *Directory of Research on Rajasthan* (Jaipur: Rawat Publishers for the Institute of Rajasthan Studies, no date, *circa* 1994). Colonel James Tod, whose foundational study of Rajasthan has received a very "Rajput" reading, especially by nationalist historians in search of heroes, pays more attention than is usually noted to the history of trading towns, trade routes, and trading communities, especially Jains. James Tod, *Annals and Antiquities of Rajputana*, two volumes in one (London: Routledge, 1914). Originally published in 1829 and 1832. Two seminars hosted by the South Asian Studies Center and the Political Science Department of the University of Rajasthan in 1995–1996 saw attempts to critique the prevailing Rajputization of Rajasthan history: "Honor and Power in Rajasthan and Tamil Nadu: A

Research Proposal," presented by Professor N.K. Singhi and Dr P.C. Mathur, February 10, 1996, and "People and Rajasthan," presented by Dr P.C. Mathur, February 19, 1996.

3. See Barbara N. Ramusack, "The Indian Princes as Fantasy: Palace Hotels, Palace Museums, and Palace on Wheels," in Carol Breckenridge, editor, *Consuming Modernity* (Delhi: Oxford University Press, 1996), 66–89.

4. For a conceptualization of Rajput politics over the long *duree*, see Iqbal Narain and P.C. Mathur, "The Thousand Year Raj: Regional Isolation and Rajput Hinduism in Rajasthan Before and After 1947" in Francine Frankel and M.S.A. Rao, editors, *Dominance and State Power in India: Decline of a Social Order*, vol. II (Delhi: Oxford University Press, 1990), 1–58.

5. Norbert Elias, *The Court Society*, translated by Edmund Jephcott (New York: Pantheon Books, 1983), 2–3. For a detailed account of the ritual and political practices of the Rajasthan courts, see R.P. Kathuria, *Life in the Courts of Rajasthan* (New Delhi: S. Chand and Co., 1987). The marriage practices that created and sustained court society are reviewed in Varsha Joshi, *Polygamy and Purdah: Women and Society among Rajputs* (Jaipur: Rawat Publishers, 1995).

6. For a systematic discussion of the ways in which kingly power creates status and honor, see Nicholas Dirks, "The Original Caste: Power, History and Hierarchy in South Asia," *Contributions to Indian Sociology* 23:1 (1989): 59–77. Many British commentators, inspired by an essentialist theory of status, regarded as fraudulent any status-making process that is visible (e.g. beer-barons) but considered authentic those decently hidden by the veil of elapsed time (mobile Normans).

7. India's 562 princely states, chiefships, and other entities encompassed 40 percent of Indian territory and included 25 percent of India's population. Parshotam Mehra, *A Dictionary of Modern Indian History 1707–1947* (Delhi: Oxford University Press, 1985), 540.

8. For raj hegemony, see Susanne Hoeber Rudolph and Lloyd I. Rudolph, "Setting the Table: Amar Singh Aboard the *SS Mohawk*," *Common Knowledge* 3:1 (1994):158–177, where we observe that "Cultural projects are potentially constitutive . . . for those who rule states, cultural and ideological control is cheaper and more reliable than force. Apologists of the British empire, for example, expended significant treasure and talent on arts of cultural creation . . . [that] won the willing compliance of the lower and working classes at home and of the subject peoples abroad to an order in which their place was that of dignified and contented inferiors. Recent literature on the British raj has addressed the ways its agents invented social categories and rituals that served to control colonial subjects" (see footnote 2). "Setting the Table" tells the story of Amar Singh's subversion of these categories and rituals.

9. The 1818 treaties were signed in the context of competing strategic concepts, the balance of power framework established by Warren Hastings, the Company's first and longest serving governor general (1774–1785), and the pursuit of subcontinental hegemony as successor of the Mughal empire.Hastings had held that the Company "should aim to exert, from behind its ring fence of subordinate states, a stabilizing and responsible influence as one among several of the subcontinent's powers." The treaty of Salbai (1782), designed to establish a stable balance of power among the subcontinent's leading powers, was hailed as one of Hastings' "crowning achievements."The treaty of Salbai was soon subverted by Governor-General Hasting's putative subordinates in Bombay. See John Keay, *The Honourable Company: A History of the English East India Company* (New York: Macmillan, 1991), 445.

10. See Michael H. Fisher, editor, *The Politics of the British Annexation of India, 1757–1857* (Delhi: Oxford University Press, 1993). For outstanding accounts of state

formation in eighteenth-century India, see Stewart Gordon, *Marathas, Marauders, and State Formation in Eighteenth Century India* (Delhi: Oxford University Press, 1994) and Andre Wink, *Land and Sovereignty in India: Agrarian Society and Politics under the Eighteenth-century Maratha Swarajya* (Cambridge: Cambridge University Press, 1986).

11. For Lord Lytton's 1877 Delhi durbar, see Bernard S. Cohn, "Representing Authority in Victorian India," in Eric Hobsbawm and Terence Ranger, editors, *The Invention of Tradition* (Cambridge: Cambridge University Press, 1983), 185–207.

12. That this claim was far off the mark is made clear by both Andre Wink's *Land and Sovereignty in India* and Stewart Gordon's *Marathas*. C.A. Bayly's *Rulers, Townsmen and Bazaars: North Indian Society in the Age of Expansion, 1770–1870* (Cambridge: Cambridge University Press, 1983), argues that the "time of troubles"—the late eighteenth and early nineteenth centuries—was also a time of political stability, economic growth, relative prosperity, and cultural innovation.

13. *Two Historic Trials in Red Fort: An Authentic Account of the Trial . . . by a European Military Commission of Emperor Bahadur Shah* (New Delhi: Moti Ram, 1946), 388.

14. The academic debate over sovereignty was launched by F.W. Buckler in his 1922 essay, "The Political Theory of the Indian Mutiny." Buckler argued that "to account for the rise of the British in India . . . the theory here suggested is the continuity of the Mughal empire down to the deposition of Bahadur Shah II in 1858, as an effective source of political authority and as the suzerain *de jure* of the East India Company in the capacity of *diwan* of Bengal, arrogating the title of the British Government of India. In short, the source of the Company's authority in India lay, not in the Charters of the King of England nor in Acts of Parliament, nor in the sword, but in the *farmans* of the Mughal Emperor." The quotation is from Buckler's essay as it appears in M.N. Pearson, editor, *Legitimacy and Symbols: The South Asian Writings of F.W. Buckler*, Michigan Papers on South and Southeast Asia, Center for South and Southeast Asian Studies, Number 26 (Ann Arbor, MI: 1985), 45. Buckler's theory was disputed soon after it appeared in essays by S.M. Edwards and by Douglas Dewar and H.L. Garrett that are reprinted in M.N. Pearson's *Legitimacy and Symbols*. Edwards argues that "no writer who has lived in India . . . could solemnly suggest that up to 1857 the Indian territorial leaders and the general body of the people suffered themselves to be misled by the alleged duplicity of the Company . . . [to] actually believe that for some years prior to 1857 the Company still regarded itself in fact, and wished to be regarded, as the vassal of the Mughal Emperor" (75). The dispute raises many questions, not least the relationship between legal and ritual sovereignty and the legitimacy of sovereignty exercised on the basis of conquest and coercion. The 1857 revolt suggested that at least some leaders and some people did not regard Company rule, particularly its use of the doctrine of lapse to annex kingdoms, as legitimate.

15. See Terence Creagh Coen, *The Indian Political Service: A Study in Indirect Rule* (London: Chatto and Windus, 1971).

16. Sir William Lee-Warner suggests that muddling through was itself a strategy for strengthening British rule and weakening the subject princes: "There are no collections of political rules, and no authoritative treatises to guide the inquirer. These matters are, according to some opinions, best left alone as the mysteries of the trade. . . . [T]he absence of any definite interstatal law must be recognized as depriving the states united to the Indian Empire of the safeguard which all law or system provides." *The Native States of India*, revised edition (London: Macmillan, 1910), 2–3. Other accounts which cast light on the ambiguous legal and *de facto* meanings of paramountcy as it was understood in the early years of the twentieth century are "Reports of the Committee on the Relationship Between the Paramount Power and the States," (Butler Committee), *Parliamentary Papers* (Great

Britain, Reports of commissioners, 1928–1929), vol. VI, Cd. 3302; K.M. Panikkar, *Introduction to the Study of the Relations of Indian States with the Government of India* (London: Hopkinson, 1927); and Robin Jeffrey, editor, *People, Princes and Paramount Power: Society and Politics in the Indian Princely States* (Delhi: Oxford University Press, 1979). Our 1966 essay, "Rajputana Under British Paramountcy: The Failure of Indirect Rule," *Journal of Modern History* 38:2 (1966): 138–160, takes a more evolutionary view and expresses greater enthusiasm for state centralization than we do here. Two additional earlier essays of ours on princely state administration based on the Kanota Family Archive examine interactions among residents, British bureaucrats in princely state service, and Rajput princes and their Indian officers: "A Bureaucratic Lineage in Princely India: Elite Formation and Conflict in a Patrimonial System," *Journal of Asian Studies* 34:3 (1975): 717–753 and "Oligopolistic Competition among State Elites in Princely India" in George Marcus, editor, *Elites: Ethnographic Issues* (Albuquerque: New Mexico, 1983), 193–220. All three essays appear in our *Essays on Rajputana: Reflections on History, Culture and Administration* (New Delhi: Concept Publishing House, 1984). Barbara Ramusack's account, inter alia, of paramountcy is forthcoming in the new Cambridge History of India, *The Indian Princes and Their States*.

17. See, for example, Muzaffar Alam's volume, *The Crisis of Empire in Mughal North India* (Delhi: Oxford University Press, 1986), which argues that claims to regional autonomy advanced by many eighteenth-century kingdoms were an intensification of earlier Mughal practices.

18. Both Ian Copland and James Manor argue that British policy in the 1930s and 1940s was to interfere as little as possible in order not to drive the princes into the arms of the nationalist movement and that the absence of interference left the states unprepared for self-government at independence in 1947. Ian Copland, "The Other Guardians: Ideology and Performance in the Indian Political Service" and James Manor, "The Demise of the Princely Order: A Reassessment," in Jeffrey, editor, *People Princes and Paramount Power.* For a quasi-official account of policy and practice with respect to interference see Coen, *The Indian Political Service,* Part II, "The Indian States."

19. For an important recent account of pre-proclamation indirect rule that explores its theoretical implications and is based on an empirical investigation of the phenomenon in Awadh, see Michael Fisher, *Residents and the Residency System 1764–1857* (Delhi: Oxford University Press, 1991). For accounts of post-proclamation indirect rule, see Jeffrey, editor, *Princes,* Ian Copland, *The British Raj and the Indian Princes: Paramountcy in Western India, 1857–1930* (Bombay: Orient Longmans, 1982); and Coen, *The Indian Political Service.* A classic statement of the British conception of indirect rule by one of its inventors is Frederick D. Lugard, *The Dual Mandate in British Tropical Africa,* 3rd edition (Edinburgh: William Blackwood and Sons, 1926), 20.

20. As quoted from Lady Minto's *India and Morley 1905–1910* in Coen, *The Indian Political Service,* 94.Writing in the shadow of the 1857 rebellion and its cautionary lessons, Colonel W.F. Eden insisted that the intent was "not to revolutionize the old system of Government, bad as it undoubtedly was, but simply to improve it and remove the more manifest defects and imperfections." Eden in "Mewar" in *Report of the Political Administration of the Rajputana States, 1865–1866,* 160. Publication of these annual reports begins from 1865. Published at Bombay (1865–1967) and Calcutta (1868–1907), they represent the summing up of reports by political agents and residents of particular states to the AGG for Rajputana.

21. Eden, cited in "Mewar" in *Report of the Political Administration of the Rajputana States,* 161.

22. Copland, "The Other Guardians," 285.

23. Maharaja Ganga Singh of Bikaner succeeded to the throne in 1887 at the age of seven. Maharaja Man Singh of Jaipur succeeded in 1922 at the age of eleven. Government of India, *Rajputana and Ajmer: List of Ruling Princes, Chiefs and Leading Personages*, 6th edition (Calcutta: Government of India Central Publications Branch, 1931).

1: Court Society at Jodhpur

1. Sources for the administration and politics of Jodhpur include the annual *Report on the Administration of the Jodhpur State* published annually from various locations, Calcutta (1884–1885), Madras (1885–1886), Jodhpur (1886–1918); Archibald Adams, *The Western Rajputana States: a Medico-Topographical and General Account of Marwar, Sirohi, Jaisalmer* (London: Junior Army and Navy Stores, 1899); N.K. Acharya, "Administration of the Jodhpur State, 1800 to 1947" (Ph.D. dissertation University of Rajasthan, 1961); R.B. van Wart, *The Life of Lieut.-General H.H. Sir Pratap Singh* (London: Oxford University Press, 1926).

2. Tod's report, valid for the 1820s, shows the income from *khalsa*, lands subject to revenue collection by the Jodhpur maharajas, at one-fifth the income from the nobles' estates. Tod, *Annals and Antiquities of Rajasthan*, 131. In the 1940s, the khalsa lands constituted 13 percent of the Jodhpur territory. *Jodhpur Report, 1945–1946*, 19–20. This was despite Sir Pratap's energetic resolve to deprive nobles without direct issue of their lands under the *mori sala* legislation (see below).

3. No less than 1,400,000 cattle, according to the hides exported from Marwar, must have died. *Jodhpur Report, 1899–1900*, 6.

4. Among the more prominent eponymous clans descended from Rinmal's many sons (thought to be 26) are the descendents of Champa (Champawat clan); Karna (Karnot clan); Patta (Pattawat clan); Rupa (Rupawat clan).

5. For an account of the relationship, see Introduction, 3.

6. For a fuller account, see Introduction, 3.

7. Sir Robert Crosthwaite, speaking at the induction of Sardar Singh as maharaja. *Jodhpur Report, 1897–1898*, 3, as quoted in Acharya, "Administration of Jodhpur State," 106. The report for Marwar—another name for Jodhpur—in *Rajputana Report, 1881–1882* asserts: "He deserves the credit of having cleared off much debt" and "no one charges him with taking advantage of his position to amass money or spend it on private objects, and perhaps he is the only Marwar Minister of whom this can be said." The citation is from Percy W. Powlett, the resident.

8. To Sir Pratap's request that he be rescued from being made Maharaja of Idar, a little backwater of a state, "Lord Curzon, who was certainly not one of his greatest admirers, had said, 'To Idar I have sent him, and in Idar he will remain.'" Van Wart, *Sir Pratap Singh*, 171–172.

9. Percy Powlett who served first as agent and then as resident to the western Rajputana states (Marwar/Jodhpur, Sirohi and Jaisalmer) in 1880, 1884, 1886, 1889, 1892, took the lead in starting the nobles school that Amar Singh attends from 1888 to 1896. He is listed in the annual *Jodhpur Report*, which begins in 1884. His career is reported in van Wart, *Sir Pratap Singh*, and briefly in Adams, *The Western Rajputana States*.

10. Sukhdeo Prasad's office, known as the "Musahib Ala's [first minister's] English Office," handles the correspondence with and, where relevant, the accounts of, the British resident for the western Rajputana states, the British manager of the Jodhpur-Bikaner Railroad, the residency surgeon, again British, and other departments of Jodhpur state whose business is conducted in English, e.g. public works and forests. In the 1880s, Sukhdeo oversaw the revenue settlement of all khalsa villages. *Jodhpur Report, 1896–1897*,

130; *1898–1899*, 9. Competent bureaucrats like Sukhdeo not only "reformed" princely state administration but also helped the raj to extend its influence and control over the princely states by enhancing the "subordinate cooperation" and strengthening the suzerainty of Britain's paramountcy relations.

11. A frank account of Sardar Singh's life is given in Dhananajaya Singh's *The House of Marwar* (New Delhi: Roli Books/Lotus Collection, 1994), the writing of which was entrusted to the author by Maharaja Gaj Singh II. We are told that Sir Pratap "failed" his nephew because he was "too much of a disciplinarian and too harsh on his gentle and weak ward" (131). We learn of the adolescent Sardar Singh's "wild parties" at the Sardar Club; of his and his maharani's "life of ease and pleasure" after being invested with full powers in 1898; and of "excesses which rendered him a near invalid in his twentieth year [1900] and indebted the exchequer by over two million rupees" (132). In 1901 the Political Department tries to change Sardar Singh's ways by sending him on "European holiday." "Unfortunately, he returned untamed" (133). In 1902 he is "compelled to leave Jodhpur again," this time for the Imperial Cadet Corps (ICC) at Dehra Dun where he joins Amar Singh as a member of its first batch. The ICC too "failed to discipline" him. He is deprived of his powers in 1903, "the sharpest ever personal humiliation borne by a Rathore ruler," and is exiled for two years to Panchmari, a hill station in the present-day state of Madhya Pradesh. Sardar Singh returns to Jodhpur in 1908, is vested again with full powers in 1908 and dies in 1911 at the age of 31 (133).

12. These events can be followed in *Jodhpur Report*, various years and in Dhananajaya Singh's chapter on "Of Boy-Kings and a Grand Old Man" in his *House of Marwar*.

13. Sardar Singh was born on February 11, 1880. He is twenty at the time this is written.

14. Sir Pratap's biographer writes of Maharaja Sardar Singh: "The pity was that he allowed himself to be surrounded by men of the wrong type, desirous of gain and self-advancement. . . . [B]efore long it was deemed advisable to remove him [the maharaja] from such influences for evil, and he was for some time with the Imperial Cadet Corps at Dehra Dun, and afterwards in Europe." Van Wart, *Sir Pratap Singh*. Van Wart has reversed the order of events.

15. Matter between asterisks has been transferred from the entry *Jodhpore, Friday, 3rd February, 1899.*

16. The reorganization of the police was carried out by an officer deputed from British India, M.R. Rokhawala (a Parsi), and Sukhdeo Prasad as judicial secretary. Sukhdeo here and elsewhere seems more than willing to collaborate with British efforts to reform Jodhpur's administration. In 1905, the Jodhpur Lancers, the unit Sir Pratap had raised for imperial service and that had distinguished itself in China during the Boxer Rebellion, was merged with the police, a move Sir Pratap cannot have appreciated. Acharya, "Administration of the Jodhpur State," 150 and 157–158.

17. Takhat Singh ruled from 1843–1872. He died in 1873. He had been the Maharaja of Ahmednagar (Idar), a small state in Gujarat ruled by Rathores, the same clan/lineage as Jodhpur's royal house. When Maharaja Man Singh of Jodhpur died issueless, Takhat Singh, who belonged to a senior branch of the Rathores, was adopted and recognized as heir to the Jodhpur throne. He was not popular with his nobles, in part because he brought his own people with him from Ahmednagar (Idar) and they were unfamiliar with Jodhpur customs and patronage patterns. Van Wart, *Sir Pratap Singh*, 131–132.

18. Sumer Singh, Sardar Singh's son, was born in 1898 and died in 1918. He succeeded in 1911, at the age of thirteen. His regency council was presided over by Sir Pratap. Sumer Singh was succeeded by his fifteen-year-old brother, Umaid Singh with Sir Pratap again acting as regent.

19. Sir Pratap had no sons by his wives. Amar Singh mentions Sir Pratap's natural son, Narpat Singh, "who looks a promising boy." He is educated in England. In the 1930s Narpat Singh becomes Maharaja Umaid Singh of Jodhpur's private secretary, a member of council, and comptroller of the household. *Jodhpur Report*, various years.

20. In the diary Amar Singh tends to use the term maharaja for a ruling prince and maharaj for a brother or son of the ruler. To avoid confusion for the reader, our editing has consistently followed this practice. Sir Pratap and Ram Nathji employ the same practice.

21. Candidates for high office in the princely states in the eighteenth and nineteenth centuries, and even earlier were often drawn from "bureacratic lineages," i.e. a pool of families that had established some presumptive right to serve the state. In Udaipur in the nineteenth century several local lineages of Oswal (indigenous trading and banking community) *mutsaddis* (service lineages among Oswals) competed for office. At Jaipur, a lineage of English-educated Bengalis displaced the Champawats, Amar Singh's Jodhpur lineage, who earlier had replaced two Rajput lineages, the thakurs of Samod and Chomu. See our "Oligopolistic Competition among State Elites in Princely India," in Marcus, editor, *Elites: Ethnographic Issues*, and "A Bureaucratic Lineage in Princely India."

22. After Maharaja Sumer Singh's death in 1918 Sukhdeo serves under Sir Pratap, who heads the regency council for Umaid Singh, Sumer Singh's brother and successor. Umaid Singh's is Sir Pratap's third regency. At Sir Pratap's death in 1922, Sir Sukhdeo Prasad becomes chief member of the maharaja's council. He is forced into retirement in 1924–1925 by the combined efforts of Narpat Singh, Sir Pratap's natural son and Umaid Singh's confidant, and of the newly emergent states' peoples freedom movement.

23. The Elgin school was opened by Sir Pratap in 1896 on (the occasion of Lord Elgin's visit to Jodhpur. It was Sir Pratap's second founding, the first being the Powlett Nobles School established ten years earlier, which Amar Singh attended. The Elgin Rajpoot School gave instruction in Marwari and English, and provided training in surveying, police administration, agriculture, and the civil, ceremonial, and revenue codes. It declined in the early part of the century, and was revived in 1911 when Sir Pratap returned from Idar again to become regent of Jodhpur.

24. The mori sala rule had some standing for at least ten years. Acharya reports it being applied in a succession case in 1891. See his "Administration of the Jodhpur State," 255.

25. There is no radical change. Captain William Loch, settlement officer since 1881 ("Marwar" in *Rajputana Report, 1881–1882*), and W. Home, Manager of the Jodhpur Railway since 1884, have been with the Jodhpur administration for many years. The notable addition for 1902–1903 is G.D. Goyder, who had previously served as auditor for the Jodhpur Railway, and is now employed to organize a state auditing report.

26. *Jodhpur Report, 1901–1902*, 1, 26.

27. "From His Excellency General Sir O'Moore Creagh, G.C.B., V.C., Commander in Chief in India," in Appendices to Government of India, *Report of the Committee on Proposals for Commissioning Indians*, July 24, 1911, 64, 68. For a full discussion of the various interpretations of the ICC, especially the view in the Indian Army that the "politicals," i.e. political service officers serving as residents and agents in the princely states, had used the corps to further their purposes at the expense of those of the Indian Army, see Chapter III, "The Rise and Fall of the Imperial Cadet Corps," of Chandra Sundaran's excellent dissertation, "A Grudging Concession: The Origins of the Indianization of the Indian Army's Officer Corps, 1817–1917" (Ph.D. dissertation, Department of History, McGill University, 1996).

28. Continued June 25, 29, and July 3.

29. See Sir Walter Lawrence, *The India We Served* (London: Cassel and Co., 1928). Sir Walter was Sir Pratap's most important and influential friend at the viceregal lodge in these years.

30. Government of India (Calcutta: Central Publications Branch, Calcutta 1931), 103.

31. Maharaj Kumar Sumer Singh does not succeed to the gaddi until 1911 when his father, Sardar Singh, dies at the age of 31. Van Wart, *Sir Pratap Singh*, 172, and Dhananajaya Singh, *House of Marwar*.

32. Stripping an officer of his uniform was an act of ceremonial profanation that had achieved a certain notoriety seven years earlier when Captain Alfred Dreyfus was stripped of his. For a recent study of this much analyzed case, see Emile Zola, *The Dreyfus Affair: 'J'Accuse' and Other Writings*, edited by Alain Pages and translated by Eleanor Livieux (New Haven: Yale University Press, 1996). This decision is probably Viceroy Lord Curzon's. He prided himself on his unbending standards—which he asserted, at some political cost, against the decisions of military courts that let off British soldiers who had murdered or raped Indians, and against indolent maharajas. "In the banqueting hall of Gwalior," Nayana Goradia writes, "with its mirrors shimmering across the walls and ceiling, an aghast company of princes was made to listen to a viceregal homily they had rarely heard before. . . ." "'He [the Indian prince] cannot remain . . .'" he told them, "'a frivolous and irresponsible despot . . . his 'gaddi' is not intended to be a divan of indulgence, but the stern seat of duty. His figure should not merely be known on the polo ground, or on the race-course, or in the European hotel.'" Nayana Goradia, *Lord Curzon: The Last of the British Moghuls* (Delhi: Oxford University Press, 1993), 154–155. Curzon's speech at Gwalior on November 29, 1899, is quoted by Goradia from Curzon's *Indian Speeches*, vol. 1 (Calcutta: 1900–1906), 168.

2: Court Society at Kishengarh and Idar

1. The 1903 Delhi durbar, sometimes referred to as the "Curzonation" because Lord Curzon used it to showcase himself, marked the succession of Edward VII as King Emperor of India. Amar Singh participates as a cadet of the ICC.

2. Lytton to Queen Victoria, April 21, 1876, I.O.L.R., E218/518/1, as quoted in Bernard S. Cohn, "Representing Authority in India," 187–188.

3. Stanley Tambiah uses the concept of "replication" to theorize the "galactic polity," "a design that coded in a composite way cosmological, topographical, and politico-economic features." Tambiah draws on Max Weber as well as Hindu-Buddhist thought in theorizing "replication of the center on a progressively reduced scale by the satellites that were the major characteristic of the polity's territorial arrangements." Central to Weber's patrimonial authority ideal type is the concept of *typification*, which contrasts with the rationalization found in the bureaucratic functional specialization of rational-legal authority. Stanley J. Tambiah, *Culture, Thought and Social Action in Anthropological Perspective* (Cambridge, MA: Harvard University Press, 1985), 276.

4. The princely states were hierarchically ordered by gun salutes according to loyalty and service to the raj, size, ancient pedigree, and other criteria. At Independence in 1947 there were 118-gun-salute states: five 21-gun-salute states (Baroda, Gwalior, Hyderabad, Kashmir, and Mysore); six 19-gun-salute states (Bhopal, Indore, Kalat, Kolhapur, Travancore, and the Rajputana state of Udaipur); thirteen 17-gun-salute states, eight from Rajputana, Bharatpur, Bikaner, Bundi, Jaipur, Jodhpur, Karauli, Kotah, and Tonk; seventeen 15-gun-salute states, including six Rajputana states, Alwar, Banswara, Dungarpur, Jaisalmer, Kishengarh, Partabgarh, and Sirohi; sixteen 13-gun-salute states, including one Rajputana

state, Jhalawar; thirty-one 11 gun-salute states; and thirty 9-gun-salute states. Coen, *The Indian Political Service*, 262–265.

5. The new German Empire of 1871 had twenty-five component units of which four were "kingdoms," five grand duchies, thirteen duchies and principalities, and three free cities, plus Alsace-Lorraine, a "Reichsland," "common property" to all the states. William Langer, editor, *An Encyclopaedia of World History* (Boston: Houghton-Mifflin, 1872), 736.

6. Government of India, Secretary of State. *The Imperial Gazetteer of India*, new edition, vols XIII and XIV (Oxford: Clarendon, 1908).

7. Van Wart, *Sir Pratap Singh*, 138–139. Below, Amar Singh estimates the debt at Rs 1.5 million.

8. Lawrence, *The India We Served*, 207.

9. The quotation is attributed to Lord Curzon by van Wart, *Sir Pratap Singh*, 170.

10. Amar Singh's library of 2,400 books and periodicals at Kanota Fort is one of the better gentlemen's libraries in Rajasthan.

11. Lawrence, *The India We Served*, 206.

12. Amar Singh frequently wears this medal on his *sapha* (turban), even as Sir Pratap wears such a cameo of Queen Victoria on his. The medal is now worn on the sapha of Kanota grooms; it appeared most recently at the engagement of Prithvi Singh Kanota on January 24, 1996.

13. There seem to have been a lot of *roothi* ranis about. A palace above Jaisamand, a very large lake in southern Udaipur, bears that name, as does one of the towers of the Kumbhalgarh fort, also in Udaipur. See also, Munshi Devi Prasad, *Roothi Rani* (Calcutta: Bharatmitra, 1906) (Hindi).

14. Bukhtawar Singh and Kishore Singh are younger brothers of Sheonath Singh of Bera, Sir Pratap's son-in-law, and officers of the Jodhpur Lancers, whom Sir Pratap has brought with him from Jodhpur.

15. According to the 1908 *Imperial Gazetteer*, vol. XIII, the ordinary gross revenue of Idar was six lakhs, and the state treasury's share 4.5 lakhs. Published by Government of India at Calcutta.

16. According to Mohan Singh it is unlikely that she had leprosy. She may have had skin discoloration, which was sometimes mistaken for leprosy.

17. According to Sir Pratap's biographer, Sir Pratap did not contract an additional marriage after arriving at Idar. Van Wart, *Sir Pratap Singh*, 182.

18. For extended discussions of the practice of hypergamy in Rajasthan, see Varsha Joshi, *Polygamy* and Frances Taft, "Honor and Alliance; Reconsidering Mughal-Rajput Marriages," in Schomer et al., editors, *The Idea of Rajasthan*, 217–241.

19. According to the *List of Ruling Princes, Chiefs and Leading Personages, Rajputana and Ajmer*, 6th edn. (Calcutta: GOI Publications Branch, 1931). Maharao Raja Raghubir Singh of Bundi (born 1869; succeeded 1889; died 1927) had ten wives, including the first and second daughters of Maharaja Takhat Singh of Jodhpur, Sir Pratap's father (59).

20. Continued on July 25, 26, 31, 1905.

21. See van Wart, *Sir Pratap Singh*, 148. Sir Pratap built a palace there and subsequently renamed the city Himmatnagar (171).

22. Ahmed Shah made numerous military sorties into Mewar and Marwar (Jodhpur), invading Idar and Kelwara in 1427 and Nagaur and Mewat as well as Ahad, Eklingji, and Delwara in 1432. R.V. Somani, *History of Mewar* (Jaipur: Champalal Ranka, 1976), 118–119.

23. Van Wart reports that Ahmed Shah surrounded the city with a stone wall, which took seven years to build but that the wall was in ruins by the time of Sir Pratap. *Sir Pratap Singh*, 148.

24. Sir Pratap's severity during the minority of his nephew, Maharaja Sardar Singh of Jodhpur, is said by some to have led him to rebel by living a dissolute life. His severe standards in rearing his charges are much reported. See for example van Wart, *Sir Pratap Singh*, 181–182, and Singh, *The House of Marwar*, 131–132.

25. This must be a retrospective account pertaining to 1900 or 1901, because Babu Kanti Chander died in 1901.

26. Matter between asterisks is from later on in the same entry.

27. The charges are puzzling. Maharaja Madho Singh himself went to England in 1902, after the attack on Khetri, admittedly with great precautions against pollution. As far as concubines are concerned, practice and opinions varied. Madho Singh kept a great many but may not have kept any Muslim concubines. That Maharaja Jaswant Singh of Jodhpur, Sir Pratap's brother, kept a Muslim concubine, Nunni, was widely reported.

28. Alexander Kinloch Forbes (1821–1864), *Ras Mala, Hindoo Annals of the Province of Goozerat in Western India*, edited by H.G. Rawlinson (London: Oxford University Press).

3: H. H. Kishengarh Marries at Udaipur

1. The other three are the marriage of his cousin Pratap Singh Naila, of his sister to the Thakur of Garhi and of his sister-in-law from Satheen. The five accounts provide an interesting insight into Rajput marriage practices.

2. Hypergamy in the diary means getting daughters married into wealthier, higher status Rajput houses. In the seventeenth century, marriages of Rajput princesses to Mughal nobles or princes counted as hypergamy. See Taft, "Honor and Alliance," 217–241.

3. Akbar pursued political marriages with women of lesser sovereigns to extend and strengthen his empire, but his successors were more reluctant. Both the Mughals and Mewar rulers resorted to marriages with collaterals, e.g. eligible courtiers and noblemen, even though doing so involved the risk of the "son-in-law" problem, i.e. ambitious sons-in-law who, aspiring to rule, plot against the throne. Another consequence was not marrying daughters. Yet another was female infanticide.

4. See Taft's "Honor and Alliance," where Table I shows seventeen Mughal-Rajput marriages during Akbar's reign (1556–1605); five during Jahangir's reign (1605–1627); one during Shahjahan's reign (1627–1658); three during Aurangzeb's reign (1627–1658) and one after Aurangzeb, 218–220. Taft confirms the fact that Manbhavati, the daughter of the Jodhpur ruler Mota Raja Udai Singh, was Shahjahan's mother but raises doubts about whether Jahangir's mother was the daughter of Raja Bharmal of Amber (Jaipur). See her endnote 19, 217–218.

5. See Taft, "Honor and Alliance," 231–232 and endnote 21, 238. James Tod in *Annals and Antiquities of Rajasthan* denounces "those Rajputs who bartered their daughters, and thus their honour, for Mughal wealth and power."

6. Examples of historians ignoring or suppressing evidence of hypergamous marriages by Rajput kingdoms with Mughal ruling families are analyzed or mentioned by Taft in "Honor and Alliance."

7. Eighteen years after Rana Pratap's death, Amar Singh, Rana Pratap's successor as Maharana of Udaipur, negotiated a settlement with the Mughals in 1614. Unlike other Rajput rulers—Jodhpur, Jaipur, Bikaner—he was exempted from personal service at the Mughal court or with the Mughal armies. Although enrolled among the servants to the court he was allowed to send his son to stand in for him. G.N. Sharma, *Mewar and the Mughal Emperors, 1526–1707* (Agra: Shiva Lal Agarwala, 1962), 120. Conventional nationalist historiography of Rajasthan interprets these arrangements and the understanding that Udaipur would not marry a daughter to the Mughals (as does Sharma's account, which otherwise

does not adopt nationalist patterns) as exemptions from onerous and degrading duties rather than as opportunities spurned, e.g. the opportunity to conclude advantageous hypergamous marriages and to acquire status, wealth, and power through service as commanders of the imperial armies and as governors of Mughal provinces. The "nationalist" reading of Udaipur's special relationship to the Mughals was initiated by Tod in his *Annals and Antiquities of Rajasthan*. Post-Independence historiography has begun to include more differentiated readings; some recognize that Jaipur particularly, and Jodhpur and Bikaner as well, benefited from the Mughal relationship without losing their honor and identity and that Mewar engaged in exchange marriages with Rajput kingdoms, which married daughters to Mughal ruling families.

8. See our introduction, "Representing Rana Pratap," of Kesri Singh's *The Hero of Haldighati* (Jodhpur: Book Treasure, 1996), 1–7.

9. For a history of Mewar and the Mughals that is immune to the excessive politicization of Mewar history in the nationalist era, see Sharma, *Mewar*.

10. For the rise of "medievalism" in Britain in the second half of the nineteenth century see Florence Boos, editor, *History and Communalism: Essays in Victorian Medievalism* (New York: Garland, 1992).

11. Udaipur's ruling lineage is the oldest of the Rajput ruling houses. The Guhilots, from whom the Mewar house claims descent, appear on inscriptions in the Mewar region in the sixth century. Somani, *History of Mewar*. It is not evident how much importance this claim had prior to Tod's celebration of it. Most important to the Shishodia ruling lineage was the claim that Shishodias descended from Lav, one of Lord Rama's two sons. The dignity of ancient lineage was also a significant claim for legitimacy for Mughal rulers whose culture impacted on Rajputana; Babur, the first Mughal emperor claimed descent from Timur [Tamerlane] and through him to Ghengis Khan. See Stephen Frederic Dale, "Steppe Humanism: The Autobiographical Writings of Zahir Al-Din Muhammad Babur, 1483–1530," in Mariola Offredi, editor, *Literature, Language and the Media in India* (New Delhi: Manohar, 1992), 3–33.

12. For an account of Fateh Singh and his reign, see Devilal Paliwal, *Mewar and the British: 1857 to 1921* (Jaipur: Bafna Prakashan, 1971).

13. Paliwal, *Mewar and the British*, 191, 193, 201.

14. Repetition of the Roman numeral is Amar Singh's mistake.

15. For example, money scattered at marriages and on other festive occasions or money presented to a musician or entertainer by a circular gesture of the arm and hand over the head of the recipient followed by dropping the money from the hand to the ground.

16. Matter between asterisks from the entry *Delhi, Friday, 6th November, 1903*, "Notes About My Cousin's Marriage."

17. He touched the money with his fingers, as a courteous form of recognition, without taking it.

18. The ritual precautions taken by the maharaja to avoid the pollution conveyed by *jootha*—food touched by saliva—exceed the precautions practiced by very orthodox north Indian Hindus.

19. The Udaipur wall is now mostly dismantled, unlike the Jaipur walls, which survived the destructive urge for urban efficiency. In the 1990s, however, Jaipur's walls were disappearing behind billboards, shops, and cinemas.

20. Sardar Singh married the sister of Maharao Raja Raghubir Singh of Bundi.

21. This entry is an out-of-sequence insert from *Dehra Doon, Tuesday, 26th April, 1904*, "Notes About My Last Vacation," which serves to round out the story given above. The normal sequence resumes at XXXII.

4: Imperial Ritual at Alwar

1. Jai Singh, born June 14, 1882, at ten succeeded as minor to the throne of Alwar on May 23rd, 1892. He was declared maharaja on June 14, 1902, and invested with full powers at Alwar by Lord Curzon, the viceroy, on December 1903.

2. The Political Department already has some concerns about Jai Singh's character. "Since his return to Alwar from Mayo College in 1897, Jai Singh had been deprived of effective power within the state and all authority had been retained by the bureaucracy, the Council and the Political Agent. . . . As the end of Jai Singh's minority approached . . . it was feared his ambitions might later disturb" these carefully constructed arrangements. As a result "the Government of India decided to place restrictions on the powers that would be transferred . . ." on December 10, 1903. Edward S. Haynes, "Alwar, Bureaucracy versus Traditional Rulership: Raja, *Jagirdars* and New Administrators, 1892–1910," 45, in Jeffrey, *Princes*, 32–64. No administrative institutions or appointments could be altered without the approval of the political agent, whose sanction was also required for the annual budgets that governed his personal expenditure. For five years a willful and ambitious maharaja, who believed that he had an obligation to rule on behalf of his subjects, struggled against a paramount power that had taken *de facto* control of the administration of Alwar state. On January 1, 1909, when Jai Singh was twenty-six, all restrictions on his powers were removed.

3. For Alwar's size compared to Jaipur, see Jadunath Sarkar, *A History of Jaipur, 1503 to 1938*, revised and edited by Raghubir Singh (Hyderabad: Orient Longmans, 1984) 260; for its population, see *Jaipur, 30th June, 1919*. A "Table of Salutes to Ruling Princes" can be found in Coen, *The Indian Political Service*, 264–265.

4. Curzon-Wyllie was killed in London on July 1, 1909, by a bomb intended for John Morley; the attempt was made by the "terrorist" Madan Lal Dhingra. This use of terrorism for nationalist purposes, which occurred just prior to a visit to London from South Africa by Mohandas K. Gandhi, helped to determine the argument in his most notable early writing, *Hind Swaraj, or Indian Home Rule*. This tract argued against violent nationalism, for nonviolent means and offered a critique of and alternative to "modern civilization." See Anthony Parel, editor, *M.K. Gandhi Hind Swaraj and Other Writings* (Cambridge: Cambridge University Press, 1997). "Hundreds of Bengali terrorists were behind bars at the time, and . . . the most notorious of Maharashtra's young revolutionaries . . . Ganesh Damodar [Veer] Savarkar had just been transported for 'life' to the Andaman Islands for waging war against the King.'" Stanley Wolpert, *A New History of India* (New York: Oxford University Press, 1977), 283.

5. See Herbert Sherring, *The Mayo College, "The Eton of India": A Record of Twenty Years, 1875–1895*, two volumes (Calcutta: Thacker, Spink and Co., 1897). The British viewed the education of princes, via special schools, Imperial Cadet Corps, or tutors as a key element in legitimating Britain's "imperial monarchy" over loyal vassals. See also Ian Barrow, "Toward New Histories of the Princely States," South Asia History Seminar, University of Chicago, March 1993.

6. Anne Norton's ongoing work on Jai Singh judges British efforts to educate model princes in the historical context of their cultural concerns about "manliness" and in the philosophic context of classical and Renaissance and early modern texts on educating princes.

7. The Imperial Conference is composed of representatives of the dominion and colonial governments. The Chamber of Princes was intended as a permanent consultative body representative of the princes.

8. For Jai Singh's honors, see Government of India, *Rajputana and Ajmer: List of Ruling Princes*, 10, and for his role in the Chamber of Princes see, M.S. Jain, *Concise History of Modern Rajasthan* (New Delhi: Wishwas Prakashan, 1993), 162.

9. Urdu, which had previously been taught in primary schools, was replaced by Hindi; Hindi was also made the official language and Hindi examinations were required for all state officials. Alwar Administrative Report, 1907–1908, 2, in *Rajasthan District Gazetteers, VI. Alwar* (Jaipur: 1968), 580, as cited in Haynes, "Alwar," Endnote 53, 63. Haynes's discussion of Jai Singh's language policy concludes by observing that it "discriminated against a sizeable sector of the population, the Muslims, who had begun to define their religious and cultural identity in terms of the Urdu language" (55–56). For a pathbreaking account of the formation of Meo identity, and of how Jai Singh's agrarian policies helped to trigger the Meo revolt, see Shail Mayaram, *Resisting Regimes: Myth, Memory and the Shaping of a Muslim Identity* (Delhi: Oxford University Press, 1997). Mayaram critiques the colonial ethnography of the Meos or Mevs as a "criminal tribe." They are better understood, she argues, as cultivators with a syncretic or hybrid culture that combines Muslim and Hindu beliefs and practices.

10. Meo resistance in 1932–1933 to enhanced revenue extractions followed repeated monsoon failures and a steep downward trend in prices following the world depression, a trend that was more pronounced in Alwar than in neighboring districts. Jai Singh ignored warnings by local British administrators to deal with the peasant question, and burned the report of an Agrarian Grievances Commission that he had constituted. British military intervention in January 1933, in response to Jai Singh's request led to violence. Alwar state acknowledged that 80 had died; a Foreign and Political Department report says 282 were killed. Jai Singh's throne is saved by the paramount power whose troops contain the Meos. But his conflicting relations with the British and his subjects, combined with dark aspects of his private life that remain obscure, lead to his being deposed and exiled.M.S. Jain argues that the Meo rebellion was "a communal movement [that] was given an agrarian garb" and that the reduced revenue demand that followed the restoration of order "was a political reward given to the Meos for rendering service in enabling the British to exile Jai Singh, the ruler of Alwar." *Concise History*, 148.

11. We are indebted to Anne Norton's research in London for this finding.

12. Jai Singh married three times. On December 8, 1897, at the age of fifteen, he married the daughter of Maharaja Sardul Singh of Kishengarh. She died on May 20, 1921. On April 17, 1914, he married the daughter of the Jareja family of Khersara in Kathiawar, a niece of the Jam of Jamnagar. She died on March 23, 1919. Jai Singh married a third time on December 7, 1919, the daughter of the Jareja family of Rajpura in Kathiawar, presumably again a relative of the Jam of Jamnagar. The record of marriages is taken from *Rajputana and Ajmer: List of Ruling Princes*, 10–11.

13. According to a "Confidential demi-official dated Bharatpur, the 15th March 1919," from C.C. Watson, Esq., C.I.E., political agent in the Eastern States of Rajputana, to Major G.D. Ogilivie, Deputy Secretary to the Government of India in the Foreign and Political Department, Delhi: "The circumstances . . . of the death of the Junior Maharani of His Highness of Alwar . . . were tragic, as the Maharani who is said to have been ailing for some time shot herself in the head with a revolver on the night of the 23rd instant. The unfortunate lady was a niece of the Jam of Jamnagar who, together with her brother, was staying at Alwar at the time. Her mother was also there on a visit and was sleeping in the next room where the tragedy occurred." *Foreign and Political, 1919* (National Archives of India), 5. We are grateful to Anne Norton for this reference. Subsequent questions were raised about why the cremation occurred so abruptly; whether medical or autopsy reports were available; whether it was true that she was shot in the middle of the forehead.

14. See the *Hindustan Times*, May 20, 1933, where it is reported that H.H. Alwar was "externed," given notice to quit Alwar within forty-eight hours and not to return for a period of two years, an exile that stretched to four by the time of his death in 1937.

15. Continued on December 18, 20, 22, 24.

16. These officials constitute the establishment through which the viceroy in relationships of shared sovereignty known as "paramountcy" or "subordinate cooperation" "indirectly" rules the princely states.

17. Narain Singh serves as a member of council for military affairs from 1906. Discontented over his perquisites, he resigns in 1913. In 1916, after being offered a substantially higher salary and other benefits, he returns formally as member for military affairs and informally as an adviser to Jai Singh. Narain Singh, who leaves Alwar service in 1921 to return to Jaipur, does not advise on the policy and acts that lead to Meo discontent and eventual rebellion and to Jai Singh's exile. The Jaipur maharaja, Madho Singh, sick, without a legitimate son and concerned about the succession, is in need of an adviser who can maneuver on his behalf in the murky and turbulent waters of Jaipur and raj politics. Overcoming his suspicion of Narain Singh, Madho Singh recalls him to Jaipur, to organize support for his controversial succession plan among other princes, Jaipur court nobles, and raj officials. The succession that Madho Singh has in mind violates the terms of his own adoption and succession at the death of Maharaja Ram Singh in 1880, when he pledged not to adopt again from his own branch of the Kachhawa royal lineage, Isarda. The succession by-passed the claims of the Jhalai lineage, the branch closest to the royal line. Jhalai claims were again bypassed in 1921–1922 when Madho Singh adopted Mor Mokut Singh, second son of the then Thakur of Isarda, and arranged for his succession as Man Singh II. The Political Department favored the adoption and succession of the ten-year-old Mor Mukut because it promised a long minority during which the young prince could be educated and the state administered under raj auspices. Narain Singh's skillful maneuvering on behalf of Madho Singh's adoption of Mor Mukut is laid out in detail in the diary for 1921. Quentin Crewe, who gives a vivid account of Man Singh's contested adoption and the succession that followed in *The Last Maharaja: A Biography of Sawai Man Singh II, Maharaja of Jaipur* (London: Michael Joseph, 1985), draws extensively on Amar Singh's diary volumes. Madho Singh dies in 1922. In 1922, the British-dominated minority administration appoints Narain Singh inspector general of police, the post he held before being exiled by Madho Singh to Alwar. Narain Singh dies in 1924.

18. *Jaipore, 30th June, 1919*, "Notes About My Last Leave of 10 Days."

5: Paramountcy and Corruption

1. During Maharaja Madho Singh's minority, which began in 1880 after the death of Maharaja Ram Singh in that year, Bannerman served as "joint president" of the council of state, a weak cabinet, and was in frequent correspondence with Narain Singh, at the time Jaipur state's nazim (governor) in the northern province of Shekhawati.For Bannerman's role in the case against Thakur Fateh Singh of Naila, see Munshi Triloki Chand, private secretary to Thakur Fateh Singh of Naila, *Thakur Fateh Sigh's Case* (Ajmer: 1901), 1. In 1899, Bannerman served as assistant to the AGG, and later as officiating political agent at Kotah and Jhalawar.

2. We include here entries of August 1901, to throw light on the allegation of a bribe being paid to Captain Bannerman.

3. Son of Roop Singh, Thakur of Naila, Amar Singh's uncle.

4. For the cultural history and politics of the *Ramayana* in north India, particularly for how and why recitation performances of Tulsi's version affected evolving "Hindu" consciousness in nineteenth and twentieth centuries, see Philip Lutgendorf, *The Life of a Text: Performing the Ramcaritmanas* (Berkeley: University of California Press, 1991).

5. According to the diary, the governor general's annual salary in 1899 was Rs 22,000 and that of a Resident First Class, chief British officer in a princely state, Rs 4,000.

6. This entry has been inserted out of sequence to elaborate further the possibilities of illegal gratification in the political service.

7. While we have no independent evidence to support Amar Singh's charge, £218,000 in 1903 was an enormous amount of money. An estate of that size on a political officer's salary would require explaining by some other source of income such as great family wealth. The amount is ten times the annual salary of the then viceroy. Beynon was resident at the time of Maharaja Ram Singh's death and Madho Singh's adoption and succession, historical moments, which offered especially lucrative possibilities for persons in a position to influence or legitimize decisions and outcomes with respect to adoption, the conduct of the transition, and appointments.

8. For the historic Morley-Minto reforms of 1909 granting a measure of responsible government to India, see Mehra, *Dictionary of Modern Indian History 1707–1947*, 451–453.

9. See Babu Kanti Chander Mukerjee's letter to W.H. Curzon-Wyllie, October 18, 1900. Wyllie's subsequent reply confirms this version. Wyllie to Mukerjee, October 21, 1900. Copies in Kanota Family Archive.

10. "Memo Concerning the Jagir Case of the Thikanas of Goneer, Kanauta and Naila," *circa* 1903, Kanota Family Archive.

11. What Curzon-Wyllie may have in mind is the story of Ajja, the founding ancestor of the Raj Ranas of Bari Sadri, who rank first among the *solah* (sixteen), a term used to designate the first rank among Mewar's nobility. The Sadri lineage are Jhala Rajputs in a kingdom whose rulers are Shishodias. In 1527, at the battle of Khanua against Babur, a descendant of Timur who is regarded as the founder of the Mughal empire in India, the Mewar ruler, Rana Sangram Singh I, was wounded and taken insensible to his camp. Ajja assumed the insignia of royalty at the request of all Mewar nobles present and died fighting gallantly. The Sadri thikana was conferred on his successors with the title Raj Rana. The Sadri narrative, which includes subsequent deaths in battle by Ajja's descendants, tends to overshadow grants of thikanas for other forms of service such as those performed by the Kanota, Gondher, and Naila families. Curzon-Wyllie seems to imply that "death in battle" is the only form of service worthy of a secure land grant.

12. In Udaipur some of the most prestigious and honored jagirdars are ganayats, not Shishodias, the ruling clan. Among these is the Raj Rana of Bari Sadri, a Jhala Rajput (see previous note). Also prominent in court society and state administration have been the Rao of Bedla and the Rawat of Kotharia, both Chauhans. Other Jhala, Punwar, and Chauhan families are among the solah, the "sixteen" highest ranking noblemen of the Udaipur court. See listing of leading Udaipur nobles in *Rajputana and Ajmer: List of Ruling Princes*, 178–183. The term ganayat also deals with marriage relations. Under the Rajput rules of exogamy, a Rajput male must marry into a ganayat clan and may not marry into his own clan.

13. The viceroy's office asked Sir Griffith Evans—a barrister of Lincoln's Inn and additional member for law and regulations of the viceroy's council—to review the case. Sir Griffith's decision of February 12, 1901, found the ruling of the Jaipur court against the family unlikely (see Part II): Copy of "Opinion of Sir Griffith Evans, February 12, 1901," in Kanota Family Archive, cited in Rudolph's, "A Bureaucratic Lineage in Princely India," in Rudolph's, *Essays on Rajputana*, 116. The decision is a good example of raj micromanagement, and of the way in which local families sought to manipulate the raj process in their favor.

GLOSSARY I:
Names of Persons and Places

Ordering our subjects by name defies the usual principles of sequence or hierarchy. Our format reflects English usage for ordering English names and Indian usage for Indian names. English persons are alphabetized according to their surnames. Indians are alphabetized in three styles: (1) in the case of jagirdars (estate holders) or maharajas, they are sorted by the name of the estate or state; (2) where no estate is part of the name, we sort by "given" name; (3) where the name encompasses caste, community or other suffixes or prefixes, we use those.

To illustrate (1), Amar Singh, Thakur of Kanota, is found under "K" for Kanota, his estate. To illustrate (2), his younger brother Barisal Singh, who does not become master of the estate and has no estate suffix, is found under "B" for Barisal Singh, the given name. No one is found under "Singh," a suffix for all Rajput names, and not adequate for distinguishing persons in this diary. To illustrate (3), Bhandari Hanut Chand is found under "Bhandari," a community name that would today, under the influence of anglicization, be placed at the end, Hanut Chand Bhandari. Barath Ram Nathji Ratnu is found under "Ratnu," the suffix that distinguishes him.

While the diary has many variations on names (e.g. Balji Durji, Balji Khawas, Khawasji, Bala Bux) we have referred all variation to one standard version (in the given instance, Bux). Other variations are cross-referenced.

The diary speaks (or writes) in two voices for words and names, current English usage and Amar Singh's antique English usage. Thus Amar Singh writes Jodhpore, we write Jodhpur, Amar Singh writes Ram Nathjee, we write Ram Nathji. In this part of the glossary, we adopt current English usage. The information in this glossary is taken from the annual administrative reports of the Jodhpur, Jaipur and Udaipur states, from the Kanota Family Archive, from *Rajputana and Ajmer: List of Ruling Princes, Chiefs and Leading Personages* (Calcutta: Government of India, 1931) and from the oral recollections of members of the Kanota, Naila and Gondher families.

Abhai Singh, Thakur of Peelva See Peelva.
Achrol, Thakur Kesri Singh of Husband of Amar Singh's cousin, the daughter of Bhim Singh who was brother of Narain Singh of Kanota. Kesri Singh's daughter married Maharana Bhupal Singh of Udaipur, who succeeded to the Udaipur throne in 1930. Achrol is head of the Balbhadrots, one of the twelve kotris (leading lineages), of the Kachhawas, the ruling lineage of Jaipur state.
Adams, Archibald, Lt.-Colonel, I.M.S., M.D. Administrative medical officer in Rajputana. Dr Adams, of the Indian Medical Service, resided many years at Jodhpur, and wrote *The Western Rajputana States: A Medico-Topographical and General Account of Marwar, Sirohi, Jaisalmer* (London: Army and Navy Stores, 1899). He was residency surgeon at Jodhpur, from 1881 to his death twenty years later. He officiated as resident at Jodhpur, in 1895. Sir Pratap Singh is shown in the diary as much affected by his death of cholera at Abu in 1900.
Aga Kasim Shah Nephew of the Aga Khan. Joining the Imperial Cadet Corps in 1902, he is one of the four who finished the first course successfully. He is commissioned with Amar Singh in 1905, and is also one of the first nine Indians to receive a king's commission in 1917.

Agunta, Jaswant Singh of Having become a dacoit early in his career, after the confiscation of his estate, Agunta was reclaimed and became deputy superintendent of police, Jaipur. He was a friend and colleague of Narain Singh, the diarist's father.

Ahmednagar Rathore princely state in western India, from which Maharaja Takhat Singh was adopted to Jodhpur in 1843. Ahmednagar subsequently became part of Idar state, another Rathore lineage state ruled by Maharaja Sir Pratap Singh after 1902.

Ajmer City located in the midst of the area known as Rajputana. Ajmer was under direct British control even while the surrounding princely states were under indirect rule. In this respect, the British followed the practice of the Mughals, who had used Ajmer as an imperial control point. The city is one of the oldest in Rajasthan, with many buildings from both imperial eras. It was a cosmopolitan center; under the British, it was the focus for political groups and educational institutions, offering a less restrictive civil rights atmosphere than the surrounding princely states. Dissidents from the states often found exile and asylum at Ajmer, and a resting place for their printing presses.

Akhai Singh, Maharaj (Maharaj, without a terminal a, is often used by the diarist for royal sons who do not inherit the throne. We have standardized that usage.) Fourth son of Maharaj Zorawar Singh, who was second son of Maharaja Takhat Singh of Jodhpur, and who revolted against his father in 1872. Akhai Singh was a friend and age-mate of Amar Singh; the two are together in China as native lieutenants and staff to Sir Pratap Singh, and as cadets at the ICC. Born in 1879, and educated, like Amar Singh, at the Powlett Nobles School, Akhai Singh lived at the family estate at Raoti, in Jodhpur. After serving in France with the Jodhpur Lancers in World War I, he became ADC to the Maharaja of Jodhpur, his nephew.

Alexander, Lieutenant Officer with the Jodhpur Lancers, 1900–1901, in China during the Boxer Rebellion. He belonged to the 6th Bombay Cavalry.

Alwar, Maharaja Jai Singh of K.C.S.I., K.C.I.E., G.C.I.E., G.C.S.I. Born June 14, 1882, he succeeded to the Alwar throne in 1892 and received his full powers in 1903. He was a Naruka Rajput of the Kachhawa clan. The diarist's father, Narain Singh, was guardian to the Maharaja from 1898 to 1903, and served at his court until 1913, and again in 1916–1921. Jai Singh had a reputation for great brilliance and eccentricity. As a young man he was an outstanding polo player. In later years, he became very orthodox and supported Hindu causes generously. He was expelled from his state by the British in the 1930s, in consequence of a series of charges, including provoking the Meo rebellion by his anti-Urdu and anti-Muslim religious policies and his anti-agriculturalist policy—a policy in which the British were also implicated.

Amanat Ullah, Sahibzada Class fellow of Amar Singh at the ICC, son of the prime minister of Tonk. According to the diary, he was expelled from the Cadet Corps for not meeting his debts.

Amar Singh, Rao Raja Natural son of Maharaj Kishore Singh, a younger son of Maharaja Takhat Singh of Jodhpur. He lived at Alwar, where he served the state. One of the best polo players of his time, he was military secretary at Alwar, an influential officer, and married the natural daughter of the Maharaja of Karauli.

Amar Singh of Kanota See Kanota.

Ambala Cantonment in Punjab.

Apollo Bunder A well-known wharf at Bombay.

Aravalli Mountain range in Rajasthan running from the southeast to the northwest of the area.

Bakat Sagaur Lake near Jodhpur where Amar Singh often hunted.

Bukhtawar Singh   A native officer, subedar (a native rank "equivalent" to a captain) of the Jodhpur Lancers. He goes to China with the Lancers, where he serves with Amar Singh as staff to Sir Pratap Singh. Having been adjutant of the first regiment of the Lancers, he hoped to be made commandant when Hurjee declined to serve, but was superseded by Jasji. He is second brother of Thakur Sheonath Singh of Bera, who was married to the daughter of Sir Pratap Singh, regent of Jodhpur. He was appointed military secretary and commander in chief at Idar state when Sir Pratap Singh became its maharaja in 1902.

Balji Durji   See Bux, Bala.

Balji Khawas   See Bux, Bala.

Bannerman, Captain A.D.'A.G.   Assistant to the Agent to the Governor General (AGG) in Rajputana, October 1899, then officiating political agent in Kotah and Jhalawar. His home regiment was the 31st Lancers. He served at Jodhpur, as guardian to the minor Maharaja Sardar Singh, and as assistant inspecting officer for the Imperial Service Troops. According to the diarist, he was paid illegal gratifications and forced to retire from the political service. His explanation is that he was too favorable to Maharaja Sardar Singh of Jodhpur, who was out of favor with the Government of India.

Barath Ram Nathji   See Ratnu.

Bario   See Burio.

Barisal Singh (Kanota)   Born November 30, 1890; died July 4, 1964. Fourth son of Narain Singh, Thakur of Kanota, by his second wife, he was brother to the diarist. He served in the princely state services of Kashmir, Idar, and Udaipur. He married a wife from Moahar of the Kachhawa clan.

Basant Kanwar   Daughter of Mehtab Singh, the estate steward and cousin of Thakur Fateh Singh of Naila. She married the Thakur of Danta, a major thikana of Jaipur state.

Beatson, Major General Sir Stuart   Inspector, Imperial Service Troops, Jodhpur, 1980; inspector general, Imperial Service Troops, 1900. As a captain and major, Sir Stuart supervised the training at Jodhpur of the Jodhpur Lancers (Sardar Rissala) which were first raised in 1889. He also worked with Sir Pratap Singh to found polo at Jodhpur, and played in the victorious Jodhpur team that took the Indian championship in 1893.

Bera, Thakur Sheonath Singh of   Son-in-law of Sir Pratap Singh, whose only daughter he married. Shishodia Rajput of the Ranawat clan. His estate consisted of twelve villages and yielded an annual income of Rs 20,000.

Beynon, W.H   Political agent, Jaipur, 1877–1881. Said to have acquired a questionable fortune.

Bhandari Hanut Chand   Born 1838. Member of council at Jodhpur, and superintendent of the appellate court, he served as Marwar residency vakil (lawyer, agent) and vakil to the Agent to the Governor General.

Bhaboot Singh   Squadron commander with the Jodhpur Lancers in China.

Bhatis   Rajput lineage; lineage of the ruling family of Jaisalmer state. The diarist is interested in the fact that the Rawalot Bhatis have severe standards of hypergamy, marrying their daughters to ruling princes only, while the Urjanot Bhatis, the division to which Amar's wife belonged, are less demanding.

Bharon Singh, Rao Raja   (Also known as Bharji). Champawat Rathore Rajput, holding Loroli in Jodhpur in jagir (small thikana of 3,000); he was the first rissaldar major (native officer rank) when the Sardar Rissala was organized at Jodhpur, He commanded the first squadron of the 1st Jodhpur regiment in 1900.

Bhim Singh (Kanota)   Born January 18, 1853; died October 19, 1917. Uncle of Amar Singh, second son of Zorawar Singh of Kanota, he served in the bodyguard of Maharaja Ram Singh at Jaipur, and after Ram Singh's death in 1880, as deputy inspector general of police, Jaipur. His first wife was from Bharathla, of the Rajawat branch of the Kachhawas. The second, from Dhanata, was of the Shekhawat lineage.

Bhojpura, Kanwar Zorawar Singh of   Fellow cadet and friend of the diarist at the Imperial Cadet Corps, and one of the four (including Amar Singh) who completed the first course and received a king's commission in the Native Indian Land Forces in 1905. He was one of the first nine to receive a regular king's commission in the Indian Army in 1917 in response to pressure to Indianize the Army. He had, says the diarist, an FA degree from the University of Bombay and usually stood first in the corps. (FA stands for Faculty of Arts, i.e. two years of college.) His home was Bhavnagar, Khatiawad.

Bhoj Raj Singh, Kunwar (heir apparent) of Gondher   See Gondher.

Bhur Singh   Born November 28, 1886; died November 24, 1950. Second son of Jawahar, who was second son of Thakur Abhai Singh of Peelva (the ancestral estate of the Kanota family). He served in the Jaipur cavalry and was in charge of Nahargarh fort overlooking Jaipur. Married wife from Mohaswas of the Nathawat branch of the Kachhawas.

Bhupal Singh, Maharana of Udaipur   See Udaipur.

Bhutera, Zadav Kanwar from   First wife of Narain Singh of Kanota, Amar Singh's father. Her family were of the Nathawat branch of the Kachhawas. She bore him two sons and one daughter, all of whom died young. Narain Singh married at Kochore after her death.

Bikaner   Rathore Rajput princely state in northwest Rajasthan; the area was gradually conquered after 1465 by Bikaji, son of Jodha, the founder of Jodhpur. Its revenue in 1926 was Rs 9,158,115, larger than that of Udaipur or Jaipur, though its population was smaller, 659,685, than that of these other states.

Bikaner, Maharaja Ganga Singh of   Born in 1880, succeeded in 1887, died in 1943. The maharaja became a leading figure in imperial politics and a favorite of the British government in India and London. He led his state forces to the Boxer Rebellion in China in 1900 and to France and Egypt in 1914; represented the Indian princes at the Imperial War Conference in 1917, and the peace conference at Versailles in 1918; served as the first chancellor of the Chamber of Princes; led the Indian delegation to the 11th assembly of the League of Nations, and was a representative of the princely states at the Round Table Conference. Beginning in 1925, he built the Gang canal, then regarded as the most significant economic development in the twentieth century prior to Partition. It was the first concrete lined irrigation canal, and extends 84 miles.

Budh Singh   Servant of Amar Singh. A Rajput from the Kanota family's ancestral estate at Peelva. When the famine brought scarcity to Peelva thikana at the turn of the century, the estate was unable to feed its retainers, and sent Budh Singh to Amar Singh. He became important in Kanota thikana administration.

Bulloji   Champawat Rathore, historical/mythical hero.

Bundi   State ruled by Hara Chauhan Rajputs in eastern Rajasthan, and its capital.

Burio   Servant of Amar Singh. Accompanied him to China in 1900–1901.

Bux, Bala   Also Balji Khawas, Balji Durji, or Khawasji. Personal companion, servant and favorite of Maharaja Madho Singh of Jaipur. The Khawasji, who regulated access to Madho Singh, was envied and disliked by both civil servants and thakurs for his great influence, which was said to be a source of income. The diary refers to him as Balji Durji, that is, Balji the tailor, a reference to his alleged origins. "On the demise of H.H. [Madho Singh] in September, 1922, the State Treasury was inspected by the Resident at Jaipur and Members of the Mahkma Khas. . . . As a result of the inquiries, Rai Bahadur Khawas Bala Bux who had been appointed Muntazim of the Kapadwara [Keeper of the Wardrobe] in 1894 and enjoyed the confidence of the late Maharaja, and Kesar Lal Mushraf and Birdhi Chand Tahvildar were sent up for trial before a Special Tribunal

... on various charges of embezzlement [and] ... were convicted and sentenced ... "
(*Jaipur Administration Report, 1922–1926*, p. 95).

Cameron, Captain D.H   Captain Cameron was the adjutant at the ICC and Amar Singh's teacher. He came to know the diarist's father, Narain Singh, when he was guardian to the Nawab of Jaora while Narain Singh was (native) guardian to the Maharaja of Alwar. Cameron and the diarist gradually became close friends at the ICC. His home regiment was 1st Lancers, Central Indian Horse. In 1904, he married Miss Pilkington.

Champawat   Descendants of Champa, brother to Jodha, founder of Jodhpur city. Subclan of the Rathores to which Amar Singh belongs.

Chander Kunwari   Amar Singh's sister. In 1902 she married Thakur Karan Singh of Garhi in Alwar.

Chapman, Sergeant A   Instructor at the ICC. His home regiment was the 15th Hussars.

Chauhan   Rajput lineage name.

Chhiman Singh (Gondher)   Second son of Thakur Shambhu Singh of Gondher, he was brother of Thakur Mukend Singh and uncle of the diarist. He served in the Jaipur state cavalry. His son Kalyan Singh succeeded to the estate of Santha (formerly Gondher) when Mukend Singh's only son, Bhoj Raj Singh, failed to produce issue.

Chittar Palace   Chitur Dungri (Chitur hill) is now the site of Umaid Bhavan, an enormous palace built by Maharaja Umaid Singh in the mid-twenties. It is sometimes referred to as Chittar Palace.

Chitorgarh   Located in contemporary Udaipur, Chitor fort is one of the most renowned hill forts in India. It was in existence in A.D. 728 when Bappa Rawal, the first of the Shishodia rulers of Udaipur, seized it from the Mori Rajputs. It sustained three famous sieges, the first from Ala-ud-din Khilji, the Pathan king of Delhi, in 1303; the second from Bahadur Shah, then Sultan of Gujarat, in 1535; and the third in 1567 from Akbar. In each siege the Rajputs were defeated, and their women performed jauhar, ritual selfimmolation. The fort was restored to the maharanas of Udaipur in 1616.

The Hill fortress is 500 feet high and three and a half miles long. Until 1568 it contained the city of Chitor. The defeats are memorialized in bardic songs known throughout Rajasthan, and by the nineteenth-century historical ethnographer, Colonel James Tod, in his *Annals and Antiquities of Rajasthan*, 1829 and 1832.

Chomu, Thakur Devi Singh of   Belonging to the Nathawat branch of Kachhawa Rajputs, he was a leading nobleman of Jaipur state. Chomu supported the claims of the family of Jhalai rather than Isarda in the succession to the Jaipur throne in 1921; he was removed from the maharaja's council and punished when Isarda succeeded.

Cobb, H.V.   Resident at Jaipur, 1900–1902. The Kanota family believed that Cobb, who succeeded G.R. Irwin, was less friendly to the family than the latter had been. Knowing that the family had won a case against Maharaja Madho Singh of Jaipur who had sought to seize their estate villages on a charge of fraudulent acquisition, he yet advised Roop Singh of Naila, cousin to the Kanota family, to accept an exchange of villages in order to save the maharaja's face by compromise. The exchange resulted in an especially heavy loss to Gondher, one of the three related lineages at Jaipur.

Commeline, Captain F.H.B.   His home regiment was the 2nd Bengal Lancers. In 1898 and 1889, he assisted Major Henry H.F. Turner, then training the Sardar Rissala at Jodhpur. In 1901, he was inspecting officer of Imperial Service Troops in Rajputana, and traveled with the Jodhpur Lancers from Calcutta on their return from China.

Cooch Behar, Maharaj Kunwar Raj Rajendra Narain of   Educated at Mayo and Eton, Lieutenant in the yeomanry. Cadet at the ICC in Amar Singh's time. He is referred to as Rajji in the diary.

Craster, Major   Probably S.L. Craster, R.E., India Public Works Department, executive engineer. He was deputed to the military works department and saw field service in China in 1901.

Creagh, General Sir Garret O'Moore   Born 1848, died 1943. In 1901, he became commander, British Expeditionary Field Force in China; in 1904, commander, 5th division Western Army Corps of the Indian Army. In 1909, he succeeded Lord Kitchener as commander in chief in India. Amar Singh served on his staff with the 5th division at Mhow, in central India.

Dalip Singh (Naila)   Born October 17, 1888; died December 6, 1944. Second son of Roop Singh, Thakur of Naila. Married a wife from Singhason of the Shekhawat lineage.

Dalpat Singh   Son of Hurjee, outstanding polo player and favorite of Sir Pratap. Sir Pratap sponsored Dalpat Singh's education in England. He died in the battle of Haifa in World War I, and is said to be one of the three figures depicted in the "Teen Murti" World War I memorial statue in Delhi, near the Nehru Memorial Library.

Danta   Large estate in Jaipur state. The daughter of Mehtab Singh, cousin and estate agent of Roop Singh of Naila, married the Thakur of Danta.

Daulat Singh, Maharaj   Son of Maharaj Bhopal Singh, sixth son of Maharaja Takhat Singh of Jodhpur. Friend of Amar Singh, he joined in his wedding and was part of the group of young men educated with Amar Singh by Sir Pratap. After attending Mayo College, he served in Patiala state and was then adopted by Maharaj Madho Singh, brother of Bhopal Singh. In 1902 he was adopted by Sir Pratap Singh when the latter became Maharaja of Idar. When Sir Pratap abdicated in 1911 to return to his home state of Jodhpur, Daulat Singh succeeded as maharaja.

Deep Singh, Wordi Major   He served as commandant of the Bikaner Camel Corps, then as first native adjutant of the ICC. He was made an honorary lieutenant in the Indian Army in 1902.

Dehra Dun. Town in Uttar Pradesh, in the Himalayan foothills. Location of the summer camp of the ICC.

Deoli, Thakur Hari Singh of (Hurjee). Favorite, life-long friend, and inseparable companion of Maharaj Sir Pratap Singh of Jodhpur. Hari Singh was celebrated as a famous polo player, member of the Jodhpur team that won the Indian championship at Poona in 1893. Amar Singh describes him as a *Daroga*, a category of personal servants attached to Rajput households, and says he came to Jodhpur as part of the dowry of Sir Pratap's wife. By virtue of his friendship with Sir Pratap, he occupied high status at Jodhpur. The viceroy, the Marquis of Lansdowne, was quartered at his bungalow in 1890. His memorial stone stands beside Sir Pratap's chattri (cenotaph) near the old parade ground at Jodhpur.

   As commandant of the first regiment of the Sardar Rissala (Jodhpur Lancers), Hurjee served in China, Tirah and the Black Mountain campaign. Amar Singh says he learned horsemanship from him.

Devi Singh, Thakur of Chomu   See Chomu.

Dhokal Singh, Rissaldar   Officer in the Jodhpur Lancers and accomplished polo player. Adopted by the Thakur of Garaon. Appointed as guardian to Maharaja Man Singh of Jaipur, whom he taught polo. The diary says he was raised by Sir Pratap Singh. He claimed to be sick when he was due to go to China as Sir Pratap's staff officer. After that event, according to the diary, he appeared to be in favor with Maharaja Sardar Singh and out of favor with Sir Pratap.

Diggi   Important thikana in Jaipur state, *head* of the Khangarote branch of the Kachhawa clan.

Duleep Singh   See Dalip Singh.

Dulpat Singh   See Dalpat Singh.

Dundhlod   Thikana in Shekhawati area of Jaipur state. A disputed adoption led to difficulty between Dundhlod and Surajgarh, another Shekhawat thikana, and between these and Jaipur state.

Elgin Nobles School   This school was opened by Sir Pratap in 1896, on the occasion of Lord Elgin's visit to Jodhpur. It was the second school besides the Powlett Nobles School, founded ten years earlier, which Amar Singh attended. It gave instruction in Marwari and English, and provided training in surveying, police practices, agriculture, civil, ceremonial and revenue codes. It declined in the early part of the century, and was revived by Sir Pratap in 1911.

Erskine, Major K D., IA   Resident at Jodhpur, 1901–1902; 1909–1911.

Evans, Sir Griffith   Barrister, Lincoln's Inn; additional member for law and regulations of the viceroy's council. He gave the final ruling against Maharaja Madho Singh of Jaipur in the case by which that ruler sought to seize Kanota and the related estates.

Fateh Karanji   An influential charan at Udaipur, friend of the diarist's father. He was originally kamdar (estate agent) at Pokran, a large estate in Jodhpur. Narain Singh, Amar Singh's father, secured him the position at Udaipur under Maharana Sajjan Singh.

Fateh Singh, Maharana of Udaipur   See Udaipur.

Fateh Singh, Thakur of Naila   See Naila.

Galta   Gorge in the hills to the east of Jaipur crowded with temples and pilgrim accommodations.

Gambhir Singh (Kanota)   Born October 3, 1863; died October 3, 1900. He was the third son of Thakur Zorawar Singh of Kanota and brother of the diarist's father. He served in the cavalry of Jaipur state and married Pratap Kanwar from Dego in Jaipur of the Chauhan lineage.

Ganga Singh, Maharaja of Bikaner   See Bikaner.

Garhi   Major thikana in Alwar. Its thakur, Mangal Singh, became friends with the diarist's father, Narain Singh of Kanota.

Garhi, Thakur Bhawani Singh of   Husband of Amar Singh's youngest daughter, who was born in 1918 (?) and died in 1967 or 68. He was inspector general of police, Alwar, and later rose to superintendent of police in the central reserve police. He arrested the Kashmiri leader Sheikh Abdullah (in Gul Marg) in 1953, and died in 1962 while serving in Poonch. He was the son of Karan Singh of Garhi's brother, and adopted as thakur when Karan Singh's marriage failed of male issue.

Garhi, Thakur Karan Singh of   Born November 1881, a Dasawat Naruka Rajput of the Kachhawa clan. The thakur held eight villages with an income of about Rs 16,000 in Alwar. Brother-in-law of Amar Singh, whose sister Chander Kunwari he married in 1902.

Garhi, Thakur Mangal Singh of   Father of Kunwar Karan Singh, who married Amar Singh's sister. Member, Alwar Council. He died while Amar Singh was in China.

Gaselee, Lt. General Sir Alfred, K.C.B., A.D.C.   Born 1844, died 1918. As commander, British contingent, China Expeditionary Field Force in 1900, he led the British column which was the first to enter Peking for the relief of the foreign legations. He was promoted to major general in 1901, and to general in 1906, commanding the northern army in India in 1907–1908. His early career took him to campaigns in Waziristan and Tirah.

Gaussen, Lt. G.R.   He was posted from his home unit, the Third Bengal Cavalry, to the Jodhpur Lancers in China in 1900–1901.

Ghanerao   First class thikana of Jodhpur state belonging to the Mertia branch of the Rathore lineage.

Ghatotguch   Amar Singh's favorite horse, given him by Sir Pratap in 1899. The horse is named after the son of Bhim, one of the five Pandava brothers, heroes of the epic *Mahabharata*.

Girdhari Singh, Daffadar   Jodha Rathore Rajput, younger son of Loadsar thikana. Daffadar ("sergeant") in Jodha squadron of the Jodhpur Lancers, he accompanied the Lancers to China in 1900. After the death of Hurjee, Sir Pratap's favorite, and Sir Pratap's becoming Maharaja of Idar, Girdhari Singh became Sir Pratap's favorite at Idar.

Gondher   See also Santha. Thikana in Jaipur state, founded by Sambhu Singh, great uncle of the diarist, and eldest of the three brothers from Peelva in Jodhpur who came to seek service at Jaipur. Gondher village, from which Thakurs Sambhu Singh and Mukend Singh took their title, was lost to the thikana in the wake of a case of fraudulent acquisition Jaipur state brought against the three related thikanas Gondher, Naila and Kanota. Although Jaipur state lost the case, the state insisted on exchanging Santha for Gondher and thereafter the Thakurs of Gondher became Thakurs of Santha.

Gondher, Thakur Bhoj Raj Singh of   Born in 1873, died February 23, 1928. Eldest son of Mukend Singh of Gondher. Cousin and close friend of the diarist, he was appointed commander of the camel cavalry of Jaipur state. He became Thakur of Santha (formerly Gondher) in 1919, joined the Jaipur state judicial service, became head of the atish (personal stables of the maharaja) in 1922, and was appointed as guardian to young Maharaja Man Singh of Jaipur in 1922. When he died issueless in 1928, he was succeeded as thakur by his cousin, Kalyan Singh. His first wife came from Balarwa and the Bhati lineage, and his second wife was from Bassi in Udaipur state, of the Chandawat branch of the Shishodias.

Gondher, Thakur Mukend Singh of   Born 1850, died October 28, 1918. Later Thakur of Santha. Uncle of the diarist, son of Thakur Shambhu Singh, eldest of the three brothers who came from Peelva, in Jodhpur to seek service at Jaipur. Father of Bhoj Raj Singh, the diarist's favorite cousin. Married wife from Mehlan of Kachhawa lineage.

Gondher, Thakur Shambhu Singh of   Born April 8, 1822; died February 22, 1885. Granduncle of the diarist. Second son of Thakur Jivraj Singh of Peelva. Eldest of the three younger brothers from Peelva thikana in Jodhpur to come to seek service in Jaipur. Arriving in Jaipur in 1854, he was appointed head of the Jagir Bakshi Khana in 1869, the office which grants estates, and member for the revenue department of the maharaja's council in 1876. He received the villages comprising Gondher thikana in 1863, 1868 and 1873. The Maharaja of Jaipur conferred the honor of tazim on him in 1873. In the wake of a dispute and court case involving Gondher, Naila and Kanota, the main thikana village of Gondher was resumed by the Jaipur state in return for new lands, including the village of Santha after which the estate was renamed. He married Ratan Kanwar from Bhudana of the Bhati lineage.

Gordhan Singh (Kanota)   Cousin of Amar Singh, second son of Bhim Singh, brother of the diarist's father. He was posted as companion to the Maharaja of Indore in 1904.

Gould, Captain Jay, I.M.S.   Gould accompanied the Jodhpur Lancers to China in 1901. He served in the Indian Medical Service.

Govind Ram-Odey Ram   Firm of photographers in Jaipur with which Amar Singh did business. In the 1980s, the name of the firm still appeared on a signboard on Mirza Ismail Road in Jaipur.

Govind Singh (Kanota) Born April 17, 1894; died June 6, 1952. Son of Narain Singh, Thakur of Kanota, by his second wife. Brother of the diarist. He married a wife from Pathroj of the Kachhawa clan.

Guman Singh (Naila) Born November 28, 1859; died 1916. Second son of Thakur Fateh Singh of Naila; brother of Thakur Roop Singh. He went over to "the enemy when our case was going on," living with Maharaja Madho Singh while the case against the family was being prosecuted. He sought reconciliation when the time came to marry off his children and he required family assistance. His wife was from Mahandwas of the Kachhawa lineage.

Haldion ka Rasta Haldion's street. The three Champawat families' original Jaipur houses are located near Haldion ka Rasta.

Hans Raj, Lala Born in 1864, died in 1938, he was headmaster of the Dayanand Anglo-Vedic High School and later principal of the D.A.V. College. He lead the "college" (more modern) section of the Arya Samaj, a Hindu reform society.

Hanut Chand Bhandari See Bhandari.

Hari Singh Ladkani of Khatu See Khatu.

Hari Singh, Thakur of Deoli See Deoli.

Hari Singh, Thakur of Mahajan See Mahajan.

Hem Singh (Kanota) Born in 1876; died in 1945. Cousin of Amar Singh, son of Bhim Singh, who was second son of Zorawar Singh, Amar Singh's grandfather. He served in judicial service in Indore and Jodhpur. He married a wife from Savandhu of the Bhati lineage about the same time that Amar Singh married.

Hendley, Dr Thomas Holbein, I.M.S. Born in 1847, he joined the Indian Medical Service in 1869 and worked in Calcutta, Allahabad and Chunar before coming to Jaipur in 1874. He served as residency surgeon at Jaipur in 1895–1896. Hendley was present at the death of Maharaja Ram Singh, and certified that the maharaja had expressed a wish to adopt Qaim Singh (Madho Singh) from Isarda rather than a possible candidate from Jhalai. Jhalai partisans charged that Hendley's decision was purchased.

Herbert, Colonel C. Resident at Jaipur in 1905–1906, 1907, 1909; acting agent to the governor general in Rajputana in 1906.

Home, W. Manager of the Jodhpur railway from at least 1884 until his retirement in 1906.

Hughes, Captain E.M. Hughes is reported at Jodhpur, as early as 1898–1899. He served as an officer of the Jodhpur Lancers in China in 1901–1902. His home regiment was the 14th Bengal Lancers, although a diary entry in April 1905 places him with Hodson's Horse. He served as inspecting officer, Imperial Service Troops in Rajputana, 1904–1905.

Hurjee See Deoli, Thakur Hari Singh of.

Idar Small state in western India, closely allied to Jodhpur state. Ahmednagar, another Rathore state from which Maharaja Takhat Singh of Jodhpur had been adopted, was merged with Idar. Its royal lineage was eligible for adoption to the Jodhpur throne and vice versa because they were Rathores, as was the Jodhpur ruling lineage. Sir Pratap Singh left Jodhpur for a time, 1902–1911, to become Maharaja of Idar. The diary says the state's normal income prior to the famine of 1899 was four lakhs (Rs 400,000) but had subsequently dropped to two lakhs. Sir Pratap was succeeded, when he abdicated in 1911 to return to Jodhpur, by his adopted heir Maharaja Daulat Singh.

Idar, Maharaja Sir Pratap Singh of See Pratap Singh.

Idar, Maharaj Kanwar Daulat Singh of See Daulat Singh.

Imperial Cadet Corps Established by Lord Curzon in 1901, to train members of "the aristocracy of birth" for service as officers. The camp, situated at Dehra Dun or Meerut, depending on the season, remained a small affair, never accommodating more than twenty-five cadets. The graduates received modified king's commissions in the Native Indian Land Forces. Several served in princely state forces, some, like Amar Singh, in staff positions in the Indian Army.

Impey, Captain Political agent at Alwar in 1900. Perhaps the same as Major L. Impey, Indian Army, who had served with the Foreign Department as political agent at Bhopal.

Indaji Woman of the Inda tribe, Amar Kanwar, was the first wife of Madan Singh, grandfather of Zorawar Singh, the diarists grandfather. She had no son, all the sons of Madan Singh being from his second wife, and hence adopted Zorawar Singh.

Indas A community ruling Marwar (Jodhpur) before it was conquered by the Rathore Rajputs. The Indas married their daughters to the Rathores; they are said to have married a daughter to the Rathore chief Chunda, and given him Mandore in dowry. Indas held no large jagirs in the nineteenth century.

Irwin, G.R., I.C.S. Resident, Jaipur, 1897–1900. A friend of the Kanota family, especially of the diarist's father, Narain Singh, he pleaded their case with the Maharaja of Jaipur and advanced it with the Political Department.

Isri Singh (Kanota) Seventh son of Narain Singh, Thakur of Kanota, by his second wife. He was not healthy and died at four years of age.

Jacob, Colonel Sir Swinton Sir Swinton advanced both architecture and planning in Rajasthan, designing numerous public buildings in "Indo-Saracenic" style, and drafting the first plan for development of water resources in Rajasthan. He took charge as a young executive engineer of the public works department in 1867 under Maharaja Ram Singh who gave him considerable encouragement in the designing of the Prince Albert Museum. He is last reported in the same position in 1903–1904, having spent thirty-six years in Jaipur. He built many public works, including sixteen dams or lakes, of which Ramgarh with its 90-foot dam is the most extensive and famous.

Jaisalmer Name of a city, capital of the desert state of the same name, ruled by a Bhati lineage.

Jai Singh, Maharaja of Alwar See Alwar.

Jaipur Princely state in former Rajputana, ruled by the Kachhawa lineage. It is conventional in Rajasthan to tell the history of the state as a continuity from the founding at Amber by Dhola Rai in 967 common era, which displaced Mina and Badgujar tribal chieftains. The diarist's estate was in Jaipur where he served with the state forces until his retirement in 1936. Jaipur's annual revenue in 1921 was Rs 8,326,000.

Jaipur city Founded by Maharaja Jai Singh II (1660–1743) who laid out the city in place of Amber, his old capital. The founding ceremony took place in 1727. The city was noted for its regular planning, its graceful architecture and its pink color. By the end of the 20th century, it had fallen victim to uncontrolled commercialization. The design was probably developed by Vidyadhar, a Bengali engineer charged with approving the building plans for private houses. For a thorough account, see A.K. Roy, *History of the Jaipur City* (New Delhi: Manohar Publishers, 1978).

Jaipur, Maharaja Madho Singh of Born on August 29, 1861, as Qaim Singh, younger son of the Thakur of Isarda. As one of the estates closest by lineage to the Maharajas of Jaipur Isarda has provided sons for adoption to the Jaipur gaddi (cushion, throne). Madho Singh succeeded to the Jaipur gaddi on September 29, 1880, received his full powers in September 1882 and died in 1922. In the diary and in the Kanota family tradition, the maharaja is pictured as inimical to the Kanota family and the related houses of Gondher (Santha) and Naila.

Madho Singh was unathletic by comparison with the active sportsmen at Jodhpur, and more particular in his observance of orthodox Hindu practices than many Rajput princes. He took extraordinary precautions to preserve the purity of his victuals on his trip to England for the coronation durbar in 1901 by providing himself with Ganges water transported in three enormous urns which may still be seen at the Jaipur city palace. He is said to have built the section of the palace complex known as Mobharak Mahal to preserve the purity of the rest of the palace by receiving Europeans there.

Jaipur, Maharaja Man Singh of   Born, 1911; died, 1970. Like Madho Singh he was adopted in 1921 from the thikana of Isarda and succeeded to the Jaipur gaddi in 1923 at the death of Madho Singh. He was a famous polo player, a relatively progressive maharaja, an active member of international society circles and friend and patron of the diarist. See Quentin Crewe, *The Last Maharaja: A Biography of Sawai Man Singh II Maharaja of Jaipur* (London: Michael Joseph, 1985).

Jaipur, Maharaja Ram Singh of   Born in 1834, he died in 1880. As patron of the three Champawat families of which Kanota is one, he raised them to high ministerial position in the state and granted them tazimi honors and gave them revenue-bearing villages. He took a lively interest in new cultural and technical developments, such as the "Parsee theatre" which he built near the city, or photography, which he pursued avidly, and introduced a council of state in 1867.

Jaora, Nawab Iftikhar Ali Khan   Fellow cadet of Amar Singh at the Imperial Cadet Corps, he and the diarist were rivals for the leadership of the small society of cadets. Ruled by Muslim Nawabs, Jaora lay in Malwa, now part of Madhya Pradesh.

Jasji   A Narawath Rathore Rajput, he was thakur of a small village, Babasar, to which he was adopted. Amar Singh says he is about thirty-six in 1899, when he is commander of Jodha squadron of the Sardar Rissala at Jodhpur. When Hurjee declines to lead the first regiment to China, Jasji is promoted to subedar major ("equivalent" to a major), and commandant of the Lancers in China under Sir Pratap and Major Turner. He speaks no English, which Amar Singh regards as a disadvantage for his career.

Jaswant Singh of Agunta   See Agunta.

Jaswant Singh, Maharaja of Jodhpur   See Jodhpur.

Jawahar Singh (Peelva)   Born August 23, 1863; died July 31, 1932. Younger brother of Thakur Sultan Singh of Peelva, the ancestral estate of the three Champawat families of which Kanota is one. He married a wife from Siddhu of the Bhati clan, sister of the wives of his two brothers.

Jennings, Colonel R.H., C.S.I.   Resident at Jodhpur, 1903–1905.

Jivaraj Singh   Brother-in-law of Hurjee, married to Hurjee's sister.

Jivraj Singh, Thakur of Peelva   See Peelva.

Jodhpore   See Jodhpur.

Jodhpur   The largest former princely state in Rajputana by area, it lies in the west of present Rajasthan. The population in 1931 was 2,115,982. The western part consists of sandy desert land, with scarce and capricious rainfall. It was ruled by the Rathores who, having come from Kanauj, first settled near Pali in the twelfth century, and took Mandore from the Indas in about 1394. In 1459, Rao Jodhaji founded the city of Jodhpur.

Jodhpur Lancers   See glossary of unfamiliar terms.

Jodhpur, Maharaja Jaswant Singh of   He ruled from 1873 to 1895. Sir Pratap, Amar Singh's patron, was a younger brother to Jaswant Singh and his prime minister from 1878.

Jodhpur, Maharaja Man Singh of   Ruled Jodhpur from 1803–1843, during the time of the establishment of British paramountcy. He had sharp confrontations with his thakurs, whom he ousted from their estates.

Jodhpur, Maharaja Sardar Singh of   Born February 11, 1880, died March 20, 1911. Seventeen months younger than Amar Singh, Sardar Singh was raised together with the diarist in the house of Sir Pratap Singh, the maharaja's uncle. At fifteen, Sardar Singh succeeded his father, Maharaja Jaswant Singh, who died October 11, 1895. A regency council, headed by Sir Pratap, ruled during Sardar Singh's minority, from 1895 to 1897. At eighteen, in February 1898, Sardar Singh was given full powers, but they were withdrawn in 1903, on allegations of extravagance and mismanagement. His powers were restored, with restrictions, in 1905, but withdrawn again in 1908. Although sickly the maharaja was a good polo player. His public reputation conforms to the weak character imputed to him by the diary. See also Dhananajaya Singh, *The House of Marwar* (New Delhi: Roh Books/Lotus Collection, 1994).

Jodhpur, Maharaja Sumer Singh of   Born in 1898; died 1918. Sumer Singh succeeded his father, Sardar Singh, in 1911 at the age of thirteen. His regency council was presided over by Sir Pratap Singh until Sir Pratap went to World War I, when the council was headed by Colonel J.C. Windham, Resident.

Jodhpur, Maharaja Takhat Singh of   Ruled Jodhpur from 1843 to 1872. Died in 1873. Takhat Singh was adopted from Ahmednagar when Maharaja Man Singh died issueless. His reign was difficult and chaotic; he was heedless of the rights of his nobles, and his import of Gujarati civil servants from Ahmednagar was much resented.

Jodhpur, Maharaja Umaid Singh of   Born in 1902, Umaid Singh succeeded his brother, Sumer Singh, in 1918, at the age of sixteen. Over the heir's objections, his regency council was headed by Sir Pratap Singh until 1922, when Sir Pratap died. Umaid Singh assumed his full powers in 1923, the first Maharaja of Jodhpur, who himself conducted a stable and effective regime since the death of Maharaja Jaswant Singh.

Johar Singh   See Jawahar Singh.

Jumna   Yamuna. One of India's principle rivers, it flows south from the Himalayas to Delhi, then east, joining the Ganges at Allahabad.

Kachhawa   Named lineage of the ruling houses of Jaipur and Alwar.

Kaim Khani Squadron   See glossary of unfamiliar terms.

Kaim Khanis   A Rajput lineage, which was converted to Islam. The late prime minister of Pakistan, Zulfikar Ali Bhutto, was a Kaim Khani.

Kaisar Singh (Kanota)   See Kesri Singh.

Kaloo   Amar Singh's head servant, he accompanied Amar Singh to China, advising him in complex social situations. By mischance, he was left behind at Amar Singh's departure for Europe in World War I. A Daroga from Neemrana, he becomes kamdar of Kanota fort. In 2000, a descendant was in service at Narain Niwas.

Kama, Thakur Pratap Singh of   The Kama family is closely related to the Jaipur princely family but was considered barred from adoption by the alleged complicity of an ancestor in the poisoning of Mirza Raja Jai Singh.

Kanota   Thikana of the diarist, 12 miles from Jaipur city. It was given to Thakur Zorawar Singh by Maharaja Ram Singh as reward for his role as court administrator.

Kanota, Thakur Amar Singh of   Born Samvat 1935 (July 25, 1878); died Samvat 1999 (November 2, 1942) according to family records. Born in 1881, according to the records of the ICC. The diarist becomes Thakur of Kanota on the death of his father in 1924. His name, "Amar," means "eternal," he who will not die.

Kanota, Thakur Narain Singh of   Father of the diarist, eldest son of Zorawar Singh. Born Magh Buddi (January, dark side of the moon), Sunday, Samvat 1907, A.D. 1850, presumably at Peelva, since Zorawar Singh had not then left Peelva. Died Asos Buddi (October) Samvat 1981, A.D. 1924. He served in the cavalry bodyguard of Maharaja Ram Singh and became its commander. In 1881, he was appointed superintendent of Girai (Police) for Jaipur, and nazim (head of the district) of Jhunjhunu. He made his headquarters in Jhunjhunu in Shekhawati, the turbulent, desertified outer marches of Jaipur state. He is credited by English officers with good work in keeping the peace. Maharaja Madho Singh, wishing to remove him in 1898 in connection with a court case brought against Kanota and its related thikanas, accused him of conspiring with the Shekhawati nobles to enhance their autonomy, a charge not credited by English officers at Jaipur. Narain Singh was the main protagonist challenging the state in the case of the three related thikanas. He was wholly out of favor from 1898, when he left Jaipur, to 1921, when he returned.

    With British intervention, he was appointed "native guardian" to Maharaja Jai Singh of Alwar in 1899. In 1906 he became member of council for military affairs at Alwar. He went with the maharaja to England in 1907; resigned from Alwar service in 1913; returned in 1916, on a pay of Rs 750 per month and other perquisites. He was effective for a time in keeping his difficult maharaja out of trouble. He left Alwar in 1921 when called to Jaipur by Maharaja Madho Singh, who, having no legitimate sons, needed help in arranging for the adoption of Man Singh of Isarda, his choice as successor to the Jaipur throne. In 1921 he was again appointed inspector general of the police and served until his death in 1924. When Narain Singh died in 1924 he was succeeded by F.C. Coventry, who took charge of Girai, Kotwali and C.I.D. Reserve. He had a reputation with his peers, the English, and his son as a man of considerable poise and natural authority. His first wife was Jadav Kanwar from Bhutera of the Nathawat branch of Kachhawas; the second was Saman Kanwar from Kochore, of the Shekhawat lineage.

Kanota, Thakur Sheo Nath Singh of   Born January 20, 1882. Second son of Thakur Narain Singh of Kanota by his second wife. Brother of the diarist. He went with the diarist to Jodhpur in 1888 as ward of Sir Pratap Singh, attended Mayo College, and entered the ICC in 1905. He was a fine sportsman, especially in riding and polo, but also played tennis, hockey and football. He served in the princely state services of Alwar (1907), Datia (1914), and Jaipur. In 1923, he was appointed head of "thirty-six departments" at Jaipur; in 1925, head of the forest department. In 1935, he became administrator of the Jaipur student hostel of Mayo College. He succeeded Amar Singh as Thakur of Kanota in 1942. His first wife was Lad Kanwar from Bagoli, of the Shekhawat lineage, and the second Ratan Kanwar from Tashin in Alwar of the Badgujar clan. He too kept a diary, presumably at Amar Singh's instance, in eight volumes from 1901 to 1926. Died 1977.

Kanota, Thakur Zorawar Singh of   Born February 24, 1827; died February 2, 1908. First Thakur of Kanota, grandfather of the diarist. Third son of Thakur Jivraj Singh of Peelva, he was the middle one of the three younger sons of Peelva thikana in Jodhpur to come to seek service in Jaipur He came to Jaipur in 1861; was appointed head of the atish (personal stables of the maharaja), and later of "thirty six departments," a miscellaneous portfolio including the manufacturing activities of Jaipur state. He succeeded his brother Shambhu Singh in 1876 as head of the Jagir Bakshi Khana (estate granting office) until 1898. He held office as a member of the maharaja's council from 1898 until his death in 1908, despite some eagerness by the maharaja to remove him in the wake of the case against the three related thikanas. "In my opinion, Zorawar Singh's experience and high character will make him a valuable member," wrote the resident,

G.R. Irwin. Zorawar Singh also carried on a brisk business of moneylending with other thikanas, which accounted for the prosperity of the estate and his reputation in the family for penuriousness. He married as his first wife Amrit Kanwar of the Inda lineage from Joilali and as second Raj Kanwar from Bhudana, of the Bhati lineage.

Karan Singh of Gurhi (Garhi)   See Garhi.

Karauli   One of the smallest of the princely states of Rajputana, located in the southeast of the area.

Kashmir   Princely state famed for its mountains and beauty, north of Delhi. Ruled by a Dogra dynasty.

Kaviraj Murardan   See Murardan.

Kesri Singh, Thakur of Achrol   See Achrol.

Kesri Singh (Kanota)   Born January 1, 1892. Fifth son of Narain Singh, Thakur of Kanota, and brother of the diarist. He attended Mayo College and served in the princely states of Kashmir and Gwalior. He attended the Agriculture College, Poona, from which he graduated with first division distinction. He became deputy inspector general of police of Jaipur state in 1925, and later head of the Shikarkhana (hunting department) of Jaipur and ADC to Maharaja Man Singh of Jaipur. He authored *The Tiger of Rajasthan; The Encyclopedia of Hunting*, and other works on animals and hunting. His first wife was from Todiyana in Jodhpur of Bhati lineage, the second from Ashti of the Nathawat lineage of Kachhawas. He introduced the Rudolphs to the diary and to Mohan Singh of Kanota. Died 1980.

Kettlewell, Major   English guardian of the Maharaja of Alwar in 1900; colleague of Narain Singh of Kanota, who was native guardian.

Khandela, Raja of   Khandela was a major thikana in Shekhawati, divided into senior and junior branches. The senior branch was married to the daughter of Sultan Singh, Thakur of Peelva, holder of the thikana whence Amar Singh's grandfather came to Jaipur. Kochore, the thikana of Narain Singh's second wife, Amar Singh's mother, was related to Khandela.

Kharia, Thakur Sawai Singh of   Third brother of Amar Singh's wife, adopted to the thikana of Kharia.

Khatri, Babu Deoki Nandan   Hindi novelist. Author of *Chandra Kanta; Chandra Kanta Santati; Booth Nath; Kusum Kumari.*

Khawasji   Title by which Bala Bux was known. See Bux, Bala. See also glossary of unfamiliar terms.

Khatu, Hari Singh Ladkani of   Bakshi fauj and superintendent of police of Jaipur after 1898, when Narain Singh, Amar Singh's father, was dismissed from that post. The two were sharp rivals. He was dismissed in 1903.

Khejarla   Major thikana in Jodhpur near kin to Satheen, the thikana of Amar Singh's wife. They are of Bhati lineage, the ruling lineage of Jaisalmer state. It was, according to Amar Singh, the only "foreign" lineage thikana among the eight first-class nobles of Jodhpur. He says they are Urjanot Bhatis, who do not generally marry their daughters to maharajas, while Rawalot Bhatis marry their daughters only to maharajas.

Khejarla, Thakur Madho Singh of   Eldest of three sons of the Thakur of Satheen who was adopted to Khejarla. He was Amar Singh's brother-in-law.

Khetri, Raja of   Powerful Shekhawat jagirdar of northern Jaipur whose thikana possessed several attributes of statehood, such as police, customs, power, and judicial competency. It was the second largest Jaipur jagir after Sikar, and larger than many states.

Khichis   A named lineage of Rajputs.

Kiam Khan   Amar Singh's Urdu teacher in 1900.

Kishengarh   Small Rathore Rajput state located between Jaipur and Jodhpur.

Kishengarh, Maharaja Madan Singh of   Fellow cadet and constant companion of Amar Singh in the early years at the ICC (1901, 2, 3). He ruled from 1900 to 1926 when he died. In 1904 he married the eldest daughter of Maharana Fateh Singh of Udaipur.

Kishore Singh, Daffadar   Friend of Amar Singh at Jodhpur, in 1898, he was brother of Thakur Sheonath Singh of Bera, who was married to the daughter of Sir Pratap Singh, regent of Jodhpur, and of Bukhtawar Singh. He became superintendent of police at Idar in 1902 when Sir Pratap went there as maharaja.

Kochore   Thikana of Amar Singh's mother, Saman Kanwar. The family is related to the large Shekhawat lineage thikana of Khandela in Jaipur. Saman Kanwar was Narain Singh's second wife, whom he married after the death of Zadav Kanwar from Bhutera.

Kotah   Founded by a Hara Rajput in 1625, Madho Singh, who received from Emperor Jehangir for good services to that emperor a grant to the territory which he had conquered.

Kumbhalgarh   A fort that stands in a mountain between Abu and Udaipur. It was built by Maharana Kumbha (fifteenth century) of Chitor (Udaipur or Mewar state) who established his rule over parts of Malwa and Gujarat. Kumbha was grandfather to Maharana Sangha.

Lachman Singh (Naila)   Born March 15, 1880; died January, 14, 1951. "Cousin" of Amar Singh; first son of Guman Singh, who was brother of Thakur Roop Singh of Naila. He was something of a poet and a bookworm, and went into Kishengarh state service. He married a wife from Bikampore of the Bhati lineage.

Ladkani, Hari Singh   See Khatu.

Lala Hans Raj   See Hans Raj.

Lall, Babu Syam Sunder   See Syam.

La Touche   Probably J.N.D. La Touche, executive engineer in the Indian public works department, and deputed as consulting engineer to the railways at Jodhpur after 1895.

Lawrence, Sir Walter   Private secretary to the viceroy, Lord Curzon (in 1902). His book, *The India We Served*, has important accounts of various persons in the diary, notably Maharaja Madho Singh and Sir Pratap, with both of whom he was on cordial terms.

Loch, Colonel W.   Civil officer deputed to assist Jodhpur state in the time of Maharaja Jaswant Singh. Defined civil and criminal powers of jagirdars and organized courts.

Madan Singh, Maharaja of Kishengarh   See Kishengarh.

Madho Singh, Thakur of Khejarla   See Khejarla.

Madho Singh, Maharaja of Jaipur   See Jaipur.

Mahajan, Thakur Hari Singh of   Brother-in-law of Amar Singh; he is married into Satheen thikana, to a sister of Amar Singh's wife. Mahajan was a leading thikana in Bikaner state, and Hari Singh member of council under Maharaja Ganga Singh.

Maharaja's College, Jaipur   See Mukerjee, Babu Kanti Chander.

Manji   Guardian of the Maharaja of Jodhpur and Amar Singh at Abu when they were young.

Man Singh, Maharaja of Jaipur   See Jaipur.

Mandawa   Rajput family belonging to the Shekhawat lineage and located in northern Jaipur. The family was connected by marriage to that of the diarist.

Mangal Singh of Gurhi   See Garhi.

Mani Ram ki Kothi ka Rasta   Street of Mani Ram's House. Location of the three Champawat families' town houses.

Manu Bhagwan   Manu is the (mythical) author of the Manusmriti, a text prescribing rules of conduct for Hindus, presumably composed prior to the third century of the common era.

Marathas   West Indian peoples who contested Mughal hegemony and expanded their military power north to Rajasthan and Delhi and eastward in the eighteenth and nineteenth centuries. Their home was the area covered by modern Maharashtra state.

Martindale, A.H.T.   Resident at Jodhpur, 1897 to 1901. Acting as AGG in Rajputana in 1899–1900.

Marwar   Another name for Jodhpur.

Mathura   City south of Delhi, sacred to Krishna.

Mayne, Captain   At Jodhpur, in 1898.

Mayo College   Princes and nobles college founded at Ajmer by Lord Mayo in 1875. Rajputana's main educational institution for her ruling classes. Founded on English public school lines, it taught revenue, accounts, and law in addition to general education. It was one of four chiefs colleges, the others being located at Rajkot, Indore and Lahore.

Meenda   Estate in Jodhpur source of political difficulty to Sir Pratap Singh in the early years of the diary.

Mehtab Singh (Peelva)   Born March 10, 1865; died November 29, 1913. Third son of Thakur Abhai Singh of Peelva; younger brother of Sultan Singh, Thakur of Peelva, the thikana in Jodhpur from which the three Champawat families (Kanota, Naila, Gondher) had come. He acted as estate steward to Roop Singh of Naila, whose favorite and close companion he was, and laid out Naila town. His income from Peelva, according to Amar Singh, was about Rs 200 per year (October 24, 1904). He married a wife from Siddha of the Bhati lineage, sister to the wives of his two brothers.

Mertias   A Rajput lineage.

Mewar   See Udaipur.

Minchin, Captain A.B.   Foreign Department, Government of India. Assistant to the AGG in Rajputana.

Mookend Singh, Thakur of Gondher (Santha)   See Gondher, Thakur Mukend Singh.

Mount Abu   Hill Station in southwestern Rajasthan.

Mukerjee, Babu Kanti Chander   Prime minister of Jaipur and chief nemesis of the Kanota family, he died in 1901. From 1898, he harassed the family with a case that threatened Kanota, Naila and Gondher estates, charging that the estates had been fraudulently acquired. In 1881, at the death of Maharaja Ram Singh, who had favored the Kanota lineage and appointed them to court posts, he replaced the Kanota ministers and served as *de facto* prime minister, directing all the activities of the young and recently adopted Maharaja Madho Singh. He was extremely industrious and capable and commanded respect in British India. Brought from Bengal by Maharaja Ram Singh, he began his Jaipur career as a school master and moved smoothly over into court administration. Appointed headmaster of Maharaja's College (founded 1844) in 1865, he reorganized the college, and in 1867 sent up the first batch of candidates to the entrance examination of Calcutta University. In 1888, the college was affiliated to Calcutta University, and opened B.A. classes in 1890.

Murardan, Kaviraj   Born in 1833, court poet of Jodhpur and chief of the state's charans; judge of the appellate court at Jodhpur, from *circa* 1884 to *circa* 1900, he became joint musahib ala (first minister) in the absence of Sir Pratap Singh in China in 1900–1901. He held various posts under the Jodhpur court, including member of the council. In 1900 he was honored by the viceroy with the title Mahamaha padyaya.

Nahar Singh (Naila)   Younger brother of Lachman Singh, son of Guman Singh, who was the younger brother of Thakur Roop Singh of Naila.

Naila   Thikana at Jaipur founded by Fateh Singh, grand-uncle of the diarist, youngest of the three brothers who came from Peelva in Jodhpur to serve in Jaipur.

Naila, Thakur Fateh Singh of   Born May 25, 1830; died November 10, 1897. Fourth son of Jivraj Singh of Peelva and first Thakur of Naila. He and his older brother, Shambhu Singh, left their home thikana of Peelva in 1854 to serve Maharaja Ram Singh at Jaipur, following their father Jivraj Singh, who had preceded them. Fateh Singh served successively as head of the zenana deorhi (zenana office handling property of the royal women), in 1867; qilazat (in charge of forts) in 1869; private secretary to Maharaja Ram Singh in 1872; prime minister in 1873. In 1863, 1868, 1873 and 1875, he received the villages that made up Naila thikana; in 1873 Maharaja Ram Singh conferred tazim (honored status among nobles) on him and his brothers. In 1881, one year after the death of Maharaja Ram Singh, Fateh Singh's formal office, vice-president of council, was abolished; he was accused, but not convicted, of serious embezzlement of funds from the treasury. The family fell into relative disfavor under Maharaja Madho Singh, whose succession Fateh Singh had favored, if not engineered. He married a first wife of the Bhati lineage from Savedavo; and a second of the Kachhawa lineage from Watka near Jaipur.

Naila, Thakur Pratap Singh of   Born 1877; died December 26, 1940. Eldest son of Roop Singh of Naila, cousin of Amar Singh, he served in the cavalry and the judicial service of Jaipur state. His first wife was Suraj Kanwar from Karansar, of the Ranawat lineage of Shishodias. His second wife was from Khatoli in Kotah and of the Hara lineage. The third was Kisan Kanwar from Tota Bogha in Jaisalmer state, of the Bhati lineage.

Naila, Thakur Roop Singh of   Born November 24, 1856; died October 13, 1934. Son of Thakur Fateh Singh of Naila, he was appointed commander of the Jaipur forts (qiledar) in 1872, a post his father held before him and entered the judicial service of the state in 1880. He served on the sardar appellate court, civil side, from at least 1905 to 1921. In 1921, when Devi Singh of Chomu was removed from the cabinet for his support of Jhalai in the succession to the Jaipur throne, Roop Singh took his place, serving at Revenue and Finance (1922), Home (1923), Military and Political (1924, 1925), and Revenue (1926 to 1931) Departments. He married a first wife from Harsoli, of the Khangerot branch of the Kachhawas; a second, Raj Kanwar, came from Bagra-ka-Bas, and was of the Nathawat branch of Kachhawas.

Narain Singh, Thakur of Kanota   See Kanota.

Narawat   Branch of the Rathores, ruling clan of Jodhpur, state.

Narpat Singh   Natural son of Sir Pratap, the regent and prime minister of Jodhpur, periodically from 1878 to 1923, he was educated in England and in the 1920s entered the personal service of Maharaja Umaid Singh of Jodhpur. He was private secretary to the maharaja in 1931, comptroller of the royal household, member-in-waiting of the council, 1928–1932, and minister-in-waiting, 1938–1946.

Nawalgarh   One of the "panchpana sardars", related large thikanas in Shekhawati. Sir Pratap took a wife from Nawalgarh, and Gambhir Singh's daughter was married there.

Nathdwara   Charitable place where the society of Naths, holy men, dwell; a town in Udaipur state.

Odeypore   See Udaipur.

Ogumji   A young Rajput, favored companion of the young Maharaja Sardar Singh of Jodhpur. Ogumji was considered a bad influence, and banished from court by the British resident.

Pabuji   Popular deity at Jodhpur, he figures in the songs and tales of the Bhopas, wandering singers who travel with a wall-hanging depicting the life of Pabuji, about which they sing, sometimes all night.

Pachmarhi   The hill station of Madhya Pradesh, 3,500 feet above sea level, on the rail line to Jabalpur.

Pank, Lieutenant Colonel Philip Durrell, I.M.S. Born 1853; joined the Indian Medical Service in 1880; served in Bombay, Bikaner, Alwar, Udaipur in 1894–1895, and Ajmer before coming to Jaipur in 1899 as Dr Hendley's successor as residency surgeon and superintendent of dispensaries and vaccination. Acting resident at Jaipur in 1899 and 1907.

Paonaskar, Professor Private tutor of the Maharaja of Kishengarh. He leaves Kishengarh to become a teacher at Mayo College in Ajmer.

Paota Residence at Jodhpur, where distinguished visitors were lodged.

Papio Amar Singh's orderly.

Patiala Largest of the Sikh states in the Punjab.

Patterson, Captain Assistant inspecting officer, July 16, 1899.

Pears, Lieutenant Colonel T.C. Resident at Jodhpur, 1898, at Nepal until 1903, at Jaipur. 1903–1904.

Peelva The small thikana in Jodhpur from which Amar Singh's grandfather and granduncles came to Jaipur, their eldest brother, Abhai Singh, remaining as thakur. Its official value in the 1920s was Rs 5,000. The thikana maintained a house in Jodhpur city which Amar Singh visited periodically while at Jodhpur. When the diary begins, Sultan Singh, Amar Singh's uncle and son of Abhai Singh, is the thakur.

Peelva, Inder Singh of Born May 11, 1884; died April 19, 1942. First son of Jawahar, second son of Thakur Abhai Singh of Peelva. (See genealogical chart.) He was eventually adopted by Thakur Sultan Singh of Peelva as his heir. He held charge of the Jaipur treasury. His first wife came from Singhason and the Shekhawat lineage. His second wife was from Kailawa in Jodhpur and the Tanwar lineage.

Peelva, Thakur Abhai Singh of Born January 13, 1818; died November 13, 1885. Eldest son of Thakur Jivraj Singh of Peelva he remained at Peelva in Jodhpur when his three brothers, Shambhu Singh, Zorawar Singh, and Fateh Singh came to serve Maharaja Ram Singh at Jaipur in the 1850s and 1860s. Relations between him and the brothers, notably Zorawar Singh, were strained by landed property questions. He was given the honor of tazim when Maharaja Ram Singh conferred it on the three younger brothers, an event which may reflect the capacity of his three brothers at Jaipur to exercise influence at both Jaipur and Jodhpur. He gained an increase of Rs 2,000 in the value of this jagir in 1873, the year the Jaipur tazim was conferred. He and his successors are considered the heads of the lineage that established Gondher, Kanota, and Naila estates. He married Daulat Kanwar, of the Bhati lineage, as his first wife, and a Bhati from Sirohi as his second wife.

Peelva, Thakur Jivraj Singh of Born September 6, 1799; died October 9, 1853. Ancestor of the Kanota, Naila and Gondher families at Jaipur, he came to Jaipur in 1849, and served Maharaja Ram Singh. He died after his return to Jodhpur. He married Amrit Kanwar of the Bhati lineage from Banna-ka-Bas.

Peelva, Thakur Sultan Singh of Born February 23, 1847; died October 30, 1910. Amar Singh's uncle, thakur of the thikana from which Amar Singh's grandfather and granduncles left for Jaipur, Sultan Singh was the eldest son of Abhai Singh, who had remained at Peelva when Shambhu Singh, Zorawar Singh, and Fateh Singh went to Jaipur. He had four daughters, no son, and adopted his nephew Inder Singh. He married a first wife from Siddha of the Bhati lineage; a second wife from Bairda-ka-Bas of the Bhati lineage.

Pilkington, Miss English lady who married Captain Cameron, Amar Singh's officer and close companion at the ICC.

Pinchard, Captain Served in China, 1900–1901, with Jodhpur Lancers.

Pinney, Captain Once a guardian of Maharaja Sardar Singh of Jodhpur. Acting adjutant of the ICC, 1903–1904.

Powlett, Colonel Percy W., C.S.I. He came to Jodhpur as resident to the Political Agency, Western States, Rajputana, later known as Political Residency, Western Rajputana States, which exercised jurisdiction over Jodhpur, Sirohi, and Jaisalmer. As resident, with some breaks, from 1880 to 1889, he worked closely with Sir Pratap, prime minister in the same years.

Powlett Nobles School Founded in 1886 by Sir Pratap working with Colonel Percy Powlett to provide education, especially in English reading and writing, to the sons of the Jodhpur nobility. A photograph of the time shows the young Maharaja of Jodhpur surrounded by young nobles (Photo I5).

Prasad, Rao Bahadur Pandit Sir Sukhdeo, Kt., C.I.E. Thakur of Jasnagar; B.A., member of council at Jodhpur, judicial secretary; eventually senior member of council (prime minister) at Jodhpur. Also chief minister at Udaipur from 1911–1918 and again in the 1930s. Sir Sukhdeo was a Kashmiri Brahmin whose family had migrated to Jodhpur and formed one of a group of professionally competent Indians who served the princely states, Babu Kanti Chander Mukerjee at Jaipur being another. Sir Pratap, the diarist's patron, regarded Sir Sukhdeo as his bitter rival for power at Jodhpur. Their power tended to alternate over a twenty-five year period, Sir Sukhdeo in charge when Sir Pratap was Maharaja at Idar or out of the state, Sir Sukhdeo out when Sir Pratap conducted several regencies at Jodhpur. Sir Sukhdeo was knighted in 1922. His final expulsion from Jodhpur was accomplished with the assistance of Sir Pratap's natural son, Narpat Singh.

In 1887–1888 he became judicial secretary to Council at Jodhpur, remaining member of council from this time forward. He was *de facto* in charge of the musahib ala's (first minister) English office in 1898 when Maharaja Sardar Singh assumed full powers; famine secretary, 1899–1900; joint musahib ala in 1900–1901 when Sir Pratap went to China; senior member mahakma khas (secretariat) 1902–1908; minister 1908–1911. With the abolition of the office of musahib ala, the senior member of the mahakma khas became the leading office in Jodhpur. He retired in 1911, at the death of Sardar Singh, when Sir Pratap returned to manage the new minority. Serving as chief minister of Mewar (Udaipur) 1911–1918, he returned to Jodhpur at the death of Maharaja Sumer Singh, and formed a new regency in 1918. After serving as revenue member and senior member, mahakma khas and judicial member until 1926, he was forced again to resign and returned as chief minister at Mewar in the 1930s.

Pratap Singh, Colonel Maharaj Dhiraj Sir G.C.S.I., K.C.B. Born 1845; died 1922. Guardian and patron of Amar Singh who lived with Sir Pratap from 1888 to 1901. Third son of Maharaja Takhat Singh of Jodhpur, Sir Pratap virtually ruled Jodhpur state from 1878 to 1922, as chief adviser or prime minister to his brother the maharaja, or as regent in the minorities of three maharajas. His rule was limited however by the authority and activity of professional civil servants like Sir Sukhdeo. "Sir P" was internationally known as a soldier and sportsman, for his polo and hunting as well as for a charming and eccentric personal style. He was a favorite in England, not least with Queen Victoria, and in Anglo-Indian society in India. He was knighted in 1885; appointed ADC to the Prince of Wales in 1895; attended Victoria's jubilees in 1885 and 1895, and received an honorary LL.D. from Cambridge in 1895. As a soldier, he joined the Mohmand campaign on the personal staff of General Elles, acted as ADC to General Lockhart in the Tirah campaign, led the Jodhpur Lancers in the Allied Expeditionary Force in the Boxer Rebellion in China, joined the Lancers in France and Egypt in World War I, and served as honorary commandant of the ICC from 1901. From 1902 to 1911 he was Maharaja of Idar, a small Rathore state to which he was adopted, but which he left when another minority lured him back to the more interesting arena of Jodhpur.

The following dates sum up his career in Jodhpur:

Prime Minister, Jodhpur 1878–1881
Musahib Ala (first minister), Jodhpur 1882–1895
President, Regency Council (minority of Sardar Singh) 1895–1897
Musahib Ala 1897–1900
Maharaja of Idar 1901–1905
President, Regency Council (minority of Sumer Singh) 1911–1914
President, Regency Council (minority of Umaid Singh) 1918–1922

Pratap Singh, Thakur of Naila   See Naila.

Rai ka Bagh Palace   Palace at Jodhpur.

Rajputana   Land of Rajputs; name of area comprising twenty-two princely states prior to Indian Independence in 1947. Jurisdiction of the AGG in Rajputana, and corresponding roughly to the subah (administrative unit), imposed on the area by the Mughals in the sixteenth to eighteenth centuries.

Ram (Rama)   Royal hero of Indian epic, the *Ramayana*.

Ram Chander   See Ram.

Ram Nathji, Barath   See Ratnu.

Ram Niwas   These public gardens at Jaipur were begun in 1868 by Maharaja Ram Singh to provide employment for the poor in the famine of that year. The original design was by Surgeon Major De Faback, I.M.S., who was principal of the Jaipur School of Art.

Ram Singh, Maharaja of Jaipur   See Jaipur.

Ram, Sushila Tahl   Indian writer brought up in England who writes English and Hindi novels much favored by Amar Singh.

Rama, Thakur Sardar Singh of   Adopted to Bhadrajoon, a large Jodhpur thikana. Friend and school fellow of Amar Singh.

Rand   Abusive term for a woman; literally, widow.

Rani Dungaris   A hill in Jodhpur.

Raoti   A village to the northwest of Jodhpur, city. Home place of Akhai Singh, Amar Singh's close friend at Jodhpur, China, and the ICC. The senior member of the Raoti family was Maharaja Fateh Singh, eldest son of Maharaj Zorawar Singh, who was second son of Maharaja Takhat Singh of Jodhpur.

Rasal Kanwar   Amar Singh's wife, married to him in September, 1901. Daughter of the Thakur of Satheen, a large thikana in Jodhpur, she was Bhati by lineage, and bore a number of daughters. Only one of them survived. She died in 1945, three years after Amar Singh.

Ratanada   A palace at Jodhpur. It lies south-east of the walled city, and was the residence of the Maharaja of Jodhpur, when he did not occupy Rai ka Bagh. The name also refers to a suburban section of Jodhpur, city.

Ratnu, Barath Ram Nath   Tutor and friend of Amar Singh and the likely instigator of the diary. A charan, the caste of court bards and historians of Rajputana, he was engaged by Sir Pratap as tutor to the young Maharaja Sardar Singh at Jodhpur, where he lives in the early years of the diary. For thirteen years headmaster of the Rajput Nobles School at Jaipur, he was knowledgeable about English public school curricula, but learned in some of the Indian classics as well. He had traveled to England in 1894, when it was very uncommon for persons from Rajputana to do so, and kept a journal of his travels. Ram Nathji gives Amar Singh assignments — Plutarch, the *Mahabharata* — while they are at Jodhpur, and they develop a strong appreciation for each other as book lovers isolated in a martial society. He helps the Kanota, Naila and Gondher families develop and present evidence in the case Maharaja Madho Singh brings against the three families. When Sir Pratap becomes Maharaja of Idar, he invites Ram Nathji to serve at the small court, as does the Maharaja of Kishengarh. Ram Nathji wrote *Rajasthane Ki Itihas* (Ajmer, Rajasthan Yantralaya, 1892), one of the first Hindi language histories of Rajasthan. Ram Nathji's home village, Singothia in Sikar district, is said to be a charan village and produced another Hindi historian, Bala Bakshji, whose books were published in a series by the Nagri Pracharni Sabha at Allahabad.

Rawalot   See Bhatis.

Reed, Major General A.I.F.   Commander, 3rd Brigade, British Contingent, China Field Force.

Rewah   Princely state in central India.

Richardson, Major General G.   Commander, Cavalry Brigade, China Expeditionary Force.

Ricketts, Captain   Guardian of H.H. Jai Singh of Alwar in 1902.

Roop Singh, Thakur of Naila   See Naila.

Rutlam, Maharaja Sajjan Singh of   Fellow cadet of Amar Singh at the ICC.

Sajjan Singh, Raja of Rutlam   See Rutlam.

Saman Kanwar from Kochore   See Kochore.

Sanganer   An important clothmaking and temple village about 8 miles from Jaipur.

Santha   See Gondher. Thikana belonging to the eldest of the three branches of the Gondher, Kanota, and Naila houses. Santha is the new name taken by the Gondher family estate when the villages and fort of Gondher were exchanged by Jaipur state for other villages. Jaipur brought a case disputing the family's rightful possession of many of its villages.

Sardar Rissala   See glossary of unfamiliar terms.

Sardar Singh, Maharaja of Jodhpur   See Jodhpur.

Sardar Singh (Kanota)   Amar Singh's brother, born January 5, 1887; died January 26, 1955. Third son of Narain Singh, he was educated at Mayo College and served as manager of Kanota estate for many years while Amar Singh was in service. On behalf of his son, he challenged Amar Singh's second brother, Sheo Nath Singh's right of succession to Kanota. While the Jaipur court ruled in his favor, Maharaja Man Singh over-ruled the verdict in favor of Sheo Nath Singh. Sardar Singh married a wife from Bagoli of the Shekhawat lineage, sister of Sheo Nath Singh's first wife. He too kept a diary, presumably at Amar Singh's instance, in thirty-seven volumes from 1903 to 1952.

Sardar Singh of Rama   See Rama.

Sardar Singh, Rajkunwar of Shahpura   See Shahpura.

Satheen   One of the three related Bhati lineage thikanas in western Jodhpur. The other two are Khejarla and Khario. The thikana at the time of Amar Singh's marriage had an income of Rs 40,000 annually and a Rekh of Rs 18,000 but fell seriously into debt.

Satheen, Thakur Kishore Singh of   Brother-in-law of Amar Singh, second son of the previous thakur, he succeeded at Satheen when his eldest brother was adopted at the related and larger Bhati thikana of Khejarla. Educated at Mayo College, he died of opium and alcohol excess. His sister married Amar Singh in 1901.

Sen, Babu Sansar Chander   Born 1846, member of a Bengali service family that came to Jaipur in the time of Maharaja Ram Singh. Entering Jaipur state service in 1866, he became headmaster of the Rajput Nobles School in 1874; in December 1880 (at the accession of Madho Singh) he became private secretary to the maharaja, a post he held until 1901. In 1901, he was appointed to the Foreign Department of the maharaja's council and then its head member (equivalent to prime minister), succeeding Babu Kanti Chander Muckerjee.

Shahpura, Rajkunwar Sardar Singh of   Second son of the ruler of Shahpura, Raja Nahar Singh. A Shishodia Rajput and class fellow of Amar Singh at the ICC in 1902.

Shambhu Singh   See Gondher.

Shan Hai Kuan   Amar Singh and the Jodhpur Lancers are stationed at this town, half-way between Mukden and Peking, which contains a famous barrier gate, constructed in 618, at the eastern extremity of the Great Wall of China. While the Allied Troops occupied the city, it is said to have enjoyed great prosperity. It had a population of about 80,000 in 1924.

Shekhawat   Descendants of Shekhaji; counted as a branch of Kachhawas, ruling lineage of Jaipur. The lineage was powerful in the desert areas of northern Jaipur and had a historical propensity to dispute the suzerainty of Jaipur state. Maharaja Madho Singh suspected Narain Singh, Amar Singh's father, of conspiring with the Shekhawats.

Shekhawati   Area of northern Jaipur settled by the Shekhawats.

Sheonath Singh, Thakur of Bera   See Bera.

Sher Singh, Maharaj   Third son of Maharaj Zorawar Singh, second son of Maharaja Takhat Singh of Jodhpur, companion of Amar Singh, and brother of the diarist's close friend Maharaj Akhai Singh.

Shishodia   Ruling Rajput lineage of Udaipur state.

Sheo Nath Singh, Thakur of Kanota   See Kanota.

Sultan Singh, Thakur of Peelva   See Peelva.

Stewart, Captain J.M.   Served in China with the British Expeditionary Force in 1900.

Stothard, C.E.   Acting executive engineer, P.W.D., 1903–1904, at Jaipur, he succeeded Sir Swinton Jacob as superintending engineer in May 1905.

Sukhdeo Prasad, Sir   See Prasad.

Sultan Singh, Thakur of Peelva   See Peelva.

Sumer Singh, Maharaj Kanwar of Jodhpur   See Jodhpur.

Sundio   Servant of Amar Singh, he accompanied him to China in 1900–1901.

Suraj Mall   Famous historian and charan of Rajputana, author of *Vans Bhaskar*. See *Vans Bhaskar*.

Sushila Tahl Ram   See Ram.

Syam Sunder Lall, Babu   Prime minister of Kishengarh state in 1902.

Takhat Singh, Maharaja of Jodhpur   See Jodhpur.

Todd, R.   Manager of the Jodhpur Railway from 1906 until at least 1910.

Turner, Major Henry Hamilton Fyers   In 1899, Jodhpur state agreed that a British officer would direct, control and manage the Jodhpur Lancers whenever they served beyond the Indian frontiers. (Aitchison, vol. III, pp. 180–181.) Turner, who serves in Jodhpur in 1898 as the British officer deputed to inspect the Imperial Service Troops, becomes the directing officer when the Jodhpur troops go to China. He assumed command of the 2nd Bengal Lancers in 1915 and was killed at the second battle of Cambrai in World War I.

Udaipur   Princely state of the Shishodia lineage, also known as Mewar. Its princes were recognized in Rajputana and by the British as the most distinguished Rajput lineage by virtue of the antiquity of their genealogical claims as well as of the historical myth of resistance which has colored their history since publication in 1829 and 1831 of the Udaipur-favoring *Annals and Antiquities of Rajasthan*, by Colonel James Tod, first resident at Udaipur. The earliest representatives of the lineage established themselves at Chitor in A.D. 734 and withstood three sacks of that city, the last by the Mughal emperor Akbar, who destroyed much of Chitor city. Their resistance to the Mughal emperors was exemplified by the fact that, unlike the other Rajput states, they did not contract marriages with the Mughals, and did not personally offer obeisance but sent their sons. The myth of Rajput resistance resurfaced as an important component of nationalist ideologies in the early twentieth century, as well as in more recent Hindu nationalist rhetorics. The state's revenue in 1926 was Rs 5,076,000 per annum, and its population 1,406,990.

Udaipur, Maharana Bhupal Singh of   Born in 1884, he succeeded his father Maharana Fateh Singh *de facto* in 1921 and *de jure* in 1930. Amar Singh's cousin, the daughter of his uncle Bhim Singh, married the thakur of Achrol, and their daughter married Bhupal Singh.

Udaipur, Maharana Fateh Singh of   Born 1849, he succeeded by adoption in 1884. In the diary, he appears as the contemptuous father-in-law of Maharaja Madan Singh of Kishengarh, the diarist's close friend at the ICC. He was chosen as successor to Maharana Sajjan Singh in 1884, and acquired a reputation for resisting the march of modernity — opposing the extension of the railways, and resisting the rationalization of Udaipur administration. He was a great hunter (and his hunts were highly rationalized), and maintained and refurbished ancient monuments — such as Kumbhalgarh fortress. He died in 1930.

Umaidji Purohit   Family priest of the Kanota family. His grandson was still in 2002 family purohit for Kanota.

Umaid Singh, Maharaja of Jodhpur   See Jodhpur.

Urjanot   See Bhatis.

Vali Uddin Khan   He was one of the four cadets at the ICC who finished the first course and were commissioned with Amar Singh in 1905. He was second son of Nawab Vicral Umrao of Hyderabad, who was Dewan of that state, and of the Piagah family, a leading service family at Hyderabad. He was educated at Eton, and Amar Singh regarded him as excessively anglicized.

Walter, Colonel C.K.M.   Resident at Jodhpur, in 1873, when Maharaja Jaswant Singh came to the throne. Moving figure in the formation of the Walter Krit Hitkarni Sabha, Rajput reform society. He was the last political agent to Mewar in 1879–1881, after which British representatives were styled residents. Returned as Jodhpur resident in 1882–1885, and again in 1886–1887.

Watson, Major W.A.   First commandant, ICC, and a dedicated teacher who pounded algebra into resisting heads. He belonged to the 1st Lancers, Central India Horse.

Wyllie, Colonel E.H.C., C.I.E.   Resident at Mewar, 1893–1894; 1894–1896; resident at Jodhpur, 1898–1899; acting AGG in 1900 and favorable to the Kanota family's case. In 1903, he became political ADC to the Secretary of State for India. He was murdered by Indian revolutionaries in England who intended to kill the secretary of state.

Zaday Kanwar from Bhutera   See Bhutera.

Zalim Singh (Khichi), Rissaldar   Amar Singh says he was his guardian at the Nobles school at Jodhpur; he helps Amar Singh to outfit himself for the Kadir Cup.

Zalim Singh, Maharaj   Born 1865; tenth and youngest son of Maharaja Takhat Singh of Jodhpur, brother to Sir Pratap Singh. He studied at Mayo College and was well versed in English. Assistant musahib ala (chief adviser) under Sir Pratap Singh until 1902. In charge of Customs and Boundary Office 1893–1903. He held a five-village jagir of Rs 24,000 annual income.

Zorawar Singh, Maharaj   Second son of Maharaj Takhat Singh, Zorawar Singh rebelled against his father in 1872 and seized Nagaur. He was defeated by state troops. He had hoped to succeed Takhat Singh as maharaja, on the plea that Jaswant Singh, his eldest brother, had been adopted at Ahmednagar.

Zorawar Singh, Thakur of Kanota   See Kanota.

GLOSSARY II:
Unfamiliar Terms

We have provided definitions for English and Indian, especially Rajasthani, terms that may not be familiar to the casual reader. The guide to pronunciation draws on Marwari and Hindi usage. The glossary has profited from Sita Ram Lalas's dictionary, *Rajasthani Saboda Kosa* (Jodhpur, 1960–1971); from the advice of Professor Kali Bahl and the poet and writer, Kesri Singh, both of whom are familiar with Hindi and Rajasthani usage; and from Henry Yule and A.C. Burnell, *Hobson-Jobson*, second edition (Delhi, 1968). Many of the Rajasthani meanings were offered by Mohan Singh who in turn profited from the advice of Devi Singh Mandawa.

Aad (Ada) Woman's neck ornament.

Asis (Asisa) Blessings, benediction from elders; prayer, making wishes to benefit another.

Achkan (Acakana) A long-fitted coat with a stand-up collar, reaching to the knees, Mughal in origin.

Adit chukker (Adita cakkara). The invisible (unseen) wheel; the wheel of fate; the divine (sacred) wrath, agitation or fickleness.

Adrithia or Adratyo (Adardtiyau). "Midnight food," given to the bride and groom on their wedding night. Amar Singh and his wife were awakened at 2 a.m. to receive it. The second meal of the new groom. Also a midnight meal taken just prior to a fast.

Agent to the Governor General (AGG) Chief political officer representing the viceroy and exercising jurisdiction over a number of princely states. He and officers subordinate to him, such as residents and political agents, exercised the British governments indirect rule over the princely states. These officers belonged to the Political Department, which was directly under the viceroy, and not subject to the viceroy's council. The AGG in Rajputana holds charge of all the twenty-two princely states and chiefships of the area known as Rajputana before Independence in 1947, and since then as Rajasthan.

AGG See Agent to the Governor General.

Akha Teej (Akha Tija). The third day of the bright half of the lunar month; month of baisakha (second month of Hindu year); a famous festival of Rajasthan, marking the completion of the harvests (rabi). Observed in Marwar, Jaisalmer and Bikaner, not in Jaipur, says Amar Singh. Consists of the giving of opium and gur (jaggery). Observed in 1905 just after Gangore, which was observed in May.

Akraa milk (Akarau dudh). Sap of a plant.

Aleen (Alina). Not fit to be eaten; inadmissible, unacceptable, unfit to be received.

Angharki (Āgarakhi). Fitted coat with fitted sleeves, deeply cut out in front; worn by men.

Arti (Arati). Lamp. In a wedding, the lamp passed around the bride and groom by the mother-in-law. Also used to designate lamp of camphor or ghee in the temple.

Arya Samaj (Arya Samaja). Hindu reform society founded in the nineteenth century following the path of Swami Dayanand Saraswati, stressing, especially in its early days, opposition to idol worship and return to the Vedic roots of Hinduism. It was strong in north India, vigorous in trying to convert Muslims to Hinduism, and gained support from a number of Rajput princes, among them Sir Pratap, Amar Singh's patron.

Asha (Asa). Powerful fermented drink common to Rajasthan. It comes in many varieties; the gulab asha, rose asha, of Udaipur was especially famous.

Assami (Asami). Client, as in patron-client relations.

Atam Sukh (Atam sukh). The happiness of the soul; contentment. Used in the diary and elsewhere for a warm robe.

Atar Pan (Atara pana). Leave giving ceremony, when betel is offered in a tray, and atar (perfume) is applied by the host to the guest's chest or shoulder. Often garlands are also presented.

Atish (Atash). Stable for horses. The head of the atish was a state officer of some importance.

Baba Mendicant. Also used to refer to the natural son of a chief.

Babu (Babu). A clerk. Also respectful term used for a literate man. Its negative meaning in Anglo-Indian literature reflects English cultural predilections.

Badaran (Badaran). Zenana servants or administrators, they perform some of the functions at Rajasthan courts of the eunuch servants who figure in Byzantine and Chinese women's quarters. They had considerable responsibility for valuables as well as for the complex family arrangements and economic logistics of the large women's quarters of major courts and thikanas. They were women.

Badha Kar lena (Badha kara lena). Refers to a function at the time of a marriage reception, when brass, silver or earthen vessels (kalas) containing water and green leaves are carried on the heads of women. Also ceremony performed for a man when he visits his wife's village.

Badmash (Badamasa). Wicked, immoral. Man of bad character.

Badnami (Badanami). Slander, disrepute; state of being known in society for one's bad deeds.

Bagar (Bagara). Hay stack; the place where grass and fodder are stored.

Bahi (Bahi). Account book. Diary, in the sense of a financial diary.

Bahu (Bahu). Daughter-in-law.

Bai ji Lal (Bai ji lala). Used to refer to the daughters of the Maharaja of Jodhpur or his sisters.

Bajot (Bajota.). Low wooden table for eating while sitting on the floor.

Bajra (Bajara). A millet. A coarse grain or its plant.

Bakshi (Baksi). Paymaster.

Bakshish (Bakasisa). Act of giving alms; presentation; a tip.

Bakshi Fauj. (Bakst fauj). Literally paymaster, army. Commander.

Bana (Bana). Auspicious marriage song. The bridegroom is also known as bana. Respectful address for a young boy. Ceremony performed at the bridegroom's house in a Rajput family before the marriage party starts out for bride's house. It is a Ganesh puja (worship of the elephant God) and involves rubbing an aromatic paste on the body.

Bandobust (Bandobast). *Hobson-Jobson* says it means, literally, tying and binding. Any form of regulation, settlement, or discipline.

Baniya (Baniya). Merchant, trader, storekeeper.

Banwar (Bamvar). A Rajput whose grandfather is alive. Grandson.

Bari haveli (Bari haveli). Literally, big house. This is the house in Mani Ram ki Kothi ka Rasta, in Haldion Ka Rasta, in Jaipur city, given by Maharaja Ram Singh to the three Champawat brothers, Amar Singh's uncles and grandfather, who came from Peelva, to Jaipur. When the two younger built their own houses, they turned over this one to Shambhu Singh, Thakur of Gondher, eldest of the three. The houses of the middle and youngest brothers are referred to, respectively as bichli haveli (middle house) and choti haveli (small house).

Baradari (Baradari). Literally, verandah with twelve pillars. Open on all four sides, on each side it has three arches connecting four pillars.

Barat   (Barat). Group of bridegroom's party accompanying him at the time of wedding.

Barath   (Barahatha). Refers to caste of bards, poets, and historians attached to Rajput houses. See also charan.

Bazaar   (Bajara). Marketplace.

Beegha   See bigha.

Beend Raja   (Bind raja). Title for a bridegroom.

Bhaba   (Bhaba). Elder brother or elder cousin.

Bhabi   (Bhabi). Elder brother's or elder cousin's wife.

Bhasha   (Bhasa). Speech.

Bhateeji   (Bhatiji). A kinship term meaning brother's daughter.

Bhatyanees   (Bhatiyani). Women of the Bhati clan of Rajputs.

Bichli haveli   (Bicali haveli). Literally, middle house; the house in Mani Ram ki Kothi ka Rasta off Haldion Ka Rasta, in Jaipur city built by Zorawar Singh, the middle one of the three Champawat brothers who came from Peelva, and the diarist's grandfather. It is the town house of the Kanota family.

Bhil   (Bhila). Forest dwelling, non-Hindu people resident in southern Rajasthan and Gujarat.

Bhishti   (Bhishti). One who carried water in a large leather bag.

Bhopa   (Bhopa). A caste of wandering singers and storytellers who sing the story of the hero Pabuji. They usually sing all night, describing the events pictured on a wall-hanging of Pabuji's life.

Bhugtuns   (Bhakatana). The term originally referred to dancers performing before the image of the deity; then, to dancing girls generally; and eventually, as social institutions and valuations changed, to prostitutes.

Bhuva   (Bhuva). Father's sister.

Bhuva Bhatiji   (Bhuva-bhatiji). Bhuva: sister of father. Bhatiji: brother's daughter; the compound phrase expresses the relationship the two bear to each other.

Bhuva Sasu   (Bhuva-sasu). Father-in-law's sister.

Bigha   (Bigha). Common measure of land area. A pakka bigha, measured by an iron chain, is 3,025 square yards. A kaccha bigha is about half a pakka. It is measured by bamboo or footsteps. The conventional wisdom has it that a bigha is five-eighths of an acre.

Borah   (Bohara). Moneylender.

Brahm Bhoj   (Brahman bhoja). Feeding of Brahmans, on festive, devout, or expiatory occasions.

Brahman   (Brahmana). Traditionally the priests and intellectuals of Hindu society, and ritually highest ranked of the four varnas.

Buggi Khana   (Baggi Khana). Carriage house.

Bund   (Band). A dam, dyke, embankment.

Casters   In the diary, the word is used in the sense of cast-off, as when Sir Pratap, wishing to send worthless horses, sends the casters of the regiment.

Chakravartin   (Cakravartin). An emperor, universal monarch.

Chanas   (Chana). Cowdung cakes.

Chand   (Chand). Moon-shaped piece of jewelry, for turban.

Chanwar   See chowar.

Charan   (Carana). Caste of bards, chroniclers and keepers of the historical and literary tradition in western India.

Chargama   (Chargama). Country saddle for horses and elephants.

Chavar   See chowar.

Chela   (Cela). Disciple.

Chinkara   A light gazelle.

Chir   (Chid). Teasing to which a person is especially vulnerable.

Choatri   (cautari). Platform for sitting, often outside.

Choti Haveli   (Choti Haveli). Literally, little house. The house built in Mani Ram ki Kothi ka Rasta of Jaipur city by Fateh Singh of Naila, Amar Singh's great uncle.

Chowar   (Carana). Hindi Chanwar, chaunri; from Sanskrit chamara, chamara. The bushy tail of the Tibetan Yak, often set in a costly decorated handle to use as a fly-flapper, in which form it was one of the insignia of ancient royalty.

Chowki Khana   (Cauki Khana). In the diary, platform with stone railing.

Chukker   (cakkara). Literally, a wheel. In daily speech, a "round" of polo. Each game of polo is divided into four chukkers of 5 minutes each, allowing players to change ponies.

Chura   (Cura). Set of arm bangles worn in some castes by new brides and in others by all married women. Among Rajputs it is always of ivory, given by the bridegroom to the bride, and she must wear it for at least a year.

Cross   In polo, a foul committed when one player crosses in front of another.

Dadeer Sasoo   (Dadi sasu). Grandmother-in-law.

Daffadar   (Daphadara). Army rank, non-commissioned officer in the cavalry, roughly equivalent to a sergeant.

Dahi   (Dahi). Curd.

Dak   (Dak). Mail.

Dak Bungalow   (Dak bungalow). Literally, "mail" bungalow. Refers to rest houses used primarily by touring government officers of the British raj, but also available to tourists.

Dal   (Dala). Pulses, such as lentils.

Dara   (Darau). Sand, ridge, dune.

Dari   (Dari). Rug.

Dari Khana   (Dari Khana). Drawing room. Literally, where one sits on a dari or rug.

Daroga   (Daroga). This word has been used as the title of various types of officers in princely states and British India. In Rajasthan it mainly referred to those bound personal servants of princes and noblemen who were given along with the dowry of a daughter. Amar Singh speaks of them as a caste. They were dependents, and not free to leave or contract marriages without permission of their master. In the diary, Hurjee, who is a socially mobile daroga, occupies an important place.

Dassera   See Dussera.

Deorhi [Deodi]   (Dyodi). Portal, gateway, foyer. To be in charge of the zenana deorhi, portal of the women's quarters, was a significant administrative post at court or in an estate.

Dera   (Dera). Camp, tent, pavillion.

Deshi   (Desi). From Hindi desh, country, meaning local or Indian, as one might order "deshi" rather than English style food for dinner.

Devar   (Devara). Younger brother of husband.

Dewan   (Divana). Minister, sometimes first minister.

Dharamshala   (Dharamasala). Resthouses, usually costless. Often these are attached to temples or other holy places, and are the gift of a patron who endows them.

Dholan   (Dholana). Woman of the Dholi caste, who sing and play the dhol (drum).

Dholi   (Dholi). A caste of singers or players, who sing often with the accompaniment of kettledrums.

Dhoti   (Dhoti). A piece of cloth, usually white cotton, that is draped into a covering for the legs.

Dipty   (Dipati). Hindi contraction of deputy used in diary to refer to the deputy superintendent of police.

Doha   (Doha, duha). Couplets such as those which Amar Singh reproduces in his diary are a characteristic form of Marwari literature.

Doob   (Duba). Turf. A kind of green grass.

Doolie   (Doli). A litter, palanquin, generally used to carry females.

Dund   (Danda). Push-ups performed with an extra sliding, swinging movement.

Durbar   (Darabara). Persian for a court or levee. "Also the Executive Government of a Native State . . . in Kattywar, by a curious idiom, the chief himself is so addressed: 'Yes, Durbar'; 'No, Durbar', being common replies to him." (*Hobson-Jobson*). The same was true in Rajputana, where Amar Singh applies the epithet to various maharajas.

Durri   See Dari.

Dusgara   (Dusgara). A game played with some 200 cowry shells; involves arithmetical calculation.

Dushala   (Dusala). Shawl; embroidered wrapper; it is often included in a siropao.

Dussera   (Dasaraha). Sanskrit dasahra (or ten days') festival in October. In Rajputana, so long as the social order was dominated by Rajputs, this holiday took on a strong martial dimension, with the worship of arms and vehicles of war. It includes celebration of the "day of victory", when the god-hero Rama, main figure of the epic *Ramayana*, defeated Ravana.

Egaris   (Igyaras). Eleventh day of the moon calendar.

Ekka   (Ikkau). Small, one man tonga.

Farash Khana   (Farash Khana). An office which kept elaborate tents, rugs, furniture and other supplies for the camps which were an ordinary part of the life of the maharajas and their households when traveling.

Farrier   A professional horseshoe-maker.

Fascine   A long bundle of sticks of wood bound together and used for such purposes as filling ditches and making parapets. Used in military fortifications.

Fauj   (Phauja). Persian for a military force.

Fauj Bakshi   (Phauja baksi). Military commander. Literally, paymaster of the army.

First spear   In pig-sticking, the privilege of delivering the first spear was often reserved for the most honored member of a hunting party.

Fulgari cloth   "Hindi phulkari, flowered embroidery" (*Hobson-Jobson*). Cloth embroidered with a white embroidery on thin white mull, native to Lucknow city; also known as chikkan work.

Gabion   A hollow wickerwork or iron cylinder filled with earth and used in building military fieldworks or in mining.

Gaddi   (Gaddi). Literally cushion. The cushion on which a maharaja is installed as a European monarch would be on a throne.

Ganayats   (Gindyata). Lineages other than one's own, into which, under Rajput rules of exogamy, one may marry. The term is also used to talk about Rajput lineages "foreign" to a particular state and its dominant lineage. Thus Kachhawas (Jaipur's ruling lineage) are ganayats in Jodhpur, where Rathores are the dominant lineage.

Ganga guru   (Ganga guru). Brahman coming from a pilgrimage place on the Ganges. Such a Brahman visited Kanota once a year, when he received charity.

Gangore   (Ganagora). Festival on third day of the bright half of the lunar month celebrated by girls wishing for husbands or women with living husbands. In Jaipur it is celebrated with a festive procession, in which the deity is carried. Amar Singh is obliged to clothe the deity for the 1905 Gangore at Kanota.

Gath Jora   (Gatha jora). literally "knot joined." The diary refers to a long piece of cloth tied to both husband and wife in a wedding.

Gayatri   (Gayatri). A sacred verse of the Rig-veda, which it is the duty of every Brahman to repeat mentally in his morning and evening devotions.

Ghat   (Ghata). A landing place; a path of descent to a river; a mountain pass—and thus, by derivation, also referring to a mountain range itself, as in Eastern and Western Ghats.

Ghee   (Ghi). Clarified butter.

Ghora siropao   (Ghora siropao). Horse and suit of clothes given as a departure present.

Ghumar   (Ghumara). A kind of dance performed by four or five girls at various functions, such as weddings. In Rajasthan, it was performed inside the women's quarters.

Girai   (Girai). Police department.

Goat cutting   Refers to the practice of hanging a live goat by the back feet, and decapitating it with a sword. "Cutting with one finger" or other variations refer to cutting with a difficult light grip that requires special skill and strength, i.e. holding the sword hilt with one finger, usually the middle, or two fingers, middle and third. "To cut clean" means the head comes off.

Gola   (Gola). Male slave.

Goli   (Goli). Literally female "slave"; in context of the diary, gola/goli is a derogatory way of referring to the household servants of the Rajputs who consider themselves Darogas.

Gomasta   (Gumasta). "From Persian, gumashtah, participle: appointed, delegated." "A native agent or factor." (*Hobson-Jobson*).

Gora   (Gora). "White man."

Gyan   (Gyana). Knowledge.

Gynaits   See ganayats.

Hakim   (Hakim). From Arabic, hakim, 'a judge, a ruler, a master'; 'the authority' (*Hobson-Jobson*). In Rajputana, head of an administrative division, equivalent to a district in British India. Jodhpur was divided into twenty-four parganas, each under one hakim.

Hakim   (Hakima). A learned man, philosopher; a Muslim physician.

Halal   (Halal). Technical Muslim phrase for the slaying of an animal according to the proper ritual—the throat is cut, to the recitation of lines from the Qu'ran. Some Sikhs and some orthodox Rajputs do not eat this meat.

Halkaras   (Halkara). "Hindi, harkara, a messenger, a courier; an emissary, a spy" (*Hobson-Jobson*). In Jaipur, sergeants at arms, available for multiple errands, especially for the maharaja. They carried silver staffs.

Hamam   (Hamama). Bathing room. Water Heater.

Hans   (Hansa). Heavy necklace.

Har-ki-Pawaris   See Har ki pedi.

Har ki Pedi   (Harakipaidi). Particular place in Hardwar said to be the "staircase" of god, used by worshippers to descend to the Ganges. It is said to be the best place to take a dip and to take water.

Havaldar   (Havaladara). Non-commissioned army rank in native infantry equivalent to a sergeant.

Haveli   (Haveli). The mansion of a nobleman or merchant or other man of wealth and status.

Hindi Tika   (Hindi Tika). Hindi "commentary" elucidating meaning of text.

Hog deer   *Axis porcinus*. Abundant in the Gangetic valley and east. Runs with its head low, and has an ungainly appearance.

Hooka   See Hukkah.

Hoondan   See Hundi.

Howdah   (Hauda). A chair or framed seat carried by an elephant.

Hundi   (Hundi). A bill of exchange in an Indian language.

Hukkah   (Hukka). Hubble bubble. Water pipe.

I.C.S.   Indian Civil Service. The senior administrative service in India under the raj. It was the first civil service in the English-speaking countries (and their empires) to be competitively recruited. It was staffed mostly by Englishmen although after 1869 it began to include a few Indians. Its numbers always remained small, expanding from below 1,000 to above 1,000 by the time the English left India. It occupied very high standing and pay as a profession.

I.M.S.   Indian Medical Service.

Imperial Service Troops   This scheme for regularizing the training and organization of the princely state forces was inaugurated in the viceroyalty of Lord Dufferin (1884–1888). Princely states were encouraged to raise and train forces according to principles enforced by an inspection system under the inspector general of Imperial Service Forces. The forces remained, for purposes of discipline, under their local commandant. The Jodhpur Lancers were such forces, and began to be raised in 1889. Major Stuart Beatson came to Jodhpur in 1890 to help organize them. The Imperial Service Troops became the Indian State Forces in 1922.

Indian Clubs   A wooden club, in appearance rather like a pin in ten pins, which is swung for gymnastic exercise.

Isarjee   (Isaraji). Iswar, male deity, considered representative of Lord Shiva, especially prominent in Gangore festival.

Jaan   (Jana). Bridegroom's party.

Jagir   (Jagira). The term refers in the first instance to a form of payment by the Mughals, who gave temporary grants of land and villages to their administrative and military officers to recruit and support soldiers or an administrative apparatus from the revenue of such villages. These grants were revocable, at least so long as the Mughal rulers were strong. In Rajputana, jagirs had a more permanent standing, and constituted the economic base of the Rajput nobility. The most important jagirs were often held by families who, as kin to the maharaja and lineage chief, had helped him conquer the land. Such kinsmen claimed their lands were not resumable because they were co-conquerors. Even lands held by direct gift of the maharaja, for services rendered, were not usually considered revocable in Rajputana until the 1930s.

Jamadar   (Jamadara). Head of a group of soldiers; person on guard; army rank, in the infantry, for a junior commissioned officer. Only Indians held this rank in the British Indian Army.

Janwai   (Jamai or jāvai). Son-in-law.

Jarokhas   (Jharaokha). Latticed window used to screen the zenana rooms while allowing the women to observe the outside. Also, a balcony.

Jat Dena   (Jata dena). Worship of family gods, after marriage or when a son is born.

Jawari   (Javari). Money given to bridegroom when he leaves the bride's house.

Jeen parade   Saddle parade.

Jeensi   (Jinasi). Garrison. Where the artillery is kept. The old jeensi ground at Jaipur near Sanganer gate is now occupied by a Muslim school on Moti Dungri Road.

Jhatka   (Jhataka). Meat from an animal killed by chopping off its head in one stroke. Eaten by Sikhs and Rajputs, but not Muslims, who eat halal, i.e. meat from an animal ritually killed by cutting its throat.

Jheel   (Jhila). Lake.

Jhulum   (Julama). Injustice, injury, crime.

Jink   A sudden change of direction. Amar Singh uses the word to describe a sudden shift by a running boar.

Jod   (Jod). A man-made pond in the desert area meant for cattle.

Jodha Squadron   A squadron of the second regiment of the two cavalry regiments constituting the Sardar Rissala, the Imperial Service Troops initially raised at Jodhpur in 1889. The squadrons were organized by Rajput lineages. Jodhas are a branch of the Rathore lineage.

Jodhpur Lancers   See Sardar Rissala.

Jowar   (Jovar). A grain.

Juna Mahals   (Juna Mahala). Old palaces.

Kaccha   (Kaccha). Unfinished; unripe; incomplete.

Kadir Cup   The Meerut Tent Club's annual pig-sticking competition. Kadir means ravine of a river.

Kaim Khani Squadron   Second squadron of the second regiment of the Jodhpur Lancers (Sardar Rissala). Kaim Khanis are a lineage of Rajputs who practice Islam.

Kair   (Kaira). Small, round, green fruit used in making a pickle. The plant on which it grows.

Kakara   (Khan Kara). "Coughs"; a form of aggressive teasing. Thus if a man is "defeated" in an exchange of teasing jokes, the winner would do a victory kakara. Its implication is, "I am a bigger man than you." A younger man would not emit a kakara in front of an elder.

Kala Gora   (Kala gora). The black white (man). In context of the diary, uncle Roop Singh uses the term to abuse Amar Singh.

Kalas   (Kalasa). Brass vessels, especially those carried on heads by women at ceremonial receptions.

Kamdar   (Kamadara). Steward of a thikana. Like the stewards of English country estates, such men often wielded great power in the economic affairs of the thikana. Their role also bears a certain analogy, especially in the case of a large thikana, to that of the diwan or minister of a state, who acts as a political agent in relation with other political units. The Kanota Kamdar occupied a very large house in Kanota village.

Kameens   (Kamina). Clients in a patron-client relationship; used to refer to all who provide menial services to a patron, such as washermen, shoe-makers, etc.

Kanats   (Kanata). Curtains stretched on poles to screen off the zenana or other tents.

Kanjarni   See Kunjurnis.

Kankan Dora   (Kānkana dora). Small string, tied on right leg and wrist of groom, left leg and wrist of the bride. Red and yellow puja (ritual) threads are used, and small silver, iron and laquer objects are attached. After the wedding, the wife unties that of the husband with both hands, but the husband is allowed only one hand. Those who want to make mischief for the husband and wife tie many knots.

Kanthla   (Kanthala). Long necklace, hanging to the waist, with pictures of family members or deities' portraits set in gold or silver.

Kanwar   (Kāvara). A Rajput whose father is alive. Used especially for oldest son.

Kapal Krya   (Kapala Kriya). Ceremony of breaking the skull of a burning corpse in order to let consciousness escape.

Kapoot   (Kaputa). Bad son; condemnatory term for a Rajput man.

Khaki   (Khaki). Hindi word meaning dusty or dustcolored, from Persian Khak, 'earth' (*Hobson-Jobson*).

Khalsa (Khalasa). The lands of a Rajputana princely state were considered as "fiscal" or "khalsa" on the one hand and jagir and other grant land on the other. Khalsa lands were under the administrative, legal, and revenue control of the state and paid revenue to the state; non-khalsa lands paid revenue to a jagirdar or other holder, and were to a considerable extent under his administrative and legal control. In Jodhpur, as late as 1945 only 13 percent of the land was khalsa.

Khankraa (Khankara). A type of large bush.

Khansama (Khanasama). Cook.

Khari Khunda A "hindusthani" game, says the diarist, played at night with lamps.

Khas Chowki (Khasa Cauki). In Jaipur title for the maharaja's infantry bodyguard. Also, designation there for second category of jagirdars who did not hold the honor of tazim.

Khas Rissala (Khasa Rissala). In Jaipur title for the maharaja's cavalry bodyguard.

Khawas (Khavasa). The personal attendant of a nobleman or a maharaja.

Khawaswal (Khavasa wal). Son or daughter of a Khawas, hereditary servant; the term was usually used to denote children of a Rajput man and a Khawaswal mistress, Khawaswals married each other or Darogas. Khawaswals generally were treated with more honor than Darogas. Sons were recognized as "natural," they were asked to sit on cushions and at a bajot, low dining table.

Kheech (Khica). Type of dish prepared from bajra (a Rajasthani grain) cooked in buttermilk.

Kheer (Khira). Dish made of rice, milk and sugar boiled together. Rice pudding.

Kherjee (Khejari). A thorny tree of the desert.

Khol Bharna (Khola bharanu). Ceremony by which a near relation of the bride's new home adopts her as his daughter. It is meant to provide someone to whom she can turn in trouble.

Khora Stocks. Pillory for the legs. It was used to discipline delinquent servants in Rajputana.

Khukree (Khukhari). A Nepalese scimitar.

Kicheree (Khicari). Dish prepared from rice and pulse boiled together. A mixture of two languages, jargon.

Kilangi (Kilangi). A tall cockade for a turban that rises above the drooping cockade which is the turrah.

Koak (Koka). The Koka Sastra is a book describing sexual practices; manual of love.

Koat (Kota). Fort, castle.

Koti (Kothi). See Kotri.

Kotri (Kothari). Depending on context, a small room or, in Marwar, the main house of the thikana.

Kuchari (Kacahari). Court of justice.

Kunjurnis (Kujarani). Women performers who do tricks, including indecent ones.

Kunthi (Kanthi). String of beads.

Kunwar See Kanwar.

Lapsi (Lapasi). Dish specially prepared from ground wheat, cooked as a sweet dish, for bride and bridegroom to feed each other.

Lawajma (Lavajamau). Procession.

Leen See Aleen,

Lines As in Civil lines, Railway lines, lines of the Jodha squadron. A expression of colonial rationalization and discipline. Refers to the lay-out of an official or military colony under the British raj, where each type of service was apt to be assigned its own road or series of roads.

Loo   (Lu). Hot wind.

Lota   (Lota). A small metal pot; a mug of brass, copper, etc.

Machan   (Macana). An elevated platform, such as was built in a tree for observing tigers.

Mahabharata   (Mahabharata). Sanskrit epic.

Mahakma Khas   Name of secretariat at Jodhpur in 1902–1911.

Mahal   (Mahala). Amar Singh uses the term to refer to rest houses Mughal emperors erected at 24-mile intervals on the Agra-Ajmer road. Can also be a palace.

Maharaj, Maharaja   (Maharaja). The word maharaja is often used in the diary for brothers of the ruler or sons of princes who do not themselves occupy the throne. We have adopted a convention of using the word maharaj for such a son or brother, and maharaja only for those occupying the throne. Amar Singh does not usually make this distinction.

Maharaj Kanwar   (Maharaja Kānvara). Son of a living maharaja. Heir apparent.

Mahdol   (Madola). A large heavy palanquin.

Mahtmee   See matmi.

Maidan   (Maidana). An open ground, plain or green around which a settled area is organized.

Mallis   (Malisa). Rubbing oil on the body; in the diary, usually massage of the horses.

Mama   (Mama). Maternal uncle.

Mamee   (Mami). Wife of a maternal uncle.

Mamla   (Mamala). Money that is paid to Jaipur state as tribute.

Mansee   (Mañsi). Mother's sister.

Manwar   (Manavara). Feeding another by hand. Also the offer of a glass of wine from both hands. The act signifies equality among the participants, except in the case of a wife, who may so serve her husband. It also signifies intimacy.

Mardana   (Mardana). Men's quarters.

Martingale   A kind of bridle.

Marwari   (Maravari). Language of Marwar (western Rajasthan).

Matira   (Matira). Watermelon. Symbolically, its sending meant, in the story of Bullooji Champawat, that the recipient is desired to leave: Mati (not) rao (stay) in Marwar.

Matmi   (Mahatmi). Procedures surrounding the succession to a thikana at the death of the thikanedar. The word is used for the condolence visit paid by the maharaja to the new chief. But as this amounts to an act of recognition of the new chiefs right in the thikana, legal procedures to test or establish the right of succession may precede the visit, and these are "matmi" proceedings. The case against Naila, Kanota, and Gondher, rose out of the "matmi proceedings" at the death of Thakur Fateh Singh of Naila.

Meena   (Mina). Tribal people in Rajasthan.

Modi   (Modi). Grain dealer, grocer, purveyor.

Mohur   (Mohar). The official name of the chief gold coin of British India.

Mokudma   (Mukadma). A legal suit.

Moond Kuti   (Mund kati). Usually the compensation extracted by a ruler or chief from the perpetrator of violence and given to subjects who have had relatives robbed or killed. "Wehr-geldt." Blood money. The diarist uses the word to refer to the origin of many jagir lands in Rajasthan, which were given to loyal followers in battle as a reward.

Morchal   (Murachala). A fan or fly whisk made of peacock feathers and used on ceremonial occasions to fan a royal personage.

Mori Sala   (Mori Sala). Literally, the original grantee. A rule specifying that adoption to a jagir (estate) must be restricted to the lineal male descendants of the original grantee; in default of such a descendant, the estate may be escheated to the khalsa (crownlands).

The rule was codified in 1895 at Jodhpur by a committee including the chief jagirdars of Jodhpur. It overrode the conventional custom of adoption.

Mujra   (Mujara). A salute performed by bowing down and saluting with both hands pressed together. Ladies in purdah may send such a salute verbally. It may be performed by a dancing girl offering song and dance. A Muslim expression.

Mundo Dekhawani   (Mudodekhavani). A ceremony in which the husband promises to give ornaments for looking at his wife's face for the first time.

Munsarim   (Munsarim). Man sent by the state to manage the affairs of a thakur who is a minor.

Naal   (Nalau). Ravine.

Nadi   (Nadi). Small water, pool or stream.

Nainaira   (Nanairau). Mother's parents' home.

Nana   (Nana). Maternal grandfather.

Nawab   (Nawab). Arabic plural of the singular Nayab or Naib. A deputy. A delegate of the supreme chief such as a regional governor under the Mughal emperor, e.g. the Nawab of Oudh. Subsequently, it became a title of rank without necessarily having an office attached to it.

Nazar   (Najara). Hindi from Arabian nazar or nazr, primarily a vow or votive offering. In ordinary use, a ceremonial present, properly an offering from an inferior to a superior, the converse of in'am.

Nazar Lagao   (Nazar lagao). Cast an evil eye.

Nazim   (Najima). Head of an administrative division.

Nichrawal   (Nicharavala). Gesture, between equals, at marriage or other functions as a mark of respect or appreciation; one person will rotate a bill of money around the head of the other, and then throw it on the ground as a gift to a servant or dancing girl.

Noara   (Nora). Stables.

Nomi   (Naumi). Ninth of the moon month.

Nota   (Notau). The invitation issued for a wedding. Also, the present (usually in money form) given at the time of that invitation. Relations especially are expected to make such presents in anticipation of the wedding.

Nullah   (Nala). Stream.

Nuth   (Natha). Woman's ornament for the nose.

Nuzzar   See Nazar.

Odi   (Odi). A thatched hut for tying cattle near a well. In the diary, it is a shooting box.

Odni   (Odni). Large square headcloth worn by women.

Pagri   (Pagari). Small turban tied with cloth wound into very thin strands. Worn especially at Udaipur.

Pagri buddal bhai   (Pagari badala bhai). Among Rajputs, two men may signify close brotherhood by exchanging pagris, turbans, and thus becoming brothers. The phrase denotes such brothers.

Pagurki   (Pagarakhi). Shoes.

Palkee   (Palaki). Palanquin, litter.

Pantia   (Pāti). Row. An arrangement for eating in which persons are fed sitting in a row on the ground.

Parcha cloth   (Parchau). Brocade.

Pargana   (Pargana). An administrative unit, about the size of a tehsil in British India.

Patar   (Patara). Caste of Hindu prostitutes (Randees are Muslim prostitutes).

Pato   (Pato). Low square platform for serving food or for sitting on at a ceremony (such as Tel sichano ceremony). A student's wooden desk.

Peel Khana (Pila khana). Elephant stable.

Peethee See pithi.

Pheras (Phera). Circumambulation of the fire by the bride and bridegroom-part of the wedding ceremony.

Pig-sticking Hunting pig on horseback with spears.

Pithi (Pithi). Paste of haldi (tumeric), which brightens and softens the skin. It is applied and then washed off, a task performed at marriage time by the bhabhis, elder brother's wives. The man so treated sits in bathing clothes, and is apt to be teased and pinched in the process. The procedure is performed for a number of days before the marriage—it is probably one of those Amar Singh is grateful to have escaped by virtue of being at Jodhpur, and not at home.

Political Department Charged with exercising the paramountcy of the Government of India over the princely states. It maintained a separate service, the political service, whose officers served as agents of the Government of India in princely states (agent to the governor general; resident; political agent), or were deputed as guardians to princes or to manage the governments of the princely states during minorities. The department was directly under the viceroy in his role as crown representative, not in his role as governor general of India. The department also supplied officers for service in the Gulf where the British exercised suzerainty.

Political Agent Designation of the British crown representative in a minor princely state.

Polo A game played with mallets on horseback. It seems to have been indigenous to India, and was played near the extreme east and west of the Himalayas, at Manipur, Ladakh, Chitral. It is known to have been played in India by Englishmen both at Calcutta and Punjab in the 1860s. Sir Pratap Singh vigorously encouraged it at Jodhpur after 1889, and the Jodhpur team, consisting of Dhokal Singh, Major Stuart Beatson, Sir Pratap and Hari Singh won the all-India championship at Poona in 1893. Each team has four players.

Poonchees (Punaci). Heavy silver or gold bracelets.

Prakurma (Parikrama). Circumambulation, going around an idol as a mark of reverence. Path around a temple for circumambulating. Circumambulating the body before lighting the funeral pyre.

Pudla (Padalau). Clothes and ornaments sent by the bridegroom for his bride on the marriage day. Also other materials used at the Ganesh Puja.

Puggree See pagri

Puja (Puja). Worship.

Pujaran (Pujarana). Worshipper, priest.

Pukka (Pukka). Ripe, clear, pure, neat, finished.

Pumpship A term used in the diary for urinating. Its origin is obscure.

Punkah (Pankha). Large, fixed, swinging fan, formed of cloth and stretched on a frame that is suspended from the ceiling. It is operated by a punkah coolie who pulls the rope.

Purdah (Pardah). From Persian parda, a curtain, especially a curtain screening women from the sight of men (*Hobson-Jobson*). The practice of female seclusion.

Purdait (Pardaita). Woman in purdah. Amar Singh uses the phrase to designate the non-married consort of Sir Pratap, mother of his extramarital sons, who lives in the shelter of the zenana.

Purohit Priest.

Racquets A game similar to squash played on a larger court.

Rajput (Rajaputa). Literally, son of a raja. Refers to the Kshatriyas, warrior lineages, of Rajputana and north India more generally. For an extended discussion, see Introduction.

Rajputana (Rajaputana). Old name for Rajasthan, area comprising twenty-two former princely states in northwest India.

Ramayana (Ramayana). Sanskrit epic.

Ran Banka Rathore (Rana Banka Rathora). Motto of the Jodhpore house: "Battle valiantly Rathore."

Rang Bantha (Ranga Batanau). Ceremony observed when the janwai (bridegroom/son-in-law) is given leave. The guests are sprayed with red colored water.

Rath (Ratha). A covered chariot driven by bullocks with two and a half domes. It was used to transport the women in purdah.

Rathore (Rathora). Ruling lineage of Jodhpur as well as Bikaner and Kishengarh states. The lineage also exists in Madhya Pradesh (Ratlam, Sitamau, Jhabua, Selana), and Gujarat (Idar).

Ravana (Ravana). According to the epic work Ramayana, he was the demon king of Lanka or Ceylon. He carried off Sita, wife of the hero Rama, who eventually defeated him with the aid of an army of monkeys headed by Sugriva and Hanuman.

Red Fort Built by the emperor Shah Jahan between 1639–1648. Amar Singh is viewing the Diwan-i-Am, Hall of Public Audience, in 1903, before the inlaid panels, originally executed by Austin of Bordeaux and recovered by Lord Curzon from the South Kensington Museum, had been restored in 1909 by a Florentine working at Curzon's direction.

Rekh (Rekha). The word may signify both valuation of a jagir and a tax. Patta rekh in Jodhpur in the nineteenth century was the arbitrarily estimated income of a village, indicated on the patta or grant given to the jagirdar. Bhantu rekh was an annual stipend the jagirdar had to pay the state. In the mid-nineteenth century it was fixed at 8 percent of the patta rekh.

Resident Designation of the British crown representative in a major state.

Residency Housing of the British resident. The residency at Jaipur was located at the head of the present Sardar Patel Marg. It lies one mile southeast of the railway station. Its oldest part was constructed in 1730 or so by the wife of Maharaja Sawai Jai Singh II. It is known as Maji ka Bagh, and was first occupied by a British political officer in 1821. Other and modern buildings have been added since, and the gardens were remodeled by the late Maharaja Man Singh, who took up residence there in the 1950s after the end of princely rule.

Riding off In polo, a permissible procedure by which one player pushes another's pony from the side to get him off the ball.

Rissala (Risala). "Arabian, risala." "A troop in one of our regiments of native (so-called) Irregular Cavalry . . . a native corps of horse, apart from English regimental technicalities." (*Hobson-Jobson.* See, also, Sardar Rissala.)

Rissaldar (Risaladara). Army rank, in the cavalry, for junior commissioned officer, approximately equivalent to a lieutenant. These ranks were reserved for Indian officers.

Rumjol (Ramajola). Broad, heavy anklet with many pendants, giving a jingling effect.

Sapha (Sapha). Large turban, so tied as to achieve a high rise in the front and a drooping loop over one ear. Especially worn in Jaipur and Jodhpur. Amar Singh usually wore a sapha.

Sagar (Sagar). Literally, ocean. Lake.

Sali (Sali). Sister-in-law; sister of wife.

Salotri (Salotri). Farrier; one who shoes horses. Country horse doctor.

Sambar (Sambar). Kind of stag.

Sambela (Sambhelau). The reception at which the bride's relations receive the bridegroom's party.

Sanathan Dharma   (Sanatana dharma). Traditional Hindu religion; also formal organization dedicated to its propagation.

Sardar   (Sardara). Persian: Leader, a commander, an officer; chief, a lord. (*Hobson-Jobson*). In Rajputana, a noble, thakur or jagirdar. Respectful address for a Sikh.

Sardar Rissala   (Sardara Risala). Named after Maharaja Sardar Singh of Jodhpur this two-regiment force was first raised at Jodhpur in 1889. Each regiment consisted of 600 sowars, or troopers, of cavalry, under Indian officers, and organized by squadrons which bore the names of Rajput lineages: Jodhas, Khichis, Mertias, Gogades, Kaim Khanis. About 1900, the force had 779 Arabs, 98 Walers, and 322 country-breds. The pay of officers ranged from Rs 250 per month for squadron officers to Rs 37 for daffadars.

The rissala served in the Boxer Rebellion in 1900–1901 and in France and the Middle East in World War I, both times under Sir Pratap Singh as commandant. In China, it was referred to (in the diary) as the 9th Lancers. The first regiment was part of the reserve brigade of the Tirah Field Force, and 194 horses were sent to the Transvaal in 1899–1900. See also Imperial Service Troops. In 1905, when the Jodhpur police department was organized, the rissala was merged with the police.

Sarkar   (Sarakara). Amar Singh so designates Sir Pratap Singh, brother of Maharaja Jaswant Singh of Jodhpur, who served as prime minister of Jodhpur and as regent of Jodhpur state. The word is Persian and means, literally, "Head of Affairs." In India it came to mean the state, the government, but also "'the Master' or head of the domestic government." (*Hobson-Jobson*).

Sasra   (Sasara). In-law's household.

Satee   (Sati). A chaste or faithful wife; extended to woman who burns herself on her husband's funeral pyre.

Sawaia   (Savaiya). A particular type of couplet, differing in form from the doha.

Seth   (Setha). Merchant, commercial agent, banker, a wealthy person, a moneylender.

Shamiana   (Samiana). An awning or tent roof, with or without sides.

Shakrant   (Sākranta). A holiday, a day of the Hindu month. A day for kite flying.

Shikari   (Sikari). Sportsman, hunter, huntsman.

Shikarkhana   (Sikara khana). Hunting department.

Silakhana   (Sili khana). Armory.

Sindur   (Siñdur). Red mercury oxide used for ritual marking.

Singhasham   (Singasana). A throne; base for image of a deity.

Single stick   For stick fighting, with lathis or quarter staffs; a sport and form of fighting.

Sinjara   (Sañjirau). Evening meal.

Siropao   (Siropava). A set of clothes given on the occasion of departures or other ceremonial events.

Sirpech   (Sirapeca). Ornament placed on turban.

Sowar   (Savara). Persian: a horseman; a native cavalry soldier; a mounted orderly.

Stretching   (A pony). The pony is made to stand with his legs extended in front and back as far as possible, in order to lower his height below the limit above which it is no longer officially a pony. No horse above 14.2 hands was then allowed to enter a polo tournament.

Subedar   (Subadar). From Persian, one holding a suba, a division or province of the Mughal empire. In the diary, it generally refers to a native officer of cavalry, as in the Imperial Service Forces of the princely states, equivalent to captain.

Subedar major   The senior most non-commissioned officer rank in the Indian Army. Until 1917, when the color line was breached and Amar Singh and eight other former Imperial Cadets were given king's commissions, subedar major was the highest rank an Indian could occupy in the Indian Army. Each regiment had only one colonel and only one subedar major. Because the subedar major could speak the relevant regional language and English while the colonel (and his English officers) often could not speak both, the subedar major constituted an essential link in the command relationship between the colonel and the men of his regiment.

In the armed forces of the princely states the rank of subedar major in the infantry (and rissaldar major in the cavalry) was often used but without the apartheid connotation that non-commissioned officer had in the Indian Army. Because in the princely state forces there were no king's commissioned officers, no color bar and no language barrier the rank of subedar major functioned as the equivalent of major. The equivalent rank in the English army military career line would be major.

Subsidiary   A lesser goal in polo, accomplished when the ball, instead of passing between the two middle ones of four flags which mark the end of the field, passes between either of these and one of the side flags.

Sutar Khana   (Sutar Khana). Camel stable.

Swagan   (Svagana). A woman whose husband is alive. Opposite of widows.

Syce   (Saisa). "From Arabic Sais, a groom." (*Hobson-Jobson*).

Syndhya   Worshipping God every day, morning and evening, according to the method prescribed in the Vedas and employing the Gayatri Mantra, an especially sacred verse.

Tajia   (Tajia). "Arabic, Persian, Hindi, ta'ziyah, mourning for the dead." (*Hobson-Jobson*). In India the word is applied to the taboot, or representations, in flimsy material, of the tombs of Hussein and Hasan which are carried about in the Muharram processions.

Tazim   (Tajimi). Honor conferred upon certain sardars; in Jaipur one so honored is entitled to wear golden anklets, and the maharaja rises when he enters the court. "Double tazim" is conferred upon those whose presence the maharaja recognizes at arrival and departure.

Tazimi Sardar   (Tajimi saradar). Chief honored by the maharaja by the conferring of tazim.

Talao   (Talao). Pool or tank of water.

Teej   (Tija). Third day of each half of the lunar month; third of each half month of Savan, a festival celebrated by women whose husbands are alive.

Teeka   (Tikau). Cash, jewels, animals, etc. given by girl's family and boy's at time of engagement just before marriage. The ceremony of giving. Also mark applied to the forehead.

Teeki   (Tiki). Mark applied to the forehead.

Tel chhadana   See tel sichano.

Tel sichano   (Tela sichano). Pouring oil on the head of a girl, a ceremony performed at the time of a wedding.

Tent-pegging   A sport in which the mounted competitors pick up with their spears pegs which are stamped into the ground. Presumably the sport was once functional as a way by which surprise attackers could trap the opposing force beneath their collapsed tents. The pegs are made of two sticks of about 6 inches each sunk in the ground 6 inches apart, and tied to each other at the top with a wire. The size of the pegs was gradually reduced to matchbox height.

Thakur   (Thakura). "From Sanskrit thakurra, 'an idol, a deity.' Used as a term of respect . . . but with a variety of different referents, of which the most familiar is as the style of Rajput nobles." (*Hobson-Jobson*). In Rajasthan the term refers to a Rajput whose father is dead. It does not necessarily imply the addressed has a landed estate, although informally the term is often used for jagirdars who do possess a jagir.

Thali　(Thalû). A flat metal platter.

Thana　(Thana). Police Station.

Thanadar　(Thanadara). Officer in charge of a police station.

Thikana　(Thikana). The estate of a nobleman in Rajasthan, usually given by the maharaja, or by the Mughals, or won by conquest and confirmed by the suzerain. The revenue of the thikana's villages was paid to the thikanedar, the estate holder. His right was limited to the revenue; he did not own the land.

Thikanedar　Holder of a thikana.

Thor　(Thora). A desert plant used for medicinal purposes. A cactus bush.

Thookrani　(Thakarani). Wife of a thakur.

Tilak　(Tilak). Mark of a red color placed on man's or woman's forehead. It may have ceremonial or ornamental meaning.

Toran　(Torana). Ceremonial decoration placed over gateway to bride's quarters at marriage ceremony. The groom touches it with a sword or stick.

Tulsikrit Ramayana　(Tulasi Krta Ramayana). Ramayana written by Tulsi.

Turrah　(Turrah). Gold thread cockade on a turban. The ends droop over.

Tushes　Term used in the diary for the tusks of a boar. The usage was common among hunters in Jaipur

Tum tum　A dog cart; a cart for one horse.

Tyag　(Tyaga). Money given as charity at the time of a wedding to charans of the bride's side by the bridegroom's father.

Unnani　(Yunani). Muslim medical system.

Vakil　(Vakila). "Arabian, Wakil; an attorney; an authorized representative" (*Hobson-Jobson*).

Vans Bhaskar　An important literary work, in Marwari, written by Suraj Mal, a charan (bard) of Rajasthan.

Waler　A rather large rugged saddle horse once exported in quantity from Australia (New South Wales) to British India for military use.

Walter Krit Hitkarni Sabha　A Rajput reform society formed at the instigation of a resident at Jodhpur, Colonel C.K.M. Walter, resident in the reign of Maharaja Jaswant Singh. He gained Sir Pratap's enthusiastic support for the endeavor.

Wordi Major　(Wardi). Title of an Indian adjutant in regiments of Indian irregular cavalry.

Zamindar　(Jamindara). Landlord, landholder.

Zenana　(janana). Women's quarters. Rajput houses were divided into zenana and mardana, men and women's quarters.

APPENDIX:
GENEALOGICAL CHARTS AND LINEAGES

Genealogical Chart I
Overview of the Champawat Lineage from Peelva.

Jiv Raj Singh. 1799–1853.
Thakur of Peelva (Jodhpur),
First to serve Jaipur state
under Maharaja Ram Singh.

Peelva Line

Abhaj Singh. 1818–1885.
Thakur of Peelva.
Remains in Jodhpur.

Jawahar Singh.

Sultan Singh. 1847–1910.
Thakur of Peelva.

Inder Singh. 1884–1942
Nephew of Sultan Singh,
adopted. In charge,
Jodhpur treasury.

Madho Singh. 1914–1964.
Thakur of Peelva.
Jodhpur State Service.
I.A.S.

Gondher/Santha Line*

Sambhu Singh. 1822–1885.
Thakur of Gondher (Jaipur).
Leaves Peelva in 1854 for
Jaipur, Minister and member,
Maharaja's Council, Jaipur.

Chiman Singh.

Mukend Singh. 1850–1918.
Thakur of Gondher, then
Santha when Gondher is
taken. Jaipur Cavalry.

Bhoj Raj Singh. 1873–1928.
Thakur of Santha.
Commander, Jaipur Camel
Cavalry. Guardian to minor
Maharaja Man Singh.

Kanota Line

Zorawar Singh. 1827–1908.
Thakur of Kanota. Leaves
Peelva in 1861 for Jaipur.
Minister and Member,
Maharaja's Council, Jaipur

Narain Singh. 1851–1924.
Thakur of Kanota. Nazim
of Jhunjhunu and I.G.
Police, Jaipur. Guardian
of Maharaja of Alwar.

Amar Singh. 1878–1942.
Thakur of Kanota.
Captain, Indian Army.
Major General, Jaipur
State Forces.

Naila Line

Fateh Singh. 1830–1897.
Thakur of Naila.
Leaves Peelva in 1854
for Jaipur. First Minister
and Member of Council,
Jaipur.

Roop Singh. 1856–1934.
Thakur of Naila.
Judicial service; Minister
and Member of Council,
Jaipur.

Pratap Singh 1877–1940.
Thakur of Naila. Judicial
Service, Jaipur.

Daulat Singh. 1905–––.
Thakur of Naila.

Ram Singh. 1926–––.
Thakur of Naila.

Shiv Nath Singh. 1882–––.
Thakur of Kanota, Brother
of Amar Singh, adopted.
Alwar and Dada State
Service. Head of "thirty-
six departments," Forest
Department, Jaipur.

Mohan Singh. 1937–––.
Thakur of Kanota.
Politics and Business.

Kalyan Singh. ––1938.
Thakur of Santha. Nephew
of Bhoj Raj Singh,
adopted.

Umaid Singh.
Thakur of Santha. Rajasthan
State Service.

* The estate village of Gondher is
  exchanged for Santha in 1902.

Gopal Singh. 1922–––.
Thakur of Peelva.
Brother of Madho Singh,
adopted. Lawyer;
Pradhan, Panchayat
Samiti Phalodi

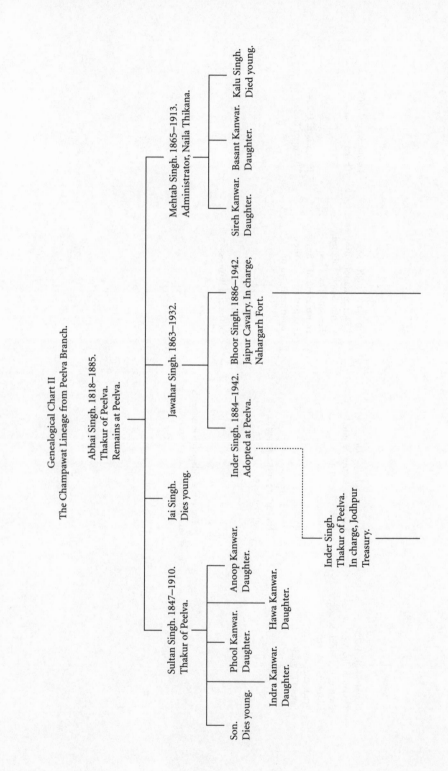

Genealogical Chart II
The Champawat Lineage from Peelva Branch.

Abhai Singh. 1818–1885.
Thakur of Peelva.
Remains at Peelva.

Mehtab Singh. 1865–1913.
Administrator, Naila Thikana.

Jawahar Singh. 1863–1932.

Sireh Kanwar.   Basant Kanwar.   Kalu Singh.
Daughter.   Daughter.   Died young.

Bhoor Singh. 1886–1942.
Jaipur Cavalry. In charge,
Nahargarh Fort.

Inder Singh. 1884–1942.
Adopted at Peelva.

Jai Singh.
Dies young.

Inder Singh.
Thakur of Peelva.
In charge, Jodhpur
Treasury.

Sultan Singh. 1847–1910.
Thakur of Peelva.

Anoop Kanwar.
Daughter.

Phool Kanwar.
Daughter.

Hawa Kanwar.
Daughter.

Indra Kanwar.
Daughter.

Son.
Dies young.

Karan Singh.
1930–.
Business.

Umaid Singh.
1923–. I.A.S.

Daughter.

Major Manohar Singh.
1919–. Indian Army.

Daughter.

Daughter.

Colonel Gulab Singh.
1912–. Sawai Man
Guards Service in
WW II.

Vijay Singh.
Pharmacy.

Sain Kanwar.
Daughter.

Gopal Singh. 1922–.
Lawyer; Pradhan,
Panchayat Samiti Phalodi.
Adopted at Peelva.

Vijay Kanwar.
Daughter.

Madho Singh. 1914–1964.
Thakur of Peelva.
Jodhpur State Service.
I.A.S.

Gopal Singh.
Thakur of Peelva.

Kishan Singh.
Border Security
Force.

Hari Singh.
Died young.

Kishore Singh.
1944–.
Indian Army.

Genealogical Chart III
The Champawat Lineage from Peelva: Gondher/Santha Branch*

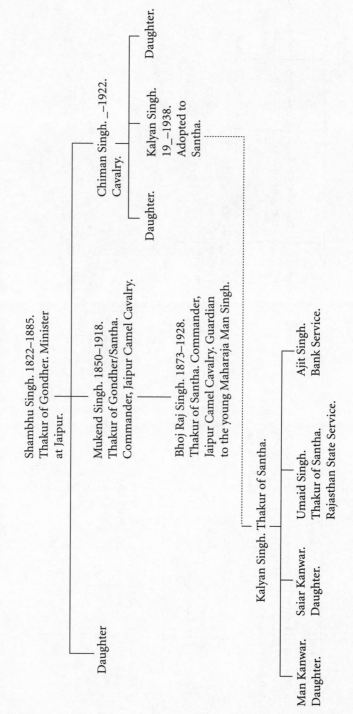

Shambhu Singh. 1822–1885.
Thakur of Gondher. Minister
at Jaipur.

Mukend Singh. 1850–1918.
Thakur of Gondher/Santha.
Commander, Jaipur Camel Cavalry.

Chiman Singh. _–1922.
Cavalry.

Daughter

Daughter.

Kalyan Singh.
19_–1938.
Adopted to
Santha.

Daughter.

Bhoj Raj Singh. 1873–1928.
Thakur of Santha. Commander,
Jaipur Camel Cavalry. Guardian
to the young Maharaja Man Singh.

Kalyan Singh. Thakur of Santha.

Man Kanwar.
Daughter.

Saiar Kanwar.
Daughter.

Umaid Singh.
Thakur of Santha.
Rajasthan State Service.

Ajit Singh.
Bank Service.

*When Gondher village is exchanged by Jaipur state for another estate village, the name of the jagir also changes, to Santha, in 1902.

Genealogical Chart IV
The Champawat Lineage from Peelva: Naila Branch.

Fateh Singh. 1830–1897.
Thakur of Naila.
First Minister, Jaipur

Guman Singh. 1859–1916.
In the service of Maharaja
Madho Singh while family
in disfavor.

Moti Singh.
1885–1944.

Devi Singh.

Hari Singh.
Sarpanch of Naila

Lachman Singh. 1889–
1951.*
In Kishengarh Service.
"Poet." "Bookworm."

Mangal Singh.

Gopal Singh.

Roop Singh. 1856–1934.
Judicial Service.
Minister of Finance,
Military, Home and
Revenue at Jaipur

Dalip Singh. 1888–1944.

Daughter.

Ranjit Singh.

Major Sumer Singh.
Indian Army, Rtd.

Pratap Singh. 1877–1940.
Jaipur Cavalry.
Judicial Service.

Man Singh.

Daughter.

Daughter.

Daughter.

Daulat Singh. 1905–__.
Thakur of Naila.

Vimal Kanwar.

Rama Kanwar.

Anand Kanwar.
Daughter.

Raghunath Singh.
1900–1920.

Ram Singh.

*Because of reticence relating to etiquette among Rajputs,
we have not been able to find out all women's names.

*Referred to as Lichman Singh in the diary.

Genealogical Chart V
The Champawat Lineage from Peelva: Kanota Branch

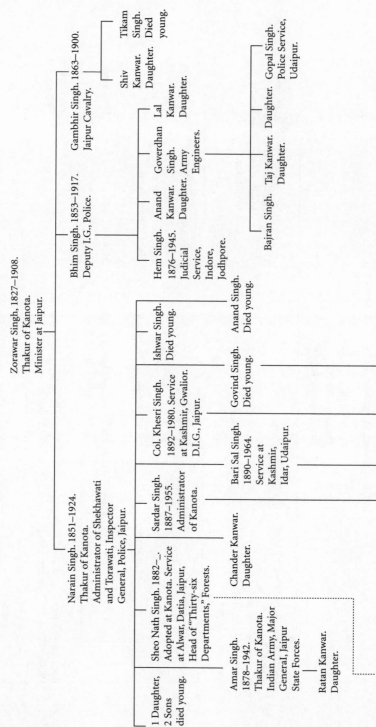

Zorawar Singh, 1827–1908.
Thakur of Kanota.
Minister at Jaipur.

Narain Singh. 1851–1924.
Thakur of Kanota.
Administrator of Shekhawati
and Torawati, Inspector
General, Police, Jaipur.

Bhim Singh. 1853–1917.
Deputy I.G., Police.

Gambhir Singh. 1863–1900.
Jaipur Cavalry.

Shiv
Kanwar.
Daughter.

Tikam
Singh. Died
young.

Anand
Kanwar.
Daughter.

Goverdhan
Singh.
Army
Engineers.

Lal
Kanwar.
Daughter.

Hem Singh.
1876–1945.
Judicial
Service,
Indore,
Jodhpore.

Bajran Singh.

Taj Kanwar.
Daughter.

Daughter.

Gopal Singh.
Police Service,
Udaipur.

Sheo Nath Singh. 1882–.
Adopted at Kanota. Service
at Alwar, Datia, Jaipur,
Head of "Thirty-six
Departments," Forests.

Sardar Singh.
1887–1955.
Administrator
of Kanota.

Col. Khesri Singh.
1892–1980. Service
at Kashmir, Gwalior.
D.I.G., Jaipur.

Ishwar Singh.
Died young.

1 Daughter,
2 Sons
died young.

Amar Singh.
1878–1942.
Thakur of Kanota.
Indian Army, Major
General, Jaipur
State Forces.

Chander Kanwar.
Daughter.

Bari Sal Singh.
1890–1964.
Service at
Kashmir,
Idar, Udaipur.

Govind Singh.
Died young.

Anand Singh.
Died young.

Ratan Kanwar.
Daughter.

Sheo Nath Singh.
Thakur of Kanota.

Ganga Kanwar.
Daughter.

Mohan Kanwar.
Daughter.

Captain Khushal Singh.
_–1948. Jaipur Cavalry.

Panna Kanwar.
Daughter.

Gajender Kanwar.
Daughter.

Daughter.

Anand Singh.
Indian Army.

Major Bhairon Singh.
_–1971. Indian Army.

Budh Kanwar.
Daughter.

Gyan Kanwar.
Daughter.

Mohan Singh.
1937–_. Hotelier.

Dhola Kanwar.
Daughter.

Lal Singh.
Revenue
Officer.

Kalu Singh.
Veterinary.

Gulab Singh.
School teacher.

Narpat Singh.
Electricity
Board.

Jatan Singh.

Rajandra Kanwar.
Daughter.

Daljeet Singh.

Khushal Kanwar.
Daughter.

Hari Singh.
_–1955.
Lieutenant,
Air Force.

Raghunath Singh.
Service, National
Engineering.

Sugan Kanwar.
Daughter.

Chatar Kanwar.
Daughter.

Laxmi Kanwar.
Daughter.

Sher Singh.
Indian Navy Retd.
Electricity
Board, Jaipur

Mool Singh.
Sheep and Wool
Department,
Jaipur

Gopal Kanwar.
Daughter.

Ganpat Singh.

Kan Singh.

Madho Kanwar.
Daughter.

Author Index

Acharya, N.K., 487n2, 512n7, 542n1, 542n7, 543n16, 544n24
Adams, Archibald, 487n2, 509n1, 512n7, 542n1, 542n9
Aitchison, Charles U., 513n9, 514n4, 515n4, 521n19
Alam, Muzaffar, 494n2, 541n17
Amyot, Jacques, 499n22, 503n22
Anstley, F., 140
Aries, Philippe, 502n7, 530nn1–2
Arnold, Edwin, 375, 534n8
Asopa, Ram Karan, 529n1
Aubrey, Frank, 375
Aurelius, Marcus, 242, 331

Babb, Alan, 538n2
Babur, Zahir Al-Din Muhammad, 497n13
Baden-Powell, R.S.S., 526n23
Bajpaee, Pandit Chander Shekhar, 375
Baldevjee, Shiv Chandra Pita, 375
Banarsi, 35
Barhat, Krishna Singh, 529n1
Barkar, A.J., 509n4
Barkawi, Tarak, 513n7
Barrow, Ian J., 489n13, 549n5
Bauer, Henry, 505n17
Bayley, C.S., 492n34, 494n2
Bayly, C.A., 540n12
Beach, Milo Cleveland, 498n18
Bell, Bruce, 505n16
Berm, J. Miram, 504n1, 518n9, 519n10, 532n4
Besant, Annie, 375
Beteille, Andre, 500n8
Bhabha, Homi K., 30
Bhag, Pritam, 375
Bharatia, Shiv Chander, 30
Blochman, Henry, 510n3
Blythe, Ronald, 495n2
Boos, Florence, 548n10
Boothby, Guy, 140
Braudel, Ferdinand., 488n5
Breckenridge, Carol, 539n3
Briggs, Asa, 505n16

Brown, John, 375
Buck, David D., 513n2
Buckler, F.W., 540n14
Buhler, Georg, 532n3
Burnell, A.C., 526n21
Butler, Arthur John, 211

Cameron, Lovett, 140
Carter, Forrest, 496n4
Chand, Barda, 490n25
Chand, Munshi Triloke, 535n19, 551n1
Chander, Harish, 375
Chandra, Nihal, 374
Chaudhuri, K.N., 488n5
Chowdhry, Prem, 538n24
Chusei, Suzuki, 513n6
Clementine-Ojha, Katherine, 538n2
Clifford, James, 500n6, 501n16
Coen, Terence Creagh, 502n9, 540n15, 541nn18–20, 549n3
Cohn, Bernard S., 439, 520n15, 520n17, 525n6, 534n17, 540n11, 545n2, 546n4
Copland, Ian, 541nn18–19, 542n22
Corbin, Alain, 497n9, 499n23, 530n2
Corelli, Marie, 375
Corelli, Mary, 60, 488n7, 503n1
Coulborn, Rushton, 491n32
Crewe, Quentin, 34, 495n6, 495n10, 497n10, 510n6, 518n3, 551n17
Crooke, William, 526n21
Cross, Victoria, 375
Cunnus, Philo, 375
Curzon, George Nathaniel (Lord), 120, 140, 514n2, 515n5, 519n1, 524n3, 527n7

Dale, Stephen Frederic, 497n13, 548n11
Dasi, Rajasundari, 498n19
Debi, Nistarini, 498n19
Defoe, Daniel, 64, 488n7
Desai, Vishaka, 34
Devee, Sunity, 499n19
Devi, Gayatri, 499n19

SUBJECT INDEX